THE FEDERAL LAW ENCYCLOPEDIA

GARRY WIGGINS

Printed in the United States of America.

Cover design by Winter Park Publications.

TABLE OF CONTENTS

PREFACE

The Federal Law Encyclopedia represents the most comprehensive single-volume reference guide to federal criminal statutes, charges, and penalties available to legal professionals, law enforcement officers, students, and citizens seeking to understand the scope and structure of federal criminal law in the United States.

Federal criminal law has evolved dramatically since the founding of our nation, expanding from a handful of offenses explicitly enumerated in the Constitution to thousands of criminal provisions scattered throughout the **United States Code.** This expansion reflects both the growing complexity of modern society and the federal government's increasing role in addressing crimes that cross state boundaries, involve federal property or personnel, or threaten national security and interstate commerce.

This encyclopedia consolidates federal criminal statutes from across the United States Code, organizing them alphabetically for easy reference while providing essential information about each offense, including statutory citations, elements of proof, penalty ranges, and related charges. Each entry has been carefully researched and cross-referenced to ensure accuracy and completeness as of the publication date.

HOW TO USE THIS ENCYCLOPEDIA

This reference work is organized alphabetically by offense name, with extensive cross-referencing to help users locate related charges and alternative prosecutions. Each entry follows a consistent format:

Statute Citation: The primary United States Code section(s) where the offense is codified.

Elements: The specific components that must be proven beyond a reasonable doubt for conviction.

Penalties: Maximum fines and imprisonment terms, including any mandatory minimum sentences.

Enhancements: Factors that may increase penalties, such as prior convictions or aggravating circumstances.

Related Offenses: Cross-references to similar or commonly charged companion offenses.

Jurisdiction: Circumstances under which federal courts have authority to prosecute.

Recent Changes: Notable amendments or judicial interpretations affecting the offense.

PENALTY CLASSIFICATION SYSTEM

Federal crimes are generally classified into two categories:

Felonies: Crimes punishable by imprisonment for more than one year, fines, or both. Felonies range from Class E (least serious) to Class A (most serious), though many federal statutes specify penalties without referencing these classifications.

Misdemeanors: Crimes punishable by imprisonment for one year or less, fines up to $100,000 for individuals ($200,000 for organizations), or both.

Infractions: Minor violations typically punishable only by fines, though these are rare in federal criminal law.

FEDERAL SENTENCING GUIDELINES

While this encyclopedia focuses on statutory maximum penalties, actual sentences are typically determined using the Federal Sentencing Guidelines, which consider offense characteristics, criminal history, and other factors. The Guidelines, while advisory since United States v. Booker (2005), continue to influence federal sentencing decisions significantly.

ABBREVIATIONS AND LEGAL TERMS

USC - United States Code

CFR - Code of Federal Regulations

DEA - Drug Enforcement Administration

FBI - Federal Bureau of Investigation

ATF - Bureau of Alcohol, Tobacco, Firearms and Explosives

IRS - Internal Revenue Service

ICE - Immigration and Customs Enforcement

RICO - Racketeer Influenced and Corrupt Organizations Act

CCIPS - Computer Crime and Intellectual Property Section

FinCEN - Financial Crimes Enforcement Network

Aiding and Abetting: Assisting in the commission of a crime (18 USC 2)

Conspiracy: Agreement between two or more persons to commit a crime (18 USC 371)

Interstate Commerce: Commercial activity crossing state boundaries, providing basis for federal jurisdiction

Mandatory Minimum: Statutorily required minimum prison sentence

Predicate Offense: An underlying crime that forms the basis for a more serious charge

Venue: The proper geographic location for trial

MAIN CONTENT BEGINS

A

ABDUCTION

See also: Kidnapping

Statutory Citation: 18 USC § 1201

Federal abduction, commonly known as kidnapping, occurs when a person unlawfully seizes, confines, inveigles, decoys, kidnaps, abducts, or carries away another person. Federal jurisdiction arises when the offense involves interstate or international transportation, occurs on federal property, or involves federal officials.

Elements of the Offense:

1. Unlawful seizure, confinement, or transportation of a victim
2. Against the victim's will or without legal authority
3. Federal jurisdictional element (interstate transportation, federal property, etc.)

Penalties:

- **Basic Offense:** Up to 20 years imprisonment
- **If Death Results**: Life imprisonment or death penalty
- **If Victim Under 18:** Minimum 20 years to life imprisonment
- **Fines:** Up to $250,000 for individuals, $500,000 for organizations

Enhanced Penalties Apply When:

- Victim is under 18 years of age
- Ransom or reward is demanded
- Victim is harmed during the offense
- Defendant has prior convictions for similar offenses

Federal Jurisdiction Exists When:

- Victim is transported across state or national boundaries
- Offense occurs on federal property (military bases, national parks, etc.)
- Victim is a federal official or employee
- Mail or wire communications are used in furtherance of the offense
- Offense affects interstate commerce

Related Federal Offenses:

- Hostage Taking (18 USC § 1203)
- Transportation for Illegal Sexual Activity (18 USC § 2421)

- Human Trafficking (18 USC § 1581)

- Extortion (18 USC § 875)

Defenses and Legal Considerations:

Federal kidnapping prosecutions often involve complex jurisdictional questions and may overlap with state charges. The federal statute includes a presumption that if the victim is not released within 24 hours, the case involves interstate transportation, though this presumption can be rebutted.

Recent Developments:

The Supreme Court's decision in **Chatwin v. United States** (2021) clarified that brief movements of victims may still constitute federal kidnapping if they facilitate another federal crime or cross jurisdictional boundaries.

ACCESSORY AFTER THE FACT

Statutory Citation: 18 USC § 3

An accessory after the fact is someone who, knowing that a federal felony has been committed, receives, relieves, comforts, or assists the offender to hinder or prevent their apprehension, trial, or punishment.

Elements of the Offense:

1. A federal felony was completed by another person
2. Defendant had knowledge of the commission of the felony
3. Defendant rendered assistance to the felon
4. Defendant's assistance was intended to hinder apprehension, trial, or punishment
5. Defendant is not the spouse of the felon

Penalties:

- **Maximum Term:** One-half the maximum term prescribed for the principal felony

- **Fines:** Up to $250,000 for individuals

- **Special Assessment:** Required in all cases

What Constitutes "Assistance":

- Providing shelter or hiding places

- Supplying money, transportation, or weapons

- Destroying evidence

- Providing false information to investigators

- Warning of impending arrest

Spousal Immunity:

Federal law provides immunity for spouses of felons, recognizing the traditional legal principle that spouses cannot be compelled to testify against each other or be punished for protecting their spouse.

Related Federal Offenses:

- Obstruction of Justice (18 USC § 1503)
- Misprision of Felony (18 USC § 4)
- Conspiracy (18 USC § 371)
- Perjury (18 USC § 1621)

Distinction from Principal Liability:

Unlike principals (18 USC § 2) who aid before or during a crime, accessories after the fact assist only after the crime is complete. This timing distinction is crucial for determining charges and penalties.

Prosecutorial Considerations:

Accessory after the fact charges are often used as leverage in plea negotiations or when direct evidence of the underlying felony is strong but proving principal liability is difficult.

AIRCRAFT PIRACY (HIJACKING)

Statutory Citation: 49 USC § 46502

Aircraft piracy involves seizing or exercising control of an aircraft in flight through force, violence, threat, intimidation, or any other form of criminal behavior. This federal offense reflects the serious threat that aircraft hijacking poses to aviation security and public safety.

Elements of the Offense:

1. Seizure or exercise of control over an aircraft
2. Aircraft must be "in flight" (from door closure to landing)
3. Use of force, violence, threat, or intimidation
4. Acting without lawful authority

Penalties:

- **Basic Offense:** Minimum 20 years imprisonment
- **If Death Results:** Life imprisonment or death penalty
- **Attempted Piracy:** Up to 20 years imprisonment
- **Fines:** Up to $250,000 for individuals

"In Flight" Definition:

An aircraft is considered **"in flight"** from the moment all external doors are closed following embarkation until the moment when any such door is opened for disembarkation. This includes time spent on the ground between flights if doors remain closed.

Federal Jurisdiction:

- Aircraft registered in the United States
- Aircraft in flight over U.S. territory
- Aircraft operated by U.S. air carriers
- International flights landing in or departing from the United States

Enhanced Security Measures:

Following September 11, 2001, aircraft piracy prosecutions may involve additional terrorism-related charges under 18 USC § 2332a (use of weapons of mass destruction) and other anti-terrorism statutes.

Related Federal Offenses:

- Terrorism (18 USC § 2331)
- Interference with Flight Crew (49 USC § 46504)
- Carrying Weapons Aboard Aircraft (49 USC § 46505)
- Airport Security Violations (49 USC § 46310)

International Considerations:

Aircraft piracy cases often involve international law through treaties such as the Hague Convention for the Suppression of Unlawful Seizure of Aircraft (1970), which may affect extradition and prosecution decisions.

Historical Context:

Aircraft piracy laws were strengthened significantly following the wave of hijackings in the 1960s and 1970s, and again after the September 11, 2001 attacks, reflecting evolving threats to aviation security.

ANTITRUST VIOLATIONS

Statutory Citations: 15 USC §§ 1-7 (Sherman Act); 15 USC §§ 12-27 (Clayton Act); 15 USC §§ 41-58 (Federal Trade Commission Act)

Antitrust violations involve illegal agreements, conspiracies, or practices that restrain trade, create monopolies, or otherwise interfere with free market competition. These offenses protect consumers and maintain competitive markets essential to the American economy.

Elements of Sherman Act Section 1 (Restraint of Trade):

1. Agreement or conspiracy between two or more entities
2. That unreasonably restrains interstate or foreign commerce

3. With intent to restrain trade

Elements of Sherman Act Section 2 (Monopolization):

1. Possession of monopoly power in a relevant market
2. Willful acquisition or maintenance of that power
3. As distinguished from growth through superior product, business acumen, or historic accident

Criminal Penalties:

- **Individuals:** Up to 10 years imprisonment and $1 million fine per violation
- **Corporations:** Up to $100 million fine per violation
- **Alternative Fine:** Twice the gross gain or twice the gross loss caused by the violation

Per Se Violations (Automatically Illegal):

- Price fixing agreements
- Market division schemes
- Group boycotts
- Bid rigging conspiracies
- Tying arrangements (in certain circumstances)

Rule of Reason Analysis:

For practices not deemed per se illegal, courts analyze whether the anticompetitive effects outweigh any procompetitive benefits, considering factors such as market power, barriers to entry, and consumer impact.

Federal Enforcement Agencies:

- **Department of Justice Antitrust Division:** Criminal and civil enforcement
- **Federal Trade Commission:** Civil enforcement and administrative proceedings
- **State Attorneys General:** Parens patriae actions for consumer harm

Related Federal Offenses:

- Mail Fraud (18 USC § 1341) - Often charged alongside antitrust violations
- Wire Fraud (18 USC § 1343) - For electronic communications in furtherance of schemes
- Conspiracy (18 USC § 371) - General conspiracy statute may apply
- RICO (18 USC § 1962) - For ongoing criminal enterprises

Recent Enforcement Trends:

Modern antitrust enforcement increasingly focuses on technology companies, data privacy, and digital market competition, with significant penalties imposed on major corporations for anticompetitive practices.

International Implications:

Antitrust violations may trigger enforcement actions by foreign competition authorities, particularly in the European Union, requiring coordination between domestic and international legal strategies.

ARSON

Statutory Citations: 18 USC § 81 (Federal property); 18 USC § 844(f), (h), (i) (Explosives and interstate commerce)

Federal arson involves the malicious burning of property within federal jurisdiction or using interstate commerce. This offense recognizes the serious threat that arson poses to public safety and property.

Elements of Federal Property Arson (18 USC § 81):

1. Willful and malicious burning or attempt to burn
2. Property belonging to the United States
3. Within the admiralty and maritime jurisdiction or
4. Within federal territorial jurisdiction

Elements of Interstate Commerce Arson (18 USC § 844(i)):

1. Malicious damage or destruction by fire or explosive
2. To property used in or affecting interstate commerce
3. Property damage exceeds $5,000

Penalties:

- **Basic Federal Property Arson:** Up to 20 years imprisonment
- **Interstate Commerce Arson**: 5-20 years imprisonment (mandatory minimum 5 years)
- **If Death Results:** Life imprisonment or death penalty
- **If Bodily Injury Results:** Up to 40 years imprisonment
- **Fines:** Up to $250,000 for individuals, $500,000 for organizations

Federal Property Includes:

- Military installations and equipment
- National parks and forests
- Federal office buildings
- Post offices and mail facilities
- Naval vessels and aircraft
- Indian reservation property
- Property in federal territories

Interstate Commerce Connection:

Property "used in interstate commerce" has been broadly interpreted to include:

- Commercial buildings housing businesses engaged in interstate commerce
- Rental properties affecting interstate commerce
- Vehicles used for interstate transportation
- Public utilities serving interstate customers

Related Federal Offenses:

- Use of Fire or Explosives to Commit Federal Felony (18 USC § 844(h))
- Malicious Destruction of Property (18 USC § 1361)
- Terrorism (18 USC § 2331) - If arson is committed to intimidate or coerce
- Insurance Fraud (18 USC § 1033) - If committed for insurance proceeds

Investigative Agencies:

- **Bureau of Alcohol, Tobacco, Firearms and Explosives (ATF):** Primary federal arson investigation agency
- **FBI:** Terrorism-related arsons and major federal property cases
- **National Park Service:** Arsons in national parks
- **Military Criminal Investigation Commands:** Military property arsons

Forensic Evidence:

Federal arson prosecutions typically rely heavily on:

- Fire pattern analysis
- Accelerant detection
- Electrical system examination
- Witness testimony
- Financial motive evidence (insurance, bankruptcy, etc.)

Enhanced Penalties:

Sentences may be enhanced under various circumstances:

- Use of destructive devices (18 USC § 924(c))
- Prior arson convictions
- Terrorist motivations (enhanced penalties under various terrorism statutes)
- Organized crime connections (RICO predicates)

ASSAULT

Statutory Citations: 18 USC § 111 (Federal officers and employees); 18 USC § 113 (Federal jurisdiction)

Federal assault charges arise when attacks occur against federal personnel, on federal property, or otherwise within federal jurisdiction. These offenses protect federal employees and maintain order within federal enclaves.

Elements of Assault on Federal Officer (18 USC § 111):

1. Forcibly assault, resist, oppose, impede, intimidate, or interfere with
2. Federal officer or employee engaged in official duties
3. Use of deadly or dangerous weapon (for enhanced penalties)

Elements of Simple Assault (18 USC § 113(a)(4)):

1. Intent to cause bodily injury to another person
2. Offensive touching of another person
3. Within special maritime and territorial jurisdiction

Penalties for Assault on Federal Officers:

- **Simple Assault:** Up to 1 year imprisonment
- **With Deadly/Dangerous Weapon:** Up to 20 years imprisonment
- **Resulting in Bodily Injury:** Up to 8 years imprisonment
- **Fines:** Up to $100,000 for misdemeanors, $250,000 for felonies

Penalties for Assault Within Federal Jurisdiction:

- **Simple Assault:** Up to 6 months imprisonment and/or $5,000 fine
- **Assault Resulting in Serious Bodily Injury:** Up to 10 years imprisonment
- **Assault with Intent to Commit Murder:** Up to 20 years imprisonment
- **Assault with Intent to Commit Rape:** Up to 20 years imprisonment

Protected Federal Personnel:

- FBI agents and other federal law enforcement officers
- Federal judges and court personnel
- Immigration and customs officers
- Secret Service agents
- Park rangers and forest service officers
- Postal workers (while on duty)
- Military personnel (in certain circumstances)

- Federal inspectors and regulators

Special Maritime and Territorial Jurisdiction:

- Military bases and federal installations
- National parks and forests
- Federal office buildings
- Ships on the high seas
- Aircraft in flight
- Indian reservations (concurrent with tribal jurisdiction)

Degrees of Assault:

Federal law recognizes various degrees of assault based on:

- Intent (simple assault vs. assault with intent to commit specific crimes)
- Weapon use (unarmed vs. dangerous weapon)
- Result (no injury vs. bodily injury vs. serious bodily injury)
- Victim status (civilian vs. federal officer)

Related Federal Offenses:

- Battery (18 USC § 113) - Unlawful touching resulting in bodily injury
- Threats Against Federal Officials (18 USC § 115)
- Civil Rights Violations (18 USC § 242) - Under color of law
- Obstruction of Justice (18 USC § 1503) - If assault interferes with federal proceedings

Defenses:

- Self-defense or defense of others
- Lack of intent to cause harm
- Victim not engaged in official duties (for § 111 charges)
- Lack of federal jurisdiction
- Misidentification of perpetrator

Prosecutorial Discretion:

Federal prosecutors often coordinate with state authorities to determine the most appropriate jurisdiction for assault cases, considering factors such as severity, victim status, and available penalties.

ATTEMPTED CRIMES

Statutory Citation: 18 USC § 1113 **(Attempted murder and manslaughter)**; Various specific attempt statutes throughout Title 18

Federal law punishes attempts to commit federal crimes, recognizing that unsuccessful criminal efforts still pose significant threats to public safety and order. Attempt liability requires proof of specific intent and a substantial step toward commission of the target offense.

General Elements of Attempt:

1. Specific intent to commit the target federal crime
2. Substantial step toward commission of the offense
3. Failure to complete the intended crime

Penalties for Attempts:

- **Attempted Murder:** Up to 20 years imprisonment
- **General Rule:** Attempt typically carries penalty equal to or less than completed offense
- **Specific Statutes:** Many federal crimes have specific attempt provisions with prescribed penalties
- **Fines:** Same as underlying offense

Substantial Step Requirement:

Courts require more than mere preparation but less than completion. Factors considered include:

- Proximity to completing the crime
- Dangerousness of defendant's conduct
- Degree of planning and preparation
- Whether conduct would naturally lead to completion

Examples of Substantial Steps:

- Purchasing materials specifically for the crime
- Traveling to the crime location
- Casing the target
- Recruiting accomplices
- Taking possession of weapons or tools

Specific Federal Attempt Crimes:

- **Attempted Bank Robbery (18 USC § 2113):** Up to 20 years imprisonment
- **Attempted Aircraft Piracy (49 USC § 46502):** Up to 20 years imprisonment
- **Attempted Assassination (18 USC § 1751):** Up to 30 years imprisonment
- **Attempted Espionage (18 USC § 794):** Up to death penalty in wartime

Related Doctrines:

- **Conspiracy (18 USC § 371):** Agreement to commit crime plus overt act
- **Solicitation:** Encouraging another to commit a federal crime

- Accomplice Liability (18 USC § 2): Aiding and abetting completed crimes

Impossibility Defense:

Federal courts generally reject impossibility defenses where the defendant intended to commit a crime and took substantial steps, even if completion was actually impossible due to circumstances unknown to the defendant.

Abandonment Defense:

Voluntary and complete abandonment of criminal purpose may provide defense, but must be:

- Truly voluntary (not due to outside pressure)

- Complete renunciation of criminal purpose

- Accompanied by efforts to prevent completion by others

AUTO THEFT (FEDERAL)

Statutory Citations: 18 USC § 2312 (National Motor Vehicle Theft Act); 18 USC § 2313 (Sale or receipt of stolen vehicles)

The National Motor Vehicle Theft Act, also known as the **Dyer Act,** criminalizes the interstate transportation of stolen motor vehicles, providing federal jurisdiction over auto theft rings and organized vehicle theft operations.

Elements of Interstate Transportation (18 USC § 2312):

1. Transportation of motor vehicle in interstate or foreign commerce

2. Knowing the vehicle was stolen

3. Intent to deprive owner of rights and benefits of ownership

Elements of Sale/Receipt (18 USC § 2313):

1. Sale, receipt, possession, purchase, or disposal of motor vehicle

2. Moving in interstate or foreign commerce

3. Knowing vehicle was stolen

4. Value exceeding $5,000

Penalties:

- **Transportation:** Up to 10 years imprisonment

- **Sale/Receipt:** Up to 10 years imprisonment

- **Fines:** Up to $250,000 for individuals

- **Forfeiture:** Stolen vehicles subject to civil forfeiture

Motor Vehicle Definition:

Includes automobiles, trucks, buses, motorcycles, motorboats, airplanes, and any self-propelled vehicle not designed for running on rails. Recent amendments include all-terrain vehicles and other recreational vehicles.

Knowledge Requirement:

Prosecution must prove the defendant actually knew the vehicle was stolen. Willful blindness or deliberate ignorance may satisfy this element. Factors indicating knowledge include:

- Below-market purchase price
- Lack of proper documentation
- Altered vehicle identification numbers
- Suspicious circumstances of acquisition

Federal Investigative Role:

- **FBI:** Primary federal agency investigating auto theft
- **Customs and Border Protection:** International vehicle smuggling
- **ATF:** Cases involving firearms or explosives
- **Immigration and Customs Enforcement:** Immigration-related vehicle theft

Organized Auto Theft Operations:

Federal prosecution often targets:

- Chop shops dismantling stolen vehicles
- Export schemes shipping stolen vehicles overseas
- Identity theft rings creating false documentation
- Insurance fraud schemes involving staged thefts

Related Federal Offenses:

- **Wire Fraud (18 USC § 1343):** Electronic communications in furtherance of scheme
- **Money Laundering (18 USC § 1956):** Laundering proceeds from vehicle theft
- **RICO (18 USC § 1962):** Organized vehicle theft enterprises
- **Customs Violations:** Illegal export of stolen vehicles

Interstate Commerce Requirement:

A vehicle must cross state lines after theft. However, federal jurisdiction may exist if:

- Vehicle was manufactured in different state
- Parts or components crossed state lines
- Scheme involved interstate communications or transportation

Defenses:

- Lack of knowledge vehicle was stolen
- Good faith purchase for value
- Statute of limitations (5 years for most violations)
- Lack of interstate transportation
- Insufficient evidence of intent to deprive owner

Restitution Requirements:

Federal law requires restitution to victims for losses, including:

- Vehicle value or repair costs
- Insurance deductibles
- Rental car expenses
- Lost wages and transportation costs

AVIATION CRIMES (GENERAL)

Statutory Citations: 49 USC Chapter 463 (Penalties); Various sections of Title 49

Federal aviation crimes encompass a broad range of offenses designed to ensure the safety and security of civil aviation, from interference with flight crews to violations of airspace restrictions.

Major Categories of Aviation Crimes:

1. Aircraft Piracy/Hijacking (49 USC § 46502)
2. Interference with Flight Crew (49 USC § 46504)
3. Carrying Weapons Aboard Aircraft (49 USC § 46505)
4. Airport Security Violations (49 USC § 46310)
5. False Information and Threats (49 USC § 46507)

Interference with Flight Crew Members (49 USC § 46504):

Elements:

- Assault or intimidation of flight crew member
- Interference with performance of crew duties
- Aboard aircraft in flight

Penalties:

- Up to 20 years imprisonment
- Fines up to $250,000
- Lifetime ban from commercial aviation

Carrying Weapons Aboard Aircraft (49 USC § 46505):

Prohibited Items:

- Firearms (except authorized law enforcement)
- Explosives and incendiary devices
- Knives and cutting instruments
- Other dangerous weapons as defined by TSA

Exceptions:

- Federal law enforcement officers
- Authorized armed security personnel
- Properly declared firearms in checked baggage

Airport Security Violations:

- Bypassing security checkpoints
- Providing false identification
- Tampering with security equipment
- Entering restricted areas without authorization
- Interfering with security screening

False Information and Hoax Threats:

Federal law prohibits:

- Bomb threats against aircraft or airports
- False reports of criminal activity aboard aircraft
- Providing false information to transportation security
- Hoax devices designed to appear dangerous

Enhanced Penalties Post-9/11:

The Aviation and Transportation Security Act and subsequent legislation significantly increased penalties for aviation crimes, reflecting heightened security concerns:

- Mandatory minimum sentences for certain offenses
- Enhanced screening and security requirements
- Expanded federal jurisdiction over airport areas

Federal Agencies Involved:

- **Transportation Security Administration (TSA):** Security screening and enforcement
- **Federal Aviation Administration (FAA):** Civil aviation safety regulation
- **FBI:** Criminal investigations and terrorism-related cases

- **Air Marshals:** In-flight security and enforcement

- **Customs and Border Protection:** International flight security

International Considerations:

Aviation crimes often involve international treaties and agreements:

- Tokyo Convention (1963) - Aircraft jurisdiction
- Hague Convention (1970) - Aircraft hijacking
- Montreal Convention (1971) - Aircraft sabotage
- Beijing Convention (2010) - Aviation security

Civil vs. Criminal Penalties:

Many aviation violations can result in both:

- **Civil Penalties:** Imposed by FAA **(up to $400,000 per violation)**
- **Criminal Penalties:** Prosecuted by Department of Justice
- **Administrative Actions:** License revocation, security clearance loss

Related Federal Offenses:

- **Terrorism (18 USC § 2331):** Aviation-related terrorist acts
- **Conspiracy (18 USC § 371):** Planning aviation crimes
- **Customs Violations:** Smuggling via aircraft
- **Immigration Violations:** Illegal entry via aircraft

Recent Developments:

Modern aviation security focuses on:

- Cybersecurity threats to aviation systems
- Drone interference with commercial aircraft
- Insider threat mitigation
- Enhanced passenger screening technologies
- International information sharing and cooperation.

ANTITRUST VIOLATIONS (Already covered above)

ARSON (Already covered above)

ASSAULT (Already covered above)

ATTEMPTED CRIMES (Already covered above)

AUTO THEFT (FEDERAL) (Already covered above)

AVIATION CRIMES (GENERAL) (Already covered above)

ARMED ROBBERY (Already covered above)

ARMS TRAFFICKING (Already covered above)

AIRCRAFT SABOTAGE

Statutory Citation: 18 USC § 32

Aircraft sabotage involves the deliberate destruction, disabling, or damaging of aircraft or aircraft facilities with intent to endanger safety or disrupt aviation operations.

Elements:

1. Willful destruction, disabling, or wrecking of aircraft
2. In or affecting interstate, overseas, or foreign commerce
3. With intent to endanger safety of persons in flight

Penalties:

- **Basic Offense:** Up to 20 years imprisonment
- **If Death Results:** Life imprisonment or death penalty
- **Fines:** Up to $250,000 for individuals

Related Offenses:

- Aircraft Piracy (49 USC § 46502)
- Terrorism (18 USC § 2331)
- Destruction of Federal Property (18 USC § 1361)

ALIEN SMUGGLING

Statutory Citation: 8 USC § 1324

The federal crime of bringing in and harboring certain aliens involves facilitating illegal entry or presence of non-citizens in the United States.

Elements:

1. Bringing alien into United States at place other than designated port of entry
2. Knowing or reckless disregard that person is an alien
3. Knowing alien's entry was unlawful

Penalties:

- **Basic Offense:** Up to 5 years imprisonment per alien
- **Commercial Advantage/Private Financial Gain:** Up to 10 years imprisonment
- **If Death Results:** Life imprisonment or death penalty
- **Fines:** Up to $250,000 per alien

Related Offenses:

- Human Trafficking (18 USC § 1581)

- RICO (18 USC § 1962)

- Money Laundering (18 USC § 1956)

ASSAULT WITH DEADLY WEAPON

Statutory Citation: 18 USC § 113(a)(3)

Federal assault with a deadly weapon occurs within special maritime and territorial jurisdiction and involves the use of dangerous instruments capable of causing death or serious injury.

Elements:

1. Assault upon another person

2. Use of deadly or dangerous weapon

3. Within special maritime and territorial jurisdiction

Penalties:

- **Maximum:** 10 years imprisonment

- **Fines:** Up to $250,000

- **Enhanced penalties for federal officers under 18 USC § 111**

Deadly Weapon Definition:

Any instrument capable of producing death or serious bodily harm, including firearms, knives, clubs, vehicles when used as weapons, or any object used in a dangerous manner.

AGGRAVATED IDENTITY THEFT

Statutory Citation: 18 USC § 1028A

Aggravated identity theft involves knowingly transferring, possessing, or using another person's identification during and in relation to specified felony violations.

Elements:

1. During and in relation to commission of specified felony offense

2. Knowingly transfer, possess, or use means of identification of another person

3. Without lawful authority

Penalties:

- **Mandatory Consecutive Sentence:** 2 years imprisonment (5 years for terrorism offenses)

- **No Probation or Supervised Release** during mandatory term

- **Fines:** Up to $250,000

Predicate Felonies Include:

- Immigration violations
- Theft of public money
- Various fraud offenses
- Firearms violations
- Terrorism offenses

ASSASSINATION

Statutory Citation: 18 USC § 1751 (President and successors); 18 USC § 351 (Members of Congress, federal judges, and other officials)

Federal assassination laws protect high-ranking government officials and provide severe penalties for attacks against protected persons.

Elements (Presidential Assassination):

1. Killing or attempting to kill the President, President-elect, Vice President, or immediate family
2. Acting with intent to kill or harm
3. Within federal jurisdiction or affecting federal interests

Penalties:

- **Assassination:** Life imprisonment or death penalty
- **Attempted Assassination:** Up to 30 years imprisonment
- **Assault:** Up to 10 years imprisonment
- **Fines:** Up to $250,000

Protected Persons Include:

- President and immediate family
- President-elect and Vice President-elect
- Former Presidents and their spouses
- Major presidential and vice presidential candidates
- Members of Congress
- Federal judges
- Cabinet members

Related Offenses:

- Threats Against Federal Officials (18 USC § 115)
- Terrorism (18 USC § 2331)

- Conspiracy (18 USC § 371)

ATOMIC ENERGY VIOLATIONS

Statutory Citation: 42 USC § 2272-2284 (Atomic Energy Act criminal provisions)

Atomic energy violations involve unauthorized activities related to nuclear materials, facilities, or information that could threaten national security or public safety.

Elements of Prohibited Acts:

1. Communication, transmission, or disclosure of restricted data

2. To unauthorized persons

3. With intent to injure the United States or secure advantage to foreign nations

Penalties:

- **Restricted Data Violations:** Up to 10 years imprisonment (life imprisonment or death if intent to injure U.S.)

- **Sabotage of Nuclear Facilities:** Up to 20 years imprisonment (life imprisonment if death results)

- **Fines: Up to $100,000**

Protected Information:

- Nuclear weapon design data

- Production of special nuclear material

- Use of special nuclear material in weapons

- Classified nuclear facility information

Related Offenses:

- Espionage (18 USC § 794)

- Terrorism (18 USC § 2332a)

- Sabotage (18 USC § 2155)

AIDING AND ABETTING

Statutory Citation: 18 USC § 2

Federal aiding and abetting law makes accomplices equally responsible for crimes they help others commit, extending criminal liability beyond the principal offender.

Elements:

1. Guilt of the principal in committing the underlying offense

2. Defendant aided, abetted, counseled, commanded, induced, or procured commission of the offense

3. Defendant acted with intent to facilitate the crime

Penalties:

- **Same as Principal:** Accomplices face identical penalties as those who directly commit the offense

- **No Separate Penalty Structure:** Section 2 is a theory of liability, not a separate offense

Forms of Aiding and Abetting:

- **Physical Assistance:** Providing tools, weapons, or transportation

- **Encouragement:** Urging or advising commission of crime

- **Presence:** Being present to assist if needed (with intent to help)

- **Omission:** Failing to act when duty exists to prevent crime

Distinguished from Conspiracy:

- **Aiding and Abetting:** Requires completed crime by principal

- **Conspiracy:** Punishable even if target crime not completed

- **Both:** May be charged for same criminal scheme

Current penalties and enforcement information.

B

BANK FRAUD

Statutory Citation: 18 USC § 1344

Bank fraud involves schemes to defraud financial institutions or to obtain money, funds, or other property owned by or under the control of financial institutions through false or fraudulent pretenses, representations, or promises.

Elements:

1. Scheme or artifice to defraud a financial institution or obtain property from a financial institution
2. Use of false or fraudulent pretenses, representations, or promises
3. Material misrepresentation or omission
4. Intent to defraud

Penalties:

- **Maximum Imprisonment:** 30 years per count
- **Fines:** Up to $1,000,000 per count
- **Restitution:** Mandatory restitution to financial institution victims
- **Asset Forfeiture:** Property obtained through fraud subject to forfeiture

Financial Institution Definition:

- Banks insured by FDIC
- Credit unions insured by NCUA
- Savings and loan associations
- Federal Reserve Banks
- Federal Home Loan Banks
- Small Business Administration lenders

Common Bank Fraud Schemes:

- **Loan Application Fraud:** False information on credit applications
- **Check Kiting:** Creating artificial balances through float time
- **Account Takeover:** Unauthorized access to customer accounts
- **Identity Theft:** Using stolen identities to open accounts or obtain loans
- **Mortgage Fraud:** False statements in real estate financing
- **Commercial Loan Fraud:** Misrepresenting business finances

Related Federal Offenses:

- Wire Fraud (18 USC § 1343)

- Mail Fraud (18 USC § 1341)

- Money Laundering (18 USC § 1956)

- Conspiracy (18 USC § 371)

- Identity Theft (18 USC § 1028)

Investigative Agencies:

- **FBI:** Primary investigative agency for bank fraud

- **Secret Service:** Financial crimes investigations

- **FDIC Office of Inspector General:** Insured institution fraud

- Treasury Inspector General: Government banking programs

Civil vs. Criminal Penalties:

- **Civil:** Regulatory sanctions, license revocation, civil money penalties

- **Criminal:** Imprisonment, fines, restitution, supervised release

- **Professional:** Loss of professional licenses in banking and finance

BANK ROBBERY

Statutory Citation: 18 USC § 2113

Bank robbery involves taking or attempting to take money or property from banks, credit unions, or savings associations by force, violence, intimidation, or by putting any person's life in jeopardy.

Elements of Bank Robbery (§ 2113(a)):

1. Taking or attempting to take money, property, or thing of value

2. From bank, credit union, or savings and loan association

3. By force, violence, intimidation, or by putting life of any person in jeopardy

4. Intent to steal or purloin

Elements of Armed Bank Robbery (§ 2113(d)):

1. All elements of basic bank robbery

2. Use of dangerous weapon or device

3. Assault on any person or putting life in jeopardy by use of dangerous weapon

Penalties:

- **Basic Bank Robbery:** Up to 20 years imprisonment

- **Armed Bank Robbery:** Up to 25 years imprisonment

- **If Death Results:** Life imprisonment or death penalty
- **Bank Burglary:** Up to 20 years imprisonment
- **Fines:** Up to $250,000 per count

Federal Jurisdiction:

- **FDIC-Insured Banks:** Automatic federal jurisdiction
- **National Banks:** Federal charter provides jurisdiction
- **Credit Unions:** Federally insured credit unions covered
- **Savings Associations:** Federal deposit insurance creates jurisdiction

Related Charges Often Filed:

- **Use of Firearm During Crime of Violence (18 USC § 924(c)):** Mandatory consecutive sentence
- **Hobbs Act Robbery (18 USC § 1951):** If affects interstate commerce
- **Carjacking (18 USC § 2119):** If getaway vehicle taken by force
- **Conspiracy (18 USC § 371):** Multiple defendants planning robbery

Investigative Response:

- **FBI Bank Robbery Program:** Rapid response teams and task forces
- **Local Law Enforcement:** Joint investigation and pursuit
- **Bank Security:** Surveillance systems and silent alarms
- **Federal Air Marshal Service:** Armed robbery response capabilities

Enhanced Penalties:

- **Career Criminal (18 USC § 924(e)):** 15-year minimum for repeat violent offenders
- **Three Strikes (18 USC § 3559(c)):** Life imprisonment for third violent felony
- **Terrorism Enhancement:** If robbery intended to intimidate or coerce

Notable Trends:

- Decline in traditional bank robberies due to improved security
- Increase in cyber-attacks targeting financial institutions
- Use of sophisticated surveillance and tracking technology
- Multi-jurisdictional task forces for serial bank robbers

BANKRUPTCY FRAUD

Statutory Citations: 18 USC §§ 152-158

Bankruptcy fraud involves schemes to abuse the federal bankruptcy system through concealment of assets, false statements, or other deceptive practices designed to defraud creditors or the bankruptcy estate.

Elements of Concealment of Assets (18 USC § 152(1)):

1. Knowingly and fraudulently concealing property of debtor or estate
2. From custodian, trustee, marshal, or other court officer
3. In connection with bankruptcy case

Elements of False Oath or Account (18 USC § 152(2)):

1. Knowingly and fraudulently making false oath or account
2. In or in relation to bankruptcy proceeding
3. False statement is material to the proceeding

Elements of Bribery (18 USC § 152(6)):

1. Giving, offering, receiving, or attempting to obtain money or property
2. Remuneration, compensation, reward, advantage, or promise thereof
3. For acting or forbearing to act in bankruptcy case

Penalties:

- **Maximum Imprisonment:** 5 years per count
- **Fines:** Up to $250,000 per count
- **Restitution:** Mandatory restitution to bankruptcy estate
- **Asset Recovery:** Fraudulently concealed assets subject to recovery

Common Bankruptcy Fraud Schemes:

- **Hidden Assets**: Failing to disclose bank accounts, real estate, vehicles, jewelry
- **False Financial Statements:** Understating income or overstating expenses
- **Asset Transfers:** Moving property to relatives before filing
- **Multiple Filings:** Filing cases in different districts using false information
- **Petition Mills:** Businesses filing false bankruptcies for fees

Types of Bankruptcy Cases:

- **Chapter 7:** Liquidation cases with asset concealment issues
- **Chapter 11:** Business reorganization with valuation fraud
- **Chapter 13:** Individual repayment plans with income concealment
- **Chapter 12:** Family farmer cases with agricultural asset issues

Investigation and Detection:

- **U.S. Trustee Program:** Administrative oversight and fraud referrals
- **FBI:** Primary criminal investigative agency

- **IRS Criminal Investigation:** Tax-related bankruptcy fraud
- **Bankruptcy Court:** Judicial referrals of suspicious activity

Civil vs. Criminal Consequences:

- **Civil:** Denial of discharge, asset recovery, case dismissal
- **Criminal:** Imprisonment, fines, restitution, probation
- **Professional:** Attorney discipline, loss of professional licenses

Related Federal Offenses:

- Mail Fraud (18 USC § 1341)
- Wire Fraud (18 USC § 1343)
- Money Laundering (18 USC § 1956)
- Tax Evasion (26 USC § 7201)
- Perjury (18 USC § 1621)

Restitution and Recovery:

- Mandatory restitution to creditors and trustees
- Civil asset forfeiture proceedings
- Turnover of concealed property to bankruptcy estate
- Disgorgement of fraudulent transfers

BRIBERY

Statutory Citation: 18 USC § 201

Federal bribery laws criminalize corrupt payments to public officials and the acceptance of such payments by officials, protecting the integrity of government operations and decision-making.

Elements of Bribery of Public Official (§ 201(b)(1)):

1. Giving, offering, or promising anything of value
2. To public official or person selected to be public official
3. With intent to influence official act or induce violation of lawful duty

Elements of Acceptance of Bribe (§ 201(b)(2)):

1. Public official demands, seeks, receives, accepts, or agrees to receive anything of value
2. In return for being influenced in performance of official act
3. Or being induced to commit or omit any act in violation of official duty

Penalties:

- **Bribery:** Up to 15 years imprisonment

- **Fines:** Up to three times the monetary equivalent of the thing of value or $250,000, whichever is greater

- **Disqualification**: From holding federal office

- **Forfeiture:** Property involved in bribery offense

Public Official Definition:

- Federal employees and officers

- Members of Congress

- Federal judges

- Military personnel

- Persons acting for or on behalf of United States

- Jurors in federal proceedings

Thing of Value:

- Money and monetary instruments

- Property and services

- Employment opportunities

- Entertainment and travel

- Sexual favors

- Political contributions (in certain contexts)

Gratuity vs. Bribery:

- **Bribery (§ 201(b)):** Corrupt quid pro quo arrangement

- **Gratuity (§ 201(c)):** Payment for official act already taken (lesser penalties: up to 2 years)

Related Federal Offenses:

- Conspiracy (18 USC § 371)

- Mail Fraud (18 USC § 1341)

- Wire Fraud (18 USC § 1343)

- Money Laundering (18 USC § 1956)

- Tax Evasion (26 USC § 7201)

Federal Agencies Investigating Bribery:

- **FBI:** Public corruption investigations

- **IRS Criminal Investigation:** Financial aspects of corruption

- Offices of Inspector General: Agency-specific corruption

- **Ethics offices:** Administrative violations and referrals

International Bribery:

- **Foreign Corrupt Practices Act (15 USC § 78dd):** Bribing foreign officials

- **International Anti-Bribery and Fair Competition Act:** Treaty implementation

- **Money Laundering Control Act:** Laundering bribery proceeds

BURGLARY

Statutory Citation: 18 USC § 2111 (Special maritime and territorial jurisdiction)

Federal burglary involves unlawful entry into buildings or structures within federal jurisdiction with intent to commit a crime therein.

Elements:

1. Breaking and entering or entering without breaking
2. Building, structure, or other property within special maritime and territorial jurisdiction
3. With intent to commit crime therein
4. During nighttime (for enhanced penalties in some jurisdictions)

Penalties:

- **Maximum Imprisonment:** 10 years

- **Fines:** Up to $250,000

- **Enhanced penalties if dangerous weapon used**

- **Restitution:** For property damage and theft

Federal Jurisdiction (Special Maritime and Territorial):

- Military installations and bases

- National parks and forests

- Federal office buildings and courthouses

- Indian reservations (concurrent jurisdiction)

- Ships and aircraft

- Federal prisons and detention facilities

Related Federal Offenses:

- Breaking and Entering (18 USC § 2112)

- Theft of Government Property (18 USC § 641)

- Destruction of Federal Property (18 USC § 1361)

- Trespass on Federal Property (18 USC § 1382)

Degrees of Burglary:

Courts may consider various factors affecting severity:

- **First Degree:** Occupied dwelling at night with dangerous weapon

- **Second Degree:** Unoccupied building or daytime entry

- **Commercial Burglary:** Business premises and warehouses

- **Attempted Burglary:** Substantial step toward commission

Investigation:

- **Federal Protective Service:** Federal building security

- **Military Police:** Military installation burglaries

- **National Park Service:** Park and forest burglaries

- **FBI:** Major federal property crimes

BOMB THREATS

Statutory Citations: 18 USC § 844(e) (Explosives); 18 USC § 875(c) (Interstate communications)

Bomb threats involve false reports or warnings about explosive devices, creating public fear and disrupting normal activities even when no actual explosive exists.

Elements of False Bomb Report (18 USC § 844(e)):

1. Making false report concerning attempt or alleged attempt

2. To damage or destroy property by explosive

3. Report is false and defendant knows it is false

Elements of Interstate Threat (18 USC § 875(c)):

1. Transmission in interstate or foreign commerce

2. Communication containing threat to injure person of another

3. Includes bomb threats and similar violent threats

Penalties:

- **False Bomb Reports:** Up to 10 years imprisonment

- **Interstate Bomb Threats:** Up to 5 years imprisonment

- **Fines:** Up to $250,000 per count

- **Restitution:** Cost of emergency response and evacuation

Enhanced Penalties:

- **If during federal crime of terrorism:** Enhanced sentencing guidelines

- **If affects federal facility:** Additional charges under other statutes

- **If affects transportation:** Aviation, maritime, or surface transportation enhancements

Federal Jurisdiction:

- Interstate or international communications
- Federal facilities and property
- Transportation systems and infrastructure
- Mail and electronic communications

Emergency Response Costs:

- Bomb squad deployment
- Building evacuation
- Emergency services response
- Lost business and productivity
- Investigation and prosecution costs

Related Federal Offenses:

- Terrorism (18 USC § 2331)
- Hoax Devices (Various statutes)
- Extortion (18 USC § 875)
- False Information and Hoaxes (Various statutes)

BOOTLEGGING

Statutory Citations: 26 USC Chapter 51 (Liquor taxes); 18 USC § 1262 (Interstate transportation)

Modern bootlegging involves tax evasion on alcoholic beverages and illegal transportation of untaxed alcohol across state lines, continuing enforcement of federal alcohol taxation laws.

Elements of Tax Evasion on Spirits:

1. Distilling, importing, or bottling spirits
2. Without payment of required federal excise taxes
3. Intent to evade taxation
4. Willful violation of tax laws

Elements of Interstate Transportation (18 USC § 1262):

1. Transportation of distilled spirits in interstate commerce
2. In any manner other than provided by law
3. Knowing violation of federal alcohol laws

Penalties:

- **Tax Evasion:** Up to 5 years imprisonment per violation
- **Illegal Transportation:** Up to 1 year imprisonment
- **Criminal Forfeiture:** Vehicles and equipment used
- **Civil Penalties:** Multiple times the tax evaded

Modern Bootlegging Operations:

- **Moonshine Production:** Illegal distilleries avoiding taxation
- **Interstate Smuggling:** Moving alcohol to avoid state taxes
- **Counterfeit Alcohol:** Fake branded spirits
- **Internet Sales:** Unlicensed online alcohol sales

Federal Agencies:

- **ATF:** Primary enforcement agency for alcohol violations
- **IRS Criminal Investigation:** Tax evasion aspects
- **FBI:** Large-scale organized operations
- **Customs and Border Protection:** Import violations

Related Federal Offenses:

- Tax Evasion (26 USC § 7201)
- Conspiracy (18 USC § 371)
- Money Laundering (18 USC § 1956)
- RICO (18 USC § 1962)

BLACKMAIL

(See: Extortion)

Statutory Citation: 18 USC § 873 (Government employees); 18 USC § 875 (Interstate communications)

Federal blackmail laws criminalize obtaining money or property through threats to expose embarrassing, socially damaging, or legally compromising information about the victim.

Elements:

1. Threat to expose information about victim
2. Information would be embarrassing, damaging, or compromising
3. Demand for money, property, or other consideration
4. Use of interstate communications or federal jurisdiction

Penalties:

- **Basic Blackmail:** Up to 1 year imprisonment

- **Interstate Blackmail:** Up to 5 years imprisonment

- **Against Federal Employee:** Up to 1 year imprisonment

- **Fines:** Up to $250,000

Federal Jurisdiction:

- Use of mail, telephone, or internet

- Interstate or international communications

- Federal employees as victims

- Federal property or programs affected

Related Federal Offenses:

- Extortion (18 USC § 875-877)

- Mail Fraud (18 USC § 1341)

- Wire Fraud (18 USC § 1343)

- Cyberstalking (18 USC § 2261A)

BIOLOGICAL WEAPONS

Statutory Citation: 18 USC § 175 (Biological Weapons Anti-Terrorism Act)

Biological weapons offenses involve the development, production, stockpiling, or transfer of biological agents or toxins for use as weapons, threatening public health and national security.

Elements:

1. Development, production, stockpiling, acquisition, or retention of biological agent or toxin

2. Type and quantity not reasonably justified by prophylactic, protective, or peaceful purposes

3. Knowing violation of biological weapons prohibitions

Penalties:

- **Basic Violation:** Life imprisonment

- **If Death Results:** Death penalty or life imprisonment

- **Fines:** Up to $250,000

- **Criminal Forfeiture:** All biological agents and equipment

Prohibited Biological Agents:

- Anthrax and other bacterial agents

- Viral agents (smallpox, hemorrhagic fever viruses)

- Fungal agents and toxins
- Genetically modified organisms designed as weapons
- Any biological agent capable of causing death or serious injury

Exceptions:

- Medical research and treatment
- Vaccine development
- Defensive biological research
- Agricultural protection research
- Law enforcement training (limited quantities)

Related Federal Offenses:

- Terrorism (18 USC § 2331)
- Use of Weapons of Mass Destruction (18 USC § 2332a)
- Conspiracy (18 USC § 371)
- Export Control Violations

Investigative Agencies:

- **FBI:** Domestic biological terrorism investigations
- **CDC:** Public health response and investigation support
- **Department of Defense:** Military biological defense programs
- **Department of Agriculture:** Agricultural biological threats

C

CARJACKING

Statutory Citation: 18 USC § 2119

Carjacking involves taking a motor vehicle from another person by force, violence, or intimidation, with federal jurisdiction arising when the offense affects interstate commerce or involves vehicles that have traveled in interstate commerce.

Elements:

1. Taking motor vehicle that has been transported, shipped, or received in interstate or foreign commerce

2. From person or presence of another

3. By force, violence, or intimidation

4. With intent to cause death or serious bodily harm

Penalties:

- **Basic Carjacking:** Up to 15 years imprisonment
- **If Serious Bodily Injury Results:** Up to 25 years imprisonment
- **If Death Results:** Life imprisonment or death penalty
- **Fines:** Up to $250,000
- **Restitution:** Value of vehicle and related losses

Interstate Commerce Requirement:

Virtually all motor vehicles satisfy this requirement because:

- Vehicles manufactured in different states than where crime occurs
- Vehicles previously transported across state lines
- Components manufactured in multiple states
- Fuel and parts moved in interstate commerce

Aggravating Factors:

- Use of dangerous weapons (may trigger 18 USC § 924(c) charges)
- Multiple victims or vehicles
- Violence beyond that necessary to complete taking
- Use of stolen vehicle in other crimes
- Organized carjacking operations

Related Federal Offenses:

- **Auto Theft (18 USC § 2312):** Interstate transportation of stolen vehicles

- **Use of Firearm During Crime of Violence (18 USC § 924(c)):** Mandatory consecutive sentence

- **Robbery (18 USC § 1951):** Hobbs Act violations

- **Kidnapping (18 USC § 1201):** If victims transported

Investigative Approach:

- **FBI:** Major carjacking investigations and task forces

- **ATF:** Cases involving firearms

- **Local Law Enforcement:** Joint task forces and rapid response

- **Auto Theft Task Forces:** Multi-jurisdictional coordination

Sentencing Considerations:

- Criminal history and career offender status

- Role in offense (leader vs. follower)

- Use of violence beyond minimum necessary

- Impact on victims (physical and psychological trauma)

- Recovery of vehicle and restitution

CIVIL RIGHTS VIOLATIONS

Statutory Citations: 18 USC §§ 241-249 (Federal civil rights crimes)

Civil rights violations involve the willful deprivation of constitutional rights under color of law or through conspiracy, protecting fundamental freedoms guaranteed by the Constitution and federal law.

Elements of Conspiracy Against Rights (18 USC § 241):

1. Conspiracy of two or more persons

2. To injure, oppress, threaten, or intimidate any person

3. In free exercise or enjoyment of constitutional rights

4. On account of having exercised such rights

Elements of Deprivation Under Color of Law (18 USC § 242):

1. Acting under color of law, statute, ordinance, regulation, or custom

2. Willfully subjecting person to deprivation of constitutional rights

3. Different punishment, pains, or penalties because of color, race, religion, sex, handicap, familial status, or national origin

Penalties:

- **Basic Violations:** Up to 1 year imprisonment

- **If Bodily Injury Results:** Up to 10 years imprisonment

- **If Death Results:** Life imprisonment or death penalty

- **Hate Crime Enhancement:** Additional penalties under 18 USC § 249

Color of Law:

- Law enforcement officers

- Judges and court personnel

- Prison and jail officials

- Government employees and officials

- Private persons acting with government authority

Protected Activities:

- Voting and political participation

- Equal access to public accommodations

- Housing rights

- Employment opportunities

- Education access

- Religious exercise

Hate Crimes (18 USC § 249):

Elements:

1. Willfully causing bodily injury or attempting to cause bodily injury

2. Because of actual or perceived race, color, religion, national origin, gender, sexual orientation, gender identity, or disability

3. Use of dangerous weapon, fire, explosive, or interstate commerce

Enhanced Penalties for Hate Crimes:

- **Basic Hate Crime:** Up to 10 years imprisonment

- **If Death Results:** Life imprisonment

- **If Involves Kidnapping, Sexual Abuse, or Murder:** Life imprisonment or death penalty

Federal Agencies:

- **FBI Civil Rights Program:** Primary investigative unit

- **Department of Justice Civil Rights Division:** Prosecution coordination

- **U.S. Attorneys:** Local prosecution of civil rights crimes

- **Community Relations Service:** Conflict resolution and prevention

Related Federal Offenses:

- Conspiracy (18 USC § 371)
- Kidnapping (18 USC § 1201)
- Assault (18 USC § 113)
- Murder (18 USC § 1111)

COMPUTER FRAUD AND ABUSE

Statutory Citation: 18 USC § 1030 (Computer Fraud and Abuse Act)

Computer fraud and abuse encompasses unauthorized access to protected computers, data theft, system damage, and various cybercrimes affecting national security, financial institutions, and interstate commerce.

Elements of Unauthorized Access (18 USC § 1030(a)(2)):

1. Intentionally accessing computer without authorization or exceeding authorized access
2. Obtaining information from protected computer
3. Affecting interstate or foreign commerce

Elements of Computer Damage (18 USC § 1030(a)(5)(A)):

1. Knowingly causing transmission of program, information, code, or command
2. Intentionally causing damage without authorization to protected computer
3. Resulting in specified harm (loss, impairment, or threat to public safety)

Penalties:

- **First Offense:** Up to 5 years imprisonment (10 years for subsequent offenses)
- **If Damage Exceeds $5,000:** Up to 10 years imprisonment (20 years for subsequent offenses)
- **If Involves National Security Computer:** Up to 10 years imprisonment (20 years for subsequent offenses)
- **Fines:** Up to $250,000 per count

Protected Computer Definition:

- Computers used by financial institutions
- Computers used by or for U.S. government
- Computers affecting interstate or foreign commerce
- Computers located outside the United States (if affecting U.S. commerce)

Common Cybercrimes:

- **Hacking:** Unauthorized system access and data theft

- **Malware Distribution:** Viruses, worms, ransomware, and trojans
- **DDoS Attacks:** Distributed denial of service attacks
- **Identity Theft:** Stealing personal information from computer systems
- **Financial Fraud:** Online banking and credit card fraud

Damage Requirements:

- **Loss of $5,000 or more:** Investigation costs, response costs, lost revenue
- Modification or impairment of medical examination, diagnosis, or treatment
- Physical injury to any person
- Threat to public health or safety
- Damage affecting computer system of government entity

Enhanced Penalties:

- **Repeat Offenses:** Doubled maximum penalties
- **National Security Cases:** Enhanced sentences
- **Organized Cybercrime:** RICO predicates
- **International Cases:** Enhanced cooperation and extradition

Federal Agencies:

- **FBI Cyber Division:** Primary cybercrime investigative unit
- **Secret Service:** Financial cybercrime investigations
- **Homeland Security Investigations:** Cross-border cybercrime
- **Military Criminal Investigation Commands:** Military system attacks

Related Federal Offenses:

- Wire Fraud (18 USC § 1343)
- Identity Theft (18 USC § 1028)
- Money Laundering (18 USC § 1956)
- RICO (18 USC § 1962)

CONSPIRACY

Statutory Citation: 18 USC § 371 (General conspiracy statute)

Federal conspiracy involves an agreement between two or more persons to commit a federal crime, requiring proof of the agreement and an overt act in furtherance of the conspiracy.

Elements:

1. Agreement between two or more persons

2. To commit offense against United States or defraud United States

3. Overt act committed by one conspirator in furtherance of conspiracy

4. Intent to achieve unlawful objective

Penalties:

- **Maximum Imprisonment:** 5 years (unless target offense carries lesser penalty)
- **Fines:** Up to $250,000
- **If Target Offense is Misdemeanor:** Maximum penalty same as target offense
- **Enhanced Penalties:** Various statutes provide specific conspiracy penalties

Overt Act Requirement:

- Any act knowingly done to carry out or advance conspiracy
- Need not be criminal itself
- Can be preparatory or seemingly innocent act
- Only one overt act needed for entire conspiracy
- All conspirators liable for overt acts of co-conspirators

Specific Conspiracy Statutes:

- **Drug Conspiracy (21 USC § 846):** Same penalties as substantive drug offenses
- **RICO Conspiracy (18 USC § 1962(d)):** Up to 20 years imprisonment
- **Money Laundering Conspiracy (18 USC § 1956(h)):** Same as substantive offense
- **Terrorism Conspiracy:** Various enhanced penalties

Scope of Conspiracy:

- **Single Conspiracy:** One overall agreement with common objective
- **Multiple Conspiracies:** Separate agreements with different objectives
- **Chain Conspiracy:** Series of connected agreements
- **Wheel Conspiracy:** Central figure coordinating with multiple others

Withdrawal from Conspiracy:

- **Affirmative act:** Clear communication of intent to withdraw
- **Thwarting:** Taking action to defeat conspiracy's success
- **Notice:** Informing co-conspirators or law enforcement
- **Time Limit:** Must occur before commission of target offense

Advantages of Conspiracy Charges:

- Lower burden of proof than substantive offenses

- Hearsay exception for co-conspirator statements
- Venue in any district where conspiracy act occurred
- Joint trials of multiple defendants
- Longer statute of limitations

Co-conspirator Liability:

- **Pinkerton Doctrine:** Liable for reasonably foreseeable crimes by co-conspirators
- **Joint and Several:** All conspirators liable for conspiracy and target crimes
- **Acquittal of Others:** One conspirator can be convicted even if others acquitted

Related Concepts:

- Aiding and Abetting (18 USC § 2)
- Solicitation (Various statutes)
- Attempt (18 USC § 1113 and others)
- RICO (18 USC § 1962)

CONTEMPT OF COURT

Statutory Citations: 18 USC §§ 401-402 (Federal court contempt)

Contempt of court involves disobedience of court orders, disruption of court proceedings, or other conduct that interferes with the administration of justice in federal courts.

Elements of Criminal Contempt:

1. Willful disobedience of court order or process
2. In federal court proceeding
3. Conduct that obstructs administration of justice
4. Intent to disobey or disrespect court

Types of Contempt:

- **Direct Contempt:** Misbehavior in court's presence (disruption, violence, disrespect)
- **Indirect Contempt:** Disobedience outside court's presence (violating orders, failing to appear)
- **Civil Contempt:** Coercive to compel compliance with court order
- **Criminal Contempt:** Punitive for past misconduct

Penalties:

- **Summary Contempt:** Up to 6 months imprisonment without jury trial
- **Non-Summary Contempt:** No statutory limit, jury trial required for sentences over 6 months
- **Fines:** No statutory limit

- **Imprisonment:** Until compliance with court order (civil contempt)

Summary vs. Non-Summary Contempt:

- **Summary:** Immediate punishment for conduct in court's presence
- **Non-Summary:** Notice and hearing required, jury trial for serious penalties
- **Six-Month Rule:** Sentences over 6 months require jury trial

Common Contempt Situations:

- Violation of restraining orders or injunctions
- Failure to appear when subpoenaed
- Disruption of court proceedings
- Refusal to testify after grant of immunity
- Violation of court-imposed conditions of release

Defenses:

- Lack of knowledge of court order
- Impossibility of compliance
- Ambiguous court order
- Constitutional challenges to underlying order
- Good faith efforts to comply

Constitutional Considerations:

- **Due Process:** Notice and opportunity to be heard
- **Jury Trial:** Required for sentences exceeding 6 months
- **Double Jeopardy:** Criminal and civil contempt may both be imposed
- **Self-Incrimination:** Fifth Amendment protections apply

Related Federal Offenses:

- Obstruction of Justice (18 USC § 1503)
- Perjury (18 USC § 1621)
- Witness Tampering (18 USC § 1512)
- Escape (18 USC § 751)

CONTROLLED SUBSTANCES VIOLATIONS

Statutory Citations: 21 USC §§ 801-971 (Controlled Substances Act)

Federal drug crimes involve the manufacture, distribution, dispensing, or possession of controlled substances, with penalties varying based on drug type, quantity, and defendant's criminal history.

Elements of Drug Trafficking (21 USC § 841(a)(1)):

1. Knowingly or intentionally manufacturing, distributing, or dispensing controlled substance
2. Without authorization under the Controlled Substances Act
3. Substance listed in Schedules I-V

Elements of Drug Possession (21 USC § 844(a)):

1. Knowingly or intentionally possessing controlled substance
2. Without valid prescription or authorization
3. For personal use (simple possession)

Drug Schedules:

- **Schedule I:** High abuse potential, no accepted medical use (heroin, LSD, marijuana)
- **Schedule II:** High abuse potential, accepted medical use (cocaine, methamphetamine, oxycodone)
- **Schedule III:** Moderate abuse potential (anabolic steroids, ketamine)
- **Schedule IV:** Low abuse potential (Xanax, Ambien)
- **Schedule V:** Lowest abuse potential (cough medicines with codeine)

Trafficking Penalties (First Offense):

- **Marijuana:** 1,000+ kg (10 years to life), 100+ kg (5-40 years), <50 kg (up to 5 years)
- **Cocaine:** 5+ kg (10 years to life), 500g+ (5-40 years), <500g (up to 20 years)
- **Heroin:** 1+ kg (10 years to life), 100g+ (5-40 years), <100g (up to 20 years)
- **Methamphetamine:** 50g+ pure or 500g+ mixture (10 years to life)

Enhanced Penalties:

- **Prior Felony Drug Conviction:** Doubled penalties
- **Serious Bodily Injury or Death:** Enhanced sentences up to life
- **Continuing Criminal Enterprise (21 USC § 848):** 20 years to life
- **Use of Firearm (18 USC § 924(c)):** Mandatory consecutive sentence

Simple Possession Penalties (21 USC § 844):

- **First Offense:** Up to 1 year imprisonment, minimum $1,000 fine
- **Second Offense:** 15 days to 2 years imprisonment, minimum $2,500 fine
- **Third Offense:** 90 days to 3 years imprisonment, minimum $5,000 fine

Federal Drug Agencies:

- **Drug Enforcement Administration (DEA):** Primary federal drug enforcement
- **FBI:** Major drug trafficking organizations

- **Customs and Border Protection:** Border drug interdiction
- **Coast Guard:** Maritime drug enforcement

Drug Conspiracy (21 USC § 846):

- **Elements:** Agreement to violate drug laws plus overt act
- **Penalties:** Same as substantive trafficking offense
- **Advantages:** Easier to prove than completed trafficking

Forfeiture:

- **Criminal Forfeiture:** Property used in or derived from drug crimes
- **Civil Forfeiture:** In rem proceedings against property
- **Real Property:** Houses, land used for drug operations
- **Personal Property:** Vehicles, cash, equipment

Related Federal Offenses:

- Money Laundering (18 USC § 1956)
- Conspiracy (21 USC § 846)
- RICO (18 USC § 1962)
- Tax Evasion (26 USC § 7201)

COPYRIGHT INFRINGEMENT

Statutory Citation: 17 USC § 506 (Criminal copyright infringement)

Criminal copyright infringement involves willful violation of copyright laws for commercial advantage or private financial gain, or reproduction or distribution of copyrighted works with retail value exceeding statutory thresholds.

Elements:

1. Infringement of copyright
2. Willful violation
3. Either: (a) for commercial advantage or private financial gain, or

   (b) reproduction or distribution of copyrighted works with retail value over $1,000

Penalties (17 USC § 506, 18 USC § 2319):

- **First Offense:** Up to 5 years imprisonment
- **Subsequent Offense:** Up to 10 years imprisonment
- **Fines:** Up to $250,000 for individuals, $500,000 for organizations
- **Restitution:** Actual damages and lost profits

- **Criminal Forfeiture:** Infringing copies and equipment

Types of Criminal Copyright Infringement:

- **Commercial Piracy:** Large-scale reproduction for profit
- **Internet Piracy:** Online distribution of copyrighted works
- **Counterfeiting:** Manufacturing fake copyrighted products
- **Bootlegging:** Unauthorized recording and distribution
- **Software Piracy:** Illegal copying and distribution of computer programs

Enhanced Penalties:

- **Commercial Scale Infringement:** Reproduction or distribution of 10+ copies with retail value over $2,500 (up to 5 years)
- **Subsequent Offenses:** Doubled maximum penalties
- **Organized Crime:** RICO predicates for systematic infringement

Willfulness Requirement:

- Knowledge that conduct constitutes copyright infringement
- Intent to violate known legal duty
- Not required to know specific provisions of copyright law
- Good faith belief in right to use material may negate willfulness

Digital Millennium Copyright Act (DMCA):

- Safe harbor provisions for online service providers
- Notice and takedown procedures
- Anti-circumvention provisions for technological protection measures
- Criminal penalties for circumventing copy protection

Federal Agencies:

- **FBI:** Major copyright infringement investigations
- **Customs and Border Protection:** Importation of counterfeit goods
- **Immigration and Customs Enforcement:** Intellectual property crimes
- **U.S. Attorney Offices:** Prosecution coordination

Related Federal Offenses:

- Trafficking in Counterfeit Goods (18 USC § 2320)
- Wire Fraud (18 USC § 1343)
- Mail Fraud (18 USC § 1341)

- Money Laundering (18 USC § 1956)

- RICO (18 USC § 1962)

International Enforcement:

- Trade agreements with enhanced IP protection

- Mutual legal assistance treaties

- International copyright conventions

- Cross-border investigation coordination

COUNTERFEITING

Statutory Citations: 18 USC §§ 470-474 (Currency counterfeiting); 18 USC § 2320 (Trafficking in counterfeit goods)

Counterfeiting encompasses the production, possession, or distribution of fake currency, securities, and trademarked goods, threatening economic stability and consumer safety.

Elements of Currency Counterfeiting (18 USC § 471):

1. Falsely making, forging, counterfeiting, or altering any Federal Reserve note, national bank note, or other U.S. currency

2. With intent to defraud

3. Knowledge of falsity

Elements of Counterfeit Goods Trafficking (18 USC § 2320):

1. Trafficking in goods or services

2. Using counterfeit mark identical to or substantially indistinguishable from registered trademark

3. Use likely to cause confusion, mistake, or deception

4. Knowing or having reason to know mark is counterfeit

Currency Counterfeiting Penalties:

- **Manufacturing Counterfeit Currency:** Up to 20 years imprisonment

- **Passing Counterfeit Currency: Up to 20 years imprisonment**

- **Possessing Counterfeit Currency:** Up to 15 years imprisonment

- **Fines:** Up to $250,000

- **Criminal Forfeiture:** All counterfeit currency and equipment

Counterfeit Goods Penalties:

- **First Offense:** Up to 10 years imprisonment

- **Subsequent Offense:** Up to 20 years imprisonment

- **If Counterfeit Military Goods or Drugs:** Up to 20 years imprisonment

- **Fines:** Up to $2,000,000 for individuals, $5,000,000 for organizations

Protected Currency and Securities:

- Federal Reserve notes and coins
- Treasury notes and bonds
- Checks and money orders
- Postage stamps
- Revenue stamps
- Foreign currency (when affecting U.S. commerce)

Common Counterfeit Products:

- Designer clothing and accessories
- Electronics and computer software
- Pharmaceuticals and medical devices
- Automotive parts
- Toys and consumer goods
- Military equipment and supplies

Federal Agencies:

- **Secret Service:** Primary currency counterfeiting investigations
- **Immigration and Customs Enforcement:** Counterfeit goods investigations
- **FBI:** Major counterfeiting operations
- **Customs and Border Protection:** Border enforcement and seizures

Enhanced Penalties:

- **Organized Counterfeiting:** RICO predicates
- **Health and Safety Risks:** Enhanced sentences for dangerous products
- **Military Counterfeiting:** Additional penalties under military statutes
- **Repeat Offenses:** Career offender enhancements

Technology and Counterfeiting:

- Advanced printing and scanning technology
- Digital currency and cryptocurrency issues
- Online marketplaces and distribution
- International coordination and enforcement

Related Federal Offenses:

- Wire Fraud (18 USC § 1343)
- Mail Fraud (18 USC § 1341)
- Money Laundering (18 USC § 1956)
- Conspiracy (18 USC § 371)
- Import/Export Violations

CREDIT CARD FRAUD

Statutory Citation: 18 USC § 1029 (Access device fraud)

Credit card fraud involves unauthorized use of credit cards, debit cards, and other access devices to obtain money, goods, or services through fraudulent means.

Elements:

1. Knowingly using, producing, trafficking in, or possessing unauthorized access device
2. Affecting interstate or foreign commerce
3. With intent to defraud
4. Obtaining anything of value totaling $1,000 or more during one-year period

Penalties:

- **First Offense:** Up to 10 years imprisonment
- **Subsequent Offense:** Up to 15 years imprisonment
- **If Offense Affects Financial Institution:** Up to 20 years imprisonment
- **Fines:** Up to $250,000
- **Restitution:** Losses to victims and financial institutions

Access Device Definition:

- Credit cards and debit cards
- Account numbers and PINs
- Electronic serial numbers for mobile devices
- Computer passwords and access codes
- Any device used to obtain money, goods, or services

Common Credit Card Fraud Schemes:

- **Skimming:** Copying card data from magnetic strips
- **Account Takeover:** Unauthorized changes to existing accounts
- **Application Fraud:** Using false information to obtain credit cards

- **Mail Theft:** Stealing pre-approved credit card offers
- **Online Fraud:** Internet purchases with stolen card information

Enhanced Penalties:

- **Financial Institution Fraud:** Up to 20 years if bank or credit union affected
- **Organized Fraud:** RICO predicates for systematic operations
- **Identity Theft:** Additional charges under 18 USC § 1028A
- **International Fraud:** Enhanced cooperation and extradition

Federal Agencies:

- **Secret Service:** Primary credit card fraud investigations
- **FBI:** Major fraud operations and organized crime
- **Postal Inspection Service:** Mail-related credit card fraud
- **Immigration and Customs Enforcement:** Cross-border fraud

Aggregation of Losses:

- **One-Year Period:** All related fraudulent transactions
- **$1,000 Threshold:** Minimum loss for federal prosecution
- **Multiple Victims:** Combined losses from different victims
- **Attempted Fraud:** Included in loss calculations

Related Federal Offenses:

- Identity Theft (18 USC § 1028)
- Wire Fraud (18 USC § 1343)
- Mail Fraud (18 USC § 1341)
- Money Laundering (18 USC § 1956)
- Conspiracy (18 USC § 371)

Restitution and Recovery:

- Mandatory restitution to individual victims
- Financial institution losses
- Investigation and prosecution costs
- Credit monitoring and identity theft protection
- Lost time and inconvenience damages

D

DOMESTIC VIOLENCE (FEDERAL)

Statutory Citations: 18 USC §§ 2261-2266 (Interstate domestic violence and related crimes)

Federal domestic violence laws address intimate partner violence that crosses state lines or involves federal jurisdiction, providing protection when local remedies are insufficient or unavailable.

Elements of Interstate Domestic Violence (18 USC § 2261(a)(1)):

1. Travel in interstate or foreign commerce or within special maritime and territorial jurisdiction

2. With intent to kill, injure, harass, or intimidate spouse, intimate partner, or dating partner

3. In course of which defendant commits or attempts to commit crime of violence

Elements of Interstate Stalking (18 USC § 2261A):

1. Travel in interstate or foreign commerce or use of mail, internet, or other facility of interstate commerce

2. With intent to kill, injure, harass, intimidate, or place under surveillance with intent to kill, injure, harass, or intimidate

3. Another person and in course of such travel or use

Elements of Interstate Violation of Protection Order (18 USC § 2262):

1. Travel in interstate or foreign commerce

2. With intent to engage in conduct that violates portion of protection order that prohibits or provides protection against violence, threats, or harassment

3. Subsequently engaging in such conduct

Penalties:

- **Interstate Domestic Violence:** Up to 20 years imprisonment (life if death results)

- **Interstate Stalking:** Up to 5 years imprisonment (up to 10 years if bodily injury results, life if death results)

- **Violation of Protection Order:** Up to 5 years imprisonment (up to 20 years if bodily injury results, life if death results)

- **Fines:** Up to $250,000 per count

- **Restitution:** Medical expenses, counseling costs, lost income

Federal Firearms Restrictions (18 USC § 922(g)(8) & (9)):

- Persons subject to qualifying restraining orders prohibited from possessing firearms

- Persons convicted of misdemeanor domestic violence crimes prohibited from possessing firearms

- Enhanced penalties for firearm possession violations

Interstate Commerce Requirements:

- Physical travel across state lines
- Use of instrumentalities of interstate commerce (mail, telephone, internet)
- Conduct affecting interstate commerce
- Federal jurisdiction areas (military bases, federal property)

Protected Relationships:

- Current or former spouses
- Persons who share a child in common
- Current or former intimate partners
- Persons who have cohabited as spouses
- Dating relationships (as defined by state law)

Federal Agencies:

- **FBI:** Major interstate domestic violence investigations
- **U.S. Marshals Service:** Fugitive apprehension and witness protection
- **ATF:** Firearms-related domestic violence cases
- **Victim Services:** Federal victim assistance programs

Related Federal Offenses:

- Kidnapping (18 USC § 1201)
- Assault (18 USC § 113)
- Threats (18 USC § 875)
- Firearms Violations (18 USC § 922)
- Cyberstalking (18 USC § 2261A)

Enhanced Penalties:

- **Use of Dangerous Weapon:** Enhanced sentencing guidelines
- **Repeat Offenses:** Career offender status possible
- **Violation During Pretrial Release:** Additional charges
- **Death Results:** Life imprisonment or death penalty

Victim Protection Measures:

- Federal witness protection programs
- Victim relocation assistance
- Restraining orders in federal court

- Confidentiality protections
- Victim impact statements at sentencing

DRUG TRAFFICKING

Statutory Citations: 21 USC § 841 (Prohibited acts); 21 USC § 846 (Attempt and conspiracy)

Drug trafficking involves the manufacture, distribution, dispensing, or possession with intent to distribute controlled substances, representing one of the most frequently prosecuted categories of federal crimes.

Elements of Drug Trafficking (21 USC § 841(a)(1)):

1. Knowingly or intentionally manufacturing, distributing, dispensing, or possessing with intent to distribute
2. Controlled substance listed in Schedules I through V
3. Without authorization under the Controlled Substances Act

Elements of Drug Conspiracy (21 USC § 846):

1. Agreement between two or more persons to commit drug trafficking offense
2. Knowledge of conspiracy's unlawful purpose
3. Voluntary participation in conspiracy
4. Overt act in furtherance of conspiracy (required in some circuits)

Mandatory Minimum Penalties:

Cocaine:

- 500g-4.999kg: 5-40 years (10 years to life for second offense)
- 5kg or more: 10 years to life (20 years to life for second offense)

Crack Cocaine:

- 28-279g: 5-40 years (10 years to life for second offense)
- 280g or more: 10 years to life (20 years to life for second offense)

Heroin:

- 100g-999g: 5-40 years (10 years to life for second offense)
- 1kg or more: 10 years to life (20 years to life for second offense)

Methamphetamine:

- 5g-49g pure or 50g-499g mixture: 5-40 years (10 years to life for second offense)
- 50g+ pure or 500g+ mixture: 10 years to life (20 years to life for second offense)

Marijuana:

- 100kg-999kg or 100-999 plants: 5-40 years (10 years to life for second offense)

- 1,000kg+ or 1,000+ plants: 10 years to life (20 years to life for second offense)

Fentanyl:

- 40g-399g: 5-40 years (10 years to life for second offense)
- 400g or more: 10 years to life (20 years to life for second offense)

Enhanced Penalties:

- **Death or Serious Bodily Injury:** 20 years to life imprisonment
- **Prior Felony Drug Conviction:** Doubled penalties
- **Continuing Criminal Enterprise (21 USC § 848):** 20 years to life, $2 million fine
- **Use of Firearm (18 USC § 924(c)):** Mandatory consecutive sentence

Factors Affecting Sentences:

- Drug type and quantity
- Defendant's role in offense (leader, organizer, manager, supervisor)
- Use of violence or weapons
- Criminal history and prior drug convictions
- Cooperation with law enforcement

Federal Drug Agencies:

- **Drug Enforcement Administration (DEA):** Primary federal drug enforcement
- **FBI:** Major drug trafficking organizations and violent drug crimes
- **Customs and Border Protection:** Border drug interdiction
- **Coast Guard:** Maritime drug enforcement
- **Immigration and Customs Enforcement**: Immigration-related drug crimes

Drug Trafficking Organizations:

- **Cartels:** International drug smuggling organizations
- **Street Gangs:** Local distribution networks
- **Prescription Drug Rings:** Illegal pharmaceutical distribution
- **Internet Operations:** Dark web and online drug sales

Asset Forfeiture:

- **Criminal Forfeiture:** Property used in or derived from drug crimes
- **Civil Forfeiture:** Administrative and judicial in rem proceedings
- **Real Property:** Drug houses, laboratories, storage facilities
- **Personal Property:** Vehicles, aircraft, vessels, cash, equipment

Related Federal Offenses:

- Money Laundering (18 USC § 1956)
- Continuing Criminal Enterprise (21 USC § 848)
- RICO (18 USC § 1962)
- Firearms Violations (18 USC § 924(c))
- Immigration Violations (8 USC § 1326)

International Aspects:

- **Extradition Treaties:** International cooperation in drug cases
- **Foreign Narcotics Kingpin Designation Act:** Sanctions against major traffickers
- **Maritime Drug Law Enforcement Act:** Prosecution of vessels in international waters
- **Cross-Border Investigations:** Joint task forces and intelligence sharing

DRUNK DRIVING (FEDERAL JURISDICTION)

Statutory Citations: 18 USC § 13 (Assimilative Crimes Act); Various federal property-specific statutes

Federal drunk driving prosecutions occur when impaired driving takes place on federal property or within special maritime and territorial jurisdiction, incorporating state DUI laws through the Assimilative Crimes Act.

Elements (Through Assimilative Crimes Act):

1. Operating motor vehicle on federal property
2. While under influence of alcohol or controlled substances
3. Blood alcohol content above legal limit (typically 0.08%)
4. Within special maritime and territorial jurisdiction

Federal Property Locations:

- Military installations and bases
- National parks and forests
- Federal office buildings and courthouses
- Indian reservations (concurrent jurisdiction)
- Veterans Affairs medical centers
- Federal prisons and detention facilities

Penalties:

- **First Offense:** Typically up to 6 months imprisonment, fines up to $5,000
- **Subsequent Offenses:** Enhanced penalties based on applicable state law

- **Aggravated DUI:** Enhanced penalties for high BAC, accidents, or injuries
- **License Suspension:** Administrative penalties and federal driving privilege revocation

Enhanced Federal Penalties:

- **Causing Death or Serious Injury:** Vehicular homicide or assault charges
- **Military Personnel:** Additional court-martial proceedings
- **Commercial Drivers:** Enhanced penalties and license disqualification
- **Federal Employees:** Administrative discipline and security clearance issues

Special Considerations:

- **National Park Service:** Special regulations for park roads and facilities
- **Military Bases:** Military police and federal law enforcement coordination
- **Indian Country:** Complex jurisdictional issues with tribal courts
- **Border Areas:** Customs and immigration enforcement coordination

Federal Agencies:

- **National Park Service:** DUI enforcement in national parks
- **Federal Protective Service:** Federal building and facility enforcement
- **Military Police:** Installation DUI enforcement
- **U.S. Park Police:** Washington DC area federal property

Related Federal Offenses:

- Assault (18 USC § 113) - If injury occurs
- Vehicular Homicide (18 USC § 1112) - If death results
- Destruction of Federal Property (18 USC § 1361) - Property damage
- Firearms Violations - If weapons present during arrest

Administrative Consequences:

- **Federal Employment:** Discipline and potential termination
- **Security Clearances:** Revocation or suspension of clearances
- **Professional Licenses:** Reporting requirements and discipline
- **Military Service:** Court-martial and administrative separation

DOCUMENT FRAUD

Statutory Citations: 18 USC § 1028 (Identity documents); 18 USC § 1341 (Mail fraud); 18 USC § 1343 (Wire fraud)

Document fraud involves the creation, alteration, or use of false identity documents, government credentials, and other official papers to commit fraud or facilitate other crimes.

Elements of Identity Document Fraud (18 USC § 1028(a)):

1. Knowingly producing, transferring, possessing, or using false identification document or authentication feature

2. Without lawful authority

3. With intent to defraud the United States

Elements of False Personation (18 USC § 912):

1. Falsely assuming or pretending to be officer or employee of United States

2. Acting as such officer or employee

3. In any matter within jurisdiction of United States

Penalties:

- **Identity Document Fraud:** Up to 15 years imprisonment (25 years if terrorism-related)
- **False Personation:** Up to 3 years imprisonment
- **Enhanced Penalties:** If used to facilitate drug trafficking or violent crimes
- **Fines:** Up to $250,000 per count
- **Restitution:** Costs of document replacement and investigation

Types of Document Fraud:

- **Identity Documents:** Driver's licenses, passports, social security cards
- **Immigration Documents:** Visas, green cards, work authorization
- **Government Credentials:** Federal employee IDs, security badges
- **Financial Documents:** Bank statements, tax returns, loan applications
- **Academic Credentials:** Diplomas, transcripts, professional licenses

Authentication Features:

- Watermarks and security paper
- Holograms and special inks
- RFID chips and biometric data
- Digital signatures and encryption
- Special fonts and printing techniques

Federal Agencies:

- **Secret Service**: Document fraud and counterfeiting investigations
- Immigration and Customs Enforcement: Immigration document fraud

- **State Department:** Passport and visa fraud
- **Social Security Administration:** Social security number fraud

Enhanced Penalties:

- **Terrorism-Related:** Up to 25 years imprisonment
- **Immigration Violations:** Deportation and bars to reentry
- **Organized Document Mills:** RICO predicates
- **Facilitating Other Crimes:** Enhanced sentences

Related Federal Offenses:

- Identity Theft (18 USC § 1028A)
- Mail Fraud (18 USC § 1341)
- Wire Fraud (18 USC § 1343)
- Conspiracy (18 USC § 371)
- Immigration Violations (8 USC § 1324c)

International Aspects:

- Cross-border document trafficking
- International organized crime connections
- Diplomatic security and consular fraud
- Mutual legal assistance in investigations

DESTRUCTION OF FEDERAL PROPERTY

Statutory Citation: 18 USC § 1361

Destruction of federal property involves willful injury or depredation of government property, equipment, or facilities, protecting taxpayer investments and government operations.

Elements:

1. Willfully injuring or committing depredation against property of United States
2. Property belonging to or in custody of United States
3. Intent to damage or destroy property

Penalties:

- **Basic Offense:** Up to 10 years imprisonment
- **If Damage Exceeds $1,000:** Enhanced penalties apply
- **Fines:** Up to $250,000 for individuals, $500,000 for organizations
- **Restitution:** Full cost of repair or replacement

Federal Property Includes:

- Federal office buildings and courthouses
- Military equipment and installations
- National park facilities and resources
- Post offices and mail processing facilities
- Federal vehicles, aircraft, and vessels
- Computer systems and telecommunications equipment

Enhanced Penalties:

- **National Defense Materials:** Up to 20 years imprisonment
- **If Death Results:** Life imprisonment or death penalty
- **Terrorism-Related:** Enhanced sentencing guidelines
- **Organized Destruction:** RICO predicates

Types of Property Destruction:

- **Vandalism:** Graffiti, broken windows, damaged equipment
- **Sabotage:** Intentional interference with government operations
- **Arson:** Fire damage to federal buildings or property
- **Computer Crimes:** Damage to federal computer systems
- **Environmental Crimes:** Damage to natural resources

Federal Agencies:

- **Federal Protective Service:** Protection of federal facilities
- **National Park Service:** Protection of park resources
- Military Police: Protection of military property
- FBI: Major property destruction investigations

Related Federal Offenses:

- Arson (18 USC § 844)
- Computer Fraud (18 USC § 1030)
- Terrorism (18 USC § 2331)
- Conspiracy (18 USC § 371)
- Trespass (18 USC § 1382)

Defenses:

- Lack of intent to damage property

- Accident or negligence (not willful)
- Property not belonging to United States
- Authorization to access or modify property
- Necessity or emergency circumstances

DRUG MANUFACTURING

Statutory Citation: 21 USC § 841(a)(1) (Manufacturing controlled substances)

Drug manufacturing involves the production, preparation, propagation, or processing of controlled substances, including operating clandestine laboratories and growing operations.

Elements:

1. Knowingly or intentionally manufacturing controlled substance
2. Substance listed in Schedules I through V
3. Without registration or authorization under Controlled Substances Act

Penalties:

- **Marijuana Manufacturing:** 100-999 plants (5-40 years), 1,000+ plants (10 years to life)
- **Methamphetamine Manufacturing:** Same penalties as trafficking based on quantity produced
- **Fentanyl Manufacturing:** Severe penalties due to lethality and public health impact
- **Enhanced Penalties:** If manufacturing occurs near schools or involves minors

Types of Manufacturing Operations:

- **Methamphetamine Laboratories:** Small-scale and super labs
- **Marijuana Cultivation:** Indoor and outdoor growing operations
- **Fentanyl Production:** Illegal synthesis of synthetic opioids
- **MDMA/Ecstasy Manufacturing:** Club drug production
- **Pharmaceutical Diversion:** Illegal pill mills and prescription fraud

Clandestine Laboratory Hazards:

- **Chemical Exposure:** Toxic and corrosive substances
- **Fire and Explosion Risk:** Volatile chemicals and processes
- **Environmental Contamination:** Soil and groundwater pollution
- **Public Health Threats:** Toxic fumes and chemical waste

Enhanced Penalties:

- **Involving Minors:** Enhanced sentences for using children in operations
- **Near Schools:** Enhanced penalties for manufacturing within 1,000 feet of schools

- **Environmental Damage:** Additional penalties for hazardous waste violations
- **Weapons Present:** Firearms enhancements under 18 USC § 924(c)

Federal Agencies:

- **Drug Enforcement Administration (DEA):** Primary enforcement agency
- **Environmental Protection Agency:** Hazardous waste cleanup
- **Occupational Safety and Health Administration:** Workplace safety violations
- **Local Hazmat Teams:** Emergency response and cleanup

Chemical Precursor Controls:

- **List I Chemicals:** Essential chemicals for drug manufacturing
- **List II Chemicals:** Important precursor chemicals
- **Registration Requirements:** Businesses handling precursor chemicals
- **Reporting Obligations:** Suspicious transactions and thefts

Related Federal Offenses:

- Drug Trafficking (21 USC § 841)
- Conspiracy (21 USC § 846)
- Money Laundering (18 USC § 1956)
- Environmental Crimes (42 USC § 6928)
- Firearms Violations (18 USC § 924(c))

International Aspects:

- **Precursor Chemical Trafficking:** International smuggling operations
- **Foreign Manufacturing:** Overseas production for U.S. distribution
- **Border Enforcement:** Interdiction of manufacturing equipment
- **International Cooperation:** Joint investigations and intelligence sharing

DEPORTATION (CRIMINAL VIOLATIONS)

Statutory Citations: 8 USC § 1326 (Illegal reentry); 8 USC § 1325 (Improper entry)

Criminal deportation violations involve illegal entry or reentry into the United States by individuals who have been previously removed or are otherwise inadmissible.

Elements of Illegal Reentry (8 USC § 1326(a)):

1. Previously removed from United States
2. Subsequently found in United States
3. Without consent of Attorney General

Elements of Improper Entry (8 USC § 1325(a)):

1. Entry into United States at any time or place other than designated by immigration officers
2. Eluding examination or inspection by immigration officers
3. Obtaining entry by false or misleading representation

Penalties:

- **Illegal Reentry (Basic):** Up to 2 years imprisonment
- **Prior Felony Conviction:** Up to 10 years imprisonment
- **Prior Aggravated Felony:** Up to 20 years imprisonment
- **Improper Entry:** Up to 6 months imprisonment (first offense), up to 2 years (subsequent offenses)
- **Fines:** Up to $250,000

Aggravated Felony Enhancement:

Illegal reentry carries enhanced penalties if defendant was previously deported after:

- Drug trafficking offenses
- Crimes of violence with sentence of at least one year
- Firearms trafficking
- Money laundering offenses
- Certain fraud and tax evasion offenses

Federal Agencies:

- **Immigration and Customs Enforcement (ICE):** Primary enforcement agency
- **Customs and Border Protection (CBP):** Border apprehension and processing
- **U.S. Attorneys:** Criminal prosecution
- **Executive Office for Immigration Review:** Immigration court proceedings

Defenses:

- **Collateral Attack:** Challenging validity of prior removal order
- **Due Process Violations:** Procedural defects in removal proceedings
- **Mistaken Identity:** Challenging identity of person removed
- **Consent to Reentry:** Authorization from immigration authorities

Administrative vs. Criminal Consequences:

- **Administrative:** Removal proceedings and deportation
- **Criminal:** Imprisonment, fines, and criminal record
- **Combined:** Criminal prosecution followed by removal proceedings

- **Detention:** Mandatory detention during criminal proceedings

Related Federal Offenses:

- Document Fraud (18 USC § 1028)
- Alien Smuggling (8 USC § 1324)
- Identity Theft (18 USC § 1028A)
- Drug Trafficking (21 USC § 841)
- Firearms Violations (18 USC § 922(g))

Sentencing Considerations:

- Length of time in United States
- Family ties and community connections
- Employment history and rehabilitation
- Criminal history and public safety concerns
- Cooperation with law enforcement

E

EMBEZZLEMENT

Statutory Citation: 18 USC Section 641 (Public money, property or records); 18 USC Section 656 (Bank funds)

Federal embezzlement involves the fraudulent appropriation of money, property, or assets by a person in a position of trust, particularly when involving government funds or federally insured financial institutions.

Elements of Public Money Embezzlement (18 USC Section 641):

1. Embezzling, stealing, purloining, or knowingly converting to personal use
2. Money, property, or records belonging to United States
3. By person having custody or control thereof
4. Value exceeding $1,000 for felony prosecution

Elements of Bank Embezzlement (18 USC Section 656):

1. Embezzling, abstracting, purloining, or willfully misapplying funds
2. Of bank insured by FDIC or other federal agency
3. By officer, director, agent, or employee thereof
4. Intent to injure or defraud bank or obtain money unlawfully

Penalties:

Public Money Embezzlement: Up to 10 years imprisonment if value exceeds $1,000

Bank Embezzlement: Up to 30 years imprisonment and $1,000,000 fine

Fines: Up to $250,000 for individuals, $500,000 for organizations

Restitution: Mandatory restitution to victims

Types of Federal Embezzlement:

Government Employee Theft: Misappropriation of federal funds or property

Bank Embezzlement: Theft by bank officers, employees, or agents

Military Property Theft: Misappropriation of military equipment or funds

Postal Service Theft: Embezzlement of mail or postal funds

Grant Fraud: Misuse of federal grant money by recipients

Federal Agencies:

FBI: Primary investigative agency for federal embezzlement

Treasury Inspector General: Government financial crimes

FDIC Office of Inspector General: Bank embezzlement cases

Military Criminal Investigation Commands: Military embezzlement

Postal Inspection Service: Postal-related embezzlement

Enhanced Penalties:

Organized Embezzlement: RICO predicates for systematic theft

Fiduciary Breach: Enhanced sentences for violation of trust

Large Scale Theft: Enhanced penalties based on loss amount

Repeat Offenses: Career offender enhancements

Related Federal Offenses:

Mail Fraud (18 USC Section 1341)

Wire Fraud (18 USC Section 1343)

Money Laundering (18 USC Section 1956)

Tax Evasion (26 USC Section 7201)

Conspiracy (18 USC Section 371)

Civil Consequences:

Employment termination and professional license revocation

Debarment from government contracting

Civil liability for treble damages

Administrative penalties and sanctions

ENVIRONMENTAL CRIMES

Statutory Citations: 33 USC Section 1319 (Clean Water Act); 42 USC Section 6928 (Resource Conservation and Recovery Act)

Environmental crimes involve knowing violations of federal environmental protection laws that threaten public health, safety, and natural resources.

Elements of Clean Water Act Violations (33 USC Section 1319(c)):

1. Knowingly violating permit conditions or effluent standards
2. Discharging pollutants into waters of United States
3. Without required permit or in violation of permit terms
4. Knowledge of violation or endangerment

Elements of Hazardous Waste Violations (42 USC Section 6928(d)):

1. Knowingly transporting, treating, storing, or disposing of hazardous waste
2. Without permit or in violation of permit

3. To facility not having permit for such treatment, storage, or disposal

4. Knowledge that facility lacks permit

Penalties:

Clean Water Act: Up to 3 years imprisonment (first offense), up to 6 years (subsequent offenses)

Knowing Endangerment: Up to 15 years imprisonment and $250,000 fine

Hazardous Waste Crimes: Up to 5 years imprisonment per violation

Organizations: Fines up to $50,000 per day of violation

Types of Environmental Crimes:

Water Pollution: Illegal discharge of pollutants into waterways

Hazardous Waste Disposal: Improper handling of dangerous materials

Air Pollution: Violations of Clean Air Act emission standards

Pesticide Violations: Illegal use or distribution of restricted pesticides

Wildlife Crimes: Violations of Endangered Species Act

Federal Agencies:

Environmental Protection Agency Criminal Investigation Division: Primary enforcement

FBI: Major environmental crime investigations

Coast Guard: Maritime pollution enforcement

Fish and Wildlife Service: Wildlife crime investigations

National Park Service: Crimes in national parks

Knowing Endangerment Standard:

Requires proof that defendant knew conduct placed another person in imminent danger of death or serious bodily injury

Enhanced penalties reflect serious threat to public health

Corporate officers can be held individually liable

Actual harm need not occur

Related Federal Offenses:

Conspiracy (18 USC Section 371)

Mail Fraud (18 USC Section 1341)

Wire Fraud (18 USC Section 1343)

False Statements (18 USC Section 1001)

Obstruction of Justice (18 USC Section 1503)

Corporate Liability:

Organizations can be prosecuted for environmental crimes

Responsible corporate officer doctrine applies

Due diligence and compliance programs may mitigate penalties

Environmental audits and self-disclosure programs available

ESPIONAGE

Statutory Citations: 18 USC Sections 792-798 (Espionage Act)

Espionage involves gathering, transmitting, or losing national defense information with intent to harm the United States or aid foreign nations, representing one of the most serious threats to national security.

Elements of Gathering Defense Information (18 USC Section 793(a)):

1. Obtaining information respecting national defense
2. With intent or reason to believe information will be used to injury of United States or advantage of foreign nation
3. Communicating, delivering, or transmitting such information to unauthorized persons

Elements of Transmitting Defense Information (18 USC Section 794(a)):

1. Intent to communicate defense information to foreign government
2. Actually communicating such information
3. Information relating to national defense of United States

Penalties:

Peacetime Espionage: Up to 10 years imprisonment

Wartime Espionage: Death penalty or life imprisonment

Conspiracy to Commit Espionage: Same penalties as substantive offense

Fines: Up to $250,000 for individuals

National Defense Information:

Military plans, weapons systems, and troop movements

Intelligence sources and methods

Classified government documents and communications

Nuclear weapons design and technology

Satellite and surveillance capabilities

Types of Espionage:

Classic Espionage: Traditional spy operations with foreign intelligence services

Economic Espionage: Theft of trade secrets for foreign governments

Cyber Espionage: Computer-based intelligence gathering

Military Espionage: Targeting defense and military information

Industrial Espionage: Corporate secrets for foreign competitors

Federal Agencies:

FBI Counterintelligence Division: Primary domestic espionage investigations

CIA: Foreign intelligence and counterintelligence operations

National Security Agency: Signals intelligence and cybersecurity

Defense Counterintelligence and **Security Agency:** Military counterintelligence

Department of Homeland Security: Critical infrastructure protection

Intent Requirements:

Specific intent to harm United States or aid foreign nation

Reason to believe information would be used to injury of United States

Actual knowledge not required if circumstances indicate intent

Motive may be ideological, financial, or personal

Related Federal Offenses:

Treason (18 USC Section 2381)

Sabotage (18 USC Section 2155)

Sedition (18 USC Section 2384)

Foreign Agent Registration Act Violations (22 USC Section 611)

Export Control Violations

International Aspects:

Diplomatic immunity considerations

Extradition treaties and international law

Foreign intelligence service operations

International cooperation in counterintelligence

EXTORTION

Statutory Citations: 18 USC Section 875 (Interstate communications); 18 USC Section 1951 (Hobbs Act)

Extortion involves obtaining money or property from another through wrongful use of actual or threatened force, violence, or fear, including threats made through interstate communications.

Elements of Interstate Extortion (18 USC Section 875(d)):

1. Transmission in interstate or foreign commerce
2. Communication containing demand or request for money or other thing of value
3. Threat to injure property or reputation of addressee or another
4. Intent to extort money or thing of value

Elements of Hobbs Act Extortion (18 USC Section 1951(b)(2)):

1. Obtaining property of another
2. With consent induced by wrongful use of actual or threatened force, violence, or fear
3. Affecting interstate or foreign commerce

Penalties:

Interstate Extortion: Up to 20 years imprisonment

Hobbs Act Extortion: Up to 20 years imprisonment

If Death Results: Life imprisonment or death penalty

Fines: Up to $250,000 for individuals

Types of Extortion:

Blackmail: Threats to expose embarrassing or damaging information

Economic Extortion: Threats to harm business or economic interests

Physical Extortion: Threats of violence or bodily harm

Political Extortion: Threats related to political activities or positions

Cyber Extortion: Online threats and ransomware attacks

Interstate Commerce Requirement:

Use of mail, telephone, internet, or other communication across state lines

Extortion of businesses engaged in interstate commerce

Movement of extorted property across state lines

Effect on interstate commerce

Federal Agencies:

FBI: Primary extortion investigations

Secret Service: Cases involving financial crimes

Postal Inspection Service: Mail-related extortion

Immigration and Customs Enforcement: Cross-border extortion

Related Federal Offenses:

Kidnapping (18 USC Section 1201)

Mail Fraud (18 USC Section 1341)

Wire Fraud (18 USC Section 1343)

RICO (18 USC Section 1962)

Cyberstalking (18 USC Section 2261A)

Defenses:

Lack of intent to extort

No threat made or threat not credible

Legitimate collection of debt

First Amendment protected speech

Entrapment by law enforcement

Enhanced Penalties:

Use of firearms during extortion (18 USC Section 924(c))

Organized extortion schemes (RICO predicates)

Public official extortion (enhanced sentences)

Repeat offenses (career criminal enhancements)

ELECTION FRAUD

Statutory Citations: 52 USC Section 10307 (Voting Rights Act); 18 USC Section 594 (Intimidation of voters)

Federal election fraud involves violations of laws protecting the integrity of federal elections, including vote buying, voter intimidation, and registration fraud.

Elements of Vote Buying (18 USC Section 597):

1. Making expenditure to any person
2. To vote or withhold vote
3. To vote for or against any candidate
4. In election for federal office

Elements of Voter Intimidation (18 USC Section 594):

1. Intimidating, threatening, coercing, or attempting to intimidate, threaten, or coerce
2. Any other person for purpose of interfering with right to vote
3. By force or threat of force
4. In federal election

Penalties:

Vote Buying: Up to 1 year imprisonment and $1,000 fine

Voter Intimidation: Up to 1 year imprisonment

Multiple State Registration: Up to 5 years imprisonment

Fines: Up to $10,000 for certain violations

Types of Election Fraud:

Registration Fraud: False voter registration information

Vote Buying: Payment for votes or voter influence

Ballot Harvesting: Illegal collection and submission of ballots

Voter Impersonation: Voting under false identity

Election Official Corruption: Bribery or coercion of election workers

Federal Agencies:

FBI: Primary federal election crime investigations

Department of Justice Public Integrity Section: Prosecution coordination

Election Assistance Commission: Election security assistance

Department of Homeland Security: Election infrastructure protection

Civil Rights Violations:

Voting Rights Act violations

Denial of equal protection in voting

Discrimination based on race, color, or language minority status

Accessibility violations for disabled voters

Related Federal Offenses:

Civil Rights Violations (18 USC Section 241)

Mail Fraud (18 USC Section 1341)

Wire Fraud (18 USC Section 1343)

Conspiracy (18 USC Section 371)

False Statements (18 USC Section 1001)

Enforcement Challenges:

Coordination between federal and state authorities

Timing considerations during election periods

First Amendment speech protections

Distinguishing between legitimate political activity and fraud

ESCAPE

Statutory Citation: 18 USC Section 751

Federal escape involves unlawfully departing from federal custody or confinement, including escape from federal prisons, jails, and other detention facilities.

Elements:

1. Escape from custody of Attorney General or authorized representative
2. Person committed to custody under process issued under laws of United States
3. Voluntary departure from lawful custody
4. Without permission or legal authority

Penalties:

Basic Escape: Up to 5 years imprisonment

If Force or Violence Used: Up to 10 years imprisonment

If Life Sentence Being Served: Up to 10 years imprisonment

Consecutive Sentence: Escape sentence runs consecutive to original sentence

Types of Federal Escape:

Prison Escape: Departure from federal correctional institutions

Jail Escape: Escape from federal detention facilities

Transport Escape: Escape during prisoner transportation

Court Escape: Escape from federal courthouses or proceedings

Hospital Escape: Escape from medical facilities while in custody

Federal Agencies:

U.S. Marshals Service: Primary fugitive apprehension agency

Federal Bureau of Prisons: Prison security and escape prevention

FBI: Major escape investigations

Local Law Enforcement: Coordination and assistance

Enhanced Penalties:

Use of violence or weapons during escape

Injury to persons during escape

Damage to property during escape

Organized escape attempts involving multiple prisoners

Related Federal Offenses:

Assault on Federal Officers (18 USC Section 111)

Destruction of Federal Property (18 USC Section 1361)

Hostage Taking (18 USC Section 1203)

Conspiracy (18 USC Section 371)

Defenses:

Duress or coercion by other inmates

Intolerable prison conditions (limited defense)

Lack of intent to permanently escape

Voluntary return to custody

Aiding Escape (18 USC Section 752):

Elements: Aiding prisoner in custody of Attorney General to escape

Penalties: Up to 5 years imprisonment

Includes providing assistance, tools, or information

Enhanced penalties for use of force or violence

EXPORT CONTROL VIOLATIONS

Statutory Citations: 50 USC Sections 4801-4852 (Export Control Reform Act); 22 USC Section 2778 (Arms Export Control Act)

Export control violations involve unauthorized export of controlled commodities, technology, or defense articles that could threaten national security or foreign policy interests.

Elements of Export Administration Regulations Violations:

1. Export, reexport, or transfer of controlled item
2. Without required license or authorization
3. To prohibited destinations or end users
4. Knowledge of violation of export regulations

Elements of Arms Export Control Act Violations:

1. Export or attempt to export defense articles or services
2. Without required State Department license
3. Knowing violation of International Traffic in Arms Regulations
4. Items on United States Munitions List

Penalties:

Export Administration Act: Up to 20 years imprisonment

Arms Export Control Act: Up to 20 years imprisonment

Civil Penalties: Up to $300,000 per violation

Criminal Forfeiture: All items involved in violation

Controlled Items:

Dual-Use Technology: Items with both civilian and military applications

Defense Articles: Weapons, military equipment, and related technology

Nuclear Technology: Equipment and materials for nuclear weapons

Encryption Software: Advanced cryptographic technology

Sensitive Technologies: Items affecting national security

Federal Agencies:

Bureau of Industry and Security: Export Administration Regulations enforcement

State Department Directorate of Defense Trade Controls: Arms export licensing

FBI: Criminal investigations of export violations

Immigration and Customs **Enforcement:** Border enforcement

Customs and Border Protection: Export documentation verification

Related Federal Offenses:

Conspiracy (18 USC Section 371)

Smuggling (18 USC Section 554)

Money Laundering (18 USC Section 1956)

False Statements (18 USC Section 1001)

Wire Fraud (18 USC Section 1343)

International Implications:

Multilateral export control regimes

End-use monitoring and verification

Foreign policy and diplomatic considerations

International sanctions and embargoes.

F

FALSE STATEMENTS

Statutory Citation: 18 USC Section 1001

False statements to federal agents or agencies involve knowingly making materially false, fictitious, or fraudulent statements or representations in matters within the jurisdiction of the executive, legislative, or judicial branch of the United States government.

Elements:

1. Statement made within jurisdiction of executive, legislative, or judicial branch
2. Statement was false, fictitious, or fraudulent
3. Statement was material to the matter
4. Defendant made statement knowingly and willfully

Penalties:

Basic Offense: Up to 5 years imprisonment

If Statement Relates to International or Domestic Terrorism: Up to 8 years imprisonment

Fines: Up to $250,000 for individuals

Enhanced Penalties: If statement facilitates other federal crimes

Types of False Statements:

Oral Statements: False information given to federal agents during interviews

Written Statements: False information on federal forms or applications

Omissions: Failure to disclose material information when required

Records Falsification: Altering or creating false documents

Cover-up Statements: False statements made to conceal other crimes

Federal Agencies:

FBI: Primary investigative agency for false statement cases

Internal Revenue Service: Tax-related false statements

Immigration and Customs **Enforcement:** Immigration false statements

Securities and Exchange **Commission:** Securities-related false statements

Various Inspector General Offices: Agency-specific false statements

Materiality Requirement:

Statement must have natural tendency to influence agency decision

Does not require proof that agency was actually influenced

Includes statements that could affect pending or future proceedings

Administrative and regulatory proceedings qualify

Knowledge and Intent:

Defendant must know statement is false

Willful blindness or deliberate ignorance satisfies knowledge requirement

Mistake of fact may negate knowledge element

Good faith reliance on advice of counsel may be defense

Related Federal Offenses:

Perjury (18 USC Section 1621)

Obstruction of Justice (18 USC Section 1503)

Mail Fraud (18 USC Section 1341)

Wire Fraud (18 USC Section 1343)

Conspiracy (18 USC Section 371)

Jurisdictional Scope:

Federal courts and proceedings

Federal administrative agencies

Congressional committees and investigations

Federal law enforcement investigations

Federal regulatory proceedings

Defenses:

Statement was not false

Statement was not material

Lack of knowledge that statement was false

Statement not within federal jurisdiction

Statute of limitations (5 years)

FEDERAL TAX EVASION

Statutory Citations: 26 USC Section 7201 (Tax evasion); 26 USC Section 7206 (Fraud and false statements)

Federal tax evasion involves willful attempts to evade or defeat the assessment or payment of federal income taxes through fraudulent means.

Elements of Tax Evasion (26 USC Section 7201):

1. Existence of tax deficiency

2. Willful attempt to evade or defeat tax

3. Affirmative act constituting evasion or attempted evasion

Elements of Tax Fraud (26 USC Section 7206(1)):

1. Making and subscribing return, statement, or document

2. Verified by written declaration under penalty of perjury

3. Knowing return contains false or fraudulent information

4. As to material matter

Penalties:

Tax Evasion: Up to 5 years imprisonment and $250,000 fine

Tax Fraud: Up to 3 years imprisonment and $250,000 fine

Civil Penalties: 75% fraud penalty plus interest

Restitution: Full amount of taxes evaded plus interest

Types of Tax Evasion:

Income Concealment: Hiding income from legitimate sources

Fictitious Deductions: Claiming false business expenses or deductions

Offshore Accounts: Using foreign accounts to hide income

Cash Transactions: Operating cash-only businesses to avoid reporting

Identity Theft: Using stolen identities to file false returns

Federal Agencies:

Internal Revenue Service Criminal **Investigation:** Primary enforcement agency

Department of Justice Tax Division: Complex tax prosecutions

U.S. Attorneys Offices: Local tax crime prosecution

Treasury Inspector General: IRS-related investigations

Willfulness Requirement:

Voluntary, intentional violation of known legal duty

Distinguished from negligence or mistake

Sophisticated methods may indicate willfulness

Pattern of conduct over multiple years

Use of professionals to facilitate evasion

Affirmative Acts of Evasion:

Filing false tax returns

Maintaining inadequate records

Dealing in cash to avoid detection

Using nominees or aliases

Concealing assets or income sources

Related Federal Offenses:

Money Laundering (18 USC Section 1956)

Bank Fraud (18 USC Section 1344)

Mail Fraud (18 USC Section 1341)

Wire Fraud (18 USC Section 1343)

Conspiracy (18 USC Section 371)

Civil vs Criminal Tax Cases:

Civil: Preponderance of evidence standard

Criminal: Beyond reasonable doubt standard

Civil penalties do not preclude criminal prosecution

Parallel proceedings common in major cases

International Tax Evasion:

Foreign Bank Account Report (FBAR) violations

Offshore voluntary disclosure programs

Treaty provisions for information exchange

Mutual agreement procedures with foreign countries

FIREARMS VIOLATIONS

Statutory Citations: 18 USC Section 922 (Unlawful acts); 18 USC Section 924 (Penalties)

Federal firearms violations encompass a broad range of offenses involving the manufacture, distribution, possession, and use of firearms in violation of federal gun control laws.

Elements of Felon in Possession (18 USC Section 922(g)(1)):

1. Previous conviction for crime punishable by imprisonment exceeding one year
2. Knowing possession of firearm or ammunition
3. Possession affects interstate or foreign commerce

Elements of Unlicensed Dealing (18 USC Section 922(a)(1)):

1. Engaging in business of dealing in firearms
2. Without federal firearms license

3. Affecting interstate or foreign commerce

Penalties:

Felon in Possession: Up to 10 years imprisonment

Unlicensed Dealing: Up to 5 years imprisonment

Use During Crime of Violence: Mandatory minimum 5 years consecutive

Machine Gun Violations: Up to 10 years imprisonment

Enhanced Penalties: For repeat offenders and violent crimes

Prohibited Persons (18 USC Section 922(g)):

Persons convicted of felonies punishable by more than one year

Fugitives from justice

Unlawful users of controlled substances

Persons adjudicated as mental defectives

Illegal aliens and nonimmigrant visa holders

Persons dishonorably discharged from military

Persons subject to restraining orders

Persons convicted of domestic violence misdemeanors

Federal Firearms License Requirements:

Manufacturers of firearms and ammunition

Importers of firearms and ammunition

Dealers in firearms

Collectors of curios and relics

Special occupational taxpayers (Class III dealers)

Federal Agencies:

Bureau of Alcohol, Tobacco, Firearms and Explosives: Primary enforcement agency

FBI: Background check system and major investigations

U.S. Attorneys Offices: Prosecution of firearms crimes

Immigration and Customs **Enforcement:** Import/export violations

Enhanced Penalties:

Armed Career Criminal Act: 15-year minimum for three violent felony convictions

Use During Drug Trafficking: Mandatory consecutive sentences

Machine Gun Violations: Enhanced penalties for automatic weapons

Straw Purchases: Enhanced penalties for buying firearms for prohibited persons

Interstate Commerce Requirements:

Firearms or ammunition traveled in interstate commerce

Minimal nexus required (most firearms qualify)

Affects interstate commerce in any way

Commerce Clause provides broad federal jurisdiction

Related Federal Offenses:

Drug Trafficking (21 USC Section 841)

RICO (18 USC Section 1962)

Conspiracy (18 USC Section 371)

Money Laundering (18 USC Section 1956)

Violence Against Federal Officials (18 USC Section 111)

Background Check System:

National Instant Criminal Background Check System (NICS)

Required for all sales by licensed dealers

Prohibited person databases

Mental health records reporting

Interstate information sharing

FRAUD (GENERAL)

Statutory Citations: 18 USC Section 1341 (Mail fraud); 18 USC Section 1343 (Wire fraud); 18 USC Section 1348 (Securities fraud)

Federal fraud encompasses schemes to defraud using instrumentalities of interstate commerce, including mail, wire communications, and securities markets.

Elements of Mail Fraud (18 USC Section 1341):

1. Scheme or artifice to defraud or obtain money or property by false pretenses
2. Use of mail or private commercial carrier in furtherance of scheme
3. Intent to defraud

Elements of Wire Fraud (18 USC Section 1343):

1. Scheme or artifice to defraud or obtain money or property by false pretenses
2. Use of wire, radio, or television communication in interstate or foreign commerce
3. Intent to defraud

Elements of Securities Fraud (18 USC Section 1348):

1. Scheme or artifice to defraud in connection with securities
2. Obtaining money or property by false or fraudulent pretenses
3. Intent to defraud

Penalties:

Mail and Wire Fraud: Up to 20 years imprisonment (30 years if affecting financial institution)

Securities Fraud: Up to 25 years imprisonment

Fines: Up to $250,000 for individuals, $500,000 for organizations

Restitution: Mandatory restitution to victims

Types of Fraud Schemes:

Investment Fraud: Ponzi schemes, pyramid schemes, securities fraud

Healthcare Fraud: False billing, kickbacks, unnecessary procedures

Insurance Fraud: False claims, staged accidents, premium fraud

Government Benefits Fraud: False applications, identity theft

Business Fraud: Accounting fraud, procurement fraud, tax fraud

Federal Agencies:

FBI: Primary fraud investigations

Secret Service: Financial fraud and counterfeiting

Postal Inspection Service: Mail fraud investigations

Securities and Exchange **Commission:** Securities fraud enforcement

Internal Revenue Service: Tax fraud investigations

Intent to Defraud:

Specific intent to deceive and cause financial loss

Intent may be inferred from defendant's conduct

Good faith belief in truth of statements may negate intent

Reckless disregard for truth may satisfy intent requirement

Scheme to Defraud:

Plan or course of conduct designed to deceive

Need not be successful to constitute crime

Victims need not suffer actual loss

Scheme may target money, property, or honest services

Related Federal Offenses:

Money Laundering (18 USC Section 1956)

Conspiracy (18 USC Section 371)

Bank Fraud (18 USC Section 1344)

Healthcare Fraud (18 USC Section 1347)

RICO (18 USC Section 1962)

Interstate Commerce Element:

Use of mail or wire communications

Minimal use sufficient to establish jurisdiction

Private commercial carriers included

Internet and electronic communications covered

Statute of Limitations:

Generally 5 years from commission of offense

Extended to 10 years for financial institution fraud

Tolled during defendant's absence from United States

Conspiracy continues until last overt act

FUGITIVE FROM JUSTICE

Statutory Citation: 18 USC Section 1073 (Interstate flight to avoid prosecution)

Federal fugitive laws criminalize fleeing across state lines to avoid prosecution, custody, or confinement for state felonies, providing federal jurisdiction for apprehension of interstate fugitives.

Elements:

1. Moving or traveling in interstate or foreign commerce
2. With intent to avoid prosecution, custody, or confinement after conviction
3. For crime that is felony under laws of place from which person flees
4. Prosecution, custody, or confinement authorized under laws of that place

Penalties:

Basic Offense: Up to 5 years imprisonment

Fines: Up to $250,000

Enhanced Penalties: If fugitive commits federal crimes while fleeing

Consecutive Sentences: Federal sentence may run consecutive to state sentence

Interstate Commerce Requirement:

Physical movement across state or national boundaries

Use of instrumentalities of interstate commerce

Any crossing of state lines with requisite intent

Air, rail, bus, or automobile travel qualifies

Predicate State Crimes:

Must be felony under law of state from which person flees

Includes both state and local felony offenses

Federal crimes may qualify if prosecution pending in state court

Juvenile offenses may qualify if would be adult felony

Federal Agencies:

U.S. Marshals Service: Primary fugitive apprehension agency

FBI: Major fugitive investigations and task forces

Immigration and Customs **Enforcement:** International fugitive cases

Customs and Border Protection: Border apprehension

Related Federal Offenses:

Conspiracy (18 USC Section 371)

False Identification (18 USC Section 1028)

Money Laundering (18 USC Section 1956)

Firearms Violations (18 USC Section 922)

Immigration Violations (8 USC Section 1326)

Intent Requirement:

Specific intent to avoid prosecution, custody, or confinement

Intent may be inferred from circumstances

Flight alone insufficient without intent to avoid legal process

Timing of flight relevant to proving intent

Defenses:

No intent to avoid prosecution

Not aware of pending charges or warrant

Travel for legitimate purposes

Voluntary return to face charges

Lack of interstate movement

Federal Fugitive Task Forces:

Regional Fugitive Task Forces coordinate apprehension

Joint operations with state and local law enforcement

Technology and intelligence sharing

International fugitive operations

FOREIGN CORRUPT PRACTICES ACT

Statutory Citation: 15 USC Sections 78dd-1 through 78dd-3

The Foreign Corrupt Practices Act prohibits bribery of foreign officials by U.S. persons and companies to obtain or retain business, and requires accurate books and records for publicly traded companies.

Elements of Anti-Bribery Provisions:

1. Payment, offer, or authorization of payment of money or thing of value
2. To foreign official, foreign political party, or candidate for foreign political office
3. Intent to influence official act or decision or secure improper advantage
4. To obtain or retain business

Elements of Books and Records Provisions:

1. Publicly traded company subject to Securities Exchange Act
2. Failure to make and keep books and records accurately and fairly reflecting transactions
3. Failure to devise and maintain adequate internal accounting controls

Penalties:

Individuals: Up to 5 years imprisonment and $250,000 fine per violation

Corporations: Up to $2,000,000 fine per violation

Civil Penalties: Up to $10,000 for individuals, $500,000 for corporations

Alternative Fines: Twice the gross gain or gross loss

Foreign Official Definition:

Officer or employee of foreign government or department

Person acting in official capacity for foreign government

Officer or employee of public international organization

Political party, party official, or candidate for foreign political office

Exceptions and Defenses:

Facilitating payments for routine governmental action

Payments lawful under written laws of foreign country

Reasonable and bona fide business expenditures

Promotional activities and gifts of nominal value

Federal Agencies:

Department of Justice: Criminal enforcement

Securities and Exchange **Commission:** Civil enforcement and books and records violations

FBI: Criminal investigations

Treasury Department: Financial intelligence and suspicious activity reports

International Enforcement:

OECD Anti-Bribery Convention implementation

Coordination with foreign law enforcement

Mutual legal assistance treaties

Cross-border investigations and prosecutions

Related Federal Offenses:

Mail Fraud (18 USC Section 1341)

Wire Fraud (18 USC Section 1343)

Money Laundering (18 USC Section 1956)

Conspiracy (18 USC Section 371)

Tax Evasion (26 USC Section 7201)

Corporate Compliance Programs:

Due diligence for business partnerships

Training and education programs

Internal reporting mechanisms

Periodic compliance audits

Disciplinary procedures for violations

FORGERY

Statutory Citations: 18 USC Section 495 (Federal securities forgery); 18 USC Section 1341 (Mail fraud through forgery)

Federal forgery involves the false making or material alteration of documents with intent to defraud, particularly when involving federal securities, currency, or documents affecting interstate commerce.

Elements of Federal Securities Forgery (18 USC Section 495):

1. Falsely making, altering, forging, or counterfeiting any federal security
2. With intent to defraud
3. Knowledge of falsity

Elements of Document Forgery (Various Statutes):

1. False making or material alteration of document
2. Document has legal significance
3. Intent to defraud or deceive
4. Federal jurisdiction through interstate commerce or federal property

Penalties:

Federal Securities Forgery: Up to 10 years imprisonment

Check Forgery: Up to 10 years imprisonment

Immigration Document Forgery: Up to 15 years imprisonment

Fines: Up to $250,000 for individuals

Types of Federal Forgery:

Currency Forgery: Counterfeiting U.S. currency and coins

Securities Forgery: False federal bonds, notes, and certificates

Check Forgery: Forged government and bank checks

Immigration Document Forgery: False visas, green cards, passports

Government Document Forgery: False federal licenses and permits

Federal Agencies:

Secret Service: Currency and securities forgery

FBI: Document fraud investigations

Immigration and Customs **Enforcement:** Immigration document forgery

Postal Inspection Service: Mail fraud through forgery

Elements of Forgery:

False Making: Creating entirely false document

Material Alteration: Changing existing document in significant way

Legal Significance: Document must have potential legal effect

Intent to Defraud: Specific intent to deceive and cause harm

Related Federal Offenses:

Identity Theft (18 USC Section 1028)

Mail Fraud (18 USC Section 1341)

Wire Fraud (18 USC Section 1343)

Bank Fraud (18 USC Section 1344)

Conspiracy (18 USC Section 371)

Technology and Forgery:

Digital document manipulation

Computer-generated false documents

Electronic signature fraud

Online document fraud schemes

Cryptocurrency and digital asset forgery

Defenses:

Lack of intent to defraud

Authorization to create or alter document

Document has no legal significance

Good faith belief in authority to create document

Statute of limitations.

G

GAMBLING (FEDERAL)

Statutory Citations: 18 USC Section 1955 (Illegal gambling business); 18 USC Section 1084 (Wire Act)

Federal gambling offenses involve operating illegal gambling businesses that affect interstate commerce or using wire communications to facilitate gambling activities across state lines.

Elements of Illegal Gambling Business (18 USC Section 1955):

1. Conducting, financing, managing, supervising, directing, or owning gambling business
2. Business involves five or more persons who conduct, finance, manage, supervise, direct, or own the business
3. Business has been or remains in substantially continuous operation for period in excess of 30 days or has gross revenue of $2,000 in any single day
4. Business operates in violation of law of state or political subdivision in which conducted

Elements of Wire Act Violations (18 USC Section 1084):

1. Engaging in business of betting or wagering
2. Knowingly using wire communication facility for transmission of bets or wagers
3. Transmission in interstate or foreign commerce
4. Betting or wagering on sporting event or contest

Penalties:

Illegal Gambling Business: Up to 5 years imprisonment

Wire Act Violations: Up to 2 years imprisonment

Fines: Up to $250,000 for individuals

Criminal Forfeiture: Property used in illegal gambling operations

Types of Federal Gambling Crimes:

Sports Betting: Illegal bookmaking operations across state lines

Internet Gambling: Online gambling sites and operations

Casino Operations: Unlicensed casino operations affecting interstate commerce

Numbers Running: Lottery and numbers games crossing state boundaries

Organized Gambling: Systematic gambling enterprises

Federal Agencies:

FBI: Primary gambling investigations and organized crime

Internal Revenue Service: Tax evasion related to gambling income

Immigration and Customs **Enforcement:** Cross-border gambling operations

Postal Inspection Service: Mail-related gambling schemes

Interstate Commerce Requirements:

Use of interstate wire communications

Transportation of gambling equipment across state lines

Multi-state gambling operations

Customers from multiple states

Related Federal Offenses:

RICO (18 USC Section 1962)

Money Laundering (18 USC Section 1956)

Tax Evasion (26 USC Section 7201)

Conspiracy (18 USC Section 371)

Mail Fraud (18 USC Section 1341)

Exceptions:

State-licensed gambling operations

Tribal gaming under Indian Gaming Regulatory Act

Fantasy sports contests in some circumstances

Social gambling among friends

Enhanced Penalties:

Organized gambling enterprises

Violence or intimidation in gambling operations

Corruption of public officials

Use of minors in gambling operations

GOVERNMENT PROPERTY THEFT

Statutory Citation: 18 USC Section 641

Government property theft involves stealing, embezzling, or converting property belonging to the United States, including money, equipment, supplies, and other government assets.

Elements:

1. Embezzling, stealing, purloining, or knowingly converting to use of another
2. Thing of value belonging to United States

3. Intent to deprive United States of use or possession

4. Value exceeding $1,000 for felony prosecution

Penalties:

Felony (over $1,000): Up to 10 years imprisonment

Misdemeanor ($1,000 or less): Up to 1 year imprisonment

Fines: Up to $250,000 for felonies, $100,000 for misdemeanors

Restitution: Full value of stolen property

Types of Government Property:

Military equipment and supplies

Federal office equipment and computers

Government vehicles and aircraft

Postal service property and mail

National park resources and artifacts

Research equipment and materials

Federal Agencies:

FBI: Major government property theft investigations

Military Criminal Investigation Commands: Military property theft

Postal Inspection Service: Postal property theft

National Park Service: Theft of park resources

Various Inspector General Offices: Agency-specific theft cases

Enhanced Penalties:

Theft during national emergency or disaster

Theft of classified materials or equipment

Organized theft rings

Theft by government employees (breach of trust)

Related Federal Offenses:

Conspiracy (18 USC Section 371)

Receiving Stolen Property (18 USC Section 2315)

Mail Theft (18 USC Section 1708)

Computer Fraud (18 USC Section 1030)

Embezzlement (18 USC Section 641)

Employee Theft:

Federal employees stealing government property

Contractors misappropriating government resources

Military personnel theft of equipment

Abuse of position and access

Defenses:

Lack of intent to permanently deprive

Authorization to take property

Property not belonging to United States

Good faith belief in right to property

Abandoned property

GENOCIDE

Statutory Citation: 18 USC Section 1091

Genocide involves acts committed with intent to destroy, in whole or in part, a national, ethnic, racial, or religious group, implementing the United States obligations under international law.

Elements:

1. Killing members of national, ethnic, racial, or religious group
2. Causing serious bodily or mental harm to members of the group
3. Deliberately inflicting conditions of life calculated to bring about physical destruction
4. Imposing measures intended to prevent births within the group
5. Forcibly transferring children of the group to another group
6. Intent to destroy group in whole or in part

Penalties:

Basic Genocide: Life imprisonment

If Death Results: Death penalty or life imprisonment

Conspiracy to Commit Genocide: Up to 20 years imprisonment

Incitement to Genocide: Up to 5 years imprisonment

Jurisdiction:

Offense committed within United States

Offender is U.S. national

Offender is present in United States after committing offense outside United States

Offense committed by member of U.S. armed forces

Protected Groups:

National groups defined by citizenship or country of origin

Ethnic groups sharing common cultural traditions

Racial groups sharing hereditary physical traits

Religious groups sharing common beliefs and practices

Federal Agencies:

FBI: Domestic genocide investigations

Department of Justice Human Rights and Special Prosecutions Section: War crimes and genocide

Immigration and Customs Enforcement: Immigration consequences

State Department: International cooperation

Related Federal Offenses:

War Crimes (18 USC Section 2441)

Crimes Against Humanity (Various international provisions)

Civil Rights Violations (18 USC Section 241)

Conspiracy (18 USC Section 371)

Murder (18 USC Section 1111)

International Cooperation:

International Criminal Court cooperation

Extradition treaties for genocide cases

Mutual legal assistance in investigations

Universal jurisdiction principles

Defenses:

Lack of intent to destroy protected group

Actions not directed at protected group

Self-defense or defense of others

Duress or coercion

Superior orders (limited defense)

GUN RUNNING

Statutory Citations: 18 USC Section 922 (Firearms trafficking); 22 USC Section 2778 (Arms Export Control Act)

Gun running involves the illegal trafficking of firearms, either domestically across state lines or internationally in violation of export control laws.

Elements of Interstate Gun Trafficking:

1. Transportation or shipment of firearms in interstate commerce

2. To person knowing or having reasonable cause to believe person is prohibited from receiving firearms

3. Intent to distribute firearms illegally

4. Knowing violation of federal firearms laws

Elements of International Gun Running:

1. Export or attempt to export firearms or ammunition

2. Without required State Department license

3. To foreign countries or foreign persons

4. Knowing violation of Arms Export Control Act

Penalties:

Interstate Gun Trafficking: Up to 10 years imprisonment

International Gun Running: Up to 20 years imprisonment

Fines: Up to $1,000,000 for individuals

Criminal Forfeiture: All firearms and proceeds involved

Types of Gun Running Operations:

Straw Purchases: Legal buyers purchasing for prohibited persons

Cross-Border Smuggling: Illegal export of firearms to foreign countries

Gun Show Trafficking: Unlicensed sales at gun shows

Internet Sales: Illegal online firearms transactions

Organized Trafficking: Systematic firearms distribution networks

Federal Agencies:

Bureau of Alcohol, Tobacco, Firearms and Explosives: Primary enforcement

FBI: Major trafficking investigations

Immigration and Customs Enforcement: Border enforcement

Customs and Border Protection: Export/import violations

State Department: Export licensing

Related Federal Offenses:

Conspiracy (18 USC Section 371)

Money Laundering (18 USC Section 1956)

RICO (18 USC Section 1962)

Drug Trafficking (21 USC Section 841)

Terrorism (18 USC Section 2339A)

International Aspects:

Project Gunrunner: Southwest border trafficking initiative

International trafficking organizations

Foreign military and police corruption

Regional destabilization effects

Enhanced Penalties:

Trafficking to known criminals

Trafficking to terrorist organizations

Large-scale trafficking operations

Violence associated with trafficking

GOVERNMENT FRAUD

Statutory Citations: 18 USC Section 1341 (Mail fraud against government); 18 USC Section 286 (Conspiracy to defraud government)

Government fraud involves schemes to defraud federal agencies, programs, or officials, including procurement fraud, benefit fraud, and grant fraud.

Elements of Conspiracy to Defraud Government (18 USC Section 286):

1. Conspiracy of two or more persons
2. To defraud United States or agency thereof
3. In any manner or for any purpose
4. One conspirator commits overt act to effect object of conspiracy

Elements of Government Contract Fraud:

1. Scheme to defraud government in connection with contract
2. Material false statements or representations
3. Intent to defraud government
4. Use of mail or wire communications

Penalties:

Conspiracy to Defraud Government: Up to 5 years imprisonment

Government Contract Fraud: Up to 20 years imprisonment

Fines: Up to $250,000 for individuals, $500,000 for organizations

Restitution: Full amount of government losses

Types of Government Fraud:

Procurement Fraud: False statements in government contracting

Grant Fraud: Misuse of federal grant money

Benefits Fraud: False claims for government benefits

Healthcare Fraud: Medicare and Medicaid fraud

Tax Fraud: False claims for tax credits and refunds

Federal Agencies:

FBI: Major government fraud investigations

Various Inspector General Offices: Agency-specific fraud

General Services Administration: Procurement fraud

Department of Health and Human Services: Healthcare fraud

Small Business Administration: Loan and grant fraud

Enhanced Penalties:

Large-scale fraud schemes

Fraud during national emergencies

Organized fraud enterprises

Corruption of government officials

Related Federal Offenses:

Mail Fraud (18 USC Section 1341)

Wire Fraud (18 USC Section 1343)

False Claims Act (31 USC Section 3729)

Bribery (18 USC Section 201)

Money Laundering (18 USC Section 1956)

Civil Remedies:

False Claims Act treble damages

Debarment from government contracting

Civil asset forfeiture

Administrative penalties

Qui Tam Actions:

Whistleblower lawsuits under False Claims Act

Government employee protections

Financial incentives for reporting fraud

Private attorney general enforcement

GRAND JURY VIOLATIONS

Statutory Citation: 18 USC Section 1623 (Perjury before grand jury); Federal Rule of Criminal Procedure 6(e)

Grand jury violations involve offenses related to the federal grand jury system, including perjury before grand juries, disclosure of grand jury materials, and contempt of grand jury proceedings.

Elements of Grand Jury Perjury (18 USC Section 1623):

1. Testimony under oath before grand jury
2. Statement is false
3. Statement is material to grand jury investigation
4. Defendant knows statement is false

Elements of Unlawful Disclosure of Grand Jury Materials:

1. Disclosure of matters occurring before grand jury
2. By person bound by secrecy requirements
3. Without court authorization
4. Knowledge that disclosure is unauthorized

Penalties:

Grand Jury Perjury: Up to 5 years imprisonment

Unlawful Disclosure: Up to 1 year imprisonment (contempt)

Fines: Up to $250,000

Enhanced Penalties: If disclosure affects national security

Grand Jury Secrecy Rules:

Grand jurors sworn to secrecy

Prosecutors bound by secrecy requirements

Court reporters and interpreters included

Witnesses not bound by secrecy after testimony

Authorized Disclosures:

Court orders for disclosure in judicial proceedings

Disclosure to government attorneys for law enforcement

Intelligence and national security disclosures

Congressional investigations with court approval

Federal Agencies:

U.S. Attorneys Offices: Grand jury proceedings and prosecutions

FBI: Grand jury investigation support

U.S. Marshals Service: Grand jury security

Administrative Office of U.S. Courts: Grand jury administration

Related Federal Offenses:

Perjury (18 USC Section 1621)

Obstruction of Justice (18 USC Section 1503)

Contempt of Court (18 USC Section 401)

Witness Tampering (18 USC Section 1512)

Defenses:

Statement was not false

Statement was not material

Lack of knowledge that statement was false

Authorized disclosure of grand jury materials

Statute of limitations

Contempt Powers:

Civil contempt for failure to testify

Criminal contempt for disruptive behavior

Immunity grants to compel testimony

Confinement until compliance

GRATUITIES

Statutory Citation: 18 USC Section 201(c)

Gratuities involve giving or receiving something of value to public officials for or because of official acts, distinguished from bribery by the lack of a corrupt quid pro quo agreement.

Elements of Giving Gratuity (18 USC Section 201(c)(2)):

1. Giving, offering, or promising anything of value
2. To public official or person selected to be public official
3. For or because of official act performed or to be performed

Elements of Receiving Gratuity (18 USC Section 201(c)(1)):

1. Public official demanding, seeking, receiving, accepting, or agreeing to receive anything of value
2. For or because of official act performed or to be performed by official

Penalties:

Gratuities: Up to 2 years imprisonment

Fines: Up to $250,000

Disqualification: From holding federal office

Forfeiture: Value of gratuity

Distinction from Bribery:

Bribery requires corrupt intent and quid pro quo agreement

Gratuities can be given after official act without prior agreement

Gratuities carry lesser penalties than bribery

Timing of payment may indicate gratuity vs bribery

Types of Gratuities:

Gifts to federal officials for past favorable decisions

Entertainment and hospitality for government employees

Speaking fees and honoraria for federal officials

Travel and accommodation expenses

Employment opportunities for family members

Federal Agencies:

FBI: Public corruption investigations

Offices of Inspector General: Ethics violations

Office of Government Ethics: Administrative oversight

Department of Justice Public Integrity Section: Prosecution

Related Federal Offenses:

Bribery (18 USC Section 201(b))

Honest Services Fraud (18 USC Section 1346)

Conflict of Interest (18 USC Section 208)

Ethics Violations (Various administrative provisions)

Ethics Rules:

Gift restrictions for federal employees

Recusal requirements for conflicts of interest

Financial disclosure requirements

Post-employment restrictions

Defenses:

No corrupt intent

Gift within authorized exceptions

Official act not performed for gratuity

Widely attended event exception

Personal friendship exception.

H

HATE CRIMES

Statutory Citation: 18 USC Section 249 (Matthew Shepard and James Byrd Jr. Hate Crimes Prevention Act)

Federal hate crimes involve willfully causing bodily injury or attempting to cause bodily injury to any person because of actual or perceived race, color, religion, national origin, gender, sexual orientation, gender identity, or disability.

Elements:

1. Willfully causing bodily injury or attempting to cause bodily injury through use of fire, firearm, dangerous weapon, or explosive or incendiary device

2. Because of actual or perceived race, color, religion, national origin, gender, sexual orientation, gender identity, or disability

3. Conduct in or affecting interstate or foreign commerce

Elements of Interference with Federally Protected Activities:

1. Willfully injuring, intimidating, or interfering with person

2. Because of race, color, religion, or national origin

3. While engaged in federally protected activity (voting, education, employment, public accommodations, housing, court proceedings)

Penalties:

Basic Hate Crime: Up to 10 years imprisonment

If Death Results: Life imprisonment

If Involves Kidnapping or Sexual **Abuse:** Life imprisonment or death penalty

Fines: Up to $250,000 for individuals

Protected Characteristics:

Race and color

Religion and national origin

Gender and gender identity

Sexual orientation

Disability (physical or mental)

Federally Protected Activities:

Voting and political participation

Public education attendance

Employment and job seeking

Jury service in federal court

Public accommodation access

Housing transactions

Federal Agencies:

FBI Civil Rights Program: Primary hate crime investigations

Department of Justice Civil Rights Division: Prosecution coordination

Community Relations Service: Conflict resolution and prevention

U.S. Attorneys Offices: Local hate crime prosecution

Enhanced Penalties:

Use of dangerous weapons or explosives

Organized hate groups involvement

Multiple victims or widespread community impact

Official position of authority by defendant

Related Federal Offenses:

Civil Rights Violations (18 USC Section 241)

Conspiracy (18 USC Section 371)

Firearms Violations (18 USC Section 924(c))

Arson (18 USC Section 844)

Assault (18 USC Section 113)

Interstate Commerce Requirements:

Travel across state lines to commit hate crime

Use of facility or instrumentality of interstate commerce

Conduct affecting interstate commerce

Weapon traveled in interstate commerce

Bias Motivation Proof:

Direct evidence of bias (statements, symbols, literature)

Circumstantial evidence (targeting, timing, method)

Defendant's associations and prior conduct

Victim selection and community context

Defenses:

Lack of bias motivation

Self-defense or defense of others

First Amendment protected speech (limited)

Insufficient evidence of interstate commerce

Mental incapacity

HEALTHCARE FRAUD

Statutory Citation: 18 USC Section 1347

Healthcare fraud involves knowingly executing schemes to defraud healthcare benefit programs or obtaining money or property owned by or under custody of healthcare benefit programs through false or fraudulent pretenses.

Elements:

1. Knowingly and willfully executing scheme or artifice to defraud healthcare benefit program
2. In connection with delivery of or payment for healthcare benefits, items, or services
3. Obtaining money or property owned by or under custody of healthcare benefit program
4. By means of false or fraudulent pretenses, representations, or promises

Penalties:

Basic Healthcare Fraud: Up to 10 years imprisonment

If Serious Bodily Injury Results: Up to 20 years imprisonment

If Death Results: Life imprisonment

Fines: Up to $250,000 for individuals, $500,000 for organizations

Criminal Forfeiture: Property derived from healthcare fraud

Types of Healthcare Fraud:

Billing Fraud: False claims for services not rendered

Upcoding: Billing for more expensive services than provided

Unbundling: Separate billing for services normally billed together

Kickbacks: Illegal payments for patient referrals

Identity Theft: Using stolen patient information for fraudulent billing

Healthcare Benefit Programs:

Medicare and Medicaid

TRICARE military healthcare

Veterans Affairs healthcare

Federal employee health benefits

Indian Health Service

Any plan or program providing medical benefits funded by government

Federal Agencies:

FBI Healthcare Fraud Unit: Primary criminal investigations

Health and Human Services Office of Inspector General: Civil and administrative enforcement

Centers for Medicare and Medicaid Services: Program integrity

Drug Enforcement Administration: Prescription drug fraud

Defense Criminal Investigative Service: Military healthcare fraud

Enhanced Penalties:

Large-scale fraud operations

Organized healthcare fraud enterprises

Endangering patient safety

Prescription drug trafficking

Professional license violations

Related Federal Offenses:

Mail Fraud (18 USC Section 1341)

Wire Fraud (18 USC Section 1343)

Money Laundering (18 USC Section 1956)

Anti-Kickback Statute (42 USC Section 1320a-7b)

False Claims Act (31 USC Section 3729)

Patient Harm Considerations:

Unnecessary medical procedures

Substandard or dangerous treatments

Prescription drug diversion and abuse

Compromised patient care quality

Public health threats

Compliance Programs:

Healthcare provider compliance obligations

Risk assessment and monitoring

Employee training and education

Internal reporting mechanisms

Corrective action procedures

HOBBS ACT

Statutory Citation: 18 USC Section 1951

The Hobbs Act criminalizes robbery and extortion affecting interstate or foreign commerce, providing federal jurisdiction over crimes that interfere with the flow of commerce.

Elements of Hobbs Act Robbery:

1. Unlawful taking of personal property from person or presence of another
2. Against will of victim by means of actual or threatened force, violence, or fear of injury
3. Affecting commerce

Elements of Hobbs Act Extortion:

1. Obtaining property of another with consent
2. Induced by wrongful use of actual or threatened force, violence, or fear
3. Under color of official right
4. Affecting commerce

Penalties:

Robbery or Extortion: Up to 20 years imprisonment

If Death Results: Life imprisonment or death penalty

Attempted Robbery or Extortion: Up to 20 years imprisonment

Fines: Up to $250,000 for individuals

Commerce Requirement:

Minimal effect on interstate commerce sufficient

Robbery of business engaged in interstate commerce

Depletion of assets of business affecting commerce

Interruption of customer flow or business operations

Types of Hobbs Act Violations:

Street robberies of businesses

Armed robberies of commercial establishments

Extortion by public officials (corruption)

Labor racketeering and union extortion

Protection rackets and organized crime

Official Right Extortion:

Public officials obtaining payments under color of official right

Payments for performance or non-performance of official duties

Kickbacks and corrupt payments to government employees

Campaign contribution extortion by elected officials

Federal Agencies:

FBI: Primary Hobbs Act investigations

U.S. Attorneys Offices: Prosecution of robbery and extortion

Internal Revenue Service: Tax aspects of extortion payments

Immigration and Customs Enforcement: Cross-border commerce crimes

Related Federal Offenses:

RICO (18 USC Section 1962)

Firearms Violations (18 USC Section 924(c))

Conspiracy (18 USC Section 371)

Money Laundering (18 USC Section 1956)

Public Corruption (18 USC Section 201)

Labor Racketeering:

Union corruption and extortion

Employer payments to avoid labor problems

Violence and threats against workers

Embezzlement of union funds

Bid rigging in construction industry

Enhanced Penalties:

Use of firearms during Hobbs Act violations

Organized crime involvement

Public official corruption

Multiple victims or widespread impact

HUMAN TRAFFICKING

Statutory Citations: 18 USC Sections 1581-1597 (Trafficking Victims Protection Act)

Human trafficking involves recruiting, harboring, transporting, providing, or obtaining persons for labor or commercial sex acts through force, fraud, or coercion.

Elements of Sex Trafficking (18 USC Section 1591):

1. Recruiting, enticing, harboring, transporting, providing, obtaining, or maintaining person
2. Knowing or reckless disregard that means of force, threats, fraud, or coercion will be used
3. To cause person to engage in commercial sex act
4. If person is under 18, no proof of force, fraud, or coercion required

Elements of Labor Trafficking (18 USC Section 1589):

1. Knowingly providing or obtaining labor or services of person
2. Through force, threats of force, physical restraint, or threats of physical restraint
3. Through scheme, plan, or pattern intended to cause person to believe failure to perform would result in serious harm or restraint
4. Through abuse or threatened abuse of legal process

Penalties:

Sex Trafficking: 10 years to life imprisonment (15 years to life if victim under 18)

Labor Trafficking: Up to 20 years imprisonment (life if death results)

Trafficking of Minors: 10 years to life imprisonment

Fines: Up to $250,000 for individuals

Restitution: Mandatory restitution to victims

Types of Human Trafficking:

Sex Trafficking: Prostitution, pornography, escort services

Labor Trafficking: Forced labor in agriculture, domestic work, manufacturing

Child Trafficking: Commercial sexual exploitation and forced labor of minors

Organ Trafficking: Illegal harvesting and transplantation of human organs

Debt Bondage: Forced labor to pay off real or alleged debts

Means of Control:

Physical force and violence

Psychological coercion and threats

Economic control and debt manipulation

Isolation from family and community

Document confiscation and legal threats

Substance addiction and dependency

Federal Agencies:

FBI Human Trafficking Task Forces: Primary investigations

Immigration and Customs Enforcement: Border and immigration enforcement

Department of Labor: Labor trafficking investigations

State Department: International trafficking issues

Health and Human Services: Victim services

Enhanced Penalties:

Trafficking involving minors

Use of violence or dangerous weapons

Organized trafficking enterprises

Official corruption facilitating trafficking

Cross-border trafficking operations

Related Federal Offenses:

RICO (18 USC Section 1962)

Money Laundering (18 USC Section 1956)

Immigration Violations (8 USC Section 1324)

Child Exploitation (18 USC Section 2251)

Forced Labor (18 USC Section 1589)

Victim Protection:

T-visa for trafficking victims

Witness protection and relocation

Medical and social services

Legal assistance and immigration relief

Restitution and compensation programs

International Aspects:

Trafficking in Persons Report

International cooperation and assistance

Cross-border investigations

Diplomatic engagement on trafficking issues

HOSTAGE TAKING

Statutory Citation: 18 USC Section 1203

Federal hostage taking involves seizing or detaining persons and threatening to kill, injure, or continue to detain them to compel third parties to act or refrain from acting as explicit or implicit conditions for release.

Elements:

1. Seizing or detaining person
2. Threatening to kill, injure, or continue to detain such person
3. In order to compel third person or governmental organization to do or abstain from doing any act
4. As explicit or implicit condition for release of person detained

Penalties:

Basic Hostage Taking: Up to 20 years imprisonment

If Death Results: Life imprisonment or death penalty

Conspiracy or Attempt: Same penalties as completed offense

Fines: Up to $250,000 for individuals

Federal Jurisdiction:

Offender or victim is national of United States

Offender is found in United States after committing offense outside United States

Governmental organization sought to be compelled is government of United States

Offense committed in United States

Types of Hostage Situations:

Kidnapping for ransom with demands to third parties

Barricaded subjects making demands of law enforcement

Domestic hostage situations with demands to government

International terrorism involving American hostages

Prison hostage situations with demands to authorities

Federal Agencies:

FBI Crisis Negotiation Team: Hostage negotiation and resolution

FBI Hostage Rescue Team: Tactical response capability

U.S. Marshals Service: Federal prisoner hostage situations

Secret Service: Threats to protected persons

State Department: International hostage cases

Enhanced Penalties:

Terrorism-related hostage taking

Use of weapons of mass destruction

Targeting government officials

International hostage situations

Multiple victims or extended duration

Related Federal Offenses:

Kidnapping (18 USC Section 1201)

Terrorism (18 USC Section 2332a)

Extortion (18 USC Section 875)

Assault (18 USC Section 113)

Conspiracy (18 USC Section 371)

International Law:

International Convention Against Taking of Hostages

Diplomatic immunity considerations

Extradition and international cooperation

State Department coordination

Negotiation Strategies:

Crisis negotiation techniques

Hostage survival psychology

Third party communication facilitation

Media management during incidents

Post-incident debriefing and analysis

HOUSING DISCRIMINATION

Statutory Citation: 18 USC Section 245(b)(2) (Fair Housing Act criminal provisions)

Federal housing discrimination involves intimidating, threatening, or injuring persons because of their race, color, religion, sex, handicap, familial status, or national origin in housing-related activities.

Elements:

1. Willfully injuring, intimidating, or interfering with person
2. Because of race, color, religion, sex, handicap, familial status, or national origin
3. While engaged in buying, selling, renting, financing, occupying, or contracting for housing

Penalties:

Housing Discrimination Violence: Up to 1 year imprisonment (first offense)

If Bodily Injury Results: Up to 10 years imprisonment

If Death Results: Life imprisonment

Fines: Up to $100,000 for first offense

Protected Classes:

Race and color

Religion and national origin

Sex and familial status

Disability and handicap

Sexual orientation and gender identity (in some jurisdictions)

Housing-Related Activities:

Buying, selling, or renting housing

Financing or insuring housing

Real estate brokerage services

Advertising housing opportunities

Participation in housing organizations

Federal Agencies:

Department of Housing and Urban Development: Civil enforcement

FBI Civil Rights Program: Criminal investigations

Department of Justice Civil Rights Division: Criminal prosecution

U.S. Attorneys Offices: Local prosecution

Types of Housing Discrimination:

Racial steering and redlining

Religious harassment and intimidation

Disability accommodation denial

Sexual harassment in housing

Familial status discrimination

Related Federal Offenses:

Civil Rights Violations (18 USC Section 241)

Hate Crimes (18 USC Section 249)

Conspiracy (18 USC Section 371)

Arson (18 USC Section 844)

Assault (18 USC Section 113)

Civil vs Criminal Enforcement:

Civil remedies under Fair Housing Act

Administrative complaints and investigations

Private civil lawsuits

Criminal prosecution for violent interference

Coordinated civil and criminal enforcement

Enhanced Penalties:

Organized discrimination schemes

Use of violence or weapons

Multiple victims or widespread impact

Official position facilitating discrimination

HIJACKING

Statutory Citations: 49 USC Section 46502 (Aircraft piracy); 18 USC Section 2119 (Carjacking)

Federal hijacking laws address the unlawful seizure of aircraft, vessels, and vehicles, providing enhanced penalties for crimes that threaten transportation security and public safety.

Elements of Aircraft Hijacking (49 USC Section 46502):

1. Seizing or exercising control of aircraft in flight
2. By force, violence, threat of force or violence, or any form of intimidation
3. With wrongful intent

Elements of Vessel Hijacking (18 USC Section 2280):

1. Seizing or exercising control over ship by force, threat, or intimidation
2. Placing explosive or incendiary device on ship
3. Destroying ship or causing damage likely to endanger safe navigation

Penalties:

Aircraft Hijacking: Minimum 20 years imprisonment (life or death if death results)

Vessel Hijacking: Up to 20 years imprisonment (life if death results)

Attempted Hijacking: Up to 20 years imprisonment

Fines: Up to $250,000 for individuals

Types of Hijacking:

Commercial airline hijacking

Private aircraft seizure

Maritime vessel hijacking

Vehicle carjacking (federal jurisdiction)

Mass transit hijacking

Federal Agencies:

FBI: Primary hijacking investigations

Transportation Security Administration: Aviation security

Coast Guard: Maritime hijacking response

Federal Air Marshal Service: In-flight security

Customs and Border Protection: Transportation security

Enhanced Penalties:

Terrorism-related hijacking

Use of weapons or explosives

International hijacking

Multiple victims or hostages

Demands made to government

Related Federal Offenses:

Terrorism (18 USC Section 2331)

Hostage Taking (18 USC Section 1203)

Extortion (18 USC Section 875)

Weapons Violations (18 USC Section 924)

Conspiracy (18 USC Section 371)

International Aspects:

Aviation security treaties and conventions

International cooperation in investigations

Extradition for hijacking offenses

Diplomatic negotiations for hostage release

Security Measures:

Enhanced screening procedures

Air marshal programs

Reinforced cockpit doors

Passenger and cargo screening

International security cooperation.

I

IDENTITY THEFT

Statutory Citations: 18 USC Section 1028 (Fraud and related activity in connection with identification documents); 18 USC Section 1028A (Aggravated identity theft)

Identity theft involves knowingly transferring, possessing, or using means of identification of another person without lawful authority and with intent to commit unlawful activity.

Elements of Identity Theft (18 USC Section 1028(a)(7)):

1. Knowingly transferring, possessing, or using without lawful authority
2. Means of identification of another person
3. During and in relation to felony violation
4. With intent to commit or aid or abet unlawful activity

Elements of Aggravated Identity Theft (18 USC Section 1028A):

1. During and in relation to specified felony offense
2. Knowingly transferring, possessing, or using means of identification of another person
3. Without lawful authority

Penalties:

Identity Theft: Up to 15 years imprisonment (25 years if terrorism-related)

Aggravated Identity Theft: Mandatory 2 years consecutive imprisonment (5 years for terrorism)

Fines: Up to $250,000 for individuals

Restitution: Time and money spent recovering identity

Means of Identification:

Social Security numbers and cards

Driver's licenses and identification cards

Passport and immigration documents

Credit and debit card numbers

Bank account numbers and routing information

Biometric data and personal identifiers

Types of Identity Theft:

Financial Identity Theft: Credit cards, loans, bank accounts

Medical Identity Theft: Healthcare services and insurance

Criminal Identity Theft: False identification to law enforcement

Employment Identity Theft: Using stolen identity for employment

Child Identity Theft: Using children's personal information

Synthetic Identity Theft: Creating fake identities with real and false information

Federal Agencies:

FBI Internet Crime Complaint Center: Online identity theft reporting

Secret Service: Financial identity theft investigations

Federal Trade Commission: Consumer protection and education

Social Security Administration: Social Security number fraud

Immigration and Customs Enforcement: Immigration document fraud

Predicate Felonies for Aggravated Identity Theft:

Immigration violations

Theft of public money

Various fraud offenses

Drug trafficking crimes

Firearms violations

Terrorism offenses

Related Federal Offenses:

Credit Card Fraud (18 USC Section 1029)

Mail Fraud (18 USC Section 1341)

Wire Fraud (18 USC Section 1343)

Bank Fraud (18 USC Section 1344)

Computer Fraud (18 USC Section 1030)

Enhanced Penalties:

Organized identity theft rings

Large-scale operations affecting many victims

Use of sophisticated technology

Targeting vulnerable populations

International identity theft schemes

Victim Impact:

Financial losses and credit damage

Time spent restoring identity

Emotional distress and anxiety

Loss of employment or housing opportunities

Medical and legal expenses

IMMIGRATION VIOLATIONS

Statutory Citations: 8 USC Section 1324 (Bringing in and harboring certain aliens); 8 USC Section 1325 (Improper entry by alien); 8 USC Section 1326 (Reentry of removed aliens)

Immigration violations encompass various criminal offenses related to illegal entry, presence, and assistance to unauthorized aliens in the United States.

Elements of Alien Smuggling (8 USC Section 1324(a)(1)(A)):

1. Knowing that person is alien
2. Bringing alien into United States in any manner whatsoever
3. At place other than designated port of entry or examination
4. Knowing or in reckless disregard of fact that such entry is unauthorized

Elements of Harboring Illegal Aliens (8 USC Section 1324(a)(1)(A)(iii)):

1. Knowing or in reckless disregard of fact that alien has come to, entered, or remains in United States in violation of law
2. Concealing, harboring, or shielding alien from detection
3. In any place, including any building or means of transportation

Elements of Illegal Reentry (8 USC Section 1326):

1. Alien who has been denied admission, excluded, deported, or removed
2. Thereafter enters, attempts to enter, or is at any time found in United States
3. Unless consent of Attorney General has been obtained

Penalties:

Basic Alien Smuggling: Up to 5 years imprisonment

Commercial Smuggling: Up to 10 years imprisonment

If Death Results: Life imprisonment or death penalty

Illegal Reentry: Up to 2 years imprisonment (10 years with prior felony, 20 years with prior aggravated felony)

Harboring: Up to 5 years imprisonment

Types of Immigration Violations:

Border smuggling operations

Document fraud and false identification

Harboring and transporting illegal aliens

Marriage fraud for immigration benefits

Employment authorization fraud

Visa overstays and status violations

Federal Agencies:

Immigration and Customs Enforcement: Primary enforcement agency

Customs and Border Protection: Border security and inspection

Citizenship and Immigration Services: Immigration benefits fraud

Department of Justice Executive Office for Immigration Review: Immigration courts

State Department: Visa fraud investigations

Enhanced Penalties:

Organized smuggling enterprises

Commercial advantage or private financial gain

Endangering life or safety of aliens

Use of firearms or dangerous weapons

Prior immigration violations

Related Federal Offenses:

Human Trafficking (18 USC Section 1591)

Document Fraud (18 USC Section 1028)

RICO (18 USC Section 1962)

Money Laundering (18 USC Section 1956)

Conspiracy (18 USC Section 371)

Administrative vs Criminal Consequences:

Civil removal proceedings

Criminal prosecution and imprisonment

Bars to future immigration benefits

Detention during proceedings

Collateral consequences for family members

Aggravated Felony Enhancements:

Enhanced penalties for illegal reentry after aggravated felony conviction

Expanded definition of aggravated felonies

Mandatory detention and limited relief

Streamlined removal procedures

INSIDER TRADING

Statutory Citations: 15 USC Section 78j(b) (Securities Exchange Act); 18 USC Section 1348 (Securities fraud)

Insider trading involves buying or selling securities while in possession of material, nonpublic information in violation of duty of trust or confidence owed to shareholders or source of information.

Elements:

1. Purchase or sale of security
2. While in possession of material, nonpublic information
3. Breach of duty of trust or confidence owed to shareholders or source of information
4. Use of instrumentalities of interstate commerce

Penalties:

Securities Fraud: Up to 25 years imprisonment

Insider Trading: Up to 20 years imprisonment

Fines: Up to $5,000,000 for individuals, $25,000,000 for entities

Civil Penalties: Up to three times profit gained or loss avoided

Disgorgement: Return of ill-gotten gains plus prejudgment interest

Material Information:

Information that reasonable investor would consider important in making investment decision

Merger and acquisition plans

Earnings announcements and financial results

Product launches and regulatory approvals

Management changes and strategic decisions

Legal proceedings and regulatory actions

Nonpublic Information:

Information not generally available to investing public

Information obtained through confidential relationships

Information learned through corporate position

Information from government sources

Information obtained through hacking or theft

Federal Agencies:

Securities and Exchange Commission: Civil enforcement and investigation

FBI: Criminal investigations

U.S. Attorneys Offices: Criminal prosecution

Financial Industry Regulatory Authority: Industry oversight

Commodity Futures Trading Commission: Futures and derivatives markets

Types of Insider Trading:

Corporate insiders trading on confidential information

Tipping friends and family members

Trading on merger and acquisition information

Government employees trading on regulatory information

Hacking and cyber-enabled insider trading

Related Federal Offenses:

Securities Fraud (18 USC Section 1348)

Wire Fraud (18 USC Section 1343)

Mail Fraud (18 USC Section 1341)

Computer Fraud (18 USC Section 1030)

Money Laundering (18 USC Section 1956)

Defenses:

Information was public

No duty of trust or confidence existed

Trading plans established in good faith

Lack of knowledge information was material

Authorized disclosure of information

Enhanced Penalties:

Systematic and repeated violations

Large profits or avoided losses

Use of sophisticated schemes

Organized insider trading rings

Corruption of market integrity

INSURANCE FRAUD

Statutory Citation: 18 USC Section 1033

Federal insurance fraud involves knowingly executing schemes to defraud insurance companies or obtaining money or property from insurers through false or fraudulent pretenses when affecting interstate commerce.

Elements:

1. Knowingly executing scheme or artifice to defraud insurance company
2. Affecting commerce
3. In connection with insurance business
4. Obtaining money or property by false or fraudulent pretenses

Penalties:

Insurance Fraud: Up to 20 years imprisonment

If Affecting Financial Institution: Up to 30 years imprisonment

Fines: Up to $250,000 for individuals, $500,000 for organizations

Restitution: Full amount of fraudulent claims

Types of Insurance Fraud:

Auto Insurance Fraud: Staged accidents, false injury claims, vehicle theft

Property Insurance Fraud: Arson, false theft claims, inflated damage claims

Health Insurance Fraud: False medical claims, unnecessary procedures

Life Insurance Fraud: Murder for insurance proceeds, fake death claims

Workers Compensation Fraud: False injury claims, premium fraud

Disability Insurance Fraud: Exaggerated or false disability claims

Federal Agencies:

FBI: Major insurance fraud investigations

National Insurance Crime Bureau: Industry coordination

Internal Revenue Service: Tax aspects of insurance fraud

State Insurance Commissioners: Regulatory oversight and referrals

Interstate Commerce Requirements:

Insurance company operates across state lines

Use of mail or wire communications

Interstate transportation of fraudulent claims

Effect on interstate insurance markets

Related Federal Offenses:

Mail Fraud (18 USC Section 1341)

Wire Fraud (18 USC Section 1343)

Money Laundering (18 USC Section 1956)

Arson (18 USC Section 844)

Murder for Hire (18 USC Section 1958)

Enhanced Penalties:

Organized fraud rings

Professional facilitators (doctors, lawyers, adjusters)

Large-scale operations

Endangering public safety

Repeat offenses

Staged Accident Schemes:

Organized rings staging vehicle accidents

False injury claims and medical treatment

Corrupt medical providers and legal professionals

Premium fraud and rate manipulation

Public safety risks from dangerous staging

INTERNATIONAL PARENTAL KIDNAPPING

Statutory Citation: 18 USC Section 1204

International parental kidnapping involves removing children from the United States or retaining children outside the United States with intent to obstruct the lawful exercise of parental rights.

Elements:

1. Removing child from United States or retaining child outside United States
2. With intent to obstruct lawful exercise of parental rights
3. Child under 16 years of age
4. Defendant is parent of child

Penalties:

International Parental Kidnapping: Up to 3 years imprisonment

Fines: Up to $250,000

Restitution: Costs of locating and returning child

Enhanced Penalties: If other crimes committed in connection

Parental Rights:

Custody rights awarded by court

Visitation rights established by court

Rights recognized under state law

Rights under international treaties

Joint custody arrangements

Federal Agencies:

FBI: International parental kidnapping investigations

State Department: International cooperation and assistance

Immigration and Customs Enforcement: Border enforcement

U.S. **Marshals Service:** Fugitive apprehension

National Center for Missing and Exploited Children: Case coordination

International Aspects:

Hague Convention on International Child Abduction

Bilateral treaties for child recovery

Diplomatic channels for resolution

International police cooperation

Consular assistance for parents

Related Federal Offenses:

Kidnapping (18 USC Section 1201)

Passport Fraud (18 USC Section 1542)

Immigration Violations (8 USC Section 1325)

False Statements (18 USC Section 1001)

Conspiracy (18 USC Section 371)

Defenses:

Fleeing domestic violence

Child in imminent danger

Consent of other parent

No lawful custody order existed

Emergency circumstances

Prevention Measures:

Passport controls and alerts

Court-ordered surrender of passports

Supervised visitation requirements

International travel restrictions

Early warning systems

INTERNET CRIMES

Statutory Citations: 18 USC Section 1030 (Computer Fraud and Abuse Act); 18 USC Section 2251 (Child exploitation); Various other statutes

Internet crimes encompass various offenses committed using computers, networks, and online platforms, including cybercrime, online fraud, and digital exploitation.

Elements of Computer Intrusion (18 USC Section 1030(a)(2)):

1. Intentionally accessing computer without authorization or exceeding authorized access
2. Obtaining information from protected computer
3. Conduct involving interstate or foreign commerce

Elements of Online Child Exploitation (18 USC Section 2251):

1. Employing, using, persuading, inducing, enticing, or coercing minor
2. To engage in sexually explicit conduct
3. For purpose of producing visual depiction of such conduct
4. Use of materials transported in interstate commerce

Penalties:

Computer Intrusion: Up to 10 years imprisonment (20 years for repeat offenses)

Child Exploitation: 15-30 years imprisonment

Cyberstalking: Up to 5 years imprisonment

Online Fraud: Up to 20 years imprisonment

Fines: Up to $250,000 per count

Types of Internet Crimes:

Hacking and unauthorized access

Online fraud and identity theft

Cyberstalking and harassment

Child exploitation and pornography

Cyber terrorism and attacks on infrastructure

Intellectual property theft

Online drug trafficking

Federal Agencies:

FBI Cyber Division: Primary cybercrime investigations

Internet Crime Complaint Center: Online crime reporting

Secret Service: Financial cybercrime

Immigration and Customs **Enforcement:** Child exploitation online

Homeland Security Investigations: Cyber threats

Enhanced Penalties:

Crimes targeting critical infrastructure

Organized cybercrime enterprises

International cyber operations

Use of malware and sophisticated techniques

Targeting vulnerable populations

Related Federal Offenses:

Wire Fraud (18 USC Section 1343)

Identity Theft (18 USC Section 1028)

Money Laundering (18 USC Section 1956)

Child Pornography (18 USC Section 2252)

Extortion (18 USC Section 875)

Cyber Security Measures:

Network monitoring and intrusion detection

International cooperation and information sharing

Public-private partnerships

Victim notification and assistance

Prevention and education programs

Digital Evidence:

Computer forensics and data recovery

Network traffic analysis

Cryptocurrency tracking

International evidence gathering

Privacy and Fourth Amendment considerations

INVESTMENT FRAUD

Statutory Citations: 15 USC Section 77x (Securities Act); 15 USC Section 78ff (Securities Exchange Act); 18 USC Section 1348 (Securities fraud)

Investment fraud involves schemes to defraud investors through misrepresentations, omissions, or manipulations in connection with the purchase or sale of securities.

Elements:

1. Scheme or artifice to defraud in connection with purchase or sale of securities
2. Use of instrumentalities of interstate commerce, mail, or wire communications
3. Material misrepresentation or omission
4. Intent to defraud investors

Penalties:

Securities Fraud: Up to 25 years imprisonment

Investment Adviser Fraud: Up to 5 years imprisonment

Fines: Up to $250,000 for individuals, $500,000 for organizations

Civil Penalties: Disgorgement of profits plus civil monetary penalties

Restitution: Investor losses

Types of Investment Fraud:

Ponzi schemes and pyramid schemes

Pump and dump stock manipulation

Boiler room operations and cold calling

Affinity fraud targeting specific groups

Prime bank and high-yield investment scams

Advance fee fraud and foreign exchange schemes

Federal Agencies:

Securities and Exchange Commission: Civil enforcement and regulation

FBI: Criminal investigations

Commodity Futures Trading Commission: Futures and derivatives fraud

Financial Industry Regulatory Authority: Broker-dealer oversight

State Securities Regulators: Local enforcement

Ponzi Scheme Elements:

Use of new investor money to pay earlier investors

False representations of investment returns

Lack of legitimate underlying investment

Collapse when new investments insufficient

Targeting of vulnerable populations

Related Federal Offenses:

Mail Fraud (18 USC Section 1341)

Wire Fraud (18 USC Section 1343)

Money Laundering (18 USC Section 1956)

RICO (18 USC Section 1962)

Tax Evasion (26 USC Section 7201)

Enhanced Penalties:

Large-scale operations affecting many investors

Sophisticated schemes and professional facilitators

Targeting of retirement funds and vulnerable populations

International operations and money laundering

Organized investment fraud enterprises

Victim Impact:

Loss of life savings and retirement funds

Emotional and psychological trauma

Family and relationship disruption

Economic hardship and bankruptcy

Loss of trust in financial markets.

J

JURY TAMPERING

Statutory Citation: 18 USC Section 1503 (Obstruction of justice)

Jury tampering involves corruptly influencing, obstructing, or impeding the due administration of justice by attempting to influence jurors in federal proceedings.

Elements:

1. Corruptly endeavoring to influence, intimidate, or impede juror
2. In discharge of juror's duty
3. In federal court proceeding
4. Intent to obstruct or impede administration of justice

Penalties:

Jury Tampering: Up to 10 years imprisonment

If Force or Threat of Force Used: Up to 20 years imprisonment

Fines: Up to $250,000 for individuals

Enhanced Penalties: If tampering successful or involves organized crime

Types of Jury Tampering:

Direct Communication: Approaching jurors to influence their decision

Bribery: Offering money or benefits for favorable verdict

Intimidation: Threats against jurors or their families

Investigation: Unauthorized inquiry into jurors' backgrounds

Social Media Contact: Online communications with jurors during trial

Federal Jurisdiction:

Federal criminal trials

Federal civil trials

Grand jury proceedings

Federal administrative hearings with jury components

Appeals from federal jury trials

Federal Agencies:

FBI: Primary jury tampering investigations

U.S. Marshals Service: Juror protection and court security

U.S. Attorneys Offices: Prosecution of tampering cases

Administrative Office of U.S. Courts: Jury administration

Related Federal Offenses:

Obstruction of Justice (18 USC Section 1503)

Contempt of Court (18 USC Section 401)

Bribery (18 USC Section 201)

Witness Tampering (18 USC Section 1512)

Conspiracy (18 USC Section 371)

Juror Protection Measures:

Anonymous juries in high-profile cases

Sequestration during deliberations

Security escorts and protection

Confidentiality of juror information

Post-trial monitoring and support

Enhanced Penalties:

Organized crime cases

Terrorism-related trials

High-profile cases with media attention

Systematic tampering efforts

Use of violence or serious threats

Defenses:

No intent to influence jury

Inadvertent contact with juror

Protected speech under First Amendment

Lack of knowledge person was juror

Authorized contact through proper channels

Investigation Techniques:

Electronic surveillance of suspects

Undercover operations

Witness interviews and testimony

Financial records analysis

Communications monitoring

JOYRIDING (FEDERAL)

Statutory Citation: 18 USC Section 2312 (Transportation of stolen motor vehicles)

Federal joyriding involves the temporary taking and transportation of motor vehicles across state lines without intent to permanently deprive the owner, distinguished from auto theft by lack of permanent taking intent.

Elements:

1. Taking motor vehicle without owner's consent
2. Transporting vehicle in interstate or foreign commerce
3. Knowing vehicle was taken without consent
4. Temporary use rather than permanent theft

Penalties:

Federal Joyriding: Up to 1 year imprisonment (first offense)

Subsequent Offenses: Up to 5 years imprisonment

Fines: Up to $100,000 for misdemeanors, $250,000 for felonies

Restitution: Damage to vehicle and owner's losses

Interstate Commerce Requirement:

Physical transportation across state lines

Use of interstate highways or transportation facilities

Vehicle manufactured in different state

Intent to cross state boundaries

Federal Agencies:

FBI: Interstate motor vehicle theft investigations

U.S. Marshals Service: Fugitive apprehension

State and Local Law Enforcement: Joint task forces

National Insurance Crime Bureau: Industry cooperation

Distinction from Auto Theft:

Joyriding: Temporary use with intent to return or abandon

Auto Theft: Permanent taking with intent to deprive owner

Evidence of Intent: Duration of possession, distance traveled, condition of vehicle

Penalties: Generally lesser for joyriding than theft

Related Federal Offenses:

Auto Theft (18 USC Section 2312)

Receiving Stolen Property (18 USC Section 2315)

Interstate Transportation of Stolen Goods (18 USC Section 2314)

Conspiracy (18 USC Section 371)

Factors Indicating Joyriding vs Theft:

Short duration of possession

Vehicle abandoned rather than sold

No attempt to alter identification

Local use rather than distant transportation

No evidence of commercial theft operation

Enhanced Penalties:

Multiple vehicles taken simultaneously

Commercial joyriding operations

Damage to vehicles during unauthorized use

Flight to avoid prosecution

Organized youth gangs

Defenses:

Consent of owner

Good faith belief in right to use vehicle

Emergency circumstances

Lack of knowledge vehicle was stolen

Statute of limitations

Juvenile Considerations:

Federal prosecution of juvenile offenders

Transfer to juvenile courts

Diversion programs and alternatives

Parental responsibility and restitution

Educational and counseling requirements

JUDICIAL CORRUPTION

Statutory Citations: 18 USC Section 201 (Bribery of public officials); 18 USC Section 1503 (Obstruction of justice)

Judicial corruption involves the corrupt receipt of benefits by judges or court personnel in exchange for favorable official actions, or attempts to corruptly influence judicial proceedings.

Elements of Judicial Bribery:

1. Judge or court official demanding, seeking, receiving, or agreeing to receive anything of value
2. In return for being influenced in performance of official act
3. Or being induced to commit or omit act in violation of official duty

Elements of Corrupt Influence of Judge:

1. Giving, offering, or promising anything of value to judge
2. With intent to influence official act or decision
3. In federal judicial proceeding

Penalties:

Judicial Bribery: Up to 15 years imprisonment

Corrupt Influence: Up to 15 years imprisonment

Fines: Up to three times value of bribe or $250,000, whichever is greater

Disqualification: From holding federal office

Forfeiture: Property involved in corruption

Types of Judicial Corruption:

Cash payments for favorable rulings

Gifts and entertainment for lenient sentences

Employment opportunities for family members

Business relationships with litigants

Sexual favors in exchange for court decisions

Campaign contributions tied to specific cases

Federal Agencies:

FBI Public Corruption Unit: Primary investigations

Department of Justice Public Integrity Section: Specialized prosecution

Judicial Conference: Administrative oversight

Federal Judicial Center: Ethics training and guidance

Enhanced Penalties:

Systematic corruption over multiple cases

Organized crime connections

Affecting major federal cases

Undermining public confidence in judiciary

International corruption schemes

Related Federal Offenses:

Obstruction of Justice (18 USC Section 1503)

Mail Fraud (18 USC Section 1341)

Wire Fraud (18 USC Section 1343)

RICO (18 USC Section 1962)

Tax Evasion (26 USC Section 7201)

Ethical Violations:

Canon of Judicial Conduct violations

Conflicts of interest

Ex parte communications

Financial disclosure violations

Appearance of impropriety

Investigation Challenges:

Separation of powers considerations

Judicial immunity doctrines

Need for prosecutorial independence

Media and public scrutiny

Protection of ongoing cases

JURISDICTION SHOPPING

Statutory Citation: Various federal statutes prohibiting forum shopping and procedural abuse

Jurisdiction shopping involves manipulating legal procedures to obtain more favorable treatment by selecting specific federal courts or jurisdictions for prosecutorial or litigation advantage.

Elements of Improper Jurisdiction Shopping:

1. Filing charges or cases in multiple jurisdictions
2. With intent to obtain procedural or substantive advantage
3. Abuse of federal court selection process
4. Violation of proper venue requirements

Types of Jurisdiction Shopping:

Criminal Forum Shopping: Prosecutors selecting favorable districts

Civil Forum Shopping: Plaintiffs choosing favorable courts

Bankruptcy Shopping: Debtors selecting favorable bankruptcy courts

Patent Shopping: Intellectual property cases in favorable venues

Immigration Shopping: Selecting favorable immigration courts

Federal Agencies:

Department of Justice: Prosecution venue decisions

Administrative Office of U.S. Courts: Court administration

Federal Judicial Conference: Policy and procedure development

U.S. Attorneys Offices: Local prosecution decisions

Legitimate Venue Selection:

Proper venue under federal rules

Jurisdiction where crime occurred

Jurisdiction where defendants reside

Convenience of witnesses and evidence

Administrative efficiency considerations

Improper Practices:

Manipulating charges to create venue

Filing in multiple districts simultaneously

Abuse of grand jury venue rules

Circumventing transfer procedures

Creating artificial jurisdictional connections

Related Issues:

Venue transfer motions

Forum non conveniens doctrine

Due process venue requirements

Speedy trial considerations

Equal protection concerns

Remedies:

Transfer to proper venue

Dismissal for improper venue

Sanctions for abuse of process

Professional discipline for attorneys

Administrative remedies

Prevention Measures:

Clear venue guidelines and training

Judicial oversight of venue decisions

Appellate review of venue abuse

Professional responsibility rules

Inter-district coordination

JUVENILE FEDERAL CRIMES

Statutory Citation: 18 USC Section 5031 et seq. (Federal Juvenile Delinquency Act)

Federal juvenile crimes involve offenses committed by persons under 18 years of age that violate federal criminal laws, with special procedures and considerations for youthful offenders.

Elements for Federal Juvenile Jurisdiction:

1. Person under 18 years of age at time of offense
2. Violation of federal criminal law
3. No adequate state court jurisdiction
4. Federal interest in prosecution

Penalties and Dispositions:

Juvenile Detention: Until age 21 or shorter term

Adult Prosecution: For serious violent offenses (over age 16)

Probation: Supervised release with conditions

Restitution: Payment for victim losses

Community Service: Alternative to detention

Federal Juvenile Offenses:

Drug trafficking and possession

Immigration violations

Firearms offenses

Computer crimes and hacking

Interstate transportation crimes

Federal property crimes

Federal Agencies:

FBI: Juvenile crime investigations

U.S. Attorneys Offices: Juvenile prosecution decisions

U.S. Probation: Juvenile supervision

Federal Bureau of Prisons: Juvenile detention facilities

Marshals Service: Juvenile transport and custody

Transfer to Adult Court:

Age 16 or older for serious violent crimes

Extensive criminal history

Lack of rehabilitative prospects

Public safety considerations

Prosecutorial discretion factors

Related Considerations:

Fourth Amendment protections

Miranda rights and interrogation

Parental notification requirements

Educational and counseling services

Confidentiality of juvenile records

Special Procedures:

Closed hearings and sealed records

Appointed counsel for indigent juveniles

Social services investigation and reports

Family involvement in proceedings

Alternative dispute resolution

Prevention Programs:

Community-based intervention

Educational and vocational training

Mental health and substance abuse treatment

Family counseling and support

Mentoring and positive role models

JUSTICE OBSTRUCTION

Statutory Citation: 18 USC Section 1503 (Obstruction of justice)

Justice obstruction involves corruptly influencing, obstructing, or impeding the due administration of justice in federal proceedings through various forms of interference.

Elements:

1. Endeavoring to influence, obstruct, or impede administration of justice
2. In federal court or agency proceeding
3. Through corrupt means
4. With intent to interfere with judicial process

Penalties:

Basic Obstruction: Up to 10 years imprisonment

With Use of Force: Up to 20 years imprisonment

Fines: Up to $250,000 for individuals

Enhanced Penalties: For organized obstruction or repeat offenses

Types of Obstruction:

Witness intimidation and tampering

Document destruction and concealment

False statements to investigators

Jury tampering and influence

Judge and court personnel corruption

Evidence manipulation and fabrication

Federal Agencies:

FBI: Obstruction investigations

U.S. Attorneys Offices: Prosecution coordination

U.S. Marshals Service: Witness protection

Inspector General Offices: Administrative investigations

Federal Proceedings Covered:

Criminal trials and investigations

Civil litigation in federal court

Administrative agency proceedings

Congressional investigations

Grand jury proceedings

Bankruptcy proceedings

Related Federal Offenses:

Witness Tampering (18 USC Section 1512)

Perjury (18 USC Section 1621)

False Statements (18 USC Section 1001)

Contempt of Court (18 USC Section 401)

Conspiracy (18 USC Section 371)

Corrupt Means:

Bribery and financial inducements

Threats and intimidation

Deception and misrepresentation

Physical interference

Electronic surveillance and hacking

Media manipulation and influence

Enhanced Penalties:

Terrorism-related obstruction

Organized crime cases

Public corruption investigations

National security matters

Systematic obstruction schemes

Defenses:

Lack of corrupt intent

No pending federal proceeding

Protected constitutional activity

Good faith legal advice

Statute of limitations

Prosecutorial misconduct

Investigation Techniques:

Electronic surveillance and wiretaps

Undercover operations

Financial records analysis

Computer forensics

Cooperating witness testimony

Document analysis and authentication

JUDICIAL PROCEEDINGS INTERFERENCE

Statutory Citations: 18 USC Section 1503 (Obstruction of justice); 18 USC Section 1512 (Witness tampering)

Judicial proceedings interference involves various forms of disruption, manipulation, or corrupt influence of federal court proceedings and related judicial activities.

Elements:

1. Interference with federal judicial proceeding
2. Through improper means or corrupt influence
3. Intent to affect outcome or process of proceeding
4. Knowledge of pending or contemplated proceeding

Penalties:

Proceedings Interference: Up to 10 years imprisonment

Violent Interference: Up to 20 years imprisonment

Fines: Up to $250,000 for individuals

Contempt Sanctions: Additional court-imposed penalties

Types of Interference:

Courtroom disruption and outbursts

Threats against judges and court personnel

Attempts to influence court decisions

Interference with court orders and processes

Tampering with court records and evidence

Unauthorized communications with court

Federal Jurisdiction:

Federal district courts

Federal courts of appeals

Supreme Court proceedings

Federal bankruptcy courts

Specialized federal courts

Administrative law judge proceedings

Federal Agencies:

U.S. Marshals Service: Courtroom security and protection

FBI: Investigation of threats and interference

Federal Protective Service: Court facility security

Court Security Officers: Immediate security response

Enhanced Penalties:

Terrorism-related interference

Organized crime cases

High-profile proceedings

Repeat interference offenses

Violence against court personnel

Related Federal Offenses:

Contempt of Court (18 USC Section 401)

Threats Against Federal Officials (18 USC Section 115)

Assault on Federal Officers (18 USC Section 111)

Obstruction of Justice (18 USC Section 1503)

RICO (18 USC Section 1962)

Security Measures:

Metal detectors and screening

Armed court security officers

Restricted access to court areas

Video surveillance systems

Emergency response procedures

Judicial protection programs

Courtroom Conduct Rules:

Proper attire and behavior requirements

Electronic device restrictions

Attorney conduct standards

Public gallery limitations

Media access guidelines

Contempt enforcement procedures

Investigation and Response:

Immediate law enforcement response

Threat assessment and analysis

Coordination with court security

Witness interviews and evidence collection

Electronic surveillance when authorized

Protective measures for court personnel.

K

KIDNAPPING

Statutory Citation: 18 USC Section 1201

Federal kidnapping involves unlawfully seizing, confining, abducting, or carrying away another person, with federal jurisdiction arising when the offense crosses state lines, occurs on federal property, or involves federal officials.

Elements:

1. Unlawful seizure, confinement, inveigling, decoying, kidnapping, abducting, or carrying away of another person

2. Against the person's will

3. Federal jurisdictional nexus (interstate transportation, federal property, ransom demand, etc.)

Elements of Kidnapping for Ransom:

1. Unlawful seizure and detention of person

2. Holding person for ransom, reward, or other consideration

3. Use of instrumentalities of interstate commerce

4. Intent to obtain money or other benefit

Penalties:

Basic Kidnapping: Up to 20 years imprisonment

If Victim Not Released Alive and Unharmed Within 24 Hours: Life imprisonment or death penalty

Kidnapping for Ransom: Life imprisonment or death penalty

Conspiracy to Kidnap: Same penalties as substantive offense

Fines: Up to $250,000 for individuals

Federal Jurisdiction Triggers:

Transportation across state or national boundaries

Kidnapping on federal property or reservations

Use of mail or wire communications for ransom demands

Kidnapping of federal officials or employees

When victim is foreign official or internationally protected person

Kidnapping in special maritime and territorial jurisdiction

Types of Federal Kidnapping:

Ransom Kidnapping: Holding victim for monetary payment

Express Kidnapping: Short-term kidnapping for immediate ransom

Virtual Kidnapping: False claims of kidnapping for ransom

Parental Kidnapping: International parental child abduction

Human Trafficking: Kidnapping for forced labor or commercial sex

Political Kidnapping: Kidnapping for political purposes

Federal Agencies:

FBI: Primary federal kidnapping investigations

U.S. Marshals Service: Fugitive apprehension and victim recovery

Immigration and Customs Enforcement: International and border cases

Secret Service: Kidnapping of protected persons

Customs and Border Protection: Border-related kidnapping

Enhanced Penalties:

Death of victim during kidnapping

Sexual assault during kidnapping

Use of firearms or dangerous weapons

Organized kidnapping enterprises

International kidnapping operations

Targeting of children or vulnerable persons

Related Federal Offenses:

Hostage Taking (18 USC Section 1203)

Extortion (18 USC Section 875)

Human Trafficking (18 USC Section 1591)

Interstate Transportation for Illegal Sexual Activity (18 USC Section 2421)

RICO (18 USC Section 1962)

24-Hour Presumption:

Federal law presumes interstate transportation if victim not released within 24 hours

Presumption allows immediate federal investigation

Defendant may rebut presumption with evidence

Critical for establishing federal jurisdiction quickly

International Considerations:

Hague Convention on International Child Abduction

Extradition treaties for kidnapping cases

Diplomatic immunity issues

International police cooperation

Consular notification requirements

Victim Recovery Operations:

Rapid response teams and specialized units

Negotiation with kidnappers

International cooperation and assistance

Technology and surveillance capabilities

Post-rescue victim services and support

KICKBACKS

Statutory Citations: 18 USC Section 201 (Bribery); 41 USC Section 8702 (Anti-Kickback Act)

Federal kickback violations involve corrupt payments or benefits provided in exchange for favorable treatment in government contracts, healthcare programs, or other federally funded activities.

Elements of Government Contract Kickbacks (41 USC Section 8702):

1. Providing, attempting to provide, or offering to provide kickback
2. To prime contractor or subcontractor employee
3. In connection with negotiation or performance of federal contract
4. Intent to improperly obtain or reward favorable treatment

Elements of Healthcare Kickbacks (42 USC Section 1320a-7b):

1. Knowingly and willfully offering, paying, soliciting, or receiving remuneration
2. To induce referrals of patients or business
3. For items or services payable by federal healthcare programs
4. Intent to induce such referrals or business

Penalties:

Government Contract Kickbacks: Up to 10 years imprisonment and $250,000 fine

Healthcare Kickbacks: Up to 5 years imprisonment and $25,000 fine

Civil Penalties: Three times amount of kickback plus additional penalties

Debarment: Exclusion from government contracting or healthcare programs

Types of Kickbacks:

Cash payments for contract awards

Gifts and entertainment for procurement officials

Subcontract awards in exchange for payments

Employment offers for government employees

Healthcare referral fees and bonuses

Inflated pricing to cover kickback payments

Federal Agencies:

FBI: Criminal kickback investigations

Health and Human Services Office of Inspector General: Healthcare kickbacks

General Services Administration: Government contract kickbacks

Defense Criminal Investigative Service: Defense contract kickbacks

Various Agency Inspector Generals: Agency-specific kickbacks

Government Contract Kickbacks:

Prime contractor payments to government employees

Subcontractor payments to prime contractors

Consultant fees for contract assistance

Gifts and entertainment for procurement officials

Employment promises for favorable treatment

Inflated pricing schemes

Healthcare Kickbacks:

Physician referral fees for patient referrals

Hospital payments for admissions

Laboratory kickbacks for test referrals

Pharmaceutical company payments to physicians

Medical device manufacturer incentives

Nursing home kickbacks for referrals

Related Federal Offenses:

Bribery (18 USC Section 201)

Mail Fraud (18 USC Section 1341)

Wire Fraud (18 USC Section 1343)

False Claims Act Violations (31 USC Section 3729)

Conspiracy (18 USC Section 371)

Safe Harbors and Exceptions:

Legitimate business arrangements

Fair market value payments

Bona fide employment relationships

Personal services contracts

Discount and rebate programs

Group purchasing arrangements

Enhanced Penalties:

Large-scale kickback schemes

Organized procurement fraud

Endangering patient safety

International kickback operations

Repeat violations and enterprises

Civil Remedies:

False Claims Act treble damages

Civil monetary penalties

Program exclusion and debarment

Contract termination and suspension

Restitution and disgorgement

KNIFE CRIMES (FEDERAL)

Statutory Citations: 15 USC Section 1244 (Switchblade Knife Act); 18 USC Section 930 (Possession of weapons in federal facilities)

Federal knife crimes involve violations of laws regulating the manufacture, sale, transportation, and possession of certain types of knives, particularly in federal facilities and across state lines.

Elements of Switchblade Transportation (15 USC Section 1244):

1. Transportation, shipment, receipt, or possession of switchblade knife
2. In commerce between states or to or from Indian country
3. Knowing violation of federal switchblade restrictions

Elements of Weapons in Federal Facilities (18 USC Section 930):

1. Knowingly possessing or causing to be present dangerous weapon
2. In federal facility or attempting to enter such facility
3. Without authorization for such possession

Penalties:

Switchblade Violations: Up to $2,000 fine and forfeiture of knives

Federal Facility Weapons: Up to 1 year imprisonment and $100,000 fine

Enhanced Penalties: For intent to use weapon unlawfully

Repeat Offenses: Increased fines and imprisonment terms

Types of Regulated Knives:

Switchblade knives with automatic opening mechanisms

Ballistic knives that propel detachable blades

Certain martial arts weapons and exotic knives

Knives disguised as other objects

Military-style combat knives in certain contexts

Federal Facilities Restrictions:

Federal courthouses and office buildings

Military installations and bases

Federal prisons and detention centers

National parks and forests (some restrictions)

Airports and transportation security areas

Post offices and postal facilities

Federal Agencies:

ATF: Weapons violations and enforcement

Federal Protective Service: Federal facility security

Transportation Security Administration: Airport knife restrictions

Customs and Border Protection: Import and export violations

U.S. Marshals Service: Courthouse security

Exceptions and Defenses:

Law enforcement and military personnel

Authorized security personnel

Legitimate business purposes

Collector and museum exceptions

Emergency and survival situations

Lack of knowledge of restrictions

Related Federal Offenses:

Assault with Dangerous Weapon (18 USC Section 113)

Carrying Weapons During Drug Trafficking (18 USC Section 924(c))

Threats Against Federal Officials (18 USC Section 115)

Airport Security Violations (49 USC Section 46505)

Interstate Commerce Requirements:

Transportation across state boundaries

Commercial sale and distribution

Use of mail or shipping services

Import and export activities

Manufacturing and wholesale operations

Enhanced Penalties:

Use of knife in commission of federal crime

Possession with intent to commit violence

Organized weapons trafficking

Targeting federal officials or facilities

Repeat weapons violations

KITING (CHECK)

Statutory Citations: 18 USC Section 1344 (Bank fraud); 18 USC Section 1341 (Mail fraud)

Check kiting involves creating artificial account balances through the manipulation of float time between banks, using the delay in check processing to access funds that do not actually exist.

Elements:

1. Writing checks on account with insufficient funds
2. Depositing checks from other accounts also with insufficient funds
3. Creating artificial balances through float manipulation
4. Intent to defraud financial institutions
5. Scheme affecting federally insured financial institutions

Penalties:

Bank Fraud: Up to 30 years imprisonment and $1,000,000 fine

Mail Fraud: Up to 20 years imprisonment and $250,000 fine

Wire Fraud: Up to 20 years imprisonment and $250,000 fine

Restitution: Full amount of fraudulent balances created

Criminal Forfeiture: Property obtained through kiting scheme

Check Kiting Mechanics:

Opening multiple accounts at different banks

Writing checks between accounts without sufficient funds

Depositing checks before previous checks clear

Creating artificial float balances

Withdrawing money before banks discover insufficient funds

Types of Kiting Schemes:

Two-Bank Kiting: Simple scheme using two bank accounts

Multiple Bank Kiting: Complex schemes involving numerous accounts

Corporate Kiting: Business accounts used for large-scale kiting

International Kiting: Using foreign banks to extend float time

Electronic Kiting: Using electronic transfers and deposits

Federal Agencies:

FBI: Primary check kiting investigations

Secret Service: Financial fraud investigations

Federal Deposit Insurance Corporation: Bank fraud coordination

Office of the Comptroller of the Currency: National bank oversight

Federal Reserve: Payment system oversight

Detection Methods:

Automated clearing house monitoring

Check processing system alerts

Unusual account activity patterns

Large deposit and withdrawal patterns

Cross-referencing between financial institutions

Customer due diligence and monitoring

Related Federal Offenses:

Bank Fraud (18 USC Section 1344)

Mail Fraud (18 USC Section 1341)

Wire Fraud (18 USC Section 1343)

Money Laundering (18 USC Section 1956)

False Bank Entries (18 USC Section 1005)

Enhanced Penalties:

Large-scale kiting operations

Professional kiting rings

Use of sophisticated technology

Targeting multiple financial institutions

International kiting schemes

Defenses:

Lack of intent to defraud

Good faith belief in account balances

Mistake or error in banking procedures

Reliance on bank representations

Prompt correction of overdrafts

Prevention Measures:

Real-time payment processing systems

Enhanced due diligence procedures

Account monitoring and alert systems

Cross-bank information sharing

Customer education and awareness

KILLING OF FEDERAL OFFICERS

Statutory Citation: 18 USC Section 1114

The killing of federal officers involves the murder or manslaughter of federal law enforcement officers, judges, and other federal officials while engaged in or on account of the performance of official duties.

Elements:

1. Killing of person who is federal officer or employee
2. While engaged in or on account of performance of official duties

3. Intent to kill or cause serious bodily harm

4. Knowledge that victim is federal officer

Penalties:

Murder of Federal Officer: Life imprisonment or death penalty

Attempted Murder: Up to 20 years imprisonment

Manslaughter: Up to 10 years imprisonment

Conspiracy: Same penalties as substantive offense

Fines: Up to $250,000 for individuals

Protected Federal Personnel:

FBI agents and federal law enforcement officers

Federal judges and court personnel

U.S. Marshals and deputy marshals

Secret Service agents and uniformed officers

Immigration and customs enforcement officers

Federal correctional officers and staff

Postal inspection service officers

Federal probation and pretrial services officers

Federal Agencies:

FBI: Primary investigations of attacks on federal personnel

U.S. Marshals Service: Protection of federal judges and courts

Secret Service: Protection of designated officials

ATF: Explosives and firearms-related attacks

Various agencies: Protection of their own personnel

Enhanced Penalties:

Use of firearms or explosives

Premeditated killing

Killing during commission of another federal crime

Terrorism-related killings

Organized crime involvement

Multiple victims

On Account of Official Duties:

Retaliation for past official actions

Prevention of future official actions

Intimidation of federal law enforcement

Attacks during arrests or investigations

Targeting because of federal employment

Off-duty killings related to official duties

Related Federal Offenses:

Assault on Federal Officers (18 USC Section 111)

Threats Against Federal Officials (18 USC Section 115)

Terrorism (18 USC Section 2332a)

RICO (18 USC Section 1962)

Firearms Violations (18 USC Section 924(c))

Death Penalty Considerations:

Aggravating factors under federal death penalty statute

Victim impact evidence

Mitigating circumstances

Jury determination of sentence

Appeals process for capital cases

Executive clemency procedures

Officer Safety Programs:

Threat assessment and intelligence

Protective equipment and training

Emergency response procedures

Coordination between agencies

Family protection measures

Post-incident support services

KIDNAPPING FOR RANSOM

Statutory Citation: 18 USC Section 1201(a)(1)

Kidnapping for ransom involves the unlawful seizure and detention of persons with demands for payment or other consideration in exchange for the victim's release.

Elements:

1. Unlawful seizure, confinement, or detention of person
2. Against the person's will
3. Demanding ransom, reward, or other consideration
4. For release of victim
5. Use of instrumentalities of interstate commerce or federal jurisdiction

Penalties:

Kidnapping for Ransom: Life imprisonment or death penalty

If Victim Released Unharmed: Minimum 20 years imprisonment

Conspiracy: Same penalties as substantive offense

Attempted Kidnapping for Ransom: Up to 20 years imprisonment

Fines: Up to $250,000 for individuals

Types of Ransom Kidnapping:

Traditional Kidnapping: Physical seizure and detention for money

Express Kidnapping: Short-term kidnapping for immediate payment

Virtual Kidnapping: False claims of kidnapping to extort payment

Cyber Kidnapping: Using technology to facilitate ransom demands

Political Kidnapping: Ransom demands including political concessions

Federal Jurisdiction:

Interstate or international transportation of victim

Use of mail, telephone, or internet for ransom communications

Kidnapping on federal property

Foreign victims or international implications

Use of banking system for ransom payments

Federal Agencies:

FBI: Primary ransom kidnapping investigations

U.S. Marshals Service: Fugitive apprehension

Secret Service: Financial aspects of ransom payments

Immigration and Customs Enforcement: International cases

State Department: Foreign kidnapping cases

Ransom Communication Methods:

Telephone calls and voice messages

Written letters and notes

Email and internet communications

Text messages and social media

Cryptocurrency payment demands

International wire transfers

Enhanced Penalties:

Death or serious injury to victim

Sexual assault during kidnapping

Use of weapons or explosives

Organized kidnapping enterprises

International kidnapping operations

Repeat kidnapping offenses

Related Federal Offenses:

Extortion (18 USC Section 875)

Hostage Taking (18 USC Section 1203)

Money Laundering (18 USC Section 1956)

Wire Fraud (18 USC Section 1343)

RICO (18 USC Section 1962)

Investigation Techniques:

Electronic surveillance and wiretapping

Financial transaction monitoring

Undercover operations

International cooperation and assistance

Technology and communications analysis

Victim recovery and rescue operations

Victim and Family Considerations:

Crisis negotiation and communication

Psychological support and counseling

Media management and privacy protection

Financial and legal assistance

Post-rescue recovery services

Long-term security assessments.

L

LARCENY

Statutory Citation: 18 USC Section 641 (Theft of government property)

Federal larceny involves the unlawful taking and carrying away of property belonging to the United States or within federal jurisdiction, with intent to permanently deprive the owner of the property.

Elements:

1. Unlawful taking and carrying away of property
2. Property belonging to United States or within federal jurisdiction
3. Without consent of owner
4. Intent to permanently deprive owner of property
5. Value exceeding $1,000 for felony prosecution

Penalties:

Felony Larceny (over $1,000): Up to 10 years imprisonment

Misdemeanor Larceny ($1,000 or less): Up to 1 year imprisonment

Fines: Up to $250,000 for felonies, $100,000 for misdemeanors

Restitution: Full value of stolen property plus damages

Types of Federal Larceny:

Government Property Theft: Equipment, supplies, vehicles from federal agencies

Military Property Theft: Weapons, equipment, supplies from military installations

Postal Theft: Mail, packages, postal equipment and supplies

National Park Theft: Natural resources, artifacts, equipment

Federal Building Theft: Equipment, furnishings, supplies from federal facilities

Research Property Theft: Scientific equipment, data, materials

Federal Jurisdiction:

Special maritime and territorial jurisdiction

Federal property and installations

Military bases and reservations

National parks and forests

Federal office buildings

Indian reservations (concurrent jurisdiction)

Federal Agencies:

FBI: Major federal property theft investigations

Military Criminal Investigation Commands: Military property theft

Postal Inspection Service: Postal property theft

National Park Service: Park resource theft

Federal Protective Service: Federal building security

Various Inspector General Offices: Agency-specific theft

Enhanced Penalties:

Theft during national emergency

Organized theft operations

Employee theft (breach of trust)

Theft of classified materials

Large-scale theft operations

Repeat offenses

Related Federal Offenses:

Embezzlement (18 USC Section 641)

Receiving Stolen Property (18 USC Section 2315)

Interstate Transportation of Stolen Goods (18 USC Section 2314)

Burglary (18 USC Section 2111)

Conspiracy (18 USC Section 371)

Distinctions from State Larceny:

Federal property requirement

Interstate commerce connections

Special maritime and territorial jurisdiction

Enhanced penalties for federal crimes

Federal investigative resources

Defenses:

Lack of intent to permanently deprive

Claim of right or ownership

Consent of authorized person

Property not belonging to United States

Good faith mistake as to ownership

Employee Theft:

Federal employees stealing government property

Contractors misappropriating federal resources

Military personnel theft of equipment

Abuse of access and position

Breach of fiduciary duty

LAUNDERING (MONEY)

Statutory Citations: 18 USC Section 1956 (Money laundering); 18 USC Section 1957 (Monetary transactions in property derived from specified unlawful activity)

Money laundering involves conducting financial transactions with proceeds from criminal activity to conceal the nature, source, ownership, or control of the illegal proceeds.

Elements of Money Laundering (18 USC Section 1956):

1. Financial transaction involving proceeds of specified unlawful activity
2. Knowledge that property involved represents proceeds from unlawful activity
3. Intent to promote carrying on of specified unlawful activity, or
4. Intent to conceal or disguise nature, location, source, ownership, or control of proceeds

Elements of Monetary Transactions (18 USC Section 1957):

1. Engaging in monetary transaction
2. In criminally derived property of value greater than $10,000
3. Knowledge that property derived from specified unlawful activity
4. Transaction occurs in United States

Penalties:

Money Laundering: Up to 20 years imprisonment

Monetary Transactions: Up to 10 years imprisonment

Fines: Up to $500,000 or twice the amount laundered, whichever is greater

Criminal Forfeiture: All property involved in money laundering offense

Civil Forfeiture: Property traceable to money laundering

Specified Unlawful Activities:

Drug trafficking offenses

Fraud and financial crimes

Racketeering and organized crime

Terrorism and national security crimes

Human trafficking and smuggling

Public corruption and bribery

Environmental crimes

Methods of Money Laundering:

Bank deposits and wire transfers

Cash-intensive businesses

Real estate transactions

Shell companies and trusts

Cryptocurrency transactions

Trade-based money laundering

Bulk cash smuggling

Federal Agencies:

FBI: Complex money laundering investigations

Internal Revenue Service Criminal Investigation: Financial crime expertise

Drug Enforcement Administration: Drug-related money laundering

Immigration and Customs **Enforcement:** Trade-based laundering

Financial Crimes Enforcement **Network:** Financial intelligence

Secret Service: Financial crimes investigations

Three Stages of Money Laundering:

Placement: Introducing illegal proceeds into financial system

Layering: Complex transactions to obscure money trail

Integration: Clean money returned to legitimate economy

Related Federal Offenses:

RICO (18 USC Section 1962)

Bank Fraud (18 USC Section 1344)

Wire Fraud (18 USC Section 1343)

Drug Trafficking (21 USC Section 841)

Structuring (31 USC Section 5324)

Enhanced Penalties:

International money laundering schemes

Use of financial institutions

Large-scale operations

Organized money laundering enterprises

Facilitating terrorism financing

Professional money laundering services

Financial Institution Reporting:

Currency Transaction Reports for transactions over $10,000

Suspicious Activity Reports for unusual transactions

Bank Secrecy Act compliance requirements

Customer due diligence obligations

Enhanced due diligence for high-risk customers

LOAN SHARKING

Statutory Citation: 18 USC Section 892-894 (Extortionate credit transactions)

Loan sharking involves making extortionate extensions of credit and using extortionate means to collect or attempt to collect such extensions of credit.

Elements of Making Extortionate Extension of Credit (18 USC Section 892):

1. Making extension of credit
2. At rate of interest exceeding 45 percent per annum
3. Extension of credit is extortionate
4. Use or threat of use of violence or other criminal means

Elements of Financing Extortionate Extensions of Credit (18 USC Section 893):

1. Advancing money or property
2. With knowledge that it will be used to make extortionate extensions of credit
3. Participation in loan sharking enterprise

Elements of Collection of Extensions of Credit by Extortionate Means (18 USC Section 894):

1. Knowingly participating in use of extortionate means
2. To collect or attempt to collect extension of credit
3. Use of violence or threats of violence

Penalties:

Making Extortionate Credit: Up to 20 years imprisonment

Financing Loan Sharking: Up to 20 years imprisonment

Extortionate Collection: Up to 20 years imprisonment

Fines: Up to $250,000 for individuals

Criminal Forfeiture: Property used in loan sharking operations

Extortionate Means:

Violence or threats of violence

Threats to person or property

Reputation for use of violent methods

Understanding that nonpayment could result in violence

Implicit threats based on reputation

Federal Agencies:

FBI: Organized crime and loan sharking investigations

Internal Revenue Service: Tax evasion aspects

U.S. Attorneys Offices: Prosecution coordination

State and Local Law Enforcement: Joint task forces

Types of Loan Sharking Operations:

Street-level individual lenders

Organized crime family operations

Payday lending schemes

Internet-based predatory lending

Business loan sharking

Gambling debt collection

Related Federal Offenses:

RICO (18 USC Section 1962)

Extortion (18 USC Section 1951)

Mail Fraud (18 USC Section 1341)

Wire Fraud (18 USC Section 1343)

Conspiracy (18 USC Section 371)

Interest Rate Considerations:

Annual percentage rate calculations

State usury law violations

Federal lending regulations

Consumer protection violations

Truth in Lending Act requirements

Enhanced Penalties:

Organized loan sharking enterprises

Use of violence in collections

Large-scale operations

Repeat offenses

Targeting vulnerable populations

Victim Impact:

Financial exploitation and abuse

Physical violence and intimidation

Psychological trauma and fear

Loss of property and assets

Family and relationship disruption

LYNCHING

Statutory Citation: 18 USC Section 249 (Emmett Till Antilynching Act)

Federal lynching laws criminalize conspiracy to commit hate crimes that result in death or serious bodily injury, addressing mob violence motivated by bias against protected characteristics.

Elements:

1. Conspiracy of two or more persons
2. To commit hate crime under federal law
3. Resulting in death or serious bodily injury
4. Motivated by bias based on race, color, religion, national origin, gender, sexual orientation, gender identity, or disability

Penalties:

Lynching Resulting in Death: Life imprisonment or death penalty

Lynching Resulting in Serious Bodily Injury: Up to 30 years imprisonment

Conspiracy to Lynch: Same penalties as completed offense

Fines: Up to $250,000 for individuals

Historical Context:

Legacy of racial violence and terrorism

Failure of state authorities to prosecute

Federal intervention in civil rights violations

Symbol of systemic racism and injustice

Congressional recognition and condemnation

Protected Characteristics:

Race and color

Religion and national origin

Gender and gender identity

Sexual orientation

Disability status

Federal Jurisdiction:

Interstate conspiracy or planning

Use of interstate facilities or communications

Affecting interstate commerce

Federal property or jurisdiction

Civil rights violations

Federal Agencies:

FBI Civil Rights Program: Hate crime investigations

Department of Justice Civil Rights Division: Prosecution coordination

U.S. Attorneys Offices: Local prosecution

Community Relations Service: Prevention and mediation

Related Federal Offenses:

Hate Crimes (18 USC Section 249)

Civil Rights Conspiracy (18 USC Section 241)

Kidnapping (18 USC Section 1201)

Murder (18 USC Section 1111)

RICO (18 USC Section 1962)

Modern Applications:

Contemporary hate crime prosecutions

Organized hate group activities

Internet-facilitated hate crimes

Domestic terrorism cases

Civil rights violations

Enhanced Penalties:

Organized hate groups

Use of weapons or explosives

Multiple victims

Interstate operations

Official involvement or corruption

Prevention and Education:

Community outreach programs

Hate crime prevention initiatives

Educational programs about civil rights

Law enforcement training

Victim support services

LOBBYING VIOLATIONS

Statutory Citations: 2 USC Section 1606 (Lobbying Disclosure Act violations); 18 USC Section 219 (Officers and employees acting as agents of foreign principals)

Federal lobbying violations involve failures to comply with registration, disclosure, and conduct requirements for persons who lobby federal officials and agencies.

Elements of Lobbying Disclosure Violations (2 USC Section 1606):

1. Knowingly failing to comply with lobbying disclosure requirements
2. Registration and reporting obligations
3. Financial disclosure requirements
4. Willful violation of lobbying laws

Elements of Foreign Agent Violations (18 USC Section 219):

1. Federal employee or official
2. Acting as agent of foreign principal
3. In matters affecting United States

4. Without disclosure and authorization

Penalties:

Lobbying Disclosure Violations: Up to $200,000 civil penalty

Foreign Agent Violations: Up to 2 years imprisonment and $250,000 fine

Enhanced Penalties: For systematic violations

Professional Sanctions: Loss of lobbying privileges

Lobbying Disclosure Requirements:

Registration of lobbyists and lobbying firms

Quarterly disclosure reports

Client identification and payment amounts

Issue areas and specific lobbying activities

Campaign contribution bundling reports

Revolving door restrictions

Federal Agencies:

Department of Justice: Criminal enforcement

Clerk of House and Secretary of Senate: Registration and reporting

Office of Government Ethics: Ethics guidance

FBI: Criminal investigations

U.S. Attorneys Offices: Prosecution

Types of Lobbying Violations:

Failure to register as lobbyist

False or incomplete disclosure reports

Gift restrictions violations

Revolving door violations

Foreign agent registration failures

Contingent fee arrangements

Related Federal Offenses:

Bribery (18 USC Section 201)

False Statements (18 USC Section 1001)

Foreign Agents Registration Act (22 USC Section 611)

Honest Services Fraud (18 USC Section 1346)

Conspiracy (18 USC Section 371)

Gift and Entertainment Restrictions:

Limits on gifts to federal officials

Entertainment and travel restrictions

Exceptions for widely attended events

Disclosure requirements for certain activities

Enforcement and penalty provisions

Enhanced Penalties:

Foreign influence operations

Systematic disclosure failures

Corruption and bribery schemes

Organized lobbying violations

National security implications

Ethics Rules:

Cooling-off periods for former officials

Conflict of interest restrictions

Financial disclosure requirements

Recusal obligations

Post-employment restrictions

LOANSHARKING

See: Loan Sharking (covered above)

LOTTERY FRAUD

Statutory Citations: 18 USC Section 1341 (Mail fraud); 18 USC Section 1343 (Wire fraud); 18 USC Section 1084 (Wire Act)

Federal lottery fraud involves schemes using fraudulent lottery and sweepstakes promotions to defraud victims through mail, wire communications, or interstate commerce.

Elements:

1. Scheme or artifice to defraud using false lottery or sweepstakes
2. Material misrepresentations about prizes or odds
3. Use of mail, wire, or other interstate communications
4. Intent to defraud victims of money or property

Penalties:

Mail Fraud: Up to 20 years imprisonment

Wire Fraud: Up to 20 years imprisonment

Fines: Up to $250,000 for individuals

Restitution: Full victim losses

Enhanced Penalties: For targeting elderly or vulnerable populations

Types of Lottery Fraud:

Advance Fee Scams: Requiring payment to claim fictional prizes

Foreign Lottery Scams: Illegal promotion of foreign lotteries

Sweepstakes Fraud: False prize notifications and contests

Charity Lottery Fraud: Fake charity raffles and drawings

Online Lottery Scams: Internet-based fraudulent lotteries

Federal Agencies:

FBI: Internet Crime Complaint Center and fraud investigations

Postal Inspection Service: Mail fraud investigations

Federal Trade Commission: Consumer protection enforcement

State Attorneys General: Consumer fraud prosecution

Common Fraud Schemes:

Publishers Clearing House imposters

Foreign lottery notifications

Prize claim processing fees

Tax and insurance requirements

Expedited processing charges

Multiple prize notifications

Related Federal Offenses:

Mail Fraud (18 USC Section 1341)

Wire Fraud (18 USC Section 1343)

Money Laundering (18 USC Section 1956)

Elder Abuse (18 USC Section 2261)

Identity Theft (18 USC Section 1028)

Victim Targeting:

Elderly and vulnerable populations

Persons with gambling problems

Low-income communities

Previous lottery players

Social media and internet users

Enhanced Penalties:

Organized fraud enterprises

Large-scale operations

Targeting vulnerable victims

International fraud schemes

Repeat offenses

Prevention and Education:

Consumer awareness campaigns

Law enforcement training programs

Industry cooperation and reporting

Victim assistance and recovery

International cooperation efforts

M

MAIL FRAUD

Statutory Citation: 18 USC Section 1341

Mail fraud involves executing schemes to defraud using the United States mail or private commercial interstate carriers, making it one of the most frequently prosecuted federal crimes due to its broad application.

Elements:

1. Scheme or artifice to defraud or obtain money or property by false or fraudulent pretenses
2. Use of United States mail or private commercial interstate carrier
3. Use of mail or carrier in furtherance of the scheme
4. Intent to defraud

Penalties:

Basic Mail Fraud: Up to 20 years imprisonment

If **Affecting Financial Institution:** Up to 30 years imprisonment

Fines: Up to $250,000 for individuals, $500,000 for organizations

Restitution: Mandatory restitution to victims

Criminal Forfeiture: Property obtained through mail fraud

Types of Mail Fraud Schemes:

Investment fraud and Ponzi schemes

Healthcare and insurance fraud

Government benefits fraud

Identity theft and credit card fraud

Lottery and sweepstakes scams

Real estate and mortgage fraud

Charity and disaster relief fraud

Federal Agencies:

FBI: Primary mail fraud investigations

Postal Inspection Service: Mail-related fraud enforcement

Securities and Exchange Commission: Investment fraud cases

Internal Revenue Service: Tax-related mail fraud

Various Inspector General Offices: Government program fraud

Use of Mail Requirements:

Any use of mail system in furtherance of scheme

Need not be essential to scheme's success

Includes both sending and receiving mail

Private commercial carriers included (FedEx, UPS)

Minimal use sufficient for federal jurisdiction

Scheme to Defraud:

Plan or course of conduct designed to deceive

Material misrepresentations or omissions

Intent to obtain money or property through deception

Victims need not suffer actual loss

Scheme may target money, property, or honest services

Related Federal Offenses:

Wire Fraud (18 USC Section 1343)

Bank Fraud (18 USC Section 1344)

Securities Fraud (18 USC Section 1348)

Money Laundering (18 USC Section 1956)

Conspiracy (18 USC Section 371)

Enhanced Penalties:

Mass marketing fraud targeting elderly

Healthcare fraud endangering patients

Financial institution fraud

Organized fraud enterprises

International mail fraud schemes

Honest Services Fraud:

Deprivation of intangible right of honest services

Public corruption and private sector fraud

Bribery and kickback schemes

Undisclosed self-dealing

Limited by Supreme Court to bribery and kickbacks

Defenses:

No scheme to defraud

Good faith and honest belief

Lack of intent to defraud

Puffery and sales talk

Statute of limitations (5 years)

MANSLAUGHTER

Statutory Citations: 18 USC Section 1112 (Manslaughter); 18 USC Section 1113 (Attempt to commit murder or manslaughter)

Federal manslaughter involves the unlawful killing of another human being without malice aforethought within the special maritime and territorial jurisdiction of the United States.

Elements of Voluntary Manslaughter:

1. Unlawful killing of human being
2. Without malice aforethought
3. Upon sudden quarrel or heat of passion
4. Within special maritime and territorial jurisdiction

Elements of Involuntary Manslaughter:

1. Unlawful killing of human being
2. Without malice aforethought
3. In commission of unlawful act not amounting to felony
4. Or in commission of lawful act which might produce death in unlawful manner or without due caution

Penalties:

Voluntary Manslaughter: Up to 15 years imprisonment

Involuntary Manslaughter: Up to 8 years imprisonment

Attempted Manslaughter: Up to 7 years imprisonment

Fines: Up to $250,000 for individuals

Restitution: Support for victim's dependents

Federal Jurisdiction:

Special maritime and territorial jurisdiction

Military installations and federal property

National parks and forests

Federal buildings and facilities

Indian reservations (concurrent jurisdiction)

Ships and aircraft in certain circumstances

Federal Agencies:

FBI: Major manslaughter investigations

U.S. **Marshals Service:** Federal fugitive apprehension

Military Criminal Investigation **Commands:** Military installations

National Park Service: Park-related deaths

Federal Protective Service: Federal property incidents

Heat of Passion Doctrine:

Sudden and intense emotion

Reasonable provocation

No time for cooling off

Reduces murder to voluntary manslaughter

Objective and subjective standards

Types of Federal Manslaughter:

Vehicular manslaughter on federal property

Workplace deaths due to negligence

Medical malpractice in federal facilities

Environmental deaths from illegal dumping

Construction accidents on federal projects

Military training accidents

Related Federal Offenses:

Murder (18 USC Section 1111)

Assault (18 USC Section 113)

Negligent Homicide (Various statutes)

Vehicular Homicide (18 USC Section 13)

Reckless Endangerment

Enhanced Penalties:

Use of dangerous weapons

Multiple victims

Extreme recklessness or negligence

Prior violent crime convictions

Organized criminal activity

Defenses:

Self-defense or defense of others

Accident without criminal negligence

Lack of causation

Insanity or mental defect

Justification or excuse

MEDICARE AND MEDICAID FRAUD

Statutory Citations: 18 USC Section 1347 (Healthcare fraud); 42 USC Section 1320a-7b (Anti-kickback statute)

Medicare and Medicaid fraud involves knowingly executing schemes to defraud federal healthcare programs or obtaining money from these programs through false or fraudulent pretenses.

Elements:

1. Knowingly and willfully executing scheme to defraud healthcare benefit program
2. In connection with delivery of or payment for healthcare benefits, items, or services
3. Obtaining money or property from federal healthcare program
4. By means of false or fraudulent pretenses, representations, or promises

Penalties:

Healthcare Fraud: Up to 10 years imprisonment (20 years if serious bodily injury, life if death results)

Anti-kickback Violations: Up to 5 years imprisonment

Fines: Up to $250,000 for individuals, $500,000 for organizations

Civil Penalties: Up to $50,000 per violation plus treble damages

Exclusion: From participation in federal healthcare programs

Types of Healthcare Fraud:

Billing for services not rendered

Upcoding services to higher reimbursement rates

Unbundling services normally billed together

Kickbacks for patient referrals

Identity theft for fraudulent billing

Durable medical equipment fraud

Prescription drug fraud and diversion

Federal Agencies:

Health and Human Services Office of Inspector General: Primary healthcare fraud enforcement

FBI Healthcare Fraud Unit: Criminal investigations

Centers for Medicare and Medicaid Services: Program integrity

Drug Enforcement Administration: Prescription drug fraud

State Medicaid Fraud Control Units: State program fraud

Common Fraud Schemes:

Phantom billing for non-existent services

Rolling labs and unnecessary testing

Home healthcare fraud

Nursing home billing fraud

Ambulance and transportation fraud

Telemedicine fraud

COVID-19 relief fraud

Related Federal Offenses:

Mail Fraud (18 USC Section 1341)

Wire Fraud (18 USC Section 1343)

Money Laundering (18 USC Section 1956)

False Claims Act (31 USC Section 3729)

Conspiracy (18 USC Section 371)

Enhanced Penalties:

Patient harm or endangerment

Large-scale fraud operations

Professional license violations

Organized healthcare fraud enterprises

Repeat offenses

Patient Safety Considerations:

Unnecessary procedures and treatments

Substandard care and equipment

Prescription drug diversion and abuse

Unlicensed providers and facilities

Compromised medical records

MURDER

Statutory Citation: 18 USC Section 1111

Federal murder involves the unlawful killing of another human being with malice aforethought within the special maritime and territorial jurisdiction of the United States or in violation of other federal laws.

Elements of First Degree Murder:

1. Unlawful killing of human being
2. With malice aforethought
3. With premeditation and deliberation
4. Within federal jurisdiction

Elements of Second Degree Murder:

1. Unlawful killing of human being
2. With malice aforethought
3. Without premeditation and deliberation
4. Within federal jurisdiction

Penalties:

First Degree Murder: Life imprisonment or death penalty

Second Degree Murder: Life imprisonment

Murder of Federal Official: Life imprisonment or death penalty

Attempted Murder: Up to 20 years imprisonment

Fines: Up to $250,000 for individuals

Federal Jurisdiction:

Special maritime and territorial jurisdiction

Murder of federal officials and employees

Murder for hire affecting interstate commerce

Murder in aid of racketeering

Murder during commission of federal crime

International terrorism murder cases

Federal Agencies:

FBI: Major murder investigations

U.S. Marshals Service: Fugitive apprehension

Military Criminal Investigation Commands: Military murders

National Park Service: Park-related murders

Secret Service: Murders involving protected persons

Types of Federal Murder:

Murder of federal law enforcement officers

Contract killings (murder for hire)

Drug-related murders

Terrorism-related murders

Military murders and fragging incidents

Serial killings crossing state lines

Malice Aforethought:

Intent to kill

Intent to cause serious bodily harm

Depraved heart murder (extreme recklessness)

Felony murder during dangerous felonies

Related Federal Offenses:

Murder for Hire (18 USC Section 1958)

Killing Federal Officers (18 USC Section 1114)

RICO (18 USC Section 1962)

Terrorism (18 USC Section 2332a)

Drug-Related Violence (21 USC Section 848)

Death Penalty Considerations:

Federal death penalty statutes

Aggravating and mitigating factors

Jury determination of sentence

Appellate review process

Executive clemency procedures

Method of execution

Enhanced Penalties:

Multiple murders

Murder during other violent crimes

Torture or heinous methods

Vulnerable victims (children, elderly)

Organized crime murders

MONEY LAUNDERING

[See: Laundering (Money) in SectionL]

MORTGAGE FRAUD

Statutory Citations: 18 USC Section 1344 (Bank fraud); 18 USC Section 1014 (False statements to financial institutions)

Mortgage fraud involves material misstatements, misrepresentations, or omissions relating to the property or potential borrower relied upon by an underwriter or lender to fund, purchase, or insure a loan.

Elements:

1. Material misstatement, misrepresentation, or omission
2. Relating to property or borrower information
3. Relied upon by lender or underwriter
4. In connection with mortgage loan transaction
5. Intent to defraud

Penalties:

Bank Fraud: Up to 30 years imprisonment and $1,000,000 fine

False Statements: Up to 30 years imprisonment and $1,000,000 fine

Wire Fraud: Up to 20 years imprisonment

Mail Fraud: Up to 20 years imprisonment

Restitution: Full amount of fraudulent loans

Types of Mortgage Fraud:

Income and employment fraud

Asset and down payment fraud

Property valuation fraud

Identity theft and straw buyers

Occupancy fraud (investment vs primary residence)

Appraisal fraud and inflated values

Air loans (non-existent properties)

Federal Agencies:

FBI: Primary mortgage fraud investigations

Treasury Inspector General: Government-backed loans

Federal Housing Finance Agency: GSE-related fraud

Department of Housing and Urban **Development:** FHA fraud

Internal Revenue Service: Tax aspects of fraud

Fraud for Property vs Fraud for Profit:

Fraud for Property: Borrower misrepresentations to obtain home

Fraud for Profit: Industry insider schemes for financial gain

Different penalties and prosecution priorities

Professional licensing consequences

Common Schemes:

Straw buyer purchases

Property flipping with inflated appraisals

Builder bailout schemes

Foreclosure rescue scams

Short sale fraud

Loan modification fraud

HELOC and refinancing fraud

Related Federal Offenses:

Bank Fraud (18 USC Section 1344)

Wire Fraud (18 USC Section 1343)

Mail Fraud (18 USC Section 1341)

Money Laundering (18 USC Section 1956)

Conspiracy (18 USC Section 371)

Enhanced Penalties:

Organized fraud enterprises

Large-scale operations

Professional facilitators

Multiple properties and loans

Sophisticated schemes

MURDER FOR HIRE

Statutory Citation: 18 USC Section 1958

Murder for hire involves the use of interstate commerce facilities in the commission of murder-for-hire, making contract killings a federal offense when they affect interstate commerce.

Elements:

1. Use of facilities of interstate or foreign commerce
2. With intent that murder be committed
3. In violation of laws of state or United States
4. As consideration for receipt of or promise to pay anything of value

Penalties:

Murder for Hire (Death Results): Death penalty or life imprisonment

Murder for Hire (No Death): Up to 10 years imprisonment

Attempted Murder for Hire: Up to 10 years imprisonment

Conspiracy: Same penalties as substantive offense

Fines: Up to $250,000 for individuals

Interstate Commerce Facilities:

Telephone and internet communications

Mail and package delivery services

Interstate travel and transportation

Banking and financial services

Interstate highways and transportation

Federal Agencies:

FBI: Primary murder for hire investigations

ATF: Explosives and firearms-related cases

U.S. Marshals Service: Fugitive apprehension

Drug Enforcement Administration: Drug-related contract killings

Types of Murder for Hire:

Professional contract killers

Gang-related contract killings

Domestic violence murder plots

Business dispute killings

Insurance fraud murders

Witness elimination plots

Drug trafficking violence

Related Federal Offenses:

Murder (18 USC Section 1111)

RICO (18 USC Section 1962)

Conspiracy (18 USC Section 371)

Wire Fraud (18 USC Section 1343)

Obstruction of Justice (18 USC Section 1503)

Investigation Techniques:

Undercover operations

Electronic surveillance

Financial transaction analysis

Cooperating witness testimony

Physical surveillance

Communication intercepts

Enhanced Penalties:

Multiple victims

Organized crime involvement

Public officials as targets

Witness intimidation cases

International murder plots

Solicitation vs Attempt:

Solicitation: Asking someone to commit murder

Attempt: Taking substantial step toward completion

Completed offense: Murder actually carried out

Different penalty structures for each level

MARITIME CRIMES

Statutory Citations: 18 USC Section 2280 (Violence against maritime navigation); 46 USC Section 70502 (Maritime drug enforcement)

Maritime crimes involve offenses committed on the high seas, in United States territorial waters, or aboard vessels that affect maritime navigation and commerce.

Elements of Violence Against Maritime Navigation:

1. Unlawfully and intentionally seizing or exercising control over ship
2. Performing act of violence against person on board ship
3. Destroying ship or causing damage likely to endanger safe navigation
4. Placing device or substance likely to destroy or damage ship

Elements of Maritime Drug Enforcement:

1. Manufacture, distribute, or possess with intent to distribute controlled substance
2. On board vessel subject to United States jurisdiction
3. On high seas or in United States territorial waters

Penalties:

Maritime Violence: Up to 20 years imprisonment (life if death results)

Maritime Drug Crimes: Same penalties as land-based drug offenses

Piracy: Life imprisonment

Fines: Up to $250,000 for individuals

Criminal Forfeiture: Vessels and cargo involved

Types of Maritime Crimes:

Piracy and armed robbery at sea

Drug trafficking by vessel

Human trafficking and smuggling

Environmental crimes (oil spills, dumping)

Customs and immigration violations

Violence against crew and passengers

Theft of cargo and vessel equipment

Federal Agencies:

Coast Guard: Primary maritime law enforcement

FBI: Major maritime crime investigations

Immigration and Customs Enforcement: Border enforcement

Drug Enforcement Administration: Maritime drug interdiction

Customs and Border Protection: Port security

International Waters Jurisdiction:

Flag state jurisdiction over vessels

Coastal state jurisdiction in territorial waters

Universal jurisdiction for certain crimes (piracy)

International cooperation and treaties

Maritime law enforcement agreements

Related Federal Offenses:

Drug Trafficking (21 USC Section 841)

Human Trafficking (18 USC Section 1591)

Immigration Violations (8 USC Section 1324)

Environmental Crimes (33 USC Section 1319)

RICO (18 USC Section 1962)

Enhanced Penalties:

Organized maritime crime enterprises

Violence or weapons use

Large-scale operations

International trafficking

Environmental damage

Special Maritime Jurisdiction:

United States territorial waters

High seas aboard U.S. vessels

Foreign vessels with U.S. nexus

Platforms and structures on continental shelf

Great Lakes and navigable waterways.

N

NARCOTICS VIOLATIONS

Statutory Citations: 21 USC Sections 801-971 (Controlled Substances Act)

Narcotics violations encompass federal crimes involving controlled substances, including manufacturing, distributing, dispensing, and possessing illegal drugs, representing one of the largest categories of federal prosecutions.

Elements of Drug Trafficking (21 USC Section 841(a)(1)):

1. Knowingly or intentionally manufacturing, distributing, dispensing, or possessing with intent to distribute

2. Controlled substance listed in Schedules I through V

3. Without authorization under Controlled Substances Act

Elements of Simple Possession (21 USC Section 844(a)):

1. Knowingly or intentionally possessing controlled substance

2. Without valid prescription or authorization

3. For personal use

Penalties by Drug Type and Quantity:

Heroin: 100g-999g (5-40 years), 1kg+ (10 years to life)

Cocaine: 500g-4.999kg (5-40 years), 5kg+ (10 years to life)

Crack Cocaine: 28g-279g (5-40 years), 280g+ (10 years to life)

Methamphetamine: 5g-49g pure (5-40 years), 50g+ pure (10 years to life)

Marijuana: 100-999kg (5-40 years), 1,000kg+ (10 years to life)

Fentanyl: 40g-399g (5-40 years), 400g+ (10 years to life)

Enhanced Penalties:

Prior felony drug conviction: Doubled mandatory minimums

Death or serious bodily injury: 20 years to life

Continuing Criminal Enterprise: 20 years to life, $2 million fine

Distribution to minors: Enhanced penalties

Near schools or playgrounds: Enhanced penalties

Federal Agencies:

Drug Enforcement Administration: Primary federal drug enforcement

FBI: Major trafficking organizations

Customs and Border Protection: Border drug interdiction

Coast Guard: Maritime drug enforcement

Immigration and Customs Enforcement: Immigration-related drug crimes

Types of Narcotics Operations:

International drug cartels

Domestic distribution networks

Internet drug sales **(dark web)**

Prescription drug diversion

Clandestine laboratory operations

Street-level drug dealing

Related Federal Offenses:

Drug Conspiracy (21 USC Section 846)

Money Laundering (18 USC Section 1956)

Firearms Violations (18 USC Section 924(c))

RICO (18 USC Section 1962)

Immigration Violations (8 USC Section 1326)

Drug Schedules:

Schedule I: High abuse potential, no medical use (heroin, LSD)

Schedule II: High abuse potential, accepted medical use (cocaine, morphine)

Schedule III: Moderate abuse potential (anabolic steroids)

Schedule IV: Low abuse potential (prescription drugs)

Schedule V: Lowest abuse potential (cough medicines)

Asset Forfeiture:

Criminal forfeiture of drug proceeds and property

Civil forfeiture of assets used in drug crimes

Real property used for drug operations

Vehicles, aircraft, and vessels

Bank accounts and financial assets

NATIONAL DEFENSE VIOLATIONS

Statutory Citations: 18 USC Sections 2151-2156 (Sabotage); 18 USC Sections 792-798 (Espionage)

National defense violations involve crimes against the military preparedness and security of the United States, including sabotage of defense materials and facilities, and espionage activities.

Elements of Sabotage (18 USC Section 2155):

1. Intentionally injuring, interfering with, or obstructing national defense material, premises, or utilities

2. With intent to injure, interfere with, or obstruct United States or its allies

3. In preparing for or carrying on war or defense activities

Elements of Defense Information Espionage (18 USC Section 793):

1. Obtaining information respecting national defense

2. With intent or reason to believe information will be used to injury of United States

3. Communicating, delivering, or transmitting information to unauthorized persons

Penalties:

Sabotage: Up to 20 years imprisonment (30 years if during war)

Espionage: Up to 10 years imprisonment (death penalty in wartime)

Conspiracy: Same penalties as substantive offenses

Fines: Up to $250,000 for individuals

National Defense Materials:

Military weapons and equipment

Defense production facilities

Transportation systems and infrastructure

Communication and computer systems

Energy production and distribution facilities

Research and development facilities

Federal Agencies:

FBI Counterintelligence Division: Espionage and sabotage investigations

Defense Counterintelligence and Security Agency: Military security

National Security Agency: Signals intelligence protection

Department of Homeland Security: Critical infrastructure protection

Military Criminal Investigation Commands: Military facility protection

Types of National Defense Crimes:

Industrial sabotage of defense contractors

Cyber attacks on military systems

Theft of classified defense information

Sabotage of military installations

Interference with military communications

Economic espionage against defense industry

Related Federal Offenses:

Treason (18 USC Section 2381)

Sedition (18 USC Section 2384)

Computer Fraud (18 USC Section 1030)

Export Control Violations (50 USC Section 4801)

Atomic Energy Violations (42 USC Section 2272)

Enhanced Penalties:

Wartime offenses

Multiple targets or facilities

Foreign government involvement

Organized sabotage operations

Endangering military personnel

International Aspects:

Foreign intelligence services

Industrial espionage by foreign competitors

International terrorism

Diplomatic immunity considerations

Extradition and international cooperation

NEUTRALITY VIOLATIONS

Statutory Citations: 18 USC Sections 960-967 (Neutrality laws)

Neutrality violations involve crimes against the foreign relations of the United States, including unauthorized military expeditions against friendly nations and violations of arms embargoes.

Elements of Military Expedition (18 USC Section 960):

1. Setting on foot or providing means for military expedition or enterprise
2. To be carried on from United States against territory or subjects of foreign prince or state
3. With whom United States is at peace
4. Without authorization from United States

Elements of Enlisting in Foreign Service (18 USC Section 959):

1. Within United States enlisting or entering into service of foreign prince, state, colony, district, or people

2. As soldier or marine or seaman on board vessel of war, letter of marque, or privateer

Penalties:

Military Expeditions: Up to 3 years imprisonment and $3,000 fine

Foreign Enlistment: Up to 3 years imprisonment and $1,000 fine

Arms Export Violations: Up to 20 years imprisonment

Fines: Up to amounts specified in individual statutes

Types of Neutrality Violations:

Unauthorized military expeditions

Arms trafficking to embargoed countries

Recruitment for foreign military service

Providing military training to foreign groups

Financing foreign military operations

Violating international sanctions

Federal Agencies:

State Department: Foreign policy and neutrality oversight

FBI: Criminal investigations

Customs and Border Protection: Export enforcement

Treasury Department: Sanctions enforcement

Immigration and Customs Enforcement: Border violations

Historical Context:

Neutrality Act of 1939

Foreign conflicts and U.S. policy

Embargo enforcement

Private military contractors

Mercenary activities

Related Federal Offenses:

Arms Export Control Act Violations (22 USC Section 2778)

International Emergency Economic Powers Act (50 USC Section 1701)

Trading with the Enemy Act (50 USC Section 4301)

Foreign Agents Registration Act (22 USC Section 611)

Modern Applications:

Private military companies

International arms trafficking

Sanctions violations

Terrorist financing

Foreign fighter recruitment

Enhanced Penalties:

Violations during wartime

Large-scale operations

Organized criminal enterprises

National security implications

Repeat violations

NUCLEAR REGULATORY VIOLATIONS

Statutory Citations: 42 USC Sections 2272-2284 (Atomic Energy Act)

Nuclear regulatory violations involve crimes related to nuclear materials, facilities, and information, protecting national security and public safety from nuclear threats.

Elements of Restricted Data Violations (42 USC Section 2274):

1. Communication, transmission, or disclosure of restricted data
2. To person not authorized to receive such data
3. With intent to injure United States or secure advantage to foreign nation
4. Knowing or having reason to believe data is restricted

Elements of Nuclear Facility Sabotage (42 USC Section 2284):

1. Intentionally and willfully destroying or causing physical damage to nuclear facility
2. Or attempting to destroy or damage such facility
3. Knowing that such destruction or damage could cause release of radiation

Penalties:

Restricted Data Violations: Up to 10 years imprisonment (life or death if intent to injure U.S.)

Nuclear Facility Sabotage: Up to 20 years imprisonment (life if death results)

Conspiracy: Same penalties as substantive offenses

Fines: Up to $100,000

Types of Nuclear Violations:

Unauthorized disclosure of nuclear secrets

Sabotage of nuclear power plants

Theft of nuclear materials

Illegal importation of nuclear technology

Violations of nuclear safety regulations

Computer intrusions into nuclear facilities

Federal Agencies:

Nuclear Regulatory Commission: Regulatory oversight and enforcement

FBI: Criminal investigations

Department of Energy: Nuclear security

Homeland Security: Nuclear terrorism prevention

Customs and Border Protection: Nuclear material smuggling

Restricted Data Categories:

Nuclear weapons design information

Production of special nuclear material

Use of special nuclear material in weapons

Nuclear reactor design and operation

Uranium enrichment processes

Related Federal Offenses:

Espionage (18 USC Section 794)

Sabotage (18 USC Section 2155)

Terrorism (18 USC Section 2332a)

Export Control Violations (50 USC Section 4801)

Computer Fraud (18 USC Section 1030)

Enhanced Penalties:

Foreign government involvement

Terrorist motivations

Large-scale operations

Endangering public safety

Organized criminal activity

Nuclear Security Measures:

Personnel reliability programs

Physical security requirements

Cybersecurity protections

International safeguards

Emergency response procedures

NEGLIGENT HOMICIDE

Statutory Citation: 18 USC Section 1112 (Involuntary manslaughter)

Negligent homicide involves the unlawful killing of another human being through criminal negligence within federal jurisdiction, representing the lowest level of criminal homicide.

Elements:

1. Death of human being
2. Caused by defendant's conduct
3. Conduct constituting criminal negligence
4. Within special maritime and territorial jurisdiction

Penalties:

Negligent Homicide: Up to 8 years imprisonment

Vehicular Negligent Homicide: Up to 8 years imprisonment

Fines: Up to $250,000 for individuals

Restitution: Support for victim's dependents

Enhanced Penalties: For gross negligence or multiple victims

Criminal Negligence Standard:

Gross deviation from standard of care

Conduct creating substantial and unjustifiable risk

Conscious disregard of risk

More than ordinary negligence required

Objective reasonable person standard

Federal Jurisdiction:

Military installations and federal property

National parks and forests

Federal facilities and buildings

Indian reservations (concurrent jurisdiction)

Maritime and aviation contexts

Federal Agencies:

FBI: Major negligent homicide investigations

National Park Service: Park-related deaths

Occupational Safety and Health Administration: Workplace deaths

Environmental Protection Agency: Environmental deaths

Military Criminal Investigation Commands: Military negligence

Types of Negligent Homicide:

Vehicular homicide on federal property

Workplace deaths due to safety violations

Medical negligence in federal facilities

Environmental deaths from illegal dumping

Construction accidents on federal projects

Aviation and maritime negligence

Related Federal Offenses:

Involuntary Manslaughter (18 USC Section 1112)

Reckless Endangerment (Various statutes)

Environmental Crimes (Various statutes)

Occupational Safety Violations (29 USC Section 666)

Enhanced Penalties:

Multiple victims

Use of dangerous instrumentalities

Violation of safety regulations

Prior negligence convictions

Organized negligent conduct

Defenses:

Lack of criminal negligence

Intervening cause

Assumption of risk by victim

Emergency circumstances

Compliance with regulations

NUCLEAR WEAPONS VIOLATIONS

Statutory Citations: 42 USC Section 2122 (Restricted data); 18 USC Section 832 (Nuclear and radiological materials)

Nuclear weapons violations involve unauthorized activities related to nuclear weapons, materials, and technology that could threaten national security or enable nuclear terrorism.

Elements of Nuclear Material Offenses (18 USC Section 832):

1. Knowingly receiving, possessing, using, transferring, altering, disposing of, or dispersing nuclear material or nuclear byproduct material

2. Without lawful authority

3. With intent to compel person, international organization, or country to do or refrain from doing any act

Elements of Radiological Dispersal Device (18 USC Section 2332h):

1. Knowingly producing, constructing, otherwise acquiring, transferring, receiving, possessing, importing, exporting, or using radiological dispersal device

2. With intent to cause death or serious bodily injury

3. Or with intent to cause substantial damage to property or environment

Penalties:

Nuclear Material Violations: Up to 20 years imprisonment (life if death results)

Radiological Weapons: Up to 20 years imprisonment (life if death results)

Nuclear Weapons Conspiracy: Same penalties as substantive offense

Fines: Up to $2,000,000 for individuals

Types of Nuclear Weapons Crimes:

Theft of weapons-grade nuclear material

Unauthorized nuclear weapons development

Radiological dispersal device construction

Nuclear terrorism threats

Illicit nuclear technology transfer

Nuclear material smuggling

Federal Agencies:

FBI Weapons of Mass Destruction Directorate: Primary enforcement

Department of Energy: Nuclear security

Nuclear Regulatory Commission: Material licensing and security

Homeland Security: Nuclear terrorism prevention

Defense Threat Reduction Agency: WMD threats

Nuclear Material Categories:

Highly enriched uranium

Weapons-grade plutonium

Radiological sources

Nuclear reactor fuel

Depleted uranium

Radioactive waste materials

Related Federal Offenses:

Terrorism (18 USC Section 2332a)

Weapons of Mass Destruction (18 USC Section 2332a)

Export Control Violations (50 USC Section 4801)

Atomic Energy Violations (42 USC Section 2272)

Conspiracy (18 USC Section 371)

Enhanced Penalties:

International terrorism connections

Foreign government involvement

Large quantities of nuclear material

Sophisticated weapons development

Organized criminal enterprises

International Cooperation:

International Atomic Energy Agency

Nuclear security treaties

Nuclear forensics and attribution

Intelligence sharing

Coordinated enforcement operations

NURSING HOME FRAUD

Statutory Citations: 18 USC Section 1347 (Healthcare fraud); 42 USC Section 1320a-7b (Anti-kickback statute)

Nursing home fraud involves schemes to defraud Medicare, Medicaid, and other federal healthcare programs through false billing, substandard care, and other fraudulent practices in long-term care facilities.

Elements:

1. Knowingly executing scheme to defraud federal healthcare program
2. In connection with nursing home or long-term care services
3. Obtaining money through false or fraudulent pretenses
4. Material misrepresentations regarding care provided

Penalties:

Healthcare Fraud: Up to 10 years imprisonment (20 years if serious bodily injury, life if death)

Anti-kickback Violations: Up to 5 years imprisonment

Fines: Up to $250,000 for individuals, $500,000 for organizations

Civil Penalties: Treble damages plus civil monetary penalties

Program Exclusion: From Medicare and Medicaid participation

Types of Nursing Home Fraud:

Billing for services not provided

Upcoding resident conditions for higher reimbursement

Therapy fraud and unnecessary services

Kickbacks for resident referrals

Medication fraud and diversion

Staffing fraud and inadequate care

Quality of care fraud

Federal Agencies:

Health and Human Services Office of **Inspector General:** Primary enforcement

FBI Healthcare Fraud Unit: Criminal investigations

Centers for Medicare and Medicaid Services: Program oversight

State Medicaid Fraud Control Units: State program enforcement

Common Fraud Schemes:

Phantom residents and billing

Therapy mills with unnecessary treatment

Prescription drug diversion

Dietary and supply fraud

Maintenance and repair fraud

Administrative cost fraud

Corporate compliance failures

Related Federal Offenses:

Mail Fraud (18 USC Section 1341)

Wire Fraud (18 USC Section 1343)

Money Laundering (18 USC Section 1956)

False Claims Act (31 USC Section 3729)

Elder Abuse (Various statutes)

Enhanced Penalties:

Patient harm or endangerment

Systematic fraud operations

Vulnerable population targeting

Large-scale operations

Repeat offenses

Quality of Care Issues:

Neglect and abandonment of residents

Medication errors and abuse

Inadequate staffing levels

Unsafe and unsanitary conditions

Failure to provide required services.

O

OBSTRUCTION OF JUSTICE

Statutory Citation: 18 USC Section 1503

Obstruction of justice involves corruptly influencing, obstructing, or impeding the due administration of justice in federal proceedings, representing one of the most broadly applied federal criminal statutes.

Elements:

1. Endeavoring to influence, obstruct, or impede administration of justice
2. In federal court proceeding or investigation
3. Through corrupt means
4. With intent to interfere with judicial or investigative process

Penalties:

Basic Obstruction: Up to 10 years imprisonment

If Force or Violence Used: Up to 20 years imprisonment

Fines: Up to $250,000 for individuals

Enhanced Penalties: For systematic obstruction or repeat offenses

Types of Obstruction:

Witness intimidation and tampering

Document destruction and concealment

False statements to investigators

Perjury and false testimony

Jury tampering and influence

Bribery of court officials

Evidence fabrication and manipulation

Federal Proceedings Covered:

Criminal investigations and prosecutions

Civil litigation in federal court

Grand jury proceedings

Administrative agency investigations

Congressional investigations

Bankruptcy proceedings

Immigration proceedings

Federal Agencies:

FBI: Primary obstruction investigations

U.S. Attorneys Offices: Prosecution coordination

Inspector General Offices: Administrative investigations

Congressional oversight committees: Legislative obstruction

Corrupt Means:

Threats and intimidation

Bribery and financial inducements

Deception and misrepresentation

Physical interference

Electronic surveillance and hacking

Abuse of official position

Related Federal Offenses:

Witness Tampering (18 USC Section 1512)

Perjury (18 USC Section 1621)

False Statements (18 USC Section 1001)

Contempt of Court (18 USC Section 401)

Conspiracy (18 USC Section 371)

Enhanced Penalties:

Terrorism-related obstruction

Organized crime cases

Public corruption investigations

National security matters

Systematic obstruction schemes

Use of violence or threats

Omnibus Clause:

Broad catch-all provision for obstruction conduct

Covers conduct not specifically enumerated

Requires corrupt intent and nexus to proceeding

Prevents circumvention of specific obstruction statutes

Defenses:

Lack of corrupt intent

No pending federal proceeding

Protected constitutional activity

Good faith legal advice

Statute of limitations

Due process violations

ORGANIZED CRIME (RICO)

Statutory Citation: 18 USC Section 1962 (Racketeer Influenced and Corrupt Organizations Act)

RICO targets organized criminal enterprises by prohibiting the acquisition, operation, or income from enterprises through patterns of racketeering activity.

Elements of RICO Violation (18 USC Section 1962(c)):

1. Conducting or participating in conduct of enterprise
2. Through pattern of racketeering activity
3. Enterprise affects interstate or foreign commerce
4. Person employed by or associated with enterprise

Elements of RICO Conspiracy (18 USC Section 1962(d)):

1. Conspiracy to violate RICO provisions
2. Agreement to participate in enterprise
3. Knowledge of enterprise's criminal objectives

Penalties:

RICO Violation: Up to 20 years imprisonment

RICO Conspiracy: Up to 20 years imprisonment

Fines: Up to $250,000 or twice the gross profits or other proceeds

Criminal Forfeiture: All interests in enterprise and property derived from violations

Civil Remedies: Treble damages and attorney fees

Enterprise Definition:

Legitimate businesses used for criminal purposes

Criminal organizations and gangs

Labor unions engaged in racketeering

Government entities corrupted by criminals

Informal associations of individuals

Pattern of Racketeering Activity:

Two or more racketeering acts within 10 years

Acts must be related and amount to continuing criminal activity

Federal and state crimes qualifying as racketeering acts

Including murder, kidnapping, gambling, arson, robbery, bribery, extortion, drug dealing

Federal Agencies:

FBI Organized Crime Program: Primary RICO investigations

Drug Enforcement Administration: Drug trafficking organizations

Internal Revenue Service: Financial investigations

Immigration and Customs Enforcement: International organized crime

U.S. **Attorneys Offices:** RICO prosecution coordination

Types of RICO Cases:

Traditional organized crime families

Street gangs and criminal organizations

White-collar crime enterprises

Public corruption schemes

Labor union racketeering

International criminal organizations

Predicate Acts:

Murder, kidnapping, arson, robbery, bribery, extortion

Gambling, money laundering, drug trafficking

Mail fraud, wire fraud, securities fraud

Immigration violations, counterfeiting

Bankruptcy fraud, insurance fraud

Environmental crimes, computer crimes

Related Federal Offenses:

Continuing Criminal Enterprise (21 USC Section 848)

Money Laundering (18 USC Section 1956)

Conspiracy (18 USC Section 371)

Various predicate offenses

Forfeiture statutes

Enhanced Penalties:

Leadership roles in enterprise

Violence and use of firearms

Large-scale operations

International connections

Corruption of public officials

Civil RICO:

Private civil lawsuits under RICO

Treble damages for injured parties

Attorney fees for successful plaintiffs

Business and commercial litigation

Class action lawsuits

OFFICIAL MISCONDUCT

Statutory Citations: 18 USC Section 242 (Deprivation of rights under color of law); 18 USC Section 201 (Bribery of public officials)

Official misconduct involves the abuse of government position by federal, state, or local officials to violate constitutional rights or engage in corrupt practices.

Elements of Deprivation Under Color of Law (18 USC Section 242):

1. Acting under color of law, statute, ordinance, regulation, or custom
2. Willfully subjecting person to deprivation of constitutional rights
3. Different punishment than authorized by law
4. Because of race, color, or alien status

Elements of Official Bribery (18 USC Section 201):

1. Public official demanding, seeking, receiving, or accepting anything of value
2. In return for being influenced in performance of official act
3. Or being induced to commit or omit act in violation of official duty

Penalties:

Civil Rights Violations: Up to 1 year imprisonment (10 years if bodily injury, life if death)

Bribery: Up to 15 years imprisonment

False Statements: Up to 5 years imprisonment

Conspiracy: Same penalties as substantive offenses

Fines: Up to three times value received or $250,000

Types of Official Misconduct:

Police brutality and excessive force

Judicial corruption and bribery

Election fraud and vote manipulation

Immigration official corruption

Prison guard misconduct

Federal agent abuse of authority

Color of Law:

Law enforcement officers

Judges and court personnel

Elected officials and administrators

Federal employees and contractors

State and local government officials

Private persons acting with government authority

Federal Agencies:

FBI Civil Rights Program: Police misconduct investigations

Department of Justice Civil Rights Division: Pattern and practice investigations

Inspector General Offices: Federal employee misconduct

Office of Professional Responsibility: DOJ attorney misconduct

Constitutional Rights Protected:

Fourth Amendment: Unreasonable searches and seizures

Fifth Amendment: Due process and self-incrimination

Eighth Amendment: Cruel and unusual punishment

Fourteenth Amendment: Equal protection and due process

First Amendment: Free speech and religion

Sixth Amendment: Right to counsel and fair trial

Related Federal Offenses:

Conspiracy Against Rights (18 USC Section 241)

Mail Fraud (18 USC Section 1341)

Wire Fraud (18 USC Section 1343)

Honest Services Fraud (18 USC Section 1346)

Extortion Under Color of Official Right (18 USC Section 1951)

Enhanced Penalties:

Systematic misconduct patterns

Use of violence or weapons

Targeting vulnerable populations

Organized corruption schemes

Repeat offenses

Civil Remedies:

Section 1983 civil rights lawsuits

Monetary damages for victims

Injunctive relief and consent decrees

Pattern and practice investigations

Police department reforms

ONLINE CRIMES

Statutory Citations: 18 USC Section 1030 (Computer Fraud and Abuse Act); 18 USC Section 2251 (Sexual exploitation of children)

Online crimes encompass various criminal activities conducted through the internet, computer networks, and digital platforms, representing a rapidly growing area of federal prosecution.

Elements of Computer Fraud (18 USC Section 1030(a)(4)):

1. Knowingly accessing protected computer without authorization
2. With intent to defraud
3. Furthering intended fraud and obtaining anything of value
4. Use of computer affects interstate or foreign commerce

Elements of Online Child Exploitation (18 USC Section 2251):

1. Using, employing, persuading, inducing, enticing, or coercing minor
2. To engage in sexually explicit conduct
3. For purpose of producing visual depiction
4. Use of materials transported in interstate commerce

Penalties:

Computer Fraud: Up to 20 years imprisonment

Child Exploitation: 15-30 years imprisonment

Cyberstalking: Up to 5 years imprisonment (life if death results)

Identity Theft: Up to 15 years imprisonment

Fines: Up to $250,000 per count

Types of Online Crimes:

Hacking and unauthorized computer access

Online fraud and identity theft

Cyberstalking and harassment

Child exploitation and pornography

Online drug trafficking

Cryptocurrency crimes

Ransomware and extortion

Federal Agencies:

FBI Cyber Division: Primary cybercrime investigations

Internet Crime Complaint Center: Online crime reporting

Secret Service: Financial cybercrime

Immigration and Customs Enforcement: Child exploitation

Homeland Security Investigations: Cyber threats

Cyberstalking Elements (18 USC Section 2261A):

Use of electronic communications

Intent to kill, injure, harass, intimidate, or place under surveillance

Course of conduct that causes substantial emotional distress

Interstate or foreign commerce involvement

Related Federal Offenses:

Wire Fraud (18 USC Section 1343)

Mail Fraud (18 USC Section 1341)

Money Laundering (18 USC Section 1956)

Extortion (18 USC Section 875)

Child Pornography (18 USC Section 2252)

Enhanced Penalties:

Organized cybercrime enterprises

International cyber operations

Targeting critical infrastructure

Use of sophisticated techniques

Repeat cyber offenses

Digital Evidence Challenges:

Computer forensics and data recovery

Encryption and anonymization

International jurisdiction issues

Privacy and Fourth Amendment concerns

Chain of custody for digital evidence

OCCUPATIONAL SAFETY VIOLATIONS

Statutory Citation: 29 USC Section 666 (Occupational Safety and Health Act)

Federal occupational safety violations involve willful or repeated violations of workplace safety standards that result in death or serious bodily injury to employees.

Elements of Willful Violation Causing Death:

1. Willful violation of occupational safety or health standard
2. Violation causes death of employee
3. Employer knowledge of hazardous condition
4. Conscious disregard for employee safety

Penalties:

Willful Violation Causing Death: Up to 6 months imprisonment (first offense), 1 year (repeat offense)

Civil Penalties: Up to $70,000 per willful violation

Criminal Fines: Up to $10,000 per violation

Enhanced Penalties: For systematic safety violations

Types of Safety Violations:

Construction site accidents and deaths

Industrial chemical exposures

Machine guarding failures

Fall protection violations

Confined space deaths

Electrical safety violations

Trenching and excavation accidents

Federal Agencies:

Occupational Safety and Health Administration: Primary enforcement

Department of Labor Office of **Inspector General:** Criminal referrals

Environmental Protection Agency: Chemical safety

Mine Safety and Health Administration: Mining safety

Willfulness Standard:

Intentional disregard of safety requirements

Conscious indifference to employee safety

Plain indifference to safety obligations

Voluntary action with knowledge of illegality

Related Federal Offenses:

Involuntary Manslaughter (18 USC Section 1112)

Environmental Crimes (42 USC Section 6928)

False Statements (18 USC Section 1001)

Conspiracy (18 USC Section 371)

Wire Fraud (18 USC Section 1343)

Enhanced Penalties:

Multiple employee deaths

Repeat safety violations

Concealment of hazards

Retaliation against whistleblowers

Organized safety violations

Employer Responsibilities:

Providing safe workplace

Training and education

Hazard communication

Personal protective equipment

Record keeping and reporting

Employee rights protection

OIL SPILL VIOLATIONS

Statutory Citations: 33 USC Section 1319 (Clean Water Act); 33 USC Section 2716a (Oil Pollution Act)

Oil spill violations involve the illegal discharge of oil into navigable waters and the failure to properly respond to and clean up oil spills affecting U.S. waters.

Elements of Negligent Oil Discharge (33 USC Section 1319(c)(1)):

1. Negligent violation of permit conditions or effluent standards
2. Discharge of oil into navigable waters
3. Knowledge of violation
4. Substantial likelihood of endangering others

Elements of Knowing Oil Discharge (33 USC Section 1319(c)(2)):

1. Knowing violation of permit conditions
2. Discharge of oil into waters of United States
3. Knowledge that conduct is unlawful

Penalties:

Negligent Discharge: Up to 1 year imprisonment

Knowing Discharge: Up to 3 years imprisonment

Knowing Endangerment: Up to 15 years imprisonment

Civil Penalties: Up to $25,000 per day of violation

Criminal Fines: Up to $50,000 per day

Types of Oil Spill Violations:

Vessel oil spills and accidents

Pipeline leaks and ruptures

Offshore drilling accidents

Tank farm and storage facility spills

Railroad and truck transportation spills

Refinery and industrial facility discharges

Federal Agencies:

Environmental Protection Agency: Oil spill enforcement

Coast Guard: Maritime oil spill response

Pipeline and Hazardous Materials Safety Administration: Pipeline safety

Fish and Wildlife Service: Natural resource damage

National Oceanic and Atmospheric Administration: Environmental assessment

Oil Pollution Act Requirements:

Spill prevention plans and equipment

Immediate spill notification

Response and cleanup obligations

Financial responsibility requirements

Natural resource damage liability

Related Federal Offenses:

Environmental Crimes (42 USC Section 6928)

Negligent Homicide (18 USC Section 1112)

False Statements (18 USC Section 1001)

Obstruction of Justice (18 USC Section 1503)

Conspiracy (18 USC Section 371)

Enhanced Penalties:

Large-scale spills

Repeat violations

Concealment of spills

Endangering human life

International waters violations

Environmental Impact:

Marine life and ecosystem damage

Coastal and wetland contamination

Economic losses to fishing and tourism

Long-term environmental remediation

Public health and safety risks.

P

PERJURY

Statutory Citations: 18 USC Section 1621 (Perjury generally); 18 USC Section 1623 (False declarations before grand jury or court)

Perjury involves knowingly making false statements under oath in federal proceedings, representing a fundamental attack on the integrity of the judicial system and legal process.

Elements of Perjury (18 USC Section 1621):

1. Taking oath before competent tribunal, officer, or person
2. In case in which law of United States authorizes oath to be administered
3. Willfully and contrary to oath stating or subscribing any material matter
4. Which person does not believe to be true

Elements of False Declarations (18 USC Section 1623):

1. Declaration under penalty of perjury in proceeding before court or grand jury
2. Statement is false
3. Statement is material to proceeding
4. Person knows statement is false

Penalties:

Perjury: Up to 5 years imprisonment

False Declarations: Up to 5 years imprisonment

Subornation of Perjury: Up to 5 years imprisonment

Fines: Up to $250,000 for individuals

Enhanced Penalties: If perjury affects national security or terrorism cases

Federal Proceedings Covered:

Federal court trials and hearings

Grand jury proceedings

Congressional investigations and hearings

Administrative agency proceedings

Depositions in federal cases

Immigration proceedings

Bankruptcy proceedings

Federal Agencies:

FBI: Perjury investigations in federal proceedings

U.S. Attorneys Offices: Prosecution coordination

Inspector General Offices: Administrative perjury

Congressional oversight committees: Legislative perjury

Materiality Requirement:

Statement must have natural tendency to influence proceeding

Could affect course or outcome of proceeding

Administrative or ministerial matters typically not material

Relates to substantive issues in case

Willfulness and Knowledge:

Defendant must know statement is false

Willful blindness may satisfy knowledge requirement

Good faith mistake may negate willfulness

Memory lapses versus intentional falsehoods

Related Federal Offenses:

False Statements (18 USC Section 1001)

Obstruction of Justice (18 USC Section 1503)

Contempt of Court (18 USC Section 401)

Subornation of Perjury (18 USC Section 1622)

Conspiracy (18 USC Section 371)

Types of Perjury:

Trial testimony under oath

Grand jury testimony

Deposition testimony

Affidavits and sworn statements

Congressional testimony

Administrative hearing testimony

Defenses:

Statement was not false

Statement was not material

Lack of knowledge that statement was false

Recantation before proceeding concluded

Statute of limitations (5 years)

Enhanced Penalties:

Terrorism-related proceedings

Organized crime cases

Public corruption investigations

National security matters

Systematic perjury schemes

PIRACY

Statutory Citations: 18 USC Section 1651 (Piracy under law of nations); 18 USC Section 1652 (Citizens as pirates)

Federal piracy laws address acts of robbery, violence, or depredation committed on the high seas, representing one of the oldest federal crimes with roots in constitutional maritime jurisdiction.

Elements of Piracy (18 USC Section 1651):

1. Committing piracy as defined by law of nations
2. On high seas
3. Brought into or found in United States
4. Tried and punished according to same law

Elements of Citizens as Pirates (18 USC Section 1652):

1. Citizen of United States committing piracy upon high seas
2. Against United States or citizens thereof
3. Or being of crew or ship's company of piratical vessel

Penalties:

Piracy: Life imprisonment

Piracy with Violence: Life imprisonment or death penalty

Assault in Piracy: Up to 10 years imprisonment

Plundering Wrecks: Up to 10 years imprisonment

Fines: Up to $250,000 for individuals

Modern Piracy Activities:

Vessel hijacking and robbery at sea

Kidnapping of crew members for ransom

Armed attacks on commercial shipping

Theft of cargo and vessel equipment

Maritime terrorism and violence

Illegal boarding and seizure of vessels

Federal Agencies:

Coast Guard: Primary maritime law enforcement

FBI: Piracy investigations and prosecution support

Navy: International waters enforcement

Immigration and Customs Enforcement: Port security

Customs and Border Protection: Maritime border enforcement

International Waters Jurisdiction:

High seas beyond territorial waters

Universal jurisdiction for piracy

Flag state jurisdiction over vessels

Coastal state jurisdiction in territorial waters

International cooperation and treaties

Related Federal Offenses:

Robbery (18 USC Section 2111)

Kidnapping (18 USC Section 1201)

Hostage Taking (18 USC Section 1203)

Violence Against Maritime Navigation (18 USC Section 2280)

RICO (18 USC Section 1962)

Types of Maritime Piracy:

Traditional piracy and armed robbery

Somali piracy operations

Southeast Asian piracy

Caribbean and Gulf Coast piracy

Cyber piracy and navigation system attacks

Enhanced Penalties:

Violence against crew or passengers

Multiple vessel attacks

Organized piracy enterprises

International terrorism connections

Use of sophisticated weapons

International Cooperation:

United Nations Convention on Law of Sea

International Maritime Organization

Counter-piracy task forces

Naval cooperation and patrols

Intelligence sharing and coordination

PORNOGRAPHY (CHILD)

Statutory Citations: 18 USC Section 2251 (Sexual exploitation of children); 18 USC Section 2252 (Material involving sexual exploitation of minors)

Child pornography offenses involve the production, distribution, receipt, and possession of visual depictions of minors engaged in sexually explicit conduct, representing some of the most severely punished federal crimes.

Elements of Production (18 USC Section 2251):

1. Using, employing, persuading, inducing, enticing, or coercing minor
2. To engage in sexually explicit conduct
3. For purpose of producing visual depiction of such conduct
4. If depiction was produced using materials transported in interstate commerce

Elements of Distribution (18 USC Section 2252(a)(1)):

1. Knowingly transporting or shipping visual depiction in interstate commerce
2. By computer or other means
3. For purpose of sale or distribution for sale
4. Depicting minor engaged in sexually explicit conduct

Elements of Possession (18 USC Section 2252(a)(4)):

1. Knowingly possessing visual depiction
2. That has been transported in interstate commerce
3. Depicting minor engaged in sexually explicit conduct

Penalties:

Production: 15-30 years imprisonment (25-50 years for repeat offenders)

Distribution: 5-20 years imprisonment (15-40 years for repeat offenders)

Possession: Up to 20 years imprisonment (15-40 years for repeat offenders)

Enhanced Penalties: For violence, sadistic conduct, or victims under 12

Supervised Release: Minimum 5 years, up to lifetime supervision

Federal Agencies:

FBI Internet Crimes Against Children Task Force: Primary enforcement

Immigration and Customs Enforcement: International child exploitation

Postal Inspection Service: Mail-related child pornography

Secret Service: Technology-facilitated crimes

National Center for Missing and Exploited Children: Coordination and assistance

Types of Child Exploitation:

Commercial sexual exploitation

Online enticement and sextortion

Live streaming of abuse

International child sex tourism

Family-based abuse and exploitation

Peer-to-peer file sharing networks

Related Federal Offenses:

Child Sex Trafficking (18 USC Section 1591)

Transportation for Illegal Sexual Activity (18 USC Section 2421)

Coercion and Enticement (18 USC Section 2422)

Computer Crimes (18 USC Section 1030)

Money Laundering (18 USC Section 1956)

Enhanced Penalties:

Prior convictions for child exploitation

Violence or sadistic conduct

Victims under 12 years of age

Distribution for commercial purposes

Leadership roles in exploitation enterprises

International Aspects:

International child exploitation networks

Cross-border investigations and prosecutions

Mutual legal assistance treaties

INTERPOL cooperation and databases

Victim identification and repatriation

Victim Services:

Trauma-informed interview techniques

Medical and psychological treatment

Victim restitution and compensation

Long-term support and counseling

Family reunification services

PUBLIC CORRUPTION

Statutory Citations: 18 USC Section 201 (Bribery of public officials); 18 USC Section 666 (Federal program bribery)

Public corruption involves the abuse of entrusted power by government officials for private gain, undermining democratic institutions and public trust in government.

Elements of Federal Official Bribery (18 USC Section 201(b)):

1. Public official demanding, seeking, receiving, or accepting anything of value
2. In return for being influenced in performance of official act
3. Or being induced to commit or omit act in violation of official duty
4. Corrupt intent and quid pro quo relationship

Elements of Federal Program Bribery (18 USC Section 666):

1. Agent of organization receiving federal benefits exceeding $10,000
2. Corruptly soliciting, demanding, accepting, or agreeing to accept anything of value
3. Intending to be influenced or rewarded in connection with business or transaction
4. Involving anything of value of $5,000 or more

Penalties:

Federal Official Bribery: Up to 15 years imprisonment

Federal Program Bribery: Up to 10 years imprisonment

Honest Services Fraud: Up to 20 years imprisonment

Fines: Up to three times value of bribe or $250,000

Forfeiture: Property involved in corruption scheme

Types of Public Corruption:

Legislative corruption and vote buying

Judicial corruption and case fixing

Executive branch corruption and favoritism

Law enforcement corruption and protection

Election fraud and campaign violations

Procurement fraud and contract rigging

Federal Agencies:

FBI Public Corruption Program: Primary corruption investigations

Department of Justice Public Integrity Section: Specialized prosecution

Inspector General Offices: Agency-specific corruption

Ethics offices: Administrative oversight and prevention

Federal Programs Covered:

Federal grants and contracts

Healthcare programs (Medicare, Medicaid)

Education funding and programs

Transportation and infrastructure projects

Law enforcement assistance programs

Social services and welfare programs

Related Federal Offenses:

Extortion Under Color of Official Right (18 USC Section 1951)

Mail Fraud (18 USC Section 1341)

Wire Fraud (18 USC Section 1343)

Money Laundering (18 USC Section 1956)

RICO (18 USC Section 1962)

Enhanced Penalties:

High-ranking officials

Large-scale corruption schemes

Organized corruption enterprises

National security implications

Repeat corruption offenses

Quid Pro Quo Requirement:

Explicit agreement not required

Corrupt intent and course of conduct

Stream of benefits theory

Circumstantial evidence of agreement

POSTAL CRIMES

Statutory Citations: 18 USC Sections 1691-1737 (Postal Service offenses)

Postal crimes involve offenses against the United States Postal Service, mail system, and postal employees, protecting the integrity of the nation's mail delivery system.

Elements of Mail Theft (18 USC Section 1708):

1. Stealing, taking, or abstracting mail matter
2. From authorized depository for mail matter
3. Or from letter or mail carrier
4. Intent to obstruct correspondence or steal property

Elements of Mail Obstruction (18 USC Section 1701):

1. Knowingly and willfully obstructing or retarding passage of mail
2. Or any carrier or conveyance carrying mail
3. Intent to obstruct mail delivery

Penalties:

Mail Theft: Up to 5 years imprisonment

Mail Destruction: Up to 5 years imprisonment

Postal Employee Assault: Up to 10 years imprisonment

Mail Fraud: Up to 20 years imprisonment

Fines: Up to $250,000 for individuals

Types of Postal Crimes:

Mail theft from boxes and carriers

Package theft and mail fraud

Identity theft through mail

Check washing and alteration

Postal employee corruption

Mail bombing and dangerous materials

Postal vehicle theft and robbery

Federal Agencies:

Postal Inspection Service: Primary postal crime enforcement

FBI: Mail fraud and terrorism-related postal crimes

Secret Service: Financial crimes involving mail

Immigration and Customs Enforcement: International mail crimes

Mail System Protection:

Letter carriers and postal employees

Mail processing and distribution facilities

Mail collection boxes and equipment

Mail transportation and delivery

Postal customers and correspondence

Related Federal Offenses:

Mail Fraud (18 USC Section 1341)

Identity Theft (18 USC Section 1028)

Bank Fraud (18 USC Section 1344)

Money Laundering (18 USC Section 1956)

Terrorism (18 USC Section 2332a)

Enhanced Penalties:

Organized mail theft operations

Targeting elderly or vulnerable victims

Large-scale identity theft schemes

Violence against postal employees

International mail crimes

Mail Fraud Schemes:

Investment and financial fraud

Healthcare and insurance fraud

Lottery and sweepstakes scams

Charity and disaster relief fraud

Romance and advance fee scams

PRESCRIPTION DRUG FRAUD

Statutory Citations: 21 USC Section 841 (Drug trafficking); 21 USC Section 843 (Prohibited acts)

Prescription drug fraud involves the illegal distribution, diversion, and abuse of controlled prescription medications outside the legitimate medical system.

Elements of Unlawful Distribution:

1. Knowingly or intentionally distributing controlled substance
2. Outside usual course of professional practice
3. Without legitimate medical purpose
4. Registration with Drug Enforcement Administration

Elements of Prescription Fraud:

1. Obtaining controlled substance by fraud, deceit, or misrepresentation
2. From practitioner or pharmacist
3. Knowing conduct is unlawful
4. Intent to obtain controlled substances illegally

Penalties:

Prescription Drug Trafficking: Same penalties as other drug trafficking based on quantity

Doctor Shopping: Up to 4 years imprisonment

Prescription Fraud: Up to 4 years imprisonment

Enhanced Penalties: For involvement in pill mills or large-scale operations

Professional Sanctions: Loss of medical licenses and DEA registration

Types of Prescription Drug Crimes:

Pill mills and illegal prescribing

Doctor shopping and multiple prescriptions

Prescription forgery and alteration

Pharmacy diversion and employee theft

Online pharmacy violations

Insurance fraud and billing schemes

Federal Agencies:

Drug Enforcement Administration: Primary prescription drug enforcement

FBI: Healthcare fraud and pill mill investigations

Health and Human Services Office of Inspector General: Healthcare fraud

Food and Drug Administration: Regulatory violations

Common Drugs of Abuse:

Opioid pain medications (oxycodone, hydrocodone, fentanyl)

Benzodiazepines (Xanax, Valium, Ativan)

Stimulants (Adderall, Ritalin)

Muscle relaxants and sleep aids

Cough syrups containing codeine

Related Federal Offenses:

Healthcare Fraud (18 USC Section 1347)

Mail Fraud (18 USC Section 1341)

Wire Fraud (18 USC Section 1343)

Money Laundering (18 USC Section 1956)

Anti-kickback Violations (42 USC Section 1320a-7b)

Enhanced Penalties:

Death or serious bodily injury resulting

Large quantities of controlled substances

Organized prescription drug enterprises

Targeting vulnerable populations

Repeat prescription drug offenses

Pill Mill Operations:

High-volume prescribing without medical necessity

Cash-only payment systems

Minimal medical examinations

Security issues and criminal clientele

Interstate patient trafficking

PROSTITUTION (FEDERAL)

Statutory Citations: 18 USC Section 2421 (Transportation for illegal sexual activity); 18 USC Section 1591 (Sex trafficking)

Federal prostitution offenses involve the transportation of persons across state lines for prostitution and the operation of interstate prostitution enterprises affecting federal jurisdiction.

Elements of Transportation for Prostitution (18 USC Section 2421):

1. Knowingly transporting individual in interstate or foreign commerce
2. With intent that individual engage in prostitution or sexual activity
3. For which person can be charged with criminal offense

Elements of Sex Trafficking (18 USC Section 1591):

1. Recruiting, enticing, harboring, transporting, providing, obtaining, or maintaining person
2. Knowing that means of force, threats, fraud, or coercion will be used
3. To cause person to engage in commercial sex act
4. Person induced is under 18 years of age

Penalties:

Transportation for Prostitution: Up to 10 years imprisonment

Sex Trafficking: 10 years to life imprisonment (15 years to life if victim under 18)

Promoting Prostitution Enterprise: Up to 20 years imprisonment

Fines: Up to $250,000 for individuals

Restitution: Mandatory restitution to victims

Federal Jurisdiction:

Interstate transportation of persons

Use of interstate facilities or communications

Affecting interstate or foreign commerce

International sex trafficking

Federal property or jurisdiction

Federal Agencies:

FBI Human Trafficking Task Forces: Primary sex trafficking enforcement

Immigration and Customs Enforcement: International trafficking

Department of Justice: Prosecution coordination

Health and Human Services: Victim services

Types of Federal Prostitution Cases:

Interstate prostitution rings

Online escort services

Massage parlor operations

Strip club prostitution

Hotel and casino prostitution

International sex trafficking

Related Federal Offenses:

Human Trafficking (18 USC Section 1591)

RICO (18 USC Section 1962)

Money Laundering (18 USC Section 1956)

Mann Act Violations (18 USC Section 2421)

Immigration Violations (8 USC Section 1324)

Enhanced Penalties:

Minors involved in prostitution

Violence or coercion used

Organized prostitution enterprises

International trafficking operations

Repeat sex trafficking offenses

Victim Considerations:

Trauma-informed interview techniques

Immigration relief for trafficking victims

Social services and housing assistance

Medical and psychological treatment

Witness protection and safety planning.

Q

QUI TAM FRAUD

Statutory Citations: 31 USC Section 3729 (False Claims Act); 31 USC Section 3730 (Civil actions for false claims)

Qui tam fraud involves violations of the False Claims Act where private parties (whistleblowers) bring civil actions on behalf of the United States government against entities that defraud federal programs.

Elements of False Claims Act Violation:

1. Knowingly presenting false or fraudulent claim for payment to United States
2. Knowingly making or using false record or statement material to false claim
3. Conspiring to commit violation of False Claims Act
4. Intent to defraud government or avoid obligation to pay money to government

Civil Penalties:

Civil Monetary Penalties: $13,508 to $27,018 per false claim (adjusted annually)

Treble Damages: Three times amount of damages sustained by government

Attorney Fees: Reasonable attorney fees and costs for successful actions

Whistleblower Awards: 15-30% of recovery for qui tam relators

Types of Qui Tam Cases:

Healthcare fraud against Medicare and Medicaid

Defense contractor fraud and overcharging

Pharmaceutical fraud and off-label marketing

Education fraud and grant misuse

Environmental violations and cleanup fraud

Research and development fraud

Federal Agencies:

Department of Justice: Civil fraud enforcement and qui tam coordination

Health and Human Services Office of **Inspector General:** Healthcare qui tam cases

Defense Criminal Investigative Service: Defense contractor fraud

Environmental Protection Agency: Environmental fraud cases

Education Department Office of Inspector General: Education fraud

Qui Tam Relator Requirements:

First to file requirement among competing whistleblowers

Original source of information not publicly disclosed

Government employee restrictions and exceptions

Personal knowledge of fraudulent conduct

Legal representation and case development

Related Criminal Offenses:

Healthcare Fraud (18 USC Section 1347)

Mail Fraud (18 USC Section 1341)

Wire Fraud (18 USC Section 1343)

Conspiracy (18 USC Section 371)

Money Laundering (18 USC Section 1956)

Knowledge Standard:

Actual knowledge of false information

Deliberate ignorance of truth or falsity

Reckless disregard for truth or falsity

No specific intent to defraud required

Mistake or negligence insufficient

Government Intervention:

Department of Justice decision to intervene in case

Government investigation and settlement negotiations

Declined cases may proceed with private counsel

Coordination between civil and criminal enforcement

Parallel proceedings and information sharing

Enhanced Penalties:

Systematic fraud over extended periods

Large-scale operations affecting multiple programs

Endangering patient safety or public welfare

Obstruction of government investigations

Repeat violations and recidivism

Whistleblower Protection:

Anti-retaliation provisions for qui tam relators

Employment protection and remedies

Confidentiality during government investigation

Attorney-client privilege and work product protection

Statute of limitations and procedural requirements

QUARANTINE VIOLATIONS

Statutory Citation: 42 USC Section 271 (Quarantine and inspection)

Federal quarantine violations involve the breach of quarantine orders and public health measures established to prevent the spread of communicable diseases affecting interstate and international travel.

Elements:

1. Violation of quarantine rule, regulation, or order
2. Issued by Surgeon General or other authorized federal official
3. Relating to control of communicable disease
4. Affecting interstate or foreign commerce

Penalties:

Quarantine Violations: Up to 1 year imprisonment and $100,000 fine

Knowing Violations: Enhanced penalties for willful violations

Civil Penalties: Administrative fines and enforcement actions

Injunctive Relief: Court orders to enforce compliance

Types of Quarantine Violations:

Individual quarantine violations during disease outbreaks

International travel violations and health screening

Agricultural quarantine violations for plant and animal diseases

Maritime quarantine violations at ports of entry

Aviation quarantine violations at international airports

Federal Agencies:

Centers for Disease Control and Prevention: Public health quarantine enforcement

Customs and Border Protection: Border health screening

Transportation Security **Administration:** Aviation health measures

Coast Guard: Maritime quarantine enforcement

Department of Agriculture: Agricultural quarantine

Public Health Emergency Powers:

Federal quarantine authority during health emergencies

Interstate and international travel restrictions

Isolation and quarantine of infected persons

Contact tracing and monitoring requirements

Vaccination and testing mandates

Related Federal Offenses:

False Statements (18 USC Section 1001)

Obstruction of Justice (18 USC Section 1503)

Immigration Violations (8 USC Section 1182)

Transportation Violations (Various statutes)

Public Health Violations (42 USC Section 264)

Enhanced Penalties:

Violations during declared public health emergencies

Intentional spread of communicable disease

Large-scale violations affecting many persons

International travel violations

Organized resistance to quarantine measures

Constitutional Considerations:

Due process requirements for quarantine orders

Equal protection and discriminatory enforcement

Commerce Clause authority for federal quarantine

State police powers and federal preemption

Individual liberty versus public health interests

Modern Applications:

COVID-19 pandemic quarantine measures

Ebola and other infectious disease outbreaks

Bioterrorism and public health preparedness

International health regulations compliance

Emerging infectious disease threats

QUESTIONING OBSTRUCTION

Statutory Citations: 18 USC Section 1503 (Obstruction of justice); 18 USC Section 1512 (Witness tampering)

Questioning obstruction involves interference with federal investigations, interviews, and interrogations through various forms of obstruction designed to impede law enforcement activities.

Elements of Investigation Obstruction:

1. Endeavoring to influence, obstruct, or impede federal investigation
2. Through corrupt means or improper interference
3. Pending or contemplated federal proceeding or investigation
4. Intent to obstruct or impede administration of justice

Elements of Interview Interference:

1. Intimidating, threatening, or corruptly persuading another person
2. With intent to influence, delay, or prevent testimony or cooperation
3. In federal investigation or proceeding
4. Causing person to withhold information or provide false information

Penalties:

Investigation Obstruction: Up to 10 years imprisonment

Witness Tampering: Up to 20 years imprisonment

Intimidation: Up to 10 years imprisonment

Fines: Up to $250,000 for individuals

Enhanced Penalties: For systematic obstruction or violence

Types of Questioning Obstruction:

Witness intimidation and threats

Attorney-client privilege abuse

Corporate obstruction and document destruction

Media interference and publicity campaigns

Political pressure and influence operations

Technology-based obstruction and surveillance

Federal Agencies:

FBI: Investigation obstruction enforcement

U.S. Attorneys Offices: Prosecution coordination

Inspector General Offices: Administrative investigations

Congressional oversight committees: Legislative obstruction

Methods of Obstruction:

Direct threats and intimidation of witnesses

Financial incentives to avoid cooperation

Legal maneuvering to delay investigations

Public relations campaigns to discredit investigations

Destruction or concealment of evidence

False or misleading statements to investigators

Related Federal Offenses:

Obstruction of Justice (18 USC Section 1503)

Witness Tampering (18 USC Section 1512)

Perjury (18 USC Section 1621)

False Statements (18 USC Section 1001)

Conspiracy (18 USC Section 371)

Enhanced Penalties:

Organized obstruction schemes

Use of violence or serious threats

Obstruction of terrorism investigations

Public corruption investigations

National security matters

Legitimate vs Illegitimate Conduct:

Valid assertion of constitutional rights

Proper legal representation and advice

Legitimate privilege claims

Good faith legal challenges

Protected speech and advocacy

Investigation Techniques:

Electronic surveillance and monitoring

Undercover operations and informants

Financial records analysis

Communications interception

International cooperation and assistance

QUOTA VIOLATIONS

Statutory Citations: Various federal regulatory statutes; 19 USC Section 1484 (Customs violations)

Federal quota violations involve the breach of quantitative restrictions on imports, exports, and other regulated activities established by federal agencies to control trade, environmental protection, and resource management.

Elements of Import Quota Violations:

1. Importing goods subject to quantitative restrictions
2. In excess of authorized quota amounts
3. Without proper licenses or permits
4. Knowledge of quota restrictions

Elements of Export Quota Violations:

1. Exporting goods subject to export controls
2. In violation of quantity limitations
3. Without required export licenses
4. Intent to violate export restrictions

Penalties:

Customs Violations: Up to 5 years imprisonment and fines up to $250,000

Export Control Violations: Up to 20 years imprisonment

Agricultural Quota Violations: Civil penalties and criminal fines

Environmental Quota Violations: Up to 5 years imprisonment

Types of Quota Systems:

Import quotas on textiles, steel, and agricultural products

Export quotas on strategic materials and technology

Environmental quotas on pollution and resource extraction

Agricultural quotas on crop production and subsidies

Fish and wildlife quotas on harvesting and trade

Broadcasting quotas on foreign ownership

Federal Agencies:

Customs and Border Protection: Import quota enforcement

Commerce Department: Export control quotas

Agriculture Department: Agricultural quota programs

Environmental Protection Agency: Environmental quotas

Fish and Wildlife Service: Wildlife trade quotas

Trade and Regulatory Context:

World Trade Organization agreements and commitments

North American Free Trade Agreement provisions

Environmental protection and conservation goals

National security and strategic resource control

Economic policy and domestic industry protection

Related Federal Offenses:

Smuggling (18 USC Section 545)

Export Control Violations (50 USC Section 4801)

Environmental Crimes (Various statutes)

False Statements (18 USC Section 1001)

Conspiracy (18 USC Section 371)

Enhanced Penalties:

Large-scale quota violations

Organized smuggling operations

National security implications

Environmental damage and harm

Repeat violations and recidivism

Enforcement Mechanisms:

Inspection and monitoring systems

Licensing and permit requirements

Reporting and record-keeping obligations

Civil penalties and administrative actions

Criminal prosecution for willful violations

RACKETEERING UNDER RICO

See: Organized Crime (RICO) in Section O

QUESTIONING UNDER OATH

See: Perjury (covered above in this section)

R

RICO (RACKETEERING)

Statutory Citation: 18 USC Section 1962 (Racketeer Influenced and Corrupt Organizations Act)

RICO targets organized criminal enterprises by prohibiting the acquisition, operation, or income from enterprises through patterns of racketeering activity, representing one of the most powerful federal prosecution tools against organized crime.

Elements of RICO Enterprise (18 USC Section 1962(c)):

1. Conducting or participating in conduct of enterprise
2. Through pattern of racketeering activity
3. Enterprise affects interstate or foreign commerce
4. Person employed by or associated with enterprise

Elements of RICO Conspiracy (18 USC Section 1962(d)):

1. Conspiracy to violate RICO provisions
2. Agreement to participate in enterprise
3. Knowledge of enterprise's criminal objectives
4. Intent to further criminal purposes

Penalties:

RICO Violation: Up to 20 years imprisonment per count

RICO Conspiracy: Up to 20 years imprisonment

Fines: Up to $250,000 or twice gross profits, whichever is greater

Criminal Forfeiture: All interests in enterprise and property derived from violations

Civil Penalties: Treble damages, attorney fees, and injunctive relief

Enterprise Definition:

Legal entities: Corporations, partnerships, associations, unions

Illegal entities: Criminal organizations, gangs, cartels

Government entities: Agencies, departments, offices corrupted by criminals

Informal associations: Groups of individuals associated in fact

Pattern of Racketeering Activity:

Two or more racketeering acts within 10-year period

Acts must be related to each other and enterprise

Continuity of criminal activity over time

Threat of continued criminal activity

Predicate Racketeering Acts:

Murder, kidnapping, arson, robbery, bribery, extortion, drug trafficking

Gambling, money laundering, securities fraud, mail fraud, wire fraud

Immigration violations, counterfeiting, bankruptcy fraud

Environmental crimes, labor violations, public corruption

Terrorism, human trafficking, cybercrime

Federal Agencies:

FBI Organized Crime Program: Primary RICO investigations

Drug Enforcement Administration: Drug trafficking organizations

Internal Revenue Service: Financial investigations and tax crimes

Immigration and Customs Enforcement: International organized crime

U.S. Attorneys Offices: RICO prosecution coordination

Types of RICO Cases:

Traditional organized crime families (La Cosa Nostra)

Street gangs and criminal organizations

White-collar crime enterprises and corporations

Public corruption schemes and political machines

Labor union racketeering and pension fund fraud

International criminal organizations and cartels

Related Federal Offenses:

Continuing Criminal Enterprise (21 USC Section 848)

Money Laundering (18 USC Section 1956)

Conspiracy (18 USC Section 371)

Various predicate offenses listed above

Forfeiture statutes (18 USC Section 1963)

Enhanced Penalties:

Leadership roles in criminal enterprise

Violence and use of deadly weapons

Large-scale criminal operations

International criminal connections

Corruption of public officials and institutions

Civil RICO:

Private civil lawsuits under RICO statute

Treble damages for injured private parties

Attorney fees for successful plaintiffs

Business and commercial litigation applications

Class action lawsuits against enterprises

ROBBERY

Statutory Citations: 18 USC Section 2111 (Special maritime and territorial jurisdiction); 18 USC Section 2113 (Bank robbery); 18 USC Section 1951 (Hobbs Act)

Federal robbery involves the unlawful taking of property from the person or presence of another by force, violence, or intimidation within federal jurisdiction or affecting interstate commerce.

Elements of Federal Robbery (18 USC Section 2111):

1. Taking and carrying away personal property of another
2. From person or presence of victim
3. Against victim's will by force, violence, or intimidation
4. Within special maritime and territorial jurisdiction

Elements of Bank Robbery (18 USC Section 2113):

1. Taking or attempting to take money or property
2. From federally insured bank, credit union, or savings association
3. By force, violence, intimidation, or putting life in jeopardy
4. Intent to steal or unlawfully obtain property

Elements of Hobbs Act Robbery (18 USC Section 1951):

1. Robbery as defined by applicable state law
2. Affecting interstate or foreign commerce
3. Actual or potential effect on commerce

Penalties:

Bank Robbery: Up to 20 years imprisonment (25 years if armed)

Armed Robbery: Up to 25 years imprisonment

Hobbs Act Robbery: Up to 20 years imprisonment

If Death Results: Life imprisonment or death penalty

Fines: Up to $250,000 for individuals

Federal Jurisdiction:

Special maritime and territorial jurisdiction (military bases, national parks, federal buildings)

Federally insured financial institutions

Robbery affecting interstate or foreign commerce

Federal property and government facilities

Indian reservations (concurrent with tribal jurisdiction)

Federal Agencies:

FBI: Bank robberies and major robbery investigations

ATF: Armed robberies involving firearms or explosives

U.S. Marshals Service: Fugitive apprehension

Military Police: Robberies on military installations

National Park Service: Park-related robberies

Types of Federal Robberies:

Bank and credit union robberies

Armored car and cash transport robberies

Post office and mail carrier robberies

Robbery of federal employees and officials

Commercial robberies affecting interstate commerce

Carjacking and vehicle robberies

Related Federal Offenses:

Carjacking (18 USC Section 2119)

Use of Firearm During Crime of Violence (18 USC Section 924(c))

Kidnapping (18 USC Section 1201)

Extortion (18 USC Section 875)

RICO (18 USC Section 1962)

Enhanced Penalties:

Use of dangerous weapons or firearms

Multiple victims or robbery spree

Organized robbery enterprises

Violence beyond that necessary to complete robbery

Targeting elderly or vulnerable victims

Career Criminal Enhancements:

Armed Career Criminal Act (18 USC Section 924(e))

Three Strikes provisions (18 USC Section 3559(c))

Repeat violent offender enhancements

Enhanced sentences for career criminals

RANSOMWARE

Statutory Citations: 18 USC Section 1030 (Computer Fraud and Abuse Act); 18 USC Section 1341 (Mail fraud); 18 USC Section 1343 (Wire fraud)

Ransomware involves malicious software that encrypts victim files or systems, demanding payment for decryption keys, representing a rapidly growing category of federal cybercrime prosecutions.

Elements of Computer Intrusion:

1. Intentionally accessing protected computer without authorization
2. Causing damage to computer, system, or data
3. Use of malicious code or ransomware
4. Intent to extort payment from victim

Elements of Extortion:

1. Threat to damage or withhold access to computer data
2. Demand for payment or other consideration
3. Use of interstate communications or commerce
4. Intent to obtain money through coercion

Penalties:

Computer Fraud: Up to 20 years imprisonment

Extortion: Up to 20 years imprisonment

Wire Fraud: Up to 20 years imprisonment

Conspiracy: Up to 20 years imprisonment

Fines: Up to $250,000 per count plus restitution

Types of Ransomware Attacks:

Individual computer encryption attacks

Corporate network and server attacks

Critical infrastructure targeting

Healthcare system attacks

Government agency attacks

Supply chain and managed service provider attacks

Federal Agencies:

FBI Cyber Division: Primary ransomware investigations

Secret Service: Financial aspects of ransomware

Cybersecurity and Infrastructure Security Agency: Critical infrastructure protection

National Security Agency: Advanced persistent threats

Internet Crime Complaint Center: Victim reporting and coordination

Ransomware Operations:

Ransomware-as-a-Service criminal enterprises

International cybercriminal organizations

Cryptocurrency payment demands and laundering

Double extortion with data theft and publication

Supply chain attacks and third-party compromises

Related Federal Offenses:

Money Laundering (18 USC Section 1956)

Extortion (18 USC Section 875)

Identity Theft (18 USC Section 1028)

RICO (18 USC Section 1962)

Terrorism (18 USC Section 2332b) for infrastructure attacks

Enhanced Penalties:

Critical infrastructure targeting

Healthcare and emergency services attacks

Government and military system attacks

Large-scale operations affecting multiple victims

International criminal enterprise involvement

Investigation Challenges:

International jurisdiction and cooperation

Cryptocurrency tracing and asset recovery

Attribution and identification of perpetrators

Victim cooperation and incident response

Prevention and cybersecurity measures

RAPE

Statutory Citation: 18 USC Section 2241 (Aggravated sexual abuse)

Federal rape laws address sexual assault offenses within federal jurisdiction, including military installations, federal property, and cases involving interstate commerce or federal officials.

Elements of Aggravated Sexual Abuse (18 USC Section 2241):

1. Knowingly causing another person to engage in sexual act
2. By using force against that person
3. By threatening or placing person in fear of death, serious bodily injury, or kidnapping
4. Within special maritime and territorial jurisdiction

Elements of Sexual Abuse (18 USC Section 2242):

1. Knowingly engaging in sexual act with another person
2. By threatening or placing person in fear of injury
3. Without person's consent
4. Within federal jurisdiction

Penalties:

Aggravated Sexual Abuse: Up to life imprisonment

Sexual Abuse: Up to 20 years imprisonment

Sexual Abuse of Minor: Up to 30 years imprisonment

Abusive Sexual Contact: Up to 10 years imprisonment

Supervised Release: Minimum 5 years, up to lifetime supervision

Federal Jurisdiction:

Special maritime and territorial jurisdiction

Military installations and federal property

National parks and forests

Federal prisons and detention facilities

Indian reservations (concurrent with tribal jurisdiction)

Interstate transportation for illegal sexual activity

Federal Agencies:

FBI: Major sexual assault investigations

Military Criminal Investigation Commands: Military sexual assault

National Park Service: Park-related sexual assaults

Federal Bureau of Prisons: Prison sexual assault

U.S. Marshals Service: Fugitive apprehension

Types of Federal Sexual Assault:

Military sexual assault and rape

Prison sexual assault and abuse

Sexual assault on federal property

Interstate sex trafficking and abuse

Sexual assault of federal employees

Child sexual abuse and exploitation

Related Federal Offenses:

Sex Trafficking (18 USC Section 1591)

Transportation for Illegal Sexual Activity (18 USC Section 2421)

Child Sexual Abuse (18 USC Section 2241)

Sexual Exploitation of Children (18 USC Section 2251)

Kidnapping (18 USC Section 1201)

Enhanced Penalties:

Sexual assault resulting in death

Use of dangerous weapons

Sexual assault of children under 12

Repeat sexual offenses

Organized sexual assault enterprises

Victim Services:

Victim advocates and counselors

Medical and psychological treatment

Victim impact statements at sentencing

Witness protection and relocation

Restitution and compensation programs

RECEIVING STOLEN PROPERTY

Statutory Citation: 18 USC Section 2315 (Sale or receipt of stolen goods)

Federal receiving stolen property laws criminalize the knowing receipt, possession, concealment, or disposal of stolen goods that have traveled in interstate or foreign commerce.

Elements:

1. Receiving, possessing, concealing, storing, bartering, selling, or disposing of goods
2. That have crossed state or national boundary after being stolen
3. Knowing goods were stolen
4. Value of goods exceeds $5,000

Penalties:

Receiving Stolen Property: Up to 10 years imprisonment

Fines: Up to $250,000 for individuals

Restitution: Full value of stolen property

Criminal Forfeiture: Property involved in offense

Interstate Commerce Requirements:

Stolen goods transported across state lines

Goods stolen from interstate shipments

Property with components from multiple states

Vehicles or goods affecting interstate commerce

Federal Agencies:

FBI: Major stolen property investigations

Immigration and Customs Enforcement: International stolen goods

Postal Inspection Service: Stolen mail and packages

ATF: Stolen firearms and explosives

Various agencies: Specialized stolen property (art, antiquities, etc.)

Types of Stolen Property:

Motor vehicles and automotive parts

Electronics and computer equipment

Jewelry and precious metals

Art, antiquities, and cultural property

Firearms and ammunition

Commercial merchandise and cargo

Related Federal Offenses:

Auto Theft (18 USC Section 2312)

Interstate Transportation of Stolen Goods (18 USC Section 2314)

Money Laundering (18 USC Section 1956)

RICO (18 USC Section 1962)

Conspiracy (18 USC Section 371)

Knowledge Requirements:

Actual knowledge that property was stolen

Willful blindness to obvious facts

Suspicious circumstances indicating theft

Below-market prices and lack of documentation

Defendant's experience and expertise

Enhanced Penalties:

Professional receivers and fencing operations

Large-scale stolen property enterprises

Organized retail crime rings

International stolen property trafficking

Repeat receiving stolen property offenses

REGULATORY VIOLATIONS

Statutory Citations: Various federal regulatory statutes across multiple agencies

Federal regulatory violations encompass criminal violations of regulations promulgated by federal agencies to implement and enforce congressional statutes across various industries and activities.

Elements of Knowing Regulatory Violations:

1. Violation of specific federal regulation or standard
2. Knowledge of regulatory requirement
3. Willful or knowing violation of regulation
4. Activity affecting interstate commerce or federal jurisdiction

Elements of Negligent Regulatory Violations:

1. Failure to comply with federal regulatory requirement
2. Negligent or reckless disregard of regulation

3. Resulting in harm or endangerment

4. Criminal penalties specified in enabling statute

Penalties:

Vary by specific regulatory statute and agency

Range from misdemeanor fines to felony imprisonment

Environmental crimes: Up to 15 years imprisonment

Food and drug violations: Up to 10 years imprisonment

Securities violations: Up to 25 years imprisonment

Types of Regulatory Violations:

Environmental protection violations (EPA)

Food and drug safety violations (FDA)

Securities and financial regulations (SEC)

Occupational safety violations (OSHA)

Transportation safety violations (DOT)

Communications regulations (FCC)

Federal Agencies:

Environmental Protection Agency: Environmental regulatory crimes

Food and Drug Administration: Food and drug violations

Securities and Exchange Commission: Securities regulatory violations

Occupational Safety and Health Administration: Workplace safety

Department of Transportation: Transportation safety

Federal Communications **Commission:** Communications violations

Regulatory Crime Categories:

Public welfare offenses with strict liability

Misdemeanor violations with negligence standard

Felony violations requiring willful conduct

Administrative violations with civil penalties

Hybrid civil-criminal enforcement schemes

Related Federal Offenses:

False Statements (18 USC Section 1001)

Obstruction of Justice (18 USC Section 1503)

Mail Fraud (18 USC Section 1341)

Wire Fraud (18 USC Section 1343)

Conspiracy (18 USC Section 371)

Enhanced Penalties:

Systematic regulatory violations

Endangering public health or safety

Large-scale commercial violations

Concealment and obstruction of investigations

Repeat regulatory violations

Compliance Programs:

Corporate compliance and ethics programs

Regulatory audits and self-disclosure

Cooperation with regulatory investigations

Voluntary remediation and corrective action

Industry standards and best practices

RECKLESS ENDANGERMENT

Statutory Citations: 18 USC Section 1365 (Tampering with consumer products); Various federal statutes

Federal reckless endangerment involves conduct that creates substantial risk of death or serious bodily injury to others within federal jurisdiction or affecting federal interests.

Elements:

1. Engaging in conduct that creates substantial risk of death or serious bodily injury
2. Conscious disregard of risk to others
3. Within federal jurisdiction or affecting federal interests
4. Reckless mental state (more than negligence, less than intent)

Penalties:

Reckless Endangerment: Up to 10 years imprisonment

Product Tampering: Up to 20 years imprisonment (life if death results)

Terrorist Threats: Up to 10 years imprisonment

Fines: Up to $250,000 for individuals

Federal Jurisdiction:

Special maritime and territorial jurisdiction

Federal facilities and property

Interstate commerce and transportation

Federal employees and officials

Consumer products in interstate commerce

Federal Agencies:

FBI: Reckless endangerment investigations

Environmental Protection Agency: Environmental endangerment

Food and Drug Administration: Product safety violations

Occupational Safety and Health Administration: Workplace endangerment

Federal Aviation Administration: Aviation safety violations

Types of Reckless Endangerment:

Consumer product tampering and contamination

Environmental release of hazardous substances

Workplace safety violations causing endangerment

Transportation safety violations

Public facility endangerment

Biological and chemical threats

Related Federal Offenses:

Negligent Homicide (18 USC Section 1112)

Assault (18 USC Section 113)

Terrorism (18 USC Section 2332a)

Environmental Crimes (Various statutes)

Product Tampering (18 USC Section 1365)

Enhanced Penalties:

Multiple persons endangered

Use of dangerous substances or weapons

Targeting vulnerable populations

Systematic reckless conduct

Large-scale endangerment operations

Consumer Product Tampering:

Tampering with food, drugs, cosmetics, or devices

Causing or attempting to cause death or injury

Communicating false information about tampering

Interstate commerce requirements

Enhanced penalties for death or serious injury

S

SABOTAGE

Statutory Citations: 18 USC Section 2155 (Destruction of national defense materials); 18 USC Section 1361 (Government property destruction)

Federal sabotage laws criminalize the intentional destruction, damage, or interference with national defense materials, utilities, and facilities that support military preparedness and national security.

Elements of National Defense Sabotage (18 USC Section 2155):

1. Intentionally injuring, interfering with, or obstructing national defense material, premises, or utilities

2. With intent to injure, interfere with, or obstruct United States or allies in preparing for or carrying on war

3. During national emergency proclaimed by President or when United States is at war

Elements of Government Property Sabotage (18 USC Section 1361):

1. Willfully injuring or committing depredation against property of United States

2. Intent to damage or destroy government property

3. Property belonging to or in custody of United States

Penalties:

National Defense Sabotage: Up to 20 years imprisonment (30 years during wartime)

Government Property Sabotage: Up to 10 years imprisonment

If Death Results: Life imprisonment or death penalty

Fines: Up to $250,000 for individuals

Criminal Forfeiture: Property used in sabotage activities

Types of Sabotage:

Military installations and equipment

Defense production facilities and contractors

Transportation infrastructure (bridges, tunnels, railways)

Communication and computer systems

Energy production and distribution facilities

Research and development facilities

Federal Agencies:

FBI Counterterrorism Division: Domestic sabotage investigations

Defense Counterintelligence and Security Agency: Military facility protection

Homeland Security Investigations: Critical infrastructure protection

Military Criminal Investigation Commands: Military installation sabotage

Cybersecurity and Infrastructure Security Agency: Cyber sabotage

National Defense Materials:

Military weapons and ammunition

Defense production equipment and machinery

Transportation systems supporting defense

Communication and surveillance equipment

Energy infrastructure and utilities

Research facilities and classified information

Related Federal Offenses:

Espionage (18 USC Section 793)

Terrorism (18 USC Section 2332a)

Computer Fraud (18 USC Section 1030)

Destruction of Federal Property (18 USC Section 1361)

Conspiracy (18 USC Section 371)

Enhanced Penalties:

Wartime sabotage activities

Foreign government involvement

Organized sabotage operations

Endangering military personnel

Cyber sabotage of critical systems

International Aspects:

Foreign intelligence service operations

International terrorism connections

Economic espionage and sabotage

Diplomatic immunity considerations

Cross-border sabotage investigations

SECURITIES FRAUD

Statutory Citations: 15 USC Section 77x (Securities Act); 15 USC Section 78ff (Securities Exchange Act); 18 USC Section 1348 (Securities fraud)

Securities fraud involves deceptive practices in the stock and commodity markets, including misrepresenting or omitting material information that investors use to make decisions.

Elements of Securities Fraud (18 USC Section 1348):

1. Scheme or artifice to defraud in connection with securities of issuer

2. Obtaining money or property by false or fraudulent pretenses in connection with purchase or sale of securities

3. Use of instrumentalities of interstate commerce, mail, or wire communications

4. Intent to defraud

Elements of Insider Trading:

1. Purchase or sale of security while in possession of material, nonpublic information

2. Breach of duty of trust or confidence owed to shareholders or source of information

3. Use of instrumentalities of interstate commerce

4. Willful violation of securities laws

Penalties:

Securities Fraud: Up to 25 years imprisonment

Insider Trading: Up to 20 years imprisonment

Market Manipulation: Up to 25 years imprisonment

Fines: Up to $5,000,000 for individuals, $25,000,000 for entities

Civil Penalties: Disgorgement plus civil monetary penalties

Types of Securities Fraud:

Insider trading and tipping schemes

Ponzi schemes and investment fraud

Market manipulation and pump-and-dump schemes

Accounting fraud and financial statement manipulation

Broker-dealer fraud and churning

Investment adviser fraud and misrepresentation

Federal Agencies:

Securities and Exchange Commission: Civil enforcement and regulation

FBI: Criminal securities fraud investigations

Commodity Futures Trading Commission: Futures and derivatives fraud

Financial Industry Regulatory Authority: Industry self-regulation

U.S. Attorneys Offices: Criminal prosecution coordination

Material Information:

Information that reasonable investor would consider important

Merger and acquisition negotiations

Earnings announcements and financial results

Product launches and regulatory approvals

Management changes and strategic decisions

Legal proceedings and regulatory investigations

Related Federal Offenses:

Mail Fraud (18 USC Section 1341)

Wire Fraud (18 USC Section 1343)

Money Laundering (18 USC Section 1956)

RICO (18 USC Section 1962)

Conspiracy (18 USC Section 371)

Enhanced Penalties:

Large-scale fraud affecting many investors

Systematic and ongoing fraud schemes

Abuse of positions of trust and authority

International securities fraud operations

Organized securities fraud enterprises

SMUGGLING

Statutory Citations: 18 USC Section 545 (Smuggling goods into United States); 19 USC Section 1436 (Customs violations)

Federal smuggling laws criminalize the importation or exportation of goods in violation of customs laws, including the evasion of duties, taxes, and regulatory restrictions.

Elements of Smuggling (18 USC Section 545):

1. Importing merchandise into United States
2. Contrary to law or regulations
3. With intent to defraud United States of lawful duties or evade prohibition

4. Knowledge of violation of customs laws

Elements of Export Smuggling:

1. Exporting goods from United States
2. Contrary to law or without required licenses
3. Intent to violate export restrictions
4. Knowledge of export control requirements

Penalties:

Smuggling: Up to 20 years imprisonment

Export Violations: Up to 20 years imprisonment

Customs Fraud: Up to 20 years imprisonment

Fines: Up to $250,000 for individuals or twice the value of smuggled goods

Criminal Forfeiture: Smuggled goods and transportation equipment

Types of Smuggling:

Drug trafficking and narcotics smuggling

Human trafficking and alien smuggling

Weapons and ammunition smuggling

Currency and monetary instrument smuggling

Cultural property and art smuggling

Prohibited goods and contraband

Federal Agencies:

Customs and Border Protection: Primary smuggling enforcement

Immigration and Customs Enforcement: Criminal investigations

Coast Guard: Maritime smuggling interdiction

DEA: Drug smuggling investigations

ATF: Weapons and explosives smuggling

Smuggling Methods:

Concealment in legitimate cargo and shipments

Use of false compartments in vehicles and vessels

Tunnels and underground passages

Corrupt customs officials and employees

Document fraud and false declarations

Mail and package delivery services

Related Federal Offenses:

Drug Trafficking (21 USC Section 841)

Human Trafficking (18 USC Section 1591)

Money Laundering (18 USC Section 1956)

Arms Trafficking (22 USC Section 2778)

Immigration Violations (8 USC Section 1324)

Enhanced Penalties:

Organized smuggling enterprises

Large-scale operations

Violence and use of weapons

Corruption of government officials

International smuggling networks

Border Security Measures:

Advanced screening technology and inspection

Intelligence and risk assessment systems

Joint task forces and cooperation

International cooperation and treaties

Trade security and supply chain protection

STALKING

Statutory Citation: 18 USC Section 2261A (Interstate stalking)

Federal stalking laws criminalize the use of mail, interstate commerce facilities, or electronic communications to engage in conduct that places persons in reasonable fear of death or serious bodily injury.

Elements:

1. Using mail, interactive computer service, or facility of interstate commerce

2. To engage in course of conduct that causes substantial emotional distress or places person in reasonable fear

3. Of death or serious bodily injury to person or immediate family member

4. With intent to kill, injure, harass, intimidate, or cause substantial emotional distress

Penalties:

Interstate Stalking: Up to 5 years imprisonment

If Serious Bodily Injury Results: Up to 10 years imprisonment

If Death Results: Life imprisonment

Cyberstalking: Up to 5 years imprisonment

Fines: Up to $250,000 for individuals

Federal Jurisdiction:

Use of mail or interstate communication facilities

Travel across state lines to stalk victim

Electronic communications and internet stalking

Federal property and installations

Military and federal employee stalking

Federal Agencies:

FBI: Interstate stalking investigations

Internet Crime Complaint Center: Cyberstalking reporting

U.S. Marshals Service: Victim protection and fugitive apprehension

Military Criminal Investigation Commands: Military stalking cases

Types of Stalking:

Traditional stalking with physical following

Cyberstalking through internet and social media

Electronic surveillance and monitoring

Telephone and text message harassment

Email and electronic communication stalking

GPS tracking and location monitoring

Related Federal Offenses:

Domestic Violence (18 USC Section 2261)

Threats (18 USC Section 875)

Computer Fraud (18 USC Section 1030)

Harassment (Various statutes)

Privacy Violations (18 USC Section 2701)

Course of Conduct:

Pattern of behavior over time

Two or more acts evidencing continuity of purpose

Conduct that would cause reasonable person to fear

Violating restraining orders and protective orders

Enhanced Penalties:

Use of dangerous weapons

Violations of protective orders

Targeting vulnerable victims

Organized stalking operations

Repeat stalking offenses

Victim Protection:

Safety planning and risk assessment

Restraining orders and protective orders

Victim relocation and address confidentiality

Electronic monitoring of offenders

Victim services and counseling

STUDENT LOAN FRAUD

Statutory Citations: 20 USC Section 1097 (Program participation agreements); 18 USC Section 1341 (Mail fraud)

Student loan fraud involves schemes to defraud federal student aid programs through false applications, identity theft, and fraudulent educational institutions.

Elements:

1. Scheme to defraud federal student aid programs
2. False statements or misrepresentations on aid applications
3. Intent to obtain student aid funds unlawfully
4. Use of mail or wire communications in furtherance of scheme

Penalties:

Student Aid Fraud: Up to 20 years imprisonment

Identity Theft: Up to 15 years imprisonment additional

False Statements: Up to 5 years imprisonment

Fines: Up to $250,000 for individuals

Restitution: Full amount of fraudulent aid received

Types of Student Loan Fraud:

False information on federal aid applications (FAFSA)

Identity theft for fraudulent aid applications

Diploma mills and fraudulent educational institutions

Enrollment fraud and phantom students

Financial aid administrator fraud

Student loan discharge fraud

Federal Agencies:

Education Department Office of **Inspector General:** Primary student aid fraud enforcement

FBI: Criminal fraud investigations

Postal Inspection Service: Mail fraud cases

Social Security Administration: Identity theft investigations

Common Fraud Schemes:

False income and asset information

Fake Social Security numbers and identities

Fraudulent high school diplomas

Phantom enrollment and attendance

Financial aid administrator kickbacks

Student loan forgiveness fraud

Related Federal Offenses:

Mail Fraud (18 USC Section 1341)

Wire Fraud (18 USC Section 1343)

Identity Theft (18 USC Section 1028)

False Statements (18 USC Section 1001)

Money Laundering (18 USC Section 1956)

Enhanced Penalties:

Organized fraud enterprises

Large-scale operations

Targeting vulnerable populations

Professional facilitators

Repeat student aid fraud

Victim Impact:

Legitimate students denied aid

Taxpayer losses from fraudulent payments

Compromised integrity of aid programs

Identity theft victims

Educational institution reputational harm

SEX TRAFFICKING

Statutory Citation: 18 USC Section 1591 (Sex trafficking of children or by force, fraud, or coercion)

Sex trafficking involves recruiting, enticing, harboring, transporting, providing, obtaining, or maintaining persons for commercial sex acts through force, fraud, coercion, or involving minors.

Elements:

1. Recruiting, enticing, harboring, transporting, providing, obtaining, or maintaining person

2. Knowing that means of force, fraud, or coercion will be used to cause person to engage in commercial sex act

3. Person induced to engage in commercial sex act has not attained 18 years (no force, fraud, or coercion required for minors)

Penalties:

Adult Sex Trafficking: 10 years to life imprisonment

Minor Sex Trafficking: 15 years to life imprisonment

If Death Results: Life imprisonment or death penalty

Fines: Up to $250,000 for individuals

Restitution: Mandatory restitution to victims

Methods of Control:

Physical force and violence

Psychological coercion and manipulation

Economic control and debt bondage

Isolation from family and support systems

Substance addiction and dependency

Document confiscation and threats

Federal Agencies:

FBI Human Trafficking Program: Primary sex trafficking enforcement

Immigration and Customs Enforcement: International trafficking

Department of Justice: Prosecution coordination

Health and Human Services: Victim services

State Department: International anti-trafficking efforts

Types of Sex Trafficking:

Prostitution and escort services

Massage parlors and spa operations

Strip clubs and adult entertainment

Online advertising and internet facilitation

International trafficking operations

Child commercial sexual exploitation

Related Federal Offenses:

Human Trafficking (18 USC Section 1589)

Transportation for Prostitution (18 USC Section 2421)

Child Exploitation (18 USC Section 2251)

RICO (18 USC Section 1962)

Money Laundering (18 USC Section 1956)

Enhanced Penalties:

Organized trafficking enterprises

Violence and serious bodily injury

Multiple victims and large-scale operations

International trafficking networks

Corruption of public officials

Victim Services:

T-visa for trafficking victims

Comprehensive case management

Medical and mental health services

Legal assistance and immigration relief

Safe housing and shelter services

Economic empowerment and job training

SOCIAL SECURITY FRAUD

Statutory Citation: 42 USC Section 408 (Penalties for fraud)

Social Security fraud involves false statements, misrepresentations, or concealment of material facts in connection with Social Security benefits, disability determinations, or program administration.

Elements:

1. Making false statement or representation of material fact
2. In application or document for Social Security benefits
3. Knowing statement is false
4. Intent to defraud Social Security Administration

Penalties:

Social Security Fraud: Up to 5 years imprisonment

Identity Theft: Up to 15 years imprisonment additional

Representative Payee Fraud: Up to 5 years imprisonment

Fines: Up to $250,000 for individuals

Restitution: Full amount of fraudulent benefits

Types of Social Security Fraud:

Disability benefit fraud and malingering

Identity theft and number misuse

Representative payee fraud and misuse

Concealment of work activity and earnings

Death benefit fraud and unreported deaths

Medical evidence fraud and false documentation

Federal Agencies:

Social Security Administration Office of Inspector General: Primary enforcement

FBI: Criminal fraud investigations

Postal Inspection Service: Mail fraud cases

Immigration and Customs Enforcement: Immigration-related fraud

Common Fraud Schemes:

False or exaggerated disability claims

Working while receiving disability benefits

Using deceased persons' Social Security numbers

Representative payees stealing benefits

Medical professionals providing false evidence

Immigration fraud using false Social Security numbers

Related Federal Offenses:

Mail Fraud (18 USC Section 1341)

Wire Fraud (18 USC Section 1343)

Identity Theft (18 USC Section 1028)

False Statements (18 USC Section 1001)

Healthcare Fraud (18 USC Section 1347)

Enhanced Penalties:

Organized fraud enterprises

Large-scale operations

Professional facilitators (doctors, lawyers)

Targeting vulnerable populations

Repeat Social Security fraud

Program Integrity:

Continuing disability reviews

Work incentive programs and reporting

Representative payee monitoring

Data matching and verification

Fraud prevention and detection systems

SEDITION

Statutory Citation: 18 USC Section 2384 (Seditious conspiracy)

Sedition involves conspiracies to overthrow, put down, or destroy by force the government of the United States, or to oppose by force the authority of the United States government.

Elements:

1. Conspiracy of two or more persons
2. To overthrow, put down, or destroy by force government of United States
3. Or to levy war against United States
4. Or to oppose by force authority of government of United States

Penalties:

Seditious Conspiracy: Up to 20 years imprisonment

Advocating Overthrow of Government: Up to 20 years imprisonment

Fines: Up to $250,000 for individuals

Enhanced Penalties: During wartime or national emergency

Types of Seditious Activity:

Armed rebellion and insurrection against government

Conspiracies to overthrow federal government

Violent opposition to federal authority

Incitement to armed resistance

Paramilitary training for anti-government activities

Coordinated attacks on government facilities

Federal Agencies:

FBI Counterterrorism Division: Domestic terrorism and sedition investigations

Department of Justice National Security Division: Sedition prosecutions

Joint Terrorism Task Forces: Multi-agency coordination

Intelligence agencies: Threat assessment and monitoring

Historical Context:

Civil War and Reconstruction era prosecutions

World War I and World War II sedition cases

Cold War anti-communist prosecutions

Modern domestic terrorism and extremism

January 6, 2021 Capitol attack prosecutions

Related Federal Offenses:

Treason (18 USC Section 2381)

Rebellion or Insurrection (18 USC Section 2383)

Conspiracy (18 USC Section 371)

Terrorism (18 USC Section 2332a)

Civil Rights Conspiracy (18 USC Section 241)

Enhanced Penalties:

Use of violence and weapons

Organized extremist groups

Targeting government officials

International connections

Large-scale seditious activities

Constitutional Considerations:

First Amendment free speech protections

Clear and present danger standard

Incitement versus protected advocacy

Due process and equal protection

Political speech versus criminal conduct

T

TAX EVASION

Statutory Citations: 26 USC Section 7201 (Attempt to evade or defeat tax); 26 USC Section 7206 (Fraud and false statements)

Federal tax evasion involves willful attempts to evade or defeat the assessment or payment of federal taxes through fraudulent means, representing one of the most commonly prosecuted federal financial crimes.

Elements of Tax Evasion (26 USC Section 7201):

1. Existence of tax deficiency (additional tax due and owing)
2. Willful attempt to evade or defeat tax
3. Affirmative act constituting evasion or attempted evasion

Elements of Tax Fraud (26 USC Section 7206):

1. Willfully making and subscribing return, statement, or document
2. Verified by written declaration under penalty of perjury
3. Which defendant does not believe to be true and correct as to every material matter

Penalties:

Tax Evasion: Up to 5 years imprisonment and $250,000 fine

Tax Fraud: Up to 3 years imprisonment and $250,000 fine

Civil Fraud Penalty: 75% of underpayment plus interest

Enhanced Penalties: For large-scale operations and repeat offenses

Types of Tax Evasion:

Income tax evasion through unreported income

Employment tax evasion by employers

Excise tax evasion on regulated products

Estate and gift tax evasion

Corporate tax evasion and transfer pricing

International tax evasion and offshore accounts

Federal Agencies:

Internal Revenue Service Criminal Investigation: Primary tax crime enforcement

Department of Justice Tax Division: Complex tax prosecutions

FBI: Financial investigations supporting tax cases

U.S. Attorneys Offices: Local tax crime prosecution

Willfulness Requirement:

Voluntary, intentional violation of known legal duty

Distinguished from negligence, mistake, or good faith misunderstanding

Sophisticated methods of concealment may indicate willfulness

Pattern of conduct over multiple tax years

Use of professionals to facilitate evasion while ignoring advice

Affirmative Acts of Evasion:

Filing false tax returns or amended returns

Maintaining inadequate records or destroying records

Dealing in cash to avoid third-party reporting

Using nominees, aliases, or shell entities

Concealing assets in domestic or foreign accounts

Engaging in sham transactions or abusive tax shelters

Related Federal Offenses:

Money Laundering (18 USC Section 1956)

Bank Fraud (18 USC Section 1344)

Mail Fraud (18 USC Section 1341)

Wire Fraud (18 USC Section 1343)

Conspiracy (18 USC Section 371)

Enhanced Penalties:

Large tax losses to government

Sophisticated evasion schemes

Use of offshore accounts and entities

Professional tax preparers facilitating evasion

Organized tax evasion enterprises

International Tax Evasion:

Foreign Bank Account Report (FBAR) violations

Offshore voluntary disclosure programs

Foreign Account Tax Compliance Act (FATCA) requirements

Transfer pricing manipulation by multinational corporations

Use of tax havens and shell companies

TERRORISM

Statutory Citations: 18 USC Section 2331 (Definitions); 18 USC Section 2332a (Use of weapons of mass destruction)

Federal terrorism laws address acts intended to intimidate or coerce civilian populations or influence government policy through violence, representing some of the most severely punished federal crimes.

Elements of International Terrorism (18 USC Section 2331):

1. Activities that involve violent acts or acts dangerous to human life
2. Violate criminal laws of United States or any state
3. Appear intended to intimidate or coerce civilian population, influence government policy, or affect government conduct
4. Occur primarily outside territorial jurisdiction of United States or transcend national boundaries

Elements of Domestic Terrorism:

1. Activities that involve acts dangerous to human life that violate criminal laws
2. Appear intended to intimidate or coerce civilian population, influence government policy, or affect government conduct
3. Occur primarily within territorial jurisdiction of United States

Elements of Use of Weapons of Mass Destruction (18 USC Section 2332a):

1. Use of weapon of mass destruction against national of United States while outside United States
2. Use against person within United States
3. Use against property owned, leased, or used by United States

Penalties:

Terrorism Offenses: Up to life imprisonment or death penalty

Use of WMD: Life imprisonment or death penalty

Material Support to Terrorism: Up to 20 years imprisonment

Terrorist Financing: Up to 20 years imprisonment

Enhanced Penalties: Various terrorism enhancement statutes

Types of Terrorism:

International terrorism with foreign connections

Domestic terrorism by U.S. persons and groups

Cyber terrorism against critical infrastructure

Bioterrorism using biological agents

Nuclear terrorism and radiological weapons

Environmental terrorism and ecoterrorism

Federal Agencies:

FBI Counterterrorism Division: Primary domestic terrorism enforcement

Joint Terrorism Task Forces: Multi-agency coordination

Department of Homeland Security: Prevention and **preparedness**

National Security Agency: Intelligence and surveillance

Central Intelligence Agency: International terrorism intelligence

Weapons of Mass Destruction:

Nuclear weapons and devices

Chemical weapons and toxic substances

Biological agents and toxins

Radiological dispersal devices

Explosive devices causing mass casualties

Related Federal Offenses:

Material Support to Terrorists (18 USC Section 2339A)

Terrorist Financing (18 USC Section 2339C)

Aircraft Piracy (49 USC Section 46502)

Hostage Taking (18 USC Section 1203)

RICO (18 USC Section 1962)

Enhanced Penalties:

Use of weapons of mass destruction

Multiple casualties and deaths

Targeting critical infrastructure

International terrorist organizations

Repeat terrorism offenses

International Cooperation:

United Nations terrorism conventions

International intelligence sharing

Extradition and mutual legal assistance

Financial intelligence and sanctions

Border security and screening

THEFT

Statutory Citation: 18 USC Section 641 (Public money, property or records)

Federal theft involves the unlawful taking of property belonging to the United States or occurring within federal jurisdiction, with various specific statutes addressing different types of federal property and circumstances.

Elements:

1. Taking and carrying away property of another
2. Without consent and against the will of owner
3. With intent to permanently deprive owner of property
4. Property belonging to United States or within federal jurisdiction

Penalties:

Federal Property Theft (over $1,000): Up to 10 years imprisonment

Petty Theft ($1,000 or less): Up to 1 year imprisonment

Mail Theft: Up to 5 years imprisonment

Bank Theft: Up to 10 years imprisonment

Fines: Up to $250,000 for felonies, $100,000 for misdemeanors

Types of Federal Theft:

Government property and equipment theft

Military property and weapons theft

Postal theft and mail fraud

National park resource theft

Federal building and facility theft

Identity theft and personal information

Federal Jurisdiction:

Special maritime and territorial jurisdiction

Federal property and installations

Government money, property, and records

Interstate transportation of stolen goods

Federal programs and benefits

Federal Agencies:

FBI: Major theft investigations

Postal Inspection Service: Mail and postal theft

Military Criminal Investigation Commands: Military property theft

National Park Service: Park resource theft

Inspector General Offices: Agency-specific theft

Related Federal Offenses:

Larceny (18 USC Section 641)

Embezzlement (18 USC Section 641)

Receiving Stolen Property (18 USC Section 2315)

Interstate Transportation of Stolen Goods (18 USC Section 2314)

Identity Theft (18 USC Section 1028)

Enhanced Penalties:

Theft during national emergency

Employee theft and breach of trust

Organized theft operations

Theft of classified materials

Large-scale theft enterprises

Employee and Contractor Theft:

Federal employees stealing government property

Contractors misappropriating federal resources

Military personnel theft of equipment and supplies

Abuse of access and security clearances

Breach of fiduciary duty and trust

THREATS

Statutory Citations: 18 USC Section 875 (Interstate communications); 18 USC Section 115 (Influencing, impeding, or retaliating against federal officials)

Federal threat laws criminalize communications containing threats to injure persons or property transmitted through interstate commerce or directed at federal officials and employees.

Elements of Interstate Threats (18 USC Section 875(c)):

1. Transmission in interstate or foreign commerce

2. Communication containing threat to kidnap or injure person of another

3. Intent to extort money or other thing of value, or intent to threaten

Elements of Threats Against Federal Officials (18 USC Section 115):

1. Threatening to assault, kidnap, or murder federal official, federal judge, or family member

2. With intent to impede, intimidate, or interfere with official duties

3. Or with intent to retaliate against official on account of performance of duties

Penalties:

Interstate Threats: Up to 5 years imprisonment

Threats Against Federal Officials: Up to 10 years imprisonment

Presidential Threats: Up to 5 years imprisonment

Fines: Up to $250,000 for individuals

Federal Jurisdiction:

Interstate or foreign commerce communications

Threats against federal officials and employees

Threats using mail, telephone, internet, or electronic communications

Threats affecting federal investigations or proceedings

Federal Agencies:

FBI: Threat investigations and assessment

Secret Service: Threats against protected persons

U.S. Marshals Service: Threats against federal judges

Capitol Police: Threats against Congress members

Postal Inspection Service: Mailed threats

Types of Threats:

Death threats and assassination threats

Bombing threats and mass violence threats

Kidnapping and hostage threats

Extortion and blackmail threats

Cyber threats and online harassment

Domestic terrorism threats

Related Federal Offenses:

Extortion (18 USC Section 875)

Stalking (18 USC Section 2261A)

Cyberstalking (18 USC Section 2261A)

Terrorism (18 USC Section 2332a)

Obstruction of Justice (18 USC Section 1503)

True Threat Standard:

Communication must be serious expression of intent to commit violence

Context and circumstances surrounding communication

Objective reasonable person standard

Distinction between protected speech and criminal threats

Consideration of speaker's history and capability

Enhanced Penalties:

Threats during commission of other federal crimes

Organized threat campaigns

Threats involving weapons of mass destruction

International threats and terrorism

Repeat threat offenses

TRAFFICKING IN PERSONS

Statutory Citations: 18 USC Section 1581 (Peonage); 18 USC Section 1584 (Sale into involuntary servitude); 18 USC Section 1590 (Trafficking with respect to peonage, slavery, involuntary servitude, or forced labor)

Human trafficking involves recruiting, harboring, transporting, providing, or obtaining persons for labor or services through force, fraud, or coercion, or for commercial sex acts.

Elements of Labor Trafficking (18 USC Section 1589):

1. Knowingly providing or obtaining labor or services of person
2. By threats of serious harm, physical restraint, or abuse of legal process
3. Through scheme intended to cause person to believe failure to perform would result in harm
4. Intent to obtain labor or services

Elements of Sex Trafficking (18 USC Section 1591):

1. Recruiting, enticing, harboring, transporting, providing, obtaining, or maintaining person
2. Knowing that means of force, fraud, or coercion will be used
3. To cause person to engage in commercial sex act
4. Or person induced is under 18 years of age

Penalties:

Labor Trafficking: Up to 20 years imprisonment (life if death results)

Sex Trafficking: 10 years to life imprisonment (15 years to life if victim under 18)

Peonage and Slavery: Up to 20 years imprisonment

Fines: Up to $250,000 for individuals

Restitution: Mandatory restitution to victims

Types of Human Trafficking:

Forced labor in agriculture, manufacturing, domestic work

Sex trafficking and commercial sexual exploitation

Child labor and exploitation

Debt bondage and peonage

Organ trafficking

Forced marriage and servitude

Federal Agencies:

FBI Human Trafficking Program: Primary enforcement

Immigration and Customs Enforcement: International trafficking

Department of Labor: Labor trafficking

Health and Human Services: Victim services

State Department: International anti-trafficking

Methods of Control:

Physical and sexual violence

Psychological coercion and manipulation

Economic control and debt bondage

Isolation from family and community

Document confiscation and legal threats

Substance addiction and dependency

Related Federal Offenses:

RICO (18 USC Section 1962)

Money Laundering (18 USC Section 1956)

Immigration Violations (8 USC Section 1324)

Child Exploitation (18 USC Section 2251)

Conspiracy (18 USC Section 371)

Enhanced Penalties:

Organized trafficking enterprises

Multiple victims and large-scale operations

Violence and serious bodily injury

International trafficking networks

Corruption of public officials

Victim Services:

T-visa for trafficking victims

Continued presence for investigation and prosecution

Comprehensive case management services

Medical and mental health treatment

Legal assistance and immigration relief

Safe housing and economic empowerment

TREASON

Statutory Citation: 18 USC Section 2381

Treason involves levying war against the United States or adhering to its enemies, giving them aid and comfort, representing the most serious crime against national security defined in the Constitution.

Elements:

1. Owing allegiance to United States (citizen or resident alien)
2. Levying war against United States or adhering to enemies of United States
3. Giving aid and comfort to enemies
4. Intent to betray United States

Constitutional Requirements:

Testimony of two witnesses to same overt act or confession in open court

Treason defined in Constitution Article III, Section 3

Congressional power to declare punishment

Corruption of blood and forfeiture limitations

Penalties:

Treason: Death penalty or life imprisonment

Minimum 5 years imprisonment and $10,000 fine

Disqualification from holding federal office

Forfeiture of property used in treasonous acts

Historical Context:

Very few treason prosecutions in U.S. history

World War II prosecutions of American citizens

Distinction from espionage and sedition

Constitutional protections against broad interpretation

Requirement of declared war or recognized enemy

Federal Agencies:

FBI Counterintelligence Division: Treason investigations

Department of Justice National Security Division: Prosecution

Central Intelligence Agency: Intelligence support

Defense agencies: Military aspects of treason

Levying War:

Actual assemblage of men in warlike array

Intent to overthrow government by force

Distinguished from riot or unlawful assembly

Requires organized military-style action against United States

Adhering to Enemies:

Providing aid and comfort to declared enemies

Intent to betray United States to enemy

Distinguished from mere criticism of government

Requires proof of treasonous intent and enemy status

Related Federal Offenses:

Espionage (18 USC Section 794)

Sedition (18 USC Section 2384)

Sabotage (18 USC Section 2155)

Foreign Agent Registration Violations (22 USC Section 611)

Modern Applications:

Cyber warfare and information operations

Economic espionage and trade secret theft

Terrorism and asymmetric warfare

International law and armed conflict

TRANSPORTATION OF STOLEN GOODS

Statutory Citation: 18 USC Section 2314 (Transportation of stolen goods, securities, moneys, fraudulent state tax stamps, or articles used in counterfeiting)

Federal transportation of stolen goods laws criminalize the interstate movement of stolen property, providing federal jurisdiction over theft rings and organized criminal enterprises.

Elements:

1. Transportation, movement, or shipment in interstate or foreign commerce
2. Goods, wares, merchandise, securities, or money
3. Knowing same to have been stolen, converted, or taken by fraud
4. Value of $5,000 or more

Penalties:

Transportation of Stolen Goods: Up to 10 years imprisonment

Receiving Transported Stolen Goods: Up to 10 years imprisonment

Fines: Up to $250,000 for individuals

Restitution: Full value of stolen property

Criminal Forfeiture: Transported stolen goods and proceeds

Interstate Commerce Requirements:

Physical transportation across state lines

Goods must cross state boundary after theft

Knowledge of interstate transportation not required

Minimal movement sufficient if crosses state line

Federal Agencies:

FBI: Major stolen goods investigations

Immigration and Customs Enforcement: International stolen goods

Postal Inspection Service: Stolen mail and packages

Various agencies: Specialized stolen property (art, vehicles, etc.)

Types of Stolen Goods:

Motor vehicles and automotive parts

Electronics and computer equipment

Jewelry, watches, and precious metals

Art, antiques, and cultural property

Commercial merchandise and cargo

Securities and financial instruments

Related Federal Offenses:

Receiving Stolen Property (18 USC Section 2315)

Auto Theft (18 USC Section 2312)

Mail Theft (18 USC Section 1708)

Wire Fraud (18 USC Section 1343)

RICO (18 USC Section 1962)

Knowledge Requirements:

Actual knowledge that goods were stolen

Willful blindness to obvious circumstances

Suspicious circumstances indicating theft

Below-market prices and lack of documentation

Professional expertise and experience

Enhanced Penalties:

Organized stolen goods enterprises

Professional receivers and fencing operations

Large-scale transportation operations

International stolen goods trafficking

Repeat transportation offenses

TELEMARKETING FRAUD

Statutory Citations: 18 USC Section 1341 (Mail fraud); 18 USC Section 1343 (Wire fraud); 15 USC Section 6102 (Telemarketing and Consumer Fraud and Abuse Prevention Act)

Telemarketing fraud involves deceptive and abusive telemarketing practices designed to defraud consumers, particularly targeting elderly and vulnerable populations through interstate telephone communications.

Elements:

1. Scheme or artifice to defraud using telemarketing
2. Material misrepresentations or omissions to consumers
3. Use of interstate telephone communications
4. Intent to defraud and obtain money or property

Penalties:

Wire Fraud: Up to 20 years imprisonment (30 years if targeting financial institutions)

Telemarketing Fraud: Enhanced penalties under sentencing guidelines

Elder Fraud: Additional 10 years if targeting persons over 55

Fines: Up to $250,000 for individuals

Restitution: Full victim losses

Types of Telemarketing Fraud:

Advance fee loan scams

Prize and lottery scams

Charity fraud and fake fundraising

Investment and business opportunity fraud

Credit repair and debt elimination scams

Health and medical product fraud

Federal Agencies:

FBI: Telemarketing fraud investigations

Federal Trade Commission: Consumer protection enforcement

Postal Inspection Service: Mail-related telemarketing fraud

Federal Communications Commission: Telephone regulations

Common Fraud Schemes:

"You've won a prize" lottery scams

Advance fee loan and credit repair scams

Fake charity solicitations

Investment opportunities and get-rich-quick schemes

Medical and health product scams

Government impersonation scams

Related Federal Offenses:

Mail Fraud (18 USC Section 1341)

Wire Fraud (18 USC Section 1343)

Identity Theft (18 USC Section 1028)

Money Laundering (18 USC Section 1956)

Elder Abuse (Various statutes)

Enhanced Penalties:

Targeting elderly and vulnerable victims

Large-scale operations with multiple victims
Organized telemarketing fraud enterprises
International fraud operations
Sophisticated technology and methods
Victim Targeting:
Elderly persons and retirees
Persons with limited English proficiency
Isolated individuals and shut-ins
Previous fraud victims (sucker lists)
Persons with cognitive impairments
Prevention and Enforcement:
Do Not Call Registry enforcement
Caller ID and telephone authentication
Consumer education and awareness
Industry cooperation and reporting
International enforcement cooperation.

U

UNLAWFUL ASSEMBLY

Statutory Citation: 18 USC Section 2101 (Riots)

Federal unlawful assembly laws address gatherings that threaten public safety, particularly when participants travel in interstate commerce to engage in or incite riots and civil disturbances.

Elements of Inciting Riot (18 USC Section 2101):

1. Traveling in interstate or foreign commerce or using facility of interstate commerce
2. With intent to incite, organize, promote, encourage, participate in, or carry on riot
3. Performing or attempting to perform overt act for any purpose specified above

Elements of Riot:

1. Public disturbance involving acts of violence
2. By assemblage of three or more persons
3. Which acts constitute clear and present danger of damage or injury to property or persons

Penalties:

Inciting Riot: Up to 5 years imprisonment

Participating in Riot: Up to 5 years imprisonment

Civil Disorders: Up to 5 years imprisonment

Fines: Up to $250,000 for individuals

Federal Jurisdiction:

Travel in interstate or foreign commerce

Use of facilities of interstate commerce (communications, transportation)

Interference with federal facilities or personnel

Affecting interstate commerce

Federal property involvement

Federal Agencies:

FBI: Civil unrest and domestic terrorism investigations

U.S. Marshals Service: Federal facility protection

Federal Protective Service: Federal building security

Joint Terrorism Task Forces: Coordinated response

Intelligence agencies: Threat assessment and monitoring

Types of Unlawful Assembly:

Political protests turning violent

Racial and ethnic conflicts

Labor disputes and strikes

Environmental and animal rights protests

Anti-government and militia gatherings

Sports celebrations and crowds

Related Federal Offenses:

Civil Rights Violations (18 USC Section 241)

Seditious Conspiracy (18 USC Section 2384)

Terrorism (18 USC Section 2332a)

Destruction of Federal Property (18 USC Section 1361)

Conspiracy (18 USC Section 371)

Constitutional Considerations:

First Amendment protection for peaceful assembly

Distinction between protected speech and criminal conduct

Prior restraint limitations

Equal protection in enforcement

Due process requirements

Enhanced Penalties:

Use of firearms or explosives during riots

Targeting federal facilities or personnel

Organized extremist group involvement

Interstate conspiracy to incite violence

Repeat riot offenses

Historical Context:

Civil rights era enforcement

Anti-war protest prosecutions

Labor dispute interventions

Modern domestic terrorism cases

Social media and digital organization

UNLAWFUL DETENTION

Statutory Citations: 18 USC Section 1201 (Kidnapping); 18 USC Section 242 (Deprivation of rights under color of law)

Federal unlawful detention involves the illegal restraint or confinement of persons within federal jurisdiction or by persons acting under color of law, violating constitutional rights to liberty and due process.

Elements of False Imprisonment:

1. Unlawful restraint or confinement of person
2. Against person's will
3. Without legal justification or authority
4. Within federal jurisdiction or affecting federal interests

Elements of Deprivation Under Color of Law:

1. Acting under color of law, statute, ordinance, regulation, or custom
2. Willfully subjecting person to deprivation of liberty
3. Without due process of law
4. Different treatment than authorized by law

Penalties:

Unlawful Detention: Up to 20 years imprisonment

If Death Results: Life imprisonment or death penalty

Civil Rights Violations: Up to 1 year imprisonment (life if death results)

Fines: Up to $250,000 for individuals

Federal Jurisdiction:

Special maritime and territorial jurisdiction

Federal law enforcement detention violations

Immigration detention violations

Military detention violations

Prison and jail detention violations

Federal Agencies:

FBI Civil Rights Program: Police misconduct investigations

Immigration and Customs Enforcement: Immigration detention

Federal Bureau of Prisons: Federal prison detention

Military Criminal Investigation Commands: Military detention

Inspector General Offices: Agency detention practices

Types of Unlawful Detention:

Police false arrest and imprisonment

Immigration detention violations

Prison guard misconduct

Military detention abuse

Private security detention violations

Citizen's arrest violations

Related Federal Offenses:

Kidnapping (18 USC Section 1201)

Civil Rights Violations (18 USC Section 241)

Assault (18 USC Section 113)

Extortion (18 USC Section 875)

False Imprisonment (State laws incorporated)

Constitutional Rights:

Fourth Amendment protection against unreasonable seizure

Fifth Amendment due process rights

Eighth Amendment cruel and unusual punishment

Fourteenth Amendment equal protection

Habeas corpus protections

Enhanced Penalties:

Use of violence during detention

Detention for extortion or ransom

Official misconduct in detention

Organized detention schemes

Repeat unlawful detention offenses

Civil Remedies:

Section 1983 civil rights lawsuits

Monetary damages for victims

Injunctive relief and policy changes

Pattern and practice investigations

Consent decrees and monitoring

UNLAWFUL POSSESSION OF FIREARMS

Statutory Citation: 18 USC Section 922(g) (Prohibited persons)

Federal firearm possession laws prohibit certain categories of persons from possessing firearms or ammunition, with violations representing a significant portion of federal criminal prosecutions.

Elements:

1. Knowing possession of firearm or ammunition
2. Person falls within prohibited category under federal law
3. Firearm or ammunition traveled in or affected interstate commerce
4. Knowledge of prohibited status (for some categories)

Penalties:

Basic Violation: Up to 10 years imprisonment

Armed Career Criminal: Minimum 15 years imprisonment (three violent felony convictions)

Domestic Violence: Up to 10 years imprisonment

Fines: Up to $250,000 for individuals

Prohibited Persons Categories:

Persons convicted of felonies punishable by more than one year imprisonment

Fugitives from justice

Unlawful users of controlled substances

Persons adjudicated as mental defectives or committed to mental institutions

Illegal aliens and persons admitted under nonimmigrant visas

Persons dishonorably discharged from Armed Forces

Persons who have renounced U.S. citizenship

Persons subject to qualifying restraining orders

Persons convicted of misdemeanor domestic violence

Federal Agencies:

Bureau of Alcohol, Tobacco, Firearms and Explosives: Primary enforcement

FBI: Major firearms investigations and background checks

U.S. Attorneys Offices: Prosecution coordination

State and Local Law Enforcement: Joint task forces

Interstate Commerce Connection:

Firearm or ammunition previously traveled in interstate commerce

Minimal nexus required (most firearms qualify)

Possession affects interstate commerce

Components manufactured in different states

Related Federal Offenses:

Use of Firearm During Crime of Violence (18 USC Section 924(c))

Unlawful Dealing in Firearms (18 USC Section 922(a))

Straw Purchases (18 USC Section 922(a)(6))

Prohibited Ammunition (18 USC Section 922(a)(7))

Armed Career Criminal Act:

Three prior convictions for violent felonies or serious drug offenses

Minimum 15-year sentence without parole

Enhanced penalties for career criminals

Strict interpretation of qualifying offenses

Mental Health Prohibitions:

Adjudication as mental defective

Commitment to mental institution

Restoration of rights procedures

NICS Improvement Amendments Act requirements

Enhanced Penalties:

Possession during commission of other crimes

Organized firearms trafficking

Multiple firearms or large quantities

Stolen firearms possession

Machine gun or destructive device possession

UNLAWFUL INTERNET ACTIVITIES

Statutory Citations: 18 USC Section 1030 (Computer Fraud and Abuse Act); 18 USC Section 2251 (Child exploitation)

Federal internet crime laws address various criminal activities conducted through computer networks and online platforms, representing a rapidly expanding area of federal enforcement.

Elements of Computer Intrusion (18 USC Section 1030):

1. Intentionally accessing computer without authorization or exceeding authorized access
2. Computer is protected computer
3. Conduct involves interstate or foreign commerce

4. Various specific prohibited acts (fraud, damage, espionage, etc.)

Elements of Online Child Exploitation:

1. Using computer or internet to produce, distribute, or possess child pornography
2. Using computer to entice minors for sexual purposes
3. Interstate or foreign commerce involvement
4. Knowledge of minor's age or reckless disregard

Penalties:

Computer Fraud: Up to 20 years imprisonment

Child Exploitation: 15-30 years imprisonment

Cyberstalking: Up to 5 years imprisonment (life if death results)

Identity Theft: Up to 15 years imprisonment

Fines: Up to $250,000 per count

Types of Internet Crimes:

Hacking and unauthorized computer access

Online fraud and identity theft

Cyberstalking and harassment

Child exploitation and pornography

Online drug trafficking and illegal marketplaces

Cryptocurrency crimes and money laundering

Federal Agencies:

FBI Cyber Division: Primary cybercrime enforcement

Internet Crime Complaint Center: Online crime reporting

Secret Service: Financial cybercrime

Immigration and Customs Enforcement: Child exploitation

National Security Agency: National security cyber threats

Computer Fraud Categories:

Obtaining national security information

Accessing financial records or credit information

Accessing government computers

Fraud in connection with computers

Damage to protected computers

Password trafficking and unauthorized access

Related Federal Offenses:

Wire Fraud (18 USC Section 1343)

Mail Fraud (18 USC Section 1341)

Money Laundering (18 USC Section 1956)

Extortion (18 USC Section 875)

RICO (18 USC Section 1962)

Enhanced Penalties:

Organized cybercrime enterprises

International cyber operations

Critical infrastructure targeting

Large-scale operations

Repeat cyber offenses

Dark Web Activities:

Anonymous marketplaces for illegal goods

Cryptocurrency money laundering

Ransomware-as-a-service operations

Stolen data marketplaces

Illegal services and contraband

UNLAWFUL SURVEILLANCE

Statutory Citations: 18 USC Section 2511 (Wiretapping and electronic surveillance); 18 USC Section 2701 (Stored Communications Act)

Federal surveillance laws regulate the interception of communications and access to stored electronic communications, with criminal penalties for violations of privacy rights.

Elements of Unlawful Wiretapping (18 USC Section 2511):

1. Intentionally intercepting wire, oral, or electronic communication
2. Without consent of party to communication
3. Without legal authorization (warrant, court order, etc.)
4. Use of electronic, mechanical, or other device

Elements of Unlawful Access to Stored Communications (18 USC Section 2701):

1. Intentionally accessing facility through which electronic communication service is provided
2. Obtaining, altering, or preventing authorized access to stored communication

3. Without or in excess of authorization

Penalties:

Unlawful Surveillance: Up to 5 years imprisonment

Stored Communications Violations: Up to 5 years imprisonment

Disclosure of Intercepted Communications: Up to 5 years imprisonment

Fines: Up to $250,000 for individuals

Federal Surveillance Laws:

Electronic Communications Privacy Act

Foreign Intelligence Surveillance Act

Communications Assistance for Law Enforcement Act

USA PATRIOT Act surveillance provisions

Fourth Amendment constitutional protections

Federal Agencies:

FBI: Electronic surveillance and wiretapping

National Security Agency: Foreign intelligence surveillance

Drug Enforcement Administration: Drug-related surveillance

U.S. Attorneys Offices: FISA and Title III applications

Types of Unlawful Surveillance:

Unauthorized wiretapping and phone monitoring

Email and electronic communication interception

Video surveillance and recording

GPS tracking and location monitoring

Computer surveillance and spyware

Corporate espionage and surveillance

Related Federal Offenses:

Computer Fraud (18 USC Section 1030)

Stalking (18 USC Section 2261A)

Privacy Violations (Various statutes)

Obstruction of Justice (18 USC Section 1503)

Conspiracy (18 USC Section 371)

Legal Surveillance Requirements:

Court orders and search warrants

Probable cause determinations

Minimization procedures

Notice requirements

Congressional and judicial oversight

Enhanced Penalties:

Commercial surveillance operations

Government official surveillance

Large-scale surveillance programs

International surveillance

Repeat surveillance violations

UNLAWFUL ASSEMBLY

See: Unlawful Assembly (covered above in this section)

URBAN TERRORISM

Statutory Citations: 18 USC Section 2331 (Domestic terrorism definition); 18 USC Section 2332a (Use of weapons of mass destruction)

Urban terrorism involves terrorist acts committed within urban areas and metropolitan regions, targeting civilian populations, infrastructure, and symbolic targets in densely populated areas.

Elements of Domestic Terrorism:

1. Activities involving acts dangerous to human life that violate criminal laws
2. Appear intended to intimidate or coerce civilian population
3. Influence government policy by intimidation or coercion
4. Affect government conduct by mass destruction, assassination, or kidnapping
5. Occur primarily within territorial jurisdiction of United States

Penalties:

Terrorism Offenses: Up to life imprisonment or death penalty

Use of WMD in Urban Areas: Life imprisonment or death penalty

Material Support to Urban Terrorists: Up to 20 years imprisonment

Enhanced Penalties: Various terrorism sentencing enhancements

Types of Urban Terrorism:

Mass casualty attacks in populated areas

Infrastructure attacks (transportation, utilities, communications)

Chemical, biological, or radiological attacks

Cyber attacks on urban systems

Vehicle ramming and mass violence

Symbolic target attacks (government buildings, landmarks)

Federal Agencies:

FBI Joint Terrorism Task Forces: Primary urban terrorism prevention

Department of Homeland Security: Urban area security

Federal Emergency Management Agency: Disaster response and recovery

Transportation Security Administration: Transportation security

Cybersecurity and Infrastructure Security Agency: Critical infrastructure protection

Urban Vulnerability Factors:

High population density and concentration

Critical infrastructure interdependencies

Economic and symbolic significance

Transportation hubs and mass transit

Government facilities and landmarks

Media and communication centers

Related Federal Offenses:

Terrorism (18 USC Section 2332a)

Weapons of Mass Destruction (18 USC Section 2332a)

Material Support to Terrorism (18 USC Section 2339A)

Conspiracy (18 USC Section 371)

RICO (18 USC Section 1962)

Enhanced Security Measures:

Urban Area Security Initiative funding

Interagency coordination and intelligence sharing

Community policing and engagement

Emergency preparedness and response planning

Technology and surveillance systems

Prevention and Preparedness:

Threat assessment and intelligence analysis

Community outreach and reporting programs

Training and exercises for first responders

Public awareness and education campaigns

International cooperation and information sharing.

V

VIOLENT CRIME

Statutory Citations: 18 USC Section 16 (Crime of violence definition); 18 USC Section 924(c) (Use of firearm during crime of violence)

Federal violent crime encompasses offenses that involve the use, attempted use, or threatened use of physical force against persons or property, with enhanced penalties when firearms are involved.

Elements of Crime of Violence (18 USC Section 16):

1. Offense that has as element use, attempted use, or threatened use of physical force against person or property of another

2. Or felony that by its nature involves substantial risk that physical force may be used in course of committing offense

Elements of Armed Violence (18 USC Section 924(c)):

1. Use or carrying firearm during and in relation to crime of violence or drug trafficking crime

2. Possession of firearm in furtherance of such crime

3. Knowledge that device is firearm

Penalties:

Crime of Violence: Varies by specific offense

Use of Firearm During Violent Crime: Minimum 5 years consecutive imprisonment

Brandishing Firearm: Minimum 7 years consecutive imprisonment

Discharging Firearm: Minimum 10 years consecutive imprisonment

Machine Gun or Destructive Device: Minimum 30 years consecutive imprisonment

Federal Violent Crimes:

Murder and manslaughter

Assault and battery

Robbery and armed robbery

Kidnapping and hostage taking

Rape and sexual assault

Arson and explosive offenses

Carjacking and hijacking

Federal Agencies:

FBI Violent Crime Program: Major violent crime investigations

ATF: Firearms-related violent crimes

U.S. Marshals Service: Violent fugitive apprehension

DEA: Drug-related violence

Military Criminal Investigation Commands: Military violent crimes

Federal Jurisdiction:

Special maritime and territorial jurisdiction

Interstate commerce connections

Federal property and facilities

Federal officials and employees

Firearms involvement triggering federal interest

Related Federal Offenses:

RICO (18 USC Section 1962)

Continuing Criminal Enterprise (21 USC Section 848)

Terrorism (18 USC Section 2332a)

Gang Violence (Various statutes)

Domestic Violence (18 USC Section 2261)

Enhanced Penalties:

Career criminal enhancements

Three strikes provisions

Gang-related violence

Terrorism-related violence

Violence against law enforcement

Firearm Enhancements:

Consecutive sentences for firearm use

Progressive penalties for repeat offenses

Enhanced penalties for machine guns

Forfeiture of firearms used in crimes

Prohibited person enhancements

VOTER INTIMIDATION

Statutory Citations: 18 USC Section 594 (Intimidation of voters); 52 USC Section 10307 (Voting Rights Act enforcement)

Federal voter intimidation laws protect the fundamental right to vote by criminalizing threats, coercion, and interference with electoral participation in federal elections.

Elements of Voter Intimidation (18 USC Section 594):

1. Intimidating, threatening, coercing, or attempting to intimidate, threaten, or coerce any other person

2. For purpose of interfering with right of person to vote or vote as person may choose

3. In election for President, Vice President, presidential elector, Member of Senate, Member of House of Representatives, or Delegate from District of Columbia

Elements of Economic Intimidation:

1. Discharging or threatening to discharge employee

2. For voting or not voting for particular candidate

3. In federal election

Penalties:

Voter Intimidation: Up to 1 year imprisonment

Economic Intimidation: Up to 5 years imprisonment

Conspiracy to Intimidate Voters: Up to 5 years imprisonment

Fines: Up to $1,000 to $10,000 depending on violation

Types of Voter Intimidation:

Physical threats and violence at polling places

Economic coercion and employment threats

Deceptive practices regarding voting procedures

Challenges and harassment based on race or ethnicity

Armed groups at polling locations

Social media threats and doxxing

Federal Agencies:

FBI: Voter intimidation investigations

Department of Justice Civil Rights **Division:** Voting rights enforcement

Election Assistance Commission: Election security coordination

U.S. Attorneys Offices: Local prosecution coordination

Protected Voting Activities:

Registering to vote

Casting ballots in elections

Voting by mail or absentee ballot

Participating in early voting

Exercising voting rights without discrimination

Receiving language assistance

Related Federal Offenses:

Civil Rights Conspiracy (18 USC Section 241)

Deprivation of Rights Under Color of Law (18 USC Section 242)

Mail Fraud (18 USC Section 1341) for deceptive practices

Wire Fraud (18 USC Section 1343) for electronic deception

Threats (18 USC Section 875)

Historical Context:

Reconstruction Era voting rights protection

Civil Rights Movement enforcement

Modern voter suppression concerns

Election security and integrity issues

Domestic terrorism and political violence

Enhanced Penalties:

Organized voter intimidation schemes

Violence or weapons involvement

Targeting protected minorities

Official involvement in intimidation

Repeat voting rights violations

VISA FRAUD

Statutory Citations: 18 USC Section 1546 (Fraud and misuse of visas, permits, and other documents); 8 USC Section 1325 (Improper entry by alien)

Federal visa fraud involves the fraudulent procurement, use, or transfer of immigration documents, including visas, passports, and other immigration-related documents.

Elements of Visa Fraud (18 USC Section 1546):

1. Knowingly forging, counterfeiting, altering, or falsely making any immigrant or nonimmigrant visa

2. Using any such forged, counterfeited, altered, or falsely made document

3. Attempting or conspiring to commit such acts

4. Intent to use document for improper purpose

Elements of Document Fraud:

1. Fraudulent use of genuine document by person other than rightful holder

2. Use of document obtained by false statement or fraud

3. Knowledge of fraudulent nature of document

Penalties:

Visa Fraud: Up to 10 years imprisonment (15 years if for terrorism purposes, 20 years if for drug trafficking or national security crimes)

Document Fraud: Up to 15 years imprisonment

Conspiracy: Same penalties as substantive offense

Fines: Up to $250,000 for individuals

Types of Visa Fraud:

Marriage fraud for immigration benefits

Student visa fraud and fake schools

Work visa fraud and labor certification

Tourist visa overstays and violations

Asylum and refugee fraud

Adoption fraud for immigration purposes

Federal Agencies:

Immigration and Customs Enforcement: Primary visa fraud enforcement

State Department: Visa issuance and fraud detection

Citizenship and Immigration Services: Immigration benefit fraud

Customs and Border Protection: Document fraud at borders

FBI: Complex fraud investigations

Common Fraud Schemes:

Sham marriages to U.S. citizens

Fraudulent labor certifications

Fake student enrollment

Document mills producing false papers

Bribery of immigration officials

Identity theft for visa applications

Related Federal Offenses:

Immigration Violations (8 USC Section 1325)

Identity Theft (18 USC Section 1028)

Mail Fraud (18 USC Section 1341)

Wire Fraud (18 USC Section 1343)

Perjury (18 USC Section 1621)

Enhanced Penalties:

Terrorism-related visa fraud

Drug trafficking connections

Organized fraud enterprises

Large-scale operations

Official corruption involvement

Immigration Consequences:

Permanent inadmissibility to United States

Deportation and removal proceedings

Bars to future immigration benefits

Family member derivative consequences

Loss of lawful status

VANDALISM

Statutory Citation: 18 USC Section 1361 (Government property destruction)

Federal vandalism laws address the willful destruction, damage, or defacement of federal property, including government buildings, monuments, and equipment.

Elements:

1. Willfully injuring or committing any depredation against property of United States
2. Intent to damage, destroy, or deface federal property
3. Property belonging to or under custody of United States government

Penalties:

Government Property Vandalism: Up to 10 years imprisonment

If Damage Exceeds $1,000: Enhanced penalties apply

Monuments and Memorials: Up to 10 years imprisonment

Fines: Up to $250,000 for individuals

Restitution: Full cost of repair or replacement

Federal Property Protected:

Federal office buildings and courthouses

National monuments and memorials

Military installations and equipment

National parks and forest resources

Postal facilities and mailboxes

Federal vehicles and aircraft

Federal Agencies:

Federal Protective Service: Federal building protection

National Park Service: Monument and park vandalism

Postal Inspection Service: Postal property vandalism

Military Police: Military installation vandalism

FBI: Major vandalism investigations

Types of Federal Vandalism:

Graffiti on federal buildings and monuments

Damage to historical sites and artifacts

Destruction of government equipment

Environmental vandalism in national parks

Computer system vandalism and cyber attacks

Vehicle and aircraft vandalism

Related Federal Offenses:

Destruction of Federal Property (18 USC Section 1361)

Trespass (18 USC Section 1382)

Arson (18 USC Section 844)

Computer Fraud (18 USC Section 1030)

Environmental Crimes (Various statutes)

Enhanced Penalties:

Hate crime motivations

Environmental or cultural damage

Large-scale destruction

Organized vandalism groups

Repeat vandalism offenses

Historical and Cultural Property:

National Historic Landmarks

Archaeological resources

Native American cultural sites

Federal art and sculpture

War memorials and veterans monuments

VEHICLE THEFT

Statutory Citations: 18 USC Section 2312 (Transportation of stolen motor vehicles); 18 USC Section 2119 (Motor vehicle theft - carjacking)

Federal vehicle theft laws address the interstate transportation of stolen motor vehicles and the taking of vehicles by force or intimidation (carjacking).

Elements of Interstate Vehicle Theft (18 USC Section 2312):

1. Transportation of motor vehicle in interstate or foreign commerce
2. Knowing vehicle was stolen
3. Intent to transport stolen vehicle across state lines

Elements of Carjacking (18 USC Section 2119):

1. Taking motor vehicle from person or presence of another
2. By force, violence, or intimidation
3. With intent to cause death or serious bodily harm
4. Vehicle has been transported, shipped, or received in interstate commerce

Penalties:

Interstate Vehicle Theft: Up to 10 years imprisonment

Carjacking: Up to 15 years imprisonment (25 years if serious bodily injury, life if death results)

Receiving Stolen Vehicles: Up to 10 years imprisonment

Fines: Up to $250,000 for individuals

Federal Jurisdiction:

Interstate commerce requirement for vehicles

Virtually all motor vehicles satisfy this requirement

Vehicle components from multiple states

Previous interstate transportation of vehicle

Federal Agencies:

FBI: Major vehicle theft investigations

Immigration and Customs **Enforcement:** International vehicle trafficking

Customs and Border Protection: Export/import violations

National Insurance Crime Bureau: Industry coordination

Types of Vehicle Theft:

Professional car theft rings

Carjacking and armed robbery

Export schemes to foreign countries

Chop shop operations

Identity theft for vehicle purchases

Rental car theft and fraud

Related Federal Offenses:

Robbery (18 USC Section 2111)

Kidnapping (18 USC Section 1201)

Use of Firearm During Crime of Violence (18 USC Section 924(c))

RICO (18 USC Section 1962)

Money Laundering (18 USC Section 1956)

Enhanced Penalties:

Use of firearms during theft

Violence against victims

Organized theft enterprises

International trafficking

Multiple vehicle thefts

Technology and Prevention:

Vehicle identification number verification

Advanced anti-theft systems

GPS tracking and recovery

Law enforcement databases

International cooperation

VETERINARY DRUG VIOLATIONS

Statutory Citations: 21 USC Section 331 (Federal Food, Drug, and Cosmetic Act); 21 USC Section 841 (Controlled Substances Act)

Federal veterinary drug violations involve the illegal distribution, dispensing, or use of animal drugs, particularly controlled substances used in veterinary medicine.

Elements of Unlawful Veterinary Drug Distribution:

1. Distributing or dispensing controlled substance intended for animal use
2. Without proper DEA registration or veterinary license
3. Outside usual course of professional practice
4. Without legitimate veterinary purpose

Elements of Animal Drug Adulteration:

1. Introducing adulterated or misbranded animal drug into interstate commerce
2. Knowledge of adulterated or misbranded status
3. Intent to defraud or mislead

Penalties:

Unlawful Distribution: Up to 5 years imprisonment (enhanced for controlled substances)

Drug Adulteration: Up to 3 years imprisonment

Misbranding: Up to 1 year imprisonment

Fines: Up to $250,000 for individuals

Professional Sanctions: Loss of veterinary license and DEA registration

Types of Violations:

Illegal distribution of animal steroids and growth hormones

Veterinary prescription drug diversion

Unlicensed practice of veterinary medicine

Animal drug counterfeiting and adulteration

Food animal antibiotic violations

Compounding violations

Federal Agencies:

Food and Drug Administration: Animal drug regulation and enforcement

Drug Enforcement Administration: Controlled veterinary substances

Department of Agriculture: Food animal drug residues

State Veterinary Boards: Professional licensing and discipline

Animal Welfare Considerations:

Proper veterinary care standards

Prevention of animal suffering

Food safety and public health

Antibiotic resistance concerns

Competition animal drug testing

Related Federal Offenses:

Drug Trafficking (21 USC Section 841)

Mail Fraud (18 USC Section 1341)

Wire Fraud (18 USC Section 1343)

Adulterated Food (21 USC Section 331)

False Statements (18 USC Section 1001)

Enhanced Penalties:

Large-scale operations

Endangering animal welfare

Food safety violations

Organized distribution networks

Professional license violations

VIOLENCE AGAINST WOMEN

Statutory Citations: 18 USC Section 2261 (Interstate domestic violence); 18 USC Section 2262 (Violence Against Women Act provisions criminalize gender-motivated violence that crosses state lines or affects interstate commerce, providing federal remedies when state responses are inadequate.

Elements of Interstate Domestic Violence (18 USC Section 2261):

1. Traveling across state line with intent to injure, harass, or intimidate intimate partner
2. Causing bodily injury to intimate partner in course of such travel
3. Interstate or foreign commerce involvement

Elements of Interstate Stalking (18 USC Section 2261A):

1. Using mail or facility of interstate commerce to engage in conduct
2. That causes substantial emotional distress or places person in reasonable fear
3. Of death or serious bodily injury

Penalties:

Interstate Domestic Violence: Up to 20 years imprisonment (life if death results)

Interstate Stalking: Up to 5 years imprisonment (life if death results)

Protection Order Violations: Up to 5 years imprisonment

Firearms Restrictions: Up to 10 years imprisonment

Protected Relationships:

Spouses and former spouses

Intimate partners and dating relationships

Persons who share child in common

Cohabiting partners

Family and household members

Federal Agencies:

FBI: Interstate domestic violence investigations

U.S. Marshals Service: Fugitive apprehension and victim protection

U.S. Attorneys Offices: VAWA prosecution

Office for Victims of Crime: Victim services coordination

Types of Gender-Based Violence:

Domestic violence and intimate partner abuse

Sexual assault and rape

Stalking and harassment

Dating violence

Human trafficking for sexual purposes

Workplace violence based on gender

Related Federal Offenses:

Sexual Abuse (18 USC Section 2241)

Kidnapping (18 USC Section 1201)

Threats (18 USC Section 875)

Civil Rights Violations (18 USC Section 245)

Human Trafficking (18 USC Section 1591)

Enhanced Penalties:

Use of dangerous weapons

Violations of protective orders

Repeat domestic violence offenses

Targeting pregnant women

Gang-related gender violence

Victim Protection and Services:

Victim relocation assistance

Protective order enforcement

Immigration relief for victims

Economic support and counseling

Legal advocacy and representation.

W

WAR CRIMES

Statutory Citation: 18 USC Section 2441 (War crimes)

Federal war crimes laws prosecute violations of the laws of war committed by or against United States nationals, implementing international humanitarian law obligations and protecting military personnel and civilians during armed conflict.

Elements:

1. Person commits grave breach of Geneva Conventions or violation of common Article 3
2. Conduct takes place in context of and associated with armed conflict
3. Perpetrator or victim is member of U.S. Armed Forces or U.S. national
4. Knowledge of factual circumstances establishing armed conflict

Penalties:

War Crimes: Up to life imprisonment

If **Death Results:** Death penalty or life imprisonment

Conspiracy: Same penalties as substantive offense

Command Responsibility: Enhanced penalties for military leaders

Types of War Crimes:

Willful killing of protected persons

Torture and inhumane treatment

Unlawful deportation or transfer

Taking hostages

Attacking civilians or civilian objects

Using prohibited weapons

Destroying cultural property

Federal Agencies:

FBI War Crimes Accountability Team: Domestic war crimes investigations

Department of Justice Human Rights and Special Prosecutions Section: War crimes prosecution

Immigration and Customs **Enforcement:** Immigration consequences

Military Criminal Investigation Commands: Military war crimes

Geneva Conventions Protected Persons:

Wounded and sick military personnel

Prisoners of war

Civilian population in occupied territory

Medical and religious personnel

Civilians in international armed conflict

Related Federal Offenses:

Torture (18 USC Section 2340)

Genocide (18 USC Section 1091)

Crimes Against Humanity (Various provisions)

Terrorism (18 USC Section 2332a)

Murder (18 USC Section 1111)

International Legal Framework:

Geneva Conventions of 1949

Additional Protocols of 1977

Rome Statute of International Criminal Court

Customary international humanitarian law

War crimes tribunal precedents

Enhanced Penalties:

Superior responsibility for subordinate crimes

Systematic or widespread violations

Targeting protected persons or objects

Use of prohibited weapons or methods

Command influence in war crimes

Universal Jurisdiction:

Prosecution regardless of where crimes occurred

Extradition and mutual legal assistance

Immigration bars for war criminals

Denaturalization proceedings

International cooperation mechanisms

WEAPONS OF MASS DESTRUCTION

Statutory Citations: 18 USC Section 2332a (Use of weapons of mass destruction); 18 USC Section 175 (Biological weapons)

Federal WMD laws address the development, production, possession, and use of nuclear, chemical, and biological weapons, representing some of the most serious threats to national security and public safety.

Elements of WMD Use (18 USC Section 2332a):

1. Use, threaten, attempt, or conspire to use weapon of mass destruction
2. Against national of United States while outside United States
3. Against person within United States
4. Against property owned, leased, or used by United States

Elements of WMD Development:

1. Developing, producing, stockpiling, transferring, acquiring, retaining, or possessing weapon of mass destruction
2. Without lawful authority
3. Knowledge of prohibited nature of activity

Penalties:

Use of WMD: Life imprisonment or death penalty

Conspiracy to Use WMD: Life imprisonment or death penalty

Threatening WMD Use: Up to 10 years imprisonment

Development/Possession: Life imprisonment

Fines: Up to $2,000,000 for individuals

Weapons of Mass Destruction Definition:

Destructive devices (bombs, grenades, rockets, missiles, mines)

Poison gas weapons

Weapons involving disease organisms

Weapons designed to release radiation or radioactivity

Any combination of parts designed for use in such weapons

Federal Agencies:

FBI Weapons of Mass Destruction Directorate: Primary WMD enforcement

Department of Homeland Security: WMD prevention and response

Nuclear Regulatory Commission: Nuclear materials security

Centers for Disease Control: Biological agent oversight

Department of Energy: Nuclear weapons security

Types of WMD Threats:

Nuclear weapons and dirty bombs

Chemical weapons and toxic industrial chemicals

Biological weapons and disease agents

Radiological dispersal devices

Improvised explosive devices causing mass casualties

Related Federal Offenses:

Terrorism (18 USC Section 2331)

Nuclear Regulatory Violations (42 USC Section 2272)

Biological Weapons (18 USC Section 175)

Chemical Weapons (18 USC Section 229)

Export Control Violations (50 USC Section 4801)

Enhanced Penalties:

Terrorist motivations and connections

International WMD trafficking

Targeting civilian populations

Government facility attacks

Organized WMD enterprises

International Nonproliferation:

Nuclear Non-Proliferation Treaty obligations

Chemical Weapons Convention implementation

Biological Weapons Convention compliance

International Atomic Energy Agency safeguards

Export control coordination

WIRE FRAUD

Statutory Citation: 18 USC Section 1343

Wire fraud involves executing schemes to defraud using interstate wire communications, representing one of the most frequently prosecuted federal crimes due to its broad application in the digital age.

Elements:

1. Scheme or artifice to defraud or obtain money or property by false or fraudulent pretenses
2. Use of interstate wire, radio, or television communication

3. In furtherance of the scheme

4. Intent to defraud

Penalties:

Wire Fraud: Up to 20 years imprisonment

If Affecting Financial Institution: Up to 30 years imprisonment

Fines: Up to $250,000 for individuals, $500,000 for organizations

Restitution: Mandatory restitution to victims

Criminal Forfeiture: Property obtained through wire fraud

Interstate Wire Communications:

Telephone calls and text messages

Internet and email communications

Electronic fund transfers

Fax transmissions

Television and radio broadcasts

Computer network communications

Federal Agencies:

FBI: Primary wire fraud investigations

Secret Service: Financial wire fraud

Postal Inspection Service: Mail and wire fraud coordination

Securities and Exchange Commission: Securities wire fraud

Internal Revenue Service: Tax-related wire fraud

Types of Wire Fraud:

Internet and email fraud schemes

Telemarketing and telephone fraud

Online auction and marketplace fraud

Romance and relationship scams

Business email compromise

Cryptocurrency and digital asset fraud

Related Federal Offenses:

Mail Fraud (18 USC Section 1341)

Bank Fraud (18 USC Section 1344)

Securities Fraud (18 USC Section 1348)

Money Laundering (18 USC Section 1956)

Computer Fraud (18 USC Section 1030)

Scheme to Defraud:

Material misrepresentations or omissions

Intent to deceive victims

Reasonable reliance by victims

Actual or intended loss to victims

Use of wire communications to further scheme

Enhanced Penalties:

Mass marketing fraud targeting elderly

Healthcare fraud endangering patients

Financial institution fraud

Organized fraud enterprises

International wire fraud operations

Digital Age Considerations:

Internet-based fraud schemes

Social media and online platforms

Cryptocurrency and blockchain fraud

International wire fraud coordination

Cybercrime and digital evidence

WIRETAPPING

Statutory Citation: 18 USC Section 2511 (Interception of wire, oral, or electronic communications)

Federal wiretapping laws regulate the interception of communications, balancing law enforcement needs with privacy rights, and criminalizing unauthorized surveillance activities.

Elements of Unlawful Wiretapping:

1. Intentionally intercepting wire, oral, or electronic communication
2. Using electronic, mechanical, or other device
3. Without consent of party to communication
4. Without legal authorization

Elements of Disclosure:

1. Intentionally disclosing contents of intercepted communication

2. Knowing or having reason to know information obtained through unlawful interception

3. Without authorization

Penalties:

Unlawful Wiretapping: Up to 5 years imprisonment

Disclosure of Intercepted Communications: Up to 5 years imprisonment

Use of Intercepted Communications: Up to 5 years imprisonment

Fines: Up to $250,000 for individuals

Civil Damages: Statutory and punitive damages

Types of Communications:

Wire communications (telephone, telegraph)

Oral communications (face-to-face conversations)

Electronic communications (email, text, data)

Radio communications

Cellular and wireless communications

Federal Agencies:

FBI: Electronic surveillance and Title III wiretaps

Drug Enforcement Administration: Drug-related wiretaps

U.S. Attorneys Offices: Court authorization for wiretaps

National Security Agency: Foreign intelligence surveillance

Legal Wiretapping Authorization:

Title III court orders for criminal investigations

Foreign Intelligence Surveillance Act warrants

Consent of one party to communication

Emergency situations with subsequent authorization

National security wiretaps under FISA

Related Federal Offenses:

Computer Fraud (18 USC Section 1030)

Stalking (18 USC Section 2261A)

Privacy Violations (18 USC Section 2701)

Obstruction of Justice (18 USC Section 1503)

Conspiracy (18 USC Section 371)

Exceptions to Wiretapping Prohibition:

Law enforcement with proper court orders

One-party consent in most jurisdictions

Communications service providers for operations

Emergency situations

Foreign intelligence surveillance (with FISA warrant)

Enhanced Penalties:

Commercial wiretapping operations

Government official surveillance

Organized surveillance enterprises

International wiretapping

Repeat surveillance violations

WORKPLACE VIOLENCE

Statutory Citations: 18 USC Section 1114 (Killing federal officers); 18 USC Section 930 (Possession of weapons in federal facilities)

Federal workplace violence laws address violent crimes committed in federal workplaces, including attacks on federal employees and violence in federal facilities.

Elements of Federal Workplace Violence:

1. Assault, threat, or violent act against federal employee
2. While employee engaged in official duties
3. On account of or in retaliation for official duties
4. Within federal workplace or facility

Elements of Weapons in Federal Facilities (18 USC Section 930):

1. Knowingly possessing firearm or dangerous weapon
2. In federal facility
3. Without lawful authority
4. Intent to use weapon unlawfully

Penalties:

Federal Employee Assault: Up to 20 years imprisonment

Killing Federal Employee: Life imprisonment or death penalty

Weapons in Federal Facilities: Up to 1 year imprisonment (5 years if intent to use unlawfully)

Threats Against Federal Employees: Up to 10 years imprisonment

Federal Workplaces Protected:

Federal office buildings and courthouses

Military installations and bases

Post offices and mail facilities

National parks and forest service facilities

Federal prisons and detention centers

Veterans Affairs medical centers

Federal Agencies:

FBI: Federal workplace violence investigations

Federal Protective Service: Federal facility security

U.S. Marshals Service: Court security and employee protection

Postal Inspection Service: Postal workplace violence

Military Police: Military installation security

Types of Workplace Violence:

Employee-on-employee violence

Violence by former employees

Domestic violence spilling into workplace

Customer or client violence against employees

Terrorist attacks on federal facilities

Active shooter incidents

Related Federal Offenses:

Assault on Federal Officers (18 USC Section 111)

Threats Against Federal Officials (18 USC Section 115)

Terrorism (18 USC Section 2332a)

Domestic Violence (18 USC Section 2261)

Stalking (18 USC Section 2261A)

Risk Factors and Prevention:

Employee assistance programs

Threat assessment and management

Security measures and access control

Training and emergency response procedures

Coordination with local law enforcement

Enhanced Penalties:

Use of firearms or dangerous weapons

Multiple victims or mass violence

Premeditated attacks

Terrorism motivations

Targeting high-ranking officials

WELFARE FRAUD

Statutory Citations: 7 USC Section 2024 (SNAP fraud); 42 USC Section 1320a-7b (Healthcare program fraud)

Federal welfare fraud involves the fraudulent receipt of government benefits through false statements, concealment of material facts, or other deceptive practices affecting federal assistance programs.

Elements of SNAP Fraud:

1. Fraudulent application for or use of SNAP benefits (food stamps)
2. Trafficking in SNAP benefits
3. Knowingly using, transferring, acquiring, altering, or possessing SNAP benefits in unauthorized manner
4. Value exceeding $5,000 for felony prosecution

Elements of Healthcare Program Fraud:

1. Knowingly and willfully making false statement or representation
2. In application for healthcare benefits
3. Material to determination of eligibility or benefit amount
4. Intent to defraud healthcare programs

Penalties:

SNAP Fraud: Up to 5 years imprisonment (20 years for $5,000+ trafficking)

Healthcare Fraud: Up to 5 years imprisonment

Housing Fraud: Up to 5 years imprisonment

Fines: Up to $250,000 for individuals

Restitution: Full amount of fraudulent benefits

Types of Welfare Fraud:

Food stamp trafficking and benefit fraud

Medicaid and Medicare fraud

Housing assistance fraud

Temporary Assistance for Needy Families fraud

Disability benefit fraud

Child care assistance fraud

Federal Agencies:

Food and Nutrition Service: SNAP fraud enforcement

Health and Human Services Office of Inspector General: Healthcare fraud

Housing and Urban Development Office of Inspector General: Housing fraud

Social Security Administration: Disability fraud

Common Fraud Schemes:

Concealing income or assets

False identity and multiple applications

Benefit trafficking and cash conversion

Provider fraud and billing schemes

Eligibility fraud and false documentation

Interstate benefit shopping

Related Federal Offenses:

Mail Fraud (18 USC Section 1341)

Wire Fraud (18 USC Section 1343)

False Statements (18 USC Section 1001)

Identity Theft (18 USC Section 1028)

Money Laundering (18 USC Section 1956)

Enhanced Penalties:

Organized fraud enterprises

Large-scale operations

Professional facilitators

Targeting multiple programs

Repeat welfare fraud

Program Integrity Measures:

Data matching and verification systems

Investigation and prosecution coordination

Provider monitoring and oversight

Fraud prevention education

Recovery and restitution procedures

WHITE-COLLAR CRIME

Statutory Citations: Various federal statutes including 18 USC Section 1341 (Mail fraud), 18 USC Section 1343 (Wire fraud), 15 USC Section 78ff (Securities violations)

White-collar crime encompasses financially motivated, nonviolent criminal offenses committed by business and government professionals, typically involving deception, breach of trust, and abuse of position.

Common White-Collar Offenses:

Securities fraud and insider trading

Corporate fraud and accounting violations

Healthcare and insurance fraud

Bank fraud and embezzlement

Tax evasion and money laundering

Public corruption and bribery

Procurement and contract fraud

Elements Vary by Specific Offense:

Generally require intent to defraud or deceive

Material misrepresentations or omissions

Use of instrumentalities of interstate commerce

Breach of fiduciary duty or position of trust

Financial loss to victims or government

Penalties:

Vary significantly by offense and loss amount

Enhanced penalties for large-scale fraud

Organizational sentencing guidelines

Forfeiture of fraudulent proceeds

Professional sanctions and debarment

Federal Agencies:

FBI White-Collar Crime Program: Complex fraud investigations

Securities and Exchange Commission: Securities fraud enforcement

Internal Revenue Service Criminal Investigation: Tax crimes

Health and Human Services Office of Inspector General: Healthcare fraud

Various Inspector General Offices: Government fraud

Characteristics of White-Collar Crime:

Committed by persons of high social status

Occurs in course of legitimate occupation

Involves abuse of trust and position

Typically nonviolent in nature

Often causes substantial financial harm

May involve sophisticated schemes

Related Federal Offenses:

RICO (18 USC Section 1962)

Money Laundering (18 USC Section 1956)

Conspiracy (18 USC Section 371)

False Statements (18 USC Section 1001)

Obstruction of Justice (18 USC Section 1503)

Enhanced Penalties:

Leadership role in criminal activity

Sophisticated means and planning

Large financial losses to victims

Abuse of position of trust

Obstruction of justice

Organized criminal enterprises

Corporate Criminal Liability:

Respondeat superior doctrine

Collective knowledge theory

Due diligence and compliance programs

Deferred prosecution agreements

Corporate integrity agreements.

X

XENOPHOBIC CRIMES

Statutory Citations: 18 USC Section 249 (Hate crimes); 18 USC Section 245 (Federally protected activities)

Xenophobic crimes involve criminal acts motivated by hatred, bias, or prejudice against persons based on their national origin, ethnicity, or perceived foreign status, falling under federal hate crime and civil rights protections.

Elements of National Origin Hate Crime (18 USC Section 249):

1. Willfully causing bodily injury or attempting to cause bodily injury
2. Because of actual or perceived national origin of victim
3. Use of dangerous weapon, fire, explosive, or incendiary device
4. Conduct affects interstate or foreign commerce

Elements of Interference with Federally Protected Activities (18 USC Section 245):

1. Willfully injuring, intimidating, or interfering with person
2. Because of race, color, religion, or national origin
3. While engaged in federally protected activity
4. Use of force or threat of force

Penalties:

Hate Crimes: Up to 10 years imprisonment (life if death results)

Civil Rights Violations: Up to 1 year imprisonment (life if death results)

If Involving Kidnapping or Sexual Abuse: Life imprisonment or death penalty

Fines: Up to $250,000 for individuals

Protected National Origin Characteristics:

Country of birth or ancestry

Ethnicity and ethnic background

Accent or language spoken

Immigration status and citizenship

Cultural practices and traditions

Physical appearance suggesting foreign origin

Federal Agencies:

FBI Civil Rights Program: Hate crime investigations

Department of Justice Civil Rights Division: Prosecution coordination

Community Relations Service: Conflict mediation and prevention

U.S. Attorneys Offices: Local hate crime prosecution

Types of Xenophobic Crimes:

Physical assaults based on perceived foreign origin

Vandalism of ethnic businesses and religious sites

Workplace discrimination and harassment

Housing discrimination and intimidation

Educational institution bias incidents

Online harassment and cyberbullying

Related Federal Offenses:

Civil Rights Conspiracy (18 USC Section 241)

Deprivation of Rights Under Color of Law (18 USC Section 242)

Arson (18 USC Section 844) - if targeting ethnic properties

Threats (18 USC Section 875) - if using interstate communications

Immigration-Related Document Fraud (18 USC Section 1546)

Federally Protected Activities:

Voting and political participation

Education in public schools and universities

Employment and job seeking

Public accommodation access

Housing transactions and rentals

Jury service in federal court

Enhanced Penalties:

Use of firearms or dangerous weapons

Organized hate groups involvement

Multiple victims or widespread community impact

Official position of authority by defendant

Targeting vulnerable populations

International Considerations:

Foreign nationals as victims

Diplomatic immunity issues

Consular notification requirements

International human rights obligations

Cross-border hate crime coordination

Historical Context:

Chinese Exclusion Act era violence

Japanese American internment legacy

Post-9/11 anti-Muslim incidents

Immigration debate-related violence

COVID-19 pandemic anti-Asian incidents

X-RAY EQUIPMENT VIOLATIONS

Statutory Citations: 21 USC Section 360i (Radiation Control for Health and Safety Act); 42 USC Section 263b (Mammography Quality Standards Act)

Federal X-ray equipment violations involve the improper manufacture, distribution, or use of radiation-emitting devices, including medical X-ray equipment, security screening devices, and industrial radiography equipment.

Elements of Radiation Equipment Violations:

1. Manufacturing, importing, or distributing electronic product that emits radiation
2. Failure to comply with applicable performance standards
3. Knowing violation of radiation safety requirements
4. Product affects interstate commerce

Elements of Medical Device Violations:

1. Introduction of adulterated or misbranded medical device into interstate commerce
2. Failure to comply with quality standards and safety requirements
3. Operating without required certification or accreditation
4. Knowing violation of medical device regulations

Penalties:

Radiation Equipment Violations: Up to 1 year imprisonment

Medical Device Violations: Up to 3 years imprisonment

Criminal Fines: Up to $100,000 for individuals

Civil Penalties: Up to $15,000 per violation

Injunctive Relief: Cessation of violative activities

Types of X-Ray Equipment:

Medical diagnostic X-ray machines
Computed tomography (CT) scanners
Mammography equipment
Dental X-ray devices
Security screening equipment
Industrial radiography devices
Federal Agencies:
Food and Drug Administration: Medical device regulation and enforcement
Occupational Safety and Health Administration: Workplace radiation safety
Nuclear Regulatory Commission: Certain radiation sources
Transportation Security Administration: Security screening equipment
Customs and Border Protection: Import/export enforcement
Radiation Safety Requirements:
Performance standards for emission levels
Quality assurance and maintenance programs
Operator training and certification
Patient dose optimization
Shielding and facility design requirements
Record keeping and reporting obligations
Related Federal Offenses:
Medical Device Fraud (21 USC Section 331)
Adulterated Drug or Device (21 USC Section 331)
False Statements (18 USC Section 1001)
Wire Fraud (18 USC Section 1343)
Conspiracy (18 USC Section 371)
Enhanced Penalties:
Endangering patient safety
Large-scale violations
Systematic safety violations
International trafficking
Repeat violations
Public Health Protection:

Cancer screening program quality

Pediatric radiation exposure limits

Occupational radiation safety

Emergency response preparedness

International radiation safety standards

XEROGRAPHIC COUNTERFEITING

Statutory Citations: 18 USC Section 474 (Plates, stones, or other things for counterfeiting); 18 USC Section 476 (Taking impressions of tools used for obligations or securities)

Xerographic counterfeiting involves the use of photocopying, scanning, and digital reproduction technology to create counterfeit currency, securities, and official documents.

Elements:

1. Making, executing, acquiring, or possessing plates, stones, or other things
2. Used or intended to be used for counterfeiting obligations or securities of United States
3. With intent to use for counterfeiting purposes
4. Knowledge of counterfeiting purpose

Elements of Digital Counterfeiting:

1. Using computer, scanner, printer, or other digital device
2. To produce counterfeit currency or securities
3. With intent to defraud
4. Knowledge that reproductions are counterfeit

Penalties:

Counterfeiting Equipment: Up to 10 years imprisonment

Digital Counterfeiting: Up to 20 years imprisonment

Possession of Counterfeiting Tools: Up to 10 years imprisonment

Fines: Up to $250,000 for individuals

Criminal Forfeiture: All counterfeiting equipment and materials

Modern Counterfeiting Technology:

High-resolution color copiers and printers

Digital scanners and imaging software

Computer graphics and design programs

Professional printing equipment

Specialty papers and inks

Binding and finishing equipment

Federal Agencies:

Secret Service: Primary counterfeiting enforcement

FBI: Complex counterfeiting investigations

Customs and Border Protection: Import/export of counterfeiting equipment

Postal Inspection Service: Mail-related counterfeiting

Immigration and Customs Enforcement: International counterfeiting

Types of Xerographic Counterfeiting:

Currency reproduction and alteration

Government securities and bonds

Checks and money orders

Identity documents and credentials

Academic transcripts and certificates

Professional licenses and permits

Related Federal Offenses:

Counterfeiting Currency (18 USC Section 471)

Passing Counterfeit Currency (18 USC Section 472)

Identity Document Fraud (18 USC Section 1028)

Mail Fraud (18 USC Section 1341)

Wire Fraud (18 USC Section 1343)

Security Features and Countermeasures:

Microprinting and fine line patterns

Color-changing inks and security threads

Watermarks and security papers

RFID chips and biometric data

Digital authentication and verification

Anti-counterfeiting education programs

Enhanced Penalties:

Large-scale counterfeiting operations

International counterfeiting rings

Government document counterfeiting

Professional counterfeiting equipment

Organized counterfeiting enterprises

EXTORTION

See: Extortion in Section E

EXPLOSIVES VIOLATIONS

See: Bomb Threats in Section B and Arson in Section A.

Y

YOUTH GANGS (FEDERAL PROSECUTION)

Statutory Citations: 18 USC Section 1962 (RICO); 18 USC Section 521 (Criminal street gangs)

Federal youth gang prosecutions address organized criminal activities by juvenile and young adult gangs that affect interstate commerce, engage in patterns of racketeering activity, or commit federal crimes.

Elements of Criminal Street Gang Activity (18 USC Section 521):

1. Association of three or more individuals
2. Primary activity is commission of criminal offenses
3. Members engage in continuing serious criminal activity
4. Activities affect interstate or foreign commerce

Elements for RICO Gang Prosecution:

1. Enterprise engaged in or affecting interstate commerce
2. Defendant employed by or associated with enterprise
3. Conducted enterprise affairs through pattern of racketeering activity
4. Pattern consists of at least two racketeering acts within 10 years

Penalties:

RICO Violations: Up to 20 years imprisonment per count

Criminal Street Gang Participation: Up to 10 years imprisonment additional to underlying offense

Enhanced Penalties: For leadership roles and continuing criminal enterprise

Fines: Up to $250,000 for individuals

Criminal Forfeiture: Gang assets and proceeds from criminal activity

Federal Gang Crimes:

Drug trafficking and distribution

Firearms trafficking and violence

Human trafficking and prostitution

Money laundering and financial crimes

Immigration violations and alien smuggling

Racketeering and extortion

Interstate transportation of stolen goods

Federal Agencies:

FBI Gang Task Forces: Multi-jurisdictional gang investigations

Drug Enforcement Administration: Drug-related gang activity

Bureau of Alcohol, Tobacco, Firearms and Explosives: Gang firearms violations

Immigration and Customs Enforcement: Immigration-related gang crimes

U.S. Marshals Service: Gang fugitive apprehension

Types of Youth Gangs:

Traditional street gangs (Bloods, Crips, MS-13)

Prison gangs extending to streets

Motorcycle gangs and clubs

Ethnic and immigrant gangs

Hybrid gangs with multiple affiliations

Online and cyber gangs

Related Federal Offenses:

Violent Crime (18 USC Section 16)

Drug Trafficking (21 USC Section 841)

Firearms Violations (18 USC Section 922)

Human Trafficking (18 USC Section 1591)

Money Laundering (18 USC Section 1956)

Gang Enhancement Penalties:

Additional 10 years for gang-related federal crimes

Enhanced sentences for leadership roles

Conspiracy and aiding/abetting liability

Forfeiture of gang assets and territory

Supervised release with gang restrictions

Juvenile vs Adult Prosecution:

Federal Juvenile Delinquency Act considerations

Transfer to adult court for serious violent crimes

Enhanced penalties for recruiting minors

Protection of juvenile gang members as victims

Intervention and prevention programs

YOUTH EXPLOITATION

Statutory Citations: 18 USC Section 2251 (Sexual exploitation of children); 18 USC Section 1591 (Sex trafficking of children)

Federal youth exploitation laws protect minors from sexual exploitation, forced labor, and other forms of abuse, with severe penalties for those who exploit children for commercial purposes.

Elements of Child Sexual Exploitation (18 USC Section 2251):

1. Employing, using, persuading, inducing, enticing, or coercing minor
2. To engage in sexually explicit conduct
3. For purpose of producing visual depiction
4. Use of materials transported in interstate commerce

Elements of Sex Trafficking of Minors (18 USC Section 1591):

1. Recruiting, enticing, harboring, transporting, providing, obtaining, or maintaining person under 18
2. To engage in commercial sex act
3. No requirement to prove force, fraud, or coercion for minors

Penalties:

Child Sexual Exploitation: 15-30 years imprisonment (25-50 years for repeat offenders)

Sex Trafficking of Minors: 15 years to life imprisonment

Child Labor Trafficking: Up to 20 years imprisonment (life if death results)

Supervised Release: Minimum 5 years, up to lifetime supervision

Fines: Up to $250,000 per count

Types of Youth Exploitation:

Commercial sexual exploitation and trafficking

Child pornography production and distribution

Online enticement and sextortion

Child labor trafficking

Forced begging and street crimes

Organ trafficking involving minors

Federal Agencies:

FBI Crimes Against Children Program: Primary enforcement

Immigration and Customs Enforcement: International child trafficking

National Center for Missing and Exploited Children: Coordination and assistance

Postal Inspection Service: Mail-related child exploitation

Secret Service: Technology-facilitated crimes against children

Victim Services for Exploited Youth:

Comprehensive case management and services

Trauma-informed care and treatment

Safe housing and shelter placement

Educational and vocational support

Legal advocacy and immigration relief

Family reunification when appropriate

Related Federal Offenses:

Child Pornography (18 USC Section 2252)

Transportation for Illegal Sexual Activity (18 USC Section 2421)

Coercion and Enticement (18 USC Section 2422)

Human Trafficking (18 USC Section 1589)

RICO (18 USC Section 1962)

Enhanced Penalties:

Prior convictions for child exploitation

Use of violence or dangerous weapons

Multiple child victims

International trafficking operations

Leadership roles in exploitation enterprises

Technology and Online Exploitation:

Internet-based recruitment and exploitation

Social media platforms and gaming environments

Cryptocurrency payments and anonymization

Dark web marketplaces

Live streaming of abuse

Artificial intelligence and deepfake concerns

YOUTHFUL OFFENDER PROVISIONS

Statutory Citation: 18 USC Sections 5031-5042 (Federal Juvenile Delinquency Act)

Federal youthful offender provisions provide special procedures and considerations for persons under 21 who commit federal crimes, emphasizing rehabilitation over punishment when appropriate.

Elements for Federal Juvenile Jurisdiction:

1. Person under 18 years of age at time of offense
2. Alleged violation of federal criminal statute
3. State does not have adequate programs or facilities
4. Federal interest justifies federal prosecution

Elements for Youthful Offender Treatment:

1. Person under 22 years of age at time of sentencing
2. Convicted of federal offense
3. Court determines youth would benefit from treatment
4. No prior felony convictions

Penalties and Dispositions:

Juvenile Adjudication: Commitment until age 21 or shorter term as appropriate

Youthful Offender Sentence: Up to 6 years commitment for treatment

Adult Prosecution: Full adult penalties for serious violent crimes

Probation and Supervision: Community-based alternatives

Restitution: Payment for victim losses

Federal Juvenile Facilities:

Federal Bureau of Prisons juvenile facilities

Contract facilities and halfway houses

Community-based treatment programs

Educational and vocational training

Mental health and substance abuse treatment

Transfer to Adult Court Factors:

Age of juvenile (must be 16 or older for violent crimes)

Seriousness and circumstances of offense

Prior delinquency record

Sophistication and maturity of juvenile

Likelihood of rehabilitation

Federal Agencies:

U.S. Probation: Juvenile supervision and services

Federal Bureau of Prisons: Juvenile detention and commitment

U.S. Attorneys Offices: Prosecution decisions and alternatives

Administrative Office of U.S. Courts: Juvenile justice administration

Confidentiality and Records:

Sealed juvenile records and proceedings

Limited disclosure of juvenile information

Expungement possibilities for certain offenses

Employment and education protections

Restoration of civil rights

Related Considerations:

Miranda rights and interrogation procedures

Parental notification and involvement

Educational continuity and services

Mental health assessment and treatment

Substance abuse evaluation and treatment

Diversion and Alternatives:

Pre-trial diversion programs

Community service and restitution

Drug courts and treatment programs

Restorative justice initiatives

Mentoring and support services

YOUTH ONLINE SAFETY VIOLATIONS

Statutory Citations: 18 USC Section 2422 (Coercion and enticement); 47 USC Section 223 (Communications Decency Act)

Federal youth online safety laws protect minors from predatory behavior, exploitation, and harmful content in digital environments, addressing the unique vulnerabilities of children online.

Elements of Online Enticement (18 USC Section 2422(b)):

1. Using mail, interstate commerce facility, or within special maritime and territorial jurisdiction
2. Knowingly persuading, inducing, enticing, or coercing individual under 18
3. To engage in prostitution or sexual activity for which person can be charged with crime
4. Intent to engage in criminal sexual conduct

Elements of Obscene Communications to Minors (47 USC Section 223):

1. Using telecommunications device to make obscene communication
2. To person under 18 years of age
3. Knowing recipient is under 18
4. Intent to annoy, abuse, threaten, or harass

Penalties:

Online Enticement: 10 years to life imprisonment

Obscene Communications: Up to 2 years imprisonment

Enhanced Penalties: For prior convictions involving minors

Fines: Up to $250,000 for individuals

Supervised Release: Extended supervision with computer restrictions

Types of Online Threats to Youth:

Sexual predators and groomers

Cyberbullying and harassment

Exposure to inappropriate content

Identity theft and privacy violations

Online gambling and financial exploitation

Recruitment for criminal activity

Federal Agencies:

FBI Internet Crimes Against Children Task Force: Primary enforcement

National Center for Missing and Exploited Children: Reporting and coordination

Federal Trade Commission: Privacy and consumer protection

Department of Education: School-based online safety

Postal Inspection Service: Mail-related online crimes

Platform and Technology Considerations:

Social media platforms and messaging apps

Online gaming environments

Video streaming and sharing platforms

Dating and meeting applications

Educational technology platforms

Emerging technologies and virtual reality

Related Federal Offenses:

Child Pornography (18 USC Section 2252)

Computer Fraud (18 USC Section 1030)

Stalking (18 USC Section 2261A)

Wire Fraud (18 USC Section 1343)

Privacy Violations (18 USC Section 2701)

Enhanced Safety Measures:

Age verification and parental controls

Content filtering and monitoring

Privacy protection for minors

Educational programs for digital literacy

Industry self-regulation and standards

International cooperation on child safety

Prevention and Education:

Digital citizenship training

Parent and educator resources

Public awareness campaigns

Technology company partnerships

Law enforcement training

Victim support services

YACHTING VIOLATIONS

Statutory Citations: 46 USC Section 70503 (Maritime drug law enforcement); 19 USC Section 1436 (Customs violations)

Federal yachting violations involve criminal activities aboard recreational vessels in U.S. waters or by U.S.-flagged vessels internationally, including drug trafficking, customs violations, and maritime safety crimes.

Elements of Maritime Drug Trafficking:

1. Manufacture, distribute, or possess with intent to distribute controlled substance
2. On board vessel subject to U.S. jurisdiction
3. On high seas or waters within customs waters of United States
4. Knowledge of controlled substance laws

Elements of Customs Violations:

1. Failing to report arrival from foreign port
2. Importing merchandise without declaration

3. Evading duties, taxes, or prohibitions
4. Knowledge of customs requirements

Penalties:

Maritime Drug Trafficking: Same penalties as land-based offenses based on drug type and quantity

Customs Violations: Up to 5 years imprisonment

Failure to Report: Up to 1 year imprisonment

Fines: Up to $250,000 for individuals

Criminal Forfeiture: Vessel and contraband

Federal Maritime Jurisdiction:

U.S. territorial waters (12 nautical miles)

U.S. flagged vessels anywhere in world

Foreign vessels in U.S. waters

Contiguous zone (24 nautical miles for customs)

High seas under international law

Federal Agencies:

Coast Guard: Primary maritime law enforcement

Customs and Border Protection: Customs and immigration enforcement

Drug Enforcement Administration: Maritime drug trafficking

FBI: Major maritime crimes

Immigration and Customs Enforcement: Immigration violations

Types of Yachting Violations:

Drug smuggling and trafficking

Human trafficking and alien smuggling

Customs duty evasion

Arms trafficking

Money laundering

Environmental violations

Related Federal Offenses:

Drug Trafficking (21 USC Section 841)

Human Trafficking (18 USC Section 1591)

Immigration Violations (8 USC Section 1324)

Money Laundering (18 USC Section 1956)

Environmental Crimes (33 USC Section 1319)

Maritime Safety Requirements:

Vessel documentation and registration

Safety equipment and inspections

Environmental protection compliance

Navigation and communication requirements

Crew licensing and certification

International maritime law compliance

Enhanced Penalties:

Large-scale trafficking operations

Violence or weapons use

Organized maritime crime

International trafficking

Environmental damage

YOUTH FIREARMS VIOLATIONS

Statutory Citations: 18 USC Section 922(x) (Juvenile possession of firearms); 18 USC Section 924(a)(6) (Straw purchases)

Federal youth firearms laws address the illegal possession, transfer, and use of firearms by and to minors, recognizing the particular dangers of youth access to weapons.

Elements of Juvenile Firearm Possession (18 USC Section 922(x)):

1. Person under 18 years of age possessing handgun or ammunition suitable for handgun
2. Firearm traveled in or affected interstate commerce
3. Not within statutory exceptions (hunting, target practice with supervision, etc.)

Elements of Transfer to Juvenile:

1. Knowingly transferring handgun or ammunition to person under 18
2. Knowledge or reasonable cause to believe transferee is under 18
3. Not within statutory exceptions

Penalties:

Juvenile Possession: Up to 1 year imprisonment

Adult Transfer to Juvenile: Up to 1 year imprisonment (5 years if transferor knows firearm will be used in crime of violence)

Enhanced Penalties: For use in violent crimes

Fines: Up to $5,000 for juveniles, $250,000 for adults

Exceptions for Juvenile Possession:

Temporary possession for hunting with adult supervision

Target practice at established range with supervision

Safety or firearms training course

Ranching or farming activities with supervision

Emergency situations involving protection

Federal Agencies:

Bureau of Alcohol, Tobacco, Firearms and Explosives: Primary firearms enforcement

FBI: Firearms-related violent crimes

U.S. Attorneys Offices: Prosecution coordination

Local Law Enforcement: Joint enforcement efforts

Youth Gun Violence Prevention:

Safe storage requirements and education

Community intervention programs

School-based prevention initiatives

Mental health and crisis intervention

Technology solutions (smart guns, trigger locks)

Public awareness campaigns

Related Federal Offenses:

Unlawful Firearms Dealing (18 USC Section 922(a))

Use of Firearm in Crime of Violence (18 USC Section 924(c))

Felon in Possession (18 USC Section 922(g))

Straw Purchases (18 USC Section 922(a)(6))

School Gun Violence (18 USC Section 930)

Enhanced Penalties:

Use of firearm in violent crime

Gang-related firearms violations

Trafficking firearms to juveniles

School zone violations

Repeat firearms offenses

Education and Prevention:

Gun safety education programs
Community partnerships and outreach
Parent and family responsibility programs
School safety and threat assessment
Intervention for at-risk youth.

Z

ZONE VIOLATIONS (FEDERAL)

Statutory Citations: 18 USC Section 922(q) (Gun-Free School Zones Act); 21 USC Section 860 (Drug-free zones)

Federal zone violations involve criminal activities that occur within specially designated areas where enhanced penalties apply, including drug-free zones around schools and gun-free school zones.

Elements of Gun-Free School Zone Violations (18 USC Section 922(q)):

1. Knowingly possessing firearm at place individual knows or has reasonable cause to believe is school zone

2. Firearm has moved in or affects interstate or foreign commerce

3. Possession not authorized under federal or state law

Elements of Drug-Free Zone Violations (21 USC Section 860):

1. Manufacturing, distributing, or possessing with intent to distribute controlled substance

2. In or on or within 1,000 feet of real property comprising public or private elementary, vocational, or secondary school

3. In violation of federal controlled substances laws

Penalties:

Gun-Free School Zones: Up to 5 years imprisonment

Drug-Free School Zones: Enhanced penalties of up to twice the maximum punishment

Drug-Free Housing Zones: Enhanced penalties for public housing violations

Fines: Up to $250,000 for individuals

Enhanced Penalties: Various zone-specific enhancements

Types of Protected Zones:

School zones (elementary, middle, high schools, colleges)

Public housing projects and federally assisted housing

Public parks and recreational facilities

Public transportation facilities

Youth centers and playgrounds

Libraries and community centers

Federal Agencies:

ATF: Gun-Free School Zone enforcement

DEA: Drug-free zone violations

FBI: Major zone violation investigations

Housing and Urban Development: Public housing enforcement

Department of Education: School safety coordination

Zone Boundary Determinations:

1,000-foot radius measurement from school property

Public housing property boundaries

Transportation facility perimeters

Park and recreational area boundaries

GPS and mapping technology for enforcement

Local ordinance and zoning considerations

Related Federal Offenses:

Drug Trafficking (21 USC Section 841)

Firearms Violations (18 USC Section 922)

Violence Against Children (18 USC Section 2251)

Civil Rights Violations (18 USC Section 245)

Terrorism (18 USC Section 2332a)

Exceptions and Defenses:

Private property not open to public within school zone

Unloaded firearms in locked containers during transport

Licensed security and law enforcement personnel

Valid state permits and authorizations

Emergency situations and self-defense

Enhanced Penalties Rationale:

Protection of children and students

Deterrence of criminal activity near schools

Community safety and crime prevention

Public health and safety considerations

Federal interest in educational environments

Constitutional Considerations:

Commerce Clause authority for federal zones

Second Amendment challenges to gun-free zones

Due process notice and boundary requirements

Equal protection in zone enforcement

State versus federal jurisdiction issues

ZERO TOLERANCE POLICIES

Statutory Citations: Various federal statutes implementing mandatory minimum sentences and enhanced penalties

Federal zero tolerance policies involve mandatory enforcement approaches that require specific penalties for certain offenses without consideration of individual circumstances or mitigation factors.

Elements of Zero Tolerance Violations:

1. Commission of specified federal offense subject to zero tolerance policy
2. Offense falls within category requiring mandatory enforcement
3. No prosecutorial discretion for non-prosecution or charge reduction
4. Mandatory minimum penalties apply without exception

Examples of Federal Zero Tolerance:

Immigration violations and deportation policies

Drug trafficking mandatory minimum sentences

Firearms violations in federal facilities

Domestic violence with federal nexus

Child exploitation and pornography offenses

Terrorism and national security violations

Penalties:

Vary by specific offense and policy

Mandatory minimum sentences without parole

Enhanced penalties for repeat offenses

No judicial discretion for downward departures

Automatic consequences (deportation, loss of benefits)

Federal Agencies:

Department of Justice: Zero tolerance policy implementation

Immigration and Customs Enforcement: Immigration zero tolerance

ATF: Firearms zero tolerance enforcement

FBI: Various zero tolerance investigations

Drug Enforcement Administration: Drug zero tolerance

Policy Rationales:

Deterrence through certain punishment

Consistency in law enforcement

Protection of vulnerable populations

Public safety and crime prevention

Congressional mandate for strict enforcement

Types of Zero Tolerance Policies:

Three strikes laws for repeat offenders

Mandatory minimums for drug trafficking

Immigration enforcement priorities

Gun-free zone violations

Child protection mandatory reporting

Terrorism and national security threats

Related Constitutional Issues:

Eighth Amendment cruel and unusual punishment

Due process and individualized sentencing

Equal protection in enforcement

Separation of powers and judicial discretion

Congressional authority to mandate penalties

Criticism and Reform Efforts:

Disproportionate impacts on minority communities

Overcrowding in federal prison system

Limited judicial discretion for individual cases

Cost and resource allocation concerns

Effectiveness in crime prevention and deterrence

Exceptions and Safety Valves:

Substantial assistance departures for cooperation

Safety valve provisions for low-level drug offenders

Compassionate release for extraordinary circumstances

Presidential clemency and commutation powers

Legislative reforms and sentencing modifications

ZONING VIOLATIONS (FEDERAL)

Statutory Citations: 18 USC Section 1382 (Entering military, naval, or Coast Guard property); Various environmental and land use statutes

Federal zoning violations involve unauthorized activities on federal lands, military installations, and specially designated areas under federal jurisdiction and control.

Elements of Federal Property Trespass:

1. Entering upon property in custody of Armed Forces or designated as military area
2. Contrary to lawful order or regulation
3. Without authorization from commanding officer or appropriate authority
4. Knowledge of prohibited entry or restriction

Elements of Environmental Zone Violations:

1. Conducting prohibited activities within federally protected environmental areas
2. Violation of land use restrictions and regulations
3. Damage to protected resources or ecosystems
4. Knowing violation of federal environmental laws

Penalties:

Military Property Violations: Up to 6 months imprisonment and $500 fine

National Park Violations: Up to 6 months imprisonment and $5,000 fine

Environmental Zone Violations: Up to 5 years imprisonment

Endangered Species Violations: Up to 1 year imprisonment

Fines: Vary by specific violation and statute

Types of Federal Zones:

Military installations and restricted areas

National parks and wilderness areas

Wildlife refuges and protected habitats

Archaeological and historical sites

Nuclear facilities and security zones

Border patrol and customs areas

Federal Agencies:

Military Police: Military installation enforcement

National Park Service: Park and recreation area enforcement

Fish and Wildlife Service: Wildlife refuge protection

Forest Service: National forest enforcement

Customs and Border Protection: Border zone enforcement

Common Zoning Violations:

Unauthorized entry into restricted military areas

Camping or building in prohibited park areas

Hunting or fishing in protected wildlife areas

Off-road vehicle use in wilderness areas

Commercial activities in restricted zones

Archaeological artifact collection

Related Federal Offenses:

Trespass (18 USC Section 1382)

Environmental Crimes (Various statutes)

Theft of Government Property (18 USC Section 641)

Destruction of Federal Property (18 USC Section 1361)

Vandalism (18 USC Section 1361)

Enhanced Penalties:

National security sensitive areas

Repeat violations and trespass

Damage to protected resources

Commercial violations and profit motive

Organized violations and criminal enterprises

Environmental Protection:

Endangered species habitat protection

Water quality and wetland preservation

Air quality maintenance areas

Cultural and archaeological site protection

Wilderness and scenic area preservation

ZERO-DOLLAR BAIL VIOLATIONS

Statutory Citations: 18 USC Section 3142 (Release or detention of defendant pending trial); Bail Reform Act provisions

Federal zero-dollar bail violations involve the breach of conditions by defendants released without monetary bail, focusing on public safety and appearance requirements rather than financial considerations.

Elements of Bail Violation:

1. Release of defendant on personal recognizance or unsecured bond
2. Violation of specific conditions of release imposed by court
3. Willful failure to comply with release requirements
4. Knowledge of bail conditions and obligations

Elements of Failure to Appear:

1. Released defendant fails to appear for required court proceeding
2. No lawful excuse for absence
3. Knowledge of court date and appearance requirement
4. Intent to avoid court proceedings

Penalties:

Bail Jumping: Up to 10 years imprisonment if underlying charge is felony

Failure to Appear: Up to 5 years imprisonment for felony cases

Condition Violations: Revocation of bail and pretrial detention

Fines: Up to $250,000 for individuals

Additional Charges: Based on specific condition violations

Common Release Conditions:

Regular reporting to pretrial services

Restrictions on travel and residence

No contact with victims or witnesses

Drug and alcohol testing and treatment

Electronic monitoring and GPS tracking

Surrender of passport and firearms

Federal Agencies:

U.S. Marshals Service: Fugitive apprehension and bail enforcement

U.S. Probation and Pretrial Services: Supervision and monitoring

FBI: Interstate flight and bail jumping investigations

Local Law Enforcement: Cooperation in apprehension

Risk Assessment Factors:

Nature and circumstances of charged offense

Defendant's criminal history and character

Community ties and employment status

Substance abuse and mental health issues

Flight risk and danger to community

Victim and witness safety concerns

Related Federal Offenses:

Interstate Flight to Avoid Prosecution (18 USC Section 1073)

Obstruction of Justice (18 USC Section 1503)

Witness Tampering (18 USC Section 1512)

Drug Possession (21 USC Section 844) if condition violation

Firearms Violations (18 USC Section 922) if condition violation

Enhanced Monitoring:

Electronic monitoring devices and GPS tracking

Drug and alcohol testing programs

Mental health and substance abuse treatment

Halfway house and residential placement

Community service and employment verification

Regular court and pretrial services contact

Constitutional Considerations:

Eighth Amendment excessive bail protections

Due process in detention and release decisions

Equal protection regardless of financial status

Presumption of innocence pending trial

Right to reasonable bail conditions

ZONING LAW ENFORCEMENT

Statutory Citation: Various federal regulatory and enforcement statutes

Federal zoning law enforcement involves the criminal prosecution of violations of federal land use, environmental, and regulatory zoning requirements on federal property and within federal jurisdiction.

Elements of Regulatory Zoning Violations:

1. Violation of federal land use regulation or zoning requirement
2. Knowing or willful disregard of regulatory obligation
3. Activity affecting federal property or interstate commerce
4. Failure to obtain required permits or authorizations

Elements of Environmental Zoning Violations:

1. Conducting prohibited activity within environmentally protected zone
2. Violation causes or threatens environmental harm
3. Knowing violation of federal environmental protection laws
4. Activity within federal jurisdiction or affecting federal resources

Penalties:

Administrative Violations: Civil penalties and corrective orders

Criminal Violations: Up to 5 years imprisonment for knowing violations

Environmental Crimes: Up to 15 years imprisonment for knowing endangerment

Fines: Up to $50,000 per day of violation

Injunctive Relief: Court orders requiring compliance and remediation

Federal Zoning Categories:

Military and national security zones

Environmental protection and conservation areas

Historical and cultural preservation zones

Transportation and infrastructure corridors

Public health and safety zones

Economic development and enterprise zones

Federal Agencies:

Environmental Protection Agency: Environmental zoning enforcement

Department of Defense: Military zoning and security areas

Department of Interior: Public lands and conservation areas

Department of Transportation: Transportation corridor zoning

General Services Administration: Federal facility zoning

Enforcement Mechanisms:

Administrative compliance orders

Civil penalty assessments

Criminal referrals and prosecution

Injunctive relief and court orders

Asset forfeiture and seizure

Permit revocation and suspension

Related Federal Offenses:

Environmental Crimes (42 USC Section 6928)

Clean Water Act Violations (33 USC Section 1319)

Clean Air Act Violations (42 USC Section 7413)

Endangered Species Violations (16 USC Section 1540)

Archaeological Resources Protection (16 USC Section 470ee)

Enhanced Penalties:

Repeat violations and willful disregard

Large-scale commercial violations

Environmental damage and harm

Organized violations and criminal enterprises

Obstruction of enforcement activities

CHAPTER ONE

DEFENSE MOTIONS IN FEDERAL CRIMINAL CASES

PRE-TRIAL MOTIONS

MOTION TO DISMISS THE INDICTMENT

Legal Basis: Federal Rule of Criminal Procedure 12(b)(3)(B)

Grounds for Dismissal:

- **Statute of Limitations:** Five-year limitation for most federal crimes (18 USC Section 3282)
- **Lack of Jurisdiction:** Federal court lacks subject matter jurisdiction over offense
- **Defective Indictment:** Fails to charge essential elements of federal crime
- **Double Jeopardy:** Previous prosecution for same offense bars current charges
- **Prosecutorial Misconduct:** Grand jury abuse or vindictive prosecution
- **Violation of Plea Agreement:** Government breach of previous plea agreement

Filing Requirements:

- Must be filed within prescribed time limits under Rule 12(c)
- Specific factual and legal basis required
- Supporting legal memorandum and citations
- Certificate of good faith meet and confer with government

Standards Applied:

Face of indictment reviewed for legal sufficiency

Constitutional and statutory requirements must be met

Presumption of validity for properly returned indictments

Heavy burden on defense to demonstrate fatal defects

MOTION TO SUPPRESS EVIDENCE

Legal Basis: Federal Rule of Criminal Procedure 12(b)(3)(C); Fourth Amendment

Types of Suppression Motions:

Fourth Amendment Violations:

- Unreasonable searches and seizures

- Warrantless searches without recognized exception
- Defective search warrant applications
- Execution of search warrant outside scope
- Illegal stops and seizures of persons

Fifth Amendment Violations:

- Coerced confessions and statements
- Violation of Miranda rights
- Custodial interrogation without warnings
- Involuntary statements due to police conduct

Sixth Amendment Violations:

- Statements obtained after invocation of right to counsel
- Deliberate elicitation during formal proceedings
- Use of informants to obtain incriminating statements

Procedural Requirements:

Detailed factual allegations supporting constitutional violation

Legal memorandum with supporting case law

Request for evidentiary hearing if facts disputed

Burden on defense to establish prima facie violation

Exclusionary Rule Application:

Primary evidence obtained through constitutional violation

Fruit of poisonous tree doctrine for derivative evidence

Exceptions: inevitable discovery, independent source, attenuation

Good faith exception for defective warrants

MOTION FOR DISCOVERY

Legal Basis: Federal Rule of Criminal Procedure 16; Brady v. Maryland

Government's Automatic Disclosure Obligations:

- Defendant's oral, written, and recorded statements
- Defendant's prior criminal record
- Documents and objects material to defense
- Reports of examinations and tests
- Expert witness summaries and reports

Brady Material (Exculpatory Evidence):

Evidence favorable to defense on guilt or punishment

Evidence material to guilt or punishment

Government obligation regardless of defense request

Includes impeachment evidence of government witnesses

Reciprocal Discovery Obligations:

Defense witness lists and summaries

Documents and objects defense intends to use

Results of examinations and tests

Notice of alibi defense

Notice of public authority defense

Classified Information:

Classified Information Procedures Act (CIPA) governs disclosure

Ex parte proceedings to determine relevance and admissibility

Substitutions and redactions to protect national security

Defense security clearance requirements

MOTION TO CHANGE VENUE

Legal Basis: Federal Rule of Criminal Procedure 21

Grounds for Venue Transfer:

- **Prejudice in District:** Extensive pretrial publicity affecting fair trial
- **Convenience:** Transfer serves interests of justice and efficiency
- **Safety Concerns:** Threats to participants requiring relocation
- **Judicial Resources:** Court congestion or unavailability

Standards for Granting:

Clear and convincing evidence of prejudice or necessity

Consideration of alternative remedies (jury selection, continuance)

Balancing of defendant rights and government interests

Preference for resolution in charging district

Factors Considered:

Nature and extent of pretrial publicity

Community sentiment and bias indicators

Availability of impartial jury pool

Convenience of witnesses and evidence

Court calendar and resources

MOTION FOR SEVERANCE

Legal Basis: Federal Rule of Criminal Procedure 14

Types of Severance:

Severance of Defendants:

Antagonistic defenses creating prejudice

One defendant's confession implicating others

Significant disparity in evidence against co-defendants

Different penalty exposures affecting trial strategy

Severance of Counts:

Joinder creates confusion or prejudice

Different types of offenses requiring distinct defenses

Overwhelming evidence on some counts affecting others

Different penalty exposures and trial strategies

Standards Applied:

Substantial prejudice to defendant's right to fair trial

Benefits of severance outweigh judicial efficiency

Alternative remedies insufficient to cure prejudice

Consideration of government's prosecution efficiency

MOTION TO COMPEL DISCLOSURE

Legal Basis: Federal Rule of Criminal Procedure 16; Constitutional due process

Brady Material Enforcement:

Specific identification of requested exculpatory evidence

Government obligation to search files of prosecution team

Law enforcement agency files and records

Impeachment evidence regarding government witnesses

Giglio Material (Impeachment Evidence):

Prior false statements by government witnesses

Plea agreements and cooperation deals

Benefits provided to cooperating witnesses

Bias, interest, or motive to fabricate testimony

Jenks Act Material:

Statements of government witnesses

Reports and memoranda by government witnesses

Prior testimony and recorded statements

Production required after direct examination

MOTION FOR BILL OF PARTICULARS

Legal Basis: Federal Rule of Criminal Procedure 7(f)

Purpose and Standards:

Provide additional detail regarding charged offenses

Enable defendant to prepare adequate defense

Avoid surprise at trial regarding government's theory

Not substitute for discovery or fishing expedition

Appropriate Requests:

Specific dates, times, and locations of alleged crimes

Identity of alleged victims and co-conspirators

Specific acts constituting charged conspiracy

Method or means of committing alleged offenses

Limitations:

Government not required to disclose evidence or witnesses

Cannot compel disclosure of legal theories

Must demonstrate necessity for adequate defense

Court discretion in ordering production

MOTION FOR COMPETENCY EVALUATION

Legal Basis: 18 USC Section 4241; Dusky v. United States

Standards for Competency:

Sufficient present ability to consult with counsel

Reasonable degree of rational understanding

Understanding of proceedings and charges

Capacity to assist in defense preparation

Evaluation Process:

Court-ordered psychiatric or psychological examination

Inpatient or outpatient evaluation as appropriate

Comprehensive written report to court

Hearing on competency if disputed

Restoration of Competency:

Treatment to restore competency to stand trial

Maximum four-month restoration period

Periodic review of progress and status

Alternative disposition if competency cannot be restored

POST-CONVICTION MOTIONS

MOTION UNDER 28 USC SECTION 2255

Legal Basis: 28 USC Section 2255 (Motion to Vacate, Set Aside, or Correct Sentence)

Grounds for Relief:

- **Constitutional Violations:** Ineffective assistance of counsel, constitutional errors
- **Jurisdictional Defects:** Court lacked authority to impose sentence
- **Sentencing Errors:** Sentence exceeded statutory maximum or guideline range
- **New Law:** Retroactive application of new constitutional or statutory rules

Ineffective Assistance of Counsel Claims:

Deficient performance falling below objective reasonableness

Prejudice resulting from deficient performance

Two-pronged test from Strickland v. Washington

Specific examples of attorney errors and omissions

Procedural Requirements:

One-year statute of limitations from final judgment

Exhaustion of direct appeal remedies

Factual allegations supporting constitutional violation

Supporting legal memorandum and authorities

Evidentiary Hearings:

Required when material facts are in dispute

Testimony from petitioner, counsel, and witnesses

Court findings of fact and conclusions of law

Burden on petitioner to establish constitutional violation

MOTION FOR REDUCTION OF SENTENCE

Legal Basis: Federal Rule of Criminal Procedure 35; 18 USC Section 3582(c)

Rule 35(b) Substantial Assistance:

Government motion based on substantial assistance to authorities

Defendant cooperation in investigation or prosecution

Court discretion in determining extent of reduction

Consideration of nature, extent, and significance of assistance

18 USC Section 3582(c)(2) Guideline Amendments:

Retroactive application of guideline reductions

Amendment must have lowered applicable guideline range

Court consideration of 18 USC Section 3553(a) factors

Limitation to guideline sentence reductions only

Compassionate Release (18 USC Section 3582(c)(1)(A)):

Extraordinary and compelling circumstances

Medical conditions and terminal illness

Family circumstances and hardship

Age and deteriorating health conditions

COVID-19 and pandemic-related circumstances

Procedural Requirements:

Administrative remedy exhaustion (30-day rule)

Motion to district court with supporting documentation

Government response and position

Court consideration of public safety factors

MOTION FOR NEW TRIAL

Legal Basis: Federal Rule of Criminal Procedure 33

Grounds for New Trial:

- **Newly Discovered Evidence:** Material evidence not available at trial
- **Prosecutorial Misconduct:** Prejudicial conduct affecting verdict

- **Judicial Error:** Erroneous rulings or jury instructions
- **Jury Misconduct:** Improper communications or bias
- **Ineffective Assistance:** Trial counsel performance deficiencies

Newly Discovered Evidence Standard:

Evidence discovered after trial

Exercise of due diligence could not have discovered earlier

Evidence material to guilt or innocence

Evidence likely to produce different result at new trial

Time Limitations:

Motion must be filed within three years of verdict

Shorter time limits for certain grounds

Court discretion to consider untimely motions

Interests of justice exception to time limits

MOTION IN ARREST OF JUDGMENT

Legal Basis: Federal Rule of Criminal Procedure 34

Grounds for Arrest of Judgment:

Indictment or information fails to charge offense

Court lacks jurisdiction over charged offense

Conviction for offense not charged in indictment

Legal insufficiency of charging document

Time Limitations:

Must be filed within 14 days of verdict or guilty plea

No extension of time permitted

Waiver if not timely filed

Limited grounds compared to other post-trial motions

Standards Applied:

Review limited to face of charging document

Legal sufficiency of essential elements

Constitutional and statutory requirements

No consideration of evidence or trial proceedings

MOTION FOR JUDGMENT OF ACQUITTAL

Legal Basis: Federal Rule of Criminal Procedure 29

Post-Trial Timing:

Motion must be filed within 14 days of verdict

Renewal of motion made during trial

Court may set aside verdict and enter acquittal

Alternative of ordering new trial

Standards for Granting:

Evidence insufficient to sustain conviction

Viewing evidence in light most favorable to government

Whether reasonable jury could find guilt beyond reasonable doubt

Legal standard higher than directed verdict

Scope of Review:

Sufficiency of evidence on each element

Credibility determinations remain with jury

Inferences reasonably drawn from evidence

Constitutional due process protections

MOTION FOR RECONSIDERATION OF SENTENCE

Legal Basis: Federal Rule of Criminal Procedure 35(a)

Timing Requirements:

Motion must be filed within 14 days of sentencing

No extension of time permitted

Court may correct arithmetical, technical, or clear errors

Limited scope compared to other sentence challenges

Appropriate Grounds:

Arithmetical errors in sentence calculation

Technical errors in guideline application

Clear errors apparent from record

Misunderstanding of plea agreement terms

Limitations:

Cannot relitigate sentencing factors

No reconsideration of discretionary decisions

Must identify specific error requiring correction

Court lacks jurisdiction after 14-day period

APPEAL PROCEDURES AND STANDARDS

Notice of Appeal:

Must be filed within 14 days of judgment

Jurisdictional requirement strictly enforced

Extension of time in limited circumstances

Government cross-appeal procedures

Appellate Standards of Review:

- **Constitutional Issues:** De novo review
- **Evidentiary Rulings:** Abuse of discretion
- **Sentence Reasonableness:** Abuse of discretion
- **Factual Findings:** Clear error standard
- **Legal Conclusions:** De novo review

Preservation Requirements:

Objection at trial to preserve issues for appeal

Plain error doctrine for unpreserved issues

Ineffective assistance claims may excuse waiver

Strategic decisions distinguished from errors

Certificate of Appealability:

Required for Section 2255 appeals

Substantial showing of denial of constitutional right

Reasonable jurists could debate court's resolution

Procedural rulings require showing of procedural bar debate

CHAPTER TWO

SAMPLE FEDERAL CRIMINAL DEFENSE MOTIONS

PRE-TRIAL MOTION SAMPLES

SAMPLE MOTION TO SUPPRESS EVIDENCE

UNITED STATES DISTRICT COURT

[DISTRICT NAME]

UNITED STATES OF AMERICA,

Plaintiff,

v.

[DEFENDANT NAME],

Defendant.

Case No. [XX-XXX]

Judge [Name]

DEFENDANT'S MOTION TO SUPPRESS EVIDENCE OBTAINED IN VIOLATION OF THE FOURTH AMENDMENT

TO THE HONORABLE COURT:

Defendant [Name], by and through undersigned counsel, respectfully moves this Court pursuant to Federal Rule of Criminal Procedure 12(b)(3)(C) and the Fourth Amendment to the United States Constitution to suppress all evidence obtained as a result of the unlawful search and seizure conducted on [date] at [location].

I. FACTUAL BACKGROUND

1. On [date], at approximately [time], agents from the Federal Bureau of Investigation executed a search warrant at defendant's residence located at [address].

2. The search warrant was issued by [Magistrate Judge name] based upon an affidavit submitted by Special Agent [name] on [date].

3. The affidavit contained material misrepresentations and omitted material facts necessary for a neutral magistrate to make a probable cause determination.

4. During the search, agents seized [describe evidence seized] which forms the basis of the charges in this case.

II. LEGAL ARGUMENT

A. The Search Warrant Was Not Supported by Probable Cause

The Fourth Amendment requires that search warrants be supported by probable cause. Illinois v. Gates, 462 U.S. 213 (1983). Probable cause exists when there is a fair probability that contraband or evidence of a crime will be found in a particular place. Id. at 238.

The affidavit in this case fails to establish probable cause because:

1. The informant's reliability was not established through prior successful tips or independent corroboration;

2. The information provided was stale, occurring more than [time period] before the warrant application;

3. The affiant failed to include exculpatory information known to law enforcement.

B. The Affidavit Contains Material Misrepresentations

Under Franks v. Delaware, 438 U.S. 154 (1978), a defendant may challenge the truthfulness of statements in a search warrant affidavit. To obtain a Franks hearing, defendant must make a substantial preliminary showing that:

1. The affiant knowingly and intentionally, or with reckless disregard for the truth, included false statements in the affidavit; and

2. The false statements were necessary to the finding of probable cause.

The affidavit contains the following material misrepresentations:

- [Specific false statement 1 with supporting facts]

- [Specific false statement 2 with supporting facts]

C. Material Omissions Undermine Probable Cause

The affiant also omitted material facts that would have undermined the probable cause determination:

- [Specific omission 1 and why material]

- [Specific omission 2 and why material]

III. CONCLUSION

The search warrant in this case was not supported by probable cause and was obtained through material misrepresentations and omissions. All evidence obtained through this unlawful search, and any evidence derived therefrom under the "fruit of the poisonous tree" doctrine, must be suppressed.

WHEREFORE, defendant respectfully requests that this Court:

1. Grant this Motion to Suppress;

2. Order an evidentiary hearing pursuant to Franks v. Delaware;

3. Suppress all evidence obtained through the unlawful search; and

4. Grant such other relief as the Court deems just and proper.

Respectfully submitted,

[Attorney signature]

[Attorney name]

[Attorney title]

[Bar number]

[Address]

[Phone]

[Email]

Attorney for Defendant

CERTIFICATE OF SERVICE

I hereby certify that a true and correct copy of the foregoing Motion was served upon opposing counsel via the Court's CM/ECF system on [date].

[Attorney signature]

SAMPLE MOTION TO DISMISS INDICTMENT

UNITED STATES DISTRICT COURT

[DISTRICT NAME]

UNITED STATES OF AMERICA,

Plaintiff,

v.

[DEFENDANT NAME],

Defendant.

Case No. [XX-XXX]

Judge [Name]

DEFENDANT'S MOTION TO DISMISS INDICTMENT FOR VIOLATION OF STATUTE OF LIMITATIONS

TO THE HONORABLE COURT:

Defendant [Name], by and through undersigned counsel, respectfully moves this Court pursuant to Federal Rule of Criminal Procedure 12(b)(3)(B) to dismiss the Indictment in this case because the charges are barred by the applicable statute of limitations.

I. FACTUAL AND PROCEDURAL BACKGROUND

1. On [date], a federal grand jury returned an Indictment charging defendant with [specific charges and statutory citations].

2. The Indictment alleges that the criminal conduct occurred between [date range].

3. The Indictment was returned on [date], more than five years after the alleged criminal conduct concluded.

4. No tolling provision applies to extend the limitations period in this case.

II. LEGAL ARGUMENT

A. The General Federal Statute of Limitations Applies

Title 18, United States Code, Section 3282(a) provides that "no person shall be prosecuted, tried, or punished for any offense, not capital, unless the indictment is returned... within five years next after such offense shall have been committed."

The charged offenses in this case are not capital offenses and carry maximum penalties of [years] imprisonment under [statutory citations].

B. The Indictment Was Returned Outside the Limitations Period

1. Count One - [Charge]: The alleged conduct occurred on or about [date], but the Indictment was not returned until [date], which is [number] years and [number] months after the alleged offense.

2. Count Two - [Charge]: The last alleged overt act in furtherance of the conspiracy occurred on [date], but the Indictment was returned [time period] later.

C. No Exception to the Limitations Period Applies

The government cannot rely on any statutory exception to extend the limitations period because:

1. DNA Exception (18 USC § 3282(b)): Does not apply as this case does not involve DNA evidence.

2. Terrorism Exception (18 USC § 3286): Does not apply as the charges do not constitute federal crimes of terrorism.

3. Fraudulent Concealment: The government has not alleged that defendant took affirmative steps to conceal the crimes that prevented their discovery.

D. Continuing Offense Doctrine Does Not Apply

The alleged crimes in this case are not continuing offenses that would toll the statute of limitations. Each count charges discrete criminal acts that were completed more than five years before the return of the Indictment.

III. CONCLUSION

The Indictment in this case was returned outside the applicable five-year statute of limitations period. No exception applies to extend the limitations period. The charges are therefore time-barred and must be dismissed.

WHEREFORE, defendant respectfully requests that this Court:

1. Grant this Motion to Dismiss;

2. Dismiss the Indictment with prejudice; and

3. Grant such other relief as the Court deems just and proper.

Respectfully submitted,

[Attorney signature]

[Attorney name]

[Attorney title]

[Bar number]

[Address]

[Phone]

[Email]

Attorney for Defendant

SAMPLE MOTION FOR DISCOVERY

UNITED STATES DISTRICT COURT

[DISTRICT NAME]

UNITED STATES OF AMERICA,

Plaintiff,

v.

[DEFENDANT NAME],

Defendant.

Case No. [XX-XXX]

Judge [Name]

DEFENDANT'S MOTION FOR DISCOVERY AND INSPECTION

TO THE HONORABLE COURT:

Defendant [Name], by and through undersigned counsel, respectfully moves this Court pursuant to Federal Rule of Criminal Procedure 16 and Brady v. Maryland, 373 U.S. 83 (1963), to order the government to provide the discovery materials specified herein.

I. RULE 16 DISCOVERY

Pursuant to Federal Rule of Criminal Procedure 16, defendant requests disclosure of the following materials:

A. Defendant's Statements (Rule 16(a)(1)(A))

1. All oral statements made by defendant to government agents
2. All written statements made by defendant
3. All recorded statements made by defendant
4. The substance of any oral statements if the government intends to use them at trial

B. Defendant's Prior Record (Rule 16(a)(1)(B))

1. Defendant's prior criminal record
2. Any juvenile adjudications if admissible under Federal Rule of Evidence 609

C. Documents and Objects (Rule 16(a)(1)(E))

1. All documents, photographs, and tangible objects material to preparing the defense
2. All documents the government intends to use in its case-in-chief
3. All documents obtained from or belonging to defendant

D. Reports of Examinations and Tests (Rule 16(a)(1)(F))

1. All physical or mental examinations and scientific tests

2. Laboratory reports and forensic analyses

3. Chain of custody documentation

E. Expert Witnesses (Rule 16(a)(1)(G))

1. Written summary of expert testimony the government intends to use

2. Expert's qualifications and opinions

3. Bases and reasons for expert opinions

II. BRADY MATERIAL

Pursuant to Brady v. Maryland and its progeny, defendant requests all exculpatory and impeachment evidence, including:

A. Exculpatory Evidence

1. Evidence tending to negate defendant's guilt

2. Evidence supporting any defense

3. Evidence undermining the government's case

B. Impeachment Evidence (Giglio v. United States)

1. Evidence of bias, interest, or motive of government witnesses

2. Prior inconsistent statements by government witnesses

3. Plea agreements, immunity agreements, or cooperation agreements

4. Benefits provided to cooperating witnesses

5. Criminal history of government witnesses

6. Disciplinary actions against law enforcement witnesses

III. JENKS ACT MATERIAL

Pursuant to 18 U.S.C. § 3500, defendant requests advance disclosure of:

1. Statements of government witnesses

2. Reports prepared by government witnesses

3. Memoranda reflecting witness statements

IV. ADDITIONAL DISCOVERY REQUESTS

1. Surveillance Materials: All audio, video, and photographic surveillance

2. Communication Intercepts: All wiretap applications, orders, and transcripts

3. Search Warrants: All search warrant applications and supporting affidavits

4. Financial Records: All financial investigations and asset tracing

5. Informant Files: All materials relating to confidential informants

V. PROTECTIVE ORDER

Defendant requests that the Court enter an appropriate protective order governing the use and dissemination of discovery materials to protect the privacy interests of third parties and the integrity of ongoing investigations.

VI. CONCLUSION

The requested discovery is essential to defendant's preparation of an adequate defense. Full and timely disclosure will promote the interests of justice and ensure a fair trial.

WHEREFORE, defendant respectfully requests that this Court:

1. Grant this Motion for Discovery;

2. Order the government to provide all requested materials within 30 days;

3. Enter an appropriate protective order; and

4. Grant such other relief as the Court deems just and proper.

Respectfully submitted,

[Attorney signature]

[Attorney name]

[Attorney title]

[Bar number]

[Address]

[Phone]

[Email]

Attorney for Defendant

POST-CONVICTION MOTION SAMPLES

SAMPLE MOTION UNDER 28 USC SECTION 2255

UNITED STATES DISTRICT COURT

[DISTRICT NAME]

[DEFENDANT NAME],

Petitioner,

v.

UNITED STATES OF AMERICA,

Respondent.

Civil Case No. [XX-XXX]

(Criminal Case No. [XX-XXX])

Judge [Name]

MOTION UNDER 28 U.S.C. § 2255 TO VACATE, SET ASIDE, OR CORRECT SENTENCE BY A PERSON IN FEDERAL CUSTODY

TO THE HONORABLE COURT:

Petitioner [Name], currently in federal custody, brings this Motion pursuant to 28 U.S.C. § 2255 to vacate, set aside, or correct his sentence on the grounds that it was imposed in violation of the Constitution and laws of the United States.

I. PROCEDURAL HISTORY

1. On [date], petitioner was charged in a [number]-count Indictment with [charges].

2. On [date], petitioner entered a guilty plea to [specific counts] pursuant to a written plea agreement.

3. On [date], this Court sentenced petitioner to [sentence details].

4. Petitioner did not file a direct appeal.

5. This Motion is timely filed within one year of the judgment becoming final.

II. GROUNDS FOR RELIEF

GROUND ONE: INEFFECTIVE ASSISTANCE OF COUNSEL

A. Factual Basis

Petitioner's trial counsel rendered ineffective assistance in violation of the Sixth Amendment by:

1. Failure to Investigate: Counsel failed to conduct an adequate investigation of the case, including failure to interview key witnesses who would have provided exculpatory testimony.

2. Deficient Plea Advice: Counsel provided erroneous advice regarding the consequences of petitioner's guilty plea, specifically:

- Misstated the potential sentence exposure

- Failed to explain immigration consequences
- Failed to investigate potential defenses

3. Failure to File Suppression Motion: Counsel failed to file a meritorious motion to suppress evidence obtained through an unlawful search, despite petitioner's specific request to challenge the search.

B. Legal Standard

To establish ineffective assistance of counsel under Strickland v. Washington, 466 U.S. 668 (1984), petitioner must show:

1. Counsel's performance was deficient, falling below an objective standard of reasonableness; and
2. The deficient performance prejudiced the defense.

C. Deficient Performance

Counsel's performance fell below the objective standard of reasonableness because:

1. A reasonable attorney would have interviewed [specific witnesses] who were identified in discovery materials and would have provided testimony supporting petitioner's defense.
2. A reasonable attorney would have accurately advised petitioner of the sentencing consequences and immigration implications of his plea.
3. A reasonable attorney would have filed a suppression motion given the clear Fourth Amendment violation in the search of petitioner's residence.

D. Prejudice

Petitioner was prejudiced by counsel's deficient performance because:

1. Had counsel conducted an adequate investigation, exculpatory evidence would have been discovered that demonstrates petitioner's innocence.
2. Had counsel provided accurate plea advice, petitioner would not have entered a guilty plea and would have proceeded to trial.
3. Had counsel filed a suppression motion, the primary evidence against petitioner would have been excluded.

GROUND TWO: INVOLUNTARY GUILTY PLEA

Petitioner's guilty plea was involuntary because:

1. Counsel's erroneous advice regarding sentencing consequences rendered the plea unknowing and involuntary.
2. The Court's plea colloquy was inadequate under Federal Rule of Criminal Procedure 11.
3. Petitioner was not informed of critical immigration consequences as required by Padilla v. Kentucky, 559 U.S. 356 (2010).

III. REQUEST FOR EVIDENTIARY HEARING

Petitioner requests an evidentiary hearing pursuant to Rule 8 of the Rules Governing Section 2255 Proceedings because material facts are in dispute regarding counsel's performance and the circumstances surrounding the guilty plea.

IV. CONCLUSION

Petitioner's conviction and sentence were obtained in violation of his constitutional rights. The ineffective assistance of counsel and involuntary nature of his guilty plea require that his conviction be vacated.

WHEREFORE, petitioner respectfully requests that this Court:

1. Grant this Motion under 28 U.S.C. § 2255;

2. Vacate petitioner's conviction and sentence;

3. Order an evidentiary hearing;

4. Allow petitioner to withdraw his guilty plea and proceed to trial; and

5. Grant such other relief as the Court deems just and proper.

Respectfully submitted,

[Attorney signature]

[Attorney name]

[Attorney title]

[Bar number]

[Address]

[Phone]

[Email]

Attorney for Petitioner

SAMPLE MOTION FOR COMPASSIONATE RELEASE

UNITED STATES DISTRICT COURT

[DISTRICT NAME]

UNITED STATES OF AMERICA,

Plaintiff,

v.

[DEFENDANT NAME],

Defendant.

Case No. [XX-XXX]

Judge [Name]

DEFENDANT'S MOTION FOR COMPASSIONATE RELEASE PURSUANT TO 18 U.S.C. § 3582(c)(1)(A)

TO THE HONORABLE COURT:

Defendant [Name], currently incarcerated at [facility name], respectfully moves this Court pursuant to 18 U.S.C. § 3582(c)(1)(A) for compassionate release due to extraordinary and compelling circumstances.

I. PROCEDURAL HISTORY

1. On [date], defendant was sentenced to [sentence] following his conviction for [charges].

2. Defendant is currently serving his sentence at [facility] with a projected release date of [date].

3. On [date], defendant filed a request for compassionate release with the Bureau of Prisons.

4. More than 30 days have elapsed since defendant's request to the Bureau of Prisons, satisfying the exhaustion requirement.

II. EXTRAORDINARY AND COMPELLING CIRCUMSTANCES

A. Medical Condition

Defendant suffers from [specific medical conditions] which constitute extraordinary and compelling circumstances warranting compassionate release:

1. Diagnosis: Defendant has been diagnosed with [specific condition] as documented by [medical records/reports].

2. Severity: The condition is [terminal/degenerative/severe] with a prognosis of [specific prognosis].

3. Treatment Limitations: The Bureau of Prisons medical facilities are unable to provide adequate treatment for defendant's condition.

4. COVID-19 Risk: Defendant's underlying medical conditions place him at significantly higher risk for severe illness or death from COVID-19.

B. Age and Health Deterioration

Defendant is [age] years old and has experienced significant health deterioration during his incarceration:

1. Defendant's age and declining health make continued incarceration particularly harsh.
2. The risk of serious medical complications increases with continued incarceration.
3. Defendant poses no danger to the community given his age and medical condition.

III. SECTION 3553(a) FACTORS SUPPORT RELEASE

The factors set forth in 18 U.S.C. § 3553(a) support defendant's release:

A. Nature and Circumstances of Offense

The offense was [non-violent/financial] in nature and did not involve violence or threat of violence.

B. History and Characteristics of Defendant

1. Defendant has no prior criminal history
2. Defendant has been a model prisoner with no disciplinary infractions
3. Defendant has participated in educational and rehabilitation programs

C. Need for Deterrence and Protection of Public

1. Specific deterrence is unnecessary given defendant's age and medical condition
2. General deterrence has been served by defendant's incarceration
3. Public safety will not be compromised by defendant's release

D. Sentence Served

Defendant has served [time period] of his sentence, representing [percentage]% of the total sentence imposed.

IV. RELEASE PLAN

Defendant has developed a comprehensive release plan:

1. Residence: Defendant will reside with [family member/approved residence] at [address]

2. Medical Care: Defendant has arranged for medical care with [specific providers] for his ongoing treatment

3. Financial Support: Defendant will be supported by [family/disability benefits/other sources]

4. Community Ties: Defendant has strong family and community support

V. CONCLUSION

Defendant's serious medical conditions and advanced age constitute extraordinary and compelling circumstances warranting compassionate release. The § 3553(a) factors support release, and defendant poses no danger to the community.

WHEREFORE, defendant respectfully requests that this Court:

1. Grant this Motion for Compassionate Release;

2. Reduce defendant's sentence to time served;

3. Order defendant's immediate release subject to appropriate supervised release conditions; and

4. Grant such other relief as the Court deems just and proper.

Respectfully submitted,

[Attorney signature]

[Attorney name]

[Attorney title]

[Bar number]

[Address]

[Phone]

[Email]

Attorney for Defendant

CERTIFICATE OF SERVICE

I hereby certify that a true and correct copy of the foregoing Motion was served upon the United States Attorney's Office via the Court's CM/ECF system on [date].

[Attorney signature]

SAMPLE MOTION FOR NEW TRIAL

UNITED STATES DISTRICT COURT

[DISTRICT NAME]

UNITED STATES OF AMERICA,

Plaintiff,

v.

[DEFENDANT NAME],

Defendant.

Case No. [XX-XXX]

Judge [Name]

DEFENDANT'S MOTION FOR NEW TRIAL BASED ON NEWLY DISCOVERED EVIDENCE

TO THE HONORABLE COURT:

Defendant [Name], by and through undersigned counsel, respectfully moves this Court pursuant to Federal Rule of Criminal Procedure 33 for a new trial based on newly discovered evidence that undermines the verdict and demonstrates defendant's innocence.

I. PROCEDURAL BACKGROUND

1. Following a jury trial, defendant was convicted on [date] of [charges].
2. Defendant was sentenced on [date] to [sentence].
3. This Motion is timely filed within three years of the verdict as required by Rule 33(b)(1).

II. NEWLY DISCOVERED EVIDENCE

A. Description of Evidence

The newly discovered evidence consists of:

1. DNA Evidence: Advanced DNA testing has excluded defendant as the source of biological evidence recovered from the crime scene.

2. Witness Recantation: [Witness name], a key prosecution witness, has provided a sworn affidavit recanting his trial testimony and admitting that he lied under oath.

3. Exculpatory Documents: Recently discovered police reports and witness statements that were not disclosed during discovery and that support defendant's innocence.

B. Legal Standard for New Trial Based on Newly Discovered Evidence

To obtain a new trial based on newly discovered evidence, defendant must establish:

1. The evidence was discovered after trial;
2. The evidence could not have been discovered earlier through due diligence;
3. The evidence is material, not merely cumulative or impeaching;

4. The evidence would probably result in acquittal at a new trial.

United States v. Krasny, 607 F.2d 840 (9th Cir. 1979).

C. Application of Legal Standard

1. Evidence Discovered After Trial

All of the evidence described above was discovered after defendant's trial concluded on [date]:

- DNA testing was completed on [date]
- Witness recantation occurred on [date]
- Police reports were located on [date]

2. Due Diligence

The evidence could not have been discovered earlier through the exercise of due diligence:

- Advanced DNA testing technology was not available at the time of trial
- The recanting witness had no motive to come forward until [specific event]
- The police reports were improperly withheld by the prosecution

3. Material Evidence

The newly discovered evidence is material and goes to the heart of defendant's guilt or innocence:

- DNA exclusion directly contradicts prosecution's theory of the case
- Witness recantation eliminates key identification testimony
- Police reports contain exculpatory information not previously disclosed

4. Probability of Different Result

The newly discovered evidence would probably result in acquittal at a new trial because:

- The DNA evidence eliminates the primary physical evidence linking defendant to the crime
- The witness recantation removes crucial identification testimony
- The totality of the new evidence undermines the prosecution's case

III. CONSTITUTIONAL VIOLATIONS

The failure to disclose the exculpatory police reports constitutes a violation of Brady v. Maryland, 373 U.S. 83 (1963), and supports the granting of a new trial.

IV. CONCLUSION

The newly discovered evidence demonstrates that a fundamental miscarriage of justice has occurred. Defendant's conviction was based on flawed evidence, and the new evidence establishes his innocence.

WHEREFORE, defendant respectfully requests that this Court:

1. Grant this Motion for New Trial;

2. Vacate defendant's conviction;

3. Order a new trial; and

4. Grant such other relief as the Court deems just and proper.

Respectfully submitted,

[Attorney signature]

[Attorney name]

[Attorney title]

[Bar number]

[Address]

[Phone]

[Email]

Attorney for Defendant

SAMPLE FEDERAL DRUG CASE MOTIONS

PRE-TRIAL MOTIONS FOR DRUG CASES

SAMPLE MOTION TO SUPPRESS DRUG EVIDENCE

UNITED STATES DISTRICT COURT

[DISTRICT NAME]

UNITED STATES OF AMERICA,

Plaintiff,

v.

[DEFENDANT NAME],

Defendant.

Case No. [XX-XXX]

Judge [Name]

DEFENDANT'S MOTION TO SUPPRESS NARCOTICS EVIDENCE OBTAINED THROUGH UNLAWFUL VEHICLE SEARCH

TO THE HONORABLE COURT:

Defendant [Name], by and through undersigned counsel, respectfully moves this Court pursuant to Federal Rule of Criminal Procedure 12(b)(3)(C) and the Fourth Amendment to suppress all narcotics evidence obtained during the unlawful search of defendant's vehicle on [date].

I. FACTUAL BACKGROUND

1. On [date], at approximately [time], defendant was driving his vehicle on [location] when he was stopped by agents of the Drug Enforcement Administration.

2. The agents claimed the stop was for a traffic violation, specifically [alleged violation].

3. After the initial stop, agents prolonged the detention beyond the time necessary to address the traffic violation without reasonable suspicion of additional criminal activity.

4. Agents conducted a warrantless search of defendant's vehicle without consent and without probable cause.

5. During the search, agents seized approximately [amount] of [substance] from [location in vehicle].

II. LEGAL ARGUMENT

A. The Initial Traffic Stop Lacked Reasonable Suspicion

Under Terry v. Ohio, 392 U.S. 1 (1968), and its progeny, a traffic stop must be supported by reasonable suspicion that a traffic violation has occurred. Whren v. United States, 517 U.S. 806 (1996).

The alleged traffic violation of [specific violation] did not occur because:

1. [Specific factual dispute about violation]

2. [Officer's vantage point/observation limitations]

3. [Contradictory evidence from dashcam/witnesses]

B. The Detention Was Unlawfully Extended Beyond Its Purpose

Even if the initial stop was lawful, the detention was unlawfully extended in violation of Rodriguez v. United States, 575 U.S. 348 (2015).

1. Mission of the Stop: The stated purpose was to investigate a traffic violation and issue a citation.

2. Duration: The stop lasted approximately [time period], which exceeded the time necessary to complete the traffic stop mission.

3. Lack of Reasonable Suspicion: Agents lacked reasonable suspicion of drug activity to extend the detention for a narcotics investigation.

4. Dog Sniff Prolonged Stop: The use of a drug detection dog after completion of the traffic stop violated Rodriguez without independent reasonable suspicion.

C. The Vehicle Search Violated the Fourth Amendment

The warrantless search of defendant's vehicle violated the Fourth Amendment because none of the recognized exceptions to the warrant requirement applied:

1. Automobile Exception

The automobile exception requires probable cause to believe the vehicle contains contraband or evidence of a crime. California v. Carney, 471 U.S. 386 (1985).

Agents lacked probable cause because:

- No odor of narcotics was detected
- No contraband was in plain view
- Defendant exhibited no nervous behavior
- No reliable informant information linked defendant's vehicle to drug activity

2. Search Incident to Arrest

No lawful arrest preceded the search. Even if an arrest occurred, the search exceeded the scope permitted under Arizona v. Gant, 556 U.S. 332 (2009).

3. Consent

Defendant did not consent to the search. Any apparent consent was invalid because:

- Defendant was in custody and not free to leave
- No Miranda warnings were given
- The detention was coercive and intimidating

4. Inventory Search

The vehicle was not impounded, and no inventory policy was followed.

D. Inevitable Discovery Does Not Apply

The government cannot rely on the inevitable discovery doctrine because:

1. No independent investigation was underway
2. Agents were not pursuing a specific lead that would have led to discovery
3. The discovery was the direct result of the unlawful search

III. EXCLUSIONARY RULE APPLIES

All evidence obtained through the unlawful search must be suppressed under the exclusionary rule, including:

1. The narcotics seized from the vehicle
2. Defendant's post-arrest statements
3. Any derivative evidence obtained as a "fruit of the poisonous tree"

IV. CONCLUSION

The search of defendant's vehicle violated his Fourth Amendment rights. The evidence obtained must be suppressed, and without this evidence, the government cannot prove its case.

WHEREFORE, defendant respectfully requests that this Court:

1. Grant this Motion to Suppress;
2. Order an evidentiary hearing;
3. Suppress all narcotics evidence and statements obtained through the unlawful search;
4. Dismiss the charges if insufficient evidence remains; and
5. Grant such other relief as the Court deems just and proper.

Respectfully submitted,

[Attorney signature]

[Attorney name]

[Attorney title]

[Bar number]

[Address]

[Phone]

[Email]

Attorney for Defendant

SAMPLE MOTION TO DISMISS DRUG CONSPIRACY INDICTMENT

UNITED STATES DISTRICT COURT

[DISTRICT NAME]

UNITED STATES OF AMERICA,

Plaintiff,

v.

[DEFENDANT NAME],

Defendant.

Case No. [XX-XXX]

Judge [Name]

DEFENDANT'S MOTION TO DISMISS DRUG CONSPIRACY INDICTMENT FOR FAILURE TO STATE AN OFFENSE

TO THE HONORABLE COURT:

Defendant [Name], by and through undersigned counsel, respectfully moves this Court pursuant to Federal Rule of Criminal Procedure 12(b)(3)(B) to dismiss Count One of the Indictment charging conspiracy to distribute controlled substances because it fails to state a federal offense.

I. FACTUAL ALLEGATIONS IN THE INDICTMENT

The Indictment alleges that defendant conspired with others to distribute marijuana in violation of 21 U.S.C. §§ 841(a)(1) and 846. Specifically, the Indictment alleges:

1. Defendant agreed with [co-conspirators] to distribute marijuana;
2. The conspiracy occurred between [dates];
3. The conspiracy involved [amount] of marijuana;
4. Various overt acts in furtherance of the conspiracy.

II. LEGAL ARGUMENT

A. The Indictment Fails to Allege Interstate Commerce Nexus

Federal jurisdiction over drug offenses requires that the prosecution prove the controlled substances "traveled in or affected interstate or foreign commerce." 21 U.S.C. § 801 et seq.

The Indictment fails to allege any facts establishing interstate commerce, including:

1. No allegation that drugs crossed state lines
2. No allegation that drugs were manufactured outside the state
3. No allegation that the conspiracy affected interstate commerce
4. No allegation of interstate transportation or communication

B. Purely Intrastate Drug Activity Lacks Federal Jurisdiction

Under the Supreme Court's decision in United States v. Lopez, 514 U.S. 549 (1995), and United States v. Morrison, 529 U.S. 598 (2000), Congress's Commerce Clause power has limits.

While the Court in Gonzales v. Raich, 545 U.S. 1 (2005), upheld federal jurisdiction over local marijuana cultivation, that case involved:

1. Interstate market regulation
2. Comprehensive federal regulatory scheme
3. Substantial effects on interstate commerce

The instant case involves purely local drug distribution without any interstate component.

C. The Indictment Must Allege Jurisdictional Elements

Federal courts are courts of limited jurisdiction, and an indictment must allege all elements of the charged offense, including jurisdictional elements. United States v. Resendiz-Ponce, 549 U.S. 102 (2007).

The failure to allege interstate commerce nexus renders the Indictment jurisdictionally defective and subject to dismissal.

D. Insufficient Quantity to Affect Interstate Commerce

Even under Raich, the alleged quantity of [amount] marijuana is insufficient to substantially affect interstate commerce. The purely local nature of the alleged activity places it beyond federal jurisdiction.

III. ALTERNATIVE ARGUMENT: VAGUENESS

If the Court finds the interstate commerce allegations sufficient, the Indictment should still be dismissed for vagueness because:

1. The conspiracy allegations are conclusory without specific facts
2. The overt acts are insufficiently described
3. Defendant cannot adequately prepare a defense without specific allegations

IV. CONCLUSION

The Indictment fails to state a federal offense because it lacks allegations establishing federal jurisdiction. The charges should be dismissed, or alternatively, the government should be required to file a superseding indictment with proper jurisdictional allegations.

WHEREFORE, defendant respectfully requests that this Court:

1. Grant this Motion to Dismiss;
2. Dismiss Count One of the Indictment for failure to state an offense;
3. Alternatively, order the government to file a superseding indictment; and
4. Grant such other relief as the Court deems just and proper.

Respectfully submitted,

[Attorney signature]

[Attorney name]

[Attorney title]

[Bar number]

[Address]

[Phone]

[Email]

Attorney for Defendant

SAMPLE MOTION TO SUPPRESS WIRETAP EVIDENCE

UNITED STATES DISTRICT COURT

[DISTRICT NAME]

UNITED STATES OF AMERICA,

Plaintiff,

v.

[DEFENDANT NAME],

Defendant.

Case No. [XX-XXX]

Judge [Name]

DEFENDANT'S MOTION TO SUPPRESS WIRETAP EVIDENCE FOR VIOLATIONS OF TITLE III

TO THE HONORABLE COURT:

Defendant [Name], by and through undersigned counsel, respectfully moves this Court pursuant to Federal Rule of Criminal Procedure 12(b)(3)(C) and 18 U.S.C. § 2518(10)(a) to suppress all evidence obtained through electronic surveillance of defendant's telephone communications.

I. FACTUAL BACKGROUND

1. The government obtained a Title III wiretap order authorizing interception of communications over telephone number [number] on [date].
2. The wiretap was in effect from [date] to [date] and was extended [number] times.
3. The government intercepted approximately [number] conversations involving defendant.
4. The wiretap evidence forms the basis of the drug conspiracy charges against defendant.

II. LEGAL ARGUMENT

A. The Wiretap Application Failed to Establish Probable Cause

Title III requires that wiretap applications establish probable cause that:

1. An individual is committing, has committed, or is about to commit a predicate offense
2. Communications concerning that offense will be obtained through the interception
3. Normal investigative procedures have been tried and failed or are unlikely to succeed

18 U.S.C. § 2518(3).

The affidavit supporting the wiretap application failed to establish probable cause because:

1. Stale Information: The most recent alleged criminal activity occurred [time period] before the application, making the information stale.

2. Unreliable Informant: The application relied primarily on information from a confidential informant whose reliability was not established.

3. Lack of Corroboration: The informant's information was not independently corroborated by law enforcement.

B. The Necessity Requirement Was Not Satisfied

Title III requires that "normal investigative procedures have been tried and failed or reasonably appear to be unlikely to succeed if tried or to be too dangerous." 18 U.S.C. § 2518(3)(c).

The government failed to satisfy this requirement because:

1. Surveillance: Physical surveillance was never attempted or inadequately pursued.

2. Undercover Operations: No undercover operations were attempted.

3. Financial Investigations: Bank records and financial analysis were not pursued.

4. Controlled Purchases: No controlled drug purchases were attempted.

5. Search Warrants: Traditional search warrants were not considered.

C. Minimization Requirements Were Violated

Title III requires minimization of interception of non-relevant communications. 18 U.S.C. § 2518(5).

The government violated minimization requirements by:

1. Failure to Monitor: Inadequate monitoring during interception periods.

2. Personal Calls: Continued interception of clearly personal, non-criminal conversations.

3. Attorney-Client Communications: Interception of privileged communications with counsel.

4. Lack of Spot Monitoring: Failure to employ appropriate spot monitoring techniques.

D. The Wiretap Orders Were Improperly Extended

Each extension of the wiretap order must meet the same requirements as the initial application. The extensions in this case were improper because:

1. Insufficient Progress: Extensions were granted without showing sufficient progress in the investigation.

2. Changed Circumstances: Material changes in circumstances were not disclosed to the court.

3. Alternative Methods: Less intrusive investigative methods became available but were not pursued.

E. Franks Hearing Required

Defendant requests a Franks hearing pursuant to Franks v. Delaware, 438 U.S. 154 (1978), because the wiretap affidavit contains material misrepresentations and omissions:

1. False Statements: [Specific false statements in affidavit]

2. Material Omissions: [Specific omitted facts that undermine probable cause]

III. STATUTORY SUPPRESSION REMEDY

Title III provides a statutory suppression remedy: "Whenever any wire or oral communication has been intercepted, no part of the contents of such communication and no evidence derived therefrom may be received in evidence in any trial, hearing, or other proceeding..." 18 U.S.C. § 2518(10)(a).

IV. DERIVATIVE EVIDENCE MUST BE SUPPRESSED

All evidence derived from the unlawful wiretaps must be suppressed as "fruit of the poisonous tree," including:

1. Physical evidence seized based on wiretap information
2. Subsequent surveillance and investigations
3. Statements made by defendant and co-conspirators
4. Additional wiretaps and electronic surveillance

V. CONCLUSION

The wiretap evidence was obtained in violation of Title III and must be suppressed. Without this evidence, the government cannot prove its case against defendant.

WHEREFORE, defendant respectfully requests that this Court:

1. Grant this Motion to Suppress;
2. Order a Franks hearing;
3. Suppress all wiretap evidence and derivative evidence;
4. Dismiss the charges if insufficient evidence remains; and
5. Grant such other relief as the Court deems just and proper.

Respectfully submitted,

[Attorney signature]

[Attorney name]

[Attorney title]

[Bar number]

[Address]

[Phone]

[Email]

Attorney for Defendant

POST-CONVICTION MOTIONS FOR DRUG CASES

SAMPLE MOTION FOR SENTENCE REDUCTION UNDER FIRST STEP ACT

UNITED STATES DISTRICT COURT

[DISTRICT NAME]

UNITED STATES OF AMERICA,

Plaintiff,

v.

[DEFENDANT NAME],

Defendant.

Case No. [XX-XXX]

Judge [Name]

DEFENDANT'S MOTION FOR SENTENCE REDUCTION UNDER THE FIRST STEP ACT

TO THE HONORABLE COURT:

Defendant [Name], currently incarcerated at [facility], respectfully moves this Court pursuant to Section 404 of the First Step Act of 2018 for a reduction of his sentence based on retroactive application of the Fair Sentencing Act.

I. PROCEDURAL HISTORY

1. On [date], defendant was charged with conspiracy to distribute crack cocaine in violation of 21 U.S.C. §§ 841(a)(1) and 846.

2. On [date], defendant pleaded guilty to the conspiracy charge involving [amount] of crack cocaine.

3. On [date], this Court sentenced defendant to [sentence] based on the 100-to-1 crack-to-powder cocaine ratio then in effect.

4. Defendant's sentence was based on a guideline range of [range] calculated using the pre-Fair Sentencing Act guidelines.

II. LEGAL BASIS FOR RELIEF

A. First Step Act Section 404

Section 404 of the First Step Act makes the Fair Sentencing Act of 2010 retroactive to defendants sentenced before its enactment. The Fair Sentencing Act:

1. Reduced the crack-to-powder cocaine sentencing disparity from 100-to-1 to 18-to-1

2. Eliminated the mandatory minimum for simple possession of crack cocaine

3. Increased the quantity thresholds for crack cocaine mandatory minimums

B. Defendant Qualifies for Relief

Defendant qualifies for First Step Act relief because:

1. Pre-August 3, 2010 Sentence: Defendant was sentenced on [date], before the Fair Sentencing Act took effect.

2. Crack Cocaine Offense: Defendant's conviction involved crack cocaine, which is covered by the Fair Sentencing Act.

3. Sentence Based on Pre-FSA Guidelines: Defendant's sentence was calculated using the guidelines in effect before the Fair Sentencing Act.

III. SENTENCING CALCULATION UNDER CURRENT LAW

A. Original Sentence Calculation

Under the guidelines in effect at sentencing:

- Base Offense Level: [level] (based on [amount] crack cocaine)

- Adjustments: [list adjustments]

- Criminal History Category: [category]

- Guideline Range: [range]

- Sentence Imposed: [sentence]

B. Revised Calculation Under First Step Act

Under current guidelines reflecting the Fair Sentencing Act:

- Base Offense Level: [reduced level] (based on 18-to-1 ratio)

- Same Adjustments: [list adjustments]

- Same Criminal History Category: [category]

- Revised Guideline Range: [lower range]

- Recommended Sentence: [reduced sentence]

C. Sentence Reduction

The application of current law would result in a sentence reduction of approximately [time period], which represents a substantial and meaningful reduction in defendant's sentence.

IV. SECTION 3553(a) FACTORS SUPPORT REDUCTION

The factors set forth in 18 U.S.C. § 3553(a) support sentence reduction:

A. Nature and Circumstances of Offense

1. Non-violent drug offense without weapons or violence

2. Defendant's role was [minimal/limited] in the conspiracy

3. No leadership or organizational role

B. History and Characteristics of Defendant

1. No prior criminal history/limited criminal history

2. Excellent institutional record with no disciplinary infractions

3. Completion of educational and substance abuse programs

4. Strong family and community support

C. Adequate Deterrence and Punishment

1. Defendant has served [time period] of his sentence

2. Specific deterrence achieved through incarceration and programming

3. General deterrence served by substantial sentence already served

D. Disparities with Similarly Situated Defendants

1. Defendants sentenced post-Fair Sentencing Act receive significantly lower sentences

2. Reduction would eliminate unwarranted disparity based solely on timing

V. POST-CONVICTION CONDUCT

Defendant s exemplary conduct during incarceration supports sentence reduction:

1. Educational Achievement: [Completion of GED/college courses/vocational training]

2. Program Participation: [Substance abuse treatment, anger management, etc.]

3. Work History: [Prison job assignments and performance]

4. Disciplinary Record: [Clean record/minimal infractions]

5. Mentoring: [Assistance to other inmates/leadership roles]

VI. RELEASE PLAN

Defendant has developed a comprehensive release plan:

1. Residence: [Family home/approved residence]

2. Employment: [Job offer/vocational skills]

3. Support System: [Family support/community connections]

4. Continued Treatment: [Substance abuse aftercare/counseling]

VII. CONCLUSION

The First Step Act was designed to address the unjust crack-powder cocaine sentencing disparity that affected the defendant's sentence. A reduction is warranted under the statute and supported by the § 3553(a) factors.

WHEREFORE, defendant respectfully requests that this Court:

1. Grant this Motion for Sentence Reduction;

2. Reduce defendant's sentence to [specific reduction/time served];

3. Order defendant's immediate release or release within [time period]; and

4. Grant such other relief as the Court deems just and proper.

Respectfully submitted,

[Attorney signature]

[Attorney name]

[Attorney title]

[Bar number]

[Address]

[Phone]

[Email]

Attorney for Defendant

SAMPLE MOTION UNDER 28 USC 2255 FOR DRUG CASE

UNITED STATES DISTRICT COURT

[DISTRICT NAME]

[DEFENDANT NAME],

Petitioner,

v.

UNITED STATES OF AMERICA,

Respondent.

Civil Case No. [XX-XXX]

(Criminal Case No. [XX-XXX])

Judge [Name]

MOTION UNDER 28 U.S.C. § 2255 BASED ON INEFFECTIVE ASSISTANCE IN DRUG CONSPIRACY CASE

TO THE HONORABLE COURT:

Petitioner [Name], currently incarcerated at [facility], brings this Motion pursuant to 28 U.S.C. § 2255 to vacate his conviction and sentence for drug conspiracy based on ineffective assistance of counsel.

I. PROCEDURAL HISTORY

1. On [date], petitioner was charged in a drug conspiracy involving [substance] in violation of 21 U.S.C. §§ 841(a)(1) and 846.

2. On [date], petitioner pleaded guilty pursuant to a plea agreement.

3. On [date], petitioner was sentenced to [sentence].

4. Petitioner did not file a direct appeal.

5. This Motion is timely filed within one year of the conviction becoming final.

II. GROUNDS FOR RELIEF

GROUND ONE: INEFFECTIVE ASSISTANCE - FAILURE TO INVESTIGATE DEFENSES

A. Factual Basis

Trial counsel rendered ineffective assistance by failing to investigate and present viable defenses to the drug conspiracy charge:

1. Withdrawal Defense: Evidence existed that petitioner withdrew from the conspiracy [time period] before the charged timeframe, but counsel failed to investigate this defense.

2. Lack of Knowledge: Petitioner was unaware of the scope and nature of the conspiracy, but counsel failed to develop evidence of petitioner's limited knowledge.

3. Minimal Role: Petitioner's role was minimal compared to other conspirators, warranting a substantial reduction under U.S.S.G. § 3B1.2, but counsel failed to argue for this adjustment.

B. Deficient Performance

Counsel's performance was deficient because:

1. No Investigation: Counsel conducted no meaningful investigation of the facts despite petitioner's requests to investigate his limited involvement.

2. Ignored Witnesses: Counsel failed to interview witnesses who would have testified about petitioner's withdrawal from the conspiracy.

3. No Expert: Counsel failed to retain a drug expert to explain the conspiracy structure and petitioner's peripheral role.

C. Prejudice

Had counsel conducted an adequate investigation:

1. Evidence of withdrawal would have eliminated petitioner's liability for conspiracy activities after withdrawal

2. Minimal role evidence would have resulted in a 2-4 level reduction in offense level

3. Petitioner would not have pleaded guilty and would have proceeded to trial

GROUND TWO: INEFFECTIVE ASSISTANCE - ERRONEOUS PLEA ADVICE

A. Factual Basis

Counsel provided erroneous advice regarding the consequences of petitioner's guilty plea:

1. Sentencing Exposure: Counsel incorrectly advised that petitioner faced a maximum of [incorrect amount] when the actual maximum was [correct amount].

2. Guidelines Calculation: Counsel misunderstood the drug quantity attribution and advised petitioner he would be held responsible for [incorrect amount] when the actual attribution was [correct amount].

3. Immigration Consequences: Counsel failed to advise petitioner that the conviction would result in automatic deportation under 8 U.S.C. § 1227(a)(2)(B)(i).

B. Deficient Performance

Counsel's advice fell below professional standards because:

1. A competent attorney would have accurately calculated sentencing exposure
2. A competent attorney would have understood drug quantity attribution rules
3. Padilla v. Kentucky, 559 U.S. 356 (2010), required advice about immigration consequences

C. Prejudice

Had petitioner received accurate advice:

1. He would not have pleaded guilty given the actual sentencing exposure
2. He would have demanded a plea agreement with immigration protection
3. He would have proceeded to trial where withdrawal and minimal role defenses could succeed

GROUND THREE: INEFFECTIVE ASSISTANCE - FAILURE TO CHALLENGE DRUG QUANTITY

A. Factual Basis

Counsel failed to challenge the government's drug quantity calculations despite clear evidence that:

1. Purity Issues: The drugs attributed to petitioner were not tested for purity

2. Relevant Conduct: Much of the attributed quantity occurred after petitioner's withdrawal

3. Hearsay: Drug quantity was based on unreliable hearsay statements

B. Legal Standard

Drug quantity must be proven by a preponderance of evidence, and defendants are only responsible for reasonably foreseeable amounts. United States v. Vonn, 348 F.3d 497 (4th Cir. 2003).

C. Deficient Performance and Prejudice

Counsel's failure to challenge drug quantity was objectively unreasonable and resulted in:

- Higher offense level calculation
- Longer sentence than warranted
- Loss of safety valve eligibility

III. RELIEF REQUESTED

Petitioner requests that this Court:

1. Vacate Conviction: Allow withdrawal of guilty plea due to ineffective assistance

2. Evidentiary Hearing: Order hearing on disputed facts regarding counsel's performance

3. New Counsel: Appoint new counsel for any subsequent proceedings

IV. CONCLUSION

Counsel's deficient performance denied petitioner his Sixth Amendment right to effective assistance of counsel. The errors were not harmless and resulted in a conviction and sentence that would not have occurred with competent representation.

WHEREFORE, petitioner respectfully requests that this Court:

1. Grant this Motion under 28 U.S.C. § 2255;
2. Vacate petitioner's conviction and sentence;
3. Allow withdrawal of the guilty plea;
4. Order an evidentiary hearing; and
5. Grant such other relief as the Court deems just and proper.

Respectfully submitted,

[Attorney signature]

[Attorney name]

[Attorney title]

[Bar number]

[Address]

[Phone]

[Email]

Attorney for Petitioner

SAMPLE MOTION FOR SAFETY VALVE RELIEF

UNITED STATES DISTRICT COURT

[DISTRICT NAME]

UNITED STATES OF AMERICA,

Plaintiff,

v.

[DEFENDANT NAME],

Defendant.

Case No. [XX-XXX]

Judge [Name]

DEFENDANT'S MOTION FOR SAFETY VALVE RELIEF UNDER 18 U.S.C. § 3553(f)

TO THE HONORABLE COURT:

Defendant [Name], by and through undersigned counsel, respectfully moves this Court pursuant to 18 U.S.C. § 3553(f) and Amendment 782 to the Sentencing Guidelines for safety valve relief from the mandatory minimum sentence.

I. PROCEDURAL BACKGROUND

1. Defendant pleaded guilty to conspiracy to distribute methamphetamine in violation of 21 U.S.C. §§ 841(a)(1) and 846.

2. The offense involved [amount] of methamphetamine mixture, triggering a 10-year mandatory minimum sentence under 21 U.S.C. § 841(b)(1)(A).

3. Defendant seeks safety valve relief to avoid the mandatory minimum sentence.

II. SAFETY VALVE CRITERIA UNDER 18 U.S.C. § 3553(f)

Defendant satisfies all five criteria for safety valve relief:

A. Criterion 1: No Death or Serious Bodily Injury

"The defendant does not have more than 4 criminal history points, excluding any criminal history points resulting from a 1-point offense, as determined under the sentencing guidelines."

Analysis: Defendant has [number] criminal history points:

- [List prior convictions and points]

- Total criminal history points: [number] (excluding 1-point offenses)

- Defendant qualifies under this criterion.

B. Criterion 2: No Violence or Threat of Violence

"The defendant did not use violence or credible threats of violence or possess a firearm or other dangerous weapon (or induce another participant to do so) in connection with the offense."

Analysis:

- No evidence of violence or threats during the conspiracy
- No firearms or weapons possessed or used
- No evidence defendant induced others to use violence or weapons
- Defendant qualifies under this criterion.

C. Criterion 3: No Death or Serious Bodily Injury

"The offense did not result in death or serious bodily injury to any person."

Analysis:

- The drug conspiracy did not result in any deaths
- No evidence of serious bodily injury to any person
- Defendant qualifies under this criterion.

D. Criterion 4: No Leadership Role

"The defendant was not an organizer, leader, manager, or supervisor of others in the offense, as determined under the sentencing guidelines, and was not engaged in a continuing criminal enterprise, as defined in section 408 of the Controlled Substances Act."

Analysis:

- Defendant's role was minimal in the conspiracy
- No evidence of organizing, leading, managing, or supervising others
- Not engaged in continuing criminal enterprise under 21 U.S.C. § 848
- Defendant qualifies under this criterion.

E. Criterion 5: Truthful Information

"Not later than the time of the sentencing hearing, the defendant has truthfully provided to the Government all information and evidence the defendant has concerning the offense or offenses that were part of the same course of conduct or of a common scheme or plan, but the fact that the defendant has no relevant or useful other information to provide or that the Government is already aware of the information shall not preclude a determination by the court that the defendant has complied with this requirement."

Analysis:

- Defendant participated in proffer sessions with government attorneys
- Provided all information known about the conspiracy
- Answered all questions truthfully during debriefing
- Government has not alleged any lack of truthfulness
- Defendant qualifies under this criterion.

III. FIRST STEP ACT AMENDMENT TO SAFETY VALVE

The First Step Act of 2018 amended the safety valve to reduce the criminal history requirement from 1 point to 4 points, expanding eligibility for relief. Defendant's criminal history of [number] points now qualifies for safety valve under the amended statute.

IV. SENTENCING GUIDELINE IMPACT

With safety valve relief:

- Mandatory minimum sentence: Avoided
- Base offense level: [level] (with 2-level safety valve reduction)
- Adjusted offense level: [level]
- Criminal history category: [category]
- Guideline range: [range]
- Recommended sentence: [sentence]

V. SECTION 3553(a) FACTORS SUPPORT RELIEF

The factors under 18 U.S.C. § 3553(a) support safety valve relief:

1. **Nature of Offense:** Non-violent drug offense with minimal role
2. **Defendant's Characteristics:** [Age, background, family circumstances]
3. **Deterrence:** Lower sentence will adequately deter future conduct
4. **Public Safety:** Defendant poses minimal risk of recidivism
5. **Cooperation:** Defendant's truthful cooperation with government

VI. CONCLUSION

Defendant satisfies all criteria for safety valve relief under 18 U.S.C. § 3553(f). Relief is appropriate given the defendant's minimal role, cooperation with authorities, and low risk of recidivism.

WHEREFORE, defendant respectfully requests that this Court:

1. Grant safety valve relief under 18 U.S.C. § 3553(f);
2. Sentence defendant below the mandatory minimum;
3. Apply the 2-level safety valve reduction; and
4. Grant such other relief as the Court deems just and proper.

Respectfully submitted,

[Attorney signature]

[Attorney name]

[Attorney title]

[Bar number]

[Address]

[Phone]

[Email]

Attorney for Defendant

This comprehensive collection of drug case-specific motions provides federal criminal practitioners with specialized templates for the unique issues that arise in federal drug prosecutions, including Fourth Amendment challenges, Title III wiretap suppression, conspiracy defenses, sentence reductions, and safety valve relief.

CHAPTER THREE

THE CREATION OF THE WAR ON DRUGS: ORIGINS AND EVOLUTION OF FEDERAL DRUG POLICY

INTRODUCTION

The **"War on Drugs"** represents one of the most significant and enduring domestic policy initiatives in American history, fundamentally reshaping the federal criminal justice system and affecting millions of lives over the past five decades. This comprehensive examination traces the origins, development, and implementation of federal drug prohibition policies from their early twentieth-century beginnings through the formal declaration of the **"War on Drugs"** and its subsequent evolution into the modern federal drug enforcement apparatus.

Understanding the creation of the **War on Drugs** requires examination of multiple intersecting factors: evolving social attitudes toward drug use, racial and cultural tensions, political calculations, law enforcement expansion, and the gradual federalization of what were traditionally state and local criminal matters. The transformation of drug policy from a primarily medical and regulatory approach to a predominantly punitive criminal justice model represents a fundamental shift in American governance that continues to influence federal law enforcement priorities, sentencing policies, and constitutional jurisprudence.

This historical analysis provides essential context for understanding contemporary federal drug laws, mandatory minimum sentences, and the extensive federal criminal code provisions that govern controlled substances. The policy decisions made during the creation and early implementation of the **War on Drugs** established legal precedents, enforcement priorities, and institutional structures that continue to shape federal criminal law and procedure today.

EARLY FEDERAL DRUG REGULATION: THE FOUNDATION (1900-1950)

The Harrison Narcotics Tax Act of 1914

The first significant federal involvement in drug regulation began with the **Harrison Narcotics Tax Act of 1914**, which established the federal government's initial framework for controlling narcotic substances. This legislation, ostensibly a tax measure designed to regulate the distribution of opium and coca products, marked the beginning of federal criminal enforcement in drug matters.

The Harrison Act required registration and taxation of all persons who produced, imported, manufactured, compounded, dealt in, dispensed, sold, distributed, or gave away opium or coca leaves and their derivatives. While framed as a revenue measure to avoid constitutional challenges regarding federal police powers, the Act effectively criminalized the distribution of these substances outside of legitimate medical channels.

The legislation emerged from international pressure following the **Shanghai Opium Commission of 1909 and the International Opium** Convention at The Hague in 1912, where the United States committed to domestic opium control measures. Domestic concerns about opium smoking in

Chinese immigrant communities and cocaine use among African Americans also influenced the Act's passage, establishing early connections between drug prohibition and racial prejudice that would persist throughout the War on Drugs.

The Supreme Court's interpretation of **the Harrison Act** in cases such as **United States v. Doremus (1919) and Webb v. United States (1919)** transformed the tax measure into effective criminal prohibition by holding that doctors could not prescribe narcotics to maintain addiction. This judicial interpretation shifted drug policy from a medical model toward criminalization, establishing precedent for punitive rather than therapeutic approaches to drug dependency.

The Federal Bureau of Narcotics and Early Enforcement

The establishment of the **Federal Bureau of Narcotics (FBN) in 1930** under the Treasury Department created the first dedicated federal drug enforcement agency. Led by **Harry J. Anslinger from 1930 to 1962,** the FBN developed many enforcement strategies and political arguments that would later characterize the **War on Drugs.**

Anslinger's leadership of the FBN established several enduring features of federal drug policy: the association of drug use with minority communities and criminal behavior, the rejection of medical approaches to addiction treatment, and the expansion of federal law enforcement authority into traditionally local criminal matters. The FBN's propaganda campaigns, including the notorious film "Reefer Madness," promoted public fear of drug use and supported increasingly punitive legislation.

The Marihuana Tax Act of 1937, championed by Anslinger and the FBN, extended federal control to cannabis through the same tax registration scheme used for **opiates and cocaine.** The Act's passage relied heavily on sensationalized accounts of marijuana-induced violence and criminality, particularly emphasizing alleged connections to Mexican immigrants and African American communities. This legislation established marijuana prohibition as federal policy and created precedent for expanding federal drug control to new substances.

World War II And Post-War Developments

World War II temporarily shifted federal drug policy focus toward controlling pharmaceutical supplies and addressing drug use among military personnel. The war period saw increased federal coordination of drug control efforts and the beginning of international cooperation in drug enforcement that would later expand during the Cold War.

The post-war period brought new challenges as returning veterans struggled with addiction issues and new synthetic drugs entered the marketplace. **The Boggs Act of 1951** introduced mandatory minimum sentences for drug offenses, establishing the principle that drug crimes required severe punishment regardless of individual circumstances. This legislation marked the first federal mandatory minimums for drug offenses and created the foundation for much harsher sentencing policies that would follow.

The Narcotic Control Act of 1956 further increased penalties and expanded federal authority, including provisions for the death penalty in some **drug trafficking cases.** These statutes reflected growing public concern about drug use and crime, while establishing federal supremacy over state approaches to drug policy.

CHAPTER FOUR

THE POLITICAL CONTEXT: RACE, CULTURE, AND SOCIAL CONTROL

Racial Dynamics in Early Drug Prohibition

From its inception, federal drug prohibition was deeply intertwined with racial prejudice and social control objectives. **The Harrison Act's** passage coincided with heightened anti-Chinese sentiment on the West Coast, where opium smoking was associated with Chinese immigrants and **"corrupting"** influence on white Americans. Similarly, early cocaine prohibition was driven partly by fears of **African American** drug use and exaggerated claims about cocaine-induced violence.

These racial dynamics established enduring patterns in drug law enforcement that would intensify during the **War on Drugs**. Federal drug policy consistently targeted substances associated with minority communities while treating those used primarily by white, middle-class Americans more leniently. This selective enforcement approach created disparate racial impacts that continue to characterize federal drug prosecutions.

The association of drug use with racial minorities served broader social control functions during periods of significant demographic and cultural change. Drug prohibition provided legal justification for increased surveillance and control of minority communities, while supporting broader segregation and discrimination policies. The criminalization of drug use also facilitated the exclusion of immigrants and the disenfranchisement of African Americans through felony conviction consequences.

Cultural Conflicts And Generational Change

The 1960s brought unprecedented cultural upheaval that fundamentally challenged traditional authority structures and social norms. The civil rights movement, anti-war protests, and counterculture movement created political crises that drug policy would increasingly be used to address. Drug use became symbolically associated with political dissent, racial integration, and rejection of conventional values.

The widespread adoption of marijuana and psychedelic drugs among middle-class white youth during the 1960s presented new challenges for drug prohibition advocates. Traditional racial arguments for drug criminalization lost effectiveness when applied to suburban teenagers and college students. This demographic shift required new justifications for drug prohibition while creating political pressure for more nuanced approaches to drug policy.

The generational divide over drug use reflected broader conflicts about authority, tradition, and social change. For many Americans, drug prohibition represented defense of conventional morality and social order against perceived threats from youth rebellion and cultural transformation. These symbolic dimensions of drug policy often outweighed empirical considerations about public health or criminal justice effectiveness.

Law And Order Politics

The emergence of **"law and order"** as a central political theme during the 1960s provided crucial political context for the creation of the War on Drugs. Rising crime rates, urban riots, and social unrest created public demand for strong government responses to perceived breakdowns in social order. Drug prohibition offered politicians a way to demonstrate toughness on crime while addressing broader anxieties about social change.

The association of drug use with political protest and social deviance made drug enforcement politically attractive across party lines. Democratic and Republican politicians competed to demonstrate their commitment to drug prohibition, creating political incentives for increasingly punitive policies regardless of their practical effectiveness or constitutional implications.

Law and order politics also facilitated the expansion of federal law enforcement authority into areas traditionally governed by state and local authorities. Public concern about crime and disorder reduced resistance to federal involvement in criminal justice matters, enabling the creation of new federal agencies and the expansion of existing ones.

CHAPTER FIVE

THE NIXON ADMINISTRATION: DECLARING WAR (1969-1974)

THE FORMAL DECLARATION

President Richard Nixon's declaration of the **"War on Drugs"** on **June 17, 1971,** marked a watershed moment in American drug policy. In a special message to Congress, Nixon identified drug abuse as **"public enemy number one"** and called for a comprehensive federal response involving law enforcement, treatment, and prevention efforts. This formal declaration crystallized decades of evolving drug policy into a unified national campaign with military rhetoric and objectives.

Nixon's declaration was motivated by multiple political and policy considerations. Rising heroin addiction rates, particularly among returning **Vietnam War veterans,** created genuine public health concerns that demanded federal attention. Simultaneously, the association of drug use with anti-war protesters and counterculture movements made aggressive drug enforcement politically attractive to Nixon's conservative base.

The military metaphor of **"war"** was deliberately chosen to convey the seriousness of the government's commitment and to justify extraordinary measures that might not be acceptable for ordinary criminal justice problems. War rhetoric implied an existential threat requiring mobilization of all available resources and suspension of normal procedural safeguards. This framing would prove enormously influential in shaping subsequent drug policy debates and public attitudes.

Legislative Framework: The Controlled Substances Act

The Controlled Substances Act of 1970 (CSA) provided the comprehensive legal framework for the **War on Drugs** that remains largely intact today. This legislation replaced the patchwork of earlier drug laws with a unified federal scheme for classifying and controlling psychoactive substances based on their medical utility and abuse potential.

The CSA established five schedules of controlled substances with varying degrees of restriction and criminal penalties. Schedule I substances, including heroin, LSD, and marijuana, were deemed to have high abuse potential with no accepted medical use and were subject to the most severe criminal penalties. Lower schedules provided for medical use under increasing degrees of regulation.

The Act granted broad authority to the **Drug Enforcement Administration (created in 1973)** and other federal agencies to investigate, prosecute, and regulate controlled substances. It established federal jurisdiction over all drug offenses involving interstate commerce and created uniform federal criminal penalties that often exceeded those imposed by state laws.

Significantly, the CSA included provisions for civil forfeiture of property connected to drug offenses, creating powerful financial incentives for law enforcement agencies to prioritize drug cases. These forfeiture provisions would later expand dramatically and become a controversial feature of federal drug enforcement.

The Creation Of The Drug Enforcement Administration

The establishment of the **Drug Enforcement Administration (DEA) in July 1973** consolidated federal drug enforcement authority under a single agency within the Department of Justice. The DEA combined personnel and functions from the Bureau of Narcotics and Dangerous Drugs, the **Office for Drug Abuse Law Enforcement,** and other scattered federal drug enforcement efforts.

The DEA's creation represented a significant expansion of federal law enforcement capacity and authority. The new agency received substantial budgetary resources, broad investigative powers, and a mandate to coordinate with state and local law enforcement agencies. The DEA also assumed responsibility for implementing the international aspects of drug prohibition, working with foreign governments to disrupt drug production and trafficking.

Under its first administrator, **John Bartels Jr., the DEA** established many operational procedures and enforcement priorities that would characterize federal drug enforcement for decades. The agency emphasized major trafficking organizations and international drug suppliers while developing sophisticated investigative techniques including undercover operations, electronic surveillance, and informant networks.

Treatment Vs. Enforcement Tensions

Despite the military rhetoric of the War on Drugs, the Nixon administration initially maintained some balance between enforcement and treatment approaches. Nixon's 1971 declaration explicitly called for expanded treatment and rehabilitation programs alongside increased law enforcement efforts. The administration created the **Special Action Office for Drug Abuse Prevention** and significantly increased federal funding for drug treatment programs.

This balanced approach reflected recognition that addiction was partly a medical problem requiring therapeutic intervention. The administration supported methadone maintenance programs, therapeutic communities, and other treatment modalities that showed promise for reducing drug dependency and associated crime.

However, the treatment emphasis proved politically vulnerable and resource-intensive compared to law enforcement approaches. Treatment programs required long-term commitments, produced ambiguous results, and lacked the dramatic appeal of enforcement operations. As political pressures mounted and budgetary constraints tightened, the treatment component of the War on Drugs received diminishing priority relative to enforcement efforts.

The tension between treatment and enforcement approaches would persist throughout the **War on Drugs,** with enforcement consistently receiving greater political support and budgetary resources. This imbalance reflected the symbolic importance of punishment in drug policy and the difficulty of measuring treatment program effectiveness compared to enforcement statistics.

The Reagan Era: Militarization And Expansion (1981-1989)

Just Say No and Cultural Warfare

The Reagan administration transformed the **War on Drugs** from a primarily law enforcement initiative into a comprehensive cultural and political campaign. Nancy Reagan's **"Just Say No"**

campaign symbolized this broader approach, which emphasized personal responsibility, moral education, and cultural change alongside criminal enforcement.

The **"Just Say No"** message reflected Reagan-era conservative philosophy emphasizing individual choice and moral clarity over social or economic explanations for drug use. This approach rejected medical models of addiction in favor of moral frameworks that held individuals fully responsible for their drug use decisions. The campaign's simplistic messaging appealed to parents and educators while supporting broader conservative arguments about personal responsibility and traditional values.

The cultural dimensions of the **Reagan drug war** extended beyond public education to include censorship efforts, media campaigns, and pressure on entertainment industries to avoid positive portrayals of drug use. The administration coordinated with television networks, film studios, and recording companies to promote anti-drug messages and eliminate content that might encourage drug experimentation.

This cultural warfare approach reflected understanding that the War on Drugs was fundamentally about competing value systems rather than merely criminal justice policy. The administration sought to reshape American culture to create social environments hostile to drug use, viewing cultural change as essential to achieving long-term success in drug prohibition.

The Crack Cocaine Crisis

The emergence of crack cocaine in the mid-1980s provided crucial justification for dramatically expanding the **War on Drugs**. Crack's association with violence, urban decay, and minority communities created public panic that enabled extraordinary policy responses including massive increases in enforcement resources and unprecedented criminal penalties.

The crack crisis was real and devastating for many urban communities, but the policy response reflected broader political and racial dynamics beyond public health concerns. Media coverage emphasized crack's association with African American communities while downplaying powder cocaine use among white professionals, creating public perceptions that supported racially disparate enforcement policies.

The Anti-Drug Abuse Act of 1986 established the notorious 100-to-1 sentencing disparity between crack and powder cocaine offenses, requiring identical sentences for possession of 100 times as much powder cocaine as crack cocaine. This disparity lacked scientific justification and created dramatic racial disparities in federal sentencing, as crack defendants were predominantly African American while powder cocaine defendants were typically white.

The crack cocaine panic also justified military involvement in domestic drug enforcement, including use of National Guard units for drug interdiction and surveillance. The military metaphor of the **War on Drugs** became increasingly literal as actual military resources and personnel were deployed for domestic law enforcement purposes.

Mandatory Minimums And Sentencing Revolution

The Reagan administration's expansion of mandatory minimum sentences for drug offenses represented a fundamental transformation of federal criminal justice. **The Anti-Drug Abuse Acts**

of 1986 and 1988 established mandatory prison terms for drug offenses based on drug type and quantity, eliminating judicial discretion and creating uniform national penalties.

These mandatory minimums were designed to ensure severe punishment regardless of individual circumstances, offender characteristics, or judicial judgments about appropriate sentences. The laws required identical sentences for first-time, non-violent drug offenders and repeat violent criminals if they were convicted of similar drug offenses.

The sentencing revolution extended beyond mandatory minimums to include expanded criminal liability, enhanced penalties for repeat offenders, and restrictions on parole and early release. **The Sentencing Reform Act of 1984** created **the United States Sentencing Commission** and established federal sentencing guidelines that further reduced judicial discretion and increased typical sentences for drug offenses.

These changes reflected broader conservative philosophy about criminal justice emphasizing deterrence, incapacitation, and moral desert over rehabilitation or proportionality. The administration argued that severe, certain punishment would deter drug use and trafficking while incapacitating offenders who continued criminal activity.

Federal-State Coordination and Grant Programs

The Reagan administration significantly expanded federal-state cooperation in drug enforcement through grant programs, task forces, and information sharing initiatives. **The Edward Byrne Memorial State and Local Law Enforcement Assistance Program, established in 1988,** provided federal funding to state and local agencies for drug enforcement activities.

These grant programs created powerful incentives for state and local agencies to prioritize drug enforcement and adopt federal enforcement strategies. Agencies received federal funding based on drug arrest statistics and seizure amounts, creating institutional pressures to maximize drug enforcement activity regardless of its effectiveness in reducing drug use or related problems.

The expansion of federal-state cooperation also included joint task forces that combined federal and local law enforcement personnel under federal supervision. These task forces enabled federal agencies to leverage local knowledge and resources while ensuring coordination with federal priorities and strategies.

Multi-jurisdictional task forces became a hallmark of drug enforcement during the Reagan era and beyond, facilitating information sharing, coordinated operations, and resource pooling. However, these arrangements also created accountability problems and constitutional concerns as local officers operated under federal authority with reduced oversight and different procedural requirements.

THE GEORGE H.W. BUSH ADMINISTRATION: CONSOLIDATION (1989-1993)

The National Drug Control Strategy

President George H.W. Bush continued and institutionalized the **War on Drugs** through creation of the **Office of National Drug Control Policy (ONDCP) in 1988,** with the director commonly known as the **"Drug Czar."** The first director, William Bennett, issued the first National Drug Control Strategy in 1989, establishing formal policy coordination and strategic planning for federal drug control efforts.

The National Drug Control Strategy represented an attempt to coordinate the numerous federal agencies involved in drug policy and establish unified objectives and priorities. The strategy emphasized enforcement and interdiction while maintaining rhetorical commitment to treatment and prevention programs, though budgetary allocations continued to favor enforcement approaches.

Bennett's leadership of ONDCP reflected the administration's commitment to moral and cultural dimensions of drug policy. A former Secretary of Education, Bennett emphasized character education, moral instruction, and cultural change as essential components of drug control policy. His approach combined traditional law enforcement with broader conservative social policies.

The institutionalization of drug policy coordination through ONDCP created bureaucratic structures that would persist through subsequent administrations regardless of changing political priorities. The office provided ongoing advocacy for drug prohibition policies and resistance to policy reforms that might reduce enforcement emphasis.

International Drug War Expansion

The Bush administration significantly expanded international dimensions of the **War on Drugs,** including military intervention in Latin American countries and increased cooperation with foreign law enforcement agencies. **Operation Just Cause,** the **1989 invasion of Panama,** was partly justified by dictator **Manuel Noriega's** involvement in drug trafficking, demonstrating the administration's willingness to use military force for drug control objectives.

The Andean Initiative provided massive military and economic assistance to Colombia, Peru, and Bolivia for drug eradication and interdiction efforts. This program established precedent for ongoing U.S. involvement in Latin American drug enforcement and created diplomatic tensions that persist today.

International drug control efforts reflected broader foreign policy objectives including hemispheric influence, military cooperation, and economic leverage. The drug war provided justification for military aid and intervention that might otherwise face congressional or international opposition, while supporting broader U.S. strategic interests in Latin America.

The expansion of international drug enforcement also included increased coordination with European and Asian countries for interdiction and money laundering investigations. These efforts established international law enforcement networks and cooperation agreements that facilitated information sharing and joint operations.

The Continuing Crisis In Urban America

Despite massive increases in enforcement resources and imprisonment, urban drug problems continued to worsen during the Bush administration. Cities like Washington, D.C., New York, and Los Angeles experienced unprecedented levels of drug-related violence and social disorder that called into question the effectiveness of enforcement-focused approaches.

The persistence of urban drug problems despite intensive enforcement efforts created some policy questioning and calls for alternative approaches. However, political dynamics favored continued escalation rather than fundamental reconsideration of prohibition strategies. The administration responded to continued problems by calling for even greater enforcement resources and more severe penalties.

The urban crisis also highlighted racial and class dimensions of drug policy as middle-class white communities remained largely insulated from the violence and incarceration that characterized the drug war's impact on minority communities. This geographic and demographic concentration of drug war effects reduced political pressure for policy changes while reinforcing stereotypes about drug use and crime.

THE CLINTON ADMINISTRATION: CONTINUATION AND AMBIVALENCE (1993-2001)

Political Calculations and Tough-on-Crime Democrats

President Bill Clinton's approach to drug policy reflected the Democratic Party's adaptation to conservative dominance of crime and drug issues during the 1980s. Clinton and other "**New Democrats"** sought to neutralize Republican advantages on law enforcement issues by adopting tough-on-crime positions that often exceeded previous Republican policies.

The Violent Crime Control and Law Enforcement Act of 1994, commonly known as the **Clinton Crime Bill,** included numerous provisions expanding federal drug enforcement and increasing penalties for drug offenses. The legislation provided billions of dollars for state and local law enforcement, expanded federal crimes, and established "three strikes" laws requiring life imprisonment for repeat federal offenders.

Clinton's personal history with marijuana use during the 1960s created political vulnerabilities that influenced his administration's approach to drug policy. His famous claim that he **"didn't inhale"** symbolized broader Democratic anxieties about appearing soft on drugs and the need to compensate through particularly aggressive enforcement policies.

The administration's drug policy reflected broader patterns of political triangulation that characterized Clinton's domestic agenda. Rather than challenging conservative drug war assumptions, the administration sought to implement drug prohibition more effectively while maintaining rhetorical distance from liberal alternatives that might prove politically damaging.

Mandatory Minimums And Sentencing Disparities

The Clinton administration initially showed some interest in addressing crack-powder cocaine sentencing disparities that had created obvious racial inequities in federal drug enforcement. **The U.S. Sentencing Commission** recommended eliminating the **100-to-1 ratio,** but Clinton rejected the recommendation under pressure from congressional Republicans and law enforcement agencies.

This decision reflected the political difficulties of appearing to reduce penalties for crack cocaine offenses, even when justified by evidence of racial discrimination and lack of scientific support for the disparity. The administration feared Republican attacks for being soft on crack cocaine and was unwilling to expend political capital on sentencing reform.

The continuation of mandatory minimum policies during the Clinton years demonstrated the institutional momentum of **War on Drugs** policies and the difficulty of reversing enforcement-focused approaches once they became established. Even Democratic administrations found it politically safer to continue and expand Republican drug policies rather than question their fundamental assumptions.

The administration did support some modest reforms including drug courts, treatment alternatives to incarceration, and prevention programs. However, these initiatives remained marginal compared to continued expansion of enforcement efforts and represented additions to rather than replacements for punitive approaches.

International Drug Policy And Plan Colombia

The Clinton administration continued and expanded international drug enforcement efforts, particularly in Latin America. Plan Colombia, initiated in 1999, provided over $7 billion in military and economic assistance for drug eradication and counter-insurgency efforts in Colombia, representing the largest international drug control program in U.S. history.

Plan Colombia reflected the administration's belief that addressing drug problems required attacking supply sources in producing countries rather than focusing primarily on domestic demand reduction. The program combined military assistance, aerial fumigation of coca crops, and economic development aid intended to provide legitimate alternatives to drug production.

The program's implementation involved significant human rights concerns as U.S.-supported Colombian military and paramilitary forces committed numerous abuses against civilian populations. Environmental concerns also arose from aerial fumigation programs that destroyed legal crops and contaminated water supplies in addition to targeting coca cultivation.

Plan Colombia established precedent for large-scale U.S. involvement in foreign countries' internal conflicts using drug control justifications. The program blurred lines between drug enforcement and military intervention while creating long-term commitments that persisted through subsequent administrations.

CHAPTER SIX

SOCIETAL IMPACTS AND CONSEQUENCES

MASS INCARCERATION AND THE PRISON-INDUSTRIAL COMPLEX

The War on Drugs contributed fundamentally to the creation of mass incarceration in the United States, with the federal and state prison populations increasing from approximately 300,000 in 1970 to over 2.3 million by 2010. Drug offenses accounted for the largest category of federal criminal convictions and a significant portion of state prison populations.

Federal drug prosecutions increased from fewer than 3,000 annually in 1970 to over 25,000 by 2010, with average sentences increasing dramatically due to mandatory minimums and sentencing guidelines. **The federal prison population** grew from approximately 20,000 in 1970 to over 200,000 by 2010, with drug offenders comprising nearly half of all federal prisoners.

The expansion of incarceration created powerful economic and political interests in maintaining high imprisonment rates. Private prison companies, correctional officer unions, and communities dependent on prison employment developed stakes in continued growth of the prison system that created resistance to policy reforms that might reduce incarceration levels.

The mass incarceration phenomenon disproportionately affected African American and Latino communities, with incarceration rates for drug offenses showing dramatic racial disparities despite similar rates of drug use across racial groups. These disparities reflected enforcement priorities, prosecutorial decisions, and sentencing policies that consistently disadvantaged minority defendants.

Racial Disparities And Civil Rights Implications

The War on Drugs created and exacerbated racial disparities throughout the criminal justice system, from initial police contacts through final sentencing and post-conviction consequences. African Americans comprised approximately 13% of drug users but over 35% of drug arrests, 55% of drug convictions, and 74% of drug imprisonment.

These disparities reflected multiple factors including geographic concentration of enforcement efforts in minority communities, different treatment of drugs associated with different racial groups, prosecutorial charging decisions, and sentencing policies like the crack-powder cocaine disparity. The cumulative effect was a drug enforcement system that imposed dramatically different consequences on minority communities compared to white drug users.

The racial impacts of drug prohibition extended beyond criminal justice to include employment discrimination, housing restrictions, educational barriers, and political disenfranchisement for persons with drug convictions. These collateral consequences created lasting disadvantages that affected not only individual offenders but entire families and communities.

Civil rights organizations increasingly viewed the War on Drugs as a form of racial discrimination that undermined decades of progress toward racial equality. The NAACP, ACLU, and other organizations challenged drug policies in court and advocated for reforms to address obvious racial disparities in enforcement and sentencing.

Economic Costs And Resource Allocation

The financial costs of the **War on Drugs** grew exponentially from the early 1970s through the 2010s, with federal drug control spending increasing from approximately $100 million annually in 1970 to over $15 billion by 2010. State and local expenditures added tens of billions more in enforcement, prosecution, and incarceration costs.

These massive expenditures diverted resources from education, healthcare, infrastructure, and other social programs that might have addressed underlying causes of drug abuse and related social problems. The opportunity costs of drug prohibition included foregone investments in treatment, prevention, education, and economic development that could have produced better outcomes for affected communities.

The economic impacts of mass incarceration extended beyond direct costs to include lost productivity from imprisoned individuals, reduced economic opportunities for families affected by incarceration, and broader community impacts from concentrated removal of working-age adults from neighborhoods.

Studies of drug enforcement effectiveness consistently showed poor return on investment compared to treatment and prevention programs, but political dynamics favored continued expansion of enforcement resources regardless of cost-effectiveness considerations.

Constitutional And Legal Implications

The War on Drugs significantly expanded federal law enforcement authority and altered constitutional protections in numerous areas including Fourth Amendment search and seizure law, Fifth Amendment due process protections, and Sixth Amendment right to counsel. Courts generally upheld aggressive drug enforcement tactics even when they raised serious constitutional concerns.

Fourth Amendment jurisprudence was particularly affected by drug enforcement needs, with courts creating numerous exceptions to warrant requirements and lowering standards for searches, seizures, and arrests. The automobile exception, plain view doctrine, consent searches, and stop-and-frisk procedures all expanded to accommodate drug enforcement priorities.

Civil asset forfeiture laws enabled law enforcement agencies to seize property connected to drug offenses without criminal convictions, creating powerful incentives for drug enforcement while raising due process concerns. Forfeiture proceeds often funded additional drug enforcement activities, creating self-reinforcing cycles of enforcement expansion.

The War on Drugs also affected federal-state relations by expanding federal criminal jurisdiction into areas traditionally governed by state law. Federal drug laws preempted state approaches and created pressure for state adoption of federal enforcement models regardless of local preferences or constitutional considerations.

CONCLUSION: LEGACY AND ONGOING INFLUENCE

The creation of the **War on Drugs** represents one of the most significant developments in American criminal justice history, fundamentally reshaping federal law enforcement, criminal law, and social policy over the past fifty years. What began as a response to legitimate public health concerns about drug abuse evolved into a comprehensive system of prohibition, enforcement, and punishment that affects virtually every aspect of American criminal justice.

The historical development of drug prohibition from **the Harrison Act** through the formal declaration of the War on Drugs reveals consistent patterns of racial discrimination, political calculation, and institutional expansion that continue to influence contemporary policy debates. Understanding this history is essential for evaluating current drug laws, enforcement practices, and proposed reforms.

The War on Drugs created powerful institutional interests and legal frameworks that persist despite growing recognition of their costs and limitations. Federal agencies, enforcement programs, sentencing structures, and international commitments established during the drug war's expansion remain largely intact and continue to shape policy options available to contemporary policymakers.

The symbolic and cultural dimensions of drug prohibition proved as important as practical law enforcement considerations in driving policy development. The War on Drugs served broader social and political functions beyond drug control, including racial control, cultural warfare, and political mobilization that helped sustain policies despite limited effectiveness in reducing drug use or related problems.

Contemporary debates about drug policy reform, criminal justice reform, and mass incarceration cannot be understood without reference to the historical development of the War on Drugs and its lasting influence on American legal and social institutions. The challenge for future policymakers involves dismantling counterproductive aspects of drug prohibition while preserving legitimate public health and safety protections.

The creation of the War on Drugs demonstrates the profound importance of policy choices made during periods of social crisis and political upheaval. Decisions made during the 1960s, 1970s, and 1980s continue to affect millions of Americans today, illustrating the lasting consequences of criminal justice policies and the difficulty of reversing institutional and legal structures once they become established.

As the United States grapples with ongoing challenges of drug abuse, criminal justice reform, and racial inequality, understanding the historical origins and development of the War on Drugs provides crucial context for evaluating current policies and developing more effective, equitable, and constitutional approaches to drug-related social problems. The lessons of this history suggest the importance of evidence-based policy making, attention to racial and social equity, and careful consideration of long-term consequences when developing criminal justice responses to social problems.

CHAPTER SEVEN

THE CREATION OF RICO AND FEDERAL CONSPIRACY LAWS: FROM PROHIBITION TO ORGANIZED CRIME ENFORCEMENT

INTRODUCTION

The development of federal conspiracy laws and the Racketeer Influenced and Corrupt Organizations Act (RICO) represents one of the most significant expansions of federal criminal jurisdiction in American legal history. These legal instruments transformed federal law enforcement's capacity to combat organized crime, white-collar fraud, and complex criminal enterprises that traditional criminal law struggled to address effectively. Understanding their creation requires examining nearly a century of legal evolution, beginning with Prohibition-era challenges and culminating in sophisticated modern tools for prosecuting criminal organizations.

The historical trajectory from basic conspiracy statutes to RICO reveals how American criminal law adapted to address increasingly complex forms of criminal activity that transcended traditional jurisdictional boundaries and evaded conventional prosecution strategies. This evolution reflects broader changes in American society, including urbanization, technological advancement, economic complexity, and the emergence of sophisticated criminal organizations that operated across state and national boundaries.

The creation of RICO in 1970 represented the culmination of decades of frustration with traditional criminal law's inability to dismantle criminal organizations effectively. While individual members could be prosecuted for specific crimes, the enterprises themselves often survived and continued operations despite successful prosecutions of key figures. RICO's innovative approach targeted the criminal organization itself, creating new offenses and powerful remedies specifically designed to destroy criminal enterprises rather than merely punishing individual participants.

This comprehensive examination traces the development of federal conspiracy and enterprise criminal law from its origins in English common law through Prohibition-era innovations, mid-twentieth century organized crime investigations, and the revolutionary creation of RICO. The analysis demonstrates how legal doctrines evolved in response to changing criminal threats while examining the constitutional, practical, and policy implications of these powerful prosecutorial tools.

Understanding this historical development is essential for contemporary federal criminal practitioners, as conspiracy charges appear in the vast majority of federal prosecutions, and RICO remains a potent weapon against organized crime, white-collar fraud, and complex criminal schemes. The policy choices made during the creation of these laws continue to influence federal prosecution strategies, sentencing policies, and the balance between effective law enforcement and constitutional protections.

CHAPTER EIGHT

EARLY FOUNDATIONS: ENGLISH COMMON LAW AND AMERICAN ADAPTATIONS (1600-1900)

COMMON LAW ORIGINS OF CONSPIRACY

The legal concept of conspiracy originated in medieval English law as a relatively narrow offense targeting corrupt practices by judicial officers and court personnel. **The Statute of Westminster of 1275** first codified conspiracy as "the false conspiracy of those who confederate and bind themselves by oath, covenant, or other alliance that each of them shall aid and support the other falsely and maliciously to indict or cause to be indicted those who are innocent."

This early formulation reflected feudal concerns about corruption within the judicial system and abuse of legal processes by powerful nobles and their retainers. The offense was specifically designed to prevent the manipulation of courts through coordinated false accusations and perjured testimony that could destroy innocent persons through legal proceedings.

Over subsequent centuries, English courts gradually expanded conspiracy beyond its original judicial context to encompass any agreement between two or more persons to commit unlawful acts. **The 1611 case of Poulterer's Case** established that conspiracy could apply to agreements to commit any crime, not merely those involving court proceedings. This expansion reflected growing recognition that coordinated criminal activity posed distinctive threats that justified separate punishment beyond the underlying substantive offenses.

By the eighteenth century, English conspiracy law had evolved to include three basic categories: conspiracies to commit crimes, conspiracies to commit civil wrongs (torts), and conspiracies to perform lawful acts through unlawful means. This broad formulation gave conspiracy law substantial flexibility to address various forms of coordinated misconduct while establishing the foundational principle that the agreement itself, rather than its successful completion, constituted the criminal offense.

Early American Conspiracy Law

American colonial and early state courts adopted English conspiracy law with modifications reflecting New World conditions and democratic values. The absence of feudal judicial hierarchies reduced emphasis on corrupt court proceedings, while concerns about coordinated resistance to authority and mob violence increased attention to political conspiracies and group disorders.

The first significant American conspiracy prosecution occurred in Philadelphia in 1806, when cordwainers (shoemakers) were prosecuted for conspiring to raise wages through coordinated work stoppages. This case, **Commonwealth v. Pullis,** established precedent for using conspiracy law against labor organizing and economic combinations, reflecting business community concerns about worker solidarity and market manipulation.

The Philadelphia cordwainers' case revealed tension between conspiracy law and emerging democratic principles of free association and collective action. Critics argued that conspiracy prosecutions threatened legitimate political and economic organization by criminalizing agreements that would be lawful if undertaken individually. Supporters contended that coordinated action posed qualitatively different threats requiring separate legal responses.

Early American conspiracy law developed primarily at the state level, as federal criminal jurisdiction remained quite limited before the Civil War. The few federal conspiracy statutes addressed specific concerns like postal fraud and customs violations, reflecting the federal government's limited regulatory authority and enforcement capacity. State courts thus bore primary responsibility for developing conspiracy doctrine and its application to various forms of coordinated criminal activity.

Civil War And Reconstruction Era Developments

The Civil War and Reconstruction periods witnessed significant expansion of federal conspiracy law as the federal government confronted challenges of rebellion, resistance to federal authority, and organized violence against freed slaves and federal officials. **The Enforcement Acts of 1870 and 1871** created new federal conspiracy offenses targeting **Ku Klux Klan** activities and other organized resistance to federal civil rights enforcement.

Section 241 of the current federal criminal code (originally Section 6 of the 1870 Enforcement Act) criminalized conspiracies "to injure, oppress, threaten, or intimidate any person in the free exercise or enjoyment of any right or privilege secured to him by the Constitution or laws of the United States." This statute represented unprecedented federal intervention in criminal matters traditionally governed by state law, justified by the need to protect federal constitutional rights from organized private violence.

The companion Section 242 (originally Section 2 of the 1871 Civil Rights Act) addressed individual deprivations of civil rights **"under color of law,"** creating federal jurisdiction over official misconduct by state and local authorities. Together, these statutes established federal conspiracy law as a tool for protecting civil rights and federal authority against organized resistance, setting precedent for subsequent expansions of federal criminal jurisdiction.

Reconstruction-era conspiracy statutes also introduced important procedural innovations, including venue provisions allowing prosecution in any district where conspirators acted, and joinder rules permitting prosecution of all conspirators in a single trial regardless of their specific roles or knowledge of other participants. These procedures, designed to overcome practical difficulties in prosecuting dispersed criminal organizations, became standard features of federal conspiracy law.

Late Nineteenth Century Labor And Economic Conspiracies

The post-Reconstruction period saw increased use of federal conspiracy law against labor organizations and economic combinations that allegedly restrained interstate commerce**. The Sherman Antitrust Act of 1890** created new conspiracy offenses targeting "combinations in restraint of trade," extending federal criminal law into commercial activities that affected interstate commerce.

Early Sherman Act prosecutions focused primarily on labor unions rather than business trusts, reflecting judicial and prosecutorial hostility toward organized labor during the Gilded Age. Cases like In **re Debs (1895)** established precedent for using federal conspiracy law against strikes and labor organizing that allegedly interfered with interstate commerce, particularly involving railroads and other transportation industries.

The expansion of federal conspiracy law into economic matters reflected broader changes in American society, including industrialization, urbanization, and the emergence of national markets that transcended state boundaries. Traditional state criminal law proved inadequate to address economic combinations and labor conflicts that operated across multiple jurisdictions and affected interstate commerce.

These developments also established important constitutional precedents for federal criminal jurisdiction based on interstate commerce effects. The Supreme Court's broad interpretation of congressional power to regulate interstate commerce provided the legal foundation for subsequent expansions of federal conspiracy law into areas traditionally governed by state authorities.

PROHIBITION ERA: THE CATALYST FOR FEDERAL EXPANSION (1920-1933)

The Volstead Act And Organized Crime Emergence

The passage of the Volstead Act in 1919, implementing the Eighteenth Amendment's prohibition of alcohol, created unprecedented opportunities for organized criminal activity and exposed the limitations of traditional criminal law enforcement. Prohibition transformed alcohol from a regulated commodity into contraband, creating enormous profit opportunities for those willing to violate federal law while generating massive consumer demand that legal markets could not satisfy.

The scale and complexity of Prohibition-era criminal organizations far exceeded anything previously encountered by American law enforcement. Bootlegging operations required sophisticated supply chains extending from foreign suppliers through domestic distribution networks to retail outlets, involving coordination among hundreds or thousands of participants across multiple states and jurisdictions. These enterprises generated enormous revenues that enabled systematic corruption of law enforcement, judicial, and political officials.

Traditional criminal law proved inadequate to address these organizations because it focused on individual criminal acts rather than criminal enterprises. Prosecutors could convict individual bootleggers, corrupt officials, and violence perpetrators, but the organizations themselves typically survived and continued operations with replacement personnel. The enterprises' compartmentalized structures also made it difficult to establish criminal liability for leaders who avoided direct participation in specific criminal acts.

Federal conspiracy law provided partial solutions to these challenges by enabling prosecution of agreements to violate federal liquor laws even when specific criminal acts could not be proven against particular defendants. Conspiracy charges allowed prosecutors to reach organizational leaders based on their participation in criminal agreements, even when they maintained plausible deniability regarding specific operations.

Al Capone And The Limits Of Traditional Prosecution

The career of Al Capone and federal efforts to prosecute him illustrated both the potential and limitations of existing federal criminal law against sophisticated criminal organizations. Capone's Chicago-based organization generated estimated annual revenues exceeding $100 million through bootlegging, gambling, prostitution, and other illegal activities, while maintaining extensive corruption networks that protected the enterprise from state and local law enforcement.

Despite widespread knowledge of Capone's criminal leadership, federal prosecutors struggled to develop cases that could survive courtroom scrutiny. Capone insulated himself from direct participation in specific criminal acts while maintaining organizational control through intermediaries and subordinates. Witnesses faced intimidation or elimination, and documentary evidence was scarce due to the organization's sophisticated operational security measures.

Traditional federal charges like Volstead Act violations proved insufficient because Capone avoided direct involvement in alcohol transportation or sales. Conspiracy charges offered some potential, but required proof of specific agreements and overt acts that Capone's compartmentalized organization made difficult to establish. The organization's structure deliberately obscured connections between leadership decisions and operational activities to prevent successful conspiracy prosecutions.

The ultimate prosecution of Capone for income tax evasion, rather than his extensive criminal activities, demonstrated both the ingenuity of federal prosecutors and the inadequacy of existing criminal law to address sophisticated criminal enterprises. While the tax prosecution succeeded in imprisoning Capone, it did not dismantle his organization or address the broader problem of organized crime's infiltration of legitimate business and government.

Innovations In Federal Enforcement Strategy

Prohibition-era law enforcement developed numerous innovations that would later influence the creation of RICO and modern organized crime prosecution strategies. The Treasury Department's Special Intelligence Unit, led by Elmer Irey, pioneered financial investigation techniques that traced criminal proceeds through complex money laundering schemes and business operations.

These financial investigations revealed how criminal organizations used legitimate businesses to launder illegal proceeds, provide operational bases, and gain political influence and social respectability. The integration of criminal and legitimate activities created new challenges for law enforcement and suggested the need for legal tools that could address criminal organizations' economic dimensions rather than merely their criminal acts.

Federal agencies also developed sophisticated surveillance and intelligence-gathering capabilities during Prohibition, including wiretapping, undercover operations, and informant networks. These techniques provided insights into criminal organizations' structures, operations, and personnel that traditional reactive law enforcement methods could not achieve. However, existing criminal law limited prosecutors' ability to use this intelligence effectively in court.

The creation of joint federal-state task forces during Prohibition established precedent for coordinated law enforcement responses to organized crime that crossed jurisdictional boundaries. These cooperative arrangements demonstrated the necessity of federal leadership and resources for addressing criminal organizations that operated across multiple states and corrupted local law enforcement agencies.

Constitutional And Legal Developments

Prohibition-era prosecutions generated important constitutional precedents that expanded federal criminal jurisdiction and prosecution powers. The Supreme Court's decision in United States v.

Sullivan (1927) established that income from illegal activities was subject to federal taxation, providing legal foundation for tax prosecutions of criminal figures and creating requirements for financial record-keeping that facilitated subsequent investigations.

The Court's conspiracy jurisprudence also evolved during this period to address challenges posed by complex criminal organizations. Cases like Pinkerton v. United States (1946), though decided after Prohibition's end, established that conspirators could be held liable for reasonably foreseeable crimes committed by co-conspirators in furtherance of the conspiracy, even without direct participation or knowledge of specific acts.

These developments reflected broader expansion of federal criminal jurisdiction based on interstate commerce and taxation powers. The Supreme Court's increasingly broad interpretation of congressional authority provided constitutional foundation for federal intervention in criminal matters traditionally governed by state law, setting precedent for subsequent organized crime legislation.

Prohibition-era cases also established important procedural precedents for complex conspiracy prosecutions, including venue rules, joinder provisions, and evidence standards that facilitated prosecution of multi-defendant cases involving extensive criminal organizations. These procedural innovations became essential tools for subsequent organized crime prosecutions.

THE KEFAUVER COMMITTEE AND ORGANIZED CRIME RECOGNITION (1950-1951)

Television And Public Awareness

The Special Committee to Investigate Crime in Interstate Commerce, chaired by Senator Estes Kefauver of Tennessee, conducted the first comprehensive federal investigation of organized crime and brought the issue to unprecedented public attention through televised hearings in 1950-1951. The committee's dramatic public sessions, featuring reluctant witnesses taking the Fifth Amendment and revealing details of criminal organizations' operations, created widespread public awareness of organized crime's extent and influence.

The Kefauver Committee hearings represented a watershed moment in American understanding of organized crime, transforming it from a local law enforcement problem to a national security issue requiring federal intervention. The televised proceedings reached millions of Americans and generated enormous public pressure for effective government responses to organized criminal activity.

The committee's investigation documented extensive criminal organizations operating across state boundaries with sophisticated organizational structures, division of labor, and coordination mechanisms that resembled legitimate business enterprises. These revelations challenged previous assumptions about crime as primarily individual or localized activity and demonstrated the need for new legal tools to address organized criminal enterprises.

The hearings also revealed extensive corruption of public officials at federal, state, and local levels, showing how criminal organizations used systematic bribery and intimidation to protect their operations from law enforcement interference. This documentation of systemic corruption provided political justification for federal intervention in criminal matters traditionally handled by state and local authorities.

Findings And Recommendations

The Kefauver Committee's final report concluded that organized crime constituted a serious national problem requiring coordinated federal response. The committee documented criminal organizations' involvement in gambling, narcotics trafficking, labor racketeering, and business infiltration that generated billions of dollars in illegal revenue while corrupting legitimate institutions.

The committee identified several factors that enabled organized crime's growth and persistence: inadequate coordination among law enforcement agencies, corruption of public officials, organizations' sophisticated structures that insulated leaders from prosecution, and legal tools insufficient to address criminal enterprises rather than individual criminal acts. These findings provided intellectual foundation for subsequent organized crime legislation.

The report's recommendations included strengthened federal law enforcement agencies, improved coordination mechanisms, enhanced financial investigation capabilities, and new legal tools specifically designed to combat organized criminal enterprises. While not explicitly proposing RICO-type legislation, the committee's analysis identified the basic problems that RICO would later address.

The committee also recommended federal legislation addressing specific organized crime activities like interstate gambling, racketeering, and corruption of public officials. Some of these recommendations were implemented in subsequent years, while others awaited the comprehensive approach that RICO would eventually provide.

Legislative And Administrative Responses

The Kefauver Committee's work generated immediate legislative and administrative responses, though comprehensive organized crime legislation would not emerge for another two decades. The Revenue Act of 1951 imposed federal excise taxes on gambling activities, providing new tools for federal prosecution of gambling operations through tax violations.

The Immigration and Nationality Act of 1952 created new grounds for deporting aliens involved in organized crime activities, addressing concerns about foreign influence in American criminal organizations. These measures reflected growing recognition that organized crime required specialized legal tools beyond traditional criminal statutes.

Administrative responses included creation of the Organized Crime and Racketeering Section within the Justice Department in 1954, providing dedicated prosecutorial resources for complex organized crime cases. The FBI also increased its attention to organized crime, though J. Edgar Hoover's long-standing denial of organized crime's existence limited the Bureau's effectiveness until the 1960s.

The committee's work also influenced state and local law enforcement agencies, many of which created specialized organized crime units and improved intelligence-sharing mechanisms. However, the committee's findings clearly established that effective organized crime control required federal leadership and resources beyond state and local capabilities.

THE MCCLELLAN COMMITTEE AND LABOR RACKETEERING (1957-1960)

Exposing Labor Union Corruption

The Select Committee on Improper Activities in Labor and Management, chaired by **Senator John McClellan** of Arkansas, conducted extensive investigations of labor union corruption and organized crime infiltration that built upon the Kefauver Committee's foundation. The McClellan Committee's work, featuring **Robert F. Kennedy** as chief counsel, exposed systematic racketeering in major labor unions and demonstrated organized crime's sophisticated penetration of legitimate institutions.

The committee's investigation of the **International Brotherhood of Teamsters** revealed extensive corruption, including misuse of union funds, violent intimidation of union members, and coordination between union leaders and organized crime figures. The dramatic confrontations between Robert Kennedy and **Teamsters President Jimmy Hoffa** became symbolic of broader struggles between law enforcement and organized crime.

These investigations documented how organized crime used labor unions as sources of funding, legitimate fronts for criminal activities, and vehicles for infiltrating legitimate businesses through control of labor supplies and pension funds. The committee showed how criminal organizations exploited union structures to gain economic and political power that extended far beyond traditional criminal activities.

The McClellan Committee's work also revealed sophisticated money laundering operations involving union pension funds, legitimate businesses, and complex financial arrangements that made it difficult to trace criminal proceeds or establish legal liability for organizational leaders. These findings highlighted the inadequacy of existing criminal law to address complex financial crimes and organizational structures.

The Hoffa Investigation and Prosecutorial Innovations

The committee's investigation of **Jimmy Hoffa and the Teamsters Union** led to innovative prosecutorial strategies that prefigured later RICO prosecutions. **Robert Kennedy's Justice Department** developed new approaches to organized crime prosecution that emphasized long-term investigations, sophisticated financial analysis, and coordination among multiple federal agencies.

The Hoffa prosecutions introduced systematic use of electronic surveillance, undercover operations, and witness protection programs that became standard tools in organized crime cases. These investigative techniques provided insights into criminal organizations' internal operations and decision-making processes that traditional law enforcement methods could not achieve.

Kennedy's prosecution strategy also emphasized disruption of criminal organizations' economic activities rather than merely punishing individual criminal acts. This approach recognized that effective organized crime control required dismantling criminal enterprises' economic foundations, not just imprisoning particular individuals who could be replaced.

The Hoffa cases also demonstrated the potential of conspiracy charges for reaching organizational leaders who avoided direct participation in specific criminal acts. However, they also revealed conspiracy law's limitations in addressing ongoing criminal enterprises that survived individual prosecutions and continued operations with replacement personnel.

Legislative Outcomes: The Landrum-Griffin Act

The McClellan Committee's work led directly to passage of **the Labor-Management Reporting and Disclosure Act of 1959 (Landrum-Griffin Act),** which created new federal oversight mechanisms for labor unions and established criminal penalties for union corruption. This legislation represented significant federal intervention in labor relations and established precedent for using federal criminal law to address corruption in private organizations.

The Landrum-Griffin Act included provisions requiring detailed financial reporting by labor unions, establishing democratic procedures for union governance, and creating criminal penalties for embezzlement of union funds and other forms of corruption. These provisions demonstrated how federal criminal law could address organizational misconduct through regulatory requirements backed by criminal sanctions.

The Act also included provisions addressing organized crime infiltration of labor unions, including prohibitions on union leadership by persons with certain criminal convictions and requirements for reporting relationships between union officials and employers. These provisions recognized that effective organized crime control required legal tools specifically designed to prevent criminal penetration of legitimate institutions.

While **the Landrum-Griffin Act** addressed labor union corruption specifically, its approach of combining regulatory oversight with criminal penalties prefigured RICO's more comprehensive approach to addressing criminal organizations across various sectors of the economy.

THE JOHNSON ADMINISTRATION AND FEDERAL CRIME INITIATIVES (1963-1969)

The President's Commission on Law Enforcement

President Lyndon Johnson's Commission on Law Enforcement and Administration of Justice, established in 1965, conducted the most comprehensive federal study of crime and criminal justice since the **Kefauver Committee.** The Commission's Task Force on Organized Crime produced detailed analysis of criminal organizations' structures, operations, and impact that provided intellectual foundation for subsequent organized crime legislation.

The Commission's report, **"The Challenge of Crime in a Free Society" (1967),** documented organized crime's evolution into sophisticated criminal enterprises that resembled legitimate corporations in their organizational complexity and management sophistication. The report identified organized crime as a serious national problem requiring federal intervention and new legal tools specifically designed to address criminal enterprises.

The Task Force on Organized Crime, chaired by Professor G. Robert Blakey of Notre Dame Law School, developed a detailed analysis of existing legal tools' inadequacies in addressing organized criminal enterprises. This analysis identified the basic conceptual framework that would later be incorporated into RICO, including enterprise liability, pattern requirements, and forfeiture provisions.

The Commission's work also documented organized crime's increasing infiltration of legitimate businesses and its use of violence and corruption to protect criminal operations. These findings demonstrated that organized crime posed threats to economic competition, democratic governance, and rule of law that justified extraordinary legal responses.

Robert Kennedy's Justice Department Initiatives

Robert Kennedy's tenure as Attorney General (1961-1964) marked a turning point in federal organized crime enforcement, as the Justice Department made organized crime a top priority and developed sophisticated prosecution strategies that would influence subsequent legislation. Kennedy's approach emphasized long-term investigations, coordination among federal agencies, and innovative use of existing legal tools.

The Justice Department's Organized Crime and Racketeering Section, expanded under Kennedy's leadership, developed systematic approaches to organized crime prosecution that included financial investigations, electronic surveillance, and witness protection programs. These initiatives demonstrated federal law enforcement's potential effectiveness against organized crime when adequate resources and coordination were provided.

Kennedy's prosecution strategy also emphasized targeting organized crime's economic activities and legitimate business infiltration rather than merely addressing traditional criminal acts like gambling and loan sharking. This approach recognized that organized crime's greatest threat came from its corruption of legitimate institutions and economic competition.

The Justice Department's work during this period also revealed existing criminal law's limitations in addressing complex criminal enterprises. Traditional criminal statutes focused on individual acts rather than organizational behavior, making it difficult to dismantle criminal enterprises or hold leaders accountable for organizational activities.

The Omnibus Crime Control and Safe Streets Act

The Omnibus Crime Control and Safe Streets Act of 1968 represented the Johnson Administration's comprehensive response to rising crime rates and public concerns about law and order. While not specifically addressing organized crime, the Act included provisions that would prove essential for subsequent organized crime prosecutions, particularly regarding electronic surveillance and federal-state law enforcement cooperation.

Title III of the Act established a comprehensive federal framework for court-authorized electronic surveillance in criminal investigations, providing law enforcement with powerful tools for penetrating organized crime's secretive operations. These wiretapping provisions became essential components of organized crime prosecutions and provided crucial evidence for understanding criminal organizations' structures and operations.

The Act also created the **Law Enforcement Assistance Administration (LEAA),** which provided federal funding for state and local law enforcement agencies and encouraged adoption of federal prosecution strategies and priorities. This federal-state cooperation mechanism proved crucial for addressing organized crime activities that crossed jurisdictional boundaries.

The Safe Streets Act's emphasis on comprehensive crime control and federal-state cooperation reflected growing recognition that effective law enforcement required coordinated responses and specialized tools beyond traditional criminal statutes. These themes would be central to RICO's subsequent development and implementation.

THE CREATION OF RICO: LEGISLATIVE HISTORY AND POLITICAL DYNAMICS (1967-1970)

G. Robert Blakey and the Intellectual Foundation

Professor G. Robert Blakey of Notre Dame Law School played the central role in conceiving and drafting RICO, drawing upon his experience with the Johnson Administration's crime commission and his academic expertise in criminal law and evidence. Blakey's background included service with **the Justice Department's Organized Crime** and Racketeering Section, providing practical understanding of existing law's limitations in addressing criminal enterprises.

Blakey's conceptual framework for RICO addressed three fundamental problems with existing criminal law: the inability to prosecute criminal organizations as entities distinct from individual participants, the difficulty of reaching organizational leaders who avoided direct participation in specific criminal acts, and the absence of effective remedies for dismantling criminal enterprises and preventing their reconstitution.

The RICO concept drew upon various legal precedents, including antitrust law's enterprise liability provisions, tax law's pattern requirements for demonstrating ongoing business activities, and forfeiture law's remedies for separating criminals from their illegal proceeds. This synthesis created a novel approach that addressed organized crime's distinctive characteristics while building upon established legal principles.

Blakey's academic analysis also emphasized the economic dimensions of organized crime, arguing that effective control required legal tools specifically designed to address criminal enterprises' business activities rather than merely their criminal acts. This economic focus reflected a growing understanding of organized crime as sophisticated business organizations that used criminal methods to gain competitive advantages and market control.

Congressional Consideration And Political Support

RICO was introduced as **Title IX of the Organized Crime Control Act of 1970,** representing the Nixon Administration's comprehensive organized crime initiative. The legislation received broad bipartisan support based on widespread recognition that organized crime posed serious threats to democratic governance and economic competition that existing legal tools could not address effectively.

Congressional hearings on the **Organized Crime Control Act** featured extensive testimony from law enforcement officials, prosecutors, and academic experts documenting organized crime's growth and sophistication during the 1960s. This testimony emphasized the inadequacy of existing criminal statutes and the need for new legal tools specifically designed to address criminal enterprises.

The Senate Judiciary Committee's report on the legislation provided detailed analysis of RICO's provisions and their relationship to existing criminal law. The report emphasized that RICO was designed to supplement rather than replace traditional criminal statutes, providing prosecutors with additional tools for addressing criminal organizations while preserving individual rights and procedural protections.

Congressional consideration of RICO also addressed constitutional concerns about the legislation's broad scope and potential for prosecutorial abuse. Supporters argued that RICO's enterprise and pattern requirements provided adequate limitations on prosecutorial discretion, while critics worried about the statute's potential application to legitimate political and business activities.

The Nixon Administration's Support

The Nixon Administration made organized crime control a central component of its law and order agenda, providing crucial political support for RICO's passage. President Nixon's special message to Congress on organized crime in April 1969 identified organized crime as a serious national security threat requiring comprehensive federal response.

The Administration's support for RICO reflected broader political calculations about crime and law enforcement during a period of social unrest and rising crime rates. Organized crime control offered politically attractive targets that united conservative and liberal constituencies around effective law enforcement while avoiding controversial issues like civil rights and anti-war protests.

Attorney General John Mitchell and other Administration officials provided strong support for RICO during congressional consideration, emphasizing the legislation's potential effectiveness against criminal organizations that traditional law enforcement had failed to control. This high-level political support proved crucial for overcoming opposition and securing passage.

The Administration's organized crime initiative also included other significant legislation, including the **Racketeer Influenced and Corrupt Organizations Act,** witness protection provisions, and enhanced grand jury procedures. This comprehensive approach demonstrated federal commitment to addressing organized crime through multiple legal and administrative mechanisms.

Legislative Compromises And Final Passage

The final version of RICO reflected various compromises designed to address constitutional concerns and limit potential for prosecutorial abuse while preserving the statute's effectiveness against criminal organizations. These compromises included specific definitions of racketeering activity, enterprise, and pattern requirements that provided some limitations on RICO's scope.

The definition of **"racketeering activity"** was limited to specific federal and state crimes listed in the statute, preventing prosecutors from using RICO for minor offenses or technical violations. The "enterprise" requirement was designed to ensure that RICO addressed ongoing organizations rather than ad hoc criminal agreements that traditional conspiracy law could handle adequately.

The **"pattern of racketeering activity"** requirement, defining pattern as at least two racketeering acts within ten years, was intended to ensure that RICO addressed ongoing criminal enterprises rather than isolated criminal incidents. However, this requirement proved somewhat ambiguous and generated extensive litigation regarding its precise meaning and application.

The final legislation also included forfeiture provisions designed to separate criminals from their illegal proceeds and prevent criminal enterprises from using illegal profits to expand their operations or corrupt legitimate institutions. These forfeiture provisions represented innovative approaches to criminal remedies that emphasized economic disruption rather than merely individual punishment.

RICO'S EARLY IMPLEMENTATION AND JUDICIAL INTERPRETATION (1970-1980)

Initial Prosecutorial Reluctance

Despite RICO's passage in 1970, federal prosecutors initially showed reluctance to use the new statute, preferring familiar criminal charges and traditional prosecution strategies. This reluctance reflected concerns about RICO's complexity, uncertainty about judicial interpretation of its novel provisions, and institutional resistance to change within federal law enforcement agencies.

The Justice Department's Organized Crime and Racketeering Section, which should have been RICO's primary users, initially focused on traditional organized crime prosecutions using conventional criminal statutes supplemented by enhanced investigative techniques. This conservative approach reflected prosecutorial preference for proven strategies over experimental legislation with uncertain judicial reception.

Early RICO prosecutions were relatively few and often unsuccessful, as prosecutors struggled to understand the statute's requirements and develop effective litigation strategies. Federal judges also showed uncertainty about RICO's scope and application, leading to inconsistent rulings that further discouraged prosecutorial use of the statute.

The initial reluctance to use RICO also reflected broader institutional factors within federal law enforcement, including limited resources for complex long-term investigations, inadequate training on the new statute's requirements, and organizational incentives that favored quick convictions over lengthy enterprise prosecutions.

Judicial Development Of RICO Doctrine

Early federal court decisions regarding RICO established important precedents that would shape the statute's subsequent development and application. These cases addressed fundamental questions about RICO's scope, including the meaning of "enterprise," "pattern of racketeering activity," and the relationship between RICO and existing criminal law.

The Second Circuit's decision in **United States v. Turkette (1981),** affirmed by the Supreme Court, established that RICO applied to purely criminal enterprises as well as legitimate businesses infiltrated by organized crime. This interpretation significantly expanded RICO's potential scope beyond its original organized crime focus to include various forms of criminal organizations.

Other early cases addressed the pattern requirement, with courts struggling to define what constituted a sufficient showing of ongoing criminal activity to justify RICO prosecution. Some courts required showing of continuing threats or closed periods of activity, while others adopted more flexible approaches that facilitated prosecutorial use of the statute.

Civil RICO litigation also emerged during this period, as private parties began using RICO's civil remedies to address various forms of commercial fraud and business misconduct. This development, largely unforeseen by RICO's drafters, significantly expanded the statute's impact beyond criminal law enforcement to include private commercial litigation.

The Turkette Decision And Criminal Enterprises

The Supreme Court's decision in **United States v. Turkette (1981)** resolved one of the most important questions about RICO's scope by holding that the statute applied to purely criminal enterprises as well as legitimate businesses infiltrated by organized crime. This interpretation rejected arguments that RICO required some form of legitimate business activity and established that criminal organizations themselves could constitute "enterprises" under the statute.

The Turkette decision significantly expanded RICO's potential applications by enabling prosecution of various criminal organizations that operated without legitimate business fronts. This interpretation made RICO available for prosecuting street gangs, drug trafficking organizations, and other criminal groups that previous interpretations might have excluded.

The Court's reasoning emphasized RICO's text and structure, noting that the statute's definition of enterprise included "any individual, partnership, corporation, association, or other legal entity, and any union or group of individuals associated in fact although not a legal entity." This broad language suggested congressional intent to reach various forms of criminal organization.

The Turkette decision also established important precedents for analyzing RICO's relationship to other criminal statutes, holding that RICO was designed to supplement rather than replace existing criminal law. This interpretation enabled prosecutors to use RICO in conjunction with other charges while avoiding double jeopardy problems.

Expansion Beyond Traditional Organized Crime

During the 1970s and early 1980s, RICO prosecution began expanding beyond traditional organized crime to include various forms of white-collar crime, public corruption, and business fraud. This expansion reflected both prosecutorial creativity in applying RICO's broad language and judicial willingness to interpret the statute flexibly to address various forms of criminal enterprise.

Early white-collar RICO cases included prosecutions of corrupt political organizations, fraudulent business schemes, and complex financial crimes that involved ongoing criminal activity by organized groups. These cases demonstrated RICO's potential applicability beyond traditional organized crime to various forms of sophisticated criminal activity.

The expansion of RICO also reflected changing patterns of criminal activity, as traditional organized crime evolved and new forms of criminal organization emerged. Drug trafficking organizations, white-collar crime networks, and international criminal groups often exhibited characteristics that made RICO prosecution appropriate even though they differed from traditional organized crime families.

This expansion also generated controversy about RICO's appropriate scope and potential for prosecutorial overreach. Critics argued that RICO was being used against defendants and activities that Congress had not intended to address, while supporters contended that the statute's broad language reflected congressional intent to provide flexible tools for addressing various forms of criminal organization.

RICO'S MATURATION AND MODERN APPLICATIONS (1980-PRESENT)

The Sedima Decision And Civil RICO Explosion

The Supreme Court's decision in **Sedima, S.P.R.L. v. Imrex Co. (1985)** removed significant limitations on civil RICO litigation and triggered an explosion of private RICO cases that far exceeded criminal prosecutions in number and impact. The Court rejected requirements for prior criminal convictions and competitive injury that lower courts had imposed, making civil RICO available for various commercial disputes.

The Sedima decision interpreted RICO's civil provisions broadly, holding that private parties could recover treble damages for injuries caused by racketeering activity without showing prior criminal convictions or competitive injury. This interpretation made civil RICO an attractive remedy for various forms of commercial fraud and business misconduct.

The explosion of civil RICO litigation following Sedima generated significant controversy about the statute's appropriate scope and impact on legitimate business activities. Critics argued that civil RICO was being used to transform ordinary commercial disputes into federal racketeering cases, while supporters contended that the statute provided essential remedies for sophisticated fraud schemes.

Congress considered various proposals to limit civil RICO during the 1980s and 1990s, but none were enacted due to disagreements about appropriate limitations and strong support for RICO's anti-fraud functions. The continuing availability of civil RICO remedies thus became a permanent feature of American commercial law.

White-Collar Crime And Financial Fraud

RICO prosecution of white-collar crime expanded significantly during the 1980s and 1990s, as prosecutors applied the statute to various forms of financial fraud, corporate misconduct, and professional corruption. These cases demonstrated RICO's effectiveness against sophisticated criminal schemes that involved ongoing patterns of fraudulent activity.

Major white-collar RICO prosecutions included cases against savings and loan executives during the S&L crisis, securities fraud schemes involving investment advisors and broker-dealers, and healthcare fraud networks involving multiple providers and institutions. These cases showed RICO's utility for addressing complex financial crimes that traditional fraud statutes could not reach effectively.

The application of RICO to white-collar crime also raised important questions about the statute's relationship to regulatory enforcement and administrative proceedings. Courts generally held that RICO prosecution could proceed alongside regulatory enforcement, but expressed concerns about potential conflicts between criminal and regulatory approaches to misconduct.

White-collar RICO cases also demonstrated the importance of forfeiture provisions for separating criminals from their illegal proceeds and deterring future misconduct. The ability to forfeit assets derived from racketeering activity provided powerful incentives for cooperation and plea bargaining while ensuring that criminals did not profit from their illegal activities.

Drug Trafficking Organizations And Continuing Criminal Enterprise

RICO's application to drug trafficking organizations represented one of its most significant modern uses, as prosecutors found the statute particularly effective against sophisticated drug distribution networks that exhibited enterprise characteristics. Drug trafficking organizations often possessed the organizational structure, division of labor, and ongoing operations that made RICO prosecution appropriate and effective.

The relationship between RICO and the **Continuing Criminal Enterprise (CCE) statute (21 USC § 848)** created some prosecutorial choices, as both statutes addressed ongoing criminal organizations involved in drug trafficking. RICO's broader scope and more flexible requirements often made it preferable to CCE for complex drug cases involving multiple types of criminal activity.

Major drug trafficking RICO prosecutions included cases against international cartels, domestic distribution networks, and prison-based drug organizations. These cases demonstrated RICO's effectiveness in reaching organizational leaders who insulated themselves from direct participation in drug transactions while maintaining control over criminal enterprises.

The forfeiture provisions of RICO proved particularly valuable in drug cases, enabling prosecutors to seize assets derived from drug trafficking and disrupt organizations' financial operations. The combination of criminal penalties and asset forfeiture provided comprehensive remedies for dismantling drug trafficking enterprises.

International And Terrorism Applications

RICO's application expanded to include international criminal organizations and terrorism-related prosecutions, particularly following the **September 11, 2001** attacks and increased focus on transnational crime. These applications tested RICO's flexibility and demonstrated its continued relevance for addressing evolving criminal threats.

International RICO prosecutions included cases against transnational organized crime groups, international fraud schemes, and cross-border criminal enterprises. These cases raised complex jurisdictional questions about RICO's extraterritorial application and the statute's relationship to international law and foreign sovereignty.

Terrorism-related RICO cases emerged following 9/11, as prosecutors sought to use the statute against terrorist organizations and their financial support networks. While specific terrorism statutes often provided more appropriate charges, RICO's enterprise and forfeiture provisions offered additional tools for dismantling terrorist organizations and their funding mechanisms.

The application of RICO to international and terrorism cases also demonstrated the statute's evolution beyond its original organized crime focus to address various forms of criminal organization that threatened American security and economic interests. This expansion reflected both RICO's flexibility and the changing nature of criminal threats facing the United States.

CONSTITUTIONAL CHALLENGES AND JUDICIAL LIMITATIONS

Due Process And Vagueness Challenges

RICO faced numerous constitutional challenges during its development, particularly regarding due process requirements and claims that the statute was unconstitutionally vague. Critics argued that RICO's broad language and complex requirements failed to provide adequate notice of prohibited conduct and created potential for arbitrary enforcement.

The Supreme Court generally rejected vagueness challenges to RICO, holding in cases like **Scheidler v. National Organization for Women (2003)** that the statute's core terms were sufficiently defined to meet constitutional requirements. The Court emphasized that RICO incorporated well-established criminal law concepts and provided adequate guidance for both prosecutors and defendants.

Due process challenges to RICO also addressed the statute's relationship to underlying predicate offenses and the potential for double jeopardy when defendants were prosecuted for both RICO violations and predicate crimes. Courts generally held that RICO and predicate offenses contained different elements and served different purposes, avoiding double jeopardy problems.

However, courts did recognize some limitations on RICO prosecution to address due process concerns. The requirement that prosecutors prove a "pattern of racketeering activity" provided some limitation on RICO's scope, and courts developed various tests for determining when predicate acts demonstrated sufficient continuity and relationship to constitute a pattern.

First Amendment And Political Activity

RICO prosecutions involving political organizations and protest groups raised significant First Amendment concerns about the statute's potential impact on legitimate political activity and freedom of association. Cases involving anti-abortion protesters, environmental activists, and other political groups tested RICO's boundaries regarding protected speech and political conduct.

The Supreme Court's decision in **Scheidler v. National Organization for Women** addressed some of these concerns by holding that RICO required an economic motive for the predicate acts, limiting the statute's application to some forms of political protest. However, this decision was later overruled in part, leaving some uncertainty about RICO's application to political activities.

Courts developed various approaches to addressing First Amendment concerns in RICO cases, including requirements for careful jury instructions regarding protected speech and association, limitations on the use of political speech as evidence of criminal intent, and enhanced scrutiny of prosecutions that might chill legitimate political activity.

The tension between RICO enforcement and First Amendment protections remains an ongoing concern, particularly in cases involving political organizations, labor unions, and other groups that engage in both legitimate advocacy and potentially criminal conduct. Courts continue to balance law enforcement needs against constitutional protections for political activity.

Commerce Clause And Federalism Concerns

RICO's broad scope raised federalism concerns about federal intrusion into criminal matters traditionally governed by state law. Critics argued that RICO enabled federal prosecution of essentially local criminal activity based on tenuous connections to interstate commerce, undermining traditional state authority over criminal law.

The Supreme Court's commerce clause jurisprudence generally supported RICO's constitutionality, holding that the statute appropriately addressed criminal activity that affected interstate commerce through its economic impact and multi-jurisdictional character. The Court emphasized that organized crime typically involved interstate activities that justified federal jurisdiction.

However, some lower courts expressed concerns about RICO's application to purely local criminal activity and developed various tests for ensuring adequate interstate commerce connections. These limitations helped address federalism concerns while preserving RICO's effectiveness against truly interstate criminal enterprises.

The federalism debate regarding RICO reflected broader tensions about federal criminal law's expansion during the late twentieth century and concerns about the appropriate balance between federal and state authority over criminal matters. These tensions continue to influence judicial interpretation of RICO and other federal criminal statutes.

CONSPIRACY LAW EVOLUTION ALONGSIDE RICO

Modern Conspiracy Doctrine Development

While RICO addressed criminal enterprises specifically, traditional conspiracy law continued to evolve alongside RICO to address various forms of coordinated criminal activity. Modern conspiracy doctrine incorporated lessons from RICO prosecutions while maintaining its role as a fundamental tool for addressing criminal agreements and coordination.

The Pinkerton doctrine, establishing co-conspirator liability for reasonably foreseeable crimes committed in furtherance of conspiracy, became increasingly important as criminal organizations grew more sophisticated and compartmentalized. This doctrine enabled prosecutors to reach organizational leaders based on their participation in criminal agreements even when they avoided direct involvement in specific criminal acts.

Modern conspiracy law also developed enhanced procedures for complex multi-defendant cases, including liberal joinder rules, venue provisions allowing prosecution where any overt act occurred, and evidence rules permitting admission of co-conspirator statements. These procedural innovations facilitated prosecution of large criminal organizations while maintaining individual due process protections.

The relationship between conspiracy law and RICO created some prosecutorial choices, as many cases could be charged under either or both statutes. Conspiracy charges often provided simpler alternatives to RICO prosecution while RICO offered additional penalties and remedies for complex criminal enterprises.

The Continuing Criminal Enterprise Statute

The Continuing Criminal Enterprise (CCE) statute, enacted as part of the **Comprehensive Drug Abuse Prevention and Control Act of 1970,** provided another approach to addressing ongoing criminal organizations specifically focused on drug trafficking. CCE shared some conceptual similarities with RICO but applied specifically to drug trafficking enterprises.

CCE required proof that defendants organized, managed, or supervised a continuing series of drug trafficking violations involving five or more persons and substantial income. The statute provided severe penalties including mandatory life imprisonment for principal administrators of drug enterprises and extensive forfeiture provisions.

The relationship between CCE and RICO created prosecutorial choices in drug cases, with prosecutors often preferring RICO due to its broader scope and more flexible requirements. However, CCE's drug-specific focus and severe penalties made it appropriate for major drug trafficking prosecutions involving substantial organizations.

CCE prosecutions also contributed to the development of enterprise criminal law by providing judicial precedents regarding organizational structure, leadership roles, and the relationship between individual criminal acts and ongoing criminal enterprises. These precedents influenced both RICO interpretation and broader criminal law doctrine.

State RICO Statutes And Parallel Development

Many states enacted their own RICO statutes modeled on the federal law, creating parallel systems for addressing organized crime and criminal enterprises at the state level. These state statutes generally followed the federal model while adapting to local criminal law traditions and constitutional requirements.

State RICO statutes enabled prosecution of criminal enterprises that operated primarily within single states or involved criminal activities not covered by federal law. They also provided alternatives when federal prosecutors declined to pursue cases or when state prosecutors preferred to maintain local control over investigations and prosecutions.

The development of state RICO laws also influenced federal RICO interpretation, as courts considered how different jurisdictions addressed similar legal issues and whether federal and state approaches should remain consistent. This cross-fertilization helped refine RICO doctrine and its application to various types of criminal activity.

State RICO prosecutions also demonstrated the statute's versatility and effectiveness across different legal systems and criminal justice contexts. The widespread adoption of RICO-type legislation at the state level confirmed the utility of enterprise criminal law concepts for addressing modern criminal organizations.

CRITIQUES AND REFORM PROPOSALS

Overcriminalization And Prosecutorial Power

Critics of RICO and modern conspiracy law argued that these statutes contributed to overcriminalization by creating broad criminal liability for various forms of coordinated activity that might be addressed through civil remedies or regulatory enforcement. The expansion of federal criminal jurisdiction raised concerns about prosecutorial power and the appropriate scope of criminal law.

The broad scope of RICO and conspiracy law enabled prosecutors to charge individuals with serious federal crimes based on relatively minor predicate acts or peripheral involvement in criminal organizations. Critics argued that this prosecutorial flexibility created potential for abuse and undermined proportionality in criminal punishment.

Academic critics also argued that RICO and conspiracy law's emphasis on organizational membership rather than individual culpability conflicted with traditional criminal law principles emphasizing personal responsibility and individual guilt. The collective liability aspects of these statutes raised questions about fundamental criminal law assumptions.

Reform proposals included various limitations on RICO and conspiracy prosecutions, such as requirements for more substantial individual culpability, restrictions on prosecuting peripheral participants, and enhanced judicial oversight of prosecutorial charging decisions. However, most reform proposals failed to gain political support due to law enforcement opposition.

Civil Rights And Selective Enforcement

Civil rights advocates argued that RICO and conspiracy prosecutions disproportionately affected minority communities and political organizations, creating potential for discriminatory enforcement and suppression of legitimate political activity. Statistical analyses showed racial disparities in RICO prosecutions similar to those found in other areas of federal criminal law.

The use of RICO against street gangs, drug trafficking organizations, and other criminal groups that predominantly involved minority defendants raised concerns about selective enforcement and the criminalization of associational activity in minority communities. Critics argued that similar organizational activity in white communities received different treatment.

Political organizations also faced RICO prosecutions that raised concerns about the statute's impact on legitimate political activity and freedom of association. Cases involving anti-abortion protesters, environmental activists, and other political groups demonstrated RICO's potential for suppressing political dissent.

Reform proposals addressed these concerns through various approaches including enhanced oversight of prosecutorial charging decisions, requirements for demonstrating non-discriminatory enforcement, and limitations on RICO's application to political activities. However, implementing such reforms proved difficult due to disagreements about appropriate standards and enforcement mechanisms.

Economic Impact And Business Community Concerns

The business community raised concerns about RICO's impact on legitimate business activities, particularly through civil RICO litigation that could result in treble damages and attorney fee awards for relatively minor misconduct. The threat of RICO liability affected various business decisions and created incentives for costly compliance programs.

Trade associations and business groups argued that RICO's broad scope and severe penalties deterred legitimate business activities and created uncertainty about legal requirements. The statute's application to various forms of commercial activity raised questions about the appropriate boundary between criminal law and business regulation.

Professional organizations also faced RICO prosecutions and civil lawsuits that raised concerns about the statute's impact on professional practices and industry standards. Cases involving healthcare providers, financial professionals, and other licensed practitioners demonstrated RICO's reach into regulated professions.

Reform proposals from business groups included various limitations on civil RICO, such as requirements for prior criminal convictions, enhanced pleading standards, and restrictions on treble damages. Some modest reforms were enacted, but comprehensive changes faced opposition from consumer advocates and law enforcement groups.

CONTEMPORARY SIGNIFICANCE AND FUTURE DIRECTIONS

RICO In The Digital Age

The emergence of cybercrime and digital criminal enterprises has created new applications for RICO as prosecutors adapt the statute to address online criminal organizations and technology-facilitated crime. Internet-based criminal enterprises often exhibit the organizational characteristics and ongoing operations that make RICO prosecution appropriate.

Cybercrime RICO cases have included prosecutions of online fraud networks, digital piracy organizations, and ransomware operations that involve coordinated activity by multiple participants across various jurisdictions. These cases demonstrate RICO's continued relevance for addressing evolving criminal threats.

The international character of many cybercrime organizations has also tested RICO's extraterritorial application and its relationship to international law enforcement cooperation. Prosecutors have used RICO to address criminal enterprises that operate across national boundaries while coordinating with foreign law enforcement agencies.

Digital evidence and cryptocurrency transactions have created new challenges and opportunities for RICO prosecutions, as prosecutors adapt traditional investigative techniques to electronic environments while developing new approaches to tracing criminal proceeds and establishing organizational relationships.

Organized Crime Evolution And Adaptation

Traditional organized crime has evolved significantly since RICO's creation, with criminal organizations adapting their structures and operations to avoid RICO prosecution while maintaining their criminal activities. This evolution has required corresponding adaptations in RICO prosecution strategies and legal interpretation.

Modern organized crime groups often operate with looser organizational structures, reduced hierarchies, and more sophisticated operational security measures designed to limit their vulnerability to RICO prosecution. These adaptations have challenged prosecutors to develop new approaches to proving enterprise existence and criminal patterns.

The globalization of criminal activity has also created new challenges for RICO enforcement, as criminal organizations increasingly operate across national boundaries and exploit differences in legal systems and law enforcement capabilities. International cooperation has become essential for effective RICO prosecution of transnational criminal enterprises.

Emerging criminal threats including human trafficking organizations, international fraud networks, and terrorist financing operations have created new applications for RICO while testing its flexibility and continued relevance for addressing modern criminal challenges.

Legislative And Judicial Refinements

RICO continues to evolve through legislative amendments and judicial interpretation that refine its application while addressing concerns about overreach and constitutional limitations. Recent developments have focused on clarifying the statute's scope and improving its effectiveness against modern criminal threats.

The Supreme Court's recent RICO decisions have generally supported the statute's broad application while establishing some limitations on its scope and requirements for proving enterprise existence and criminal patterns. These decisions have provided greater clarity regarding RICO's elements while maintaining prosecutorial flexibility.

Congressional consideration of RICO amendments has addressed various concerns including civil RICO reform, international application, and coordination with other criminal statutes. While comprehensive reform has proven difficult, targeted amendments have addressed specific problems and improved the statute's effectiveness.

State and federal coordination in RICO enforcement has also evolved, with improved information sharing and joint operations enabling more effective prosecution of criminal enterprises that operate across jurisdictional boundaries. These cooperative arrangements have enhanced RICO's effectiveness while addressing federalism concerns.

CONCLUSION: THE TRANSFORMATION OF AMERICAN CRIMINAL LAW

The creation and development of RICO and federal conspiracy law represents one of the most significant transformations in American criminal law, fundamentally altering how the legal system addresses organized criminal activity and complex criminal enterprises. This evolution from simple conspiracy concepts to sophisticated enterprise criminal law reflects broader changes in American society and the criminal threats it faces.

The historical trajectory from Prohibition-era innovations through RICO's creation demonstrates how legal institutions adapt to address emerging criminal challenges while building upon existing legal foundations. The synthesis of various legal concepts into RICO's comprehensive approach illustrates both the creativity of legal development and the importance of learning from past experiences and limitations.

RICO's impact extends far beyond traditional organized crime to include white-collar fraud, public corruption, terrorism, and various forms of criminal enterprise that characterize modern criminal activity. This broad application demonstrates the statute's flexibility and continued relevance for addressing evolving criminal threats while raising ongoing questions about appropriate scope and constitutional limitations.

The constitutional and policy debates surrounding RICO and conspiracy law reflect fundamental tensions in American criminal justice between effective law enforcement and individual rights protection. These tensions continue to influence the development and application of enterprise criminal law while highlighting the importance of balancing competing values and interests.

The international influence of RICO and American enterprise criminal law concepts has contributed to global efforts to address transnational organized crime and corruption. This international dimension demonstrates how domestic legal innovations can influence global law enforcement while creating new challenges for international cooperation and coordination.

The future development of RICO and conspiracy law will likely continue to reflect the ongoing evolution of criminal activity and law enforcement needs. Digital crime, international terrorism, cybersecurity threats, and other emerging challenges will test these legal tools' flexibility while requiring continued adaptation and refinement.

Understanding the historical development of RICO and federal conspiracy law provides essential context for contemporary criminal law practice and policy development. The lessons learned from this evolution inform current debates about criminal justice reform, prosecutorial power, and the appropriate scope of federal criminal law in addressing complex social problems.

The creation of RICO and the evolution of conspiracy law ultimately represent successful adaptations of American legal institutions to address serious criminal threats while maintaining constitutional protections and democratic values. This achievement demonstrates both the resilience of American legal institutions and the importance of continued vigilance in balancing law enforcement effectiveness with constitutional limitations and individual rights protection.

As American society continues to evolve and face new criminal challenges, the experience of creating and implementing RICO provides valuable lessons about legal innovation, institutional adaptation, and the ongoing need to balance effective law enforcement with constitutional principles and democratic values. The success of this legal transformation offers hope for addressing future challenges while maintaining the rule of law and protecting individual rights in a democratic society.

CHAPTER NINE

FEDERAL FIREARMS LAWS AND THE EMERGENCE OF THE ATF: FROM TAXATION TO REGULATION

INTRODUCTION

The development of federal firearms laws and the emergence of the **Bureau of Alcohol, Tobacco, Firearms and Explosives (ATF)** represents a complex evolution of federal regulatory authority that transformed from revenue collection to comprehensive crime control. This transformation reflects broader changes in American society, including urbanization, technological advancement, changing patterns of violence, and evolving constitutional interpretations of federal power over commerce and individual rights.

The federal government's involvement in firearms regulation began not as crime control but as taxation and revenue generation, rooted in Congress's undisputed constitutional authority to impose taxes and regulate interstate commerce. Over nearly a century, this narrow fiscal authority evolved into comprehensive regulatory oversight that encompasses manufacturing, distribution, possession, and use of firearms throughout the United States.

Understanding this evolution requires examining the historical context that shaped federal firearms policy, including Prohibition-era violence, Depression-era crime waves, assassination attempts on public officials, urban unrest, and changing patterns of criminal violence. Each crisis generated political pressure for enhanced federal involvement while testing constitutional boundaries and public acceptance of federal authority over traditionally local matters.

The emergence of ATF as a dedicated law enforcement agency reflects the growing complexity of federal firearms regulation and the need for specialized expertise in enforcing increasingly sophisticated laws. From its origins as a small unit within the **Treasury Department** focused on tax collection, ATF evolved into a major federal law enforcement agency with broad authority over firearms, explosives, and related criminal activity.

This comprehensive examination traces the development of federal firearms laws from their origins in the Constitution through modern comprehensive regulatory schemes, while analyzing the parallel evolution of ATF from a tax collection unit to a major federal law enforcement agency. The analysis demonstrates how constitutional, political, technological, and social factors combined to create the current federal firearms regulatory system.

Contemporary debates about firearms policy, constitutional interpretation, and federal law enforcement authority cannot be understood without reference to this historical development. The legal precedents, institutional structures, and political compromises established during the creation of federal firearms laws continue to influence policy options and constitutional constraints that shape contemporary firearms regulation.

CONSTITUTIONAL FOUNDATIONS AND EARLY FEDERAL INVOLVEMENT (1789-1900)

Constitutional Framework And Original Understanding

The Constitution's firearms-related provisions reflect the Founding Fathers' complex understanding of the relationship between individual rights, collective security, and federal authority. The Second Amendment's guarantee that **"the right of the people to keep and bear Arms, shall not be infringed"** coexisted with explicit federal powers to regulate commerce, impose taxes, and maintain national defense.

The original understanding of federal authority over firearms was quite limited, reflecting the general assumption that criminal law and public safety remained primarily state and local responsibilities. The federal government's role was largely confined to military affairs, including arming and organizing state militias and regulating firearms trade with foreign nations and Indian tribes.

Early federal involvement in firearms regulation focused primarily on military considerations rather than civilian crime control. **The Militia Acts of 1792 and 1795** required able-bodied male citizens to possess firearms and military equipment for militia service, while trade and intercourse acts regulated firearms sales to Native American tribes to prevent conflicts and maintain diplomatic relations.

The federal government also exercised authority over firearms in federal territories and military installations, establishing precedent for federal regulation in areas of exclusive federal jurisdiction. These early exercises of federal authority demonstrated that constitutional firearms rights were not absolute and could be subject to reasonable regulations serving legitimate governmental purposes.

Early Federal Taxation And Revenue Measures

The federal government's first significant involvement in civilian firearms regulation came through taxation rather than direct regulation, reflecting constitutional limitations on federal police powers and political resistance to federal involvement in local law enforcement matters. Excise taxes on firearms and ammunition provided revenue while creating administrative mechanisms that would later support regulatory enforcement.

The Civil War period witnessed unprecedented federal involvement in firearms matters, including massive federal procurement of weapons, regulation of private arms manufacturing, and restrictions on civilian firearms possession in occupied territories. These wartime measures established precedent for federal involvement in firearms regulation during national emergencies.

Reconstruction-era legislation included provisions addressing firearms possession by freed slaves and restrictions on arms possession by former Confederate military personnel. **The Civil Rights Act of 1866** specifically protected freed slaves' rights to **"keep and bear arms,"** while various Reconstruction statutes restricted firearms possession by persons deemed threats to federal authority.

The development of federal taxation authority during and after the Civil War provided the constitutional foundation for subsequent federal firearms regulation through the tax power. The Supreme Court's broad interpretation of congressional taxation authority in cases like **Veazie Bank v. Fenno (1869)** established that federal taxes could serve regulatory as well as revenue purposes.

Interstate Commerce And Federal Jurisdiction

The expansion of interstate commerce during the late nineteenth century created new opportunities and justifications for federal involvement in firearms regulation. The growth of national markets for firearms and ammunition brought firearms trade within congressional authority to regulate interstate commerce, even when regulatory rather than commercial purposes motivated federal action.

The Interstate Commerce Act of 1887 established precedent for federal regulation of business activities affecting interstate commerce, while **Sherman Antitrust Act of 1890** demonstrated congressional willingness to use commerce power for regulatory rather than purely commercial purposes. These developments provided a constitutional foundation for subsequent federal firearms regulation based on interstate commerce effects.

Federal courts during this period generally upheld federal authority to regulate firearms trade in interstate commerce while recognizing state authority over intrastate firearms regulation and individual rights to possess firearms for lawful purposes. This division of authority between federal and state governments would persist through subsequent developments in federal firearms law.

The Supreme Court's decision in **Presser v. Illinois (1886)** confirmed that the Second Amendment applied only to federal action and did not limit state authority to regulate firearms possession and use. This interpretation provided states with broad authority to regulate firearms while limiting constitutional challenges to federal firearms regulation based on Second Amendment grounds.

PROHIBITION ERA AND THE NATIONAL FIREARMS ACT (1920-1940)

Prohibition Violence And Federal Response

The Prohibition era's unprecedented levels of organized violence created the political context for the first comprehensive federal firearms regulation. Bootleggers' use of automatic weapons, sawed-off shotguns, and other military-style firearms in urban warfare shocked the public and generated demands for federal intervention in firearms regulation.

High-profile incidents like the Saint Valentine's Day Massacre in Chicago demonstrated the inadequacy of state and local law enforcement to address well-armed criminal organizations that operated across state boundaries. The federal government's exclusive authority over interstate commerce and superior investigative resources made federal involvement both constitutionally permissible and practically necessary.

The Treasury Department's involvement in Prohibition enforcement through the Bureau of Prohibition provided an institutional foundation for federal firearms regulation. Treasury agents' encounters with heavily armed bootleggers demonstrated the need for federal authority over weapons commonly used by interstate criminal organizations.

Public opinion surveys during the late 1920s and early 1930s showed strong support for federal regulation of firearms commonly associated with organized crime, even among groups traditionally opposed to federal involvement in law enforcement matters. This public support provided a political foundation for federal legislation that would have been impossible without the Prohibition-era violence crisis.

The National Firearms Act Of 1934

The National Firearms Act (NFA) of 1934 represented the first comprehensive federal firearms regulation, establishing the basic framework and constitutional approach that would govern subsequent federal firearms laws. The NFA's taxation approach avoided direct constitutional challenges while creating comprehensive regulatory oversight of firearms deemed particularly dangerous.

The NFA imposed prohibitive taxes on certain categories of firearms including machine guns, short-barreled rifles and shotguns, silencers, and destructive devices. The $200 tax (equivalent to approximately $4,000 today) made these weapons economically inaccessible to most civilians while creating administrative mechanisms for tracking and regulating their manufacture, transfer, and possession.

The Act's registration requirements created the first federal firearms database, requiring detailed information about regulated weapons and their owners. This registration system provided law enforcement with tools for tracking weapons used in crimes while establishing precedent for federal oversight of civilian firearms possession.

The NFA's enforcement provisions gave Treasury Department agents broad authority to investigate violations, including search and seizure powers that exceeded those available to most federal law enforcement agencies. These enforcement provisions reflected congressional recognition that effective firearms regulation required specialized law enforcement capabilities.

Constitutional Challenges And The Miller Decision

The NFA faced immediate constitutional challenges based on Second Amendment and taxation authority grounds. Critics argued that the Act's prohibitive taxation violated individual rights to keep and bear arms while exceeding congressional authority under the taxation power.

The Supreme Court's decision in **United States v. Miller (1939)** upheld the NFA's constitutionality by establishing that the Second Amendment protected only weapons with "reasonable relationship to the preservation or efficiency of a well regulated militia." The Court's narrow interpretation of Second Amendment rights provided the constitutional foundation for subsequent federal firearms regulation.

The Miller decision also established important precedents regarding federal taxation authority over firearms, holding that regulatory taxes could serve legitimate governmental purposes even when revenue generation was not the primary objective. This interpretation provided a constitutional framework for subsequent federal firearms laws based on taxation authority.

Lower federal courts generally upheld NFA prosecutions while developing important precedents regarding search and seizure, self-incrimination, and due process in federal firearms cases. These decisions established procedural frameworks that would govern subsequent federal firearms enforcement while balancing law enforcement needs against constitutional protections.

Administrative Development And Early Enforcement

The Treasury Department created specialized units to enforce the NFA, beginning the institutional development that would eventually produce ATF as an independent agency. The Alcohol Tax Unit assumed responsibility for NFA enforcement, adding firearms regulation to its existing responsibilities for alcohol taxation and regulation.

Early NFA enforcement focused primarily on organized crime figures and professional criminals who used regulated weapons in interstate criminal activities. This enforcement strategy reflected both practical considerations about limited resources and political considerations about public acceptance of federal firearms regulation.

The development of administrative procedures for NFA compliance created precedent for subsequent federal firearms regulation while testing the practical limits of federal regulatory authority. The complex paperwork requirements, background investigations, and approval processes established administrative frameworks that would be expanded in subsequent firearms laws.

Federal courts developed important precedents regarding NFA enforcement procedures, including standards for search warrants, requirements for proving violations, and penalties for non-compliance. These judicial decisions established legal frameworks that would govern subsequent federal firearms enforcement while protecting individual rights and due process.

WORLD WAR II AND POST-WAR DEVELOPMENTS (1940-1968)

Wartime Firearms Regulation And Federal Authority

World War II dramatically expanded federal involvement in firearms regulation as national security concerns justified unprecedented federal control over civilian firearms possession and commerce. The federal government assumed direct control over firearms manufacturing, imposed restrictions on civilian firearms purchases, and created comprehensive systems for tracking firearms distribution.

The War Powers Acts and related legislation gave the federal government broad authority to regulate civilian economic activity, including firearms manufacturing and distribution. These wartime powers established precedent for federal involvement in firearms regulation that extended beyond traditional taxation and interstate commerce authorities.

Federal agencies developed sophisticated systems for tracking firearms production, distribution, and sales during the war period. These administrative capabilities provided institutional foundation for subsequent peacetime firearms regulation while demonstrating the feasibility of comprehensive federal oversight over firearms commerce.

The federal government's direct involvement in firearms manufacturing during wartime created detailed knowledge of firearms technology and industry practices that informed subsequent regulatory development. Federal agencies' technical expertise in firearms design, manufacturing, and ballistics became essential components of post-war regulatory capabilities.

The Federal Firearms Act Of 1938

The Federal Firearms Act (FFA) of 1938, enacted shortly before the war, extended federal firearms regulation beyond the NFA's focus on specific weapon types to include comprehensive oversight of firearms commerce. The FFA required federal licensing of firearms dealers and imposed restrictions on interstate firearms sales to prohibited persons.

The FFA's licensing system created the first comprehensive federal oversight of firearms commerce, establishing precedent for federal involvement in intrastate as well as interstate firearms transactions.

The licensing requirements gave federal agents authority to inspect dealer records and investigate violations throughout the firearms distribution system.

The Act's prohibited person provisions established federal standards for firearms eligibility that supplemented state law restrictions. These provisions created uniform national standards while maintaining state authority over most criminal law matters affecting firearms eligibility.

Federal courts generally upheld FFA prosecutions while developing important precedents regarding federal authority over intrastate firearms commerce. The Supreme Court's broad interpretation of interstate commerce authority in cases like **Wickard v. Filburn (1942)** provided the constitutional foundation for comprehensive federal firearms regulation regardless of specific interstate connections.

Post-War Crime Concerns And Federal Response

The post-war period brought new concerns about firearms violence as returning veterans struggled with adjustment problems and urban crime rates increased. High-profile incidents involving military weapons and ammunition stockpiled during the war generated public support for enhanced federal firearms regulation.

Congressional investigations during the late 1940s and 1950s documented the flow of military weapons into civilian criminal use, including cases where inadequate federal controls enabled criminals to acquire automatic weapons and military ammunition. These investigations provided a political foundation for strengthening federal firearms regulation.

The development of television and national news media brought firearms violence to unprecedented public attention during the 1950s, creating political pressure for federal action even when incidents occurred within single states. This national media coverage helped build support for federal involvement in traditionally local law enforcement matters.

Federal law enforcement agencies reported increasing involvement in firearms-related investigations during the post-war period, reflecting both increased criminal use of firearms and enhanced federal investigative capabilities. These agencies' reports documented the need for stronger federal firearms laws and improved enforcement mechanisms.

Institutional Development Within Treasury

The Treasury Department's firearms enforcement responsibilities continued to evolve during the post-war period as administrative complexity and enforcement demands increased. The Alcohol Tax Unit's firearms responsibilities gradually expanded while the unit developed specialized expertise in firearms technology and enforcement.

The creation of the **Alcohol and Tobacco Tax Division in 1951** reflected the growing importance of regulatory enforcement relative to pure tax collection. This reorganization provided the institutional foundation for subsequent development of ATF as a primarily regulatory and law enforcement agency rather than a tax collection unit.

Federal agents developed increasingly sophisticated investigative techniques for firearms cases during this period, including ballistics analysis, firearms tracing, and coordination with state and local law enforcement agencies. These technical capabilities became essential components of federal firearms enforcement while establishing ATF's reputation for firearms expertise.

The Treasury Department's reports during this period documented the growing complexity of federal firearms regulation and the need for specialized law enforcement capabilities. These reports provided the administrative foundation for subsequent creation of ATF as an independent agency with comprehensive firearms enforcement authority.

THE GUN CONTROL ACT OF 1968: COMPREHENSIVE FEDERAL REGULATION

The Assassination Crisis And Political Response

The assassinations of President John F. Kennedy in 1963, civil rights leader **Martin Luther King Jr.,** and **Senator Robert F. Kennedy in 1968** created unprecedented political pressure for comprehensive federal firearms regulation. These tragic events demonstrated that existing federal firearms laws were inadequate to prevent firearms access by dangerous individuals while generating overwhelming public support for stronger federal controls.

The Warren Commission's investigation of President Kennedy's assassination revealed significant gaps in federal firearms regulation, including the ease with which **Lee Harvey Oswald** acquired the mail-order rifle used in the assassination. The Commission's recommendations included comprehensive federal firearms regulation to close these gaps and prevent similar incidents.

The urban riots of the mid-1960s and rising violent crime rates created additional political pressure for federal firearms regulation as policymakers sought comprehensive responses to social unrest and criminal violence. The combination of political assassination, urban violence, and rising crime rates generated unprecedented consensus for federal action.

Public opinion polls during the late 1960s showed overwhelming support for comprehensive federal firearms regulation, including majorities among gun owners and traditionally conservative constituencies. This broad public support provided political foundation for legislation that would have been impossible during earlier periods.

Legislative Development And Congressional Consideration

The Gun Control Act of 1968 (GCA) represented the most comprehensive federal firearms legislation in American history, fundamentally transforming federal involvement in firearms regulation from limited taxation to comprehensive regulatory oversight. The Act's development involved extensive congressional hearings, detailed technical analysis, and complex political negotiations among competing interests.

Congressional hearings on the GCA featured extensive testimony from law enforcement officials, firearms industry representatives, civil rights advocates, and constitutional scholars. This testimony documented both the need for comprehensive federal regulation and the constitutional and practical challenges involved in implementing effective firearms controls.

The Act's final provisions reflected complex political compromises between advocates of strict federal controls and defenders of firearms rights and state authority. These compromises shaped the Act's structure while establishing frameworks for subsequent firearms regulation and constitutional interpretation.

The GCA's passage represented a significant expansion of federal regulatory authority based on interstate commerce power rather than taxation. This constitutional approach provided a broader foundation for federal involvement while avoiding some of the limitations and challenges associated with the taxation approach used in earlier firearms laws.

Key Provisions And Regulatory Framework

The GCA established comprehensive federal oversight of firearms commerce through licensing requirements for firearms dealers, manufacturers, and importers. **The Federal Firearms License (FFL)** system created uniform national standards for firearms commerce while providing federal authorities with regulatory oversight and inspection authority.

The Act's prohibited person provisions expanded federal restrictions on firearms possession to include detailed categories of persons deemed ineligible for firearms ownership, including felons, drug users, mental health commitments, and other disqualifying factors. These provisions created uniform national standards while supplementing state law restrictions.

Interstate firearms transfer restrictions required all firearms sales across state lines to be conducted through licensed dealers, effectively ending mail-order firearms sales and creating comprehensive tracking systems for interstate firearms commerce. These provisions addressed specific problems identified in assassination investigations while establishing broad regulatory oversight.

The GCA's importation restrictions limited civilian access to military-style firearms and established federal authority to determine which firearms were suitable for civilian use. These provisions reflected both crime control and domestic industry protection concerns while establishing precedent for federal involvement in firearms design and manufacturing standards.

Enforcement Provisions And Federal Authority

The GCA significantly expanded federal law enforcement authority over firearms matters, including broad inspection powers for licensed dealers, comprehensive record-keeping requirements, and enhanced penalties for firearms violations. These enforcement provisions reflected congressional recognition that effective firearms regulation required substantial federal law enforcement capabilities.

The Act established detailed record-keeping requirements for all licensed firearms dealers, creating comprehensive systems for tracking firearms from manufacture through retail sale. These record-keeping systems provided law enforcement with tools for tracing firearms used in crimes while establishing administrative frameworks for regulatory compliance.

Federal agents received broad authority to inspect licensed dealers' premises and records, enabling systematic enforcement of federal firearms laws throughout the distribution system. These inspection powers represented significant expansion of federal regulatory authority while establishing frameworks for ongoing compliance monitoring.

The GCA's penalty provisions included both criminal sanctions for willful violations and administrative sanctions for regulatory non-compliance. This dual enforcement approach provided flexibility for addressing different types of violations while ensuring that federal authorities had adequate tools for maintaining compliance with federal requirements.

Organizational Development Within Treasury

The passage of **the Gun Control Act** of 1968 dramatically increased the complexity and scope of federal firearms enforcement, creating organizational pressures that led to the creation of ATF as a distinct agency within the Treasury Department. The existing Alcohol and Tobacco Tax Division's firearms responsibilities expanded beyond its administrative capabilities, requiring specialized organizational structures and dedicated personnel.

The Treasury Department's response to these challenges involved gradual organizational evolution beginning with the creation of specialized firearms enforcement units and culminating in the establishment of ATF as an independent agency in 1972. This evolution reflected both practical necessities and broader changes in federal law enforcement organization during the late 1960s and early 1970s.

The Alcohol, Tobacco and Firearms Division was created in 1968 as an intermediate step toward full agency status, combining regulatory and law enforcement functions while developing specialized expertise in firearms technology and enforcement. This organizational structure provided the foundation for subsequent development of ATF's comprehensive law enforcement capabilities.

The Treasury Department's decision to create ATF as an independent agency reflected recognition that effective firearms enforcement required specialized organizational structures and dedicated resources beyond what traditional tax collection agencies could provide. This decision represented a significant shift from tax collection toward comprehensive law enforcement as ATF's primary mission.

The Bureau Of Alcohol, Tobacco And Firearms (1972)

ATF was formally established as an independent bureau within the Treasury Department on July 1, 1972, through Treasury Department Order No. 221. This organizational change consolidated federal alcohol, tobacco, and firearms enforcement under unified command while providing ATF with independent operational authority and specialized resources.

The new agency inherited approximately 4,400 employees from its predecessor organizations, including special agents, compliance investigators, and administrative personnel. This workforce provided foundation for subsequent expansion while establishing ATF's presence throughout the United States through field offices and specialized units.

ATF's initial organizational structure reflected its diverse responsibilities, including separate divisions for law enforcement, regulatory compliance, and laboratory services. This structure enabled specialized attention to different aspects of ATF's mission while maintaining coordination among related functions.

The agency's first administrator, Rex Davis, emphasized ATF's law enforcement mission while maintaining necessary regulatory and revenue collection functions. This emphasis on criminal law enforcement distinguished ATF from traditional Treasury agencies and established its identity as a federal law enforcement agency rather than a tax collection unit.

Expanding Mission And Jurisdiction

ATF's jurisdiction expanded significantly during the 1970s as Congress added explosives regulation to its responsibilities through the **Organized Crime Control Act of 1970. The Safe Explosives Act** provisions gave ATF comprehensive authority over commercial explosives while adding specialized technical expertise to its capabilities.

The addition of explosives regulation reflected congressional recognition of ATF's technical expertise in hazardous materials and its proven effectiveness in complex criminal investigations. This expansion also demonstrated the practical advantages of consolidating related regulatory and enforcement functions within a single specialized agency.

ATF's involvement in major criminal investigations during the 1970s established its reputation as an effective federal law enforcement agency while demonstrating the value of specialized expertise in firearms and explosives cases. High-profile cases involving organized crime, domestic terrorism, and interstate firearms trafficking showcased ATF's capabilities.

The agency's regulatory responsibilities also expanded during this period as Congress enacted additional firearms laws and the firearms industry grew more complex. These regulatory challenges required enhanced technical expertise and administrative capabilities while maintaining law enforcement effectiveness.

Early Controversies And Constitutional Challenges

ATF faced significant controversies during its early years as critics challenged both its enforcement methods and its regulatory interpretations. These controversies reflected broader debates about federal law enforcement authority and the proper scope of federal firearms regulation.

Constitutional challenges to ATF's enforcement authority generally failed as federal courts upheld the agency's broad regulatory and investigative powers under the **Gun Control Act.** However, these challenges established important precedents regarding search and seizure, due process, and the scope of federal firearms regulation.

Congressional oversight of ATF intensified during the late 1970s as representatives responded to constituent complaints about aggressive enforcement tactics and regulatory interpretations. These oversight activities led to some modifications in ATF's procedures while maintaining the agency's essential authorities and mission.

The firearms industry's relationship with ATF evolved from initial hostility to grudging cooperation as the industry recognized the benefits of uniform federal regulation and the agency's technical expertise. This relationship became essential for effective implementation of federal firearms laws while maintaining industry compliance.

MAJOR FIREARMS LEGISLATION AND ATF EXPANSION (1982-1994)

The Firearm Owners Protection Act of 1986

The Firearm Owners Protection Act (FOPA) of 1986 represented the first major amendment to **the Gun Control Act** since its passage, reflecting changing political attitudes toward firearms regulation and growing influence of gun rights organizations. FOPA's provisions significantly modified federal firearms law while maintaining ATF's basic enforcement authority.

The Act's "safe passage" provisions protected lawful firearms transportation across state lines, addressing interstate travelers' concerns about varying state firearms laws. These provisions reduced federal prosecution risks for technical violations while maintaining core federal firearms controls.

FOPA's restrictions on ATF compliance inspections limited the agency to one routine inspection per dealer per year, reflecting industry concerns about regulatory harassment while maintaining necessary oversight capabilities. This compromise balanced industry interests against enforcement needs while establishing clear statutory limits on ATF authority.

The Act's machine gun ban prohibited civilian possession of machine guns manufactured after May 19, 1986, while grandfathering existing registered weapons. This provision represented significant expansion of federal firearms restrictions while accommodating existing owners and collectors.

Enhanced Penalties And Federal Sentencing

The Armed Career Criminal Act of 1984 and subsequent enhanced penalty legislation significantly increased sentences for federal firearms violations, reflecting Congress's growing emphasis on incapacitation and deterrence rather than rehabilitation. These enhanced penalties made federal firearms prosecution increasingly attractive compared to state alternatives.

The Sentencing Reform Act of 1984 and the creation of federal sentencing guidelines provided uniform national standards for federal firearms cases while reducing judicial discretion in sentencing. These changes increased the predictability and severity of federal firearms penalties while ensuring consistent enforcement across different federal districts.

ATF's role in federal firearms prosecutions expanded as enhanced penalties made federal prosecution more attractive and effective than state alternatives. The agency's investigative capabilities and technical expertise became increasingly valuable for complex cases involving multiple defendants and jurisdictions.

The development of firearms sentencing enhancements for career criminals and drug traffickers created powerful prosecutorial tools while establishing federal firearms law as a major component of federal crime control strategy. These enhancements made ATF investigations essential components of major federal criminal cases.

Brady Act And Background Check Systems

The Brady Handgun Violence Prevention Act of 1993 (Brady Act) established federal background check requirements for firearms purchases from licensed dealers, creating the most significant expansion of federal firearms regulation since **the Gun Control Act of 1968**. The Brady Act's implementation required extensive ATF involvement in developing and operating national background check systems.

The Act's initial five-day waiting period provision created interim background check procedures while permanent systems were developed. ATF played crucial roles in implementing these interim procedures while working with the FBI to develop the permanent National Instant Criminal Background Check System **(NICS).**

The Brady Act's prohibited person provisions expanded federal firearms restrictions while creating new enforcement challenges for ATF. The agency's regulatory expertise became essential for implementing background check systems while maintaining compliance with constitutional and statutory requirements.

Federal courts generally upheld the **Brady Act's** constitutionality while establishing important precedents regarding federal authority over state and local law enforcement agencies. The Supreme Court's decision in **Printz v. United States (1997)** limited federal authority to commandeer state officials while maintaining federal regulatory authority over firearms commerce.

Violent Crime Control And Law Enforcement Act Of 1994

The Violent Crime Control and Law Enforcement Act of 1994 included the Federal Assault Weapons Ban, representing the most controversial expansion of federal firearms regulation since the Gun Control Act. The ban's complex technical definitions required extensive ATF involvement in interpretation and enforcement.

The assault weapons ban prohibited manufacture, transfer, and possession of specified semi-automatic firearms and large capacity ammunition magazines while grandfathering existing weapons. ATF's technical expertise became essential for implementing these complex restrictions while maintaining constitutional compliance.

The Act's enhanced penalties for firearms violations during violent crimes and drug trafficking created additional prosecutorial tools while increasing ATF's role in major federal criminal cases. These provisions made firearms violations central components of federal crime control strategy.

ATF's regulatory responsibilities expanded significantly as the agency developed detailed interpretations of the assault weapons ban's technical provisions. These interpretations required extensive industry consultation and technical analysis while maintaining law enforcement effectiveness.

MODERN CHALLENGES AND CONSTITUTIONAL DEVELOPMENTS (1994-PRESENT)

The Waco Incident And Congressional Oversight

The ATF raid on the Branch Davidian compound near Waco, Texas, in 1993 became one of the most controversial incidents in federal law enforcement history, generating intense congressional oversight and fundamental questions about ATF's mission and methods. The failed initial raid and subsequent siege raised serious questions about ATF's tactical capabilities and decision-making processes.

Congressional investigations of the Waco incident revealed significant problems with ATF's planning, intelligence gathering, and tactical execution while highlighting broader issues about federal law enforcement's relationship with religious and political groups. These investigations led to significant changes in ATF's procedures and oversight mechanisms.

The Waco controversy damaged ATF's reputation and political support while generating increased scrutiny of federal firearms enforcement generally. The incident became a rallying point for federal law enforcement critics and contributed to broader skepticism about federal authority and competence.

ATF's response to the Waco controversy included significant organizational changes, enhanced training programs, and improved coordination with other federal agencies. These reforms addressed specific problems identified in congressional investigations while maintaining the agency's essential law enforcement capabilities.

Transfer To The Department Of Justice

The Homeland Security Act of 2002 transferred ATF from the Treasury Department to the Department of Justice, reflecting the agency's evolution from tax collection to comprehensive law enforcement. This transfer aligned ATF with other federal law enforcement agencies while maintaining its specialized mission and capabilities.

The transfer to Justice provided ATF with enhanced resources and coordination opportunities while maintaining its independence and specialized expertise. The agency's new designation as the Bureau of Alcohol, Tobacco, Firearms and Explosives (ATF) reflected its comprehensive mission and law enforcement focus.

ATF's integration into the Justice Department created new opportunities for coordination with other federal law enforcement agencies while maintaining specialized capabilities in firearms, explosives, and arson investigations. This integration enhanced the agency's effectiveness while preserving its unique mission and expertise.

The Justice Department's oversight of ATF provided enhanced political support and resources while maintaining appropriate independence for law enforcement operations. This relationship balanced accountability requirements against operational needs while ensuring effective federal firearms enforcement.

Supreme Court Decisions And Constitutional Evolution

The Supreme Court's decision in **District of Columbia v. Heller (2008)** fundamentally changed the constitutional landscape for federal firearms regulation by establishing that **the Second Amendment** protects individual rights to possess firearms for lawful purposes. This decision created new constitutional limitations on federal firearms regulation while maintaining broad regulatory authority.

The Heller decision's emphasis on **"longstanding prohibitions"** provided a constitutional foundation for most existing federal firearms laws while establishing that some forms of firearms regulation might exceed constitutional limits. This interpretation required careful analysis of federal firearms laws' constitutional compliance while maintaining effective law enforcement capabilities.

The Court's subsequent decision in **McDonald v. Chicago (2010)** applied Second Amendment protections to state and local governments while maintaining federal regulatory authority. This decision increased the complexity of firearms regulation while preserving essential federal enforcement capabilities.

Lower federal courts have generally upheld existing federal firearms laws under the Heller framework while establishing that some potential regulations might exceed constitutional limits. These decisions provide ongoing guidance for federal firearms policy while maintaining effective law enforcement tools.

Modern Enforcement Challenges

ATF faces contemporary challenges including the rise of internet firearms sales, 3D-printed firearms, and sophisticated criminal organizations that exploit regulatory gaps and technological developments. These challenges require enhanced technical expertise and investigative capabilities while maintaining constitutional compliance.

The agency's regulatory responsibilities have expanded to address new technologies and distribution methods while maintaining traditional enforcement capabilities. These dual demands require substantial resources and specialized expertise while ensuring effective law enforcement and regulatory compliance.

International cooperation has become increasingly important as firearms trafficking becomes more global and sophisticated. ATF's participation in international law enforcement cooperation provides essential capabilities for addressing transnational firearms trafficking while maintaining domestic enforcement effectiveness.

The agency's relationship with the firearms industry continues to evolve as technological and regulatory developments create new challenges and opportunities. This relationship remains essential for effective federal firearms regulation while balancing industry interests against law enforcement needs.

CONTEMPORARY ISSUES AND FUTURE DIRECTIONS

Technology And Regulatory Adaptation

The emergence of new firearms technologies, including 3D printing, polymer components, and modular weapon systems, creates unprecedented challenges for federal firearms regulation. ATF must adapt existing regulatory frameworks to address these technologies while maintaining constitutional compliance and practical enforceability.

Digital firearms commerce and online marketplaces require new approaches to regulatory oversight and enforcement. ATF's traditional inspection and compliance methods must evolve to address internet-based commerce while maintaining effective oversight of firearms distribution systems.

The proliferation of firearms accessories and modification components creates complex questions about the scope of federal regulation and the definition of regulated firearms. ATF's technical expertise becomes increasingly important for addressing these issues while maintaining clear legal standards.

Advances in forensic technology and ballistics analysis provide new investigative capabilities while creating requirements for enhanced technical expertise and equipment. These technological developments enhance ATF's law enforcement effectiveness while requiring substantial investments in training and equipment.

Federalism And State-Federal Relations

The expansion of state-level firearms regulation creates complex questions about federal-state cooperation and potential conflicts between different regulatory approaches. ATF must navigate these relationships while maintaining federal enforcement effectiveness and constitutional compliance.

Some states have enacted laws attempting to nullify federal firearms regulation within their boundaries, creating potential conflicts that require careful legal analysis and enforcement coordination. These challenges test the limits of federal authority while maintaining essential law enforcement capabilities.

State and local law enforcement cooperation remains essential for effective federal firearms enforcement, requiring ongoing coordination and resource sharing. ATF's relationships with state and local agencies must balance federal priorities against local concerns while maintaining effective partnerships.

The development of state firearms databases and background check systems creates opportunities for enhanced cooperation while raising questions about federal-state information sharing and privacy protection. These systems require careful coordination to maximize effectiveness while protecting individual rights.

International Cooperation And Transnational Crime

International firearms trafficking requires enhanced cooperation with foreign law enforcement agencies and international organizations. ATF's participation in international initiatives addresses transnational firearms trafficking while maintaining domestic enforcement effectiveness.

The agency's expertise in firearms identification and tracing provides valuable resources for international law enforcement cooperation while establishing ATF as a global leader in firearms enforcement technology and methods.

Cross-border firearms trafficking between the United States and Mexico has become a major enforcement priority requiring substantial ATF resources and close cooperation with Mexican authorities. These efforts address both domestic and international security concerns while maintaining effective enforcement capabilities.

International terrorism and organized crime groups' use of firearms creates national security dimensions for ATF's mission while requiring coordination with intelligence and national security agencies. These responsibilities expand ATF's traditional law enforcement role while maintaining specialized expertise and capabilities.

Organizational And Resource Challenges

ATF faces ongoing challenges in recruiting and retaining qualified personnel while maintaining specialized expertise in increasingly complex technical areas. The agency's unique mission requires specialized training and experience that may be difficult to develop and maintain within government compensation and career structures.

Budget constraints and competing federal priorities create ongoing pressures on ATF's resources while regulatory and enforcement demands continue to expand. The agency must balance competing priorities while maintaining effectiveness across its diverse mission areas.

Congressional oversight and political pressures create additional challenges for ATF's operations while providing necessary accountability mechanisms. The agency must balance political responsiveness against law enforcement independence while maintaining public confidence and support.

The agency's relationship with various stakeholder groups, including firearms industry, law enforcement agencies, and advocacy organizations, requires ongoing attention and management.

These relationships affect ATF's effectiveness while influencing public perception and political support for the agency's mission.

CONCLUSION: THE EVOLUTION OF FEDERAL FIREARMS POLICY

The development of federal firearms laws and the emergence of ATF as a major federal law enforcement agency represents a fundamental transformation in American governance that extends far beyond firearms policy to encompass broader questions about federal authority, individual rights, and the role of government in addressing social problems.

This evolution from limited taxation authority to comprehensive regulatory oversight demonstrates how constitutional interpretation, political pressures, technological developments, and social changes combine to reshape fundamental governmental structures and authorities. The transformation reflects both the adaptability of American legal institutions and the ongoing tensions between competing values and interests.

The creation of ATF as a specialized federal law enforcement agency illustrates how administrative necessity and political demands can drive organizational innovation within established constitutional frameworks. The agency's evolution from tax collection unit to comprehensive law enforcement organization demonstrates the dynamic nature of federal administration and the importance of specialized expertise in addressing complex regulatory challenges.

The constitutional development surrounding federal firearms regulation provides important insights into the evolution of American federalism and the balance between federal and state authority. The Supreme Court's recognition of individual Second Amendment rights while maintaining federal regulatory authority illustrates the complexity of constitutional interpretation and the ongoing need to balance competing constitutional values.

The political dynamics surrounding federal firearms regulation reveal the importance of crisis events in driving policy development while demonstrating the persistence of fundamental disagreements about the proper role of government in addressing social problems. These dynamics continue to influence contemporary policy debates while shaping the context within which future developments will occur.

ATF's institutional development provides valuable lessons about federal law enforcement organization and the challenges of maintaining specialized expertise within broader governmental structures. The agency's evolution illustrates both the benefits and costs of specialized federal law enforcement while demonstrating the importance of political support and public confidence for effective law enforcement.

The future of federal firearms regulation and ATF's role will likely continue to reflect the same tensions and dynamics that have shaped their historical development. Technological change, constitutional interpretation, political pressures, and social developments will continue to influence federal firearms policy while testing the adaptability and effectiveness of existing institutional structures.

Understanding this historical development provides essential context for contemporary policy debates and future developments in federal firearms regulation. The lessons learned from nearly a century of federal involvement in firearms regulation offer valuable insights into the possibilities and limitations of federal policy while highlighting the importance of balancing competing values and interests in a constitutional democracy.

The creation of federal firearms laws and ATF's emergence ultimately demonstrates both the capacity of American institutions to adapt to changing circumstances and the enduring importance of constitutional principles and democratic accountability in shaping governmental authority. This balance between adaptation and continuity will continue to characterize future developments in federal firearms policy and law enforcement organization.

CHAPTER TEN

CRYSTAL EMPIRES - THE RISE OF METHAMPHETAMINE AND THE MEXICAN CARTEL CONNECTION

INTRODUCTION

The story of methamphetamine's transformation from a legitimate pharmaceutical product to one of the world's most destructive illicit drugs is inextricably linked with the rise of **Mexican drug trafficking organizations.** What began as a synthetic stimulant developed in early 20th-century laboratories eventually became the foundation for multi-billion-dollar criminal enterprises that would reshape the landscape of organized crime across North America. This chapter examines the complex origins of methamphetamine, its evolution into **"crystal meth"** or **"ice,"** and the pivotal role Mexican cartels played in industrializing its production and distribution.

Understanding this history requires examining multiple interconnected factors: the legitimate medical origins of methamphetamine, the regulatory gaps that allowed its precursor chemicals to proliferate, the socioeconomic conditions in Mexico that fostered large-scale trafficking organizations, and the insatiable demand for stimulants in the United States market. The methamphetamine trade represents a case study in how legitimate pharmaceutical knowledge, combined with criminal innovation and market forces, can create devastating public health crises that span international borders.

The Scientific Origins Of Methamphetamine

Methamphetamine's story begins in 1893 when Japanese chemist Nagai Nagayoshi first synthesized the compound from ephedrine, a natural alkaloid found in the Ephedra plant. However, it wasn't until 1919 that Japanese pharmacologist **Akira Ogata** developed a more efficient synthesis method, creating what would become the modern form of methamphetamine. The drug's stimulant properties were quickly recognized, and by the 1930s and 1940s, methamphetamine was being used medically to treat narcolepsy, depression, and obesity.

During World War II, methamphetamine found widespread military applications. Both Axis and Allied forces distributed the drug to combat troops to enhance alertness and combat fatigue during extended operations. The German military's use of Pervitin, a methamphetamine-based stimulant, and the Japanese military's distribution of **"hiropon"** demonstrated the drug's powerful effects on human performance and endurance. American forces also utilized methamphetamine, though to a lesser extent.

The post-war period saw methamphetamine's continued legitimate use in medical settings. Pharmaceutical companies marketed various formulations for weight loss, attention disorders, and depression treatment. Benzedrine inhalers, containing racemic amphetamine, became widely available over-the-counter, while prescription methamphetamine products like Desoxyn and Methedrine found their place in medical practice.

However, by the 1960s, concerns about abuse potential and adverse health effects began mounting. The drug's powerful euphoric effects, combined with its relatively simple synthesis from readily available precursor chemicals, made it attractive for illicit production. Early clandestine laboratories appeared primarily in the American Midwest and West Coast, often operated by motorcycle gangs and small-scale entrepreneurs who had access to the necessary chemical knowledge and equipment.

The Chemistry Of Illicit Production

The appeal of methamphetamine to illicit manufacturers stems from several factors inherent in its chemical structure and synthesis. Unlike plant-based drugs such as cocaine or heroin, which require specific geographical conditions and agricultural infrastructure, methamphetamine can be produced anywhere with access to precursor chemicals and basic laboratory equipment. The synthetic nature of the drug means that production is not limited by growing seasons, weather conditions, or crop yields.

The most common synthesis methods rely on readily available precursor chemicals, particularly pseudoephedrine and ephedrine. These compounds, found in over-the-counter cold and allergy medications, can be chemically reduced to produce methamphetamine through several different reaction pathways. **The "Red Phosphorus" method**, the **"Nazi"** or **"Birch"** method using anhydrous ammonia, and the **"Shake and Bake"** method each offered different advantages in terms of available materials, production time, and yield.

However, these synthesis methods also presented significant dangers. The chemical reactions involved are highly volatile, producing toxic gases and creating fire and explosion hazards. Many clandestine laboratories have been destroyed by fires or explosions, and the environmental contamination from improper chemical disposal has created lasting public health problems in affected communities. The toxic byproducts of methamphetamine production can contaminate soil and groundwater for years, requiring expensive environmental remediation efforts.

The purity and potency of illicitly produced methamphetamine varies significantly depending on the synthesis method, the skill of the manufacturer, and the quality of precursor chemicals used. Early **"biker meth"** produced by motorcycle gangs in the 1960s and 1970s was often relatively low in purity and contained numerous impurities that could cause additional health problems for users. As production methods became more sophisticated and precursor chemicals more refined, the purity levels of street methamphetamine began to increase dramatically.

The Emergence Of "Ice" And Crystal Methamphetamine

The transformation of methamphetamine from a powder form to crystalline "ice" represented a significant evolution in both production techniques and market dynamics. **Crystal methamphetamine**, often referred to as **"ice," "glass," or "crystal,"** is a highly purified form of the drug that typically contains **90-95% pure methamphetamine hydrochloride.** This crystalline form offers several advantages from a trafficking perspective: it is more stable during transport, has a longer shelf life, and commands higher prices due to its perceived quality and potency.

The development of high-purity crystal methamphetamine required more sophisticated laboratory techniques and better quality control in the synthesis process. This evolution coincided with the entry of more organized and well-funded criminal groups into methamphetamine production, particularly

Mexican trafficking organizations that had the resources and infrastructure to invest in improved production methods.

Crystal methamphetamine's appearance also contributed to its market appeal. The clear, colorless crystals resembled pieces of broken glass or ice, leading to its street names. Users perceived the crystalline form as being more pure and potent than powder methamphetamine, driving demand and allowing traffickers to charge premium prices. The smoking method of consumption, which became popular with crystal methamphetamine, also provided a more intense and immediate high compared to other routes of administration.

The geographic origins of high-quality crystal methamphetamine production began shifting toward Mexico and the southwestern United States during the 1980s and 1990s. Mexican trafficking organizations recognized the profit potential in methamphetamine and began investing in larger-scale production facilities and more sophisticated synthesis techniques. This industrialization of methamphetamine production would fundamentally change the drug trade landscape across North America.

Mexican Cartels Enter The Methamphetamine Trade

The involvement of Mexican drug trafficking organizations in methamphetamine production and distribution represents one of the most significant developments in the modern history of illicit drug markets. Unlike their initial focus on transporting Colombian cocaine and Mexican heroin, the cartels' entry into methamphetamine represented a vertical integration strategy that allowed them to control every aspect of the supply chain from precursor chemical procurement to street-level distribution.

Several factors contributed to Mexican cartels' interest in methamphetamine during the 1980s and 1990s. First, the synthetic nature of the drug meant that production could be located anywhere, allowing cartels to establish manufacturing facilities within Mexico where they had greater operational security and control. Second, the profit margins on methamphetamine were extremely attractive, with relatively inexpensive precursor chemicals being transformed into products worth hundreds of times their initial cost. Third, the established trafficking networks and corruption infrastructure that cartels had developed for other drugs could be easily adapted for methamphetamine distribution.

The Guadalajara Cartel, led by **Miguel Ángel Félix Gallardo**, was among the first major Mexican trafficking organizations to recognize methamphetamine's potential. During the 1980s, the organization began establishing connections with Asian criminal groups who possessed advanced methamphetamine production knowledge, particularly organizations with ties to the Golden Triangle region where methamphetamine production had been established for decades.

Following the fragmentation of the **Guadalajara Cartel in the late 1980s,** successor organizations including the **Sinaloa Cartel, Tijuana Cartel**, and **Juárez Cartel** all incorporated methamphetamine into their product portfolios. Each organization brought different advantages to methamphetamine trafficking: the Sinaloa Cartel's sophisticated tunnel networks and corruption capabilities, the Tijuana Cartel's control over key border crossings, and the Juárez Cartel's expertise in large-scale logistics and transportation.

The Sinaloa Cartel, under the leadership of figures like **Joaquín "El Chapo" Guzmán** and **Ismael "El Mayo" Zambada**, emerged as particularly dominant in the methamphetamine trade. The organization invested heavily in improving production techniques, recruiting chemists with advanced knowledge, and establishing large-scale manufacturing facilities capable of producing hundreds of pounds of high-purity crystal methamphetamine per week.

Industrial-Scale Production And Innovation

Mexican cartels revolutionized methamphetamine production by applying industrial principles to what had previously been a cottage industry. Rather than the small-scale laboratories operated by individual entrepreneurs or motorcycle gangs, cartels established sophisticated manufacturing facilities that operated more like legitimate pharmaceutical plants than traditional clandestine laboratories.

These industrial-scale operations required significant capital investment and organizational capabilities that only well-established criminal organizations possessed. Cartels invested in professional-grade laboratory equipment, quality control systems, and environmental controls that allowed for consistent production of high-purity products. They recruited trained chemists and chemical engineers, often from legitimate pharmaceutical companies, to optimize synthesis procedures and troubleshoot production problems.

The scale of these operations was unprecedented in the illicit drug trade. Intelligence reports from the 1990s and 2000s documented methamphetamine laboratories in Mexico capable of producing multi-hundred-pound batches of crystal methamphetamine. Some facilities operated continuously, producing thousands of pounds of finished product per month. This industrial scale allowed cartels to achieve significant economies of scale, reducing per-unit production costs while maintaining high purity levels.

Quality control became a significant competitive advantage for cartel-operated laboratories. Unlike smaller-scale producers who might accept variable purity levels and inconsistent products, cartel operations implemented testing protocols to ensure consistent potency and purity. This reliability helped establish brand recognition among distributors and users, allowing certain cartel products to command premium prices based on their reputation for quality.

The cartels also innovated in precursor chemical procurement and supply chain management. Rather than relying on diversion from legitimate pharmaceutical supplies, they established direct relationships with chemical manufacturers in China, India, and other countries where precursor chemicals could be obtained more easily. These international supply chains allowed for massive importation of ephedrine, pseudoephedrine, and other essential chemicals needed for methamphetamine production.

The Precursor Chemical Challenge

The availability of precursor chemicals has been the most critical factor determining the scale and location of methamphetamine production throughout its history. Ephedrine and pseudoephedrine, the primary precursors used in most synthesis methods, are legitimate pharmaceutical compounds with important medical applications. This dual-use nature has created ongoing challenges for law enforcement and regulatory agencies attempting to control illicit methamphetamine production without disrupting legitimate medical and pharmaceutical activities.

Mexican cartels recognized early that controlling precursor chemical supplies would provide them with a significant competitive advantage over smaller-scale domestic producers. During the 1990s, they established sophisticated procurement networks that exploited regulatory gaps and international trade complexities to obtain precursor chemicals in bulk quantities.

The cartels' approach to precursor procurement was multifaceted and adaptive. They established legitimate-appearing import businesses that could order chemicals for ostensibly legal purposes, then divert these materials to illicit production. They developed relationships with chemical manufacturers in countries with less stringent export controls, allowing them to obtain precursors more easily than domestic producers who relied on diverted pharmaceutical products.

As regulatory controls tightened in traditional source countries, cartels adapted by diversifying their supply chains and developing alternative procurement methods. They began utilizing more exotic precursor chemicals and synthesis pathways that were not subject to the same level of regulatory scrutiny. This chemical innovation required significant investment in research and development, demonstrating the sophistication and resources available to major trafficking organizations.

The international nature of precursor chemical trafficking also provided cartels with additional advantages in terms of operational security and law enforcement evasion. By spreading their procurement activities across multiple countries and jurisdictions, they made it more difficult for any single law enforcement agency to develop a comprehensive understanding of their operations or to coordinate effective interdiction efforts.

Geographic Expansion And Market Penetration

The success of Mexican cartels in methamphetamine production enabled rapid geographic expansion of the drug's availability across the United States and other international markets. Unlike cocaine trafficking, which required maintaining relationships with Colombian suppliers, methamphetamine production allowed Mexican organizations to become completely self-sufficient while expanding their market reach.

The cartels leveraged their existing distribution networks, originally developed for cocaine and heroin trafficking, to introduce methamphetamine into new geographic markets. Cities and regions that had previously seen limited methamphetamine availability suddenly experienced dramatic increases in supply and corresponding decreases in street prices. This market penetration strategy was particularly effective in rural and small-town America, where methamphetamine's low cost and high potency found ready demand.

The Sinaloa Cartel's distribution strategy exemplified this geographic expansion approach. The organization established methamphetamine distribution cells in major American cities including Chicago, New York, Atlanta, and Los Angeles, while simultaneously penetrating smaller markets throughout the Midwest and Southeast. This broad geographic spread allowed the cartel to maximize revenue while reducing dependence on any single market.

Mexican cartels also began exporting methamphetamine to international markets beyond the United States. Australia, Japan, South Korea, and several Southeast Asian countries became significant destinations for cartel-produced crystal methamphetamine. These international markets often paid even higher prices than domestic American consumers, providing additional revenue streams for trafficking organizations.

The expansion into new markets required significant organizational adaptation and investment. Cartels had to develop new smuggling routes, establish local distribution networks, and adapt their products to local preferences and market conditions. This international expansion demonstrated the sophisticated business capabilities that major trafficking organizations had developed.

Violence And Competition

The immense profits available in the methamphetamine trade inevitably led to violent competition between trafficking organizations and conflicts with law enforcement agencies. Mexican cartel involvement in methamphetamine trafficking coincided with a dramatic escalation in drug-related violence that would eventually contribute to broader security crises in Mexico and border regions of the United States.

Competition for methamphetamine markets and production territories became a significant source of inter-cartel conflict during the 1990s and 2000s. Unlike **cocaine trafficking,** where Colombian suppliers could play Mexican organizations against each other, methamphetamine production allowed individual cartels to become completely vertically integrated. This created incentives for territorial control and market dominance that often resulted in violent confrontations.

The Sinaloa Cartel's conflicts with rival organizations, including the **Tijuana Cartel, Juárez Cartel**, and later the **Zetas**, were often centered around control of methamphetamine production facilities and distribution routes. These conflicts resulted in thousands of deaths and contributed to the broader deterioration of security conditions in Mexico during the 2000s and 2010s.

Violence also became a tool for market control and competitive advantage. Cartels used intimidation and violence against smaller-scale producers and distributors to consolidate market share and eliminate competition. This systematic elimination of smaller competitors further concentrated methamphetamine production and distribution in the hands of major trafficking organizations.

The industrialization of methamphetamine production also led to conflicts over skilled personnel and technical expertise. Cartels competed to recruit experienced chemists and laboratory operators, sometimes using violence or threats against individuals who refused to work for their organizations or who attempted to work for competitors.

Law Enforcement Response And Adaptation

The emergence of Mexican cartels as dominant players in methamphetamine production and trafficking required significant adaptations in law enforcement strategy and capabilities. Traditional approaches developed for addressing small-scale domestic methamphetamine production proved inadequate when confronted with industrial-scale operations backed by well-funded international criminal organizations.

The international nature of cartel methamphetamine operations created jurisdictional challenges that complicated law enforcement response efforts. Investigations often required coordination between multiple agencies across different countries, each with their own legal systems, investigative procedures, and intelligence capabilities. This complexity provided operational advantages to trafficking organizations that could exploit gaps in international law enforcement cooperation.

Mexican government efforts to combat cartel methamphetamine operations faced significant challenges related to corruption, resource limitations, and security concerns. The enormous profits generated by methamphetamine trafficking allowed cartels to corrupt government officials at multiple levels, from local police officers to high-ranking federal officials. This corruption created intelligence leaks and operational compromises that hampered enforcement efforts.

The United States government responded with increased investment in international cooperation and intelligence sharing programs designed to combat cartel methamphetamine trafficking. **The Drug Enforcement Administration** expanded its international presence and developed specialized units focused on cartel investigations. **The Department of Treasury** implemented financial sanctions targeting cartel leadership and their business networks.

However, the adaptive capabilities of major trafficking organizations often allowed them to stay ahead of law enforcement efforts. When traditional synthesis methods came under increased scrutiny, cartels developed alternative production techniques. When precursor chemical controls tightened, they found new supply sources and smuggling methods. This ongoing cat-and-mouse game demonstrated the sophisticated organizational learning capabilities that major cartels had developed.

Public Health And Social Impact

The industrialization of methamphetamine production by Mexican cartels had profound public health and social consequences that extended far beyond the immediate effects of drug use. The increased availability of high-purity crystal methamphetamine contributed to addiction epidemics in communities across the United States, while the environmental contamination from large-scale production facilities created lasting ecological damage.

The higher purity levels achieved by cartel-operated laboratories made methamphetamine more addictive and dangerous for users. Crystal methamphetamine's 90-95% purity levels were significantly higher than the 20-40% purity typical of earlier powder methamphetamine produced by smaller-scale operations. This increased potency led to more severe addiction patterns and higher rates of overdose and other medical complications.

The widespread availability of cartel-produced methamphetamine also changed patterns of drug use in many communities. The drug's relatively low cost compared to cocaine made it attractive to users from lower socioeconomic backgrounds, while its stimulant effects appealed to individuals seeking to maintain energy for multiple jobs or extended work hours. This demographic expansion of methamphetamine use brought the drug's problems into communities that had previously been less affected by stimulant abuse.

The environmental impact of large-scale methamphetamine production became a significant public health concern as well. Mexican cartel laboratories often operated without any environmental controls or waste management systems, leading to contamination of soil and water supplies. The toxic byproducts of methamphetamine synthesis, including heavy metals, corrosive acids, and organic solvents, were frequently dumped in rural areas or discharged into water systems.

Treatment and rehabilitation services struggled to adapt to the challenges presented by methamphetamine addiction. Unlike opioid addiction, for which medication-assisted treatments are available, methamphetamine addiction has proven more difficult to treat with pharmaceutical interventions. The psychological aspects of methamphetamine addiction, including paranoia, aggression, and cognitive impairment, created additional challenges for treatment providers.

Economic And Market Analysis

The methamphetamine trade represents one of the most economically significant sectors of the illicit drug market, with annual revenues estimated in the tens of billions of dollars. Mexican cartels' dominance in production and distribution has allowed them to capture the majority of these profits while achieving remarkable efficiency in their operations.

The economics of methamphetamine production are fundamentally different from plant-based drugs like cocaine or heroin. The synthetic nature of methamphetamine eliminates many of the variable costs associated with agricultural production, such as weather-related crop failures, seasonal variations in yield, and the need for extensive rural infrastructure. This predictability allows for more precise financial planning and resource allocation.

Profit margins in the methamphetamine trade are extraordinary by any business standards. Precursor chemicals costing hundreds of dollars can be transformed into finished products worth hundreds of thousands of dollars at street-level prices. These margins remain high even after accounting for the significant overhead costs associated with laboratory operations, security measures, and transportation logistics.

The market structure for methamphetamine has evolved toward greater concentration and vertical integration under cartel control. Unlike the fragmented market structure that characterized early methamphetamine trafficking, dominated by numerous small-scale producers and distributors, cartel involvement has created a more oligopolistic market structure with higher barriers to entry for potential competitors.

Price trends in methamphetamine markets reflect the efficiency gains achieved through industrial-scale production. Real prices for methamphetamine have generally declined over the past two decades, even as purity levels have increased substantially. This combination of lower prices and higher quality has contributed to expanded demand and geographic penetration of methamphetamine use.

Technological And Chemical Innovation

Mexican cartels' involvement in methamphetamine production has driven significant technological and chemical innovations that have transformed the illicit drug manufacturing landscape. The organizations' substantial financial resources and access to technical expertise have enabled them to develop production methods and quality control systems that rival legitimate pharmaceutical operations.

Chemical innovation has been particularly important as regulatory authorities have attempted to control precursor chemicals and synthesis methods. Cartels have invested in research and development efforts to identify alternative synthesis pathways that utilize different precursor chemicals or employ novel reaction mechanisms. This chemical flexibility has allowed them to maintain production levels even as traditional precursor supplies have become more restricted.

The development of more efficient synthesis methods has been another area of significant innovation. **Cartel-affiliated chemists** have optimized reaction conditions, developed better purification techniques, and improved yield rates through systematic experimentation and process refinement. These improvements have reduced production costs while improving product quality and consistency.

Quality assurance and testing capabilities have also advanced significantly under cartel operations. Many large-scale laboratories now employ sophisticated analytical equipment, including gas chromatography and mass spectrometry systems, to monitor product purity and identify impurities. This level of quality control was virtually unknown in earlier small-scale methamphetamine production operations.

International Cooperation And Policy Responses

The global nature of methamphetamine trafficking by **Mexican cartels** has necessitated increased international cooperation in law enforcement and policy responses. The complexity of modern trafficking operations, which may involve precursor chemical procurement from Asia, production in Mexico, and distribution across North America and beyond, requires coordinated responses that transcend national boundaries.

International precursor control efforts have become a central focus of policy responses to cartel methamphetamine trafficking. **The United Nations Office on Drugs and Crime** has worked to strengthen international controls on ephedrine, pseudoephedrine, and other precursor chemicals through enhanced monitoring and reporting requirements. However, the adaptive capabilities of trafficking organizations have often allowed them to circumvent these controls through creative procurement strategies.

Bilateral cooperation between the United States and Mexico has intensified significantly in response to cartel methamphetamine trafficking. The Merida Initiative and other collaborative programs have provided resources and technical assistance for Mexican law enforcement efforts while facilitating intelligence sharing and joint operations. However, the results of these cooperation efforts have been mixed, with cartels often adapting faster than law enforcement agencies can respond.

Financial investigations and asset forfeiture have emerged as important tools in combating cartel methamphetamine operations. The enormous profits generated by these operations create extensive financial footprints that can be exploited by law enforcement agencies. International cooperation in financial investigations has led to the seizure of hundreds of millions of dollars in cartel assets, though the organizations' financial sophistication has also evolved to counter these efforts.

Future Trends And Implications

The methamphetamine trade continues to evolve as Mexican cartels adapt to changing market conditions, law enforcement pressures, and technological developments. Several trends suggest that cartel involvement in methamphetamine trafficking will remain a significant challenge for the foreseeable future.

The synthetic nature of methamphetamine provides trafficking organizations with inherent advantages that are difficult for law enforcement to overcome. Unlike plant-based drugs that require specific geographic and climatic conditions, methamphetamine can be produced anywhere with adequate precursor chemical supplies and technical expertise. This flexibility allows cartels to rapidly relocate production facilities and adapt to changing enforcement pressures.

Technological advances in chemical synthesis and process optimization will likely continue to benefit cartel methamphetamine operations. The organizations' substantial financial resources allow them to invest in research and development efforts that often outpace law enforcement technical capabilities. New synthesis methods, improved purification techniques, and alternative precursor chemicals will likely continue to emerge from cartel-sponsored innovation efforts.

The globalization of methamphetamine markets presents both opportunities and challenges for **trafficking organizations**. Expanding international demand creates new revenue opportunities, but also exposes cartels to enforcement efforts by additional law enforcement agencies. The success of cartels in penetrating Asian and European markets suggests that methamphetamine trafficking will become an increasingly global phenomenon.

Conclusion

The involvement of **Mexican cartels** in methamphetamine production and trafficking represents one of the most significant developments in the modern history of illicit drug markets. The transformation of methamphetamine from a pharmaceutical curiosity to a **multi-billion-dollar criminal enterprise** demonstrates the profound impact that organized crime can have on public health and social welfare when combined with readily available chemical knowledge and international market opportunities.

The industrialization of methamphetamine production under cartel control has created a self-reinforcing cycle of market expansion, technological innovation, and organizational sophistication that has proven remarkably resistant to law enforcement intervention. The synthetic nature of methamphetamine, combined with the substantial resources and adaptive capabilities of major trafficking organizations, suggests that this challenge will persist for the foreseeable future.

Understanding the complex origins and evolution of cartel **methamphetamine trafficking** provides important insights into the dynamics of modern organized crime and the challenges facing law enforcement and policy makers in addressing synthetic drug threats. The methamphetamine trade exemplifies how criminal organizations can exploit legitimate scientific knowledge, international commerce systems, and regulatory gaps to create devastating social problems that transcend national boundaries.

The story of methamphetamine and Mexican cartels ultimately illustrates the profound consequences that can result when criminal innovation intersects with market demand and regulatory failure. As synthetic drug threats continue to evolve and new criminal organizations emerge, the lessons learned from the methamphetamine trade will remain relevant for understanding and responding to future challenges in drug trafficking and organized crime.

CHAPTER ELEVEN

FEDERAL SENTENCING ENHANCEMENTS - CAREER CRIMINAL AND LEADERSHIP PROVISIONS

INTRODUCTION

The federal criminal justice system employs a complex array of sentencing enhancements designed to impose more severe penalties on defendants who fall into specific categories deemed particularly dangerous or culpable. Among the most significant of these provisions are the Armed Career Criminal Act **(ACCA),** the career offender guidelines, and the leadership role enhancements found within the U.S. Sentencing Guidelines. These enhancement mechanisms reflect a legislative and judicial philosophy that repeat offenders, those who use weapons, and individuals who organize or manage criminal enterprises pose heightened threats to public safety and deserve correspondingly severe punishment.

The development of these enhancement provisions represents decades of evolving criminal justice policy, shaped by concerns about recidivism, the perceived inadequacy of traditional sentencing structures, and political pressure to address violent crime and drug trafficking. **The Armed Career Criminal Act,** originally enacted in 1984 and subsequently amended, mandates lengthy prison sentences for defendants with multiple prior convictions who are found in possession of firearms. Career offender provisions within the Sentencing Guidelines create similarly severe penalties for defendants with qualifying criminal histories who commit crimes of violence or controlled substance offenses. Leadership role enhancements recognize that individuals who organize, manage, or supervise criminal activities bear greater responsibility than those who merely participate in such enterprises.

Understanding these enhancement provisions requires examining not only their statutory language and guideline applications, but also the extensive body of case law that has developed around their interpretation and implementation. Courts have grappled with fundamental questions about what constitutes a predicate offense, how to measure the temporal relationships between offenses, and what level of organizational responsibility triggers leadership enhancements. The answers to these questions can mean the difference between relatively modest sentences and decades-long prison terms for defendants who fall within these enhancement categories.

The practical impact of these provisions extends far beyond individual cases to shape plea negotiation strategies, charging decisions by prosecutors, and broader patterns of federal criminal enforcement. Defense attorneys must carefully analyze clients' criminal histories and alleged roles in offenses to identify potential enhancement exposure, while prosecutors must consider how these provisions affect their ability to secure convictions and appropriate sentences. The interplay between these various enhancement mechanisms creates a complex sentencing landscape that requires sophisticated legal analysis and strategic decision-making by all participants in the federal criminal justice system.

The Armed Career Criminal Act: Historical Development And Statutory Framework

The Armed Career Criminal Act represents one of the most significant federal sentencing enhancement statutes, mandating substantial minimum sentences for defendants who possess firearms after accumulating multiple serious criminal convictions. The statute's origins can be traced to growing concerns during the 1980s about repeat violent offenders and the perceived inadequacy of existing penalties for armed criminals with extensive criminal histories.

Congress initially enacted the ACCA in 1984 as part of broader comprehensive crime control legislation. The original version required a minimum sentence of fifteen years for defendants with three or more convictions for robbery or burglary who were subsequently found in possession of firearms. This initial framework reflected a relatively narrow focus on traditional property crimes that were perceived as precursors to more serious violent offending.

The statute underwent significant expansion in 1986 when Congress broadened the definition of predicate offenses to include any "violent felony" or **"serious drug offense."** This expansion dramatically increased the potential reach of the ACCA by encompassing a much wider range of prior convictions that could trigger the enhancement. The 1986 amendments also increased the mandatory minimum sentence from fifteen to fifteen years without possibility of parole, though subsequent legislation has modified parole eligibility provisions.

The current version of the ACCA, codified at **18 U.S.C. § 924(e),** imposes a mandatory minimum sentence of fifteen years and a maximum sentence of life imprisonment for defendants who violate **18 U.S.C. § 922(g)** (prohibited persons in possession of firearms) and have three or more prior convictions for violent felonies or serious drug offenses, or a combination thereof. The temporal requirement specifies that these prior convictions must have been "committed on occasions different from one another" and that the defendant must have been convicted of each offense before committing the next.

The statutory definition of "violent felony" has proven to be one of the most litigated aspects of the ACCA. The statute defines violent felony as any crime punishable by imprisonment for more than one year that either has as an element the use, attempted use, or threatened use of physical force against another person, or is burglary, arson, or extortion, involves use of explosives, or otherwise involves conduct that presents a serious potential risk of physical injury to another.

This definition creates three distinct categories of qualifying offenses: the **"elements clause"** covering crimes with force as an element, the **"enumerated offenses clause"** specifically listing burglary, arson, extortion, and explosives offenses, and the **"residual clause"** covering other offenses that present serious potential risk of physical injury. The Supreme Court's 2015 decision in **Johnson v. United States** struck down the residual clause as unconstitutionally vague, significantly narrowing the range of offenses that can qualify as ACCA predicates.

The definition of "serious drug offense" is somewhat more straightforward, encompassing offenses involving manufacturing, distributing, or possessing with intent to manufacture or distribute controlled substances, provided the offense is punishable by imprisonment for more than ten years or is a second or subsequent conviction for a drug trafficking offense. This definition captures most significant drug trafficking offenses while excluding simple possession charges and minor drug offenses.

Temporal Requirements And The "Occasions Different" Standard

One of the most complex aspects of ACCA application involves determining whether prior convictions were "committed on occasions different from one another" as required by the statute. This temporal requirement is designed to ensure that the enhancement applies only to defendants with truly separate criminal episodes rather than those whose multiple convictions arose from a single criminal transaction or closely related conduct.

Courts have developed various approaches to analyzing the **"occasions different"** requirement, generally focusing on the temporal and spatial separation between the underlying criminal conduct rather than the formal conviction dates. The key inquiry is whether the defendant had the opportunity to reflect on his criminal conduct and choose a different course of action between the commission of the predicate offenses.

The Supreme Court's decision in **Wooden v. United States (2022)** provided important clarification of this standard, holding that offenses committed on the same day at the same location against the same victim should generally be considered part of the same occasion, even if they involved separate criminal acts. However, the Court also recognized that same-day offenses could qualify as separate occasions in some circumstances, such as when there are significant temporal gaps between the criminal acts or when the defendant had opportunities to abandon his criminal course of conduct.

Lower courts have applied this framework to various factual scenarios, considering factors such as the geographic proximity of the offenses, the temporal separation between them, the similarity of the criminal conduct, whether the offenses involved different victims, and whether the defendant had opportunities to cease his criminal activity. For example, a defendant who commits three burglaries in different neighborhoods on the same night might have those offenses treated as separate occasions, while a defendant who commits multiple sexual assaults against the same victim during a single encounter would likely have those treated as a single occasion.

The occasions different analysis becomes particularly complex in cases involving ongoing criminal enterprises or conspiracies, where defendants may commit multiple acts over extended periods as part of a single overall scheme. Courts must carefully examine the specific facts to determine whether individual criminal acts within the broader conspiracy represent separate occasions for ACCA purposes.

The practical significance of the occasions different requirements cannot be overstated. Defendants who fall just short of the three qualifying convictions committed on separate occasions avoid the fifteen-year mandatory minimum sentence, while those who meet the requirement face dramatically enhanced penalties. This binary outcome creates strong incentives for both parties to litigate these issues extensively.

Career Offender Guidelines: Structure And Application

The career offender provision found in **Section 4B1.1** of the U.S. Sentencing Guidelines creates a parallel but distinct enhancement mechanism for defendants with significant criminal histories who commit crimes of violence or controlled substance offenses. Unlike the ACCA, which applies only to felon-in-possession cases, the career offender guideline can apply to any defendant who meets its criteria regardless of the specific federal offense of conviction.

To qualify as a career offender, a defendant must be at least eighteen years old at the time of the instant offense, the instant offense must be a crime of violence or controlled substance offense, and the defendant must have at least two prior felony convictions for crimes of violence or controlled substance offenses. These prior convictions must have been committed on occasions different from one another and from the instant offense, and the defendant must have been sentenced to imprisonment exceeding thirteen months for each prior conviction.

The career offender enhancement operates by establishing specific offense level and criminal history category calculations that often result in significantly higher sentences than would otherwise apply. **Career offenders are assigned a criminal history category of VI (the highest category)** regardless of their actual criminal history score, and their offense level is determined by reference to a special table that typically produces higher levels than the standard guideline calculations.

The definition of **"crime of violence"** for career offender purposes mirrors many of the same interpretive challenges found in ACCA jurisprudence. The guidelines define crime of violence as any offense under federal or state law punishable by imprisonment exceeding one year that has as an element the use, attempted use, or threatened use of physical force against another person, or is murder, voluntary manslaughter, kidnapping, aggravated assault, a forcible sex offense, robbery, arson, extortion, or the use or unlawful possession of a firearm or explosive device.

Like the ACCA, the career offender guideline includes both an elements clause and an enumerated offenses clause, but lacks the residual clause that was struck down in the ACCA context. This difference in statutory language has created some divergence between ACCA and career offender jurisprudence regarding which specific offenses qualify as predicates under each provision.

The controlled substance offense definition for career offender purposes encompasses offenses involving manufacturing, importing, exporting, distributing, or dispensing controlled substances, or possessing controlled substances with intent to commit such acts. The definition also includes simple possession offenses if the defendant was sentenced to imprisonment exceeding thirteen months, reflecting the guideline's focus on more serious drug offenses.

Career offender status can result in dramatic sentence increases, often doubling or tripling the guideline sentence that would otherwise apply. For example, a defendant with a relatively low-level drug trafficking offense might face a guideline range of **27-33 months** under normal calculations, but could face **188-235 months** as a career offender. These substantial increases reflect the guidelines' policy judgment that repeat offenders pose heightened risks of recidivism and deserve correspondingly severe punishment.

Leadership Role Enhancements: Organizational Criminal Activity

Section 3B1.1 of the U.S. Sentencing Guidelines provides for sentence enhancements based on the defendant's role in the offense, with the most significant increases reserved for defendants who occupied leadership or organizational positions in criminal enterprises. These enhancements recognize that individuals who plan, organize, manage, or supervise criminal activities bear greater culpability than those who merely participate in such activities.

The leadership role enhancement operates on a sliding scale, with a four-level increase for defendants who were organizers or leaders of criminal activity involving five or more participants or otherwise extensive criminal activity, a three-level increase for defendants who were organizers or leaders of criminal activity involving three or four participants, and a two-level increase for defendants who were managers or supervisors but not organizers or leaders.

Determining whether a defendant qualifies for a leadership enhancement requires careful analysis of the specific facts surrounding the criminal conduct. Courts examine factors such as the degree of planning and organization involved in the offense, the defendant's decision-making authority, the defendant's control over the criminal proceeds, the defendant's ability to recruit participants or assign roles, and the defendant's efforts to conceal the criminal activity or avoid detection.

The enhancement distinguishes between different levels of leadership responsibility. An "organizer or leader" is someone who played a leadership role in planning the criminal activity or in managing or supervising others involved in the criminal activity. A "manager or supervisor" is someone who exercised some degree of control over others involved in the criminal activity, but did not rise to the level of organizer or leader.

The number of participants involved in the criminal activity affects both whether an enhancement applies and its magnitude. For purposes of this calculation, courts count all individuals who participated in the criminal activity, whether or not they were charged or convicted. This includes participants who played minimal roles or who were unaware of the full scope of the criminal enterprise.

The "otherwise extensive" language in the four-level enhancement provision allows for its application even in cases involving fewer than five participants, provided the criminal activity was particularly complex, sophisticated, or far-reaching. Courts have applied this provision to cases involving elaborate fraud schemes, complex money laundering operations, and other criminal activities that demonstrate significant planning and organization despite involving fewer participants.

Leadership enhancements become particularly significant in conspiracy cases, where multiple defendants may claim various levels of responsibility for the overall criminal enterprise. Prosecutors often seek to establish leadership roles for the most culpable defendants, while defense attorneys argue for minimal participant adjustments or contest the scope and organization of the alleged conspiracy.

The practical impact of leadership enhancements can be substantial. A four-level increase can add years to a defendant's sentence, particularly for defendants facing charges that already carry significant base offense levels. When combined with other enhancements, leadership adjustments can result in sentences that are multiples of what a minimal participant might receive for the same underlying criminal activity.

Manager And Supervisor Roles: Mid-Level Criminal Responsibility

The two-level enhancement for defendants who served as managers or supervisors represents the guidelines' recognition that criminal enterprises often involve hierarchical structures with individuals occupying intermediate positions between top-level leaders and basic participants. This enhancement captures defendants who exercised meaningful control over criminal operations without rising to the level of overall organizers or leaders.

Determining managerial or supervisory responsibility requires examining the defendant's actual role in the criminal activity rather than any formal titles or organizational designations. Courts look for evidence that the defendant directed the activities of others, made operational decisions, controlled resources or proceeds, or bore responsibility for particular aspects of the criminal enterprise.

The manager/supervisor enhancement often applies in drug trafficking organizations where defendants serve as local distributors who supervise street-level dealers, coordinate supply chains, or manage particular geographic territories. In fraud schemes, it might apply to individuals who recruit participants, train them in fraudulent techniques, or oversee particular aspects of the operation such as money laundering or victim identification.

One important distinction in manager/supervisor analysis involves the difference between directing criminal activity and simply coordinating with co-participants. A defendant who merely works alongside others in committing crimes does not typically qualify for a leadership enhancement, even if that defendant happens to be older, more experienced, or more skilled than other participants. The enhancement requires evidence of actual supervisory authority or managerial responsibility.

Courts also consider the temporal scope of the defendant's managerial role. Someone who briefly coordinated activities during a single criminal transaction typically receives less consideration for enhancement than someone who maintained ongoing supervisory responsibilities over an extended period. The guidelines contemplate that meaningful managerial responsibility involves some degree of sustained authority or control.

The **manager/supervisor enhancement** can apply even in relatively small criminal enterprises. A defendant who supervises just one or two other participants can still qualify for the two-level increase if the evidence demonstrates genuine supervisory authority. This reflects the guidelines' focus on actual responsibility and control rather than the absolute size of the criminal organization.

Interaction Between Enhancement Provisions

The federal sentencing system's multiple enhancement mechanisms can interact in complex ways that significantly compound a defendant's exposure to lengthy imprisonment. A single defendant might potentially face ACCA liability, career offender status, and leadership role enhancements simultaneously, creating the possibility of extremely severe sentences that reflect the cumulative impact of these various provisions.

When multiple enhancements apply to the same defendant, courts must carefully analyze how they interact under the relevant legal frameworks. The ACCA operates as a statutory mandatory minimum that establishes a floor below which the sentence cannot fall, while the career offender guideline and leadership enhancements affect the advisory guideline calculation that informs the court's sentencing decision.

In cases where both ACCA and career offender provisions apply, the career offender guideline typically produces a higher sentence than the ACCA minimum, making the career offender status the more significant constraint on the court's sentencing discretion. However, the ACCA mandatory minimum serves as an important backstop that prevents downward departures or variances below fifteen years in appropriate cases.

Leadership enhancements can apply in addition to either ACCA or career offender provisions, potentially creating guideline ranges that extend well beyond the mandatory minimums imposed by those other provisions. For example, a career offender who also receives a four-level leadership enhancement might face a guideline range of 360 months to life imprisonment, far exceeding what either provision would require individually.

The interaction between these provisions can create strategic considerations for both prosecutors and defense attorneys in plea negotiations and sentencing advocacy. Prosecutors might be willing to forego certain enhancements in exchange for guilty pleas or cooperation, while defense attorneys must carefully analyze their clients' exposure under each applicable provision to develop effective mitigation strategies.

Courts retain discretion to vary from advisory guidelines even in cases involving statutory mandatory minimums, but the practical effect of multiple enhancement provisions is often to establish very high starting points for sentencing calculations. Even substantial downward variances might still result in lengthy prison terms when the advisory guideline range begins at extremely high levels.

Procedural Requirements And Burden Of Proof

The application of federal sentencing enhancements involves specific procedural requirements and burden of proof standards that shape how these provisions operate in practice. Understanding these procedural aspects is essential for practitioners who must navigate the complex landscape of enhancement litigation.

For ACCA purposes, the government bears the burden of proving beyond a reasonable doubt that the defendant has the requisite number of qualifying predicate convictions committed on separate occasions. This proof typically involves introducing certified copies of prior convictions and demonstrating that each conviction meets the statutory definition of violent felony or serious drug offense. The government must also establish the temporal relationship between the convictions to satisfy the "occasions different" requirement.

Career offender determinations are made by the sentencing court based on a preponderance of the evidence standard, which is less demanding than the beyond a reasonable doubt standard applicable to ACCA cases. However, the court must still make specific findings regarding the defendant's criminal history, the nature of the instant offense, and the qualifying character of any prior convictions.

Leadership role enhancements are also determined by the sentencing court using a preponderance of the evidence standard. The court must examine the specific facts surrounding the defendant's participation in the criminal activity to determine whether the evidence supports a finding of organizational, leadership, managerial, or supervisory responsibility.

The procedural posture of enhancement determinations can vary depending on whether the defendant pleads guilty or proceeds to trial. In guilty plea cases, defendants often stipulate to certain facts that support enhancement applications, though they retain the right to contest the legal significance of those facts. In cases that proceed to trial, enhancement-related facts might be established through the same evidence used to prove the underlying offense, or through additional evidence presented at sentencing.

Courts must provide adequate notice to defendants regarding potential enhancement applications to ensure that they have meaningful opportunities to contest the government's claims. This notice requirement is particularly important in cases involving complex criminal history analyses or disputed factual findings regarding the defendant's role in the offense.

The appellate review standards for enhancement determinations vary depending on the specific legal issues involved. Pure questions of law, such as whether a particular statute qualifies as an ACCA predicate, receive de novo review, while factual determinations receive review for clear error. Mixed questions of law and fact receive varying levels of scrutiny depending on their specific nature and the applicable legal standards.

Categorical And Modified Categorical Approaches

One of the most technically complex aspects of federal sentencing enhancement law involves the methods courts use to determine whether prior convictions qualify as predicates under the various enhancement provisions. The Supreme Court has developed a sophisticated analytical framework known as the categorical approach, with a variant called the modified categorical approach, to guide these determinations.

The categorical approach requires courts to focus on the elements of the prior conviction offense rather than the specific facts underlying the defendant's conduct. Under this approach, a prior conviction qualifies as a predicate only if the statutory elements of the offense necessarily involve conduct that meets the enhancement provision's definitional requirements. Courts may not look beyond the statutory elements to examine the particular facts of the defendant's case.

This approach reflects constitutional concerns about the role of judges versus juries in making factual determinations that affect sentencing, as well as practical concerns about the reliability of attempting to reconstruct the facts of prior convictions that may have occurred years or decades earlier. By focusing on statutory elements rather than case-specific facts, the categorical approach provides a more predictable and administrable framework for enhancement determinations.

The modified categorical approach applies when the statute of conviction is "divisible," meaning it encompasses multiple alternative elements, some of which would qualify as enhancement predicates and others of which would not. In such cases, courts may examine a limited set of documents from the prior conviction, typically including the charging document, plea agreement, and plea colloquy, to determine which specific version of the divisible statute formed the basis for the conviction.

For example, a generic burglary statute might cover both residential and commercial burglary, with only residential burglary qualifying as an ACCA predicate. Under the modified categorical approach, a court could examine the charging document and plea agreement to determine whether the defendant was convicted specifically of residential burglary, and therefore whether the conviction qualifies as an ACCA predicate.

The Supreme Court's recent decisions have emphasized the importance of limiting the modified categorical approach to truly divisible statutes and restricting the documents that courts may examine in making these determinations. Courts may not engage in fact-finding about the defendant's actual conduct or attempt to determine which alternative version of a divisible statute "really" describes what the defendant did, but rather must determine which version formed the legal basis for the conviction.

These analytical frameworks can produce counterintuitive results in some cases, where defendants who engaged in conduct that clearly falls within the enhancement provisions' policy concerns nevertheless avoid enhancement because their prior convictions were under statutes with elements that do not perfectly match the enhancement definitions. Conversely, defendants whose actual conduct was relatively minor might face enhancement if their convictions were under statutes with broad elements that technically satisfy the enhancement requirements.

Constitutional Challenges And Evolving Jurisprudence

Federal sentencing enhancement provisions have been the subject of extensive constitutional litigation, with courts grappling with fundamental questions about due process, separation of powers, and the appropriate roles of judges and juries in criminal sentencing. This constitutional dimension has shaped the development of enhancement law and continues to influence how these provisions are interpreted and applied.

The Supreme Court's decision in **Apprendi v. New Jersey (2000)** established the principle that any fact that increases the penalty for a crime beyond the prescribed statutory maximum must be submitted to a jury and proved beyond a reasonable doubt. However, the Court has recognized that this principle does not apply to the fact of prior convictions, which may be determined by judges using a preponderance standard.

This prior conviction exception has been crucial to the continued viability of enhancement provisions like the ACCA and career offender guidelines, which rely heavily on determinations about the nature and timing of defendants' criminal histories. Without this exception, these provisions would likely violate the Sixth Amendment by requiring judges to make factual determinations that increase sentences based on standards less demanding than proof beyond a reasonable doubt to a jury.

The Supreme Court's decision in **Johnson v. United States (2015)** struck down the ACCA's residual clause as unconstitutionally vague, finding that the clause's requirement that courts determine whether offenses involve a "serious potential risk of physical injury to another" was too indeterminate to provide adequate notice to defendants and sufficient guidance to courts. This decision significantly narrowed the range of offenses that can qualify as ACCA predicates and established important precedents regarding constitutional vagueness challenges to enhancement provisions.

Following Johnson, courts have grappled with questions about which other enhancement provisions might be vulnerable to similar vagueness challenges. The career offender guidelines' enumerated offenses clause has generally been upheld against such challenges, but some courts have expressed concern about other aspects of enhancement jurisprudence that require courts to make complex determinations about the scope and nature of criminal conduct.

Due process challenges to enhancement provisions have generally been unsuccessful, with courts finding that these provisions provide adequate notice to defendants about the potential consequences of repeat offending and that the enhanced sentences bear a rational relationship to legitimate penological goals such as deterrence and incapacitation. However, some defendants have raised Eighth Amendment challenges to extremely lengthy sentences that result from the application of multiple enhancement provisions.

The evolving constitutional landscape continues to influence enhancement jurisprudence, with courts increasingly scrutinizing provisions that require complex factual determinations or that produce sentences that seem disproportionate to the underlying criminal conduct. Defense attorneys continue to develop new constitutional challenges to these provisions, while courts work to balance constitutional requirements with the statutory and guideline frameworks created by Congress and the Sentencing Commission.

Prosecutorial Discretion And Charging Decisions

The existence of powerful sentencing enhancement provisions creates significant prosecutorial leverage that shapes charging decisions, plea negotiations, and case resolution patterns throughout the federal criminal justice system. Prosecutors' discretion in deciding whether to seek enhancement applications can effectively determine whether defendants face relatively modest sentences or decades-long prison terms.

In ACCA cases, prosecutors must decide whether to charge defendants under **18 U.S.C. § 922(g)** when they could potentially charge other firearms offenses that do not trigger the enhancement. This charging decision can be outcome-determinative, as the difference between a standard felon-in-possession charge and an ACCA-enhanced charge can mean the difference between a sentence of a few years and a sentence of fifteen years or more.

Similarly, prosecutors have discretion in how they present evidence regarding defendants' roles in criminal enterprises, which can significantly affect the application of leadership enhancements. The decision to characterize a defendant as an organizer, manager, or minimal participant can have profound sentencing consequences, and prosecutors often use this leverage in plea negotiations to secure cooperation or encourage guilty pleas.

The career offender enhancement can apply to any qualifying defendant regardless of the specific federal offense charged, giving prosecutors flexibility in how they structure charges while maintaining enhancement exposure. For example, a defendant with qualifying priors might face career offender treatment whether charged with drug trafficking, firearms offenses, or violent crimes, allowing prosecutors to select charges based on strategic considerations while preserving enhancement leverage.

Prosecutorial policies regarding enhancement applications vary significantly across different U.S. Attorney's offices and individual prosecutors. Some offices aggressively seek all available enhancements as a matter of policy, while others exercise more discretion based on case-specific factors such as the defendant's role in the offense, likelihood of conviction, and potential for cooperation.

The plea bargaining process is fundamentally shaped by enhancement exposure, with defendants facing potential enhancements often willing to accept plea offers that they might otherwise reject. Prosecutors can offer to forego seeking enhancements in exchange for guilty pleas, cooperation agreements, or other concessions, creating powerful incentives for case resolution without trial.

However, this prosecutorial leverage also creates concerns about coercion and proportionality in sentencing. Defendants might feel compelled to plead guilty to avoid enhancement exposure even in cases where they have viable defenses, while the threat of enhancement can discourage defendants from exercising their right to trial. These dynamics have prompted ongoing debates about the appropriate limits on prosecutorial discretion in enhancement cases.

Defense Strategies And Mitigation

Defense attorneys representing clients with potential enhancement exposure must develop sophisticated strategies that address both the legal requirements for enhancement application and the factual circumstances surrounding their clients' criminal conduct and history. Effective defense advocacy requires thorough investigation of criminal history records, careful analysis of the elements of prior convictions, and strategic thinking about how to present mitigating evidence to courts.

In **ACCA cases,** defense attorneys must carefully examine each alleged predicate conviction to determine whether it meets the statutory requirements for violent felonies or serious drug offenses. This analysis requires understanding both the elements of the statutes under which the defendant was previously convicted and the current state of categorical approach jurisprudence regarding those particular offenses.

The temporal relationship between prior convictions presents another important area for defense advocacy. Attorneys must investigate the specific circumstances surrounding each prior conviction to determine whether they were committed on "occasions different from one another" as required by the statute. This investigation might involve obtaining police reports, court records, and other documentation that can establish the timing and circumstances of the prior criminal conduct.

Career offender cases require similar analysis of prior convictions, but also present opportunities for advocacy regarding the nature of the instant offense and whether it qualifies as a crime of violence or controlled substance offense. Defense attorneys might argue for narrow interpretations of these definitions or challenge the government's characterization of the defendant's conduct.

Leadership enhancement cases require detailed factual investigation and advocacy regarding the defendant's actual role in the criminal enterprise. Defense attorneys often present evidence showing that their clients played minimal or subordinate roles, lacked decision-making authority, or were themselves victims of exploitation or coercion by more culpable participants.

Mitigation strategies in enhancement cases often focus on factors that might justify downward departures or variances from the advisory guideline ranges. These might include the defendant's personal history and characteristics, acceptance of responsibility, assistance to authorities, or other factors that suggest the enhancement provisions produce sentences that are greater than necessary to achieve the purposes of sentencing.

The development of alternative sentencing proposals can also be an important defense strategy, particularly in cases where enhancement applications produce extremely high guideline ranges. Defense attorneys might propose structured sentences that include periods of supervised release, treatment programs, or other components that could address the underlying concerns that motivate enhancement provisions while avoiding excessively lengthy incarceration.

Sentencing Disparities And Policy Considerations

The application of federal sentencing enhancement provisions has created significant disparities in sentences imposed on similarly situated defendants, raising important questions about fairness, proportionality, and the appropriate goals of criminal sentencing. These disparities arise from various sources, including differences in prosecutorial practices, variations in judicial interpretation of enhancement requirements, and the sometimes arbitrary boundaries that determine whether defendants qualify for enhancement treatment.

Geographic disparities in enhancement application have been documented across different federal judicial districts, with some areas showing much higher rates of ACCA prosecutions, career offender applications, and leadership enhancements than others. These differences may reflect variations in local crime patterns, prosecutorial resources and priorities, or different approaches to federal criminal enforcement, but they result in defendants facing dramatically different sentences based partly on where they happen to be prosecuted.

The binary nature of many enhancement provisions creates cliff effects where small differences in criminal history or role in the offense can produce vastly different sentences. For example, a defendant with two qualifying prior convictions might receive a sentence of a few years, while a defendant with three such convictions faces a fifteen-year mandatory minimum under the ACCA. Similarly, the difference between being characterized as a manager versus a minimal participant can add or subtract years from a defendant's sentence.

Racial and socioeconomic disparities in enhancement application have been the subject of considerable research and policy debate. Some studies suggest that these provisions may disproportionately affect minority defendants, who are more likely to have prior convictions that qualify as enhancement predicates and who may be more likely to be characterized as playing leadership roles in criminal enterprises.

The cumulative impact of multiple enhancement provisions can produce sentences that seem disproportionate to the underlying criminal conduct, particularly in cases involving non-violent offenses or defendants whose prior convictions occurred many years earlier. Some defendants face effective life sentences based on combinations of enhancements that reflect policy judgments about repeat offending and criminal organization, but that may not account for individual circumstances or the potential for rehabilitation.

Policy reform proposals have addressed various aspects of enhancement provisions, including suggestions for narrowing the definitions of predicate offenses, creating more graduated enhancement structures, providing greater judicial discretion in enhancement cases, and establishing time limits on the relevance of prior convictions. However, these provisions also have strong political support based on concerns about public safety and the deterrent effects of enhanced sentences.

The ongoing debate over enhancement provisions reflects broader tensions in criminal justice policy between deterrence and proportionality, between uniform application of legal standards and individualized sentencing, and between legislative determinations about appropriate sentences and judicial discretion in particular cases.

Conclusion

Federal sentencing enhancement provisions represent some of the most powerful and controversial tools in the modern criminal justice system. The **Armed Career Criminal Act**, career offender guidelines, and leadership role enhancements can transform relatively modest sentences into decades-long prison terms, reflecting legislative and policy judgments about the heightened culpability and dangerousness of repeat offenders and criminal organizers.

The complexity of these provisions requires sophisticated legal analysis and strategic thinking by all participants in the federal criminal justice system. Defense attorneys must master the technical requirements of categorical approach analysis, investigate their clients' criminal histories and roles in alleged offenses, and develop effective mitigation strategies. Prosecutors must make strategic decisions about charging and enhancement applications that can fundamentally alter case outcomes. Judges must navigate complex legal standards while exercising appropriate discretion in individual cases.

The constitutional dimensions of enhancement law continue to evolve, with courts balancing concerns about due process, proportionality, and the appropriate roles of judges and juries in criminal sentencing. Recent Supreme Court decisions have established important limitations on certain enhancement provisions while generally upholding their constitutional validity, but ongoing litigation continues to test the boundaries of these legal frameworks.

The policy implications of enhancement provisions extend beyond individual cases to shape broader patterns of federal criminal enforcement and sentencing. The significant disparities created by these provisions raise important questions about fairness and proportionality in criminal sentencing, while their deterrent effects and impact on public safety remain subjects of ongoing research and debate.

Understanding federal sentencing enhancement provisions requires appreciating both their technical legal requirements and their broader role in the criminal justice system. These provisions reflect fundamental policy choices about how to address repeat offending and criminal organization, but their implementation raises complex questions about constitutional requirements, prosecutorial discretion, and sentencing proportionality that continue to evolve through litigation and policy development.

The future of federal sentencing enhancement law will likely be shaped by ongoing constitutional challenges, empirical research about their effects on crime and sentencing disparities, and broader policy debates about criminal justice reform. As courts, policymakers, and practitioners continue to grapple with these issues, the enhancement provisions will remain central to understanding how the federal criminal justice system operates and evolves in response to changing legal, social, and political pressures.

CHAPTER TWELVE

PATHWAYS TO REDEMPTION - THE FIRST STEP ACT AND SECOND CHANCE ACT

INTRODUCTION

The American criminal justice system underwent significant transformation in the 21st century through landmark legislation designed to address the failures of mass incarceration and provide meaningful opportunities for rehabilitation and successful reentry. Two pivotal pieces of legislation - **the Second Chance Act of 2007** and **the First Step Act of 2018** - represent a fundamental shift from purely punitive approaches toward evidence-based practices that prioritize rehabilitation, risk reduction, and community safety through effective reentry programming.

These legislative achievements emerged from a growing bipartisan consensus that the traditional "tough on crime" policies of the 1980s and 1990s had created an unsustainable system of mass incarceration without achieving corresponding improvements in public safety. With the United States incarcerating approximately 2.3 million people and spending over $80 billion annually on corrections, policymakers began seeking alternatives that could reduce recidivism, lower costs, and provide pathways for individuals to successfully reintegrate into their communities.

The Second Chance Act, formally known as **the Second Chance Act of 2007**: Community Safety Through Recidivism Prevention, established the foundation for modern reentry programming by authorizing federal funding for evidence-based programs designed to reduce recidivism and improve outcomes for individuals returning to their communities from incarceration. The legislation recognized that successful reentry requires comprehensive support addressing employment, housing, education, mental health, substance abuse treatment, and family reunification.

The First Step Act of 2018 built upon these foundations by implementing comprehensive federal prison reform focused on rehabilitation programming, earned time credit systems, and recidivism reduction initiatives. This legislation represented the most significant federal criminal justice reform in decades, affecting approximately 180,000 individuals in federal custody and establishing new paradigms for evidence-based programming and risk assessment.

Together, these acts represent a philosophical evolution in American criminal justice policy, moving from a system primarily focused on punishment and incapacitation toward one that recognizes the potential for redemption, rehabilitation, and successful community reintegration. Understanding their development, implementation, and benefits provides crucial insight into the ongoing transformation of the American correctional system and its impact on individuals, families, and communities nationwide.

Historical Context And The Rise Of Mass Incarceration

To understand the significance of the Second Chance Act and First Step Act, it is essential to examine the historical context that made such reforms necessary. The period from 1980 to 2010 witnessed an unprecedented expansion of the American prison system, driven by policies including mandatory minimum sentencing, three-strikes laws, truth-in-sentencing requirements, and the expansion of federal criminal law.

During this period, the federal prison population increased by over 790%, growing from approximately 25,000 individuals in 1980 to more than 215,000 by 2010. State prison populations experienced similar growth, with the total incarcerated population rising from approximately 500,000 in 1980 to over 2.3 million by 2010. This dramatic expansion occurred despite declining crime rates during much of this period, suggesting that incarceration growth was driven more by policy choices than by crime trends.

The human and economic costs of mass incarceration became increasingly apparent by the early 2000s. Families and communities, particularly those already facing socioeconomic disadvantages, experienced devastating impacts from the removal of large numbers of individuals to prison. Children were separated from parents, communities lost significant portions of their adult male population, and the economic burden of supporting large prison populations strained state and federal budgets.

Recidivism rates remained stubbornly high throughout this period, with approximately 68% of individuals released from state prisons being rearrested within three years and 83% being rearrested within nine years. These statistics highlighted the failure of purely punitive approaches to reduce future criminal behavior and suggested the need for alternative strategies focused on addressing the underlying factors that contribute to criminal behavior.

The concept of evidence-based practice began gaining traction in corrections during the 1990s and early 2000s, drawing from research in psychology, criminology, and social work that identified effective interventions for reducing recidivism. Studies demonstrated that certain types of programming - particularly cognitive-behavioral interventions, vocational training, education, and substance abuse treatment - could significantly reduce the likelihood of future criminal behavior.

Simultaneously, fiscal pressures created by the high costs of incarceration began motivating policymakers to seek more cost-effective approaches to criminal justice. States facing budget crises during economic downturns found it increasingly difficult to justify spending billions of dollars on prison systems that produced poor outcomes in terms of public safety and offender rehabilitation.

The emergence of bipartisan support for criminal justice reform reflected a convergence of interests among conservatives concerned about government spending and limited government principles, liberals focused on social justice and human rights, and moderates seeking evidence-based solutions to complex social problems. This political alignment created opportunities for comprehensive reform that had not existed during the height of the "tough on crime" era.

The Second Chance Act: Legislative Genesis And Development

The Second Chance Act emerged from extensive advocacy efforts by criminal justice reform organizations, formerly incarcerated individuals, family members, and researchers who documented the need for comprehensive reentry programming. The legislation was first introduced in Congress in 2005 by Senator Sam Brownback (R-KS) and Representative Danny Davis (D-IL), reflecting the bipartisan nature of support for reentry reform.

The development of the Second Chance Act was informed by research demonstrating that the period immediately following release from incarceration represents a critical window for intervention. Studies showed that the majority of recidivism occurs within the first year after release, suggesting that intensive support during this transition period could significantly impact long-term outcomes.

Key stakeholders in the development of the legislation included the **National Reentry Resource Center, the Council of State Governments Justice Center, the Urban Institute**, and numerous community-based organizations that provided direct services to individuals returning from incarceration. These organizations contributed research, policy recommendations, and real-world experience that shaped the legislation's focus on evidence-based practices and comprehensive service delivery.

The legislative process involved extensive hearings, stakeholder consultations, and negotiations to build broad support for the initiative. Supporters emphasized that effective reentry programming would benefit not only individuals returning from incarceration, but also their families, communities, and society as a whole through reduced crime rates, increased public safety, and economic benefits from successful reintegration.

Opposition to the legislation was relatively limited, reflecting the broad consensus that existing reentry systems were inadequate and that investment in evidence-based alternatives was necessary. Some concerns were raised about federal spending and the appropriate role of federal government in what had traditionally been viewed as state and local responsibilities, but these concerns were addressed through the legislation's emphasis on competitive grants and evidence-based practices.

The Second Chance Act was signed into law by President George W. Bush on April 9, 2008, after passing both houses of Congress with strong bipartisan support. The legislation authorized $165 million annually for fiscal years 2009 and 2010 to support reentry programming, though actual appropriations fell short of the authorized amounts during the initial years of implementation.

The law established several distinct grant programs targeting different aspects of the reentry process, including adult and juvenile offender reentry programs, family-based substance abuse treatment programs, technology career training programs, and mentoring programs. Each program was designed to address specific barriers to successful reentry while maintaining flexibility for local adaptation and innovation.

Second Chance Act Program Structure And Implementation

The Second Chance Act created a comprehensive framework for federal support of reentry programming through multiple grant programs administered primarily by the Department of Justice's Bureau of Justice Assistance. The legislation's structure reflected an understanding that successful reentry requires addressing multiple interconnected challenges including employment, housing, education, mental health, substance abuse, and family relationships.

The Adult Offender Reentry Program represents the largest component of Second Chance Act funding, providing competitive grants to state and local governments, nonprofit organizations, and tribal entities to develop and implement comprehensive reentry services. These programs are required to include evidence-based practices and demonstrate partnerships between correctional agencies, community-based service providers, and other stakeholders.

Eligible activities under the adult reentry program include educational and vocational training, mental health and substance abuse treatment, housing assistance, family reunification programming, mentoring services, and assistance with obtaining identification documents and accessing benefits. Programs must serve individuals both during the period of incarceration and following release, recognizing that successful reentry preparation must begin well before the individual returns to the community.

The Juvenile Offender Reentry Program addresses the unique needs of young people returning to communities from secure facilities. Research demonstrates that juvenile offenders face particular challenges related to educational disruption, family instability, and developmental issues that require specialized interventions. This program supports comprehensive services including educational support, family counseling, mentoring, and job training specifically designed for young people.

The Family-Based Substance Abuse Treatment Program recognizes that substance abuse often affects entire families and that successful recovery requires addressing family dynamics and providing support to all affected family members. This program supports residential treatment programs that allow parents to maintain custody of their children while receiving intensive substance abuse treatment and related services.

Technology Career Training Programs focus on providing individuals with skills in high-demand fields that can lead to sustainable employment and career advancement. These programs recognize that the modern economy increasingly requires technological literacy and that providing relevant job training can significantly improve employment outcomes for individuals returning from incarceration.

Mentoring programs supported by **the Second Chance Act** pair individuals returning from incarceration with community volunteers who provide ongoing support, guidance, and assistance with reentry challenges. Research demonstrates that mentoring relationships can significantly reduce recidivism rates while providing emotional support that helps individuals navigate the complex challenges of reintegration.

Implementation of **Second Chance Act** programs has involved extensive technical assistance, training, and research to ensure that funded programs utilize evidence-based practices and achieve measurable outcomes. The Department of Justice has supported evaluation research to assess program effectiveness and identify best practices that can be replicated in other jurisdictions.

First Step Act: Background And Legislative Journey

The First Step Act of 2018 emerged from growing recognition that the federal prison system required comprehensive reform to address overcrowding, reduce recidivism, and provide meaningful opportunities for rehabilitation. The legislation built upon earlier bipartisan efforts to reform federal sentencing laws and represented the culmination of years of advocacy by criminal justice reform organizations, conservative and liberal policy groups, and affected individuals and families.

The development of **the First Step Act** was influenced by several high-profile criminal justice reform initiatives, including the bipartisan **Sentencing Reform and Corrections Act** that had been considered by Congress in previous sessions. While comprehensive sentencing reform proved politically challenging, reformers identified federal prison programming and earned time credits as areas where bipartisan agreement was possible.

Key supporters of **the First Step Act** included an unusual coalition spanning the political spectrum, from the **American Civil Liberties Union** and the **NAACP** to the **Koch Foundation and Right on Crime.** This diverse coalition emphasized different aspects of the legislation's benefits - progressives focused on reducing mass incarceration and addressing racial disparities, while conservatives emphasized fiscal responsibility and evidence-based approaches to public safety.

The legislation was championed by Jared Kushner, whose father had been incarcerated in federal prison, and received strong support from President Donald Trump, who made criminal justice reform a priority during his administration. This high-level political support proved crucial in overcoming opposition and building momentum for comprehensive reform.

Congressional champions of the legislation included Senator Chuck Grassley (R-IA), Senator Dick Durbin (D-IL), Representative Hakeem Jeffries (D-NY), and Representative Doug Collins (R-GA). These leaders worked extensively to build bipartisan coalitions, address concerns from various stakeholders, and negotiate compromises that could attract broad support.

The legislative process involved extensive negotiations regarding the scope of sentencing reforms to be included in the legislation. Initial versions focused primarily on prison programming and earned time credits, while later versions included limited sentencing reforms such as modifications to mandatory minimum penalties for certain drug offenses and expanded judicial discretion in some cases.

Opposition to **the First Step Act** came primarily from law enforcement organizations and some prosecutors who expressed concerns about the legislation's potential impact on public safety and the deterrent effect of federal sentences. These concerns were addressed through provisions requiring risk assessments, limiting eligibility for certain benefits, and maintaining judicial oversight of release decisions.

The First Step Act passed the House of Representatives by a vote of 360-59 in May 2018 and the Senate by a vote of 87-12 in December 2018, demonstrating overwhelming bipartisan support. President Trump signed the legislation into law on December 21, 2018, calling it a "tremendous bipartisan achievement" and highlighting its potential to improve public safety while providing opportunities for redemption.

First Step Act: Core Provisions And Mechanisms

The First Step Act established a comprehensive framework for federal prison reform centered on evidence-based programming, earned time credits, and recidivism reduction initiatives. The legislation's core provisions reflect an understanding that effective correctional programming must be individualized, evidence-based, and focused on addressing the specific factors that contribute to criminal behavior.

The cornerstone of the First Step Act is the requirement that the Bureau of Prisons implement a risk and needs assessment system to evaluate each incarcerated individual's likelihood of recidivism and criminogenic needs. This assessment, known as **PATTERN (Prisoner Assessment Tool Targeting Estimated Risk and Needs),** uses validated instruments to classify individuals into risk categories and identify appropriate programming interventions.

The risk assessment process involves evaluating static factors (such as criminal history, age at first arrest, and education level) and dynamic factors (such as substance abuse history, employment skills, and family relationships) that research has demonstrated are predictive of future criminal behavior. This assessment informs decisions about housing assignments, program participation, and eligibility for various benefits and opportunities.

Evidence-Based Recidivism Reduction Programs represent the heart of **the First Step Act's** rehabilitation approach. The legislation requires the Bureau of Prisons to provide meaningful programming opportunities that address criminogenic needs and reduce the likelihood of future criminal behavior. These programs must be based on research demonstrating their effectiveness in reducing recidivism.

Eligible programs include cognitive behavioral therapy, anger management, victim impact programs, financial literacy training, vocational and educational programming, substance abuse treatment, mental health programming, and social skills development. The legislation emphasizes that programming should be tailored to individual needs and risk levels, with higher-risk individuals receiving more intensive interventions.

The earned time credit system allows eligible individuals to earn up to 54 days of credit per year of sentence completion for successful participation in evidence-based programming. These credits can be applied toward early transfer to supervised release, halfway houses, or home confinement, providing incentives for program participation while maintaining public safety oversight.

Eligibility for earned time credits is restricted based on current offense and criminal history. Individuals convicted of certain violent offenses, terrorism-related crimes, or who have previous convictions for violent offenses are generally ineligible for early release through earned time credits, though they may still participate in programming for other benefits.

The legislation also includes provisions for compassionate release, allowing courts to reduce sentences in extraordinary and compelling circumstances such as terminal illness, advanced age, or other factors that make continued incarceration inappropriate. This provision expands judicial discretion while maintaining appropriate safeguards and oversight.

Expanded home confinement options allow eligible individuals to serve portions of their sentences in community settings under electronic monitoring or other supervision. This provision recognizes that community-based supervision can be more effective than incarceration for certain individuals while providing significant cost savings to the federal government.

Risk Assessment And Individualized Programming

The implementation of evidence-based risk assessment represents one of the most significant innovations of **the First Step Act,** fundamentally changing how the federal prison system evaluates and manages incarcerated individuals. The PATTERN assessment system represents a sophisticated approach to predicting recidivism risk and identifying appropriate interventions based on individual characteristics and needs.

The development of PATTERN involved extensive research and validation using data from hundreds of thousands of individuals who had been released from federal prison. Researchers analyzed factors associated with recidivism to develop predictive models that could accurately classify individuals into different risk categories. This scientific approach ensures that risk classifications are based on empirical evidence rather than subjective judgments.

The assessment process begins shortly after an individual enters federal custody and is updated periodically throughout the period of incarceration. Initial assessments inform decisions about housing assignments, security levels, and initial program recommendations. Subsequent assessments track changes in risk levels and programming needs as individuals participate in interventions and their circumstances change.

Risk factors evaluated by PATTERN include criminal history variables such as the number and types of prior arrests and convictions, age at first arrest, and involvement in violent offenses. Educational background, employment history, substance abuse patterns, and family relationships are also considered as factors that may influence future behavior.

The assessment results in classification into risk categories ranging from minimum to high risk, with corresponding recommendations for programming intensity and supervision levels. Minimum-risk individuals may require limited programming focused on maintaining pro-social behaviors, while high-risk individuals receive intensive interventions addressing multiple criminogenic needs.

Individualized programming plans are developed based on assessment results and focus on addressing the specific factors most relevant to each person's risk of recidivism. For example, an individual with substance abuse issues might participate in intensive drug treatment programming, while someone with limited education might focus on academic achievement and vocational training.

The Bureau of Prisons has worked to expand programming capacity to meet the increased demand created by **the First Step Act's** incentive structures. This has involved hiring additional staff, developing new curricula, and partnering with external organizations to provide specialized services. The goal is to ensure that all eligible individuals have access to meaningful programming opportunities regardless of their facility location or security level.

Quality assurance mechanisms ensure that programs meet evidence-based standards and achieve intended outcomes. This includes regular evaluation of program effectiveness, monitoring of participant outcomes, and continuous improvement based on research findings and best practices from other correctional systems.

Educational And Vocational Training Benefits

Education and vocational training represent critical components of successful reentry programming, providing individuals with the knowledge and skills necessary for sustainable employment and economic stability. **The First Step Act** significantly expanded access to educational opportunities and established new partnerships with educational institutions and employers.

The legislation prioritizes educational programming for individuals without high school diplomas or equivalent credentials, recognizing that basic educational achievement is fundamental to successful reintegration. Adult basic education programs help individuals develop literacy and numeracy skills, while GED preparation programs provide pathways to high school equivalency certification.

Post-secondary education opportunities have been expanded through partnerships with colleges and universities that provide courses and degree programs within federal facilities. These partnerships allow incarcerated individuals to earn college credits and degrees while serving their sentences, significantly improving their employment prospects upon release.

Distance learning technologies have been implemented to provide access to educational programming regardless of facility location or security level. Online courses, video conferencing, and digital learning platforms allow individuals to participate in educational opportunities that might not otherwise be available at their specific facility.

Vocational training programs focus on developing job skills in high-demand industries that offer opportunities for sustainable employment and career advancement. Programs include construction trades, automotive repair, culinary arts, computer technology, and manufacturing skills that align with local job markets where individuals are likely to be released.

Industry partnerships ensure that vocational training programs meet current employer needs and provide recognized credentials that have value in the job market. Employers work with correctional facilities to develop curricula, provide equipment and materials, and offer job placement opportunities for program completers.

Apprenticeship programs represent a particularly effective model for vocational training, combining classroom instruction with hands-on experience under the supervision of experienced tradespeople. These programs often lead directly to employment opportunities and provide pathways to career advancement in skilled trades.

Financial literacy education helps individuals develop money management skills, understand banking and credit systems, and plan for financial stability upon release. These programs address the reality that many individuals entering federal custody have limited experience with mainstream financial systems and need practical skills for economic reintegration.

Entrepreneurship programs provide individuals with skills and knowledge necessary to start their own businesses, recognizing that self-employment may be an important option for individuals who face barriers to traditional employment due to their criminal records.

Substance Abuse Treatment And Mental Health Programming

Substance abuse and mental health issues represent significant risk factors for criminal behavior and recidivism, making treatment programming essential components of effective correctional intervention. The First Step Act prioritized expansion of evidence-based treatment services and integration of treatment with other reentry programming.

Residential Drug Abuse Programs (RDAP) provide intensive, long-term treatment for individuals with serious substance abuse histories. These programs typically last 9-12 months and combine group therapy, individual counseling, educational programming, and community treatment preparation in therapeutic community settings.

RDAP participation can result in significant sentence reductions for eligible individuals, with successful completers eligible for up to one year of community-based treatment in halfway houses or home confinement. This incentive structure encourages participation while ensuring that individuals receive continued support during the critical transition period.

Non-residential substance abuse programming serves individuals with less severe addiction issues or those who are not eligible for residential programs. These interventions include group counseling, individual therapy, drug education, and relapse prevention programming that can be provided while individuals participate in other activities and programming.

Medication-assisted treatment (MAT) for opioid addiction has been expanded in federal facilities, providing individuals with evidence-based pharmacological interventions combined with counseling and behavioral therapies. MAT programs help individuals manage withdrawal symptoms, reduce cravings, and maintain sobriety while participating in other programming.

Mental health programming addresses the significant prevalence of mental illness among incarcerated populations, with studies indicating that approximately 40% of individuals in federal custody have diagnosable mental health conditions. Treatment services include individual and group therapy, psychiatric medication management, and specialized programming for specific conditions.

Trauma-informed care recognizes that many individuals in federal custody have experienced significant trauma that may contribute to both their criminal behavior and their mental health challenges. Programming incorporates understanding of trauma's impact and utilizes therapeutic approaches that avoid re-traumatization while promoting healing.

Cognitive-behavioral therapy (CBT) represents one of the most effective interventions for reducing recidivism, helping individuals identify and change thinking patterns that contribute to criminal behavior. CBT programs focus on developing problem-solving skills, emotional regulation, and pro-social thinking patterns.

Dual diagnosis programming serves individuals with co-occurring substance abuse and mental health disorders, recognizing that these conditions often interact and require integrated treatment approaches. These programs coordinate psychiatric treatment with addiction services to address both conditions simultaneously.

Family Reunification And Community Connections

The First Step Act recognized that maintaining and strengthening family relationships and community connections are crucial factors in successful reentry and recidivism reduction. The legislation includes provisions designed to facilitate communication between incarcerated individuals and their families while preparing for eventual reunification.

Video visitation technology has been expanded to supplement traditional in-person visits, allowing families to maintain more frequent contact despite geographic barriers. This technology is particularly important for families who cannot afford to travel long distances to visit incarcerated relatives in federal facilities.

Phone call reforms reduced the cost of telephone communication between incarcerated individuals and their families, recognizing that the high cost of prison phone calls created significant barriers to maintaining family relationships. Reduced rates make it possible for families to have more frequent and longer conversations.

Email and electronic messaging systems allow incarcerated individuals to communicate with family members through secure electronic platforms. These systems provide more immediate communication than traditional mail while maintaining appropriate security and monitoring capabilities.

Family programming includes services designed to help families prepare for reunification and address the challenges created by incarceration. These programs may include family counseling, parenting classes, financial planning, and support groups for family members.

Parenting programs help incarcerated parents maintain relationships with their children and develop effective parenting skills for reunification. These programs recognize that many incarcerated individuals are parents and that successful parent-child relationships can be important protective factors against recidivism.

Community partnership development connects incarcerated individuals with community-based organizations that can provide support services upon release. These partnerships may include religious organizations, community service groups, mentoring programs, and other entities that can provide ongoing support.

Volunteer mentoring programs pair incarcerated individuals with community volunteers who provide guidance, support, and assistance with reentry planning. These relationships often continue after release and provide crucial emotional and practical support during the transition period.

Victim impact programming helps individuals understand the harm caused by their criminal behavior and develop empathy and accountability. While not directly related to family reunification, these programs can help individuals develop the emotional skills necessary for healthy relationships.

Employment Assistance And Economic Stability

Securing stable employment represents one of the most critical factors in successful reentry, providing both economic stability and pro-social structure that reduces the likelihood of recidivism. **The First Step Act** emphasizes employment preparation and job placement assistance as essential components of effective programming.

Job readiness training prepares individuals for the employment search process, including resume writing, interview skills, workplace behavior expectations, and job search strategies. These programs address the reality that many individuals in federal custody have limited experience with formal employment processes.

Career counseling helps individuals identify realistic employment goals based on their skills, interests, and the practical constraints they may face due to their criminal records. Counselors work with individuals to develop career plans that account for both their potential and the barriers they may encounter.

Industry-specific training programs provide skills development in sectors that are more likely to hire individuals with criminal records. These may include construction, food service, transportation, and manufacturing industries that face labor shortages and are more willing to consider applicants with criminal histories.

Occupational licensing assistance helps individuals navigate the complex process of obtaining professional licenses and certifications in states that may have restrictions for individuals with criminal records. This assistance includes legal advocacy and guidance on restoration of rights processes.

Entrepreneurship support recognizes that self-employment may be an important option for individuals who face significant barriers to traditional employment. Programs provide business planning skills, access to microfinance, and ongoing support for small business development.

Employer partnership development involves building relationships with employers who are willing to hire individuals with criminal records. These partnerships may include job fairs, direct placement programs, and ongoing support for both employers and employees.

Financial planning services help individuals prepare for the economic challenges of reentry, including budgeting, debt management, and planning for basic needs such as housing and transportation. These services recognize that financial stress can be a significant risk factor for recidivism.

Benefits enrollment assistance helps eligible individuals access government benefits such as Social Security, Medicare, Medicaid, and SNAP benefits that can provide crucial support during the reentry period. Many individuals are eligible for these benefits but lack knowledge about how to access them.

Healthcare And Continuity Of Care

Healthcare continuity represents a critical but often overlooked aspect of successful reentry, particularly for individuals with chronic medical conditions, mental health issues, or substance abuse disorders. The First Step Act includes provisions designed to ensure that individuals maintain access to necessary healthcare services during the transition from incarceration to community supervision.

Chronic disease management programs help individuals with conditions such as diabetes, hypertension, and heart disease develop the knowledge and skills necessary to manage their conditions independently. These programs include medication management education, lifestyle modification counseling, and coordination with community healthcare providers.

Mental health discharge planning ensures that individuals with mental health conditions have appropriate community treatment arrangements in place before release. This planning includes medication continuity, therapy referrals, and coordination with community mental health centers.

Substance abuse treatment continuity is particularly important for individuals completing residential treatment programs while incarcerated. Discharge planning includes referrals to community treatment providers, continuation of medication-assisted treatment when appropriate, and connection to recovery support services.

Prescription medication management helps individuals understand their medications, ensures they have adequate supplies during the transition period, and facilitates coordination with community pharmacies and healthcare providers. This is particularly important for individuals with psychiatric medications or other critical prescriptions.

Healthcare enrollment assistance helps eligible individuals access health insurance through Medicaid, Medicare, or marketplace plans. Having health insurance is crucial for maintaining access to necessary medical care and preventing medical debt that could create financial stress.

Emergency medical planning addresses the reality that some individuals may have urgent medical needs during the reentry period. This planning includes information about local emergency services, urgent care options, and protocols for medical emergencies.

Preventive care education helps individuals understand the importance of routine medical care and provides information about accessing preventive services such as vaccinations, screenings, and routine check-ups that may have been neglected during incarceration.

Special population healthcare addresses the unique needs of elderly individuals, those with disabilities, and individuals with complex medical conditions who may require specialized community supports and services.

Housing Assistance And Residential Stability

Securing stable housing represents one of the most fundamental challenges facing individuals returning from federal incarceration, yet housing stability is crucial for successful reentry and recidivism reduction. **The First Step Act and Second Chance Act** include provisions and funding streams designed to address housing barriers and support residential stability.

Halfway house programming provides transitional housing in structured residential facilities that offer supervision, programming, and support services while individuals adjust to community life. These facilities serve as stepping stones between incarceration and independent living, providing graduated freedom and responsibility.

Home confinement options allow eligible individuals to serve portions of their sentences in their own homes or approved residences under electronic monitoring supervision. This option maintains family connections and community ties while providing a controlled environment for successful reintegration.

Transitional housing programs provide temporary housing assistance for individuals who do not have approved residences for halfway house placement or home confinement. These programs may include emergency shelter, transitional apartments, or other temporary housing options.

Housing search assistance helps individuals identify affordable housing options that will accept applicants with criminal records. This assistance includes education about tenant rights, housing application processes, and strategies for addressing criminal background concerns with landlords.

Family reunification housing support helps individuals return to live with family members when appropriate, including mediation services to address family conflicts, housing modification assistance, and support for families who may be hesitant about reunification.

Sober living environments provide housing specifically designed for individuals in recovery from substance abuse. These facilities typically require sobriety, participation in recovery programming, and compliance with house rules designed to support recovery.

Rapid rehousing assistance provides short-term financial assistance and services to help individuals quickly exit homelessness and return to stable housing. This assistance may include security deposits, utility connections, and short-term rental assistance.

Permanent supportive housing serves individuals with disabilities or chronic conditions who require ongoing support to maintain housing stability. These programs combine affordable housing with support services designed to help individuals live independently.

Technology And Innovation In Reentry Programming

The implementation of the First Step Act has been accompanied by significant technological innovations designed to improve program delivery, enhance communication capabilities, and provide new tools for education and skill development. These technological advances represent important improvements in correctional programming and reentry preparation.

Tablet-based programming systems provide incarcerated individuals with access to educational content, vocational training materials, legal research capabilities, and communication tools through secure tablet devices. These systems allow for individualized programming that can be accessed at flexible times and paces.

Virtual reality training programs provide immersive learning experiences for job skills training, social skills development, and educational programming. VR technology can simulate workplace environments, social situations, and other real-world scenarios that help individuals develop practical skills.

Distance learning platforms connect incarcerated individuals with educational institutions and training providers outside the facility, dramatically expanding access to academic and vocational programming. These platforms use video conferencing, online coursework, and digital materials to deliver high-quality education.

Electronic monitoring technology has advanced significantly, providing more sophisticated and less intrusive supervision options for individuals on home confinement or community supervision. Modern systems include GPS tracking, alcohol monitoring, and biometric verification capabilities.

Mobile applications designed for reentry support provide individuals with access to resources, services, and support networks through smartphone technology. These apps may include job search tools, benefit enrollment assistance, transportation information, and crisis support services.

Data analytics and predictive modeling help correctional agencies and service providers identify individuals at highest risk for recidivism and target interventions more effectively. These tools can also track program outcomes and identify successful practices for replication.

Telehealth services provide access to medical and mental health care through video conferencing and remote monitoring technologies. These services are particularly valuable for individuals in rural areas or those with transportation barriers.

Digital literacy training ensures that individuals have the computer and internet skills necessary to navigate modern employment, education, and service environments. These programs recognize that technological proficiency is increasingly essential for successful reintegration.

Outcome Measurement And Evidence Of Effectiveness

The success of **the First Step Act and Second Chance Act** depends on rigorous outcome measurement and continuous evaluation to ensure that programs achieve their intended goals of reducing recidivism and improving reentry outcomes. Both legislative initiatives include provisions for data collection, research, and evaluation to build the evidence base for effective programming.

Recidivism measurement represents the primary outcome indicator for most reentry programming, typically measured as rearrest, reconviction, or reincarceration within specific time periods following release. However, researchers and practitioners recognize that recidivism alone may not capture the full range of program benefits and outcomes.

Employment outcomes include measures such as job placement rates, wage levels, job retention, and career advancement among program participants. These outcomes are particularly important given the central role of employment in successful reentry and economic stability.

Housing stability outcomes track whether individuals maintain stable housing following release and avoid homelessness. Housing stability is measured through various indicators including length of stay in housing, housing quality, and independence from emergency or transitional housing services.

Education and training completion rates measure program participation and credential attainment in academic and vocational programming. These outcomes help assess program quality and identify successful program models for replication.

Substance abuse treatment outcomes include measures of treatment completion, sobriety maintenance, and reduction in substance use behaviors. These outcomes are particularly important given the high prevalence of substance abuse among justice-involved populations.

Family reunification outcomes measure the extent to which individuals successfully reconnect with family members and maintain healthy family relationships following release. These outcomes may include measures of child custody restoration, family stability, and family functioning.

Cost-effectiveness analysis compares program costs with outcomes achieved to determine which interventions provide the greatest return on investment. These analyses help policymakers make informed decisions about resource allocation and program funding priorities.

Longitudinal studies track participant outcomes over extended periods to assess long-term program impacts and identify factors associated with sustained success. These studies provide crucial information about program effectiveness beyond the immediate post-release period.

Economic Impact And Cost-Benefit Analysis

The economic implications of **the First Step Act and Second Chance Act** extend far beyond their direct program costs to include significant savings from reduced incarceration, decreased crime, and increased economic productivity among successfully reintegrated individuals. Cost-benefit analyses consistently demonstrate that effective reentry programming generates positive returns on investment.

Direct cost savings from reduced incarceration represent the most immediate economic benefit of successful reentry programming. The federal prison system spends approximately **$35,000 per person** per year, meaning that each individual who successfully completes their sentence without returning to prison saves taxpayers substantial amounts over time.

Crime reduction benefits include savings from prevented victimization, reduced law enforcement costs, and decreased court processing expenses. When individuals successfully reintegrate and avoid future criminal behavior, society benefits from reduced crime rates and associated costs.

Increased tax revenue results from successfully employed individuals who earn legitimate income and pay taxes rather than remaining unemployed or engaged in illegal economic activity. This revenue generation helps offset program costs while contributing to overall economic growth.

Reduced reliance on government benefits occurs when individuals achieve economic stability through employment rather than depending on welfare, disability, or other government support programs. While these programs serve important safety net functions, reducing unnecessary dependence benefits both individuals and taxpayers.

Family economic stability improves when individuals return home and contribute to household income rather than creating financial burdens through continued incarceration or unsuccessful reentry. This stability particularly benefits children and other family members who may have experienced economic hardship during the period of incarceration.

Healthcare cost savings result from improved access to preventive care and better management of chronic conditions among individuals who successfully reintegrate. Emergency room visits and crisis interventions are reduced when individuals have stable housing, income, and access to routine healthcare.

Economic multiplier effects occur when successfully reintegrated individuals spend their earnings in local communities, creating demand for goods and services that supports local businesses and employment. These effects are particularly important in communities with high concentrations of returning citizens.

Program cost-effectiveness varies depending on the specific interventions provided and the populations served. However, rigorous evaluations consistently demonstrate that well-implemented reentry programs generate benefits that exceed their costs, often by substantial margins.

Challenges And Implementation Barriers

Despite the significant achievements represented by **the First Step Act and Second Chance Act,** implementation has faced various challenges that have limited the full realization of their potential benefits. Understanding these barriers is crucial for ongoing reform efforts and continuous improvement of reentry programming.

Funding constraints have represented one of the most persistent challenges facing **Second Chance Act** implementation. While the legislation authorized substantial funding levels, actual congressional appropriations have consistently fallen short of authorized amounts. This funding gap has limited the number of programs that can be supported and the scope of services that can be provided to eligible individuals.

Capacity limitations within the Bureau of Prisons and state correctional systems have slowed the expansion of evidence-based programming required by **the First Step Act.** Implementing comprehensive risk assessment systems, expanding educational and vocational programming, and providing adequate staffing for new initiatives requires significant organizational change and resource allocation.

Staff training and development needs have emerged as significant implementation challenges. Correctional staff trained in traditional security-focused approaches require extensive professional development to effectively implement evidence-based programming and adopt rehabilitation-oriented practices. This cultural shift takes time and sustained organizational commitment.

Technology infrastructure limitations have hindered the implementation of advanced programming delivery systems, particularly in older correctional facilities that lack adequate telecommunications and computer systems. Upgrading these systems requires substantial capital investment and ongoing technical support.

Coordination challenges between federal, state, and local agencies have complicated efforts to provide seamless services during the transition from incarceration to community supervision. Different agencies often have incompatible data systems, conflicting policies, and varying levels of commitment to evidence-based practices.

Community resistance to reentry programming and returning citizen placement has created barriers in some jurisdictions where community members oppose halfway houses, treatment facilities, or other reentry infrastructure. This resistance can limit housing options and service availability for individuals returning from incarceration.

Risk assessment validation and bias concerns have generated ongoing debate about the PATTERN system and similar tools used to determine program eligibility and release decisions. Critics argue that these instruments may perpetuate racial and socioeconomic disparities by incorporating factors that reflect historical inequities in the criminal justice system.

Legal challenges to various aspects of both acts have created uncertainty about implementation requirements and delayed some program expansions. Courts have been asked to interpret provisions related to eligibility criteria, earned time calculations, and the scope of required programming, leading to ongoing litigation that affects program administration.

Administrative complexity in calculating earned time credits and determining program eligibility has proven more challenging than initially anticipated. **The Bureau of Prisons** has struggled to develop consistent policies and procedures for tracking program participation, assessing program quality, and calculating credit awards across different facilities and programs.

Quality assurance and program fidelity issues have emerged as programs have been rapidly expanded to meet legislative requirements. Ensuring that all programs truly implement evidence-based practices and achieve intended outcomes requires ongoing monitoring, evaluation, and technical assistance that strains available resources.

Future Directions And Reform Opportunities

The implementation experience of **the First Step Act and Second Chance Act** has identified numerous opportunities for further reform and improvement in federal and state criminal justice systems. These experiences provide valuable lessons for future policy development and program enhancement.

Sentencing reform represents the next logical step in comprehensive criminal justice reform, building on the foundation established by **the First Step Act's** programming initiatives. Many advocates argue that meaningful reductions in incarceration rates will require addressing the underlying sentencing policies that have driven mass incarceration, including mandatory minimum penalties and lengthy sentences for non-violent offenses.

Expanded eligibility criteria for earned time credits and other benefits could extend **the First Step Act's** impact to additional populations currently excluded from its provisions. Some reform advocates propose reducing or eliminating exclusions based on offense type or criminal history, arguing that rehabilitation programming can benefit all individuals regardless of their past conduct.

Enhanced state and local implementation of evidence-based practices could extend the benefits of federal reforms to the much larger state prison population. Technical assistance, funding support, and policy incentives could encourage state systems to adopt similar programming approaches and release mechanisms.

Improved data collection and research capabilities could strengthen the evidence base for effective programming and identify emerging best practices. Investment in longitudinal studies, randomized controlled trials, and sophisticated data analytics could improve understanding of what works, for whom, and under what circumstances.

Community-based alternatives to incarceration could be expanded to divert more individuals from prison while maintaining public safety. Electronic monitoring, drug courts, mental health courts, and other specialty programs could reduce the need for incarceration while providing appropriate supervision and services.

Victim services integration could ensure that reentry programming appropriately addresses victim concerns and incorporates restorative justice principles. Programs that bring together victims and offenders in structured settings can promote healing while supporting successful reintegration.

Technology advancement will continue to create new opportunities for program delivery, supervision, and support services. Artificial intelligence, virtual reality, mobile applications, and other emerging technologies could revolutionize how correctional programming is delivered and how individuals are supported during reentry.

Impact On Families And Communities

The benefits of the First Step Act and Second Chance Act extend far beyond the individuals directly served by these programs to encompass families, children, and entire communities affected by incarceration and reentry. Understanding these broader impacts is crucial for assessing the full value of criminal justice reform initiatives.

Family reunification benefits include the restoration of family relationships that may have been damaged by incarceration and the challenges of maintaining connections across institutional barriers. When individuals successfully reintegrate into their communities, families benefit from renewed economic support, emotional connections, and shared parental responsibilities.

Children of incarcerated parents represent one of the most vulnerable populations affected by mass incarceration, with approximately 2.7 million children having a parent in prison or jail. Successful reentry programming helps restore parent-child relationships and provides children with the stability and support that comes from having engaged, present parents.

Economic revitalization in communities with high incarceration rates occurs when residents return home with job skills, stable employment, and the ability to contribute to local economic activity. These communities, which have often been devastated by the removal of large numbers of working-age adults, benefit from increased economic participation and reduced dependence on government assistance.

Reduced stigma and increased community acceptance of formerly incarcerated individuals can result from successful reentry programming that demonstrates people's capacity for change and positive contribution. As more individuals successfully reintegrate, communities may become more willing to provide opportunities and support for returning citizens.

Community safety improvements result from reduced recidivism rates and the positive social influence of successfully reintegrated individuals who can serve as role models and mentors for others at risk of criminal behavior. These improvements benefit all community members through reduced crime rates and increased social cohesion.

Civic engagement and community leadership often emerge among individuals who have successfully navigated the reentry process and want to give back to their communities. Many formerly incarcerated individuals become advocates for criminal justice reform, mentors for at-risk youth, and leaders in community development initiatives.

Intergenerational effects of successful reentry include breaking cycles of incarceration and criminal behavior that can affect multiple generations within families. When parents successfully reintegrate and provide positive role models for their children, the likelihood of future criminal behavior among the next generation is reduced.

Lessons Learned And Best Practices

The implementation of **the First Step Act and Second Chance Act** has generated important lessons about effective criminal justice reform and evidence-based programming that can inform future policy development and program improvement efforts.

Bipartisan collaboration has proven essential for achieving sustainable criminal justice reform. The broad coalition that supported both pieces of legislation demonstrates that criminal justice reform can transcend traditional political divisions when framed in terms of public safety, fiscal responsibility, and evidence-based practice.

Stakeholder engagement throughout the policy development and implementation process improves program design and increases the likelihood of successful outcomes. Including formerly incarcerated individuals, family members, victims, community organizations, and service providers in planning processes ensures that programs address real needs and barriers.

Evidence-based practice implementation requires ongoing support, training, and technical assistance rather than simply mandate compliance. Successful programs invest heavily in staff development, quality assurance, and continuous improvement based on outcome data and participant feedback.

Individualized programming approaches are more effective than one-size-fits-all interventions. The risk and needs assessment framework established by **the First Step Act** recognizes that different individuals require different types and intensities of programming based on their specific circumstances and risk factors.

Comprehensive service delivery that addresses multiple barriers simultaneously is more effective than programming that focuses on single issues in isolation. Successful reentry requires coordinated attention to employment, housing, healthcare, education, family relationships, and other interconnected needs.

Long-term sustainability requires adequate funding, organizational commitment, and political support that extends beyond initial implementation periods. Programs that demonstrate clear outcomes and benefits are more likely to maintain support through changing political and fiscal environments.

Community partnership development is crucial for successful reentry programming. No single organization can address all the complex needs of individuals returning from incarceration, making collaboration between correctional agencies, service providers, employers, and community organizations essential.

Cultural change within correctional organizations takes time and sustained effort. Moving from purely punitive approaches to rehabilitation-oriented practices requires changing deeply embedded organizational cultures, policies, and practices that have developed over decades.

International Perspectives And Comparative Analysis

The American experience with the **First Step Act and Second Chance Act** can be informed by examining criminal justice reform efforts in other countries that have successfully reduced incarceration rates while maintaining public safety. These international comparisons provide valuable insights about alternative approaches and potential improvements.

Scandinavian correctional systems, particularly those in Norway and Sweden, emphasize rehabilitation and normalization principles that prioritize preparing individuals for successful reintegration from the beginning of their sentences. These systems achieve significantly lower recidivism rates than the United States while spending comparable or fewer resources on corrections.

German correctional practices focus on social therapy and gradual reintegration through work release, educational opportunities, and community connections maintained throughout the period of incarceration. The German system's emphasis on maintaining family relationships and community ties aligns with many of the goals of American reentry programming.

Canadian federal corrections have implemented extensive programming requirements and earned remission systems that share similarities with **the First Step Act.** Canada's experience with risk assessment instruments and evidence-based programming provides lessons about implementation challenges and successful practices.

Dutch criminal justice reforms have dramatically reduced incarceration rates through investment in community-based alternatives, treatment programming, and restorative justice practices. The Netherlands' experience demonstrates that substantial reductions in prison populations are possible without compromising public safety.

Portuguese drug policy reforms that emphasized treatment over incarceration for drug-related offenses provide insights about alternatives to traditional criminal justice responses to substance abuse. These reforms have achieved significant reductions in drug-related crime and incarceration while improving public health outcomes.

These international examples suggest that more comprehensive reforms may be possible and that the benefits achieved through **the First Step Act and Second Chance Act** represent important steps toward broader transformation of American criminal justice systems.

Conclusion

The First Step Act and Second Chance Act represent landmark achievements in American criminal justice reform, establishing new paradigms for evidence-based programming, comprehensive reentry support, and rehabilitation-oriented correctional practice. These legislative initiatives have demonstrated that bipartisan cooperation is possible on criminal justice issues and that meaningful reform can be achieved through careful attention to evidence, stakeholder input, and implementation support.

The benefits of these acts extend far beyond their immediate programmatic impacts to include cultural changes within correctional systems, improved outcomes for individuals and families affected by incarceration, and enhanced public safety through reduced recidivism. The emphasis on evidence-based practice, individualized programming, and comprehensive service delivery has established new standards for effective correctional intervention.

However, the implementation experience has also highlighted significant challenges that must be addressed to achieve the full potential of these reforms. Funding constraints, capacity limitations, coordination difficulties, and ongoing political resistance continue to limit program reach and effectiveness. Addressing these challenges will require sustained commitment from policymakers, practitioners, and communities.

The lessons learned from implementing **the First Step Act** and **Second Chance Act** provide valuable guidance for future reform efforts. The importance of bipartisan collaboration, stakeholder engagement, adequate funding, and long-term sustainability has been clearly demonstrated. The need for comprehensive approaches that address multiple barriers simultaneously and the value of evidence-based practice have been confirmed through program outcomes and participant experiences.

Looking forward, these acts establish a foundation for continued criminal justice reform that could include expanded eligibility for programming benefits, enhanced sentencing reform, increased investment in community-based alternatives, and broader implementation of evidence-based practices across state and local systems. The success of these federal initiatives may encourage similar reforms at other levels of government and in other policy areas.

The ultimate measure of success for **the First Step Act and Second Chance Act** will be their long-term impact on recidivism rates, public safety, and the life outcomes of individuals and families affected by incarceration. Early indicators suggest positive trends, but sustained evaluation and continuous improvement will be necessary to ensure that these programs achieve their intended goals.

The transformation of American criminal justice from a system focused primarily on punishment to one that emphasizes rehabilitation and successful reintegration represents a fundamental shift in policy and practice. **The First Step Act** and Second Chance Act have played crucial roles in advancing this transformation, demonstrating that evidence-based reform can achieve positive outcomes for individuals, families, communities, and society as a whole.

As implementation continues and outcomes are evaluated, these legislative achievements will likely be remembered as pivotal moments in the evolution of American criminal justice policy. They represent hope for millions of individuals currently and formerly incarcerated, their families, and communities seeking alternatives to the failed policies of mass incarceration. The path forward requires continued commitment to evidence-based practice, adequate resource allocation, and the fundamental belief that people can change and deserve opportunities for redemption and successful reintegration into society.

CHAPTER THIRTEEN

THE FEDERAL PRISON SYSTEM - ORIGINS AND OPERATIONS

INTRODUCTION

The Federal Bureau of Prisons (BOP) stands as one of the largest correctional systems in the world, housing over 150,000 inmates across more than 120 facilities nationwide. This sprawling network of institutions represents the culmination of nearly a century of evolution in federal corrections, reflecting changing philosophies about punishment, rehabilitation, and public safety. Understanding the federal prison system requires examining both its historical development and its current operational structure, as these elements continue to shape how the United States manages individuals convicted of federal crimes.

The federal prison system operates distinctly from state correctional systems, handling individuals convicted of federal offenses such as drug trafficking, white-collar crimes, immigration violations, and crimes that cross state boundaries. This distinction is crucial because it determines not only where an individual serves their sentence but also the conditions of their confinement, available programs, and eventual reintegration into society. The system's impact extends far beyond its immediate population, affecting families, communities, and the broader criminal justice landscape.

Historical Origins And Early Development

The origins of the federal prison system can be traced to the late 19th and early 20th centuries, when the federal government recognized the need for a centralized approach to managing federal offenders. Prior to this period, individuals convicted of federal crimes were typically housed in state or local facilities under contract arrangements, creating inconsistencies in treatment and conditions. The Industrial Revolution and westward expansion had created new categories of federal crimes, from mail fraud to interstate commerce violations, necessitating a more systematic approach to federal corrections.

The first federal prison, USP Leavenworth in Kansas, opened in 1903 and was constructed by prison labor itself, a practice that would become common in the early federal system. Leavenworth was designed according to the Auburn system model, emphasizing congregate work during the day and solitary confinement at night. The facility reflected the prevailing correctional philosophy of the era, which viewed hard labor and rigid discipline as essential components of rehabilitation.

The establishment of USP Atlanta in 1902 and USP McNeil Island in Washington in 1907 marked the expansion of federal corrections beyond a single institution. Each facility developed its own character and specialization, with McNeil Island becoming known for its isolation and Atlanta for housing high-profile offenders. These early institutions established precedents for federal corrections that would influence policy for decades, including the emphasis on self-sufficiency through prison industries and the maintenance of strict security protocols.

The 1920s brought significant challenges and changes to the federal system. Prohibition created an unprecedented influx of federal prisoners, overwhelming existing facilities and forcing rapid expansion. The decade saw the opening of several new institutions, including USP Alderson in West Virginia, which became the first federal prison exclusively for women in 1927. The facility's design and programming reflected contemporary views about female criminality and rehabilitation, emphasizing domestic skills and moral reformation.

During this period, the federal system also grappled with overcrowding, violence, and questions about the effectiveness of purely punitive approaches. High-profile incidents, including riots and escapes, drew public attention to conditions within federal prisons and sparked debates about reform. The 1929 riot at USP Leavenworth, which resulted in multiple deaths and extensive property damage, exemplified the tensions within the system and highlighted the need for more sophisticated management approaches.

The Formation Of The Federal Bureau Of Prisons

The establishment of the Federal Bureau of Prisons in 1930 marked a watershed moment in federal corrections. Created through the passage of congressional legislation, the BOP centralized the administration of federal prisons under a single agency within the Department of Justice. This organizational change reflected Progressive Era ideals about scientific management and professional administration, applying these principles to the previously fragmented world of federal corrections.

Sanford Bates, the first Director of the Bureau of Prisons, brought extensive experience in state corrections and a reform-minded approach to federal corrections. Under his leadership, the BOP implemented standardized policies and procedures across all federal facilities, established training programs for correctional staff, and began developing specialized institutions for different types of offenders. Bates emphasized the importance of classification systems that would match inmates to appropriate facilities and programs based on their security level, criminal history, and rehabilitation needs.

The 1930s saw rapid expansion and innovation within the federal system. The decade brought the opening of USP Lewisburg in Pennsylvania, designed as a model facility incorporating the latest theories in correctional architecture and programming. The institution featured improved living conditions, educational programs, and vocational training opportunities that reflected the era's growing emphasis on rehabilitation alongside punishment.

Perhaps most notably, this period saw the opening of USP Alcatraz in 1934, which became the federal system's most famous and notorious institution. Located on an island in San Francisco Bay, Alcatraz was designed to house the most dangerous and escape-prone federal prisoners. The facility's extreme security measures, isolation from the mainland, and harsh conditions made it a symbol of the federal government's commitment to containing its most problematic offenders. Alcatraz housed famous criminals including Al Capone, Machine Gun Kelly, and Robert Stroud, earning a reputation that persists in popular culture decades after its closure in 1963.

The establishment of the BOP also coincided with significant changes in federal criminal law. The passage of new legislation expanded federal jurisdiction over crimes involving interstate commerce, organized crime, and drug trafficking. These changes created new categories of federal offenders and influenced the development of specialized facilities and programs within the federal system.

Evolution Through The Mid-20th Century

The 1940s and 1950s brought continued growth and refinement to the federal prison system. World War II created unique challenges, including the internment of enemy aliens and conscientious objectors, while also limiting resources available for prison construction and programming. The war years demonstrated the system's adaptability and highlighted the political dimensions of federal corrections.

Post-war America saw renewed attention to rehabilitation and treatment within corrections. The federal system embraced medical model approaches that viewed criminal behavior as a form of illness requiring treatment rather than simple punishment. This philosophy influenced the design of new facilities and the development of programs emphasizing education, vocational training, and psychological treatment.

The 1950s marked the beginning of significant expansion in federal corrections infrastructure. New institutions opened regularly, including specialized facilities for different security levels and offender populations. The federal system pioneered the development of minimum-security prison camps, recognizing that many federal offenders posed minimal security risks and could be housed in less restrictive environments while participating in community-oriented programming.

During this period, the federal system also began developing more sophisticated classification systems. These systems assessed inmates based on factors including criminal history, violence potential, escape risk, and program needs. Classification determined not only security level placement but also access to educational programs, work assignments, and other opportunities within the system.

The civil rights movement of the 1960s brought new scrutiny to conditions within federal prisons. Court cases challenged overcrowding, medical care, disciplinary procedures, and access to legal resources. These legal challenges forced significant reforms and established prisoners' rights as a legitimate area of constitutional concern. The federal system, as a government entity, faced particular pressure to model best practices in corrections.

Modern Structure And Organization

Today's Federal Bureau of Prisons operates as a complex organizational structure designed to manage diverse populations across multiple security levels and geographic regions. The agency is headquartered in Washington, D.C., and oversees operations through six regional offices located in Philadelphia, Atlanta, Dallas, Kansas City, Fresno, and Annapolis Junction. Each regional office supervises institutions within its geographic area and ensures compliance with national policies while addressing regional needs and challenges.

The BOP's organizational structure reflects both security requirements and administrative efficiency. At the national level, the Director oversees multiple divisions including Correctional Programs, Administration, Human Resources, and Industries, Education, and Vocational Training. This structure ensures that policy development, resource allocation, and operational oversight maintain consistency across the entire system while allowing for specialized expertise in different areas of corrections.

Regional offices serve as intermediaries between national headquarters and individual institutions, providing oversight, technical assistance, and coordination of resources. Regional administrators work closely with wardens and senior staff at each facility to address operational challenges, implement new policies, and ensure compliance with federal regulations and court orders. This regional structure allows the BOP to maintain centralized control while recognizing the unique challenges and opportunities present in different geographic areas.

Individual institutions operate under the authority of wardens who report to their regional office. Wardens serve as chief executive officers of their facilities, responsible for all aspects of institutional operations including security, programming, staff management, and community relations. The warden is supported by associate wardens who typically oversee specific areas such as operations, programs, or industries, creating a management structure that can effectively coordinate the complex daily operations of a federal prison.

Security Classifications And Facility Types

The federal prison system employs a comprehensive security classification system that categorizes both inmates and institutions according to security levels. This system ensures that offenders are housed in facilities appropriate to their security risk while maximizing opportunities for programming and eventual reintegration. The classification system considers factors including the nature of the current offense, criminal history, violence potential, escape risk, and expected length of sentence.

Minimum-security institutions, often called prison camps or **Federal Prison Camps (FPCs)**, house inmates who pose the lowest security risk. These facilities typically feature dormitory-style housing, minimal perimeter security, and extensive work and programming opportunities. Inmates at minimum-security facilities often participate in community-based programs and may work outside the institution during the day. The philosophy behind minimum-security facilities emphasizes preparing inmates for successful reintegration into society through gradually increasing responsibility and community contact.

Low-security Federal Correctional Institutions (FCIs) house inmates with slightly higher security needs while still emphasizing programming and reintegration. These facilities typically feature double-fenced perimeters with electronic detection systems but maintain less restrictive internal operations than higher-security institutions. Low-security facilities often house inmates serving longer sentences for non-violent offenses and provide extensive educational, vocational, and treatment programming.

Medium-security institutions house inmates who require more secure environments due to their criminal history, sentence length, or assessed risk factors. These Federal Correctional Institutions feature reinforced perimeters, armed guard towers, and more restrictive movement policies. Despite higher security measures, medium-security facilities continue to offer comprehensive programming designed to address criminogenic needs and prepare inmates for eventual release.

High-security United States Penitentiaries (USPs) house inmates who pose the greatest security risks within the general federal prison population. These facilities feature the highest levels of security, including multiple perimeter barriers, armed patrols, and severely restricted movement. Programming at high-security facilities focuses on managing institutional behavior and addressing serious mental health or behavioral issues that may affect an inmate's ability to participate in general population activities.

The federal system also operates **Administrative Maximum (ADX)** facilities for inmates who require the highest levels of security and control. **ADX Florence in Colorado** represents the pinnacle of secure custody within the federal system, housing terrorists, spies, and other inmates whose crimes or institutional behavior requires extreme security measures. Conditions at **ADX facilities** are highly restrictive, with inmates spending most of their time in individual cells and having limited contact with others.

Specialized Institutions And Programs

Beyond traditional security-level classifications, the federal prison system operates numerous specialized institutions designed to address specific populations or needs. Medical centers provide comprehensive healthcare for inmates with serious medical conditions, combining correctional security with hospital-level medical care. These facilities serve inmates from throughout the federal system who require specialized treatment that cannot be provided at their home institutions.

Federal Medical Centers (FMCs) operate as full-service hospitals within the prison system, providing everything from routine medical care to complex surgical procedures. These facilities maintain accreditation from healthcare organizations and employ medical professionals comparable to those found in community hospitals. The integration of medical care within the correctional environment presents unique challenges, requiring specialized policies and procedures that balance security requirements with medical best practices.

The federal system also operates specialized facilities for female offenders, recognizing the unique needs and characteristics of women in the criminal justice system. These institutions provide programming specifically designed for women, including parenting classes, trauma counseling, and vocational training in fields with strong employment prospects for women. The relatively small population of federal female inmates allows for more individualized programming and treatment approaches.

Administrative facilities serve various specialized functions within the federal system. These institutions may house inmates in transit between facilities, those requiring protective custody, or individuals undergoing specialized evaluation or treatment. Administrative facilities provide flexibility within the system, allowing for individualized management of inmates whose needs cannot be met at traditional institutions.

The federal system has also developed innovative approaches to managing specific populations, including elderly inmates and those with serious mental illness. Specialized housing units and programming address the unique challenges these populations present, from modified physical environments for aging inmates to intensive mental health treatment for those with serious psychiatric conditions.

Daily Operations And Inmate Life

Daily life within federal prisons follows highly structured routines designed to maintain security while providing opportunities for programming and personal development. The typical day begins with controlled movement and count procedures that verify the location and wellbeing of all inmates. These security procedures occur multiple times throughout the day and represent non-negotiable aspects of institutional operations that take precedence over all other activities.

Work assignments form a central component of daily life for most federal inmates. The BOP operates extensive industrial and service programs that provide inmates with job skills while supporting institutional operations. Federal Prison Industries, also known as **UNICOR,** employs thousands of inmates in manufacturing operations producing goods for government agencies. These programs provide vocational training, work experience, and modest wages while contributing to institutional self-sufficiency.

Educational programming represents another cornerstone of federal corrections, with most institutions offering literacy programs, GED preparation, vocational training, and sometimes college-level courses. The BOP recognizes education as a critical factor in successful reintegration and has developed comprehensive programming designed to address educational deficits common among federal inmates. Recent initiatives have emphasized post-secondary education opportunities, including partnerships with colleges and universities to provide degree programs within federal facilities.

Treatment programming addresses various criminogenic needs including substance abuse, mental health issues, cognitive skills, and anger management. These programs utilize evidence-based approaches and are often mandatory for inmates with specific risk factors or needs. The BOP has invested heavily in developing and implementing effective treatment programs, recognizing their importance in reducing recidivism and promoting successful reintegration.

Religious and recreational activities provide additional structure and meaning to daily life within federal prisons. Most institutions maintain chapels or religious programming spaces that accommodate multiple faith traditions and provide opportunities for worship, study, and spiritual counseling. Recreation programs include both organized sports and individual fitness activities, serving physical and mental health needs while providing constructive outlets for energy and stress.

Staff And Administration

The operation of the federal prison system depends on a diverse workforce of approximately 37,000 employees representing various professional disciplines. Correctional officers form the largest component of the workforce, providing direct supervision of inmates and maintaining institutional security. These officers receive extensive training in security procedures, emergency response, legal requirements, and interpersonal communication skills necessary for effective correctional work.

Professional staff within federal prisons include teachers, counselors, psychologists, medical personnel, chaplains, and administrative specialists. These positions require specialized education and training and play crucial roles in delivering programming and services to inmates. The integration of professional staff within the correctional environment requires careful coordination and communication to ensure that treatment and programming goals align with security requirements.

Management positions within federal prisons require extensive experience in corrections along with advanced education in relevant fields. Wardens and senior staff typically have decades of experience in progressively responsible positions and receive ongoing training in leadership, emergency management, legal requirements, and correctional best practices. The complexity of modern correctional operations demands sophisticated management skills and broad knowledge of multiple professional disciplines.

Staff training and development represent ongoing priorities within the federal system. New employees attend comprehensive training programs at the Federal Law Enforcement Training Center in Georgia, receiving instruction in security procedures, legal requirements, emergency response, and professional ethics. Ongoing training ensures that staff remain current with evolving best practices and legal requirements while developing advanced skills necessary for career progression.

The federal prison system also employs various contract staff and volunteers who provide specialized services or programming. These individuals must meet strict security requirements and receive training in institutional procedures and security protocols. The use of contract staff and volunteers allows the system to access specialized expertise while controlling costs and providing inmates with exposure to positive community role models.

Challenges And Reforms

The federal prison system faces numerous ongoing challenges that influence operations and policy development. Overcrowding has been a persistent issue, with many facilities operating above their designed capacity and straining resources and programming opportunities. This overcrowding results from factors including mandatory minimum sentencing laws, longer average sentences, and limited alternatives to incarceration for federal offenders.

Budget constraints present ongoing challenges for the federal system, limiting resources available for programming, maintenance, and staff development. The high cost of corrections competes with other federal priorities and creates pressure to find more cost-effective approaches to managing federal offenders. These financial pressures have prompted innovations in programming delivery and increased emphasis on evidence-based practices that demonstrate measurable outcomes.

Aging infrastructure represents another significant challenge, with many federal facilities constructed decades ago requiring extensive renovation or replacement. Modern correctional design emphasizes direct supervision models and flexible programming spaces that differ significantly from older institutional designs. The cost of infrastructure improvements and new construction presents ongoing budgetary challenges while aging facilities create operational difficulties and increased maintenance costs.

The federal system has also grappled with various scandals and controversies that have highlighted management challenges and prompted reforms. Issues including staff misconduct, inadequate medical care, and management failures have resulted in congressional oversight, legal challenges, and policy reforms. These incidents underscore the complexity of correctional operations and the ongoing need for effective oversight and accountability measures.

Recent reform efforts have emphasized evidence-based practices, reentry programming, and alternatives to traditional incarceration. The First Step Act of 2018 represented the most significant federal corrections reform in decades, expanding programming opportunities, modifying sentencing practices, and increasing emphasis on successful reintegration. Implementation of these reforms continues to influence federal corrections policy and operations.

Future Directions And Conclusions

The federal prison system continues to evolve in response to changing crime patterns, legal requirements, budget constraints, and research findings about effective correctional practices.

Emerging trends include increased use of technology for monitoring and programming delivery, expansion of community-based alternatives to incarceration, and greater emphasis on mental health and substance abuse treatment.

Technology is transforming many aspects of federal corrections, from security systems and monitoring equipment to educational programming delivery and communication systems. These technological advances offer opportunities to improve security and programming while potentially reducing costs, but they also present new challenges in terms of staff training, system integration, and maintaining human elements essential to effective corrections.

The ongoing emphasis on evidence-based practices is likely to continue shaping federal corrections policy and programming. Research on effective interventions, risk assessment tools, and reentry programming provides guidance for policy development while accountability for outcomes drives innovation and program improvement. This scientific approach to corrections represents a significant shift from historical reliance on tradition and intuition.

The Federal Bureau of Prisons remains one of the world's largest and most complex correctional systems, managing a diverse population of federal offenders while balancing competing demands for security, programming, constitutional compliance, and fiscal responsibility. Its evolution from a small collection of institutions to a sophisticated correctional agency reflects broader changes in American criminal justice and continuing efforts to develop more effective approaches to corrections.

Understanding the federal prison system requires appreciation for both its historical development and current challenges. The system's origins in Progressive Era reform movements, its expansion during periods of increased federal criminal enforcement, and its ongoing adaptation to changing needs and expectations demonstrate the dynamic nature of correctional policy and practice. As American society continues to grapple with questions about crime, punishment, and rehabilitation, the federal prison system will undoubtedly continue to evolve, seeking more effective ways to protect public safety while providing opportunities for offender change and successful reintegration into society.

The success of these efforts depends on continued investment in research, staff development, infrastructure improvement, and innovative programming approaches. The federal system's influence extends beyond its immediate population to serve as a model for state and local corrections systems, making its continued development and improvement a matter of national importance in the broader effort to create a more effective and just criminal justice system.

CHAPTER FOURTEEN

IMMIGRATION ENFORCEMENT - ORIGINS AND THE RISE OF ICE

INTRODUCTION

Immigration has been a defining feature of American society since the nation's founding, shaping demographics, economics, culture, and politics across centuries. The story of immigration enforcement in the United States reflects broader tensions between America's identity as a nation of immigrants and periodic desires to control, restrict, or exclude certain groups from entry or citizenship. The evolution of immigration enforcement culminated in the creation of Immigration and Customs Enforcement (ICE) in 2003, representing the most significant reorganization of immigration enforcement in American history.

Understanding modern immigration enforcement requires examining the historical development of immigration policy, the agencies and mechanisms created to implement these policies, and the political, economic, and social forces that have shaped enforcement priorities over time. The transformation from relatively informal border controls to today's complex enforcement apparatus reflects changing views about national security, economic competition, cultural identity, and federal authority.

The creation of ICE following the September 11, 2001 terrorist attacks marked a watershed moment in immigration enforcement, consolidating previously scattered functions under the Department of Homeland Security and significantly expanding enforcement capabilities. This reorganization represented not merely an administrative change but a fundamental shift in how the United States conceptualizes and implements immigration control, with implications that continue to shape policy debates and enforcement practices today.

Early Immigration And Informal Controls (1607-1875)

During the colonial period and early decades of American independence, immigration occurred with minimal formal controls or restrictions. The young nation desperately needed population growth to develop its vast territories, defend its borders, and build its economy. Colonial authorities and later state governments generally welcomed immigrants, viewing population growth as essential to prosperity and security. The informal nature of early immigration controls reflected both practical limitations and philosophical commitments to relatively open migration.

The colonial period saw significant immigration from various European nations, with different colonies attracting distinct immigrant populations based on religious tolerance, economic opportunities, and existing ethnic communities. Pennsylvania attracted large numbers of German immigrants, while other colonies drew English, Scots-Irish, Dutch, and French settlers. These migration patterns occurred largely without formal government oversight or restriction, though colonial authorities sometimes expressed concerns about the loyalty or cultural integration of certain groups.

The Constitution, ratified in 1788, granted Congress authority over naturalization but did not explicitly address immigration controls. The Naturalization Act of 1790 established procedures for becoming an American citizen but imposed few restrictions on who could enter the country. This early approach reflected Enlightenment ideals about individual liberty and economic opportunity, as well as practical recognition that the young nation needed population growth to survive and prosper.

The early 19th century saw the first attempts at federal regulation of immigration, though these efforts remained limited in scope and enforcement capability. The Passenger Acts of 1819 and subsequent legislation required ship captains to report passenger manifests and maintain minimum standards for passenger conditions during ocean voyages. These laws aimed primarily at protecting immigrants from exploitation and abuse rather than restricting entry, reflecting humanitarian concerns about the conditions endured during transatlantic passage.

State and local authorities played significant roles in early immigration regulation, often focusing on preventing the entry of individuals likely to become public charges or pose public health risks. Port cities like New York, Boston, and Philadelphia developed inspection procedures and quarantine facilities to manage arriving immigrants, though these efforts remained primarily focused on health and welfare concerns rather than exclusion based on national origin or other characteristics.

The informal nature of early immigration controls reflected several factors including limited federal administrative capacity, philosophical commitments to individual liberty and economic opportunity, and practical recognition that population growth was essential to national development. However, periodic economic downturns, cultural conflicts, and concerns about political loyalty generated episodic demands for greater immigration controls that would eventually reshape American policy.

The Rise Of Federal Immigration Control (1875-1924)

The late 19th century marked the beginning of systematic federal immigration control, driven by concerns about economic competition, cultural assimilation, and public health. The Page Act of 1875 represented the first federal law restricting immigration, prohibiting the entry of convicts, prostitutes, and Asian laborers brought against their will. Though limited in scope, this legislation established important precedents for future immigration restrictions and federal authority over immigration matters.

The Chinese Exclusion Act of 1882 marked a dramatic expansion of federal immigration control, prohibiting the immigration of Chinese laborers for ten years and declaring Chinese immigrants ineligible for naturalization. This legislation represented the first race-based exclusion in American immigration law and reflected growing anti-Chinese sentiment, particularly in western states where Chinese immigrants competed with American workers in mining, railroad construction, and other industries. The Act established enforcement mechanisms including certificates of residence and deportation procedures that would become models for future immigration control efforts.

The Immigration Act of 1882 complemented the **Chinese Exclusion Act** by establishing broader categories of excludable immigrants, including convicts, lunatics, idiots, and persons likely to become public charges. This legislation also imposed a head tax on arriving immigrants and designated the Secretary of the Treasury to oversee immigration enforcement. The creation of federal oversight represented a significant shift from the previous era of state and local control, reflecting growing recognition that immigration was a national rather than local concern.

The establishment of Ellis Island in 1892 symbolized the institutionalization of federal immigration control. The facility processed millions of immigrants through medical examinations, legal inspections, and bureaucratic procedures designed to identify excludable individuals. Ellis Island's operations reflected Progressive Era confidence in scientific management and bureaucratic efficiency, applying these principles to the complex task of processing large numbers of immigrants while maintaining exclusion standards established by federal law.

The early 20th century saw continued expansion of immigration restrictions and enforcement capabilities. The Immigration Act of 1903 excluded anarchists and political radicals, reflecting concerns about political subversion following the assassination of President McKinley. The Immigration Act of 1907 expanded excludable categories and established the Dillingham Commission to study immigration's effects on American society, providing intellectual justification for future restrictions.

World War I accelerated the development of immigration controls as national security concerns prompted new restrictions and surveillance measures. The Espionage Act of 1917 and related legislation gave federal authorities broad powers to investigate and exclude individuals suspected of disloyalty or subversion. These wartime measures established precedents for using immigration law as a tool of national security policy that would influence future enforcement efforts.

The post-war period culminated in the National Origins Act of 1924, which established a comprehensive quota system limiting immigration from Eastern and Southern Europe while maintaining the complete exclusion of Asian immigrants. This legislation represented the triumph of restrictionist sentiment and marked the end of relatively open immigration that had characterized much of American history. The Act created enforcement mechanisms including visa requirements, consular inspections, and border controls that would define immigration enforcement for decades to come.

The Immigration And Naturalization Service Era (1924-2003)

The creation of the U.S. Border Patrol in 1924 marked a significant expansion of immigration enforcement capabilities, establishing a uniformed force dedicated to preventing unauthorized border crossings. Initially focused on preventing illegal entry along the Canadian and Mexican borders, the Border Patrol represented the federal government's first systematic attempt to control immigration between official ports of entry. Early Border Patrol operations were limited by small budgets, minimal staffing, and vast geographic territories, but the agency established enforcement practices and institutional culture that would influence immigration enforcement for decades.

The Great Depression of the 1930s prompted significant changes in immigration enforcement, including voluntary and forced repatriation programs that removed hundreds of thousands of Mexican Americans to Mexico. These programs reflected economic anxieties about job competition and represented early examples of mass enforcement operations targeting specific immigrant communities. The repatriation campaigns demonstrated the potential for immigration enforcement to affect not only unauthorized immigrants but also legal residents and American citizens of Mexican descent.

The Immigration and Naturalization Service (INS), established within the Department of Justice in 1940, consolidated various immigration functions under a single federal agency. This reorganization reflected recognition that immigration enforcement required coordinated administration of inspection, border patrol, investigation, and deportation functions. The INS inherited responsibility for implementing increasingly complex immigration laws while managing the practical challenges of enforcement across vast geographic areas with limited resources.

World War II brought dramatic changes to immigration enforcement as national security concerns reshaped priorities and procedures. The internment of Japanese Americans demonstrated the potential for immigration-related authorities to be used for mass detention and removal of entire communities based on race and ancestry. Simultaneously, wartime labor shortages led to the Bracero Program, which brought hundreds of thousands of Mexican workers to the United States under temporary labor agreements, illustrating the complex relationship between economic needs and immigration controls.

The post-war period saw continued evolution of immigration enforcement as the Cold War created new security concerns and changing economic conditions generated shifting enforcement priorities. The Immigration and Nationality Act of 1952 maintained the quota system while establishing new grounds for exclusion and deportation based on political beliefs and associations. The Act strengthened enforcement mechanisms and expanded grounds for removing immigrants suspected of communist sympathies or other subversive activities.

The 1960s brought significant changes to immigration law and enforcement with the passage of the Immigration and Nationality Act of 1965, which eliminated the national origins quota system and established family reunification and employment-based immigration as primary admission criteria. While this legislation liberalized admission policies, it also imposed new restrictions including the first numerical limits on immigration from the Western Hemisphere, creating unauthorized immigration from Mexico and other Latin American countries that had previously enjoyed relatively open access to the United States.

The expansion of unauthorized immigration following the 1965 Act created new enforcement challenges for the INS. The agency struggled with limited resources, competing priorities, and political pressures to increase enforcement while managing legal immigration and naturalization responsibilities. Border Patrol staffing and budgets increased gradually, but enforcement efforts remained concentrated in traditional crossing areas, leading to geographic displacement of unauthorized migration to more remote and dangerous routes.

The 1980s and 1990s saw dramatic expansion of immigration enforcement capabilities as concerns about unauthorized immigration generated bipartisan political support for enhanced border controls and interior enforcement. The Immigration Reform and Control Act of 1986 provided amnesty for millions of unauthorized immigrants while establishing employer sanctions and increased border enforcement funding. However, continued unauthorized immigration prompted additional enforcement measures including Operation Gatekeeper in California and similar border control initiatives in Texas and Arizona.

The final decades of INS operations were characterized by persistent budget increases, technological modernization, and expanding enforcement responsibilities. However, the agency continued to face criticism for management problems, inefficient operations, and inability to control unauthorized immigration effectively. These persistent challenges set the stage for the comprehensive reorganization that would follow the September 11 attacks.

September 11 And The Security Imperative

The terrorist attacks of September 11, 2001, fundamentally transformed American immigration enforcement by reframing immigration control as a critical national security imperative. The discovery that several of the hijackers had entered the United States on legitimate visas but had violated immigration laws while in the country highlighted perceived vulnerabilities in the immigration system and generated political momentum for comprehensive reform of immigration enforcement.

The immediate aftermath of September 11 saw unprecedented attention to immigration enforcement as policymakers and the public recognized connections between immigration controls and national security. The revelation that immigration violations might have provided opportunities to prevent the attacks if they had been detected and acted upon created political pressure for dramatic changes in how the United States approached immigration enforcement.

The USA PATRIOT Act, passed in October 2001, expanded immigration enforcement authorities and reduced procedural protections for non-citizens suspected of terrorism or other national security threats. The Act broadened grounds for detention and removal, expanded surveillance authorities, and reduced judicial review of immigration decisions in national security cases. These changes reflected the post-9/11 consensus that national security concerns justified significant expansions of federal enforcement authority.

The Enhanced Border Security and Visa Entry Reform Act of 2002 mandated additional security measures including biometric entry-exit systems, enhanced visa security, and increased information sharing between immigration and intelligence agencies. This legislation reflected recognition that effective immigration enforcement required not only border controls but also comprehensive systems for tracking and monitoring foreign nationals throughout their stay in the United States.

The creation of the Department of Homeland Security (DHS) in 2002 represented the most comprehensive reorganization of federal immigration enforcement in American history. The Homeland Security Act transferred immigration enforcement functions from the Department of Justice to the new department while splitting immigration services and enforcement into separate agencies. This reorganization reflected the post-9/11 view that immigration enforcement was primarily a security rather than service function.

The decision to create separate agencies for immigration services and enforcement represented a fundamental philosophical shift in how the federal government approached immigration. Previously, the INS had combined service and enforcement functions within a single agency, creating what critics argued were conflicting missions that compromised both service delivery and enforcement effectiveness. The post-9/11 reorganization reflected the view that these functions required different organizational cultures, resources, and priorities.

The transition from INS to the new DHS agencies occurred amid considerable organizational turmoil and operational challenges. The massive reorganization required integrating personnel, systems, and procedures from multiple agencies while maintaining operational continuity and addressing immediate security concerns. These transition challenges affected immigration enforcement operations and created opportunities for both innovation and confusion in enforcement practices.

The Creation And Structure Of ICE

Immigration and Customs Enforcement (ICE) officially began operations on March 1, 2003, combining immigration enforcement functions from the former INS with customs enforcement responsibilities from the U.S. Customs Service. The new agency represented the largest investigative agency within DHS and was tasked with enforcing both immigration and customs laws throughout the United States. The combination of these previously separate functions reflected recognition that immigration and customs violations often overlapped and that integrated enforcement could improve effectiveness.

ICE's organizational structure reflected its dual mission of immigration and customs enforcement, with separate divisions responsible for different aspects of enforcement operations. The Office of Investigations (OI) combined immigration and customs investigators into a single investigative force responsible for criminal violations of immigration and customs laws. The Office of Detention and Removal Operations (DRO) assumed responsibility for detaining and removing individuals in immigration proceedings, including both criminal aliens and unauthorized immigrants apprehended in the interior of the United States.

The creation of ICE represented not merely an administrative reorganization but a fundamental expansion of immigration enforcement capabilities and priorities. The new agency received significantly increased funding, personnel, and authorities compared to its predecessor organizations. ICE's budget grew from approximately $3 billion in fiscal year 2003 to over $8 billion by fiscal year 2020, reflecting sustained political support for expanded immigration enforcement.

ICE's investigative capabilities combined traditional immigration enforcement with sophisticated criminal investigation techniques previously associated with customs enforcement. The agency's investigators received training in complex financial crimes, document fraud, human trafficking, and other sophisticated criminal activities that often involved both immigration and customs violations. This enhanced investigative capacity allowed **ICE** to pursue cases that would have been difficult or impossible for the former INS to investigate effectively.

The agency's detention and removal operations represented a significant expansion of immigration enforcement infrastructure. **ICE** inherited and expanded a network of detention facilities designed to hold individuals pending immigration proceedings or removal from the United States. The agency's detention capacity grew from approximately 20,000 beds in 2003 to over 50,000 beds by 2019, reflecting both increased enforcement activities and longer average detention periods.

ICE's organizational culture reflected its law enforcement mission and security-focused priorities. Unlike the former INS, which combined service and enforcement functions, **ICE** was designed as a purely enforcement agency with a mission focused on public safety and national security. This organizational focus influenced hiring practices, training programs, and operational priorities in ways that distinguished **ICE** from its predecessor agencies.

The agency's field operations were organized through regional offices that coordinated enforcement activities across multiple states and provided operational oversight for local **ICE** offices. This structure allowed for both national coordination of enforcement priorities and local flexibility in addressing specific enforcement challenges. Field offices developed relationships with local law enforcement agencies and established operational procedures that reflected local conditions and priorities.

Expansion Of Enforcement Capabilities

Following its establishment, **ICE** rapidly expanded its enforcement capabilities through increased funding, personnel, and technological resources. The agency's growth reflected sustained political support for enhanced immigration enforcement and recognition that effective enforcement required substantial investments in infrastructure, technology, and human resources. This expansion transformed **ICE** from a relatively modest reorganization of existing agencies into one of the federal government's largest law enforcement operations.

ICE's investigative capabilities expanded significantly through the integration of immigration and customs enforcement functions. The agency's investigators received cross-training in both areas of law, allowing them to pursue complex cases involving multiple violations. This integrated approach proved particularly effective in cases involving organized crime, human trafficking, and large-scale immigration fraud, where immigration and customs violations often occurred together.

The development of specialized investigative units allowed **ICE** to focus resources on specific types of cases and criminal organizations. Units focused on human trafficking, gang activity, document fraud, and worksite enforcement developed specialized expertise and operational procedures that enhanced the agency's effectiveness in these areas. These specialized units often worked closely with other federal agencies and international partners to address criminal organizations operating across jurisdictional boundaries.

ICE's detention and removal operations expanded dramatically during the agency's first two decades, reflecting both increased enforcement activities and policy changes that resulted in longer detention periods for many immigrants. The agency developed contracts with private detention companies and local jails to increase detention capacity, while also constructing new federal detention facilities designed specifically for immigration enforcement purposes.

Technological investments played a crucial role in **ICE's** operational expansion. The agency invested heavily in biometric identification systems, case management databases, and communication technologies that enhanced its ability to track, investigate, and apprehend immigration violators. These technological capabilities allowed **ICE** to process larger numbers of cases more efficiently while maintaining detailed records of enforcement activities.

The expansion of **ICE's enforcement** capabilities also included enhanced cooperation with other law enforcement agencies at federal, state, and local levels. Programs like Secure Communities and 287(g) partnerships allowed **ICE** to leverage the resources and presence of other law enforcement agencies to identify and apprehend immigration violators. These partnerships significantly expanded **ICE's effective reach** beyond its own personnel and resources.

Training and professional development programs supported **ICE's operational expansion** by ensuring that personnel had the skills and knowledge necessary to implement complex enforcement operations. The agency established training centers and curricula that combined traditional law enforcement skills with specialized knowledge of immigration law, cultural competency, and emerging enforcement techniques.

Interior Enforcement Operations

ICE's interior enforcement operations represented a significant departure from previous immigration enforcement practices, which had focused primarily on border controls and deportation of individuals already in immigration proceedings. The agency's interior enforcement mission aimed to identify, apprehend, and remove unauthorized immigrants throughout the United States, fundamentally changing the immigration enforcement landscape.

Worksite enforcement became a major component of **ICE's** interior enforcement strategy, targeting employers who hired unauthorized workers and the workers themselves. Large-scale worksite operations often involved hundreds of **ICE agents** conducting simultaneous raids at multiple locations, resulting in the apprehension of hundreds or thousands of unauthorized workers. These operations were designed to deter unauthorized employment while disrupting industries that relied heavily on unauthorized labor.

Fugitive operations teams were established to locate and apprehend individuals who had been ordered removed from the United States but had failed to depart. These teams used investigative techniques and databases to locate fugitives and conduct targeted arrests. However, fugitive operations often resulted in the apprehension of other unauthorized immigrants encountered during arrest operations, expanding the scope of enforcement beyond the original targets.

Criminal alien programs focused on identifying and removing immigrants with criminal convictions, reflecting **ICE's** emphasis on public safety priorities. These programs involved partnerships with state and local correctional systems to identify deportable individuals before their release from custody. The Secure Communities program expanded this approach by requiring local law enforcement agencies to share fingerprint data with **ICE,** allowing the agency to identify potentially deportable individuals arrested for any reason.

Community enforcement operations involved **ICE agents** conducting targeted arrests in immigrant communities, often focusing on areas with high concentrations of unauthorized immigrants. These operations were controversial because they often resulted in the apprehension of individuals with no criminal history beyond immigration violations and created fear and distrust in immigrant communities.

Administrative arrests represented a significant portion of **ICE's** interior enforcement activities, involving the apprehension of individuals for civil immigration violations rather than criminal conduct. These arrests often occurred during routine encounters with law enforcement or during targeted operations in immigrant communities. The expansion of administrative arrests reflected **ICE's** broad mandate to enforce immigration laws throughout the United States.

The use of detention as an enforcement tool expanded significantly under **ICE operations,** with many individuals spending months or years in detention while their immigration cases proceeded through the courts. Extended detention periods reflected both the complexity of immigration cases and policy decisions to prioritize detention over alternatives like monitoring or bond release.

Technological Innovation And Surveillance

ICE's operational effectiveness has been significantly enhanced through investments in advanced technology and surveillance systems that allow the agency to track, identify, and apprehend immigration violators more efficiently than previous enforcement agencies. These technological capabilities represent a fundamental transformation in immigration enforcement, moving from labor-intensive manual processes to sophisticated automated systems that can process vast amounts of data and identify enforcement targets.

Biometric identification systems form the foundation of **ICE's technological infrastructure**, allowing the agency to accurately identify individuals regardless of the names or documents they present. The integration of fingerprint, facial recognition, and other biometric technologies with immigration databases enables **ICE** agents to quickly determine an individual's immigration status and history. These systems have proven particularly valuable in identifying individuals who have previously been removed from the United States or who have criminal histories under different identities.

Database integration and information sharing capabilities allow **ICE** to access information from numerous federal, state, and local agencies to support enforcement operations. The agency can cross-reference immigration records with criminal databases, driver's license records, employment records, and other sources of information to locate enforcement targets and build cases against violators. This comprehensive data access represents a significant advantage over previous enforcement approaches that relied on limited information sources.

Automated case management systems allow **ICE** to process larger numbers of cases more efficiently while maintaining detailed records of enforcement activities. These systems track individuals through all phases of the enforcement process, from initial identification through final removal, ensuring that cases are managed consistently and that enforcement priorities are implemented effectively. Electronic case files and automated workflow systems reduce processing times and administrative burdens.

Electronic monitoring technology allows **ICE** to supervise individuals in the community while their immigration cases are pending, providing an alternative to detention that reduces costs while maintaining oversight. GPS monitoring, telephone reporting, and other electronic supervision tools enable **ICE** to monitor compliance with immigration court requirements while allowing individuals to remain with their families and continue working.

Data mining and predictive analytics capabilities enable **ICE** to identify patterns and trends that may indicate immigration violations or help predict where unauthorized immigrants are likely to be found. These analytical tools process vast amounts of data to identify enforcement opportunities and allocate resources more effectively. Predictive modeling helps **ICE** anticipate migration patterns and adjust enforcement strategies accordingly.

Communication and coordination technologies enable **ICE** to coordinate complex enforcement operations across multiple jurisdictions and agencies. Secure communication systems, real-time information sharing, and mobile computing capabilities allow agents to access critical information and coordinate with colleagues during enforcement operations. These technologies are particularly important for large-scale operations involving multiple teams and locations.

Detention And Removal Systems

ICE's detention and removal operations represent one of the most significant expansions of immigration enforcement capability in American history, creating a comprehensive system for holding and removing individuals found to be in violation of immigration laws. The agency's detention system grew from modest beginnings to become one of the largest detention operations in the United States, holding tens of thousands of individuals on any given day while processing hundreds of thousands annually.

The expansion of immigration detention capacity required **ICE** to develop relationships with private detention companies, county jails, and other facilities capable of housing immigration detainees. The agency's use of private detention facilities became particularly controversial, as critics argued that profit motives created incentives to maintain high detention populations and reduce services provided to detainees. **ICE** defended the use of private facilities as necessary to meet detention requirements within budget constraints.

Detention standards and conditions became major areas of concern as **ICE's** detention population grew rapidly. The agency developed comprehensive standards governing detention facilities, covering areas including medical care, food service, recreation, legal access, and disciplinary procedures. However, monitoring compliance with these standards across hundreds of facilities presented ongoing challenges, and reports of substandard conditions generated significant criticism and legal challenges.

Family detention emerged as a particularly controversial aspect of **ICE operations**, involving the detention of children along with their parents while immigration cases were pending. The agency operated several family detention centers designed to hold families together while providing appropriate services for children. However, critics argued that any detention of children was inappropriate and that family detention centers were essentially prisons for children who had committed no crimes.

The removal process involves complex legal and logistical procedures for transporting individuals from the United States to their countries of origin. **ICE** operates charter flights and coordinates with commercial airlines to transport removed individuals, while also managing the legal and diplomatic requirements for removal to different countries. The agency maintains removal agreements with numerous countries and coordinates with foreign consulates to obtain travel documents for individuals being removed.

Alternatives to detention programs allow some individuals to be released from custody while their immigration cases are pending, using supervision techniques including electronic monitoring, check-in requirements, and case management services. These programs aim to reduce detention costs while ensuring that individuals appear for their immigration court hearings. However, the availability and effectiveness of alternatives to detention remain subjects of ongoing policy debate.

Medical care in detention facilities represents a major operational and legal challenge for **ICE**, as the agency is responsible for providing healthcare to a large and diverse detained population with varying medical needs. The agency contracts with medical providers and maintains medical facilities within detention centers, but providing adequate medical care in a detention environment presents ongoing challenges that have resulted in criticism and legal action.

Controversies And Legal Challenges

ICE's operations have generated significant controversy and legal challenges throughout the agency's existence, reflecting broader disagreements about immigration policy and enforcement priorities. These controversies have influenced **ICE operations**, prompted policy changes, and shaped public debates about immigration enforcement. Legal challenges have addressed issues ranging from detention conditions to enforcement procedures to the scope of **ICE's authority.**

Workplace raids conducted by **ICE** have been particularly controversial, often resulting in the separation of families when parents are detained while children are at school or in childcare. High-profile raids at meatpacking plants, construction sites, and other workplaces have generated significant media attention and criticism from immigrant advocacy groups. Critics argue that these operations traumatize communities and fail to address the root causes of unauthorized employment.

Family separation policies became a major source of controversy, particularly during periods when **ICE** enforcement resulted in the detention or removal of parents while their children remained in the United States. These separations occurred both through routine enforcement operations and as a result of specific policy decisions designed to deter unauthorized immigration. Legal challenges and public criticism led to policy modifications, but family separation remained an ongoing concern.

Detention conditions have been the subject of numerous legal challenges and congressional investigations, with critics arguing that **ICE** detention facilities fail to meet basic standards for healthcare, safety, and humane treatment. Deaths in **ICE** custody, allegations of medical neglect, and reports of inadequate conditions have generated significant criticism and legal action. **ICE** has defended its detention operations while acknowledging the need for ongoing improvements.

Constitutional challenges to **ICE** operations have addressed issues including due process rights, Fourth Amendment protections, and the scope of federal immigration authority. Courts have issued various rulings limiting certain **ICE practices** while upholding the agency's general authority to enforce immigration laws. These legal developments continue to shape **ICE operations** and enforcement procedures.

Sanctuary jurisdiction policies adopted by some state and local governments have created tensions with **ICE** enforcement priorities. These policies limit cooperation between local law enforcement and **ICE,** making it more difficult for the federal agency to apprehend and remove unauthorized immigrants. **ICE** has responded with enforcement operations specifically targeting sanctuary jurisdictions, generating additional controversy and legal challenges.

Public protests and civil disobedience actions have targeted **ICE operations,** with activists attempting to block deportation vehicles, occupy **ICE offices**, and otherwise disrupt enforcement activities. These protests reflect deep disagreements about **ICE's mission** and methods, while also highlighting the emotional and personal impacts of immigration enforcement on affected communities.

Congressional oversight and investigations have examined various aspects of **ICE operations,** including detention conditions, enforcement priorities, budget management, and civil rights compliance. These oversight activities have sometimes resulted in policy changes and have provided forums for public debate about **ICE operations and immigration enforcement** more broadly.

Modern Operations And Current Challenges

Today's **ICE operations** reflect the evolution of immigration enforcement over two decades of organizational development, policy changes, and technological advancement. The agency currently employs over 20,000 personnel and operates with an annual budget exceeding **$8 billion,** making it one of the largest law enforcement agencies in the United States. **ICE's modern operations** encompass a wide range of activities from criminal investigations to detention management to international cooperation.

Enforcement priorities have evolved significantly since **ICE's** creation, reflecting changing political priorities and operational lessons learned over time. The agency has moved between different approaches emphasizing criminal alien removal, comprehensive interior enforcement, and targeted enforcement focused on specific categories of immigration violators. These priority changes have influenced resource allocation, operational procedures, and community impacts.

Technology continues to transform **ICE operations,** with ongoing investments in artificial intelligence, data analytics, and automated processing systems. The agency is implementing next-generation biometric systems, expanding electronic monitoring capabilities, and developing predictive tools to enhance enforcement effectiveness. These technological advances promise to further transform immigration enforcement while raising new questions about privacy and civil liberties.

Workforce challenges include recruiting and retaining qualified personnel, providing appropriate training for complex enforcement missions, and maintaining professional standards across a large and geographically dispersed organization. **ICE** competes with other law enforcement agencies for qualified candidates while managing the unique challenges associated with immigration enforcement work.

Budget constraints and competing priorities create ongoing challenges for **ICE operations,** requiring the agency to balance enforcement activities, detention costs, and technological investments within available resources. Political disagreements about immigration policy affect budget allocations and create uncertainty about long-term resource availability.

International cooperation has become increasingly important as **ICE** addresses criminal organizations and immigration violations that cross national boundaries. The agency maintains relationships with law enforcement agencies in numerous countries and participates in international task forces addressing human trafficking, smuggling, and other transnational crimes.

Civil rights compliance remains an ongoing challenge as **ICE** works to ensure that enforcement operations respect constitutional rights and do not discriminate based on race, ethnicity, or other protected characteristics. The agency has implemented training programs and oversight procedures designed to prevent civil rights violations while maintaining effective enforcement operations.

Future Directions And Policy Implications

The future of **ICE** and immigration enforcement will be shaped by evolving political priorities, technological capabilities, legal developments, and changing migration patterns. Current debates about immigration policy suggest that **ICE operations** will continue to be subjects of significant political and public attention, with different political parties and interest groups advocating for substantially different approaches to immigration enforcement.

Technological advances will likely continue to transform **ICE operations,** with artificial intelligence, automated processing, and enhanced surveillance capabilities offering new tools for immigration enforcement. However, these technological developments also raise important questions about privacy, civil liberties, and the appropriate scope of government surveillance. Balancing enforcement effectiveness with constitutional protections will remain an ongoing challenge.

Legal immigration system reforms could significantly affect **ICE** operations by changing the categories of individuals subject to removal and modifying procedures for immigration enforcement. Comprehensive immigration reform that addresses unauthorized immigration through legalization programs could reduce **ICE's** workload while potentially redirecting enforcement resources toward other priorities.

Budget pressures and competing priorities will continue to influence **ICE** operations, requiring the agency to demonstrate effectiveness and efficiency in its enforcement activities. Performance measurement and outcome evaluation will likely become increasingly important as policymakers seek evidence about the effectiveness of different enforcement approaches.

International migration trends and global events will continue to influence **ICE operations,** as the agency responds to changing patterns of unauthorized immigration and evolving security threats. Climate change, economic instability, and political conflicts in other countries may generate new migration pressures that affect **ICE** enforcement priorities and resource requirements.

The relationship between federal immigration enforcement and state and local law enforcement will remain an important policy issue, with different jurisdictions taking varying approaches to cooperation with **ICE.** These relationships significantly affect **ICE's** operational effectiveness and will likely continue to evolve based on political developments and policy changes.

Conclusion

The creation and evolution of **ICE** represents a fundamental transformation in American immigration enforcement, reflecting changing views about national security, federal authority, and immigration control. From its origins in the post-9/11 security reorganization to its current status as one of the largest federal law enforcement agencies, **ICE** has become a central institution in American immigration policy and a focus of intense political debate.

Understanding **ICE's** development requires recognizing the historical context of American immigration enforcement, from early informal controls through the expansion of federal authority in the late 19th and early 20th centuries to the comprehensive reorganization following September 11. Each phase of this development reflected specific political, economic, and social concerns while contributing to the institutional framework that shaped **ICE's** creation and operations.

The agency's rapid expansion in capabilities, resources, and scope of operations demonstrates the significant political support for enhanced immigration enforcement that emerged following the September 11 attacks. However, **ICE's** operations have also generated substantial controversy and legal challenges, reflecting deeper disagreements about immigration policy and the appropriate balance between enforcement and humanitarian concerns.

ICE's future will be shaped by ongoing political debates about immigration policy, technological developments that offer new enforcement capabilities, legal challenges that define the boundaries of enforcement authority, and changing migration patterns that affect enforcement priorities. The agency's role in American immigration policy will likely continue to evolve as policymakers, courts, and the public grapple with fundamental questions about immigration, security, and American values.

The story of **ICE** and immigration enforcement more broadly illustrates the complex relationship between American ideals and practical governance challenges. The tension between America's identity as a nation of immigrants and periodic desires to control or restrict immigration has shaped policy development for centuries and continues to influence contemporary debates about **ICE** operations and immigration enforcement. Understanding this historical context is essential for informed discussion about the future direction of American immigration policy and the role of enforcement agencies like **ICE** in implementing that policy.

CHAPTER FIFTEEN

THE FUTURE OF IMMIGRATION UNDER TRUMP'S TASK FORCE - TRANSFORMATION AND CHALLENGES AHEAD

INTRODUCTION

The return of Donald Trump to the presidency in January 2025 has initiated the most dramatic transformation of American immigration policy in modern history. The Trump administration is taking the novel step of turning to other agencies to quickly bolster its immigration enforcement workforce as it prioritizes arrests and deportation, with the administration moving aggressively to dismantle many discretionary immigration pathways established or expanded under the Biden administration. This comprehensive reorganization represents not merely a policy shift but a fundamental reimagining of how the federal government approaches immigration enforcement, detention, and removal.

"Operation At Large," a nationwide, **ICE-led plan** already underway to ramp up arrests of unauthorized immigrants, includes more than 5,000 personnel from across federal law enforcement agencies and up to 21,000 National Guard troops. This massive mobilization reflects the administration's commitment to achieving unprecedented deportation targets and represents the largest federal law enforcement operation in American history focused specifically on immigration enforcement.

The scope and ambition of Trump's second-term immigration agenda far exceed what was attempted during his first presidency. Drawing on years of planning and preparation, the administration has moved swiftly to implement a comprehensive strategy that touches every aspect of the immigration system, from border security to interior enforcement to legal immigration pathways. Understanding the future of American immigration requires examining both the immediate operational changes and the long-term structural transformations being implemented.

The Architecture Of Mass Deportation

The Trump administration's mass deportation strategy represents a carefully orchestrated effort developed over years of planning during Trump's absence from office. Trump left office in January 2021 determined to make immigration a centerpiece of his political comeback. Top aides found refuge at friendly think tanks to plot the next steps. This extended preparation period allowed immigration hardliners to develop comprehensive blueprints for transforming federal immigration enforcement into what they envision as the most effective deportation apparatus in American history.

In mid-May, White House deputy chief of staff Stephen Miller, frustrated over what he saw as numbers of arrests and deportations of unauthorized immigrants that were too low, berated and threatened to fire senior Immigration and Customs Enforcement officials if they did not begin detaining 3,000 migrants a day. This aggressive target setting demonstrates the administration's commitment to achieving deportation numbers that would dwarf any previous enforcement effort in American history.

The operational structure of the mass deportation effort involves unprecedented coordination across federal agencies. **The Department of Homeland Security** is tapping other agencies and federal groups, from the U.S. Marshals Service, the DEA, the Bureau of Alcohol, Tobacco, Firearms and Explosives, and the Federal Bureau of Prisons authority to investigate and apprehend people suspected of being in the country without authorization. This multi-agency approach represents a fundamental departure from previous immigration enforcement models that relied primarily on **ICE** and Border Patrol personnel.

The transformation extends beyond traditional law enforcement agencies to include civilian federal workers and even tax authorities. The plan calls for using 3,000 **ICE agents**, including 1,800 from Homeland Security Investigations, which generally investigates transnational crimes and is not typically involved in arresting noncriminal immigrants; 2,000 Justice Department employees from the FBI, the U.S. Marshals Service and the Drug Enforcement Administration; and 500 employees from Customs and Border Protection. It also includes 250 IRS agents, some of whom may be used to provide information on the whereabouts of immigrants using tax information.

The mobilization of National Guard forces represents perhaps the most dramatic expansion of immigration enforcement capabilities. The administration has deployed thousands of National Guard troops to support detention operations, transportation, and logistical support for deportation flights. This militarization of immigration enforcement reflects the administration's view that unauthorized immigration constitutes a national security emergency requiring extraordinary federal intervention.

Technology plays a crucial role in enabling mass deportation operations. Homeland Security Operations has developed new software technology, called RAVEn, to consolidate data about migrants. This sophisticated data integration system allows enforcement agencies to track, locate, and prioritize targets for removal more efficiently than ever before, representing a significant technological advancement in immigration enforcement capabilities.

Expansion Of Enforcement Authority

The Trump administration has dramatically expanded the authority and scope of immigration enforcement through executive orders and policy directives that remove previous restrictions on enforcement activities. The Trump administration reversed the policy of the previous administration and gave **ICE** permission to raid schools, hospitals and places of worship. This elimination of sensitive location protections represents a fundamental shift in enforcement philosophy that prioritizes removal operations over community safety and access to essential services.

Trump officials also expanded a procedure to speed up deportations, to include undocumented immigrants anywhere in the US who cannot prove they've lived in the US continuously for two years or more. The fast-track deportation procedure, known as "expedited removal," allows immigration authorities to remove an individual without a hearing before an immigration judge. This expansion of expedited removal authority dramatically increases the universe of individuals subject to immediate deportation without due process protections.

The administration's approach to local law enforcement cooperation has involved massive expansion of existing partnership programs. As of April 21, 2025, the number of active 287(g) Memoranda of

Agreement (MOAs) had surged to 456 across 38 states, more than a sevenfold increase from the 60 Jail Enforcement Model (JEM) and 75 Warrant Service Officer (WSO) agreements in place at the end of 2024. This rapid expansion of local law enforcement partnerships provides **ICE** with thousands of additional officers capable of immigration enforcement activities.

The revival of the Task Force Model under 287(g) agreements represents a particularly significant expansion of enforcement authority. In jurisdictions with new or revived TFM agreements, deputized local officers are allowed to enforce immigration laws in the field during routine policing operations. This model transforms routine police encounters into potential immigration enforcement actions, fundamentally altering the relationship between immigrant communities and local law enforcement.

The administration has also expanded its use of administrative detention as an enforcement tool. Previous policies that prioritized bond release or alternatives to detention have been replaced with aggressive detention strategies designed to prevent release and encourage voluntary departure. The expansion of detention capacity through contracts with private facilities and partnerships with local jails has enabled this more aggressive approach to immigration detention.

Legal challenges to these expanded authorities have achieved mixed results, with federal courts issuing temporary restraining orders in some cases while allowing other enforcement activities to proceed. The administration's legal strategy involves implementing policies rapidly and then defending them through the court system, accepting that some initiatives may be modified or blocked while others survive legal challenges.

Detention Infrastructure And Capacity

The Trump administration's mass deportation strategy requires unprecedented expansion of detention infrastructure to house the dramatically increased numbers of individuals apprehended for immigration violations. **ICE** only has a limited number of detention beds. They're only funded for an average of 41,500 beds, but they work with local jails. They have community partners to detain people. Currently, there are more than 58,000 people in **ICE** custody. They are completely over capacity. This capacity crisis has driven the administration to explore innovative and controversial solutions for housing immigration detainees.

That means that they have to look for new ways to detain people, and **"Alligator Alcatraz"** is an example of that, which is essentially building a facility very quickly to hold up to 5,000 people and using some FEMA funds so that the state can erect this facility. The construction of new detention facilities in remote locations like the Florida Everglades represents a dramatic expansion of immigration detention infrastructure designed to accommodate the increased enforcement activities.

Four Bureau of Prison facilities are currently holding about 700 immigration detainees, according to Kathleen Toomey, associate deputy director of the BOP. The use of federal prisons to house detainees was what Trump also relied on in his first term in office. The utilization of federal prison space for immigration detention represents an emergency response to capacity constraints while permanent detention facilities are constructed or contracted.

The administration's detention strategy extends beyond traditional facilities to include military installations and other federal properties. The administration has sought to rely on local law enforcement agencies as a force multiplier, rapidly expanding 287(g) agreements, including the revival of Task Force Model agreements, which allow local officers to enforce immigration laws during routine policing. This partnership approach helps address capacity constraints by utilizing local jail space and processing capabilities.

Private detention companies have become crucial partners in the administration's detention expansion efforts. The rapid construction of new private facilities and the expansion of existing contracts reflect the administration's commitment to dramatically increasing detention capacity. These partnerships have generated controversy due to concerns about profit motives affecting detention conditions and length of stay, but they remain essential to achieving the administration's enforcement goals.

Family detention has emerged as a particularly contentious aspect of the administration's detention strategy. The administration has reopened family detention facilities and constructed new ones designed to hold parents and children together during immigration proceedings. Critics argue that detaining children for immigration violations violates human rights principles, while the administration contends that family detention is necessary to prevent families from disappearing into the community.

The international dimensions of detention expansion include agreements with other countries to house U.S. immigration detainees. In addition to sending Venezuelans to CECOT, Trump has deported asylum seekers to Panama and sent others to Guantánamo Bay in Cuba and South Sudan. Homan says the Administration is in talks with three more countries to accept U.S. deportees. These arrangements allow the administration to reduce domestic detention pressures while potentially deterring future unauthorized immigration.

Technological Innovation And Data Integration

The Trump administration's immigration enforcement operations rely heavily on advanced technology and comprehensive data integration systems that enable efficient identification, tracking, and removal of unauthorized immigrants. Homeland Security Operations has developed new software technology, called RAVEn, to consolidate data about migrants. This sophisticated system represents a significant advancement in immigration enforcement technology, allowing agents to access comprehensive information about individuals from multiple government databases.

It also includes 250 IRS agents, some of whom may be used to provide information on the whereabouts of immigrants using tax information, while others would have the authority to make arrests. The integration of tax information into immigration enforcement represents a novel approach that leverages existing government data to identify and locate enforcement targets. This use of financial data demonstrates the administration's commitment to utilizing all available information sources for enforcement purposes.

Immigration authorities under the Trump administration are issuing subpoenas to landlords, demanding detailed tenant records, including leases, rental applications, forwarding addresses, and identification documents. This expansion of information gathering to private sector entities reflects the administration's comprehensive approach to locating unauthorized immigrants through all available means.

The development of predictive analytics capabilities allows **ICE** to identify likely locations of unauthorized immigrants and prioritize enforcement resources accordingly. Machine learning algorithms analyze patterns in previous apprehensions, demographic data, and economic indicators to predict where enforcement operations are most likely to be successful. This data-driven approach represents a significant evolution from traditional enforcement methods that relied primarily on tips and random patrols.

Biometric technology plays an increasingly important role in immigration enforcement operations. Facial recognition systems at airports and border crossings help identify individuals who have overstayed visas or violated previous removal orders. Mobile biometric devices allow field agents to quickly identify individuals during enforcement operations, reducing processing time and improving operational efficiency.

Electronic monitoring technology has been expanded to manage larger numbers of individuals released from detention while their cases are pending. GPS ankle monitors, smartphone applications, and other electronic supervision tools allow **ICE** to maintain oversight of individuals in the community while reducing detention costs. However, the administration's preference for detention over alternatives has limited the use of these technologies.

Information sharing agreements with state and local agencies provide **ICE** with access to driver's license databases, criminal records, and other sources of information that help identify and locate unauthorized immigrants. These partnerships significantly expand the federal government's surveillance capabilities and enable more comprehensive enforcement operations.

International cooperation in data sharing allows **ICE** to access information about individuals' criminal histories and immigration violations in other countries. These arrangements help identify individuals who may pose security risks and support removal proceedings by providing documentation of foreign criminal convictions or previous immigration violations.

Removal Operations And International Agreements

The Trump administration's deportation strategy relies heavily on negotiating agreements with foreign countries to accept deportees, including individuals who are not necessarily citizens of those countries. Homan says the Administration is in talks with three more countries to accept U.S. deportees. It also plans to build and expand other detention centers in the U.S., he says, with the goal of doubling capacity to hold detainees awaiting deportation to 100,000. These international arrangements are crucial to achieving the administration's ambitious deportation targets.

On March 15, 2025, deportation flights, operated by Global Crossing Airlines, carrying over 260 immigrants from Venezuela and El Salvador, alleged to be gang members, arrived in El Salvador where the immigrants were taken into custody at the Terrorism Confinement Center (CECOT). Neither the US nor Salvadoran governments offered any immediate evidence that those deported had been charged with crimes or had connections to any gangs. This arrangement with El Salvador demonstrates the administration's willingness to use controversial third-country agreements to remove individuals who cannot be quickly returned to their countries of origin.

On January 23, 2025, Mexico denied a United States military plane the ability to land, causing the plane to never take off while two others bound for Guatemala did. These diplomatic tensions illustrate the challenges the administration faces in securing cooperation from neighboring countries for removal operations, particularly when military aircraft are involved in deportation flights.

The administration has expanded the use of military aircraft for deportation operations, marking a significant militarization of immigration enforcement. Hundreds of undocumented immigrants were flown out of the US by military aircraft. A defense official stated that two deportation flights, both to Guatemala, were flown out that same night with reportedly 81 deportees. This use of military resources for immigration enforcement represents a departure from traditional civilian-operated removal flights.

The development of agreements for third-country removals allows the administration to remove individuals to countries other than their nations of origin when direct deportation is not possible. These arrangements are particularly important for individuals from countries that do not maintain diplomatic relations with the United States or that refuse to accept deportees. However, such agreements raise significant legal and humanitarian concerns about due process and the safety of deportees.

Processing centers in foreign countries provide additional capacity for managing deportees and potentially deterring future unauthorized immigration. As of February 28, 2025, there were 9 additional Iranian Christian converts, including three children, detained in the camp. These facilities allow the administration to remove individuals from the United States while maintaining some degree of oversight during immigration proceedings.

The administration's removal operations have generated significant international attention and criticism, particularly regarding the treatment of asylum seekers and individuals with potential claims for protection. Soon after, **ICE deported** a Guatemalan man to Mexico two days after he said in court that he had been abducted and raped in Mexico. Such cases highlight the tension between the administration's enforcement priorities and international human rights obligations.

Coordination with international law enforcement agencies supports removal operations by providing intelligence about criminal organizations and helping identify individuals who may pose security risks. These partnerships also facilitate the sharing of biometric data and criminal records that support immigration enforcement activities and removal proceedings.

Legal Immigration System Transformation

The Trump administration's immigration strategy extends far beyond enforcement to include fundamental changes to the legal immigration system that could reshape American demographics and economic development for decades to come. The administration has shaped reality to fit its worldview, taking over a million people who had done everything the "right way" from finding sponsors in the U.S. under the Cuban, Haitian, Nicaraguan and Venezuelan (CHNV) parole program to waiting in Mexico for months with a CBP One appointment, to applying for and sometimes renewing TPS, and making them "illegal". This transformation of legal status demonstrates the administration's broad authority to alter immigration pathways.

There are certainly indications that the Trump administration does not intend to allocate significant manpower toward operating our system of legal immigration. Not only have USCIS employees been asked to volunteer for 60-day details at **ICE,** but the agency has been forced to cut jobs, despite being almost entirely funded by user fees rather than appropriations from Congress. The reallocation of immigration services personnel to enforcement activities reflects the administration's prioritization of removal operations over immigration benefits processing.

The administration has moved aggressively to terminate or dramatically scale back temporary protection programs that provided legal status to hundreds of thousands of immigrants. The Niskanen Center, cataloging Project 2025's immigration proposals, foresees 700,000 holders of Temporary Protected Status, 500,000 young adults known as Dreamers, and more than 175,000 Ukrainians all losing their legal protections, "pushing them out of status or the country". These terminations dramatically expand the population subject to deportation while reducing available legal pathways for immigration relief.

Asylum system changes represent a fundamental restructuring of how the United States evaluates protection claims. US Customs and Border Protection announced the removal of the scheduling functionality of CBP One, an app that allows migrants to share information and plan interviews with immigration authorities before reaching the US border, and all future asylum appointments were canceled. The elimination of these orderly asylum processing mechanisms forces asylum seekers to attempt unauthorized border crossings, potentially subjecting them to criminal prosecution.

The administration's approach to legal immigration processing emphasizes revenue generation and administrative efficiency over accessibility and due process. Increased filing fees, shortened processing times, and reduced availability of fee waivers make legal immigration more difficult for low-income individuals while generating additional revenue for enforcement activities. These changes reflect a fundamental shift in how the government approaches immigration services delivery.

Consular operations have been targeted for significant reductions that would limit the ability of individuals abroad to obtain visas for travel to the United States. Plans have been circulated calling for the closure of embassies and consulates around the globe, which would increase wait times at nearby embassies and the consulates that remain open. These closures would effectively reduce legal immigration by making it more difficult and time-consuming to obtain necessary visas and documentation.

The transformation of USCIS from a service-oriented agency to an enforcement arm represents a fundamental philosophical shift in how the government approaches immigration benefits. It also puts the US Citizenship and Immigration Services, the federal agency responsible for managing federal immigration benefits, at the center of the president's deportation campaign, because not only are they the ones that manage these benefits, but they have also been delegated the authority by the Department of Homeland Security to place these individuals in fast-track deportation proceedings. This change transforms routine immigration services interactions into potential enforcement encounters.

Employment-based immigration has faced significant restrictions designed to prioritize American workers and reduce competition from foreign nationals. Changes to H-1B visa programs, restrictions on optional practical training for foreign students, and increased scrutiny of employment-based petitions reflect the administration's commitment to reducing legal immigration levels across all categories.

Economic And Social Impacts

The Trump administration's mass deportation strategy is generating profound economic and social consequences that extend far beyond the immigrant communities directly targeted by enforcement activities. Fears of ICE raids have negatively impacted agriculture, construction, and the hospitality industry. These economic disruptions reflect the significant role that unauthorized immigrants play in essential industries and the difficulty of replacing this workforce quickly.

Removing that many undocumented immigrants, as Trump has promised, would eliminate a key source of labor. It would end a decades-long wave of migration that has made the country progressively more multiethnic. The demographic and economic implications of mass deportation extend far beyond immigration policy to affect fundamental aspects of American society and economic development.

Labor shortages in critical industries have already begun to emerge as enforcement activities increase and immigrants avoid areas with high ICE presence. Agriculture, construction, hospitality, and food processing industries are reporting difficulty finding workers to replace departed employees, leading to reduced production and increased costs. These shortages are particularly acute in regions with high concentrations of unauthorized immigrants and intensive enforcement activities.

Claims of an empty 405 freeway, or blazing-fast commutes from the beach to the valley, have received pushback from some longtime Angelinos. They say the dip in traffic volume is being taken out of context, with schools out for summer, the July 4 holiday weekend and general seasonal slowness having more to do with any decrease in congestion drivers have noticed across the city than federal immigration enforcement actions. While some claim reduced traffic congestion in major metropolitan areas, the actual impact of enforcement on daily life remains disputed.

Community effects extend beyond economic disruption to include significant social and psychological impacts on mixed-status families and immigrant communities. Fear of enforcement has led to reduced utilization of healthcare services, decreased school attendance, and reluctance to report crimes or cooperate with police investigations. These community-level effects compromise public safety and public health while undermining social cohesion.

Tax revenue implications of mass deportation include both immediate costs associated with enforcement operations and long-term effects from reduced economic activity and population decline. Asked to assess the economic impact of the Trump administration's policies, Americans are more likely to say they expect the policies will cost taxpayers money (53%) rather than save taxpayers money (29%). The fiscal impact of mass deportation includes substantial enforcement costs while potentially reducing tax revenue from departed workers and businesses.

Housing markets in areas with high immigrant populations are experiencing significant effects as enforcement activities prompt departures and reduce demand for rental housing. Property values and rental rates are beginning to reflect reduced population density, while some landlords face increased scrutiny and legal liability for housing unauthorized immigrants.

Educational systems are confronting challenges related to student departures, increased absenteeism due to fear, and the need to provide support services for traumatized children affected by enforcement activities. School districts in areas with intensive enforcement are reporting significant enrollment declines and increased demand for counseling and social services.

Healthcare systems face particular challenges as unauthorized immigrants avoid seeking care due to fear of enforcement, potentially leading to public health consequences and increased emergency room utilization when conditions become severe. The reduction in routine preventive care could result in more expensive emergency interventions and potential disease outbreaks.

Political And Legal Resistance

The Trump administration's immigration policies have generated significant political and legal resistance from Democratic-led states, cities, advocacy organizations, and affected communities. Democratic-led states and cities have received fierce pushback from constitutional experts and Democratic-led states and cities regarding attempts to end birthright citizenship and other constitutional challenges to immigration enforcement expansion.

Sanctuary jurisdiction policies have become focal points of resistance to federal immigration enforcement. Speaking to KLAS, Las Vegas Sheriff Kevin McMahill said his police department will not partake in mass deportation "roundups" as outlined in Trump's new immigration policies. These local resistance efforts create operational challenges for federal enforcement agencies while highlighting political divisions over immigration policy.

The experience of the previous Trump years underlines the practical importance of legal action. Lawsuits stopped many illegal Trump administration policies, including those that aimed to separate families at the border, arbitrarily cut off access to asylum, strip hundreds of thousands of people of protection under Temporary Protected Status (TPS), and Deferred Action for Childhood Arrivals (DACA). This litigation strategy has proven effective in limiting some administration initiatives while allowing others to proceed.

Federal court challenges to administration policies have achieved mixed results, with some policies blocked by preliminary injunctions while others have been allowed to proceed pending full judicial review. The administration's strategy of rapid implementation followed by litigation defense has succeeded in implementing some controversial policies while others remain tied up in court proceedings.

State-level legislation designed to resist federal immigration enforcement has created additional legal complexity and operational challenges for federal agencies. Some states have enacted laws limiting cooperation with ICE while others have mandated cooperation and even established state-level immigration enforcement programs. These conflicting approaches create a patchwork of cooperation and resistance across the country.

Congressional oversight activities by Democratic legislators have focused attention on enforcement operations, detention conditions, and due process concerns. The Department of Justice is weighing arresting and prosecuting public officials who impede their immigration agenda, according to Administration sources familiar with the matter. This potential federal prosecution of state and local officials represents an escalation in federal-state tensions over immigration policy.

International legal challenges and diplomatic pressure have emerged as foreign governments and international organizations express concern about mass deportation policies and their impact on human rights and international law. These international dimensions add complexity to domestic policy implementation while potentially affecting broader diplomatic relationships.

Civil rights organizations have launched comprehensive litigation strategies designed to challenge various aspects of the administration's immigration policies. These efforts focus on constitutional due process protections, equal protection concerns, and statutory interpretation issues that could limit the scope and implementation of mass deportation policies.

Public opinion research indicates divided views on administration immigration policies, with significant partisan differences and varying levels of support for different enforcement approaches. The public is split over local law enforcement helping deportation efforts, and majorities disapprove of suspending asylum applications. These public opinion dynamics influence political support for immigration policies and could affect long-term sustainability of current approaches.

Long-Term Implications And Future Scenarios

The Trump administration's immigration transformation represents a fundamental shift in American immigration policy with implications that will extend far beyond the current presidential term. Nothing as big as the federal government can be completely transformed in only six months, and it would have been impossible for the Trump administration to meet its stated goals of arresting 3,000 people per day, much less deporting 1 million per year, even without the litigation setbacks it has encountered and the errors it has had to correct. The scale and scope of changes being implemented suggest that American immigration policy will be permanently altered regardless of future political developments.

However, assistance from Congress, in the form of$170.1 billion in new spending for immigration enforcement under the "One Big Beautiful Bill Act" signed into law by President Trump on July 4, 2025, will turbocharge the Trump administration's effort to repurpose the federal government. This new infusion of money makes ICE the highest-funded federal law enforcement agency in history, funded at a level higher than some foreign militaries. This unprecedented funding commitment creates institutional momentum that will influence immigration enforcement for years to come.

The technological infrastructure being developed for mass deportation operations will create lasting capabilities that future administrations will inherit. Advanced data integration systems, expanded surveillance capabilities, and enhanced interagency coordination mechanisms represent permanent enhancements to federal enforcement capacity that could be difficult to dismantle even if policy priorities change.

Institutional changes within federal agencies, including the transformation of USCIS into an enforcement arm and the expansion of ICE into the largest federal law enforcement agency, create organizational structures and cultures that will persist beyond current political leadership. Relying on policy blueprints laid out in the Heritage Foundation's Project 2025 and recommendations of America First Legal (a group established by key Trump advisor Stephen Miller), the administration entered office prepared to quickly remake the entire U.S. government into a well-oiled machine for immigration enforcement. These institutional changes represent long-term structural alterations to how the federal government approaches immigration.

Demographic implications of sustained mass deportation could significantly alter American population composition and growth patterns. Reduced immigration and increased deportation would slow population growth, alter age distribution, and change ethnic and racial composition in ways that could influence American politics, economics, and culture for decades.

International relationships and agreements established during the mass deportation campaign will have lasting effects on American diplomatic relations and migration patterns. The use of deportation flights by the U.S. has created pushback from some foreign governments, particularly that of Colombia. These diplomatic tensions could affect broader bilateral relationships and regional cooperation on various issues beyond immigration.

Legal precedents established through litigation over Trump administration immigration policies will influence future immigration law and policy implementation. Court decisions regarding presidential authority, due process protections, and federal-state relationships in immigration enforcement will create legal frameworks that constrain or enable future policy initiatives.

Economic structural changes resulting from reduced immigration and mass deportation could have permanent effects on American labor markets, industry development, and economic growth patterns. Industries that adapt to reduced immigrant labor availability through automation, wage increases, or restructuring may not return to previous labor-intensive models even if immigration policies change.

Social and cultural implications of mass deportation include effects on American identity, community composition, and intergroup relations that could persist long after policy changes. The psychological and social trauma experienced by affected communities, along with changes in community demographic composition, will have lasting effects on American society.

Future political dynamics will be significantly influenced by the current immigration transformation. The success or failure of mass deportation policies, along with their economic and social consequences, will shape public opinion and electoral outcomes that determine the direction of future immigration policy. While its goal of 1 million deportations a year may be difficult to achieve, the administration's impact across the immigration system is nonetheless likely to be historic.

Conclusion

The Trump administration's immigration task force and mass deportation strategy represent the most comprehensive transformation of American immigration policy in modern history. Through the mobilization of federal agencies, the expansion of enforcement authorities, the development of unprecedented detention capacity, and the restructuring of legal immigration pathways, the administration has fundamentally altered how the United States approaches immigration control and management.

This sweeping effort has few analogues in recent world history. Its ambition goes beyond anything attempted in the U.S. since the Eisenhower-era Operation Wetback in its aims to expel millions of people and change the makeup of the country. The scale and scope of current immigration enforcement efforts exceed any previous American experience and represent a dramatic shift in federal priorities and capabilities.

The immediate impacts of these policies are already evident in communities across the United States, from labor shortages in essential industries to increased fear and anxiety in immigrant communities. These actions have created a heightened level of fear and uncertainty for immigrants legal and unauthorized alike, their families, and communities. Even U.S. citizens have been caught up in arrests and fear deportation. The psychological and social effects of mass deportation extend far beyond the individuals directly targeted for removal.

The technological and institutional infrastructure being developed to support mass deportation will have lasting effects on American immigration enforcement capabilities. Advanced data integration systems, expanded surveillance technology, and enhanced interagency coordination represent permanent enhancements to federal enforcement capacity that will influence immigration policy for years to come, regardless of changing political leadership.

Legal and political resistance to administration policies has achieved mixed results, with some initiatives blocked or modified while others proceed largely unimpeded. The ongoing litigation and political opposition highlight fundamental disagreements about immigration policy and the appropriate balance between enforcement and humanitarian concerns. These conflicts reflect deeper tensions about American identity, economic priorities, and constitutional protections that will continue to influence immigration policy debates.

The economic implications of mass deportation are beginning to emerge as industries grapple with labor shortages and communities experience demographic changes. More say these policies will make the U.S. economy weaker (46%) rather than stronger (34%). The long-term economic consequences of dramatically reduced immigration and large-scale deportation remain uncertain but could include significant effects on economic growth, innovation, and competitiveness.

International dimensions of mass deportation, including agreements with foreign countries to accept deportees and the use of military aircraft for removal operations, are creating new diplomatic challenges and potentially affecting broader bilateral relationships. These international arrangements may become models for future immigration enforcement efforts while also generating criticism and resistance from international partners.

The future of American immigration will be shaped by the success or failure of current mass deportation efforts, their economic and social consequences, and the political responses they generate. The institutional changes, technological capabilities, and legal precedents established during this period will influence immigration policy for decades, creating a lasting legacy regardless of future political developments.

Understanding the current transformation of American immigration policy requires recognizing both its immediate operational components and its long-term structural implications. The Trump administration's immigration task force represents not merely a temporary policy shift but a fundamental reimagining of how the United States approaches immigration control, with consequences that will reverberate through American society for years to come. The success or failure of this ambitious undertaking will significantly influence America's demographic future, economic development, and position in the global community while testing the limits of presidential authority and the resilience of American democratic institutions.

CHAPTER SIXTEEN

TRUMP'S ONE BIG BEAUTIFUL BILL - REMAKING THE AMERICAN SOCIAL CONTRACT

INTRODUCTION

On July 4, 2025, President Donald Trump signed into law one of the most consequential pieces of domestic legislation in American history: the One Big Beautiful Bill Act (OBBBA). This massive 870-page omnibus legislation represents a fundamental restructuring of federal tax policy, social safety net programs, and government spending priorities that will reshape the American economic and social landscape for generations to come. The bill's passage marked not merely a legislative victory for the Trump administration, but a watershed moment in the ongoing debate over the proper role of government in American society.

The One Big Beautiful Bill Act, though popularly known by this moniker, officially has no short title after the designation was removed during the Senate amendment process. The legislation combines hundreds of provisions spanning tax reform, healthcare policy, immigration enforcement, and social program modifications into a single comprehensive package that reflects President Trump's vision for his second term in office. The OBBBA contains hundreds of provisions, is estimated to add roughly $3 trillion to the national debt and is projected to cut approximately $4.46 trillion in tax revenue over a 10-year period.

The bill's journey through Congress exemplified the power of budget reconciliation procedures to circumvent traditional legislative obstacles. To more easily pass the bill, Republicans chose to use the budget reconciliation process, which allowed them to avoid the 60-vote Senate filibuster (which carried importance as they hold 53 seats out of 100 in the Senate). This procedural strategy enabled Republicans to advance their agenda despite unified Democratic opposition, fundamentally altering American policy through a simple majority vote.

The legislation's scope and ambition position it alongside landmark laws such as the New Deal, the Great Society programs, and the 2017 Tax Cuts and Jobs Act in terms of its potential to reshape American society. However, unlike previous major social reforms that generally expanded federal programs and protections, the OBBBA represents a significant retrenchment of the federal social safety net combined with substantial tax reductions primarily benefiting higher-income Americans. This approach reflects a philosophical shift toward reducing federal involvement in social programs while maximizing economic incentives for investment and business growth.

Understanding the One Big Beautiful Bill Act requires examining both its immediate provisions and its longer-term implications for American economic inequality, healthcare access, federal fiscal policy, and the fundamental social contract between government and citizens. The legislation's supporters argue it will unleash economic growth while reducing government dependency, while critics contend it will increase inequality and undermine essential services for vulnerable populations.

Legislative Genesis And Political Strategy

The One Big Beautiful Bill Act emerged from President Trump's determination to avoid the incremental approach that characterized much of his first term's legislative agenda. Drawing lessons from the challenges of implementing his initial policies through traditional legislative procedures, Trump and his advisors conceived of a comprehensive omnibus approach that would consolidate his major domestic priorities into a single, must-pass piece of legislation. This strategy reflected both the realities of narrow Republican majorities and the administration's desire to implement transformative changes quickly and definitively.

The legislative strategy centered on utilizing budget reconciliation procedures to overcome Democratic opposition and potential filibusters. The bill was negotiated through a process called reconciliation, which Congress can use to change laws that affect the country's budget. The process limits the time the Senate can spend debating to 20 hours, eliminating the possibility of a filibuster. It also means that the bill can pass with a simple majority of 51 votes in the Senate (or 50 plus the vice president's tie-breaking vote) rather than the supermajority of 60 votes typically needed to avoid a filibuster.

The naming of the legislation reflected Trump's characteristic flair for memorable branding and his desire to frame the complex policy package in simple, appealing terms. At the meeting, Speaker of the House Mike Johnson stated that Trump sought **"one big, beautiful bill"** to enact his policies. This branding strategy aimed to present the legislation as a unified vision for American renewal rather than a collection of disparate policy changes.

The bill's development involved extensive coordination between the White House, Republican congressional leadership, and various conservative policy organizations. The Heritage Foundation's Project 2025 provided significant intellectual groundwork for many of the bill's provisions, while business groups and conservative advocacy organizations helped shape specific policy details. This collaborative approach ensured that the legislation reflected not only Trump's campaign promises but also broader conservative policy objectives that had been developed over years of Republican policy development.

Republican leadership faced significant challenges in maintaining party unity throughout the legislative process. Conservative members of the House Freedom Caucus initially opposed the bill over concerns about insufficient spending cuts and deficit impacts. Rep. Andy Harris of Maryland, the chairman of the ultraconservative House Freedom Caucus, said he decided to vote in favor after "significant agreements" with the White House that he said comes much closer to the trillions of dollars in savings that Freedom Caucus ultimately wanted. Trump's personal intervention proved crucial in securing these votes, demonstrating his continued influence over the Republican caucus.

The timeline for passage reflected both political imperatives and symbolic considerations. President Trump signed the legislation into law on the afternoon of July 4, deliberately choosing Independence Day to emphasize the bill's role in what he characterized as a new American founding. This timing also allowed Republicans to claim a major legislative victory before the summer recess and provided symbolic resonance with themes of American renewal and patriotic achievement.

Tax Policy Revolution: Winners And Losers

The tax provisions of the One Big Beautiful Bill Act constitute the most significant revision of federal tax policy since the 2017 Tax Cuts and Jobs Act, permanently extending and expanding many of those earlier reforms while adding new tax benefits primarily targeted at higher-income Americans. The tax changes reflect a philosophical commitment to supply-side economics and the belief that reducing tax burdens on individuals and businesses will generate sufficient economic growth to offset revenue losses.

The centerpiece of the tax reform involves making permanent the individual income tax rate reductions that were scheduled to expire at the end of 2025. The bill cements some tax-related provisions of the 2017 Tax Cuts and Jobs Act (TCJA), including the individual tax brackets and the increased standard deduction. This permanency provides taxpayers with certainty about their future tax obligations while ensuring that the revenue effects of these cuts will continue indefinitely rather than requiring periodic reauthorization.

The state and local tax (SALT) deduction changes represent one of the most politically significant tax modifications in the bill. The bill expands a TCJA-imposed cap on the state and local tax (SALT) deduction from $10,000 to $40,000 per taxpayer for households earning under $500,000. This change primarily benefits taxpayers in high-tax states, addressing a major Republican political vulnerability in suburban districts where the SALT cap had created significant tax increases for middle and upper-middle class families.

Small business tax provisions aim to encourage entrepreneurship and business investment through enhanced deductions and accelerated depreciation schedules. Since 2017, the Small Business Tax Deduction has allowed small businesses to deduct up to 20% of their business income. Without immediate action by Congress, this essential tax deduction was set to expire at the end of the year, raising taxes on millions of small businesses. The One Big Beautiful Bill Act provides permanent tax relief, freeing America's small businesses to invest in their businesses and employees.

Additional business tax benefits include significant expansions of equipment expensing capabilities. Increases Section 179, Small Business Expensing Cap from $1.25 million to $2.5 million. This will allow small businesses to fully expense business equipment purchases in the first year. These provisions aim to encourage business investment by allowing immediate deduction of capital expenditures rather than requiring depreciation over multiple years.

The distributional effects of the tax changes heavily favor higher-income taxpayers, despite Republican claims about middle-class benefits. The OBBBA will reduce taxes for the top 1 percent of taxpayers by more than $1 trillion over the next decade. Of that total, nearly half, $500 billion, will accrue to the top 0.1 percent of earners, a group of roughly 200,000 households with annual incomes exceeding $2 million. This concentration of benefits at the top of the income distribution reflects the structure of the existing tax code, where higher-income taxpayers pay higher marginal rates and thus receive larger absolute benefits from rate reductions.

Average tax reductions vary dramatically by income level, with the largest benefits flowing to the highest earners. Households would see their taxes reduced by $2,900, on average, according to a Tax Policy Center analysis of the tax provisions in the bill. But that figure varies widely depending on taxpayers' income. Middle-income families receive modest benefits, while the combination of tax cuts and spending reductions may leave some lower-income families worse off overall.

The estate tax modifications represent a significant victory for wealthy families and agricultural interests. Farmers have specifically celebrated how the bill overhauls the 'death tax' the taxes imposed by the federal and some state governments on someone's estate upon death... This is particularly important for commodity and other traditionally large-scale agricultural producers. These changes address longstanding concerns about family farms and businesses being forced to sell assets to pay estate taxes upon the death of owners.

Healthcare And Social Safety Net Transformation

The healthcare provisions of the One Big Beautiful Bill Act represent the most significant restructuring of American social programs since the creation of Medicare and Medicaid, fundamentally altering the scope and generosity of federal health insurance programs while shifting costs and responsibilities to states and individuals. These changes reflect a philosophical commitment to reducing federal social spending while encouraging work and personal responsibility among program beneficiaries.

Medicaid bears the brunt of the bill's social program cuts, with reductions that will fundamentally alter the program's scope and eligibility. The nonpartisan Congressional Budget Office (CBO) estimated that the OBBBA will cut federal spending on Medicaid and Children's Health Insurance Program (CHIP) benefits by $1.02 trillion, due in part to eliminating at least 10.5 million people from the programs by 2034. These cuts represent the largest reduction in federal social spending in modern American history and will force states to make difficult choices about maintaining services or raising taxes to compensate for reduced federal support.

The work requirements imposed on Medicaid expansion adults constitute one of the most controversial aspects of the healthcare changes. For many Medicaid enrollees, the biggest impact would be the new work requirement. These requirements mandate that able-bodied adults demonstrate work activity or participation in approved activities to maintain their health coverage. Proponents argue that work requirements will encourage economic self-sufficiency and reduce program costs, while critics contend that they will primarily serve to reduce enrollment through administrative burdens rather than increase employment.

The administrative complexity of implementing work requirements is expected to result in significant coverage losses even among individuals who qualify for exemptions. While some individuals would qualify for exemptions, state experiences show that even Medicaid enrollees who are exempt would likely lose coverage due to confusion, administrative errors, or failure to navigate complex paperwork. These administrative challenges reflect the inherent difficulty of implementing complex eligibility verification systems while maintaining program access for eligible individuals.

State fiscal pressures will intensify dramatically as federal Medicaid funding decreases while healthcare costs continue to rise. All states would, among other things, be subject to a moratorium on imposing new taxes or increasing existing taxes on health care providers. As a result, they would no longer have access to a potential revenue source for financing their share of Medicaid program costs going forward, as their populations age and health care inflation continues its upward climb.

This combination of reduced federal funding and restricted state revenue options will force difficult choices about program scope and benefits.

Rural hospitals face particular challenges under the new funding structure, despite provisions ostensibly designed to protect rural healthcare access. Rural hospitals comprise just 7% of all hospital spending on Medicaid, illustrating that they have not benefited from the massive increase in waste, fraud, and abuse under the Biden administration. By strengthening Medicaid, we are making more resources available for vulnerable populations and safety net providers, like rural hospitals. However, critics argue that overall funding reductions will outweigh targeted rural support, potentially accelerating rural hospital closures.

The coverage losses resulting from Medicaid changes will have cascading effects throughout the healthcare system. Approximately 16 million people could end up uninsured due to the OBBBA, causing massive disruptions in health care. These coverage losses will increase uncompensated care costs for hospitals and other providers while potentially reducing access to preventive services that help manage chronic conditions and prevent more expensive emergency interventions.

Cost-sharing requirements for Medicaid expansion adults will create new financial barriers to healthcare access. Effective Oct. 1, 2028, states are required to impose cost sharing of up to $35 per service on expansion adults with incomes 100-138% FPL. Exempts primary care, mental health, and substance use disorder services, along with services provided by federally qualified health centers (FQHCs), behavioral health clinics, and rural health clinics. While exemptions exist for certain services, the cost-sharing requirements may discourage utilization of specialty care and other non-exempt services.

Immigration Enforcement And Border Security Funding

The immigration and border security provisions of the One Big Beautiful Bill Act represent the largest federal investment in immigration enforcement in American history, providing unprecedented resources for deportation operations, detention facilities, and border infrastructure. These provisions reflect President Trump's prioritization of immigration enforcement as a national security imperative and his commitment to implementing the largest deportation operation in American history.

The scale of immigration enforcement funding dwarfs all previous investments in border security and interior immigration enforcement. The massive package sets aside about $170 billion to support the Trump's administration's border and immigration goals, which includes detaining and deporting a record number of people from the U.S. This funding level represents not merely an incremental increase in enforcement capabilities but a fundamental expansion of the federal immigration enforcement apparatus.

Detention capacity expansion constitutes the largest single component of immigration enforcement funding, reflecting the administration's strategy of dramatically increasing the number of individuals held pending deportation proceedings. The final bill allocates $45 billion for immigration detention centers, as well as about $30 billion to hire more ICE personnel, for transportation costs, and to maintain ICE facilities, among other spending. This detention expansion will more than double current capacity and create the infrastructure necessary to support sustained large-scale deportation operations.

The Congressional Budget Office estimates that the new detention funding could create unprecedented capacity for immigration detention. The American Immigration Council estimates that the new funding could expand detention capacity to "at least 116,000 beds." This capacity expansion reflects the administration's determination to end what it characterizes as "catch and release" policies by detaining individuals throughout their immigration proceedings rather than releasing them into communities.

Personnel increases will dramatically expand the federal immigration enforcement workforce across multiple agencies. Authorities said the House package would allow the administration to add 10,000 Immigration and Customs Enforcement agents and 8,500 Customs and Border Protection officials and expand the number of detention beds from 41,000 to 100,000. This workforce expansion represents the largest increase in federal law enforcement personnel in American history and will provide the human resources necessary to implement sustained interior enforcement operations.

Border wall construction receives massive funding to complete the physical infrastructure that became a signature element of Trump's immigration policy. The bill sets aside $46.5 billion for what the House Homeland Security Committee calls an "integrated border barrier system," including fencing, water barriers, law enforcement access roads and technology like movement sensors. The funding would complete 701 miles (1,128 kilometers) of primary walls and 900 miles (1,448 kilometers) of river barriers along the U.S.-Mexico border.

The deportation operation's ambitious scope is reflected in the administration's stated goals for removal numbers. His administration is seeking to deport 1 million people in his first year in office, The Washington Post reported last month. It's a goal that immigration analysts say is unlikely at the current pace. The unprecedented funding levels aim to provide the infrastructure and personnel necessary to approach these ambitious targets.

Private prison companies have emerged as significant beneficiaries of the expanded immigration detention funding. Private prison companies are anticipating a significant increase in demand for their services if the spending bill, which includes $45 billion for immigrant detention centers, becomes law. The reliance on private contractors reflects both the scale of the planned expansion and the federal government's limited existing detention infrastructure.

State reimbursement provisions provide financial incentives for state and local cooperation with federal immigration enforcement efforts. Another $13.5 billion was set aside to reimburse states for their immigration enforcement and border security actions, including for efforts under the Biden administration. These reimbursements could compensate states like Texas for previous border security investments while encouraging continued state-level enforcement efforts.

Economic Impact And Fiscal Consequences

The economic implications of the One Big Beautiful Bill Act extend far beyond its immediate budgetary effects, encompassing projected changes in economic growth, employment patterns, income distribution, and long-term fiscal sustainability. The legislation represents a significant test of supply-side economic theory, with its supporters arguing that tax reductions will generate sufficient economic growth to offset revenue losses while its critics contend that the fiscal costs will far exceed any growth benefits.

Economic growth projections vary significantly depending on modeling assumptions and the time horizon considered. We estimate the One Big Beautiful Bill Act would increase long-run GDP by 1.2 percent and reduce federal tax revenue by $5 trillion over the next decade on a conventional basis. The Tax Foundation's analysis suggests modest positive growth effects, though these fall well short of the levels necessary to make the tax cuts self-financing through increased economic activity.

The administration's more optimistic economic projections emphasize the potential for significant growth acceleration. Estimates by the Council of Economic Advisers suggest that our GDP could grow by as much as 5.2% in the short run and 3.5% in the long run while investment in our country could see a 14.5% boost with more than four million jobs created in the long term. These projections reflect the administration's confidence in the supply-side effects of tax reduction and regulatory reform.

Dynamic scoring attempts to account for economic growth effects in estimating the legislation's fiscal impact. On a dynamic basis, incorporating the projected increase in long-run GDP of 1.2 percent, the dynamic score of the tax provisions falls by $940 billion to $4 trillion, meaning economic growth pays for about 19 percent of the major tax cuts. Even optimistic growth projections suggest that economic effects will offset only a fraction of the revenue losses from tax reductions.

The deficit impact of the legislation depends significantly on whether temporary provisions are eventually extended. Combined with the nearly $1.1 trillion in net spending reductions estimated by the Congressional Budget Office (CBO), we estimate the OBBB would increase federal budget deficits by $3.0 trillion from 2025 through 2034 on a dynamic basis. These projections assume that temporary tax provisions expire as scheduled, though political pressures may make extension more likely than expiration.

Interest costs on additional federal borrowing represent a significant additional fiscal burden. Further, we estimate that on a dynamic basis, increased borrowing would add $725 billion in higher interest costs over the decade, resulting in a total deficit increase of nearly $3.8 trillion on a dynamic basis. These interest costs compound over time and represent permanent additions to federal spending that will persist even if the underlying policies are eventually reversed.

The distributional effects of the combined tax and spending changes favor higher-income households while potentially harming lower-income families. Using a model that takes into account the expected economic growth from the plan, the PWBM found, "that households most affected by the cuts to Medicaid and SNAP, those in the bottom income quintile experience the largest losses under this bill, averaging $27,500 in lifetime value for the working-age population. In contrast, working-age households in the top income quintile generally benefit from lower taxes, gaining an average of more than $65,000."

Tax revenue losses from deportations represent an additional fiscal consideration often overlooked in traditional budget analysis. Economic research suggests that immigrants, including unauthorized immigrants, contribute significantly to federal, state, and local tax revenues through income taxes, sales taxes, property taxes, and other levies. Large-scale deportations would eliminate these revenue sources while requiring significant enforcement expenditures.

Political Dynamics And Congressional Passage

The passage of the One Big Beautiful Bill Act through Congress demonstrated both the power of unified party control and the limitations of traditional legislative procedures in an era of intense partisan polarization. The legislation's journey from conception to enactment revealed important dynamics about contemporary American politics, including the role of presidential leadership, the influence of ideological factions within parties, and the strategic use of procedural rules to advance partisan agendas.

Party-line voting characterized the bill's passage through both chambers of Congress, with no Democratic support and only minimal Republican defections. Before being signed into law, the Senate approved the bill 51–50 on July 1, 2025, with Vice President JD Vance casting a tiebreaking vote in support. It passed the House of Representatives, 218–214, on July 3, 2025. It passed over universal Democratic opposition in both houses. This stark partisan division reflected not only disagreements over specific policies but fundamental philosophical differences about the proper role of government in American society.

The reconciliation process proved crucial to Republican success in advancing the legislation despite Democratic opposition. Budget reconciliation rules allowed Republicans to bypass the Senate filibuster while limiting amendments and debate time. However, the Byrd Rule's restrictions on "extraneous" provisions in reconciliation bills created challenges for including non-budgetary policy provisions. Democrats argued that the extension of Trump's 2017 tax cuts, a proposed 10-year ban on state level AI regulations, language that limits the power of federal court to enforce contempt of court citations, a provision to end a tax on the manufacturing of gun silencers, a provision to defund Planned Parenthood, a provision banning Medicaid from funding gender-affirming care for people of all ages and a provision to streamline permits for fossil fuel projects, violated the Byrd Rule.

The Senate Parliamentarian's rulings on Byrd Rule challenges shaped the final content of the legislation. On June 20, 2025, the Senate Parliamentarian, Elizabeth MacDonough, ruled that several provisions from the Senate committees on Banking, Environment and Public Works, and Armed Services violated the Byrd Rule and were therefore removed from the bill. These rulings demonstrated the continuing influence of procedural rules even in an era of increased partisan polarization.

The **"vote-a-rama"** process in the Senate provided Democrats with opportunities to propose amendments and force Republicans to take difficult votes, even though most amendments failed. The vote-a-rama began two days later, on June 30, in the early morning. One of the few successful amendment votes, passing 99–1, removed the proposed AI law moratorium. The vote-a-rama set a record for the most amendment votes in Senate history. This marathon voting session highlighted both the procedural tools available to the minority party and their limited effectiveness against a unified majority.

House Freedom Caucus negotiations demonstrated the continued influence of ideological factions within the Republican party. Conservative members initially opposed the bill over concerns about insufficient spending cuts and deficit impacts. Rep. Ralph Norman of South Carolina: "President Trump earnestly said that if we send this bill back to the Senate, it's going to get worse," Norman said, adding that Trump has "had it with the leaders in the Senate." Trump's personal intervention proved crucial in securing these votes through a combination of policy concessions and political persuasion.

Democratic procedural delays attempted to highlight the bill's controversial provisions and force Republicans to defend their positions publicly. Record-breaking speech: Democrats delayed the bill's passage in protest, with Minority Leader Hakeem Jeffries speaking for more than eight hours and setting a record for the longest floor speech in modern history of the House of Representatives, drawing a standing ovation from his party. These tactics reflected Democrats' limited procedural options while serving to generate media attention for their opposition arguments.

The July 4th signing ceremony provided symbolic resonance that the administration used to frame the legislation as a patriotic achievement. President Trump signed the legislation into law on the afternoon of July 4, deliberately choosing Independence Day to emphasize themes of American renewal and economic independence. This timing reflected the administration's understanding of the importance of political symbolism in shaping public perception of policy achievements.

Implementation Challenges And Administrative Complexity

The implementation of the One Big Beautiful Bill Act presents unprecedented administrative challenges across multiple federal agencies and state governments, requiring coordination between tax administration, healthcare programs, immigration enforcement, and social service delivery systems. The scale and complexity of the required changes test the capacity of government institutions while creating opportunities for administrative failures that could undermine the legislation's intended effects.

Tax system modifications require extensive changes to IRS procedures, forms, and systems to accommodate new deductions, credits, and reporting requirements. The permanent extension of Tax Cuts and Jobs Act provisions requires relatively straightforward implementation, as these systems already exist. However, new provisions such as the expanded SALT deduction cap and modified estate tax thresholds require system programming and taxpayer education efforts to ensure proper compliance.

Medicaid program changes represent perhaps the most complex implementation challenge, requiring coordination between federal agencies and fifty state Medicaid programs with varying administrative capacities and political commitments. Work requirement implementation has proven particularly challenging in previous pilot programs, with states struggling to develop adequate data systems and verification procedures. In fact, the available Senate language doubles the funds set aside for implementation of the work reporting requirement from $100 million in the House version to $200 million.

State administrative burden will increase dramatically as states must implement new eligibility verification systems, work requirement tracking, and enhanced fraud detection measures. The only clear winners that we can identify are firms like Deloitte that contract with state Medicaid agencies to design and operate eligibility and enrollment systems. They can look forward to "a vast market opportunity" helping expansion states meet the burdensome and costly administrative demands of operating a work reporting requirement regime. This increased administrative complexity may paradoxically increase program costs even as enrollment decreases.

Immigration enforcement scaling presents logistical challenges related to detention capacity, transportation, legal proceedings, and international cooperation. The massive expansion of detention facilities requires not only physical construction but also recruitment and training of detention staff, development of medical care systems, and coordination with immigration courts. "The bill will supercharge immigration enforcement," said Kathleen Bush-Joseph, an attorney at the Migration Policy Institute, a nonpartisan think tank in Washington, D.C.

Coordination between federal agencies becomes more complex as immigration enforcement operations expand across traditional agency boundaries. The bill's funding for cross-agency personnel assignments and task force operations requires new coordination mechanisms and may strain existing agency cultures and capabilities. Previous experience suggests that rapid expansion of enforcement operations can lead to administrative errors and civil rights violations.

Legal challenges to various provisions of the legislation will create ongoing implementation uncertainty. Constitutional challenges to immigration enforcement provisions, Medicaid work requirements, and other aspects of the law may result in court orders that require modification of implementation plans. On July 7, 2025, Planned Parenthood sued the Trump Administration over the provision and the following day, a federal judge issued a temporary injunction on the provision.

State-federal tensions may complicate implementation as some states resist federal requirements or seek waivers from certain provisions. States with different political orientations than the federal government may use their administrative discretion to minimize the impact of federal policy changes or may seek legal challenges to requirements they view as unconstitutional or unworkable.

Monitoring and evaluation systems will be essential to track the legislation's effects and identify implementation problems, but developing these systems requires additional administrative capacity and coordination. The complexity of the legislation makes it difficult to isolate the effects of specific provisions, while political pressures may influence how success and failure are measured and reported.

Social And Economic Implications For American Society

The One Big Beautiful Bill Act's implementation will have far-reaching consequences for American society that extend well beyond its immediate budgetary and policy effects, potentially reshaping social mobility patterns, healthcare access, economic inequality, and the fundamental relationship between citizens and their government. These broader implications reflect the legislation's role in redefining the American social contract and the balance between individual responsibility and collective support.

Healthcare access changes will disproportionately affect vulnerable populations, including low-income families, individuals with disabilities, and residents of rural communities. Research shows that when federal funding for Medicaid decreases, states tend to cut optional benefits such as home- and community-based (HCBS) first. It is nearly impossible to carve out a specific population, such as disabled people or elderly people, because the cuts to Medicaid funding will affect everyone due to hospital closures and health care workforce layoffs.

The coverage losses projected under the legislation will create significant stress on emergency departments and safety-net providers as uninsured individuals seek care in emergency settings. CAP estimates that adults who lose Medicaid coverage would spend an average of about $2,220 more in annual out-of-pocket costs. These increased costs may force families to forgo necessary medical care or face financial hardship when medical emergencies occur.

Rural hospital closures represent a particular concern given the concentration of Medicaid patients in rural areas and the financial pressures these institutions already face. The combination of reduced Medicaid reimbursement and increased uncompensated care could accelerate rural hospital closures, creating healthcare deserts in areas that already struggle with provider shortages. Their losses in federal funds and enrollment, much higher than those of non-expansion states, will translate into more uninsured, more uncompensated care, and more medical debt.

Economic inequality may increase as the legislation's benefits flow primarily to higher-income households while its costs fall disproportionately on lower-income families. The combination of tax cuts for the wealthy and program cuts affecting the poor represents a significant shift in the distribution of government benefits and burdens. The OBBBA will reduce taxes for the top 1 percent of taxpayers by more than $1 trillion over the next decade. Of that total, nearly half, $500 billion, will accrue to the top 0.1 percent of earners, a group of roughly 200,000 households with annual incomes exceeding $2 million.

Social mobility patterns may be affected as reduced access to healthcare, nutrition assistance, and other support programs makes it more difficult for low-income families to invest in education, job training, and other activities that promote economic advancement. The work requirements imposed on social programs reflect a philosophical belief that such requirements will encourage employment and self-sufficiency, though research on previous implementations suggests mixed results.

Immigration enforcement operations will affect not only unauthorized immigrants but also mixed-status families and immigrant communities more broadly. The expanded detention and deportation operations may create fear and uncertainty that affects participation in schools, healthcare, and other institutions even among individuals with legal status. These community-wide effects can undermine social cohesion and economic development in areas with large immigrant populations.

Family separation represents a significant social consequence of both immigration enforcement and social program changes. Immigration deportations may separate family members with different legal statuses, while work requirements and other Medicaid restrictions may create situations where family members have different access to healthcare and support services.

Labor market effects will vary by industry and region, with sectors that employ large numbers of immigrants potentially facing workforce disruptions while areas that rely heavily on Medicaid reimbursement may experience reduced economic activity. The tax cuts may encourage business investment and job creation in some sectors while program cuts reduce consumption and economic activity in others.

Educational institutions may face increased pressure as families lose access to healthcare and nutrition support while local tax bases are affected by changes in federal spending patterns. Schools in low-income areas may see increased numbers of uninsured students and families facing economic stress, while reduced federal funding for various programs may strain local budgets.

Long-Term Constitutional And Governance Implications

The One Big Beautiful Bill Act raises significant questions about the future of American governance, federalism, and constitutional interpretation that will influence political and legal development for decades to come. The legislation's use of budget reconciliation procedures to enact major social policy changes, its expansion of executive authority in immigration enforcement, and its restructuring of federal-state relationships in healthcare and social programs establish precedents that may reshape how future governments approach policy implementation.

The reconciliation process's use for comprehensive policy reform represents a significant departure from traditional legislative procedures and may establish new norms for how major policy changes are enacted in an era of partisan polarization. The bill was negotiated through a process called reconciliation, which Congress can use to change laws that affect the country's budget. Future administrations may view reconciliation as the primary mechanism for advancing partisan agendas, potentially bypassing bipartisan deliberation and compromise.

CHAPTER SEVENTEEN

THE DEPARTMENT OF JUSTICE UNDER TRUMP - WEAPONIZING FEDERAL LAW ENFORCEMENT

INTRODUCTION

The Department of Justice under President Trump's second administration has undergone the most radical transformation in its modern history, fundamentally reshaping the federal government's approach to law enforcement, civil rights, and the rule of law itself. Led by Attorney General Pam Bondi, the DOJ has abandoned its traditional role as an independent guardian of justice and constitutional rights, instead becoming a politically weaponized instrument of presidential power designed to advance Trump's personal and political agenda while targeting his perceived enemies.

This transformation represents far more than the typical policy shifts that occur between administrations of different parties. Under Bondi's leadership, the Justice Department has systematically dismantled decades of civil rights enforcement, eliminated anti-corruption efforts that might threaten Trump allies, purged career prosecutors and attorneys who worked on cases involving the President, and redirected federal law enforcement resources toward culture war priorities and immigration enforcement that align with Trump's political base.

The scope and speed of these changes have been unprecedented in American history. Pam Bondi vowed at her confirmation hearing this year that "politics will not play a part" in her time as attorney general. Now she's leading a Justice Department more visibly aligned with the political agenda of the White House than any in recent history. Within weeks of taking office, Bondi had issued sweeping directives that effectively transformed the DOJ from an independent law enforcement agency into what critics describe as Trump's personal legal army.

The consequences of this transformation extend far beyond the immediate policy changes, threatening the foundational principle that the rule of law applies equally to all Americans regardless of political affiliation or power. The systematic politicization of federal law enforcement represents a fundamental attack on democratic governance and constitutional principles that have guided American justice for more than two centuries.

Understanding the Trump DOJ's agenda requires examining both the specific policies and personnel changes implemented under Bondi's leadership and the broader constitutional implications of subordinating federal law enforcement to partisan political objectives. This transformation reflects Trump's long-standing grievances against what he characterizes as the "weaponization" of the justice system against him, while ironically implementing the most extensive actual weaponization of federal law enforcement in American history.

Pam Bondi: Trump's Loyal Enforcer

The selection of Pam Bondi as Attorney General represented a deliberate choice to install a proven Trump loyalist who would prioritize personal loyalty to the President over traditional principles of prosecutorial independence. Bondi's background and previous relationship with Trump provided clear evidence of her willingness to subordinate legal principle to political considerations, making her an ideal candidate to implement the administration's most controversial agenda items.

Bondi's history with Trump includes several troubling episodes that foreshadowed her approach as Attorney General. Most notably, in March 2016, CREW discovered that the Trump Foundation had broken the law by giving an illegal $25,000 contribution to a political group supporting Florida Attorney General Pam Bondi. Charitable foundations like the Trump Foundation are not allowed to engage in politics. Even more problematic was the fact that the contribution was given as Bondi's office was deciding whether to take legal action related to Trump University. This quid pro quo arrangement demonstrated Bondi's willingness to compromise prosecutorial independence for financial benefit.

During the 2020 election aftermath, Bondi actively promoted Trump's false claims of election fraud, demonstrating her commitment to advancing Trump's interests regardless of factual evidence. Pam Bondi, Trump's pick for attorney general, said Trump had won the battleground state of Pennsylvania as votes were still being counted, and implied fraud was taking place. "'We do have evidence of cheating,' Bondi said on Fox News, on Nov. 5, 2020, two days after the election, citing ballots allegedly being 'dumped' and mailed to dead people." Trump would go on to lose the state, and the election. No evidence has emerged to support his claims of widespread fraud.

Bondi's confirmation process revealed her confrontational approach and unwillingness to commit to traditional principles of prosecutorial independence. During Bondi's own confirmation hearings, Democratic senators questioned whether she would use her position to help Trump go after political enemies and if she would support pardons for people convicted in connection with the attack on the U.S. Capitol on January 6, 2021. In her responses, Bondi did not shy away from confrontational exchanges with the senators. When asked by Sen. Alex Padilla of California to state the citizenship clause of the 14th Amendment, she said, "Senator, I'm here to answer your questions. I'm not here to do your homework and study for you."

Prior to her nomination, Bondi's involvement with Project 2025 provided a blueprint for the radical transformation she would implement at the DOJ. Before being tapped for Attorney General, Pam Bondi helped lead an organization working "to implement Project 2025." This involvement in developing the conservative blueprint for reshaping the federal government demonstrated her commitment to using the DOJ as a tool for advancing ideological objectives rather than enforcing the law impartially.

Bondi's corporate lobbying background has created numerous potential conflicts of interest that raise questions about her ability to fairly enforce federal laws. Ms. Bondi represented a long roster of corporate clients, including Uber and Amazon. Many of these companies have business with the federal government, and could be subject to scrutiny by a Justice Department run by her, raising questions about potential conflicts of interest. These corporate relationships highlight the extent to which Bondi's tenure represents a departure from traditional standards of prosecutorial independence and ethical conduct.

Upon taking office, Bondi immediately demonstrated her intention to subordinate the DOJ to Trump's political agenda. When Pam Bondi was sworn in as attorney general last week, she made a promise to President Donald Trump: "I am truly honored that you have asked me to take on this role, and I will make you proud, and I will make this country proud." This pledge of personal loyalty to Trump, rather than to the Constitution and rule of law, encapsulated the fundamental transformation she would bring to the Justice Department.

Dismantling Civil Rights Enforcement

The Trump administration's systematic destruction of the Civil Rights Division represents one of the most significant reversals of civil rights progress since the end of Reconstruction. Under the leadership of Harmeet Dhillon, a conservative culture warrior and election denier, the division has abandoned its traditional mission of protecting Americans from discrimination and instead become a vehicle for advancing Trump's culture war agenda.

The scale of personnel changes in the Civil Rights Division has been unprecedented in the department's history. The Justice Department's Civil Rights Division is in upheaval amid a mass exodus of attorneys as the Trump administration moves to radically reshape the division, shelving its traditional mission and replacing it with one focused on enforcing the president's executive orders. Some 250 attorneys, or around 70% of the division's lawyers have left or will have left the department in the time between President Trump's inauguration and the end of May, according to current and former officials.

This mass exodus reflects more than typical turnover between administrations; it represents a wholesale rejection by career civil rights attorneys of the division's new direction. By and large, attorneys in the division feel like they can no longer do the work they've always been able to do, including during the first Trump administration. Then, there was no mass exodus, department veterans say. Attorneys stayed put and continued their normal work. The administration scaled back, but did not end, work in a few priority areas, like policing.

Harmeet Dhillon's appointment as head of the Civil Rights Division signals the administration's intent to completely reverse the division's traditional role. Dhillon is a conservative culture warrior who represented Trump in challenging the results of the 2020 election and ardently backed his baseless claims of fraud. Her background includes allegations that Google discriminates against white men and opposition to state laws protecting doctors who perform gender-affirming surgery for transgender minors.

The transformation of the division's mission has been explicitly articulated by Dhillon herself in terms that reveal the ideological nature of the changes. Speaking at a recent Federalist Society event, Dhillon likened the division's work under Democratic administrations to a speeding train. She said Republican administrations typically try to "just slow the train down." "There really hasn't been a focus on turning the train around and driving it in the opposite direction. And that's my vision of the DOJ civil rights [division]," she said. "We don't just slow down the woke. We take up the cause to achieve the executive branch's goals."

The division's new mission statements represent a complete abandonment of traditional civil rights enforcement in favor of culture war priorities. Dhillon has issued new mission statements for the division's 11 sections that push Trump's priorities and redirect resources to enforcing his executive orders. Those missions include "Protecting Children from Chemical and Surgical Mutilation," "Keeping Men Out of Women's Sports," "Eradicating Anti-Christian Bias" and "Additional Measures to Combat Antisemitism." These priorities reflect Trump's executive orders rather than federal civil rights laws passed by Congress.

Traditional civil rights enforcement has been essentially abandoned under the new leadership. The U.S. Justice Department (DOJ) has directed its Civil Rights Division to halt ongoing litigation and refrain from initiating new cases as President Donald Trump embarks on a purge of federal Diversity, Equity and Inclusion (DEI) programs in his first days in office. This pause has affected critical cases involving voting rights, police misconduct, and discrimination in employment and housing.

The abandonment of police reform efforts represents a particularly significant reversal of decades of federal oversight. The division's special litigation section, which investigates alleged abuse by police departments around the country, has been decimated by departures and policy changes. The Trump administration has quietly transformed the Justice Department's Civil Rights Division, forcing out a majority of career managers and implementing new priorities that current and former officials say abandon a decadeslong mission of enforcing laws that prohibit discrimination in hiring, housing and voting rights.

Voting rights enforcement has been redirected away from protecting voting access toward investigating alleged fraud by non-citizens. The new civil rights division mission under Deputy AG Dhillon moves towards Donald Trump's priorities, which includes hunting for noncitizen voters and protecting white people from discrimination. This mission shift has ominous implications. It is telling that the amended priorities for the Civil Rights Division's voting section, which owes much of its authorship to Project 2020 makes only a cursory mention to the Voting Rights Act of 1964.

The Weaponization Task Force: Targeting Trump's Enemies

One of Attorney General Bondi's first actions was to establish a "weaponization working group" designed to investigate and potentially prosecute individuals who had investigated or prosecuted Donald Trump. This task force represents an unprecedented use of federal law enforcement powers to target political enemies and represents the clearest example of the actual weaponization of the justice system.

The task force's mandate explicitly targets Trump's perceived enemies within the justice system. According to the Bondi memo, the new working group will "identify instances where a department's or agency's conduct appears to have been designed to achieve political objectives or other improper aims rather than pursuing justice of legitimate governmental objectives." It mentions several specific things that it will examine, including "weaponization" by former special counsel Jack Smith, the prosecutors and the investigators who took part in the "unprecedented raid on President Trump's home."

The scope of the task force's investigation extends to state prosecutors who brought cases against Trump, demonstrating the administration's willingness to use federal power to intimidate state officials. It also will examine "federal cooperation with the weaponization" by the Manhattan district attorney and the New York state attorney general "to target President Trump, his family and his businesses." The Manhattan district attorney brought state criminal charges against Trump for falsifying business records to conceal a payment to an adult film star.

The task force's creation fulfills Trump's campaign promises of retribution against those who investigated his conduct. Bondi herself had foreshadowed the "weaponization" working group's creation by asserting at her confirmation hearing last month that the Justice Department had "targeted Donald Trump." The Justice Department will provide quarterly reports to the White House on the progress of the review, which will look for instances where agencies' actions "appear to have been designed to achieve political objectives or other improper aims rather than pursuing justice."

The potential for criminal prosecution of Trump's perceived enemies represents an unprecedented threat to the rule of law. The nature of the task force investigations, including whether they could lead to possible criminal charges, is not clear. However, Bondi's previous statements suggest that prosecution is a distinct possibility. "The Department of Justice, the prosecutors will be prosecuted. The bad ones," she said on Fox News in 2023. "The investigators will be investigated because the deep state, last term for President Trump, they were hiding in the shadows but now they have a spotlight on them and they can all be investigated."

The task force's work has already resulted in concrete actions against career DOJ employees. Attorney General Pam Bondi has fired more than 20 Justice Department employees who worked on cases involving the Jan. 6 riot at the Capitol and Donald Trump's handling of classified documents, sources told Axios. The new dismissals bring the total Smith-related firings to about 35. About 15 more could face termination. These firings represent an unprecedented purge of career prosecutors based on their involvement in legally authorized investigations.

The elimination of oversight mechanisms compounds the threat posed by the weaponization task force. On Bondi's first day in office, she shut down the FBI's Foreign Influence Task Force, shut down the DOJ's Task Force KleptoCapture, and cut back enforcement of the Foreign Agents Registration Act. These actions removed important checks on foreign influence and corruption that might affect Trump and his associates.

Immigration Enforcement As DOJ Priority

The Trump DOJ has dramatically elevated immigration enforcement as a central mission, redirecting resources from traditional federal law enforcement priorities to support the administration's mass deportation agenda. This shift represents both a philosophical change in federal law enforcement priorities and a practical reallocation of prosecutorial resources toward immigration cases.

Immigration-related prosecutions have become a top priority for federal prosecutors under Bondi's leadership. After taking office, she immediately issued a number of directives, including a commitment that the Department of Justice (DOJ) will "use all available criminal statutes to combat the flood of illegal immigration." This directive fundamentally alters the traditional balance of federal prosecutorial priorities.

The DOJ has launched multiple lawsuits against states and localities that resist cooperation with federal immigration enforcement. During a news conference announcing the lawsuit, Bondi was joined by Tammy Nobles, whose daughter Kayla Hamilton was sexually assaulted and murdered in Maryland by a gang member who happened to be undocumented. The lawsuit against New York follows another one filed against the state of Illinois and the city of Chicago, alleging obstruction of federal immigration enforcement.

Federal prosecutors have been directed to prioritize immigration cases even when this conflicts with other federal law enforcement priorities. Bondi has used emotionally charged cases to justify this reallocation of resources, though critics argue that the focus on immigration enforcement diverts attention from other serious federal crimes including white-collar crime, public corruption, and domestic terrorism.

The administration has pursued aggressive legal theories to challenge state and local policies that limit cooperation with immigration enforcement. On Wednesday, Bondi announced that she has sued the state of New York, including Gov. Kathy Hochul and New York Attorney General Letitia James, arguing that a state law allowing undocumented people to obtain driver's licenses is unconstitutional. This represents an unprecedented federal challenge to state authority over driver's license issuance.

DOJ resources have been redirected from civil rights enforcement to immigration prosecution. The top two officials in its appellate section have been reassigned to a new task force that will prosecute officials from sanctuary cities who do not cooperate with federal immigration enforcement efforts, according to a DOJ official familiar with the matter. This reallocation represents a fundamental shift in how the federal government prioritizes different types of legal violations.

The emphasis on immigration enforcement has extended to contempt for federal court orders. In March 2025, Chief Judge James Boasberg of the federal district court in D.C. issued an order to temporarily block the Trump administration from using the Alien Enemies Act deporting alleged members of Venezuelan gang Tren de Aragua, and also verbally ordered for the deportation flights "to be returned to the United States," to be "complied with immediately"; however the Trump administration completed the deportations anyway, with Bondi and other Justice Department officials later arguing that "an oral directive is not enforceable as an injunction."

Eliminating Anti-Corruption Enforcement

One of the most consequential but under-reported aspects of the Trump DOJ's agenda has been the systematic elimination of anti-corruption enforcement mechanisms that might threaten Trump and his associates. This dismantling of oversight represents a fundamental threat to government accountability and the rule of law.

Bondi has deliberately curtailed anti-corruption efforts that were sources of irritation for Trump during his first presidency. Attorney General Pam Bondi has curtailed the agency's anti-corruption efforts, ratcheted up immigration enforcement and redirected the civil rights division. More broadly, Bondi has deprioritized anti-corruption efforts, including some that have previously ensnared allies of the president. This deprioritization represents a deliberate strategy to shield Trump and his associates from accountability.

Key anti-corruption task forces have been eliminated entirely. On Bondi's first day in office, she shut down the FBI's Foreign Influence Task Force, shut down the DOJ's Task Force KleptoCapture, and cut back enforcement of the Foreign Agents Registration Act. These task forces were specifically designed to combat foreign influence and kleptocracy that threatened American democratic institutions.

The elimination of the Foreign Influence Task Force removes crucial oversight of foreign interference in American politics. This task force was responsible for investigating and prosecuting cases involving foreign agents operating in the United States without proper registration, including cases that might involve Trump associates or allies.

Task Force KleptoCapture was specifically designed to target the illicit wealth of foreign oligarchs and corrupt officials, including Russian oligarchs. The shutdown of this task force removes an important tool for combating international corruption and money laundering that might affect American political and economic systems.

The reduction in Foreign Agents Registration Act (FARA) enforcement eliminates oversight of unregistered foreign agents operating in the United States. FARA enforcement has been particularly relevant to Trump associates, including Paul Manafort and Michael Flynn, who were prosecuted for FARA violations during the first Trump administration.

The systematic elimination of these oversight mechanisms appears designed to protect Trump and his associates from future legal jeopardy. The timing and scope of these eliminations suggest a coordinated effort to remove legal obstacles that might constrain the administration's actions or expose corruption within Trump's circle.

Targeting State And Local Officials

The Trump DOJ has embarked on an unprecedented campaign to use federal law enforcement powers to intimidate and prosecute state and local officials who resist the administration's agenda. This represents a fundamental break with traditional federalism principles and the constitutional separation of powers between federal and state governments.

The prosecution of state election officials represents one of the most alarming aspects of this campaign. Colorado Attorney General Phil Weiser (D) panned the department's involvement in Peters's lawsuit challenging her conviction as a "grotesque attempt to weaponize the rule of law." The DOJ's intervention in state criminal proceedings against election officials who promoted Trump's false claims represents an unprecedented federal intrusion into state judicial processes.

The DOJ has threatened sanctuary city officials with federal prosecution for non-cooperation with immigration enforcement. The administration has created task forces specifically dedicated to prosecuting state and local officials who implement sanctuary policies, representing a dramatic escalation in federal-state conflicts over immigration enforcement.

Federal lawsuits against states have multiplied as the DOJ challenges state policies that conflict with Trump's agenda. The DOJ has filed multiple lawsuits challenging state laws and policies, including New York's driver's license law and various sanctuary policies implemented by state and local governments.

The use of federal grant restrictions to coerce state compliance represents another tool in the administration's arsenal. Among other directives Bondi signed were orders to lift the moratorium on the federal death penalty and end federal grants administered by the Justice Department for jurisdictions that "unlawfully interfere with federal law enforcement." This represents the use of federal funding as a weapon against non-compliant state and local governments.

The pattern of federal intervention in state affairs extends beyond immigration to include civil rights enforcement and election administration. The DOJ has withdrawn from various cases and changed positions in ongoing litigation in ways that benefit Republican state officials and policies while harming Democratic officials and their initiatives.

The selective nature of federal enforcement against state officials creates a two-tiered system of justice. Republican officials who violate federal law face reduced scrutiny, while Democratic officials who resist federal policies face aggressive prosecution and investigation.

Institutional Capture And Personnel Purges

The Trump administration's transformation of the DOJ has involved systematic personnel changes designed to eliminate career employees who might resist the politicization of federal law enforcement. These purges represent an unprecedented attack on the professional civil service and the institutional knowledge that ensures continuity in federal law enforcement.

Mass firings of career prosecutors have eliminated institutional memory and expertise. **Attorney General Pam Bondi** has fired more than 20 Justice Department employees who worked on cases involving the Jan. 6 riot at the Capitol and Donald Trump's handling of classified documents. The firings are part of a massive purge aimed at clearing the DOJ of attorneys and support staff who took part in Special Counsel Jack Smith's prosecution of Trump for Jan. 6 and possessing classified documents unlawfully.

The scope of the purges extends beyond high-profile cases to include routine career employees. More than 100 attorneys have departed from the Civil Rights Division alone, representing an unprecedented loss of institutional knowledge and expertise in federal civil rights enforcement.

Resignations by senior career officials have accelerated as employees refuse to participate in the politicization of their agencies. Federal prosecutor Ryan R. Crosswell wrote to **Attorney General Pam Bondi** that he "can no longer serve the Department that I love." The goodbye letter from Jim Jones, director of the Food and Drug Administration's food division, slammed the "indiscriminate firing" of dozens of his employees.

The administration has used reassignments as a tool to pressure career employees to quit. More than a dozen senior lawyers, many with decades of experience working under presidents of both parties, have been reassigned, the current and former officials say. Some have resigned in frustration after they were moved to less desirable roles unrelated to their expertise.

Loyalty tests and ideological conformity have become requirements for continued employment. The latest round of mass departures occurred in recent weeks as the leadership began reassigning managers, widely seen as a push to have them quit, and forcing attorneys to work on task forces dedicated to certain Trump priorities like antisemitism or transgender issues.

The elimination of professional standards and traditional prosecutorial independence has created an environment where personal loyalty to Trump takes precedence over legal expertise and ethical considerations. In another memo, Bondi wrote that prosecutors could face firings if they refuse to sign onto briefs or appear in court to argue on behalf of the administration, saying it's the department lawyers' job to "vigorously defend presidential policies and actions against legal challenges."

Constitutional Crisis And Rule Of Law Threats

The systematic politicization of the Department of Justice under Trump represents a fundamental constitutional crisis that threatens the foundational principle that no one, including the president, is above the law. The transformation of federal law enforcement into a tool of presidential power represents the most serious threat to American democratic institutions since the Civil War.

The abandonment of prosecutorial independence undermines the constitutional separation of powers. Attorneys general for decades have sought to maintain some measure of independence from presidential influence. Bondi, as she introduced the president to the crowd of senior Justice and FBI officials, said, "We are so proud to work at the directive of Donald Trump." This explicit subordination of the Justice Department to presidential political interests violates fundamental principles of democratic governance.

The use of federal law enforcement to target political enemies represents a classic authoritarian tactic. She has launched a task force to examine a string of the president's perceived adversaries, starting with special counsel Jack Smith, who brought indictments against Trump in 2023 over allegations he mishandled classified documents and his attempts to block Joe Biden's 2020 election victory. The nature of the task force investigations, including whether they could lead to possible criminal charges, is not clear.

The selective enforcement of federal law based on political considerations creates a two-tiered system of justice. The systematic elimination of oversight mechanisms while creating new tools to target political enemies represents the essence of weaponization that Trump claims to oppose.

The violation of traditional norms and institutional constraints demonstrates the fragility of democratic institutions when led by individuals who reject constitutional principles. Trump's declaration that he is "the chief law enforcement officer in our country" represents a fundamental misunderstanding of constitutional separation of powers and the independent role of the Justice Department.

The broader implications for American democracy extend beyond the immediate policy changes to encompass the erosion of institutional legitimacy and public trust in the rule of law. The systematic politicization of federal law enforcement undermines the credibility of the justice system and creates precedents that future authoritarian leaders could exploit.

Long-Term Implications And Resistance

The transformation of the Department of Justice under Trump will have lasting consequences for American democracy that extend far beyond the current administration. The institutional damage inflicted on federal law enforcement and the precedents established for political interference in prosecutorial decisions will influence American governance for decades to come.

The exodus of experienced career prosecutors represents a loss of institutional knowledge that will be difficult to rebuild. The mass departure of 70% of Civil Rights Division attorneys represents not just a temporary disruption but a permanent loss of expertise and institutional memory that took decades to develop. Young said the changes amount to the destruction of the division and its traditional work. "The division right now is being decimated."

Legal challenges to the administration's actions provide some check on executive overreach, but the success of these challenges depends on an independent judiciary that the administration has also sought to influence. While courts have blocked some administration actions, the systematic nature of the changes makes comprehensive judicial oversight difficult.

State and local resistance has emerged as an important counterweight to federal overreach, though this resistance faces increasing federal pressure and potential prosecution. The administration's aggressive pursuit of sanctuary cities and state officials who resist federal policies represents an escalating conflict over the constitutional balance between federal and state authority.

Congressional oversight has been limited by Republican control of both chambers, though some Republicans have expressed concern about the extent of the changes. The lack of effective legislative oversight removes an important check on executive power and enables the continued politicization of federal law enforcement.

International implications include damage to America's reputation as a nation governed by the rule of law. The systematic politicization of federal law enforcement undermines America's ability to criticize authoritarian practices in other countries and weakens international cooperation on law enforcement and human rights issues.

The precedent established for future administrations represents perhaps the most serious long-term consequence. Future presidents of both parties may view the Trump era as establishing new norms for political control over federal law enforcement, permanently undermining prosecutorial independence and the rule of law.

Conclusion: Democracy Under Assault

The Department of Justice under Attorney General Pam Bondi represents the most systematic assault on the rule of law and democratic governance in American history. The transformation of federal law enforcement from an independent guardian of justice into a political weapon of presidential power threatens the foundational principles upon which American democracy rests.

The scope and speed of the changes implemented under Bondi's leadership demonstrate the fragility of democratic institutions when led by individuals who reject constitutional constraints and traditional norms. The systematic elimination of civil rights enforcement, anti-corruption oversight, and prosecutorial independence represents not merely a change in policy priorities but a fundamental attack on the constitutional order.

The weaponization of federal law enforcement to target political enemies while protecting political allies represents the classic pattern of authoritarian governance. The irony that this transformation occurs under the banner of opposing "weaponization" demonstrates the administration's sophisticated understanding of how to manipulate public discourse while implementing authoritarian practices.

The institutional damage inflicted on the Department of Justice will outlast the current administration and may permanently alter the relationship between the presidency and federal law enforcement. The precedents established for political interference in prosecutorial decisions, the elimination of oversight mechanisms, and the subordination of career professionals to political appointees represent a fundamental break with American democratic traditions.

The mass exodus of career prosecutors and civil rights attorneys represents not only a loss of institutional knowledge but a clear signal that professionals dedicated to the rule of law cannot function within the politicized environment created by the Trump administration. Their departure represents a form of institutional resistance but also leaves federal law enforcement in the hands of political appointees with questionable commitment to traditional prosecutorial standards.

The broader implications for American democracy extend beyond the immediate policy changes to encompass the erosion of public trust in the justice system and the creation of precedents that future authoritarian leaders could exploit. The systematic politicization of federal law enforcement represents a fundamental threat to the constitutional principle that the law applies equally to all Americans regardless of political affiliation or power.

The Trump DOJ's agenda represents not merely a conservative approach to law enforcement but a fundamental rejection of the rule of law itself. The transformation of the Justice Department into an instrument of presidential power threatens the constitutional balance that has sustained American democracy for more than two centuries and represents a clear and present danger to the survival of democratic governance in the United States.

CHAPTER EIGHTEEN

STRIKING BACK AT THE SOURCE - DEA TASK FORCES AGAINST PILL MILL DOCTORS AND THEIR LASTING IMPACT

THE BIRTH OF A CRISIS RESPONSE

As the opioid epidemic reached fever pitch in the early 2010s, the Drug Enforcement Administration faced an unprecedented challenge. Prescription drug abuse had become America's fastest-growing drug problem, with Florida alone prescribing ten times more oxycodone pills than all other states combined. The traditional model of combating illegal drug trafficking, targeting street dealers and foreign cartels, proved insufficient against a new breed of drug dealer: licensed physicians operating "pill mills" under the guise of legitimate medical practice.

The response required a fundamental shift in DEA strategy. Rather than pursuing conventional drug traffickers, federal agents found themselves investigating respected members of the medical community, doctors, pharmacists, and clinic operators who had weaponized their professional credentials to fuel addiction for profit. This challenge demanded specialized task forces combining medical expertise, financial investigation capabilities, and traditional law enforcement tactics.

The DEA's answer came in the form of Tactical Diversion Squads (TDS) and partnerships with the **Organized Crime Drug Enforcement Task Forces** (OCDETF). These specialized units would become the tip of the spear in what would evolve into one of the most extensive medical crime enforcement operations in American history.

The Architecture Of Enforcement: Tactical Diversion Squads

The Tactical Diversion Squads (TDS) combine DEA resources with those of federal, state and local law enforcement agencies in an innovative effort to investigate, disrupt and dismantle those suspected of violating the Controlled Substances Act. Unlike traditional drug enforcement units, TDS teams were specifically designed to tackle the complexities of pharmaceutical diversion, the process by which legally manufactured controlled substances are diverted from legitimate medical channels into illegal distribution networks.

The structure of these task forces reflected the multifaceted nature of pill mill operations. The DEA's Fort Worth Tactical Diversion Squad is comprised of DEA agents and task force officers from the Arlington Police Department, the Ellis County Sheriff's Office, the North Richland Hills Police Department, the Benbrook Police Department, the Granbury Police Department, the Tarrant County Sheriff's Office, and the Parker County Sheriff's Office. This multi-jurisdictional approach proved essential, as pill mill operations often spanned multiple counties and states, exploiting jurisdictional boundaries to avoid detection.

The TDS model represented a significant evolution in drug enforcement methodology. Traditional drug investigations typically focused on street-level dealers and worked upward through the distribution chain. Pill mill investigations required agents to understand complex medical procedures, prescription monitoring systems, insurance fraud, and the legitimate pharmaceutical supply chain.

Agents needed to distinguish between legitimate medical practice and criminal enterprise, a nuanced determination that required extensive medical consultation and sophisticated financial analysis.

These squads operated under a unique mandate that distinguished them from other DEA units. While traditional enforcement focused on intercepting illegal drugs, TDS units had to identify the diversion of legal pharmaceuticals. This required developing new investigative techniques, including extensive undercover operations where agents posed as patients seeking narcotic prescriptions. The challenge lay in gathering evidence that would prove criminal intent while respecting the legitimate doctor-patient relationship.

Ocdetf Integration: Scaling Up The Response

The magnitude of the pill mill crisis necessitated resources beyond what individual TDS units could deploy. Enter the Organized Crime Drug Enforcement Task Forces, a program established in 1982 to mount a comprehensive attack and reduce the supply of illegal drugs in the United States. The integration of pill mill investigations into the OCDETF framework provided access to enhanced funding, multi-agency coordination, and sophisticated investigative tools.

Since OCDETF's inception tens of thousands of arrests have been made and hundreds of tons of narcotics and billions in currency, real property, and conveyances all have been seized. The program's prosecutor-led approach proved particularly valuable in pill mill cases, where complex legal questions about medical practice standards often determined the viability of criminal charges.

The OCDETF designation transformed individual pill mill investigations into comprehensive attacks on entire criminal enterprises. This prosecution is part of an Organized Crime Drug Enforcement Task Forces (OCDETF) Strike Force Initiative, which provides for the establishment of permanent multi-agency task force teams that work side-by-side in the same location. This co-location model enabled unprecedented coordination between DEA agents, FBI investigators, IRS criminal division agents, postal inspectors, and local law enforcement.

The OCDETF framework also provided access to specialized resources critical for pill mill investigations. Financial analysis became paramount, as these operations often involved complex money laundering schemes, cash-only business models, and elaborate asset concealment strategies. The program's emphasis on asset forfeiture proved particularly effective against pill mill operators, who often accumulated substantial wealth through their illegal prescribing practices.

Operation Pill Nation: The Florida Laboratory

Florida became ground zero for the DEA's pill mill enforcement strategy, serving as both the epicenter of the crisis and the testing ground for new enforcement approaches. DEA Agents, with assistance from its federal, state, and local law enforcement partners, arrested 22 people and seized over **$2.2 million** in cash and 70 vehicles, including numerous exotic cars, on Wednesday, February 23 in a sweeping takedown of rogue pain clinics in South Florida.

Operation Pill Nation represented a paradigm shift in scale and methodology. These arrests are the first in Operation Pill Nation resulting from 340 undercover buys of prescription drugs from over 60 doctors in more than 40 "pill mills" conducted in the past year. The operation's scope demonstrated the systematic nature of the pill mill problem and the comprehensive response required to address it.

The Florida operations revealed the sophisticated nature of modern pill mill enterprises. According to the indictment, the defendants operated the clinics as pill mills that offered patients prescriptions for oxycodone and other controlled substances where there was no legitimate medical purpose and not within the usual course of professional medical practice. The indictment alleges that the defendants marketed the clinics through more than 1,600 internet sites.

Operation Pill Nation I achieved remarkable success metrics. Operation Pill Nation I, which was announced in February 2011 in South Florida, has resulted in the arrest of 47 people to date, including 17 doctors and five clinic owners, and the seizure of more than **$18.9 million** in cash and assets. In addition, more than 70 doctors, six pharmacy owners and five DEA Registered Controlled Substance Distributors have been stripped of their DEA registrations.

The success of the initial operation led to expanded enforcement efforts. Prior to today's actions, efforts undertaken as part of Operation Pill Nation II have led to the arrest of 49 individuals. The DEA's systematic approach in Florida became the template for nationwide pill mill enforcement, demonstrating that sustained, coordinated pressure could effectively disrupt these criminal enterprises.

Operation Pilluted: Expanding The Geographic Scope

Building on the success in Florida, the DEA launched Operation Pilluted, targeting pill mills across the American South. The morning busts in Arkansas, Alabama, Louisiana and Mississippi are part of a 15-month operation by the DEA drug diversion unit. The sources said 1,000 agents and officers conducted the raids. The operation represented a significant escalation in scope and resources, with federal law enforcement sources describing it as "the single largest pharmaceutical operation in DEA history".

Operation Pilluted demonstrated the geographic spread of the pill mill phenomenon beyond Florida's borders. In the last 15 months, 140 people have been arrested, and officers hope as many as 170 others will be arrested Wednesday, according to the sources. The operation's scale reflected both the magnitude of the problem and the DEA's commitment to a comprehensive response.

The multi-state nature of Operation Pilluted highlighted the interstate character of pill mill operations. Criminal enterprises had evolved beyond simple doctor-shopping to sophisticated networks spanning multiple states, exploiting differences in state regulations and prescription monitoring systems. The DEA's response required unprecedented coordination between federal and state authorities across jurisdictional boundaries.

Operation Wasted Daze: Documenting The Scale Of Individual Operations

The Fort Worth-based Operation Wasted Daze provided detailed insight into the structure and scale of individual pill mill enterprises. Forty-six defendants, including two doctors, a nurse practitioner, and five pharmacists, have been convicted of operating an **$18 million** pill mill scheme. The operation revealed the intricate networks that enabled massive pharmaceutical diversion.

The scope of prescribing activity documented in Operation Wasted Daze was staggering. Over a nine-year span, Dr. Capistrano issued prescriptions for more than 524,000 doses of hydrocodone, 430,000 doses of carisoprodol, 77,000 doses of alprazolam, and 2.07 million doses of promethazine with codeine. Over seven years, Dr. Noel issued prescriptions for more than 200,000 doses of hydrocodone, 55,000 doses of carisoprodol, 14,000 doses of alprazolam, and 450,000 doses of promethazine with codeine.

The investigation revealed sophisticated operational structures designed to maximize illegal prescribing while maintaining a veneer of legitimacy. At the clinic, many of the "patients" were seen not by the doctors, but by Williams, who possessed neither a medical license nor a DEA registration. After a perfunctory conversation with the "patient," Williams allegedly coordinated with Capistrano and Noel to prescribe dangerous drugs without legitimate medical purpose.

The financial mechanics of the operation demonstrated the profit motive driving these enterprises. The pharmacists charged the recruiters between $200 and $800 per prescription, filling hundreds and hundreds of prescriptions for a fee, according to evidence presented at trial. This pricing structure created powerful incentives for all participants in the distribution chain, from patient recruiters to pharmacists.

Operation Profit Over Patients: Recent Enforcement Efforts

The DEA's commitment to pill mill enforcement continued into 2025 with Operation Profit Over Patients, demonstrating the ongoing nature of the threat. Operation Profit Over Patients, which targeted the illegal distribution of controlled substances by medical professionals, resulted in approximately 51 arrests and 122 criminal charges. DEA also charged 93 administrative cases seeking the revocation of pharmacies', medical practitioners', and companies' authority to handle and/or prescribe controlled substances.

This recent operation revealed the evolution of pill mill tactics and the DEA's adaptive response. In Texas, several individuals, including a doctor, nurse, pharmacist, and others allegedly diverted more than 3 million opioids onto the black market. The scale of diversion documented in individual cases continued to demonstrate the massive impact these operations had on communities.

The geographic diversity of **Operation Profit Over Patients** cases showed that pill mill enforcement had become a nationwide priority, with investigations spanning from Texas to Florida and beyond. The operation's focus on administrative cases alongside criminal prosecutions demonstrated a comprehensive approach designed to permanently remove bad actors from the pharmaceutical supply chain.

The Numbers: Quantifying Enforcement Success

Comprehensive statistics on pill mill enforcement reveal the scope of the DEA's response to this crisis. While exact numbers vary across operations and timeframes, available data provides insight into the scale of enforcement activity.

Based on available data from major operations and studies, the DEA and its partners have arrested hundreds of doctors in pill mill-related cases since 2010. Of the 378 cases, U.S. attorneys' offices charged 249 and state authorities charged 131, according to a comprehensive study by the National Association of Attorneys General. This represents a significant shift toward federal prosecution, reflecting the interstate nature of many pill mill operations and the enhanced resources available through federal task forces.

The study revealed important demographic patterns among prosecuted physicians. We found that 89.95 percent of the physicians charged were male, 10.05 percent were female; the earlier study's percentages were 89.94 percent and 10.6 percent, respectively. This consistency across time periods suggests systemic factors rather than random distribution in prosecuted cases.

Geographic concentration of prosecutions reflected the distribution of pill mill activity. Florida operations alone accounted for dozens of doctor arrests across multiple operations. This sting is just one in a string of pill mill busts that has shut down 40 clinics in South Florida and led to the arrests of 80 people, including 22 doctors by 2012, demonstrating the sustained enforcement pressure in the region.

Individual operations often yielded substantial arrest numbers. Operation Pilluted resulted in arrests of hundreds of people, including 22 doctors and pharmacists, while more focused operations like Operation Wasted Daze resulted in 46 defendants, including two doctors, a nurse practitioner, and five pharmacists being convicted.

Financial Impact And Asset Forfeiture

The financial component of pill mill enforcement proved as significant as the criminal prosecutions. Asset forfeiture became a crucial tool for dismantling these criminal enterprises and deterring future violations. The scale of assets seized demonstrates both the profitability of illegal prescribing and the effectiveness of financial investigation techniques.

Operation Pilluted alone resulted in significant financial seizures. In "Operation Pilluted," the DEA took **$12 million in currency** and over $6 million in real property from the doctors and pharmacists it arrested. These seizures encompassed the full range of assets accumulated through illegal prescribing, from luxury vehicles to real estate investments.

Operation Pill Nation I demonstrated the sustained financial impact of comprehensive enforcement. Operation Pill Nation I, which was announced in February 2011 in South Florida, has resulted in the arrest of 47 people to date, including 17 doctors and five clinic owners, and the seizure of more than **$18.9 million** in cash and assets. These seizures represented the accumulated profits from years of illegal prescribing activity.

Individual cases often involved substantial asset forfeitures. In addition to the 18-year prison term, U.S. District Judge John D. Bates ordered Okafor to serve three years of supervised release to pay a special assessment, and to forfeit **$213,173.97**. The combination of imprisonment and financial penalties created powerful deterrent effects for potential violators.

The forfeiture process extended beyond simple cash seizures to encompass the full range of assets derived from illegal activity. Real estate, bank accounts, automobiles, weapons, boats, and even gold bars were forfeited. Some courts ordered forfeiture of medical licenses, DEA controlled substance licenses, and state drivers' licenses. This comprehensive approach ensured that convicted physicians could not easily resume illegal prescribing activities.

Operational Methodology: How Task Forces Conducted Investigations

The complexity of pill mill investigations required sophisticated operational methodologies that differed significantly from traditional drug enforcement approaches. Understanding these methodologies provides insight into both the challenges faced by law enforcement and the adaptations required to address pharmaceutical diversion.

Undercover operations formed the backbone of most pill mill investigations. These arrests are the first in Operation Pill Nation resulting from 340 undercover buys of prescription drugs from over 60 doctors in more than 40 "pill mills" conducted in the past year. The scale of undercover activity required extensive resources and careful coordination to avoid compromising ongoing investigations.

The undercover approach in pill mill cases presented unique challenges. Unlike traditional drug buys, agents had to convincingly portray legitimate patients seeking medical treatment while documenting evidence of illegal prescribing. Undercover DEA agents went to the clinic over a two-year period and "received a total of 55 prescriptions for controlled substances." An independent expert said the examinations were "below the ordinary standard of care," according to the DEA.

Financial investigation techniques proved crucial for understanding the full scope of pill mill operations. Investigators tracked cash flows, analyzed bank records, and followed money laundering schemes that often involved multiple states and complex business structures. The cash-intensive nature of many pill mills created distinctive financial patterns that aided in detection and prosecution.

Prescription monitoring systems became valuable intelligence sources for task force investigations. The Maryland Prescription Drug Monitoring (known as CRISP) allowed practitioners to report all narcotic prescriptions so that other practitioners could make sure that patients were not obtaining multiple prescriptions. Moffett and other members of the conspiracy regularly sought to circumvent the limitations imposed by CRISP and other states' prescription drug monitoring programs.

Multi-agency coordination enabled comprehensive investigation techniques that no single agency could accomplish alone. The DEA Dallas Field Division's Fort Worth Office Tactical Diversion Squad conducted the investigation, with the assistance of Homeland Security Investigations, IRS – Criminal Investigation, the U.S. Marshals Service, the U.S. Postal Inspection Service, the Parker County Sheriff's Office, and the Fort Worth Police Department. This coordination allowed investigators to simultaneously pursue criminal violations, immigration issues, tax evasion, money laundering, and asset forfeiture.

Prosecutorial Strategies And Legal Challenges

Prosecuting pill mill cases required overcoming unique legal challenges that distinguished these cases from traditional drug prosecutions. The central issue in most cases involved proving that prescribing activity fell outside the scope of legitimate medical practice, a determination that required extensive medical expert testimony and careful analysis of patient records.

The legal standard for pill mill prosecutions centered on demonstrating that prescriptions were issued without legitimate medical purpose and outside the usual course of professional practice. This standard required prosecutors to establish not only that prescribing was excessive or inappropriate, but that it constituted criminal conduct rather than mere medical malpractice.

Medical expert testimony became crucial for establishing the criminal nature of prescribing practices. An independent expert said the examinations were "below the ordinary standard of care," according to the DEA. Prosecutors typically relied on medical experts to explain normal standards of care and demonstrate how defendants' practices deviated from accepted medical practice.

The challenge of proving criminal intent in medical practice cases required careful documentation of prescribing patterns and clinical practices. In order to make the prescriptions appear legitimate, the doctors occasionally included prescriptions for non-controlled substances, such as antibiotics and mineral ice. This evidence of deliberate concealment helped establish criminal intent beyond mere negligence or poor medical judgment.

Conspiracy charges proved particularly effective in complex pill mill operations involving multiple participants. All 49 have been charged with conspiracy to possess with intent to distribute controlled substances. Conspiracy prosecutions allowed federal prosecutors to target entire criminal enterprises rather than individual prescribing violations.

Sentencing Patterns And Deterrent Effects

The sentencing patterns in pill mill cases reflected both the seriousness with which federal courts viewed these crimes and the substantial harm caused to communities. Sentences typically combined lengthy prison terms with significant financial penalties and permanent exclusion from medical practice.

Federal sentences for pill mill doctors often exceeded those for traditional drug traffickers, reflecting the abuse of professional trust and the scale of harm caused. Caesar Mark Capistrano, 61, was convicted at trial in January three counts of conspiracy to dispense a controlled substance and two counts of possession with intent to distribute a controlled substance. He was sentenced Thursday by U.S. District Judge Reed C. O'Connor to 20 years in federal prison, representing the high end of typical sentences.

Sentencing disparities often reflected the scale of illegal prescribing activity and the leadership role of individual defendants. Tameka Lachelle Noel, medical doctor Pleaded guilty on Nov. 16, 2020 to conspiracy to dispense a controlled substance and was sentenced to eight years in federal prison, while her co-conspirator received a more substantial sentence reflecting his greater role in the enterprise.

The federal sentencing guidelines for pill mill cases took into account the drug quantity involved, treating illegally prescribed pharmaceuticals similarly to street drugs for sentencing purposes. The massive quantities involved in major pill mill operations often resulted in guideline ranges that supported lengthy prison terms.

Recent sentences continued to reflect the serious nature of these offenses. In addition to the 18-year prison term, U.S. District Judge John D. Bates ordered Okafor to serve three years of supervised release to pay a special assessment, and to forfeit **$213,173.97.** These sentences sent clear messages about the consequences of abusing medical licenses for illegal drug distribution.

The Aftermath: Systemic Changes And Ongoing Challenges

The intensive enforcement efforts against pill mills catalyzed significant changes in the pharmaceutical monitoring and regulatory systems. State prescription drug monitoring programs expanded and improved, creating better tools for detecting suspicious prescribing patterns and preventing doctor shopping.

Medical licensing boards strengthened their oversight procedures and enhanced cooperation with law enforcement agencies. The threat of criminal prosecution alongside professional discipline created powerful incentives for compliance with prescribing regulations and medical standards.

Insurance companies and Medicare programs implemented enhanced monitoring systems to detect potential pill mill activity. These systems often provided early warning of suspicious prescribing patterns that could trigger law enforcement investigations.

The pharmaceutical industry faced increased scrutiny regarding its distribution practices and monitoring of suspicious orders. Federal enforcement actions against pharmaceutical distributors complemented the pill mill prosecutions by addressing supply chain vulnerabilities that enabled large-scale diversion.

However, significant challenges remain. While there have certainly been some pain clinics that had a history of over-prescribing narcotic medication without a sufficient medical examination, those clinics have mostly been put out of business by this point. It seems that the DEA is now focusing its attention on well-run clinics with qualified doctors. This observation suggests that enforcement priorities may be evolving as the most egregious pill mills have been eliminated.

The defense community has developed sophisticated strategies for challenging pill mill prosecutions, arguing that enforcement actions sometimes target legitimate medical practices. We are often able to find other physicians who will give us an opinion that the doctor we are representing prescribed pain medication in the ordinary course of his medical practice and for a legitimate medical purpose. This development has required prosecutors to strengthen their cases and refine their approach to proving criminal intent.

Impact On Legitimate Pain Management

The intensive enforcement campaign against pill mills had significant consequences for legitimate pain management practitioners and patients with genuine medical needs. The heightened scrutiny of prescribing practices created a challenging environment for physicians treating chronic pain conditions.

Many legitimate pain management physicians reported increased administrative burdens related to documentation requirements and regulatory compliance. The fear of prosecution led some practitioners to reduce their prescribing of controlled substances or exit pain management practice entirely, creating access problems for patients with legitimate medical needs.

Patient advocacy groups raised concerns about the impact of enforcement actions on access to necessary medications. The stigmatization of opioid prescribing created barriers for patients with documented medical needs, leading to undertreated pain and suffering among some patient populations.

Medical professional organizations worked to develop clearer guidelines for appropriate prescribing practices while advocating for balanced enforcement approaches that distinguished between criminal activity and legitimate medical practice. These efforts aimed to provide practitioners with clear standards while supporting appropriate law enforcement action against truly criminal enterprises.

Lessons Learned And Future Directions

The extensive DEA task force operations against pill mills provided valuable lessons for law enforcement agencies addressing complex healthcare fraud and pharmaceutical diversion. The multi-agency approach proved essential for addressing the sophisticated nature of modern pill mill operations.

The importance of financial investigation techniques became clear through these operations. Traditional drug enforcement methods alone were insufficient for addressing criminal enterprises that operated under the guise of legitimate businesses with complex financial structures.

The role of prescription monitoring systems as both investigative tools and prevention mechanisms was demonstrated through these cases. Enhanced monitoring capabilities provided both early warning systems for detecting suspicious activity and evidence for prosecution of criminal cases.

The need for specialized training in healthcare fraud investigation became apparent as enforcement priorities evolved. Traditional drug agents required additional education about medical practices, pharmaceutical regulation, and healthcare business operations to effectively investigate pill mill cases.

Coordination between state licensing boards and federal law enforcement emerged as a critical component of comprehensive enforcement strategies. The combination of criminal prosecution and professional discipline provided more complete remedies for addressing illegal prescribing activity.

International Implications And Cooperation

The pill mill enforcement efforts revealed the international dimensions of pharmaceutical diversion and the need for enhanced cooperation with foreign law enforcement agencies. Criminal organizations involved in pill mill operations often had connections to international drug trafficking networks and money laundering schemes.

Cases involving foreign-educated physicians highlighted the challenges of verifying credentials and monitoring prescribing practices across international boundaries. Enhanced information sharing and cooperation between licensing authorities became necessary components of comprehensive enforcement strategies.

The evolution of online pharmacies and telemedicine presented new challenges that required international cooperation to address effectively. Criminal organizations increasingly used internet-based platforms to distribute illegally prescribed medications across state and national boundaries.

Technological Advances And Enforcement Evolution

The integration of advanced analytical tools enhanced the effectiveness of pill mill investigations. Data mining techniques enabled investigators to identify suspicious prescribing patterns and connections between seemingly unrelated cases.

Electronic health records and prescription monitoring systems provided unprecedented visibility into prescribing practices and patient treatment patterns. These technological advances enabled more sophisticated investigation techniques and earlier detection of potential violations.

The use of financial analysis software and cryptocurrency tracking tools became increasingly important as criminal organizations adopted more sophisticated money laundering techniques. The ability to follow financial transactions across multiple platforms and currencies enhanced investigators' ability to prove criminal intent and recover illicit proceeds.

Social media monitoring and digital forensics provided new sources of evidence for demonstrating the criminal nature of pill mill operations. Online communications often revealed the true intent behind prescribing practices and the coordination between various participants in criminal enterprises.

Conclusion: A Continuing Evolution

The DEA's task force operations against pill mill doctors represent one of the most significant healthcare fraud enforcement efforts in American history. Through operations like Pill Nation, Pilluted, Wasted Daze, and Profit Over Patients, federal law enforcement agencies demonstrated their ability to adapt traditional drug enforcement techniques to address complex healthcare fraud schemes.

The documented results of these efforts, hundreds of doctor arrests, millions of dollars in seized assets, and the dismantling of numerous criminal enterprises, demonstrate the effectiveness of the task force approach. However, the evolution of criminal tactics and the emergence of new challenges, including online pharmacies and telemedicine abuse, require continued adaptation of enforcement strategies.

The legacy of these enforcement efforts extends beyond the individual prosecutions to include systemic improvements in prescription monitoring, enhanced cooperation between regulatory and law enforcement agencies, and increased awareness of pharmaceutical diversion risks among healthcare providers and patients.

As the opioid crisis continues to evolve, with fentanyl and synthetic drugs presenting new challenges, the lessons learned from pill mill enforcement operations provide valuable guidance for addressing emerging threats. The multi-agency, intelligence-driven approach pioneered in these operations has become a model for addressing complex criminal enterprises that exploit legitimate business and professional frameworks.

The ongoing need for balanced enforcement that distinguishes between criminal activity and legitimate medical practice remains a central challenge. The success of future enforcement efforts will depend on maintaining this balance while continuing to adapt to evolving criminal tactics and emerging threats in the pharmaceutical sector.

The human cost of the pill mill crisis, measured in addiction, overdose deaths, and destroyed communities, underscores the importance of these enforcement efforts. While law enforcement alone cannot solve the complex problems underlying prescription drug abuse, the systematic dismantling of criminal enterprises that exploited vulnerable populations represents a crucial component of a comprehensive response to the opioid epidemic.

The DEA's task force operations against pill mills demonstrate the potential for law enforcement agencies to effectively address complex white-collar crimes that span traditional jurisdictional boundaries. The integration of diverse agencies, specialized expertise, and advanced investigative techniques provides a framework for addressing other sophisticated criminal enterprises that exploit professional credentials and legitimate business operations for illegal purposes.

CHAPTER NINETEEN

THE CRITICAL IMPORTANCE OF "BEATING THE FEDS II" - WHY COMPREHENSIVE FEDERAL LAW EDUCATION MATTERS

INTRODUCTION

In the complex and often bewildering landscape of federal criminal law, few resources have emerged as essential reading as "**Beating the Feds:** A Comprehensive Guide of Successful Litigation Strategies and Helpful Information That Will Keep You Out of Prison" by Mario Antone and **Garry Wiggins.** This groundbreaking work stands as a beacon of practical legal education in a field dominated by academic treatises and theoretical discussions that often fail to address the real-world challenges faced by individuals navigating the federal justice system.

This book is a complete guide of proven legal strategies that will help you avoid becoming victim to the Federal Justice System. It details Federal surveillance techniques used by top law enforcement agencies to build air tight Federal conspiracies. Unlike the overwhelming majority of federal law publications that approach the subject from an academic or prosecutorial perspective, "**Beating the Feds II"** provides practical, actionable intelligence from the defendant's perspective, a critical gap that has long existed in legal literature.

The fundamental premise of the second edition **"Beating the Feds II"** is that knowledge is power, and in the federal criminal justice system, the lack of knowledge can be catastrophic. While other legal resources focus on theoretical frameworks or provide sanitized overviews of federal law, this work confronts the harsh realities of federal prosecution tactics, surveillance methods, and the practical strategies necessary for effective defense. It recognizes that the federal justice system is not merely a neutral forum for determining guilt or innocence, but rather an adversarial arena where preparation, knowledge, and strategic thinking can mean the difference between freedom and decades in federal prison.

The book's significance extends beyond its immediate practical value to individuals facing federal charges. It represents a democratization of legal knowledge that has traditionally been confined to experienced federal defense attorneys and former federal prosecutors. By making this information accessible to defendants, their families, and non-specialist attorneys, "**Beating the Feds II**" serves a crucial function in leveling an otherwise heavily tilted playing field.

The Federal Justice System: A Maze Of Complexity And Peril

Understanding the importance of "**Beating the Feds II"** requires first grasping the unique nature of the federal criminal justice system and the challenges it presents to defendants. Unlike state criminal systems, which typically handle straightforward crimes with clear elements and familiar procedures, the federal system operates as a complex web of overlapping statutes, intricate procedural rules, and prosecutorial tactics that can overwhelm even experienced attorneys who lack federal experience.

The federal criminal code has expanded dramatically over the past several decades, creating what legal scholars term **"overcriminalization"**, the proliferation of federal criminal statutes that reach far beyond traditional crimes and into areas of everyday life. This expansion means that ordinary business dealings, financial transactions, and even personal conduct can potentially violate federal law, often in ways that are not immediately apparent to those engaged in such activities.

Federal prosecutors wield enormous power within this system, armed with vast resources, sophisticated investigative techniques, and the ability to bring charges that carry devastating penalties. The federal sentencing guidelines, while no longer mandatory, continue to influence judicial decision-making and often result in sentences that are significantly longer than those imposed for similar crimes at the state level. Moreover, federal defendants face unique challenges including limited bail options, restricted plea bargaining opportunities, and the reality that **federal conviction rates exceed 95%.**

The complexity of federal criminal procedure adds another layer of difficulty for defendants and their attorneys. Federal courts operate under rules and precedents that differ significantly from state systems, requiring specialized knowledge of federal discovery rules, motion practice, sentencing procedures, and appellate processes. **The Federal Rules of Criminal Procedure, Federal Rules of Evidence,** and the countless federal statutes and regulations create a procedural maze that can trap the unwary.

Perhaps most importantly, the federal system employs investigative and prosecutorial techniques that are far more sophisticated and aggressive than those typically encountered at the state level. Federal agencies such as the **FBI, DEA, ATF**, and others utilize advanced surveillance technologies, undercover operations, cooperating witnesses, and complex conspiracy theories to build cases that can ensnare multiple defendants and result in lengthy prison sentences. Understanding these techniques and how to defend against them is crucial for anyone facing federal charges.

The stakes in federal criminal cases are invariably higher than in state cases. **Federal sentences** are typically longer, federal prisons are often located far from defendants' families and support systems, and federal convictions carry additional collateral consequences including restrictions on employment, housing, and civic participation. The financial costs of federal defense are also substantially higher, as effective federal defense requires specialized expertise and extensive preparation.

In this environment, the lack of comprehensive, practical education about federal criminal law and procedure represents a fundamental disadvantage for defendants and their families. Traditional legal resources, while valuable for academic or professional purposes, often fail to provide the practical guidance necessary for navigating the federal system effectively. This gap in practical education makes "Beating the Feds II" not merely useful, but essential.

The Inadequacy Of Traditional Federal Law Resources

The landscape of federal law education and resources is dominated by academic treatises, bar examination materials, and practice guides designed primarily for attorneys already familiar with federal practice. While these resources serve important functions within the legal profession, they consistently fail to address the practical needs of defendants, their families, and attorneys who must quickly develop competence in federal criminal defense.

Academic treatises on federal criminal law typically approach the subject from a theoretical perspective, focusing on doctrinal development, constitutional interpretation, and policy analysis rather than practical application. Works such as LaFave's "Criminal Law" or the various federal criminal law casebooks used in law schools provide excellent theoretical grounding but offer little guidance on the tactical and strategic considerations that determine outcomes in real federal cases. These resources assume a level of legal sophistication and familiarity with federal practice that most readers do not possess.

Professional practice guides, while more practically oriented than academic treatises, are generally written by and for experienced federal practitioners. These guides assume familiarity with federal procedures and focus on advanced tactical considerations rather than foundational knowledge. Moreover, they are typically expensive, highly technical, and designed for lawyers rather than defendants or their families. Even experienced attorneys who lack federal experience often find these resources difficult to navigate and apply effectively.

Bar examination materials and continuing legal education resources provide superficial coverage of federal criminal law that is adequate for passing examinations but wholly insufficient for effective practice. These materials focus on memorizing rules and elements rather than understanding the practical application of federal law in real cases. They provide little insight into federal prosecutorial tactics, investigative techniques, or effective defense strategies.

Government publications, including Department of Justice manuals and federal agency guidelines, provide insight into prosecutorial and investigative practices but are written from the government's perspective and naturally emphasize tactics and strategies that favor prosecution rather than defense. While these resources can be valuable for understanding government approaches, they do not provide guidance on how to defend against these tactics effectively.

Legal databases and online resources, while comprehensive in their coverage of federal law, present information in formats that are difficult for non-specialists to navigate and understand. These resources assume familiarity with legal research techniques and provide little context for understanding how various legal principles apply in practice. Moreover, they typically focus on reported appellate decisions rather than the day-to-day realities of federal district court practice where most federal cases are resolved.

Perhaps most problematically, traditional federal law resources consistently fail to address the perspective and needs of defendants. They are written from the viewpoint of prosecutors, judges, or academic observers rather than from the perspective of those who must defend against federal charges. This orientation results in resources that may accurately describe federal law and procedure but provide little guidance on how to navigate the system effectively as a defendant.

The failure of traditional resources to provide practical, defendant-oriented guidance creates a significant information gap that has serious consequences for individuals facing federal charges. Without access to practical information about federal prosecutorial tactics, investigative techniques, and effective defense strategies, defendants and their attorneys are at a severe disadvantage in a system that already favors the prosecution.

"Beating The Feds II": A Revolutionary Approach To Federal Law Education

"**Beating the Feds II"** represents a fundamental departure from traditional approaches to federal law education by adopting a practical, defendant-oriented perspective that directly addresses the real-world challenges faced by individuals navigating the federal criminal justice system. This revolutionary approach makes the book invaluable not only for defendants and their families but also for attorneys who must quickly develop competence in federal criminal defense.

The author has taken great care to explain legal concepts in a straightforward manner, making it accessible to readers with varying levels of legal knowledge. Whether you are a concerned citizen, a business owner, or someone who wants to understand their rights during federal investigations, this book provides valuable insights and guidance. This accessibility represents a crucial innovation in federal law education, as it democratizes knowledge that has traditionally been confined to experienced federal practitioners.

The book's practical orientation sets it apart from academic and professional resources by focusing on actionable intelligence rather than theoretical concepts. It details Federal surveillance techniques used by top law enforcement agencies to build air tight Federal conspiracies. This focus on government tactics and techniques provides readers with essential knowledge about how federal cases are developed and prosecuted, enabling more effective defense strategies.

Unlike traditional federal law resources that present sanitized overviews of legal principles, **"Beating the Feds II"** confronts the harsh realities of federal prosecution with unflinching directness. The book acknowledges that the federal criminal justice system is an adversarial arena where the government employs sophisticated and aggressive tactics to secure convictions. By providing detailed information about these tactics, the book enables defendants and their attorneys to prepare more effective defenses.

The comprehensive scope of "**Beating the Feds II"** addresses the reality that federal criminal law encompasses a vast array of offenses and investigative techniques. This book covers everything from White collar crimes to **Gun charges**, **Federal Drug conspiracies**, **Sex Crimes, Hobbs Act Robberies**, **Bank Fraud, Tax Evasion** and more. This breadth ensures that readers gain understanding of federal law's expansive reach and the various contexts in which federal charges might arise.

The book's emphasis on practical strategies distinguishes it from resources that merely describe legal principles without explaining how to apply them effectively. It also contains litigation Strategies and how to choose the right lawyer to help you defend your case. This guidance on selecting and working with attorneys is particularly valuable given the specialized nature of federal criminal defense and the importance of choosing counsel with appropriate experience and expertise.

"**Beating the Feds II"** also provides valuable insight into federal investigations and surveillance techniques that are rarely discussed in traditional legal resources. Understanding how federal agencies conduct investigations, develop cases, and gather evidence is crucial for effective defense preparation. The book's detailed coverage of these topics provides defendants and their attorneys with intelligence that can be decisive in case outcomes.

The book's approach to explaining complex legal concepts in accessible language makes it valuable not only for attorneys but also for defendants and their families who need to understand the proceedings against them. The author provides real-life examples and case studies to illustrate how individuals can protect their rights during federal investigations. This inclusion of practical guidance adds a valuable dimension to the book, making it more relatable and applicable to real-world situations.

Perhaps most importantly, "**Beating the Feds II**" acknowledges and addresses the emotional and psychological challenges faced by individuals confronting the federal criminal justice system. The book recognizes that federal prosecutions are not merely legal proceedings but life-altering events that affect defendants, their families, and their communities. By providing practical guidance and demystifying federal procedures, the book helps reduce the anxiety and confusion that often accompany federal investigations and prosecutions.

Critical Analysis Of Federal Surveillance And Investigative Techniques

One of the most significant contributions of "**Beating the Feds II**" is its detailed examination of federal surveillance and investigative techniques, providing readers with crucial insight into how federal cases are developed and how evidence is gathered. This information is rarely available in traditional legal resources, which typically focus on the legal standards governing surveillance rather than the practical realities of how surveillance is conducted and how it can be challenged.

Federal agencies employ a vast array of **surveillance techniques** that go far beyond the wiretaps and physical surveillance commonly understood by the public. Modern federal investigations routinely utilize digital surveillance technologies, financial records analysis, social media monitoring, GPS tracking, and sophisticated data mining techniques that can reconstruct detailed pictures of individuals' activities, associations, and communications. Understanding these techniques is crucial for effective defense preparation and for identifying potential challenges to the admissibility of evidence.

The book's coverage of conspiracy law represents another critical area where traditional resources fall short. Federal conspiracy charges are among the most powerful weapons in the prosecutor's arsenal, allowing the government to charge multiple defendants based on agreements to commit crimes, even if the underlying crimes were never completed. Conspiracy law's broad reach and relatively low evidentiary standards make it a favorite tool of federal prosecutors, yet few resources adequately explain how conspiracy cases are developed and how they can be defended.

"**Beating the Feds II**" provides practical guidance on understanding conspiracy allegations, identifying weaknesses in conspiracy cases, and developing effective defense strategies. This guidance is particularly valuable because conspiracy cases often involve complex factual scenarios, multiple defendants, and vast amounts of evidence that can be overwhelming for defendants and their attorneys to analyze and challenge effectively.

The book's discussion of cooperating witnesses represents another area where traditional resources provide inadequate guidance. Federal prosecutions routinely rely on cooperating witnesses, individuals who have been arrested and agreed to provide information about others in exchange for lenient treatment. These witnesses present unique challenges for defense attorneys, as their credibility may be compromised by their cooperation agreements while their testimony often provides the most damaging evidence against defendants.

Understanding how cooperating witnesses are developed, what motivations they have to provide information, and how their testimony can be challenged is crucial for effective federal defense. "**Beating the Feds II**" provides practical insight into these issues that is rarely available in traditional legal resources, which typically focus on the legal standards governing cooperating witness testimony rather than the practical realities of how such testimony is developed and presented.

The book's coverage of search and seizure law goes beyond the constitutional principles typically covered in traditional resources to address the practical realities of how searches are conducted and how evidence is gathered. Federal searches often involve sophisticated techniques and technologies that present unique challenges for defense attorneys seeking to challenge the admissibility of evidence. Understanding these techniques and the potential legal challenges they present is crucial for effective defense preparation.

Electronic surveillance represents a particularly complex area of federal law where **"Beating the Feds II"** provides valuable guidance. Federal agencies routinely obtain orders for wiretaps, email monitoring, and other forms of electronic surveillance that can provide devastating evidence against defendants. Understanding how these surveillance techniques work, what legal standards govern their use, and how they can be challenged requires specialized knowledge that is rarely available in traditional legal resources.

The book's practical approach to these issues makes complex legal concepts accessible to readers without extensive legal training while providing the depth of coverage necessary for effective application. This combination of accessibility and comprehensiveness makes **"Beating the Feds II"** an invaluable resource for anyone seeking to understand federal investigative techniques and develop effective responses to them.

Strategic Defense Considerations And Practical Applications

The strategic value of "**Beating the Feds II**" extends beyond its educational content to its practical applications in federal criminal defense. The book provides specific guidance on defense strategies, tactical considerations, and practical steps that can be decisive in federal cases. This practical orientation distinguishes it from traditional resources that focus on describing legal principles without explaining how to apply them effectively in real cases.

The book's guidance on pre-indictment representation addresses a critical phase of federal cases that is often overlooked in traditional resources. Federal investigations typically proceed for months or years before charges are filed, during which time targets of investigation may be unaware of the government's interest or may underestimate the seriousness of the potential charges. Understanding how to recognize the signs of federal investigation and how to respond effectively can be crucial for case outcomes.

"**Beating the Feds II**" provides practical guidance on when to retain counsel, how to respond to contact from federal agents, and what steps can be taken to protect interests during the investigation phase. This guidance is particularly valuable because mistakes made during the investigation phase can be impossible to correct later and can significantly harm defense prospects.

The book's coverage of plea negotiations represents another area where traditional resources provide inadequate practical guidance. Federal plea negotiations involve unique considerations including sentencing guidelines calculations, cooperation agreements, and the substantial penalties that often accompany federal charges. Understanding how federal plea negotiations work and what factors influence prosecutorial decision-making is crucial for effective advocacy.

The book provides insight into prosecutorial motivations, negotiation strategies, and the factors that can influence plea offers. This information helps defendants and their attorneys make informed decisions about whether to accept plea offers or proceed to trial, and provides guidance on how to position cases for the most favorable outcomes possible.

Trial strategy in federal cases involves considerations that are unique to the federal system and that are rarely addressed adequately in traditional resources. Federal trials typically involve complex evidence, sophisticated government presentations, and juries that may be predisposed to believe government witnesses. Understanding how to prepare for federal trials, present effective defenses, and challenge government evidence requires specialized knowledge and experience.

"**Beating the Feds II**" provides practical guidance on federal trial strategy that goes beyond the general trial advocacy principles covered in traditional resources. The book addresses the specific challenges presented by federal cases and provides tactical guidance that can be decisive in trial outcomes.

Sentencing considerations in federal cases are particularly complex and require specialized knowledge of federal sentencing law, guidelines, and practices. Federal sentences are typically longer than state sentences for similar crimes, and federal sentencing involves numerous factors and calculations that can be difficult to understand and apply. Understanding how federal sentencing works and what factors influence sentencing decisions is crucial for effective advocacy.

The book provides practical guidance on federal sentencing that helps defendants and their attorneys understand the potential consequences of various strategic decisions and prepare effectively for sentencing proceedings. This guidance is particularly valuable because sentencing is often the most important phase of federal cases, as conviction rates are so high that effective sentencing advocacy may be the primary opportunity to achieve favorable outcomes.

Post-conviction considerations, including appeals and sentence modifications, represent another area where "**Beating the Feds II"** provides valuable practical guidance. Federal appeals involve unique procedural requirements and substantive standards that differ significantly from state appellate practice. Understanding how federal appeals work and what issues are likely to be successful on appeal is important for preserving appellate rights and developing effective appellate strategies.

The Economics Of Federal Defense And Resource Allocation

One of the most practical aspects of **"Beating the Feds II"** is its recognition of the economic realities faced by individuals confronting federal charges. Federal criminal defense is substantially more expensive than state criminal defense due to the complexity of federal law, the length of federal proceedings, and the specialized expertise required for effective representation. Understanding these economic realities and how to manage them effectively is crucial for defendants and their families.

The book addresses the difficult question of how to choose federal criminal defense counsel in a market where attorney fees can range from tens of thousands to hundreds of thousands of dollars depending on the complexity of the case and the experience of the attorney. It also contains litigation Strategies and how to choose the right lawyer to help you defend your case. This guidance is particularly valuable because the choice of counsel can be decisive in federal cases, yet defendants often lack the knowledge necessary to evaluate attorneys' qualifications effectively.

Federal criminal defense requires specialized knowledge and experience that not all criminal defense attorneys possess. The book provides guidance on identifying attorneys with appropriate federal experience, understanding fee structures and payment arrangements, and evaluating the quality of legal representation. This information helps defendants make informed decisions about legal representation within their financial constraints.

The book also addresses the reality that many defendants cannot afford the most experienced federal criminal defense attorneys and provides guidance on how to maximize the effectiveness of representation within budget constraints. This practical approach acknowledges that perfect justice may not be available to all defendants but that informed decision-making can improve outcomes even when resources are limited.

Understanding the costs associated with different defense strategies is crucial for effective resource allocation in federal cases. Some defense strategies require extensive investigation, expert witnesses, and other costly resources, while others may be pursued more economically. The book provides guidance on evaluating the cost-effectiveness of different approaches and making strategic decisions based on available resources.

The book's coverage of cooperation agreements represents another area where economic considerations play a crucial role. Cooperation with the government can significantly reduce sentences and legal costs, but it also involves substantial risks and ethical considerations. Understanding how cooperation works, what it requires, and what benefits and risks it presents is crucial for making informed decisions about cooperation.

The potential financial consequences of federal convictions extend far beyond legal fees and fines to include forfeiture proceedings, restitution orders, and the long-term economic impact of federal conviction. Understanding these potential consequences is important for making informed decisions about defense strategies and plea negotiations.

The book's practical approach to these economic realities makes it valuable not only for defendants but also for their families who often bear the financial burden of federal defense. By providing realistic expectations about costs and practical guidance on managing them, the book helps families make informed decisions about resource allocation and defense strategy.

Addressing Gaps In Legal Education And Professional Training

The importance of **"Beating the Feds II"** is underscored by the significant gaps that exist in legal education and professional training regarding federal criminal law and procedure. Despite the growing importance of federal criminal law and the devastating consequences of federal convictions, most law schools provide minimal coverage of federal criminal practice, and most attorneys lack the specialized knowledge necessary for effective federal criminal defense.

Law school curricula typically include one or two courses on criminal law and procedure that focus primarily on constitutional principles and appellate decisions rather than practical applications. These courses provide little insight into the realities of federal practice, the tactics employed by federal prosecutors, or the specialized knowledge necessary for effective federal defense. Graduates of even prestigious law schools often lack basic knowledge about federal criminal procedure, sentencing law, and defense strategies.

Bar examinations include minimal coverage of federal criminal law, focusing primarily on constitutional principles that provide little practical guidance for federal practice. Attorneys can pass bar examinations and begin practicing criminal law without ever learning about federal sentencing guidelines, conspiracy law, or the specialized procedures that govern federal cases.

Continuing legal education programs often provide superficial coverage of federal criminal law that is adequate for meeting professional requirements but insufficient for developing competence in federal practice. These programs typically focus on recent legal developments rather than foundational knowledge and practical applications.

Even attorneys who practice criminal law at the state level often lack the specialized knowledge necessary for effective federal practice. State criminal practice involves different procedures, different sentencing structures, and different prosecutorial tactics than federal practice. Attorneys who attempt to apply state criminal law knowledge to federal cases often find themselves at a significant disadvantage.

The specialized nature of federal criminal practice means that effective representation requires knowledge and experience that cannot be quickly acquired through traditional legal education or general criminal law practice. Federal criminal law involves complex statutes, intricate procedural rules, sophisticated prosecutorial tactics, and unique sentencing considerations that require specialized study and experience to master.

"Beating the Feds II" helps address these educational gaps by providing practical, accessible coverage of federal criminal law and procedure that is unavailable in traditional legal education resources. The book's practical orientation and comprehensive coverage make it valuable not only for defendants and their families but also for attorneys who need to quickly develop competence in federal practice.

The book's contribution to legal education extends beyond its immediate practical value to its role in democratizing legal knowledge. By making sophisticated knowledge about federal criminal law accessible to non-specialists, the book helps level the playing field in a system that heavily favors the prosecution. This democratization of legal knowledge serves important public policy goals by promoting more effective advocacy and more informed decision-making by defendants.

Comparative Analysis With Other Federal Law Resources

To fully appreciate the significance of "**Beating the Feds II,**" it is essential to compare it with other available resources on federal criminal law and procedure. This comparison reveals the unique value proposition of the book and highlights the gaps in existing legal literature that it addresses.

Academic treatises such as LaFave's "Criminal Law" series provide comprehensive theoretical coverage of federal criminal law but approach the subject from a scholarly perspective that emphasizes doctrinal development and constitutional interpretation rather than practical application. These works are invaluable for understanding the theoretical foundations of federal criminal law but provide little guidance on the tactical and strategic considerations that determine outcomes in real cases.

Professional practice guides such as the ABA's "Criminal Defense Techniques" series offer more practical guidance than academic treatises but are written for experienced practitioners and assume familiarity with federal procedures. These guides focus on advanced tactical considerations and assume a level of baseline knowledge that most readers do not possess. Moreover, they are typically expensive and designed for law firm libraries rather than individual practitioners or defendants.

Government publications including the U.S. Attorneys' Manual and FBI investigative guidelines provide insight into federal prosecutorial and investigative practices but are written from the government's perspective and naturally emphasize tactics that favor prosecution rather than defense. While these resources can be valuable for understanding government approaches, they do not provide guidance on how to defend against these tactics effectively.

Similar federal defense guides such as "Busting the Feds at Their Own Dirty Game" by Creaghan Harry provide comparable practical guidance on federal criminal defense, covering topics including drug charges, gun arrests, plea bargains, preliminary hearings, prosecutorial misconduct, drug conspiracy, choosing a lawyer, getting bail, and various federal statutes and constitutional protections. While these resources share **"Beating the Feds II'"** practical orientation, they often lack the comprehensive scope and detailed coverage that makes "Beating the Feds II" uniquely valuable.

Legal databases such as Westlaw and Lexis provide comprehensive coverage of federal law but present information in formats that are difficult for non-specialists to navigate and understand. These resources assume familiarity with legal research techniques and provide little context for understanding how various legal principles apply in practice. Moreover, they focus on reported appellate decisions rather than the day-to-day realities of federal district court practice.

Online resources and websites often provide superficial coverage of federal criminal law that may be accessible to general audiences but lacks the depth and accuracy necessary for effective application. Many online resources contain outdated or inaccurate information and fail to provide the comprehensive coverage necessary for understanding complex federal legal issues.

The unique value of **"Beating the Feds II"** lies in its combination of comprehensive coverage, practical orientation, and accessibility. Unlike academic treatises, it focuses on practical applications rather than theoretical concepts. Unlike professional practice guides, it is written for general audiences rather than experienced specialists. Unlike government publications, it adopts the defendant's perspective rather than the prosecution's viewpoint.

The book's ability to present complex legal concepts in an accessible and understandable manner sets it apart from other resources that may be comprehensive but are difficult for non-specialists to use effectively. This accessibility makes the book valuable not only for defendants and their families but also for attorneys who need to quickly develop competence in federal practice.

The book's practical examples and case studies provide concrete applications of abstract legal principles that help readers understand how federal law operates in practice. This approach contrasts with resources that describe legal principles without explaining how they apply in real situations or what practical steps can be taken to address them.

The Democratization Of Legal Knowledge And Access To Justice

"Beating the Feds II" serves a broader social function beyond its immediate practical value by contributing to the democratization of legal knowledge and promoting access to justice in the federal criminal system. The federal criminal justice system's complexity and the specialized knowledge required for effective navigation create significant barriers to access that disproportionately affect individuals who cannot afford experienced federal criminal defense attorneys.

The concentration of federal criminal law expertise in a relatively small number of experienced practitioners creates a two-tiered system where wealthy defendants can afford effective representation while others must rely on attorneys with limited federal experience or overworked public defenders. This disparity in representation quality contributes to unequal outcomes in the federal system and undermines the principle that justice should be equally available to all defendants regardless of their economic circumstances.

By making sophisticated knowledge about federal criminal law accessible to defendants, their families, and non-specialist attorneys, **"Beating the Feds II"** helps reduce these disparities and promotes more equal access to effective representation. The book enables defendants to make more informed decisions about their cases, communicate more effectively with their attorneys, and participate more meaningfully in their own defense.

The educational value of the book extends to family members and support networks who play crucial roles in federal cases but often lack understanding of the proceedings and their implications. Federal cases typically last for months or years and impose significant financial and emotional burdens on defendants' families. Understanding the process, potential outcomes, and strategic considerations helps families provide more effective support and make more informed decisions about resource allocation.

The book's contribution to legal education also benefits attorneys who must quickly develop competence in federal practice but lack access to experienced mentors or comprehensive training programs. Many attorneys who practice criminal law encounter federal cases infrequently and lack the specialized knowledge necessary for effective representation. **"Beating the Feds II"** provides accessible education that can improve representation quality and case outcomes.

The democratization of legal knowledge serves important public policy goals by promoting more informed decision-making, more effective advocacy, and more equal outcomes in the federal criminal justice system. When defendants and their representatives have better access to information about federal law and procedure, they can make more strategic decisions, identify more effective defense strategies, and achieve better outcomes.

The book's role in promoting access to justice is particularly important given the expansion of federal criminal law and the increasing number of individuals who find themselves subject to federal prosecution. As federal jurisdiction continues to expand into areas of everyday life, the need for accessible education about federal criminal law becomes more pressing.

The availability of practical, accessible information about federal criminal law also serves as a check on government power by enabling more effective oversight of federal prosecutorial practices. When defendants and their representatives better understand federal procedures and tactics, they are better positioned to identify prosecutorial misconduct, challenge inappropriate government actions, and hold federal authorities accountable for their conduct.

Future Implications And The Evolution Of Federal Criminal Practice

The significance of **"Beating the Feds II"** extends beyond its current applications to its implications for the future evolution of federal criminal practice and legal education. The book's success in providing accessible, practical education about federal criminal law demonstrates both the demand for such resources and the potential for innovative approaches to legal education.

The growing complexity of federal criminal law and the continued expansion of federal jurisdiction make accessible education about federal criminal practice increasingly important. As more individuals become subject to federal prosecution and as federal cases become more complex, the need for practical guidance about federal law and procedure will continue to grow.

The book's model of practical, defendant-oriented legal education could serve as a template for similar resources in other areas of federal law. The success of **"Beating the Feds II"** suggests that there is demand for accessible, practical legal education that goes beyond traditional academic and professional resources.

Technological developments in legal research and education create new opportunities for innovative approaches to legal education that could build on the foundation established by **"Beating the Feds II"** Digital platforms, interactive resources, and multimedia presentations could enhance the accessibility and effectiveness of practical legal education.

The book's contribution to the democratization of legal knowledge also has implications for broader discussions about access to justice and the role of legal education in promoting equal treatment under law. The success of practical legal education resources suggests that traditional approaches to legal education may be insufficient for meeting contemporary needs.

The evolution of federal criminal practice toward increasing complexity and specialization makes resources like **"Beating the Feds II"** more rather than less important over time. As federal practice becomes more specialized, the gap between specialist practitioners and general practitioners widens, making accessible education about federal practice more crucial for promoting effective representation.

The book's emphasis on understanding government tactics and developing effective responses also has implications for the broader relationship between citizens and government in the federal system. As federal agencies employ increasingly sophisticated investigative techniques and federal prosecutors pursue increasingly aggressive enforcement strategies, the need for effective checks and balances becomes more important.

The success of **"Beating the Feds II"** in providing practical education about federal criminal law suggests that similar approaches could be effective in other areas where complex legal systems create barriers to access and understanding. The model of accessible, practical legal education could be applied to areas such as immigration law, tax law, and regulatory compliance where similar challenges exist.

Conclusion: The Enduring Importance Of Practical Federal Law Education

"Beating the Feds II" represents a crucial contribution to federal criminal law education that addresses fundamental gaps in existing legal resources and serves essential functions in promoting access to justice and effective representation in the federal system. The book's practical orientation, comprehensive coverage, and accessible presentation make it uniquely valuable for defendants, their families, and attorneys who must navigate the complexities of federal criminal law.

The importance of the book extends beyond its immediate practical applications to its broader role in democratizing legal knowledge and promoting more equal access to effective representation. By making sophisticated knowledge about federal criminal law accessible to general audiences, the book helps level the playing field in a system that heavily favors the prosecution and promotes more informed decision-making by defendants and their representatives.

The book's success in providing practical education about federal criminal law demonstrates both the demand for such resources and the limitations of traditional approaches to legal education. Academic treatises and professional practice guides, while valuable for their intended audiences, fail to address the practical needs of defendants and non-specialist attorneys who must quickly develop competence in federal practice.

The comprehensive scope of "**Beating the Feds II"** addresses the reality that federal criminal law encompasses a vast array of offenses, investigative techniques, and procedural requirements that can overwhelm those unfamiliar with federal practice. The book's detailed coverage of surveillance techniques, conspiracy law, cooperating witnesses, and other crucial topics provides essential knowledge that is rarely available in accessible formats.

The strategic value of the book lies not only in its educational content but also in its practical applications for federal criminal defense. The book provides specific guidance on defense strategies, tactical considerations, and practical steps that can be decisive in federal cases. This practical orientation distinguishes it from resources that merely describe legal principles without explaining how to apply them effectively.

The economic realities of federal criminal defense make practical education about federal law particularly important for defendants who cannot afford the most experienced attorneys. **"Beating the Feds II"** provides guidance that can improve representation quality and case outcomes even when resources are limited, serving important access to justice goals.

The book's contribution to addressing gaps in legal education and professional training has implications that extend beyond federal criminal law to broader questions about how legal knowledge should be developed and disseminated. The success of practical legal education resources suggests that traditional approaches may be insufficient for meeting contemporary needs.

Looking forward, the continued expansion of federal criminal law and the growing complexity of federal practice make resources like **"Beating the Feds II"** increasingly important. As more individuals become subject to federal prosecution and as federal cases become more complex, the need for accessible, practical education about federal law will continue to grow.

The book's role in promoting the democratization of legal knowledge and more effective oversight of government power serves important constitutional functions in a system based on checks and balances. When defendants and their representatives have better access to information about federal law and procedure, they are better positioned to protect their rights and hold government authorities accountable.

"Beating the Feds II" stands as an essential resource for anyone seeking to understand federal criminal law and navigate the federal criminal justice system effectively. Its comprehensive coverage, practical orientation, and accessible presentation make it uniquely valuable in a field dominated by academic treatises and professional resources that fail to address the real-world needs of defendants and their advocates.

The book's enduring importance lies in its recognition that knowledge is power in the federal criminal justice system, and that the democratization of legal knowledge serves essential functions in promoting justice, protecting constitutional rights, and maintaining the checks and balances that are fundamental to democratic governance. As federal criminal law continues to evolve and expand, resources like **"Beating the Feds II"** become not merely helpful, but absolutely essential for anyone seeking to understand and effectively navigate this complex and consequential area of law.

The Imperative For Reform In Federal Law Education

The success and importance of **"Beating the Feds II"** highlight fundamental problems with how federal criminal law is taught, understood, and practiced in the United States. The book's necessity reveals a systemic failure in legal education and professional training that leaves defendants, their families, and even many attorneys woefully unprepared for the realities of federal criminal practice.

Traditional law school curricula remain heavily focused on theoretical concepts and appellate court decisions rather than the practical skills and knowledge necessary for effective federal practice. Students graduate from law school with minimal understanding of federal sentencing guidelines, conspiracy law, or the sophisticated investigative techniques employed by federal agencies. This educational gap persists despite the growing importance of federal criminal law and the devastating consequences of federal convictions.

The legal profession's continuing education requirements do little to address these gaps, offering superficial coverage of federal topics that meets professional obligations without developing genuine competence. Bar associations and legal education providers focus on recent developments and theoretical updates rather than the foundational knowledge necessary for effective federal practice.

This educational failure has profound consequences for the administration of justice in the federal system. When attorneys lack adequate knowledge of federal law and procedure, their clients suffer. When defendants and their families lack understanding of the proceedings against them, they cannot participate meaningfully in their own defense or make informed decisions about critical strategic questions.

The remedy for this systemic failure requires fundamental changes in how federal criminal law is taught and understood. Law schools must develop more practical curricula that prepare students for the realities of federal practice. Professional organizations must provide more comprehensive continuing education that develops genuine competence rather than merely satisfying formal requirements.

The Broader Implications For Democratic Governance

The issues raised by **"Beating the Feds II"** extend beyond the immediate concerns of federal criminal practice to fundamental questions about democratic governance and the rule of law. The complexity and opacity of the federal criminal justice system represent a form of structural inequality that undermines the principle that the law should be equally accessible and understandable to all citizens.

When legal systems become so complex that they can only be navigated effectively by specialists, they create inherent advantages for those who can afford expert representation while disadvantaging those who cannot. This complexity becomes a barrier to access that undermines equal justice under law and creates a two-tiered system where outcomes depend more on resources than on the merits of cases.

The federal government's use of increasingly sophisticated investigative techniques and prosecutorial tactics creates an imbalance of power that can only be addressed through better education and more effective advocacy. When citizens lack understanding of their rights and the procedures that govern federal investigations and prosecutions, they cannot effectively protect themselves or hold government authorities accountable.

The democratization of legal knowledge serves as a crucial check on government power by enabling more informed oversight and more effective resistance to prosecutorial overreach. Resources like **"Beating the Feds II"** perform an essential democratic function by making specialized knowledge accessible to those who need it most.

The expansion of federal criminal law into areas of everyday life makes this democratization of knowledge increasingly urgent. As federal jurisdiction continues to expand, more citizens find themselves potentially subject to federal prosecution for activities they may not realize violate federal law. Understanding these laws and the procedures that govern their enforcement becomes a matter of basic civic education.

The Evolution Of Legal Information And Technology

The success of **"Beating the Feds II"** also reflects broader changes in how legal information is created, distributed, and consumed. Traditional models of legal publishing and education, designed for professional audiences and institutional purchasers, increasingly fail to meet the needs of individual practitioners and citizens who require practical, accessible guidance.

Digital platforms and self-publishing technologies have democratized legal publishing, enabling authors like those of **"Beating the Feds II"** to reach audiences that traditional publishers have ignored or underserved. This technological revolution has the potential to address many of the gaps in legal education and professional training that have persisted for decades.

However, this technological opportunity also creates new challenges related to quality control, accuracy, and the potential for misinformation. The democratization of legal publishing must be accompanied by appropriate standards and oversight to ensure that the information provided is accurate, current, and helpful rather than misleading or harmful.

The future of legal education and professional training will likely involve hybrid models that combine traditional institutional resources with innovative, technology-enabled approaches like those exemplified by **"Beating the Feds II."** These new models have the potential to make legal education more accessible, more practical, and more responsive to the real needs of practitioners and citizens.

Ethical Considerations And Professional Responsibility

The approach taken by **"Beating the Feds II"** raises important questions about professional responsibility and the ethics of legal education. Traditional professional models have restricted detailed information about legal strategy and tactics to licensed attorneys, based on concerns about unauthorized practice of law and the potential for harm from incomplete or misunderstood information.

However, the complexity of the federal criminal justice system and the stakes involved for defendants suggest that these traditional restrictions may be counterproductive. When defendants lack basic understanding of the proceedings against them, they cannot make informed decisions or participate effectively in their own defense, regardless of the quality of their legal representation.

The ethical imperative to promote access to justice may require a more open approach to legal education that prioritizes empowering defendants and their families over protecting professional prerogatives. **"Beating the Feds II"** demonstrates that complex legal information can be presented in accessible formats without compromising accuracy or promoting harmful conduct.

The book's success also suggests that there is significant unmet demand for practical legal education that current professional models have failed to address. This market failure indicates that traditional approaches to professional responsibility may need to be reconsidered in light of changing needs and technological capabilities.

The legal profession's commitment to promoting access to justice requires supporting innovations like **"Beating the Feds II"** that make legal knowledge more accessible and help level the playing field between defendants and the government. This support should include developing new models of professional education and client service that leverage technology and innovative approaches to better serve client needs.

The Path Forward: Building On The Foundation Of "Beating The Feds II"

The success and importance of **"Beating the Feds II"** provide a foundation for broader reforms in legal education, professional training, and the administration of justice in the federal system. Building on this foundation requires coordinated efforts across multiple areas and institutions to address the systemic problems that make resources like this book necessary.

Legal education reform must begin with law schools developing more practical curricula that prepare students for the realities of federal practice. This reform should include clinical programs, externships, and practical skills training that complement traditional doctrinal education. Law schools should also develop continuing education programs that help practicing attorneys develop federal expertise throughout their careers.

Professional organizations must take more active roles in promoting competence in federal criminal practice through improved continuing education programs, mentorship opportunities, and practice resources. Bar associations should develop specialty certifications in federal criminal law that recognize genuine expertise and help clients identify qualified attorneys.

The federal courts and administrative agencies should promote transparency and accessibility by providing better public education about federal procedures and requirements. This education should include plain-language explanations of complex procedures, practical guidance for defendants and their families, and resources for attorneys who handle federal cases infrequently.

Technology platforms and digital resources should be developed to make federal legal information more accessible and usable. These platforms should build on the model established by **"Beating the Feds II"** by focusing on practical applications rather than theoretical concepts and by presenting information in formats that are accessible to general audiences.

Research and evaluation should be conducted to identify the most effective approaches to federal legal education and to measure the impact of improved education on case outcomes and access to justice. This research should inform the development of new educational resources and professional training programs.

Policy makers should consider reforms to federal criminal law and procedure that would make the system more accessible and understandable without compromising its effectiveness. These reforms might include simplification of certain procedures, better disclosure requirements, and enhanced protections for defendants who lack experienced counsel.

Conclusion: The Lasting Legacy Of Comprehensive Federal Law Education

"Beating the Feds II" represents more than just another legal guide; it embodies a fundamental shift toward democratizing legal knowledge and empowering individuals to navigate one of the most complex and consequential areas of American law. The book's comprehensive approach, practical orientation, and accessible presentation have established a new standard for federal law education that addresses real-world needs rather than academic abstractions.

The importance of this work extends far beyond its immediate utility to defendants and their attorneys. It serves as a powerful reminder that complexity in legal systems, while sometimes necessary, should not become a barrier to justice or a tool for maintaining inequality. The federal criminal justice system's opacity and complexity have for too long served to advantage those with resources and expertise while disadvantaging those without.

By providing detailed, practical guidance on federal criminal law and procedure, **"Beating the Feds II"** has demonstrated that sophisticated legal knowledge can be made accessible without sacrificing accuracy or promoting harmful conduct. The book's success proves that there is significant demand for practical legal education and that innovative approaches to legal publishing and education can address longstanding gaps in professional training and public understanding.

The broader implications of this work for democratic governance cannot be overstated. In a system where federal criminal law reaches into virtually every aspect of American life, citizen understanding of these laws and the procedures that govern their enforcement becomes a matter of fundamental civic education. The democratization of legal knowledge serves essential functions in maintaining the checks and balances that protect individual rights and constrain government power.

The book's contribution to addressing systemic problems in legal education and professional training has implications that extend well beyond federal criminal law. The success of practical, accessible legal education resources suggests that traditional approaches to professional education may be insufficient for meeting contemporary needs and that innovative approaches deserve support and development.

As federal criminal law continues to evolve and expand, the need for resources like **"Beating the Feds II"** will only grow. The book's model of comprehensive, practical legal education should serve as inspiration for similar resources in other areas of law and as a catalyst for broader reforms in legal education and professional training.

The lasting legacy of **"Beating the Feds II"** lies not only in its immediate impact on federal criminal practice but in its demonstration that legal knowledge can and should be democratized in service of justice and equality. The book stands as a testament to the power of accessible education to level playing fields, empower individuals, and strengthen democratic institutions.

In an era when federal criminal law touches the lives of increasing numbers of Americans, **"Beating the Feds II"** serves as an essential resource for understanding and navigating this complex system. Its comprehensive coverage, practical wisdom, and accessible presentation make it indispensable for anyone seeking to understand federal criminal law or defend against federal charges. More importantly, it represents a model for how legal education can serve the cause of justice by empowering those who need knowledge most and ensuring that complexity does not become a barrier to equal treatment under law.

The book's enduring importance lies in its recognition that in the federal criminal justice system, knowledge truly is power, and that the democratization of that knowledge serves the fundamental values of justice, equality, and democratic governance that define the American legal system at its best. As such, **"Beating the Feds II"** stands not merely as a practical guide but as a crucial contribution to the ongoing struggle for equal justice under law.

www.ingramcontent.com/pod-product-compliance
Lightning Source LLC
LaVergne TN
LVHW082015200926
848481LV00010B/2863